Reginald Sparks

EPPING FOREST THEN AND NOW

'Look into your hearts, and look into the past, and
remember that all this beauty is a gift which you can
never replace . . . you can make a town, you can make
a desert, you can even make a garden, but you can never,
never make the country, because it was made by Time.'

E. M. Forster

EPPING FOREST THEN AND NOW

An anthology compiled by Winston G. Ramsey

with Reginald L. Fowkes

Contents

Credits

EPPING FOREST THEN AND NOW
© 1986 Battle of Britain Prints International Limited. Printed in Great Britain
ISBN 0 900913 39 8
Edited and designed by Winston G. Ramsey

PUBLISHERS
Battle of Britain Prints International Limited
3 New Plaistow Road
London E15 3JA

PRINTERS
Plaistow Press Limited
3 New Plaistow Road
London E15 3JA

BINDERS
Dorstel Press
Edinburgh Way, Temple Fields
Harlow, Essex

PHOTOGRAPHS
With the passage of time, the origin of many contemporary photographs becomes lost, and the name of the photographer, in whom the copyright exists, or existed until 50 years from the date of his death, is unknown. In a great number of cases a copy of the same original, sometimes a second or third generation copy, was supplied to us by different individuals or organisations, thus blurring even further the true provenance. Included in this book is material from the following local collections: Epping Forest District Museum, Essex Record Office, Loughton Library, Passmore Edwards Museum, Redbridge Central Library, and Vestry House Museum.

FRONT ENDPAPER
A typical weekend outing for the boys. The Robin Hood junction before this notorious accident black-spot was reconstructed in 1936.

REAR ENDPAPER
The girls preferred the tranquillity of a Sunday afternoon boating on Connaught Water.

DUSTJACKET
Reproduction of a drawing made by the Royal Engineers in 1867 and now in Redbridge Library. The illustration of the copper medallion struck to commemorate the opening of Epping Forest was the seventeenth in the series of twenty-six such medallions produced by the Corporation of London to record notable civic events between 1831 and 1893. It was designed by Charles Wiener of Brussels and weighs six and a half ounces and is reproduced the same size as the original.
Front cover: Reverse of the medallion, depicting a scene in Epping Forest, with a winding pathway among the trees and herbage. On the left the City of London, with the City arms on a cloak over her right shoulder, standing with a broken fence in her hands, and facing Queen Victoria on the right, seated and crowned and holding a sceptre in her right hand. Legend: "It gives me the greatest satisfaction to dedicate this beautiful forest for the use and enjoyment of my people for all time."
Rear cover: Obverse, bearing a crowned bust of the Queen, to left, in her royal robes, within a band bearing a wreath of roses, shamrocks and thistles, surrounded by a circle of pearls.

FRONTISPIECE
Fairmead Lodge and Oak in 1898, photographed by John Bulk.

PAGES 8-9
The parish church of St Mary and All Saints', Lambourne. The church, which dates back to the twelfth century, has a fifteenth-century bell turret and spire and is classified under the Department of the Environment List of Buildings of Special Architectural or Historical Interest as Grade II*.

DEDICATION
It is sad to record that six people who helped us with their deep fund of local knowledge never lived to see the final work, and Epping Forest has lost much in their passing: Bill Bryant of Chingford, Will Francies of Loughton, Len Heasman of Woodford Bridge, Sidney Hills of Epping, Bill How of Woodford Green and Marjorie Smith of South Woodford. To you this book is dedicated.

Acknowledgements

The source of all extracts included in this anthology is quoted where known. Every effort has been made to trace the copyright holders and the Editor formally apologises for any errors or omissions while gratefully acknowledging permission received from the following authors and publishers: J. M. Dent & Sons Ltd for *Epping Forest* by (Sir) William Addison; the Conservators of Epping Forest for *Wanstead Park* by Sir William Addison and *Epping Forest* by Alfred Qvist; Cassell & Co. Ltd for *The Second World War* by Winston S. Churchill; The Bodley Head for *The Air Defence of Britain 1914-1918* by Christopher Cole and E. F. Cheesman; William Heineman Ltd for *Animals in War* by Jilly Cooper; IPC Magazines Ltd for material from *Country Life* and *London's Epping Forest* by James A. Brimble; Cyril Demarne for extracts from his *London Blitz*; Miss Winifred Eastment for extracts from *Wanstead Through the Ages* and *Wanstead Parish Church*; Georgina Green for extracts from her *Epping Forest Through the Ages*; David & Charles Ltd for *Epping Forest* by Alfred Leutscher; Penguin Books for *The Journal of Beatrix Potter* by Leslie Linder; B. T. Batsford Ltd for *First Through the Clouds* by F. W. Merriam; The Essex Field Club for *Epping Forest — the natural aspect?* by Oliver Rackham, and *Deer of Essex* by D. I. Chapman; Harrap Ltd. for *Forty Years of Murder* by Professor Keith Simpson; and Routledge & Kegan Paul for *Family and Class in a London Suburb* by Peter Willmott and Michael Young. Last but by no means least to Charles W. B. Burdett for *Gossiping Rambles in Suburban Essex, Epping Forest and Beyond*, The 'Round London' Publishing Company.

The foremost reference source for any study of the history of Essex is the *Victoria History of the Counties of England*, produced under the auspices of the Institute of Historical Research at the University of London, published by the Oxford University Press, and extracts have been included from Volumes IV and V from the County of Essex by kind permission of the General Editor, Christopher Elrington.

The Editor is also indebted to F. H. Headley for *Rambles in Epping Forest*; J. Elsden Tuffs for *Essex Coaching Days*; Sir William Addison for *Essex Heyday*; W. G. S. Tonkin for *The Lea Bridge Turnpike and Wragg Stage Coaches*; E. J. Erith for *Woodford Essex 1600-1836*; John Booker for *Essex and the Industrial Revolution*; Marjorie M. Smith for *Chigwell Transactions*; L. Robinson for *Essex House*; Stanley Tiquet for *It Happened Here*; Chris Johnson for *Victorian Buckhurst Hill*; the Claybury Hospital Management Committee; W. J. Maine for *A Glimpse of Old Chingford*; the Reverend R. Marriott for permission to quote from *The Story of Chingford Church* by Canon Douglas Grant; S. Warburton for *Chingford at War*; Bernard Ward for *The Retreats of Epping Forest*; Jack Farmer for *Theydon Bois as I Knew It*; David Phillipson for *About Theydon*; Percy Lindley for *Walks in Epping Forest*; A. F. S. Brown for *Essex at Work 1700-1815*, and the Editor and Staff of *Essex Countryside*.

A large part of this book is taken up with Press reports of the period, and grateful thanks are due to Editors past and present, known and unknown, for their contributions. We are especially indebted to London and Essex Guardian Newspapers Ltd whose newspapers have recorded the local scene since the early days of the *Epping Monthly Record*, and the Editor would like to extend his special thanks to Dennis Wood for his patience over many hours spent researching back issues at his office at Walthamstow.

Many people contributed material, information, photographs, their time or assistance during the research phase, and our appreciation is extended to: Trevor Ambrose; Mr and Mrs E. Anderson; T. W. M. Anderson; D. T. Argent; John Auld; Eric Barham; Jack W. Barnett; Mrs Trudy Barrett; Mrs K. Bayles; Mrs Crissie Bishop; Lyn Brooks; Dr Richard Brown; the late Bill Bryant and his wife Joan; Mrs E. Jacques Burrell; Margaret Campbell; Cliff Canning; Laurence Carr; Steve Casely; H. C. Casserley; Mr and Mrs C. Chambers; Mrs D. A. T. Chapman; Frank Cheesman; Alex Chiswell; Allan Church; Derek Church; Mary Clayton; Chris Cole; Mrs Beatrice Cooke; Bob Cookson; S. R. Cotton; Timothy Couzens; Dick Cramp; Arthur Crow; Bob Cumber; Joan Dalton; Bob Daniels; Margery Day; Arthur C. Dorling; Mrs J. W. Dunster; John Eborn; A. D. Elliott; Jack Farmer; Bob Forbes; Dick Foreman; Mrs Marjorie Foreman; Ray Figg; L. D. W. Francis; K. A. Frost; Ernest Fulcher; Mrs Gwen Gathercole; Tony Giblett; W. T. Glemister; Peter R. H. Gould; Ken Graham; Mrs Cath Gray; Georgina Green; Mrs Joyce M. Green; Mrs J. H. Greenwood; David O. Hale; Elizabeth Hayes; Horace Herbert; Mr D. Hicks; B. Higginson; H. F. Howson; R. W. Jacobs; Chris Johnson; the Reverend Alan Jones; Mrs N. Korte; Peter Lawrence; David Lazell; Alfred Leutscher; Liz Lloyd; Mrs R. Mackintosh; W. J. Maine; Henry Malby; Terence Mallinson; Sister Agnes Mary; John Metson; T. Middlemass; Tony Mills; Robert Mitchell; the late Wilf Nicoll and Mrs R. Nicoll; R. Norman; Andrew O'Brien; Stanley Occomore; A. K. Palmer; Howard Parkinson; Dr Robert Parkinson; Bob Pearson; Ken Penfold; Bryan Perry; Mr and Mrs David Phillipson; Dr J. Pippard; Alfred Qvist; Gerry Randall; Gordon Riley; Leading Fireman Bill Ross; Edwin Rule and his brother, the late Ernie Rule; Mrs C. Rush; Mrs Lilian Scott, MBE; Anthony Sharpe; John Silberrad; Phil Simmonds; W. Simmonds; R. McKensie Smith; Ray Stebbings; Terry Stembridge; Mrs Gladys Street; John Strong; Noel Ta'Bois; Hans Teske; Heather Thirtle; Mrs M. Thorp; PC George Timms; Arthur Tingey; Mrs E. Tomkins; Edward Treby; H. W. Tunstall; Stuart Turner; David Tyler; Bob Walker; Richard Walker; George Warner; Arthur Warren; Jack Warren; Brian and Jean Watson; R. W. Wheelhouse; Dennis Wilde; A. Read Wilkinson; Miss Grace Withers; Martin Wood.

We also wish to thank the local historical and preservation societies for their generous help: John Redfern and Bert Steel at Chigwell; George Rider and the late William G. S. Tonkin at Chingford; Reg Mason at Epping; John Priest at Theydon Bois, Kenneth Bascombe at Waltham Abbey, and the late J. Elsden Tuffs at Wanstead.

Of special assistance over a long period were the staffs of the various official bodies consulted, and we extend our thanks to: Ann Parkinson Omah, Joyce Stevens and Alisdair Wilson of the Epping Forest District Museum; Susan Kenyon, Dorothy Jeffreys and Barbara Pratt and staff at Loughton Library; Howard Bloch of the Local Studies Library, Newham Library Service; Pam Greenwood and Pat Wilkinson of Passmore Edwards Museum; John Hart and Peter Wright of Redbridge Central Library, and Sharon Cross and John Evans and staff of the Vestry House Museum.

We are indebted to the Superintendent of Epping Forest, Mr J. I. Besent, and his staff for their patience in answering many of our queries, and to Mr J. Fisher and staff of the Guildhall Library of the Corporation of the City of London.

Additional help was provided by: Christoper Allen of Aerofilms Ltd; Mr R. Gilbert of Messrs Ambrose, Estate Agents; Denis Bateman of the Air Historical Branch, RAF; the British Film Institute; Defence Audio Visual Agency, Washington; Hazel Kissoon of the Commonwealth War Graves Commission; Robin Ashman of the Eastern Regional Office of the Department of the Environment; Mr. P. Day of the Devonshire Collection at Chatsworth; Liz Willcocks, Paul and Tricia Moxey and staff of the Epping Forest Conservation Centre; Mrs Ruth Benjamin, Town Clerk, and Mr Norman Jackson and Andy Robinson of the Planning Department of Epping Forest District Council; David Corke of the Essex Field Club; Sergeant John Woodgate of the Essex Police; Graham Coombs and Jack Starr of the Gilwell Park Scout Association; the Imperial War Museum; Michael Fitzgerald of the London Transport Museum; Mrs J. Harland of the Lord Chamberlain's Office; Jim Armond of the Metropolitan Water Board; the Metropolitan Police; Mr R. Wright of Northamptonshire County Library; Mr J. West of Ordnance Survey; Messrs Poulton and Sons Ltd; Mr J. R. Palmer of the Planning Department, London Borough of Redbridge, and Councillor P. R. Goody, Chairman of the Conservation Areas Advisory Committee; Mr G. Rayment, Registrar of Births and Deaths at Epping; Flying Officer R. Longhurst of the Royal Air Force Imagery Production Flight, and Jack Eggleston of the RAF Joint School of Photography Museum; Reg Mack at the Royal Air Force Museum, Hendon; Mr A. French of Truman's Brewery; the staff of Waltham Abbey Town Hall; Mrs. E. Tull of the Development Department and Jill Norman of the London Borough of Waltham Forest; not forgetting John Fricker of Chigwell, our pilot for the aerial photography flights.

Finally to George Campbell, our artist, and Peggy Campbell, who has worked unstintingly for the Editor (her son) as researcher and query-shooter during the hectic eighteen-month production phase, and without whose dedicated help his task would have been infinitely greater.   W.G.R.

Preface

In the search for a compact title to adequately describe the scope of this book, many alternatives were considered and discarded before Reg Fowkes and I settled on the present one. 'Epping Forest and its environs' would be more correct, yet even then an arbitrary decision would have to be made on the extent of the area to be covered lest the finished work expand out of all proportion. In the end we decided that Forest Gate to Epping, and Chingford to Chigwell, form the generally accepted boundaries of the Forest area as it stands in 1986. Waltham Abbey, although now physically divorced from the forest proper, also has a special rôle to play being the focus of the ancient history of the area and, more recently, the location of the Epping Forest Museum.

The Epping Forest Act of the nineteenth century has preserved the Forest with few changes until late into the twentieth century, but unfortunately the same cannot be said for bricks and mortar, as the relentless tide of 'progress' has swept aside so many of the historic buildings known to our grandparents. For what? Conservation is a word which has only recently assumed its rightful importance; before then efforts at preservation, the more so in the southern end of the area under the camera's lens, can be summed up as 'too little too late'. Regrettably Wanstead and Woodford cannot be proud of its record in this respect; from Wanstead House, torn apart by selfish creditors a hundred years ago, to the Wilfred Lawson, wantonly destroyed in the 1970s, the developer with no sense of history has been given almost free rein to transform the area out of all recognition.

Thankfully, over the past ten years people have become more historically minded, and the word 'heritage' and the obligation on us all to pass on to our children the best of what has been bequeathed to us has led to some shining examples of preservation *in spite of* the cost, Liddle's post office at South Woodford, Wheelers at Woodford Green and Gwynne House at Woodford Bridge, springing immediately to mind. Let us hope that if anyone picks up this book a hundred years hence, they will not have further cause to reproach our generation.

In no way has it been my intention that this book should be considered a concise history of the Epping Forest area. Any book with a historical content can only tell the story up to a certain point in the calendar, and the rewriting of history loses much of its flavour with the passing of the years. Also every generation puts its own interpretation on events, be they past or present, and all historians, however hard they try to set aside their own thoughts and feelings, are biased to some degree. That is why I have chosen instead to use many contemporary quotations, extracts and accounts to try to portray the more major events *as the people who experienced them saw them at the time*, and the reader must bear in mind that some may not appear one hundred per cent correct in the light of subsequent events. History changes every day and, indeed, it has been a considerable struggle to try to keep up to date just during the gestation period of this book! It is to be hoped that this volume will be looked on more as a 'dip into history' — a glimpse at days gone by, never to return. I have tried to include a wide variety of facets of everyday life, of the incidents and happenings which have shaped and changed the area: both happy and sad; at war and peace; man and his beasts; the rich and the poor. For those who hark back to 'the good old days' the chapter covering the seamier side, which unfortunately is part and parcel of the Forest's history, may be a sobering influence that things today are not nearly as bad as they were!

Photographically recorded history can be loosely dated from the turn of the century. In presenting our 'then and now' comparisons, I was drawn to a little guide by The 'Round London' Publishing Company entitled *Gossiping Rambles in Suburban Essex, Epping Forest and Beyond*. Published in 1908, its author was Charles William B. Burdett, then resident at 6 St Margaret's Road, Wanstead, and he explained in his Foreword that it was the 'fruit of many happy days spent in Epping Forest and its vicinity during the past twenty years'. His guide gives us a marvellous description of the area at the beginning of its transformation from the village era to the urban townscape we know today; the period of change we have set out to illustrate in this publication. This book therefore is introduced by an extract from the guide (in italic type), setting the scene, as it were, as it appeared in the early 1900s. As regards this and all the other contemporary extracts some judicious editing has been necessary although I have largely retained the spelling, capitalisation and punctuation of each individual author and writer. While this has produced some inconsistencies (for example the spelling of Wanstead/Wansted, Beech/Beach and Whipps/Whip's, etc.), I felt that the rigid imposition of an overall 'modern' typographical style would have lost too much of the originality implicit in each extract — in fact, left alone, they give an interesting illustration of the development in reportage style over the last two hundred years.

WINSTON G. RAMSEY

Left: **This bridge over the Roding at Woodford was constructed in 1770-71 by John Phillips and John Heard at a cost of £4,650. 'Woodford Bridge' was a vital link on the road to Norwich and** it served the community well for nearly 200 years. *Above:* **It was unceremoniously swept away in 1962 and the river diverted from beneath it when the motorway was built.**

Introduction

Lying just over the Eastern border of London there is a land of wonder and beauty almost unknown to tens of thousands of the great city's teeming millions. It is a land full of rich historical associations, of topographical charms, of fair and pleasant prospects. Ancient ruins, stately halls, crumbling castles, the hunting grounds of kings are within its limits. Rich and varied landscapes, flowing streams, leafy glades, even a beautiful forest are among its proud possessions. A poetic fancy may discern the ghostly lineaments of many a knight and lady fair; the portly form of Bluff King Hal, or the energetic shade of good Queen Bess, toying with the courtly Leicester, or hear her with language like a trooper expressing in unmistakable terms her opinion of some unfortunate wight who has had the ill luck to offend the royal lady. Not only does this land possess the charms of the past, it teems with interests of the present. It affords the leafy walk, the afternoon ramble, the

animated scene of busy life, or the objects of antiquarian research. The ardent amateur photographer may find ample use for his camera, the cyclist can take run afer run into centres of rest and quietude, the lover of nature may revel in many a sweet beauty spot, the aimless wanderer may saunter to his heart's content. Jaded indeed, and blasé to a degree must be the one who can find no joy or relaxation in 'suburban Essex'.

When the Romans came to England Essex was for the most part covered with forest trees, stretching for many miles over its undulating surface. Its umbrageous character gave plenty of shelter to savage beasts and almost equally savage men; the red deer and the wild boar kept company in its glades with the uncouth peasant and the bloodthirsty Druid, and the forest depths often resounded with the noise of the chase or the groans of the sacrificial victim. After many a bloody battle the Romans succeeded in imposing their ways and works upon the wild inhabitants. Roads were made, morasses drained, spaces cleared, order introduced, civilization maintained. To this day

many old Roman and Saxon names linger in Essex, such as Stratford, Ilford, Romford, and numerous others, including the very name of the county itself; indeed, the philologist finds very much of great interest to him in the vernacular of the people.

As to the many changes which have occurred since those far off days, they belong to the domain of history properly so called; and may not be amplified here. We are only concerned with suburban Essex as it is today, and we hope to interest the reader sufficiently to induce him to explore the region for himself, if he has not already done so; the time thus spent will prove to be filled with pleasure and profit, he will gain a holiday at a small expense, will add to his general stores of knowledge, and we trust learn to love his native land even more deeply than before:

'This precious stone set in a silver sea . . .
This blessed plot, this earth, this realm, this England.'

C. W. B. Burdett, 1908

The most direct approach [to Epping Forest] is by the Great Eastern Railway Company's line, from Liverpool Street or from Fenchurch Street station. The Midland Railway Company also has a service of trains from either Moorgate Street or St Pancras stations via South Tottenham and Wanstead Park. Tram cars also run from Aldgate Church to Bow Bridge where they join the service of the West Ham cars, or the Leyton cars, giving direct access to Epping Forest via the Bakers Arms, or Rising Sun, etc. Of recent years, the Great Eastern Railway Company have also opened a new district by means of a loop line via Stratford, Ilford and Woodford, from Liverpool Street and Fenchurch Street, running through a very pretty stretch of forest scenery.

The large open space on the edge of the southern extremity of Epping Forest is easily reached from either Forest Gate or Manor Park stations on the Great Eastern Railway, or Manor Park on the Midland Railway. It is now under the control of the Epping Forest

The tram terminus, Wanstead Flats, Forest Gate. In 1937-40 the trams were replaced by trolley buses until they in turn were superseded by the motor bus in 1960.

Conservators, and, as a matter of fact, a pedestrian may walk from Rabbits Bridge at Manor Park, across the Flats, through Bush Wood, Snaresbrook, and so on right through the heart of the Forest itself until Epping and the Lower Forest are reached. On the further side of the Flats is the beautiful City of London Cemetery, of very large extent. Immediately adjoining this is Wanstead Park, through which a short cut leads to Cranbrook Park, Ilford. . . . As further indicating the remarkably open nature of this particular part of Essex it may be stated that a reference to a map of the world will shew that a line drawn across Wanstead Flats in a north-easterly direction does not go through any large town or even village of any considerable size, but crosses the German Ocean and the North Sea until the pole is reached; which is the first land in a direct line after leaving the shores of England. This undoubtedly tends to keep the

air of the district fresh and sweet. Electric cars from East Ham cross a corner of the Flats at Manor Park; the West Ham cars run for a short distance on the western edge, being linked up with the Leyton cars at Forest Road. This noble open space is the property of the people for ever, and is the playground of thousands.

A few years ago this great plain was quite bare of trees or shrubs, except for one or two isolated clumps, and was very boggy in patches. But, thanks to the efforts of the Epping Forest Committee, its surface is now broken up by picturesque groups of trees and shrubs, relieving its former monotony. Drainage has brought about a much better state of surface, and good paths cross the Flats in many directions. Near us is a pond known as Angel Pond, the delight of scores of happy youngsters who sail craft upon it or try to capture the furtive minnow. Within a railed

enclosure is the bandstand erected by the Corporation of West Ham whose borough boundaries extend for a short distance in a northerly direction. In the distance, on our left, we may descry the square tower of Leytonstone Church; facing us is a grassy slope, a mile away behind which we see Wanstead Church peeping above the tree tops near Bush Wood; the eye, sweeping round, sees the high trees of Wanstead Park over the tops of the houses of a small new residential estate, while on our extreme right the Flats extend across to Ilford Cemetery and to Manor Park. Their total circumference is between five and six miles, the width varying from about three-quarters of a mile to a mile and a half. Here cricket and football find many ardent supporters according to the different seasons; there are no jealous notices of 'please keep off the grass', or 'trespassers will be prosecuted'; the whole expanse is free to all at all times and seasons; here and there are beautifully verdant plots of grass, the home of certain lawn tennis clubs, where Dan Cupid often shoots a sly arrow at the moment when some fair maiden cries 'Love, fifteen', while her responsive swain doubtless thinks 'Love me' the better phrase.

Top: This postcard originally published in the IXL Series printed in Germany is undated but that *above* was posted to Mr W. A. Higginson of Borough Road College, Spring Grove, Isleworth, on November 23, 1903, thus dating the age of the trees around Angel Pond or Lake within a year or so. *Below:* The open air concerts never got going after World War II and the bandstand was demolished in 1957.

We cross the Flats by way of the Woodford Road, which is a continuation of Woodgrange Road; and on the far side we deflect a little to the left hand, in order to pay a tribute of respect to the memory of Tom Hood, who lived in the house (known as Lake House) which we see embowered amid the trees. It is in a sadly dilapidated condition, built of wood at the back and sides, with a somewhat imposing-looking portico in the Grecian style, with four or five Corinthian pillars supporting a gable. In Hood's day it must have been a very beautiful spot as far as situation went, as it is surrounded by trees, and had a small lake in front; hence the name. The insatiable maw of London has nearly swallowed it, as the land on which it stands, though surrounded by the Flats and Bush Wood, is being sold and a new street made right in the heart of this part of the district. Steps were recently taken to buy Lake House and its grounds for the use of the people but were not successful. Here Tom Wood wrote a novel called 'Tylney Hall', which was well thought of at the time. Much of the description of scenery in it was taken from the surrounding neighbourhood. Originally built as a banqueting hall or summer house in connection with the great Wanstead House near by, Lake House had fallen into sad disrepair even when Hood lived in it. His son says, 'There was a beautiful chimney piece carved in fruit and flowers by Grinling Gibbons, and the ceiling bore traces of painting. Several quaint Watteau-like pictures were pannelled on the walls, but it was all in a shocking state of repair. In the twilight the rats used to come and peep out of the holes in the wainscot. . . . From the windows one could catch lovely glimpses of forest scenery, especially one fine aspen avenue.' Tom Hood is best remembered as the author of the pathetic 'Song of the Shirt'.

Above and bottom: **Woodford Road looking north circa 1900 and in 1985.**

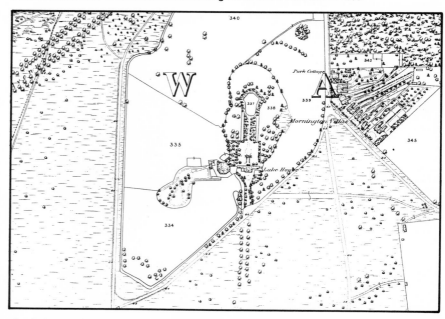

Lake House (on the northern side of Wanstead Flats) as it appeared on the Ordnance Survey of 1869. By this date the lakes had gradually dried up and had been planted with trees.

Above: Lake House pictured in an engraving of September 12, 1792. Also called Russian Farm, it served as an annexe to Wanstead House and contained a large banqueting hall with a fine fireplace by Grinling Gibbons. Thomas Hood, the poet and novelist (1799-1845) lived here from 1832-35 and his son Tom was born in the house on January 19, 1835. Towards the end of the nineteenth century a suggestion was put forward that the house should be purchased and restored for the benefit of the public as one of the amenities of Epping Forest. Nothing came of this idea and for several years it was used as a sports pavilion by several clubs in the neigbourhood. *Right:* This is the rear view pictured in January 1908 shortly before it was demolished. *Below:* The Lake House Estate now stands on the site although a part of the old lake bed now occupied by Aldersbrook Lawn Tennis Club can be seen alongside Blake Hall Road, authorised to be constructed by an Act of Parliament of 1816.

SITE OF THE SWISS CHALET

Leaving this interesting spot, we turn our steps towards the noble avenue of trees known as Evelyn Avenue, Bush Wood. This formed part of the main approach to Wanstead House, and must have been a lovely sight when in all its summer glory in the days of the Earl of Mornington. It is even yet of great beauty, and led by a grand sweeping curve to the front of Wanstead House and beyond. It is situated in what is known as Bush Wood, in

Above: **The Avenue, Bushwood in 1904. Sir Josiah Child, merchant banker and head of the East India Company who purchased the manor of Wanstead in 1667, instructed John Evelyn of Watton to plant avenues of Spanish chestnuts in quincunx formation, radiating from the house. The grandest were the three avenues through what is now Blake Hall Road to Leytonstone.** *Below:* **Our bird's-eye view clearly picks out the remains of The Avenue — three hundred years after it was planted.**

which are many fine oak, elm, and lime trees, intersected by paths in all directions. In addition to the forest trees above mentioned,

there are very many of a smaller kind, such as the hawthorn, growing in thick bushy clumps in great profusion.

After winding our way through Bush Wood we cross the Blake Hall road, which is a continuation of the Woodford Road before mentioned, entering between a pair of iron gates near the house of Sir John Bethell, M.P. This is a public road and leads us near a large pond, almost circular in shape, known as The Basin. This handsome lake stood in front of Wanstead House.

The path we are following leads to Wanstead Church, dedicated to the Virgin Mary. The present structure was built in 1790 on the site of a smaller edifice which formerly stood here.

Not so long since this church stood in the middle of a field, the nearest houses being some distance away. Today it has lost a great deal of that purely rural aspect, and is being surrounded by well-built houses of a good suburban type, isolated or semi-detached. It will always be a favourite residential spot for those who can afford to live here, as no small property is allowed to be built; there are no public-houses and no shops. The church itself is neat and pleasing in appearance, and contains a fine marble monument to the memory of Sir Josiah Child, Bart., whose memory is so bound up with Wanstead Park. He died in 1699.

At the end of the churchyard are the foundations of Wanstead house, all that now remains of what was once one of the finest structures of its kind in England, whose melancholy history forms one of the most striking chapters on record of the instability of riches and grandeur.

Then known as the Bush Gate, these massive stone pillars still stand to mark the main entrance to the Wanstead House estate. They bear the interlaced monogram of Sir Josiah. On the right stands Park House, the residence of Sir John, later Lord Bethell. In 1931 it was converted into flats but damage during the Second World War resulted in its subsequent demolition.

When Sir Josiah Child (above) died in 1699, this monument (right) was erected in the old parish church. It was taken down and re-installed in the new parish church which was built in 1787. Fingers damaged during the move were restored in 1899.

Christmas greetings to Miss V. Hulbert at 64 Capel Road, Forest Gate, in December 1908 — the Perch Pond in Wanstead Park.

Quitting the precincts of the few bricks showing the old foundations of the house we turn to the left, and either follow the legitimate pathway or make a short cut across the gravel pits to the entrance to Wanstead Park, entering by a little wicket-gate. If we take into account the fact that the Park is but six miles or so from Liverpool Street, it is a matter for wonder that so many scenes of lovely wildness can yet be found there. Shady walks and bosky dells abound; there are fine glades and open meadow-like spaces; the River Roding, small but pretty, winds its cheerful way along a pebbly channel towards the ever-waiting Thames, lying just below at the end of Barking Creek; in summer and winter, spring and autumn there is always something to attract the eye and please the fancy. When the foliage on the trees is at its best; when the ponds and lakes are full of the flush of summer life, one might easily imagine oneself to be a hundred miles away from the rush and roar of London. The air is full of sweet scents and sounds; the brilliant dragon fly in his glittering coat of fire with his gauzy wing trembling in the palpitating air; the hum of insect life, the softened sound of the cawing of the rooks, the shrill note of blackbird and thrush fill the heart with delight.

In the spring the glades are carpeted with the lowly bluebell, the honeysuckle hangs in patches here and there, while the stately heron and the ubiquitous crow may be seen busily engaged in household cares upon the swaying tops of the high trees of Lincoln Island.

It must be admitted that the distinctly rural character of the park has been to some extent affected by the rapid and indeed phenomenal growth of the suburbs of East and West Ham during the last ten or fifteen years.

Not so long ago Forest Gate was but a village, East Ham but a hamlet. Today the two join, and there are consequently many thousands of inhabitants in a district formerly but sparsely populated. Electric cars runs across Wanstead Flats in two directions, the one from Canning Town and Plaistow, the other from Beckton and North Woolwich. The former also unite with cars from Leyton and Walthamstow; and the Midland and Tottenham and Forest Gate Railway Company run a service of trains from St Pancras to Wanstead Park station. All these means of access to the park are of quite recent growth.

Ilford has developed to an enormous extent,

Fashions like the foliage change with the years; children's interests it seems do not.

sending out long tentacles of roads and avenues in every direction. A road has been made from the Cranbrook Park, Ilford, leading directly into Wanstead Park, while on the north west side Wanstead itself has begun to develop in a most surprising manner. Fortunately, Bush Wood, the Flats, and Wanstead Park cannot be interfered with by the builder; these fine open spaces are secured to the nation for ever. They are the actual beginnings of Epping Forest, and under the control of the Conservators. The history of Wanstead Park possesses many features of deep interest.

We are now in a scene of sylvan beauty the like of which it would be hard to find anywhere else in England, certainly not within many miles of the metropolis. Epping Forest has many beauty spots, which in their own

way are unrivalled, but Wanstead Park in summer time is so sweet and restful that one's senses are at once charmed and ravished by it. Let us take the path on our left hand. This leads us in a few minutes to the ornamental water in which are situated Lincoln Island, Rook Island, etc., and our ears and eyes are at once provided with sweet sounds and lovely scenes. As we saunter along the pathway we note perchance the stately heron, his long legs outspread behind him as he sails majestically over the tops of the high trees; or we see a shy moorhen silently stealing away to the safe shelter of the opposite bank. A little further along we note the flapping wings of several ducks which are chasing each other into the recesses of Rook Island. Lovely patches of water-lilies adorn the placid surface of the lake, spreading out their broad leaves to the

Sir Josiah was succeeded by his son of the same name who died in 1704 without leaving an heir. His half-brother, Richard Child, succeeded to his title and estates and was created Viscount Castlemaine in 1718 and Earl Tylney in 1733. His son John became the second earl on his father's death in 1750 and the building of the Mount or Grotto alongside the Ornamental Lake is attributed to him.

The interior consisted of artificial stalactites, sea shells, pebbles, coloured glass and ornaments.

rays of the cheerful sunlight which stream through the overhanging branches of willow, beech and chestnut.

On our extreme left is the River Roding, lurking sleepily in little pools and hollows, or hurriedly waking up to the fact that it has yet several miles to go ere it reaches Barking Creek on its way to the waiting Thames; rushing over its pebbly bed now with quite a noisy clatter, as one who should say, 'See what I can do if I really try!'

Bye and bye we cross over a pretty little meadow which is within the park, and strike into a path leading along the opposite side of the lake, until we reach a spot which all visitors stop to admire, a picture of rare beauty. It is The Grotto, now a sad ruin, an empty shell. It never was anything but a pleasure freak, and possesses no historical interest, but its splendid setting across the long stretch of water, embosomed among the trees, its quaint air of antiquity, its ruinous appearance, have made it the subject of countless pictures by pen, pencil, and camera. (Incidentally, it may be mentioned that permission to use a camera in the park must be obtained from the City of London authorities at the Guildhall, E.C.; and the right to fish in the ornamental water can be obtained from 'The Temple' in the park itself. Tickets for fishing are 2s. per day. The lakes other than the ornamental water are free. The extent of the park is about 184 acres, of which about 30 acres are water.)

In its heyday the Wanstead House Grotto, typical of the romanticism of the eighteenth century, was considered even finer than Alexander Pope's masterpiece at Twickenham. However in November 1884 a fire — reputedly caused by a careless workman using hot tar to re-caulk the boat which was stored in the boathouse below — gutted the feature. Modern-day vandals have furthered its destruction.

The garden Temple, on the other hand, still stands intact — almost the same now as in 1900.

The Heronry Lake, Wanstead Park

26. 9. 03. Many thanks for post cards. Last tennis London
tea tomorrow (weather permitting). E. S.

Formerly the Grotto was more picturesque than at present, if we may judge from photographs and written descriptions. It is improbable that any such building would be erected today, as they are no longer in vogue. But the somewhat meretricious style of that

1903 — the year of the Wright brothers' first powered flight . . . the first motor taxis in London . . . and the imposition of a 20 mph speed limit! For Mr W. Higginson of Isleworth, who received this postcard in September, it was an invitation to the last tennis tea of the year. It would appear that the photograph was actually taken beside the Ornamental Water, not the Heronry Pond as indicated. Our picture shows the same view eighty years on.

day, that of Louis XIV, was widely spread, and showed itself in many forms. Everywhere the bizarre was sought; this grotto was merely a symptom of the disease. It has the appearance of an ancient ruin, and was always designed to have that effect, so much so that strangers often think it to be at least several hundred years old. As a matter of fact its age is about 150 years. Its primary cost is said to have been £2,000, the after additions amounting to more than ten times that sum. Its roof was dome shaped, the inside being highly ornamented with pebbles, shells, crystals, and rare and costly stones. A remarkable tessellated pavement made of small deer bones, costing many thousands of pounds was one of its attractions, a fine stained glass window was another. Not less than £30,000 is said to have been spent upon its embellishment. This sum may be grossly exaggerated, but when all deductions have been made it remains a fact that quite a fortune was spent upon it. When Wanstead House was destroyed, the Grotto, either by design or accident, was left untouched. The view from its windows was most enchanting. At this point the lake opens out into lovely bays and little promontories, the banks verdant in summer or majestically stern in winter, with hundreds of trees dipping their long branches into the mirrored surface below, in which aquatic plants and birds abound.

At one time the Roding flowed directly into the lake at this spot, but was afterwards diverted into its present channel. In November 1884 a destructive fire broke out in the Grotto, and the place was wrecked. The domed roof has quite gone, the tessellated pavement is no more, the ancient glories have departed, never to return. A small waterway at the rear gives shelter to the park keepers' punt, but the boats laden with ladies in silks and satins, their bosoms glittering with precious stones are but dim memories of the past.

Having mused and rested long enough, we proceed to further investigation of the park, taking a path which leads through the undergrowth in a diagonal direction, afterwards crossing a fine open glade (of which there are several) until we reach a pretty rustic bridge leading to what is known as the Short Cut from Ilford. An inscription upon it informs us that 'The Short Cut to Wanstead Park was initiated in 1894 by the Ilford Ratepayers Associaton, and opened by W. P. Griggs, Esq., J.P. E.C.C., the donor of this bridge, on 21st June 1902'. This has been a great boon to thousands.

We retrace our steps for a few yards, entering upon a path close at hand, which winds in and out among the undergrowth, until at length we emerge close by the keepers' lodges, and 'The Temple'. Close by is the pretty little pavilion or châlet, used as a refreshment room, and forming quite a pretty picture with its deep setting of green forest trees. There is a fine open meadow-like space here, used for lawn tennis, hockey, cricket, etc., well

patronised by sundry clubs. On the right are also the links of the Wanstead Park Golf Club, but these are not actually in the park itself.

Crossing the open we have now come to the Perch Pond and Bathing lake on our left hand, with the so called Heronry Pond on our right. This latter pond was originally the home of these large birds, but they have not inhabited it for quite a number of years, preferring Lincoln Island in the ornamental

Left: **Close by the Temple once stood the chalet — in use when this picture was taken shortly after the turn of the century as a refreshment pavilion.** *Right:* **All that remains to mark its presence today — it burned down in the late 1920s.**

lake instead. They do not seem to mind the people in the park at all, but are greatly bothered by the thieving rooks, who chase them unmercifully. The Heronry Pond has recently been deepened and much altered in shape (the work of the unemployed, 1906-7) and is again a large sheet of water, but at present somewhat ugly in appearance. Nature is already smoothing away its asperities with her gentle fingers; in a few more years it will look more like her former self.

Another piece of history now no more — the rustic bridge dedicated in June 1902 to the short cut to the Park introduced by the Ilford Ratepayers Association.

Just across the way is Barkingside station, and we are fortunate enough to be in time for a train. We book to Grange Hill passing Fairlop and Hainault stations on our way. The distance is not very great, but the brief rest refreshes us. At one time these names suggested the leafy avenue and the wooded dingle, the sturdy oak and the giant elm, but the glories of Hainault have gone. As the train speeds along we see only fields and hedges of just the ordinary kind to be seen anywhere; here and there a tall tree lifts its head above the hedgerow, but the once beautiful forest of Hainault is now no more. Fairlop Oak is gone, celebrated in many a song and merry jest, and beneath whose welcome shade Queen Bess is said to have rested, and certainly beneath which many a happy group has footed the swift hour away in the jocund dance. Cultivated desolation reigns in the place of the natural wildness that formerly characterised the lovely district. The tale has often been told but never more scathingly than by the late Sir Walter Besant in his charming book 'All in a Garden Fair'. He was a devoted lover of the forest, and knew it intimately well. He describes how the good people of the neighbourhood had taken the eighth commandment out of the decalogue, as being awkward and in the way, 'and had given up their whole leisure to carving bits out of the forest, and adding them to their own gardens, sticking up palings round these bits, here a cantle and there a snippet, here a slab and there a slice; a round corner, and a square corner, a bare piece of turf, or a wooded clump: and all so neighbourly, encouraging each other the while with a "Brother, will this

Grange Hill — then a country station on the Woodford and Ilford branch of the LNER; today a commuter link on the Central Line underground system.

The renowned Fairlop Oak — the venue for the famous, or infamous, Fairlop Fair — was claimed as being over 1,800 years old but was more probably nearer 900. With a girth of 36 feet, by the eighteenth century the trunk was hollow and in about 1800 surgery was attempted by trimming the branches and the application of a patent solution to try to stop any further decay. However in June 1805 a fire caused severe damage and it was finally blown down in February 1820.

The Fairlop Fair had its beginnings in the early 1700s as a private party held annually under the Oak on the first Friday in July by a London engineer, Daniel Day. The eccentric Day travelled to Fairlop with his friends in a boat on wheels and gradually, as the years went by, more and more people joined in the revelry. By the time Day died in 1767 the custom had developed into a huge three-day public orgy at which drink and food were consumed in large quantities. In 1840 missionaries reported the presence of 108 drink stalls and 72 gaming tables with a drunken cast of thousands clogging every road to and from East London, both on foot and with horse-drawn vehicles of every description. With the de-afforestation of Hainault Forest in 1851, the venue switched to the Old Maypole but the attraction began to wane and the tradition lapsed shortly after 1900.

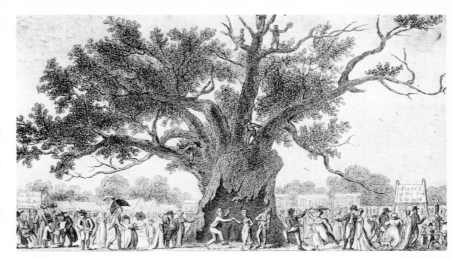

be to your mind?" or "Help yourself neighbour," and "Let me recommend, sir, another slice," or "A piece of the woody part, dear friend." 'And then in his own inimitable style Sir Walter goes on to describe the former glories of the forest, its wild animals, its trees and its flowers. But the filching and appropriation he satirises so keenly reached a climax in 1851, when a firm of agricultural implement makers acting under instructions took down gangs of men, who with steam engines, anchors, chains, and other like instruments of destruction, uprooted in the short space of six weeks about 1,000,000 trees, driving away the deer, and reducing this once lovely spot to the bare monotony of the cultivated field and paddock. Isolated patches of the original forest were left, and one of these still stands to charm and enrapture the lover of nature by its wild untrammelled beauty.

Turning to our right on leaving the station we ascend the hill towards Chigwell Row, via Manor Road. As we proceed we note the fine gardens on our left filled with splendid ash, weeping willow, copper beeches, and many other garden trees, and wonder if their fortunate owners appreciate them as highly as does the passing stranger. Presently on our right we spy a little wicket gate, telling us this is the entrance to the 'Recreation Ground'. Ye gods what a fall is here — from Hainault Forest to a recreation ground! However, it is the spot we want, so we enter. A small sheet of water just inside the gate is called Cox's Pond. We shall do well to remember this landmark, as we may require to find it again. Walking across a small green and noting the high square towers of Chigwell Row church obliquely on the left, we plunge into a path leading into the undergrowth, and follow its devious windings as best we may. To a group of happy lads whom we discover playing in a glade we put the question as to where the path leads which we are following? We soon discover these youngsters are by no means

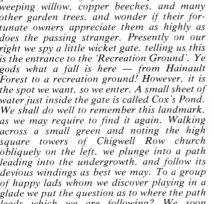

The Lake, Hainault Forest, then and now.

upon their native heath. They are genuine cockney lads, out for a holiday, perhaps making acquaintance with the wild grandeur of nature for the first time. They answer, 'We don't know, sir! we're strangers here, but if yo go a bit furder yer can't get out, 'cept on yer hands an' knees! an' then yer gets inter the cornfields.' We decide not to try that particular mode of exploration, and push on in the orthodox manner. Says Sir Walter Besant, in the book before referred to, 'There are pools in the forest, but most of them are shallow, there are marshy places and quags, but a wet foot is the worst that can happen . . . it is not a very great forest, beside the New Forest or the Forest of Dean it is small, but it is real forest, it is wild. An active lad would soon cover the whole ground.' And wild enough we find it to be. But virtue is its own reward. By pushing on, turning here and twisting there we find ourselves at length in one of the most primitive scenes possible to imagine. The interlacing boughs of horn-beam, beech, and oak, form a canopy overhead, which seems full of 'dim religious light'. Gnarled and twisted trunks meet the eye in every direction, lichen covered, moss encrusted, storm marked trees everywhere. Surely this is the forest primeval! Delicious glimpses of leafy alcoves, fitting home of gnome and faun; thickets through which only a four-footed animal could find a way, soft patches of green flooring carpeted thickly with delicate grasses, other patches still brown with the fallen leaves of yesteryear; Nature in one of her wildest and most unfettered moods. Hark!

Originally part of the Forest of Essex, Barking Abbey's wood of Hainault is first recorded by name in 1221. After the dissolution of the monasteries, the forest passed to the Crown and became known as the King's Woods. In 1793 the Commissioners of Woods, Forests and Land Revenues recommended that Hainault should be de-afforested, mainly on account of damage being caused in the forest parishes by deer. After an abortive attempt to secure permission to clear the forest in 1817, in 1851 Parliament passed an Act to eliminate 4,000 acres of forest land. Two years later gangs of men working day and night with the most modern mechanical appliances of the period grubbed up the forest in six short weeks. Forest Road on the left and Romford Road were laid down on the land thus cleared.

what noise is that? Some tragedy of the woods is taking place near at hand, a shrill, frightened scream from a terrified bird, a fierce rush of wings. Presently we arrive at the scene of the murder, for murder it is. The ground is thickly strewn with the soft white feathers from the breast of a wood pigeon, the branches round about bear traces of the sanguinary struggle which has just taken place, overhead is part of a bleeding wing, fixed high in a forking branch, doubtless dropped there by the marauder; who wings his flight to enjoy his bloodthirsty meal in solitude.

After winding in and out for some further distance we are hopelessly lost. We are in a small open glade, hemmed in on every side with blackberry bushes giving promise of thousands of the luscious berries later on in the season; tall trees overtop the brambles, but there are thickets all around. One of us boldly essays to find a path, and in one minute is completely lost to sight, so thick is the undergrowth. It is literally a question of fighting one's way through, and we realise,

however faintly, what the explorers of an Asiatic jungle have to contend with. At length we find a path and a group of small boys who are exercising forest rights by collecting a sackful of broken sticks. One of these becomes our guide, philosopher and friend, reconducts us to Cox's Pond before mentioned, and is sent away rejoicing with a small douceur. We leave this portion of the forest with regret, but time presses, we must away. The memory of its wild untamed beauty will linger with us for many a day to come; we shall often hear the echoes of the strange weird noises found in its deep recesses. Owing to this very wildness it is hardly the place for a lady, as skirts and dainty head and foot gear would get sorely mangled and torn, but for those who are not afraid of these obstacles it more than repays a visit, as it is doubtful if such a purely wild woodland spot exists anywhere else within the precincts of the whole of Epping Forest. It extends in patches from Chigwell Row to Dog Kennel Hill on the one side; and by Cabin Hill and Crabtree Hill to Lambourne End on the other.

We retrace our steps for a few hundred yards towards Grange Hill, until we reach a road running at right angles to the Manor Road, along which we are walking. This turn will take us to Chigwell, some half mile or so away. This pretty little village has been immortalised by Charles Dickens in 'Barnaby Rudge'. Writing to his friend and biographer John Forster, Dickens says in one of his playful moods: 'Chigwell, my dear fellow, is the greatest place in the world. Name your day for going. Such a delicious old inn opposite the churchyard — such a lovely ride — such beautiful forest scenery — such an out-of-the-way rural place — such a sexton! I say again, name your day.' The 'delicious old inn' is still standing, and has undoubtedly stood there for centuries. May it continue to stand for centuries yet to come! It was a famous place long before Dickens gave it an added lustre. Those who are fond of ancient hostelries should certainly see the King's Head, as the place is rightfully called. Dickens gave it the name of the Maypole in 'Barnaby Rudge'. Its many diamond-paned windows, its deep low doorways, its low ceilings crossed by massive oak beams; its walls lined with oak panels, dark with age but most carefully preserved, are just as they have been for long, long years. In the entrance hall is a mysterious looking deep recess, in which half-a-dozen men might hide. At the back of the house is a pretty little lawn, edged with parterres of gaily coloured flowers. On the left hand is an archway of green, in front of which stands a venerable old apple tree now tottering to its fall, its senile arms outspread as though in feeble expostulation with the decay which is overtaking it. Through the archway is yet another little lawn, trim, clean, circumspect; a long, high, thick hedge divides the two. Here in olden days the monks and abbotts and friars wandered in pensive mood or told their beads, for the ancient hostelry was once a religious house. Here Queen Elizabeth too has wandered, for it has been a royal resting place on more than one occasion.

The chief and particular glory of the house is in its Chester Room, which is on the floor above the present tap rooms. In this celebrated room, Elizabeth herself has slept. It stands today much as it was in her time; except that a dividing screen which formerly secured a kind of privacy for the royal sleeper has been removed. Its low ceiling and deep embrasures breathe the very air of antiquity, its diamond leaded windows give it an imposing, even regal setting. From the long window at the back a pleasing prospect is offered by the two pretty lawns before mentioned; while the front one commands the churchyard to which Dickens refers. . . . So we turn our step towards Chigwell Station.

The most important road in the area in early times was the London-Abridge road — following closely the line of an old Roman road — which also formed the main route to Epping via Theydon Bois. At Chigwell the King's Head, dating from the Stuart period, was an important coaching inn, and from 1713 or earlier it was regularly used for the meetings of the Court of Attachments of Waltham Forest. It became famous for its pigeon pie and was a favourite resort for public authority banquets in the 1850s. The twentieth century has played its part in altering the façade as the beams, said to have come from a ship of the Spanish Armada, were not exposed until 1937. Up until then plaster covered both front and back elevations but this was removed by the owners, Mann, Crossman & Paulin Limited, on the advice of George E. Clay, ARIBA.

If we detrain at Chingford we find ourselves in an open space where formerly stood a triumphal arch commemorating the visit of Her Majesty, the late Queen Victoria, to open and dedicate the forest to the people of England for ever. This was on Saturday, May 6, 1882. The archway stood until August, 1901, when having become very dilapidated it was removed. An event of such national importance as the opening of the Forest is worthy of a more lasting memorial. It is a pity that some steps are not taken to put up a suitable inscription in a conspicuous place. Many an event not nearly so well worth remembrance finds itself recorded in stone or brass. Why not this?

Chingford is possessed of many items of historic interest, but it is not our purpose to detail these on the present occasion, our immediate concern is with the forest itself.

On leaving the station we turn to the right, and after walking a few yards find ourselves upon Chingford Plain. This extensive open space, like a gigantic carpet of greensward, stretches across to the edge of the forest several hundred yards away. In the distance the dark green foliage of thousands of forest trees contrasts very prettily with the lighter green of the grass. The scene is a very animated one. Hundreds of happy children are playing at hide and seek, or riding upon patient donkeys, or chasing each other with gleeful shout in and out of the dells and glades which here abound. Their noise reaches us but

The present Chingford Station was built in 1878, a little to the north of the original one which nevertheless remained in use for the goods depot until 1953. The interior was remodelled shortly after WWII and the line electrified in 1960.

faintly; they are too far away to interfere with the enjoyment of those children of a larger growth who are also on Chingford Plain.

Below: Horse-brakes on Chingford Plain. Now this is Rangers Road but in 1900 it was called The Avenue.

which indeed is roomy enough for all. Here a flourishing golf links is provided for the votaries trove of rare and curious objects. The Corporation of London is responsible for the upkeep of the Lodge, but the exhibits are placed here by the loving care of the Essex Field Club. A portion of the exhibit was removed some few years ago to Stratford, where it may be seen in the Passmore Edwards Museum in the Romford Road, next door to the Technical Institute.

Noticing the hospitable looking Royal Forest Hotel so close at hand we determine to enter, and are met by the genial host himself. Having satisfied our modest wants, we are about to depart when our attention is arrested by a fine piece of illuminated work in the form of an address, which sets forth that the Licensed Victuallers' Association hold Mr John Brill in the highest esteem because of his eminent labours in the cause of charity, the funds of the Institute having benefited by some hundreds of pounds through his exertions. Mr Brill notices that we are looking upon it with a great deal of interest, and presently we note another, and yet a third. 'Why, you have quite a picture gallery of illuminated addresses here!' we exclaim.

'Yes,' says Mr Brill, in a modest way, 'I could have had eight more of them, but those are quite as many as I care to exhibit.'

On leaving the Lodge we make our way to Connaught Waters, which lies due north

When Charles Burdett visited the Royal Forest he could have had no idea of the devastation to befall it in May 1912 when a fire gutted most of the building. When repaired it retained the mock Tudor style.

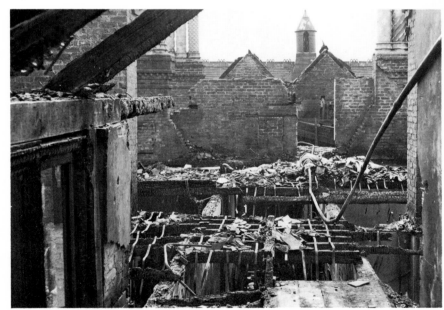

across the plain. Here we spend a pleasant half-hour in wandering around its banks watching the straining efforts of a lover who is taking his lass for a ride, and is evidently more accustomed to driving a quill than pulling an oar. But he appears very happy and his lady-love looks so too — 'All's well that ends well.' Many other equally happy swains are to be seen engaged in like pursuits; their tiny craft gliding in and out between the various wood-crowned islands with which the lake is studded; and we are more than glad that such innocent joys and pleasures are placed within the reach of all who care for them.

On leaving Connaught Waters we enter the plain again and are fortunate to drop across Keeper Butt, who has lived in the Forest thirty-two years. His bright eyes are as keen as ever, his form erect, his step strong and vigorous. To use the old familiar phrase, 'What he doesn't know about Epping Forest isn't worth knowing'; and his vast store of information is always at the disposal of all who care to ask for it. He well remembers the time when Chingford Plain was covered with waving corn, and has many a story to tell of the fight for an open forest.

'Now, Mr Butt, which do you consider the prettiest walk from here to High Beech?'

Above: **Connaught Water circa 1895 and** *below* **sometime after the turn of the century.**

The high summer of 1976 produced drought conditions in many of Britain's lakes. This picture was taken on September 3 producing a rather unusual comparison.

'Ah, that's rather a difficult question to answer! But I can direct you by a way which wants some beating! This is it. Go straight across to the far corner of the plain, take the little path you will find there. This leads you in a few yards into the Green Ride, by the Cuckoo Pits, across Almhouse Plain then across Fairmead Bottom straight into High Beech. You will find this road to be one of the finest in the forest.'

'Many thanks. Your old dog does not go far away from you!'

'Not he, he's as cunning as a fox, and knows the forest as well as I do. And he can smell a poacher a mile off.'

'You get poachers in the forest still?'

'Oh yes, but they're mostly after the rabbits. But my old dog soon roots them out.'

So we pass on our way. Mr Butt's dog being evidently of the opinion that we do not belong to the poaching fraternity, as he simply gives a quiet sniff at our calves and lies down contentedly to await his master's next move.

Presently we enter upon the Green Ride, which truly deserves its name (there are several leafy roads through the forest at various points, all known as Green Rides, which fact tends to confuse the visitor, but as they are several miles apart the confusion is more apparent than real). Lofty trees line the road on either side, and presently taking a sharp curve to the right the road is covered with a rich springy greensward, exceedingly pleasant to walk upon and to contemplate.

There is a solemn beauty in forest pathways which fills the contemplative mind with a species of awe. The overhanging branches of the trees, and the dim mysterious recesses of their inner depths, the peculiar stillness which yet seems audible with other than human voices, the faint nameless odours of new vegetable life thrusting its way through the decaying dust of the centuries, all speak to the soul of man in majestic undertones, like the sound of far away music. Every few yards brings before the charmed vision some new vista of leafy enchantment, scores of birds fly in twittering alarm from the open spaces, or

Keeper Herbert Butt with his dog.

flit silently from tree to tree; the fungi emits curious scents which mingle with those of the fern and the hawthorne, and that sweet, subtle odour of cows, impossible to define, but quite unmistakable. For there are cows here and there in the forest which stray along their own well-defined pathways, following the tinkling bell of their gentle leader, a wise old beast which plods steadily along in search of the sweet herbage or the juicy plant. Yet so great is the extent of the forest that we may wander about in it for days without coming across any of these patient animals. They are not very numerous, and belong to certain people who own farms on the edge of the

forest, or apparently in it, possessions dating from time immemorial.

We cross Almshouse Plain, which is in itself a thing of beauty and affords many a spot suitable for pencil or camera, and take shelter for a few minutes under a spreading tree while a rain-storm passes over head. This lasts only for a very brief time, and when the sun again shines forth the scene looks like fairyland, glittering sprays of diamonds hang pendulous from the edges of every leafy twig and branch, the grass sparkles with irridescent splendour; the air is filled with a new sweetness.

We cross Fairmead Bottom and ascend the hill until we reach the glorious elevation called High Beech, 343 feet above sea level. The name of this locality is variously spelt as High Beech and High Beach, it is also known as the Hill Wood. There is a solemn grandeur beneath the spreading branches of these beech trees which seems to exist nowhere else in the forest. Their massive trunks spread on high, with wide reaches of limb and leaf, resemble the aisles of a cathedral. To the right hand, to the left, all around they stand like silent sentinels guarding the secrets of the wood. The floor is thickly carpeted with the 'mast' which has fallen in thick brown layers, there is little or no grass to be seen; for the beech trees almost always kill the undergrowth, and stand in their own majestic solitudes, their smooth boles reflecting the soft quivering light which beams through the lofty splendour of the overhanging foliage.

One is awed by the silent solemnity of the scene. While we stand with bared heads as though in a cathedral, we hear a sweet sound of bells, subdued, but beautiful. This proceeds from High Beech Church near at hand, reminding us of the flight of time. As the hour rings out from the belfry we take a farewell look around the 'dim cathedral aisles' of the beeches and guided by the sound of the clock make our way to the church, pausing on arrival to admire its pretty little lych gate, its neat 'God's acre,' well cared for and very beautifully situated, in which the quiet dead are sleeping.

From this spot we proceed to the King's Oak and refresh the inner man, afterwards turning to the right over Mount Pleasant until we reach the broad new Epping Road.

Epping Town is very quiet, very clean and very pleasant. To a stranger entering Epping the appearance of the town is exceedingly pretty. The trees in their summer sheen on each side of the broad thoroughfare give it a very pleasing and delightful aspect. Rarely is there to be found such a picture of old world quaintness so charmingly combined with the modern boulevard as in Epping. There are very many beautiful towns in England where the later element is as effectively introduced, but yet wanting in that peculiar charm which surrounds these sixteenth and seventeenth century buildings. They align its broad roadway in such bizarre fashion as to form a very interesting feature.

Many of the old buildings, of the few that yet remain, and which come to mind at this moment, in other less favoured townships, are unsightly curvatures, flush with narrow and sloping streetways, and paved with rough cobbled stones to ease the descent of horse

Another of Miss Hulbert's postcards — this one posted at 5.30 p.m. on July 22, 1910 — shows the London Road at the point where it passes the Bell inn.

traffic. Nothing so objectionable prevails in the Forest capital: wide, open, level roadways — girded with Elizabethan dwellings, which did not always look down upon the well-made roads that exist here to-day. We therefore do not hesitate to make the assertion that in Epping one is confronted with a town as pretty as can be found in a day's march, combined as it is with a host of conveniences that many other are devoid of. What wonder then that the Great Eastern Railway Company should seek to keep it (as far as their railway is concerned) immune from the ruthless spoiler and to preserve its refined and unique position as a residential quarter. We need not further descant upon its healthiness, beyond what is so well-known — that the town stands upon a natural ridge, well-drained, high and bracing, and withal more invigorating than any southern or western sea-side resort. It is

situated, too, within easy walk (at either end of the street) of the upper and lower Forests, which take the name from the township.

Adjoining each end of the High Street are beautiful greenswards — large and verdant open spaces — at all times the happy sporting ground of the villagers and townsfolk. In the 'good old days', upon these commons were wont to be held the fairs and revelry so characteristically a feature of earlier times. Their ever-green and freshening appearance, so soothing always to the eye, gives an additional charm to the handsome thoroughfare that runs almost parallel (the town road being about a mile in length).

The surrounding country is equally attractive, and abounds in fine walks, drives, and charming scenery. Many views of the neighbouring counties can be seen from various eminences in the district, notably

Modernised, extended and developed to cater for the motorised business traveller of the 'eighties — the Bell Motel in 1985.

Middlesex, Hertfordshire, Kent, and Bedfordshire. Such is Epping of today — a beauty spot — and, while so easily accessible, is wonderfully free from the banefulness of many another otherwise prettily favoured sylvan spot, spoiling under the hand of some modern vandal. Its bill of health is one of the very best in the county. Here, also, once flourished many famous scholastic establishments, but why there are no public schools today is a mystery, except perhaps that they abound in the surrounding Forest border towns.

Epping hostelries were as famous at one time as its sausages, and if the town has improved and beautified under modern conditions, the animation, bustle, and activity of its busy streets have to a very large extent departed, leaving behind many reminiscences of its former glory, a fact not without many precedents on the page of history.

Like all the Forest towns, Epping has many times been honoured by visits from royalty. Among others, Charles II stopped here (in 1669) on one of his visits to Newmarket. He was accompanied by Prince Cosmo, Grand Duke of Tuscany. After resting in the quaint old town for a time they proceeded to Newmarket, and we learn the following facts about a little known exploit of his majesty and Rochester, the roué, who after a life of debauchery was converted by Bishop Burnett, and turned as great a saint as he had formerly been a sinner.

Epping town is comparatively of modern origin. The road to London from Harlow passed from Wintry Wood (so-called) across the Forest to Abridge, the present road, being then all but impassable. It was not until the year 1518, that one John Baker, a mercer, of

If Charles Burdett, who wrote his delightful description in the early 1900s, were to come back today, surely the one thing above all else that he would comment on about modern-day Epping would be the absence of trees.

Coincidentally with the taking of our comparison in May 1985, a new High Street tree planting programme had just been set in motion.

Epping, bequeathed a part of the proceeds of his estate at Coopersale (or Theydon Garnon) for the purpose of diverting the high road to Epping street (as we now know it), whereby, the inhabitants benefited very considerably, and caused the neighbourhood to vastly improve. It is interesting to note that Prince Cosmo describes the large open space at

Epping (presumably the Heath) and Bishop's Stortford as belonging to the Bishopric of London.

By way of following up the various changes which have of late years taken place in Epping, and to show its once bustling character, we may mention that no fewer than twelve stage coaches passed through to London daily,

Monday is still market day — only the goods offered for sale have changed.

and eleven from London came to the town. All these coaches had their respective Inns of call, where their horses were kept; and as each coach was driven four-in-hand, the number of horses in Epping could not be less than 200, which must have made a considerable amount of work for many grooms, stable-boys, etc. Add to these coaches the important posting business carried on here, and we may then form some slight idea of the activity and business of Epping fifty or sixty years ago.

But we must return to modern Epping, the town of today. It possesses a fine wide High Street in which a tiny cattle market is held. This is too small to interfere with the traffic of the district to any appreciable extent, and as a cattle sale happens to be in progress as we pass through, we stand for a few minutes to watch the proceedings. A few calves at one end of the little market, a few sheep, a few horses, a few cows, a few buyers, a few spectators, a few drovers, a few dogs; such is Epping Market on the day of our visit. There is an air of well-fed contentment on most of the faces of the farmers present, a kind of 'I am pretty well, thank you, hope you're the same', look on them which does one's heart

good to see. Their rosy cheeks and rotund forms bespeak a well-stocked larder, and a fairly well filled purse, a look of keen and clear intelligence in their eyes gives the lie to the arid jokes about bucolic stupidity; these men are all alive, alert, full of business. 'Now gentlemen', says the auctioneer, whose keen eye flashes over each person present, 'what shall I say for this fine young heifer? Come gentlemen, give me a start! Eleven pounds, eleven pounds only bid, dear me, dear me, eleven five, ten, fifteen, twelve, twelve five, all done, sold! Thank you sir', and so on.

We leave the little group, proceeding on our way through Epping, numerous motor cars passing us, and a dashing coach filled with passengers, the guard loudly tooting his horn as he draws near the town. This coach runs from Woodford and Chingford to Harlow during the summer months, and affords a very pleasant way of seeing the beauties of Epping Forest.

In point of population Epping is not very much larger than it was seventy-five years ago. It then had 2,440 souls, in 1907 its population is about 3,800, which considering its proximity to London, and its road and rail facilities, is very remarkable. It stands high (300 feet above sea level) has many fine walks and open spaces close at hand, has some good shops, and a very pure bracing atmosphere, and no doubt it has a big future before it in the way of suburban development.

Beyond the High Street, along which we proceed for about half-a-mile, Epping Plain is reached. While not so extensive as Chingford Plain, it yet possesses interesting features of its own, and affords a fine playground to the youth of Epping. Its sward is delightfully green and springy, sinking underfoot like an excellent pile carpet. On the day of our visit its surface is gemmed with many a wild flower, odoriferous, and pleasant to the eye. The Lesser Celandine puts forth its little flowerets in abundance. . . . Here and there are the little green squares of turf beloved by golf players, a small white flag denoting the number of the hole. Purple patches of heather beautify the landscape, and as we approach the precincts of the wood, an abundance of young oak trees is seen springing up in all directions; their green and tender foliage making a pleasing contrast with the darker green of the grass. Many clumps of the yellow gorse are noticed, dear to us in childhood's days by the familiar name of 'eggs and bacon', though why so called we never knew, famous in history as the plant à genet from which the house of the Plantagenets derived its name. Blackberry bushes are plentiful, their pretty flowers giving promise of a bounteous yield later on in the year, primroses and wild violets

The trees on Epping Plain, on the other hand, have proliferated considerably since Burdett's day.

have already made the plain beautiful at an earlier period, but their leaves still look fresh and green, forecasting the glories of another springtime to follow.

The Lower Forest which we are now entering on the left hand side is quite detached from the main portion of Epping Forest, is triangular in shape and about 300 acres in extent. It is bounded on the north-western side (the left hand as we enter) by the road leading to Bishop's Stortford and Cambridge, on the west to the east by a road leading to Chelmsford, and from the eastern corner a road runs back into Epping through a section of the Forest, making a well defined triangle. The Great Eastern Railway skirts it on the extreme right hand (or eastern side) running to Ongar.

Near Ongar is Greensted Church, un-doubtedly one of the most remarkable objects of its kind in Essex, if not indeed in all England. It is supposed to have been standing about 1,000 years, and the nave is built en-tirely of wood, smoothed inside with the adze, the marks of the chippings being still plainly visible. It is twenty-nine feet nine inches long, and fourteen feet wide. The wood is oak and chestnut, tongued together in a manner in-dicating Anglo-Saxon workmanship. Local tradition asserts that the body of St Edmund, King and Martyr lay here in 1010. He was put to death by the Danes in 870 AD for refusing to abjure the Christian religion. In 1848 an old tree at Hoxne in Suffolk fell, and an arrow head was found deeply embedded in the trunk. The annular growth of the tree showed that about 1,000 years had passed since the arrow was shot from the bow, and it may have been one of those fired at the martyr king himself.

Born in Nuremburg in 841, Edmund was crowned King of East Anglia on Christmas Day 856. For several years the Danes had been mounting raids on England, com-mitting dreadful ravages, killing whole families and burning all that stood in their path. In 865 a massive Viking invasion army landed in East Anglia with plans to remain for several years, and they first set about conquering Edmund's kingdom and equipping themselves with horses so that they could foray further afield as a mounted force. The Danes met King Edmund's supporters near Thetford where a most bloody battle was fought. Edmund fled to Framlingham pursued by Vikings who besieged the castle and finally captured it only to find that their prize had escaped. Two Danish captains, Hengar and Hubba, with thousands of troops caught up with the King in a wood at Hoxne. They demanded the King's surrender, a share of his kingdom and his agreement to worship the god Odin. Edmund, a devout Christian, refused. 'It is more honourable to defend our liberties with our lives,' retorted Edmund 'than to beg mercy with our tears. Death is preferable to servility.' Thereupon the Danes took him and bound him to a tree where he was whipped and severely beaten. Archers pierced his body with arrows before Hengar finally beheaded him. His death on November 20, 870 aged 29, brought him martyrdom and burial at Bury St Edmunds. Later, when England was again invested by the Danes, the body was removed to London for safe keeping. In 1013 it was taken back but not before it rested for a night in the little wooden chapel at Greensted, then on the main road (Green Street) from London to Suffolk. *Above left:* The original church before extensive restoration in 1848 and *right* on April 18, 1919.

Omnibuses run from Leytonstone Station to the Cuckfield House (fare 1d.) Snaresbrook; also from the Princess Alice at Forest Gate to the Eagle at Snaresbrook (fare 2d.) We stop at the George Hotel, which stands at the corner of George Lane, to inspect a queer inscription carved on a stone let into the wall of the handsome new hotel which has replaced the quaint old hostelry formerly standing here. This inscription has puzzled many, and is of no other value than that possessed by mere eccentricity. It is a kind of 'Bill Stumps, His Mark' stone, and one would like to think it the stone immortalised in 'Pickwick'. It reads as follows, in faint, almost undecipherable characters:-

    In Memory of
    A Cherrey Pey
    As cost ½ a guinney
    ye 17th of July.
    That day we had good cheere
    And hope to have it many a yeare
    1752 Th_____

No doubt it records some piece of hearty fooling, which its perpetrators desired to keep green. They themselves have long since passed away; their joke remains. Peace be to his ashes!

Our way lies to the left, up the High Street, past Hermon Hill, in which is situated a fine pile, the Seamen's Hospital, 'standing in a commanding position', as the auctioneers say, and affording a sheltering roof to many orphan children. Passing under the arch of Snaresbrook railway station, we arrive at the Eagle Hotel and the Eagle Pond, both well-known landmarks. The fine expanse of the pond is rippling and trembling in the sunshine, its glassy surface reflecting the outlines of several stately swans and quacking ducks who are being fed by a delighted little girl in charge of her nursemaid; and in the background we see the towering block of the Infant Orphan Asylum, its many windows lucent with the rays of sunlight pouring upon them.

'A pleasant old village, fast being modernised, 3 miles from Ilford across country.' An 1890s impression. The plaque on The George, out of the picture to the right, still remains.

Our road passes through very pleasant surroundings, under fine trees, and along shady walks, grass bordered and sweet scented. Here and there we note specimens of the old wooden houses at one time so common in Essex, but which are gradually giving place to the more comfortable, if less picturesque structures of brick and stone. Woodford itself is a pleasant open place, with good well paved roads, and wide spaces of greensward, quite free to the public.

On the left is the old parish church, known as St Mary's, formerly St Margaret's. It has a high square brick tower, which is considerably older than the main building. This latter was rebuilt in 1816, and is disfigured by the sort of stucco plastering outside which was so prevalent in the early years of the nineteenth century.

Near the entrance porch is a fine old yew tree, its dull green foliage offering a very marked contrast to that of the oak, elm, and other trees around. It is a famous tree, and said to be one of the largest in the kingdom. Its massive bole is practically destitute of bark, yet its branches are apparently as green and vigorous as ever they were.

Just behind us is a tall monumental shaft, indicating the family vault of the Godfreys. Thomas Godfrey left £400 to the poor of Woodford, provided the trustees, the church-wardens, would keep the tomb in perpetual repair; if not, the money was to revert to the family. In 1772 the vestry declined to do this, so the gift lapsed. Also in the churchyard lie the remains of the Rev. Thomas Maurice, friend of Sir William Jones, the great Oriental scholar. Maurice himself was a man of high attainments in Indian learning, and one of the best authorities of his day on the religion and philosophy of the Hindus. . . .

In the church itself are several monuments of an interesting character, such as John Child, son of Sir Ceasar Child, buried 1701; and special mention may be made of that of the Lee family; whose Sir Henry Lee will be familiar to all readers of Sir Walter Scott's 'Woodstock'. This worthy gentleman left forty shillings a year to the poor of Woodford in 1659, and it would be worth about £40 now,

The 'interesting old pile' of St Mary's, as she was described by Charles Burdett in 1908. The parish church of Woodford underwent major rebuilding in 1816-17 when north and south aisles were added to cope with greatly enlarged congregations of the period. A disastrous fire in 1969 led to another major reconstruction in 1971.

but it appears to belong to the things that have been rather than the things that are.

En passant we may state there are several specimens of stained glass in the windows of the church, effigies of St Peter and St Paul, also Matthew, Mark and John, but curiously enough that of St Luke is absent. However, time flies, and we must away.

Leaving this interesting old pile we pass on to the high road until we reach the Sir Wilfrid Lawson, a well-known temperance house. There are all kinds of refreshment places near here, and those who like alcholic liquids can easily gratify their taste at one of the numerous inns or hotels to be found.

By 1905 the craze of sending and collecting picture postcards reached its peak with some 7,000 million being handled by the world's post offices. Pictorial postcards originated in France and they were in common use years before they were introduced to Britain in the 1890s, German printers and publishers being in the vanguard — the Berlin firm of Deyhle & Wagner producing 200 million in 1905. The pioneer British firms were Blum & Degan of Paternoster Row, London; Messrs Stewart of Edinburgh, and The British Photographic Company of Edinburgh. In 1902 the British Post Office allowed the name and address to be written on one half of one side so that the other half could be used for correspondence and the reverse for a picture. Postcards therefore give us an ideal picture source for turn-of-the-century illustrations, like these of the Wilfrid Lawson Temperance Hotel which was opened in 1883 by Sir Wilfrid who was greatly concerned with the chronic alcoholism of the day — the evils of drink finding echoes in the drug problem of the 1980s.

477 *Wilfrid Lawson Temperance Hotel, Woodford Green*

In more recent times the Wilfrid Lawson was used by the urban district council for offices, becoming a nurses' training centre in 1951 before being demolished in 1974.

Woodford Wells (see also page 69). One problem with taking comparison photographs which show garages is that the picture can become dated within days. When motoring was in its infancy petrol cost 1/2½d per gallon; by 1945 it was still only 1/11d but by 1952 it had risen to 4/3d (about 21p). A price of 176.9p dates this picture to August 1984, yet the true comparison of its cost would be exactly the same in 1945 terms — the new £1 coin being only worth 5p!

We press on cheerfully and note with a smile as we pass Woodford Wells, a piece of unconscious humour in a public house sign. It is the Horse and Well hostelry, but there is no sign of either of these objects. There is, however, a tall post bearing the name of the house in bold letters, and this is surmounted by a fox in full flight! Perhaps the horse has stopped at the well to drink, and the fox is making the best use of the brief delay to get away into the adjacent forest!

Presently we pass the massive red brick pile of the Bancroft School maintained by the Drapers' Company, one of the famous Guilds of the City of London. The fortunate lads who are educated in such pleasant surroundings should value their privileges highly. We sincerely hope they do.

Those who feel that a little refreshment would now be acceptable cannot do better than walk as far as Riggs Retreat, Buckhurst Hill, which is close at hand. Here all kinds of eatables and many kinds of (non-intoxicating) drinkables can be obtained at very moderate charges; with quickness and cleanliness and civility thrown in, and no extra is charged in the bill for these essential, but sometimes forgotten details of a good meal.

Near here the road forks, but both branches lead to Loughton. Here are some very pleasant houses, with much to delight the eye and gladden the heart. The verderer of the forest, Mr E. N. Buxton, has a charming residence here, most pleasantly situated.

Bancroft's, founded in 1727, moved to the Tudor style buildings designed by Sir Arthur Blomfield in 1889. What would Burdett have said of the momentous change in 1977 when lassies were brought in to join 'the fortunate lads'!

On our way to Loughton Station we pass numerous little clearings, where fires are burning in the open forest. Those have been made by the keepers and their assistants, and scores of lads and lasses are at hand filling bags, baskets, sacks and perambulators with pieces of fallen and lopped wood.

Darkness is at hand: the glowing embers shine in the cleared spaces like so many fiery eyes of night; the blue haze curls slowly upward, and floats lazily away among the trees; and we at length reach the welcome railway station, tired, but not weary, for our tired feeling is but the natural outcome of a strenuous day's walking, until at length as Tennyson (himself a dweller at Loughton) says in Locksley Hall:

We at night along the dusky highway near and nearer drawn,

See in heaven the light of London flaming like a dreary dawn.

The Forest

When the Romans came to Britain, they found that much of the country was covered with primeval forest. An ancient map shows East Anglia spread with virgin woods from the Thames to the Wash, from the valley of the Lea to the Essex coast. In fact, so thick was the forest, that it was said that a squirrel freed in the Thames valley could reach the Wash by travelling from tree to tree, without coming to the ground. All this huge forest has gone. The trees have been hewn down, the roots grubbed up, the soil cultivated. Only fragments remain — one of them the few thousand acres of Epping Forest.

Epping Forest, J. A. Brimble, 1970

The Forrest of the lord and King in the county of Essex is included in meeres and bounds from the Bridge of Stratford unto the Bridge of Cattywad [at Manningtree over the River Stour] in length, and in breadth from the Thames unto the King's highway which is called Stanestreet.

Proclamation by King Edward I, 1277

By a charter of King John, dated March 25, in the fifth year of his reign, [1204] and confirmed by Edward IV, all that part of the forest which lay to the north of the road from Stortford through Dunmow to Colchester, was ordered to be disafforested. Its extent was further diminished by a perambulation made in 29 Edward I, in pursuance of the Charta de Foresta; but its boundaries were finally determined by an inquisition and perambulation taken in September, 1640, by a commission under the great seal of England, in pursuance of an Act of Parliament for settling the bounds of the forests in general. The boundaries as thus fixed include the whole of Wanstead, Leyton, Walthamstow, Woodford, Loughton, Chigwell, Lamborne, Stapleford Abbots, Waltham Holy Cross, Epping, and Nazing, and parts of Chingford, Stratford, East and West Ham, Little and Great Ilford, Barking, Dagenham, Theydon Bois, and Navestock. The extent of the forest was estimated at 60,000 acres, of which

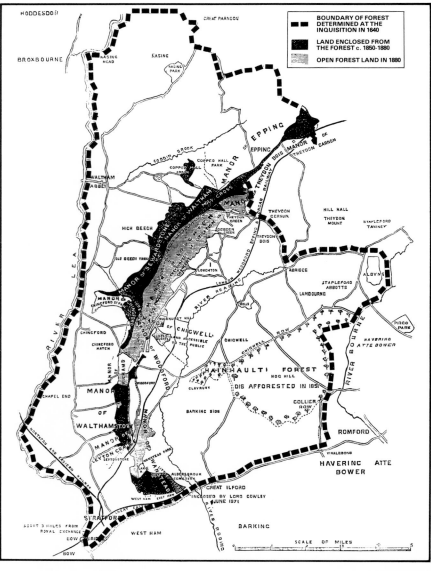

BOUNDARY OF FOREST DETERMINED AT THE INQUISITION IN 1640

LAND ENCLOSED FROM THE FOREST c. 1850-1880

OPEN FOREST LAND IN 1880

48,000 were enclosed and private property, the remaining 12,000 being unenclosed wastes and woods. What is called Henhault, or Hainault Forest is a part of this district.

The ancient bounds of the forest have been a matter of controversy from time to time, but from the days of the Long Parliament down to the year 1851, as stated above, it consisted of two parts — the Forest of Hainault and Epping Forest, the former comprising the high ground lying to the east of the Roding, and north of the high road to Romford, and the latter lying between the Roding and the Lea, and stretching northward from Stratford to Epping. Hainault Forest, in which the Crown had a more clearly-defined interest than in Epping, possessing not only rights of forest, but the soil of several large woods acquired at the dissolution of monasteries, was disafforested by Act of Parliament in 1851, and was subsequently enclosed.

The enormous tract of land which was settled under the statute of Charles I, in 1640, as the limits of Waltham Forest, doubtless included very extensive private estates, subject to rights of forest and chase; the greater part of the residue had been granted or sold by Henry VIII and succeeding sovereigns.

Greater London, Edward Walford, 1883

A very fertile and fruitful soyle; and being full of most pleasant and delightful playnes and lawnes, most useful and commodious for hunting and chasing of the game or red and fallow deer . . . Alwaies and especiallie and above all theire other fforests prized and esteemed by the Kinges Majestie and his noble progenitors the Kinges and Queenes of this Realme of England, as well for his and theire own pleasure, disport, and recreation from those pressing cares for the publique weale and safetie, which are inseparable incident to their kinglie office, as for the interteynment of foreyne Princes and Embassadors, thereby to show unto them the honor and magnificence of the Kinges and Queenes of this Realme.

Sir Robert Heath, 1628

When the Civil War broke out in 1642 most of Essex was so solidly behind Parliament that there was no fighting in the county until 1648 when a royalist force was pursued from Stratford via Romford, Brentwood and Chelmsford to Colchester. Here about 4,000 royalist troops were besieged in the town for 12 weeks, until their serious hardships and the news of Cromwell's success made them surrender. In 1649 King Charles I was beheaded. During the time of the Commonwealth it was suggested that royal hunting

forests were a luxury no longer needed and in 1653 an Act of Parliament was passed to disafforest and sell off the whole of Waltham Forest. However, the matter was put before a commission to decide on the best use of the area and fortunately no action had been taken by the time of the restoration of Charles II in 1660, so the Crown resumed the old rights over what was soon to be called Epping Forest.

Epping Forest through the Ages, Georgina Green, 1982

The management of trees in the middle ages was a long-established, systematic, and conservative art. A normal wood was managed by *coppicing*: the majority of the trees, called the *underwood*, were felled to near ground level every few years and allowed to grow again from the stump or *stool* to yield an indefinite succession of crops of poles, used for fuel and many other purposes. Scattered among the underwood were *timber* trees, usually oaks, allowed to stand for longer periods and then felled to yield structural timber. In wood-pasture, because grazing animals would eat the regrowth of coppice, it was usual instead

to manage trees by *pollarding*, otherwise called *lopping*: they were cut at 6-10ft above ground, leaving a permanent base called a *bolling*, from which successive crops of poles would sprout at a height which cattle and deer could not reach. A rare alternative was *shredding*, cutting the branches off a tree leaving a tuft at the top, in the expectation that they would grow again.

Epping Forest — the natural aspect?
Oliver Rackham, 1978

The Commonwealth put an end to all the gaiety and splendour of the royal forests. Most of the deer disappeared from them, so that they had to be restocked at the Restoration, when we find a number of English noblemen presenting to Charles II three hundred head of deer, which were divided between Windsor, Waltham and Enfield. The Forest's former proud state, however, was never restored. . . .

All the timber cut from the Forest was taken to Barking, where there was a slide into the Creek. From Barking it was transported in rafts to the dockyards at Deptford and Woolwich. . . . No doubt some of this timber found its way to the bakers in what is now the

The Forest provided not only fuel but refuge for those that desired the life of a hermit.

East End of London. Bakers are said to have abounded in this district on account of the great supply of fuel at hand in the Forest. . . . The Forest timber continued to be used for the Royal Navy up to about 1725, by which time all the best tall trees had been cut down.

Epping Forest. William Addison. 1945

Monday being the Assembly Night on Epping Forest, several Gentlemen and Ladies had ordered their Servants to attend with Fire Arms; and some of the Company staying late, the Servants diverted themselves with reconnoitring the Forest and firing their Pistols, &c. But unhappily for a Servant of Capt. Banman's, who met Mrs. Turner, and a Person whom she had hired to conduct her home; and thinking he was one of his Party, bids him stand, and fired his Pistol; upon which the Man immediately shot him, and he now lays at a House on the Forest, with very little Hopes of Recovery. A Magistrate of this City has examined the Servant, and he readily owned that his Folly had brought this Disaster upon him, and hoped the Person would not come to any trouble for what he had done, and that he forgave him heartily.

Press report, 1755

Last Sunday night the high beach tree on Epping Forest, which was a sort of mark to all people who travelled the northern roads, either Enfield or Barnet way, was blown down. This famous tree, which it is supposed has been there upwards of two hundred years, stood in the middle of High Beach Fair, about a quarter of a mile from the King's Oak, and many a lad and lass has danced round it annually.

Press report, 1758

On Thursday a Man well-dressed, booted and spurr'd, with a Watch and Money in his Pockets and two Pistols in the Side of his Great Coat, with out any Wound about him, was found dead on Epping Forest by some Higglers, who carried him to Hale-End to be own'd: A Bay Mare was likewise found grazing about a hundred Yards from him, with a very good Saddle and Bridle, marked on the Seat of the Saddle R.S. There was no Book or Memorandum found in his Pocket, so that it is conjectured he fell off his Horse in an Apoplectick Fit.

Press report, 1760

The following proposal is under consideration; viz. That Epping-Forest be cantoned into enclosures, (and those enclosures planted with oak, the chief bulwark of this nation) for the benefit of fattening lean cattle for the use of his majesty's navy; the expence would be but small, if any; for the underwood and other timber would partly, if not quite, pay the charges; or it might be burned into charcoal for the use of his majesty's powder mills.

Press report, 1761

One day last week a Reverend Clergyman and his lady riding on horseback on Epping-forest, the lady's horse took fright at the sudden sound of a puppet-shew trumpet in Woodford, unseated her, and entangling her cloaths in the pummel of the saddle, ran away with her. She was taken up for dead, and now lays dangerously ill at her house at West-Ham.

Press report, 1765

Yesterday the Body of a Man, in Boots, was found by some Higglers on Epping-Forest, supposed, as no Mark's of Violence appeared, to have fallen from a Horse in an Apoplectick Fit.

Press report, 1768

Wednesday the March at Boxing between the noted Dyer and a Country Gardener, was determined about Four o'Clock in the Afternoon, at a Place called Fairmead Bottom, about two Miles Distance from the Bald-Face Stag, near Epping-Forest. Two to One were laid, on the Parties stripping, on the Gardener, but the Dyer beat him in fifteen Minutes. A considerable Sum was collected for the Conqueror.

Press report, 1769

GREAT PEDESTRIAN PERFORMANCE.— Mr. Yates, a yeoman residing at Mitchen, started at day-break on Monday morning, to do 100 miles in 24 successive hours, which though often attempted, has scarcely ever been performed. The Pedestrian backed himself for 200 guineas, and he had undergone the necessary training for the last two months. He did the match over a 5 mile piece of ground at Martin's Grove, on a part of Epping Forest. He did 95 miles in 20 hours, 44 minutes, and 40 seconds, and was unable again to appear on the ground by a strain in the leg. This astonishing performance caused a re-measurement of the five miles, which turned out to be a full half mile short, which arose from accident, and not design. He did 40 miles in five hours and eleven minutes, and 50 (half the distance) in seven hours and 10 seconds, when he halted, from the heat of the weather, 40 minutes. It was, upon the whole, an astonishing performance, considering the great heat.

Press report, 1817

This fight took place on Wednesday, at Maze Green, on Epping Forest, for twenty sovereigns and a purse. The men had distinguished themselves as rare *glutonists*, in divers battles, and each was prodigal of his qualifications. Harris is the man who was pitted against a good one, in a match made at Epsom races, to find an untried man in the prize ring. Harris was produced, and he finished his adversary in a rare good combat. H. Ford seconded Flowers, and Barney was assisted by Joel Jacobs. Harris was backed at six to four, and a gay fight took place.

Press report, 1823

An inquest was held on Saturday at the Maypole, Chigwell Row, on an infant, named Meadowcroft, who had died on the previous Wednesday, from the bite of an adder while walking in the forest in the care of its fourteen year old sister. The constable was charged to find and destroy the noxious animal.

Kent & Essex Mercury, August 4, 1829

Mr. Montagu Burgoyne presented last Monday a petition to both houses of Parliament for the enclosure of Epping Forest, containing 12,000 acres, of which three thousand belong to the Crown.

The Observer, December 28, 1830

In the parishes of Ilford, East Ham, West Ham, Leyton, and Wansted, on the level part of Epping Forest, a great mart for cattle, brought from Wales, Scotland, and the north of England, is held annually, from the latter end of February till the beginning of May. The business between the dealers is principally transacted at the sign of the Rabbits, on the high road, in Little Ilford.

The History and Topography of the County of Essex, March 1831

ENCLOSURE OF HAINAULT FOREST.— The Commissioners in charge of her Majesty's land revenue are proceeding to enclose the Crown allotment in Hainault Forest, under the provisions of the act of Parliament passed during the last session. The consequence of this enclosure will be the future prohibition of holding the celebrated Fairlop Fair, which, for many years, was held on the first Friday in July, on the portion of the forest now to be enclosed.

Press report, 1853

The proximity of the Forest, and the pretext of procuring firewood by means of the lop-pings of the trees, which the inhabitants claim a right to cut during the winter months, encourage habits of idleness and dislike of settled labour, and in some cases give occasion for poaching, all of which are injurious to the morals of the poor. Enclosures, however, seem to be commencing in the neighbourhood, which will probably check these irregular and, to a certain extent, demoralizing tendencies.

The People's History of Essex, 1861, D. W. Coller

The apathy of the Government on the Epping Forest enclosure question is most provoking to any one who cares one fig for public health and public rights. It is not enough that 3,000 acres should have been filched from our Eastern Airing Ground further down in the forest to make rich men richer, and for the benefit of a few capitalists, but now that a slice is being taken off the most accessible portions of open ground in the neighbourhood, the play-ground of hundreds of children, and the recreation ground of thousands of smoke dried toilers in our own parish. . . . Parliament has passed a resolution declaring that Epping Forest shall be preserved, [yet] eighteen acres of Wanstead Flats were enclosed last week. . . . We are, however, glad to know that the attention we called to this encroachment has not been with-out results. As the Imperial Government will not act the Municipal Government of the City of London has already acted. The Com-missioners of Sewers of the City are copy-holders at Wanstead, and they have given notice requiring the removal of the fences, and will test the matter, if necessary, in a court of law.

The Daily News, June 24, 1871

RABBIT NETTING

Vast numbers of Rabbits are *netted*, for the London Market, in that portion of Epping Forest, known as the Warren, lying near The Roebuck, at Chingford. The mode of Netting Rabbits, *i.e.* taking them in nets, is practically as follows. On the night previous, a line of stakes is driven, usually about 300 yards in length, just facing the rabbit-holes. Next morning when the Rabbits have left their holes to feed, netting is hung upon the stakes, and men and dogs then drive the Rabbits, who, taking towards the burrows, are caught in the netting, and thus easily captured. In this way, it is not uncommon to net twelve dozen Rabbits as one morning's work.

Press report, October 9, 1849

'The new reservoir in one of the most romantic and picturesque spots on Epping Forest.' From an 1880s vintage advertisement. Staples Pond was drained in the 1930s.

The excitement prevailing in the Eastern districts of London at the prospect of losing a considerable portion [of the forest] led to a large public meeting being held on the subject on Saturday afternoon and later in the day to the forceable removal of the obnoxious fences. It was originally intended that the meeting should be held on Wanstead Flats, but on account of the review there held of the Essex Volunteers the venue was transferred to the grounds of West Ham Hall. Notice of the adjournment of the meeting was given, and with it appeals were made by very extensive circulated hand-bills to the public to refrain from any act of violence, which it was pointed out would be calculated to injure rather than promote the good cause which the people had in view. The crowd, however, who assembled at West Ham did so with a foregone conclusion to meet at Wanstead, and consequently, when Mr. C. Wingfield Baker, M.P. for South Essex, rose to speak, he was greeted with vehement cries of 'The Flats! The Flats!' several times repeated. Therefore, Dr. Alexander moved that they should adjourn to the place desired. A formal putting of the motion was hardly necessary; it was put, however, and carried unanimously. Instantly the adjournment was put into practice. The vans containing the speakers were seized before and behind, and dragged upwards of a mile over the rough and dusty roads by hundreds of men in turns, accompanied by a running crowd of some thousands more, and attended, it may be said, by considerable bodies of mounted and foot police, who regarded the transaction apparently with the utmost composure. . . . Arrived at the Flats, letters were read by the hon. sec. from Mr. Arkroyd, M.P., Mr. Baines, M.P., Mr. J. Locke, M.P., Mr. Edward North Buxton, and Alderman Lawrence, expressive of sympathy with the object of the meeting, and regret at their inability to be present; after which Sir Antonio Brady, J.P., F.G.S., having taken the chair, addressed the meeting. In the course of his remarks, the Chairman observed that the East Londoners could not have paid him a greater compliment than they had done in inviting him to take the chair. He trusted that nothing illegal would be done, because that would be merely playing into the hands of the 'enemy.'

Mr. C. W. Tanner moved the first resolution, which was to the effect 'That the meeting, seeing with deep regret the constant illegal enclosures which had taken place in Epping Forest, in consequence of the neglect of the Government to enforce the forestal rights of the Crown, resolves that an address be drawn up, entreating her Majesty, as their faithful guardian and trustee of the rights and liberties of her faithful subjects, to instruct her Ministers to take such immediate steps for the enforcement of those forestal rights as may seem to her fit, in order to stop the encroachments on the forests, and restore to her subjects the free use of and access to lands which have been their right and privilege from time immemorial.' In the course of his speech Mr. Tanner remarked that five years ago he had ventured to pull down a fence similar to that which had then roused their just indignation. He also quoted, amidst much amusement, the following lines:

'It is very wrong in man or woman
To steal a goose from off the common;
But what can be that man's excuse
That steals the common from the goose?'

A cordial vote of thanks to the Chairman terminated this part of the proceedings, and then the bulk of those present went to witness the Review on the Flats, which was at that time in progress.

The Review being over, the different corps quickly marched off the ground with bands playing, large numbers of people following; and as everything appeared to be in order, the police, who had by this time been on duty for

several hours, were withdrawn, the mounted force being the last to leave. This quiet state of things was not, however, long to continue; there was still a large number of people in the vicinity of Lord Cowley's enclosure, and from what shortly occurred it may be supposed that some of them, at any rate, had formed the intention of pulling down the fence. Be this as it may, about 9 o'clock an incident occurred, which entirely changed the aspect of affairs, and ended in the total destruction of the fence around the enclosure, close to the Foresters' Arms, and near where the meeting had been held. A man, who had seated himself on a rail of the fence, was asked by an acquaintance to get down and go home. Refusing to do so, his friend pulled at the rail, with the ostensible object of dislodging him, and that part of the fence fell to the ground. Immediately hundreds of hands were applied to the rails, and for twenty minutes the crowd tugged and pulled till the whole of the fence, forming three sides of the enclosure which is completed by the railings of Forest Lane, was down. In this way some hundreds of yards of fence were destroyed, and the whole of the ground opened; for attracted by the noise created in breaking down the rails, and shattering the woodwork into pieces, large numbers of people came from all parts of the Flats, and

out of the adjacent public houses, and seeing what was going on lent their assistance. Shortly afterwards a body of foot police arrived on the spot, receiving as they did so a large amount of badinage from the people, who jokingly recommended them to carefully guard the fragments. For some time nothing further was done, but presently a body of men essayed to take down the few remaining posts at the western end of the plot of ground; on seeing which the mounted police rode smartly to the spot and charged the people. In doing so they captured one man, and the crowd seeing this, determined to rescue him. An attempt was accordingly made; but the horsemen, riding at the crowd, succeeded in dispersing it. This *melee* occurred in Forest Lane; and the police were able, by forming a line across the narrow road and riding towards the people, to hold them in check for some minutes, during which time he was hurried off towards Ilford. In this way one man was captured, and a boy was afterwards taken prisoner, but in each case not without great difficulty. There being nothing now left to attract the crowd, it gradually melted away, and in a short time the Flats were clear of people.

The Woodford Times, July 15, 1871

'According to ancient custom', stated the caption to this 1859 woodcut depicting the beginning of the annual lop.

Alfred Willingale was imprisoned in 1866 for lopping wood from Forest land enclosed by the rector of Loughton, John Maitland.

By the mid-1850s, one William Whitaker Maitland of Loughton Hall held the manorial rights. Those rights did not, however, extend to the forest land around the village. The forest had remained Crown land, largely because of the interest of Queen Elizabeth I and other monarchs in the pastime of deer hunting.

As the kings and queens of England enjoyed the right to hunt the forest for venison, so the villagers of Loughton valued their privilege of lopping and gathering wood for their fires. Lopping rights were said to have been granted in the 16th century by Royal Charter, but they did not give the villagers carte-blanche to take just what they liked, when they liked. There were rules to be followed.

Lopping was permitted only from November until April and just one man per household was allowed to participate. Only boughs more than seven feet from the ground were to be lopped and the wood was to be carried away by the lopper himself on a single sled pulled by a maximum of two horses. Use of the wood was restricted to local domestic fires; tradesmen such as bakers or potters were not entitled to use it commercially.

Despite occasional prosecutions for infringement of lopping rights procedures, which usually resulted in fines, the system worked tolerably well. The start of the lopping season which from 1753 onwards occurred at midnight on November 11, was something of an occasion. Some ale would be consumed during the evening; the fortified loppers would then advance together into the forest to lop boughs with their long-handled axes. Punctuality was regarded as essential, for it was believed that failure to exercise the lopping rights at the very start of the season would result in their forfeiture.

In 1857, however, the Loughton commoners' lopping rights were threatened by a new development. William Whitaker Maitland was offered, by Commissioners acting for the Crown, the rights of Forest, Free Chase and Free Warren over 1,377 acres of the forest. By June 1860, those rights had been conveyed to him for a consideration in excess of £5,000.

Maitland died the following year and was succeeded by his grandson John, the rector of Loughton, who soon afterwards attempted to exclude villagers from the forest land where they had long been accustomed to grazing their livestock and lopping wood. Some villagers were tempted by inducements to give up their rights.

John Whitaker Maitland then proceeded to enclose about 1,100 acres of forest land, while similar actions were being taken by other landowners around the forest. At one stage it was estimated that all but a thousand of the forest's 6,000 acres had been enclosed. This situation disturbed not only the local residents but also the membership of the Commons Preservation Society, the body which had saved Wimbledon Common for the public.

A senior member of the Willingale family, who had lopped in Epping Forest for generations, was prosecuted by Maitland for injuring trees. Charges against the man, Thomas Willingale, were eventually dismissed, but the complicated legal situation remained, with many villagers convinced of their right to continue to cut and gather wood.

In March 1866, Thomas Willingale's son Samuel, along with cousins Alfred Willingale and William Higgins, were caught lopping and taking wood from the enclosed forest land. They were prosecuted by Maitland and fined half-a-crown with 11s costs. Having declined to pay, they spent seven days in Little Ilford jail.

David Tyler, Essex Countryside, March 1984

England changed from the Julian to Gregorian calendar in September 1752, and with the omission of eleven days (September 3 being reckoned as the 14th), the first day of lopping which had traditionally been All Saints' Day (November 1) became instead November 12. People believed that if they did not commence pollarding at midnight on the 11th they would forfeit their rights, and their source of free fuel for the winter would be lost. Lopping traditionally ended on St George's Day — April 23.

Tom Willingale originally lived in a cottage down the path to the right of the Foresters Arms on Baldwins Hill.

Epping Forest will be saved to the people, and, what is more, the thousands of acres filched away from them may be recovered, if the East-end stands to its guns, it seems monstrous that more than four thousand acres of that good and valuable land, the natural 'back garden' of the poorest parts of London, have been acquired by rich men at the average cost of £5 per acre. There are two plain duties before those who care for the health and recreation of the poor of north-east London. The first is, to hold on tenaciously by every rood of ground yet remaining; the next is, to work steadily and sternly towards an investigation of the legal title of every opulent squatter on the Forest purlieus. We are glad to see that Shoreditch, Hackney, and the neighbouring parishes keep alive this momentous question, and that sinews of war as well as speeches are forthcoming. The City Corporation has entered the field with its ancient high spirit, and the old Verderers' Court is revived with the best results. The secret embezzlement of the little land still left for popular uses seems to be effectually checkmated; and we trust that the Epping Forest movement will save many another threatened piece of waste.

Daily Telegraph, October 27, 1871

The *Daily News* informs us, in a short leader, of further legal steps taken by the Corporation of the City of London for the protection of the public rights in Epping Forest. It says:-

The Commissioners of Sewers for the City are again to be congratulated on their prompt action regarding the enclosure of Epping Forest. Among the thirteen hundred acres which have been enclosed by the lord of the manor of Loughton, the Rev. J. W. Maitland, is a piece of land near the road which leads from the village of Loughton to High Beech. On this space, as was discovered no later than

This is the spot where his home stood at the end of Wroths Path. After he was evicted he moved to Lower Road, Goldings Hill.

the 12th October last, cottages are in course of erection. Action was taken at once. The City Solicitor wrote on the Saturday to Mr. John Mills, a solicitor in the City, who was responsible with some builders for the encroachment, that, inasmuch as the land on which he was building was part of that over which the Corporation of London claims common rights, unless an assurance was received during the following Monday that the work was discontinued, an injunction would be applied for.

East London Observer, October 28, 1871

The Forest question appears likely to crop up in another phase. We notice by a Stratford contemporary that a 'party of school children excursionizing in Bushwood, under the superintendence of a Rev. Mr. Barter, were recently ordered to leave the ground, or pay a fee of one pound to a person who represented that he held a lease at 30s. a year per acre under the Lord of the Manor. By a peculiar coincidence, Sir Antonio Brady, verderer, and one or two other members of the Committee of the Forest Fund paid a visit to the party, bearing bouquets for the lady teachers and congratulations for the clergyman and school officials. Of course advice was immediately sought from the verderer in reference to the above circumstance, and he assured them they had a perfect right to use this part freely, and hoped that the time was not distant when the whole of the unsightly fences would be legally removed.

Hackney Express. July 26, 1873

Tom died in 1870 — just a year before the whole question of the Epping Forest enclosures was resolved by Act of Parliament — an event he campaigned for but failed to see fulfilled. Today his grave lies unmarked and forgotten in St John's churchyard.

EPPING FOREST
GRAND CELEBRATION OF VICTORY

Such a scene as that which took place in the beautiful woodlands of Epping Forest on Thursday, has perhaps never before been witnessed in its domains — certainly not since bluff King Hal or Queen Bess with royal retinue chased the deer, and made the Forest ring with hunter's horn and tramp of steeds. It is true the Lord Mayor's visit was made during a ceaseless downpour of October rain, but the finely conceived arrangements were so complete, and all contingencies so well provided for, that the most adverse elements could not effectually detract from the imposing character of the gathering. The object of course was the celebration of the victory won by the admirable public spirit of the Corporation in the now famous Chancery Suit, whereby the spoliation of the Forest was stayed, and some two or three thousand acres illegally enclosed thrown back into the open. For four years the suit was pending, and during that time the City authorities spared neither labour nor expense in bringing the matter to a successful issue, and the result has proved one of the grandest triumphs in the annals of the City of London.

The company invited, numbering about 600, assembled at Liverpool-street shortly after eleven o'clock, whence they were conveyed by special trains to Snaresbrook. Here there were some 160 carriages in waiting, all closed, and well equipped. The process of embarkation having been gone through, the vehicles filed off, preceded by mounted police, the Sheriffs, Aldermen, and Lord Mayor bringing up the rear. The procession extended for upwards of a mile and a large number of spectators lined portions of the route; the youths at the Merchant Seamen's Orphan Asylum forming an especial feature. At intervals, too, the bands of the various City Volunteer Regiments were stationed, and played selections of music as the procession passed. Patches of unenclosed forest were seen on either side of the road on the way to Woodford, but then to Buckhurst Hill and Loughton the Forest is almost entirely enclosed, with snug villas and large mansions standing 'in their own grounds'. Beyond Loughton ascending Goldings Hill, the Forest assumed a more open appearance, hundreds of acres lying beneath the view to the right, whilst to the left the clustering tops of the splendid trees in Great Monk Wood marked the locality of one of the finest vistas of the Forest. Still on, the way lay through fine stretches of woodland to the Wake Arms, and here the immense cavalcade turned sharp round in the direction of High Beech, past the Robin Hood, and skirting the magnificent Beech Wood, filed into the grounds of Fairmead Lodge, which was reached shortly before three o'clock.

Hackney Express and Shoreditch Observer,
October 16, 1875

One of the foremost, yet unsung, champions of the 'Forest for the People' movement was the Hackney Express and Shoreditch Observer. Leader after leader sought to promote the cause of East Londoners who used the tranquil glades as a release from the squalor of their surroundings, and the open commons as their playground. The view from Goldings Hill was mentioned in the October 16, 1875 issue — a view which has changed little in over a hundred years.

'I' THE FOREST!'

A favourite heading, some will say, this of ours. Well, it is. For ten, or more, long years have we made this and 'the Forest for the People,' a kind of slogan, first, in drawing attention to the beauties of the sylvan glades to be seen, the charming strolls to be had, and the lovely natural objects to be met with — and yet so little known to the universal public — in Epping Forest; secondly, in publishing the encroachments on its acres which we noticed from time to time, and pillorying the encroachers; and, thirdly, in ventilating the schemes whereby the 'stopper' might be put upon the plunderers, that the East-enders, who looked upon the Forest as their unalienated 'Open Space,' might not be excluded its enjoyment, or looked upon as trespassers.

It is now a matter of history, how the agitation thus commenced with us, and followed up by the rest of the Local Press, and how the necessity that something should be done to arrest a mighty wrong, to which a governmental department was lending itself by selling the birthright of the Crown for less than a mess of pottage, brought into existence the energetic body of gentlemen who banded themselves 'to do or die' for the people under the title of 'The Forest Fund Committee;' and it is, further, well known how their intervention brought other powers to the fore — Parliamentary interference — City interposition, &c., culminating in a legal decision that ensured the preservation to the people of 5,000 acres remaining intact. This glorious consummation was undoubtedly due to the power and prestige of the Corporation of the City of London, which stepped in with its money and its influence — and this from no sordid motive to come in for a share of plunder as 'big' people do sometimes, but the purest one, namely, that to preserve at any cost, and by all means in their power, Epping Forest for the purposes of recreation and enjoyment for the humble toilers of London.

The Hackney and Kingsland Gazette,
October 20, 1875

BANK HOLIDAY AT THE FOREST

The question, 'where shall we go?' found a very practical answer in every direction on Monday morning last. All the outlets of this great metropolis poured forth immense streams of excursionists, — by road, and rail, and water. But of all the journeys from this district, perhaps there was none so favoured as those to our glorious old Forest. The lines to Loughton and Chingford were positively choked, and every train carried an immense freight far in excess of the stipulated accommodation. Let us, courteous reader, take the Chingford line, with Hackney Downs as our starting point. We obtain our tickets with difficulty, and are taken a little aback to find the platform literally crammed with waiting passengers. Comparatively few leave by the 'Enfield' or 'Rye House' trains, but when the 'Walthamstow and Chingford' is announced

With the advent of the railway and its extension to the borders of the Forest (Loughton 1856, Epping 1865 and Chingford in 1873), the area was opened up to the poorer visitor without any form of personal transport. People came out to the Forest in droves, especially on the new 'Bank Holidays' after they were introduced under Sir John Lubbock's Act of 1871. The 'retreats', erected initially by John Riggs but soon copied by other enterprising businessmen, catered for teas and other non-alcoholic refreshments, and soon became part and parcel of the Forest scene.

there is a good deal of 'movement,' and blank dismay when it is found that every seat is occupied, with very little standing room to spare. Under these circumstances we will not measure our strength with the 'weaker vessels' or the troops of juveniles, so we stand aside till the process of 'packing' is completed, and the train moves off. In the course of half an hour, another Chingford train arrives, under exactly similar conditions. We determine to wait a further half hour, and to relieve the tedium, we make a mental note or two, finding abundant materials amongst the great variety of human nature by which we are surrounded. But this occupation becomes a little tiring. We resolve therefore we *must* depart by the next train, which is approaching the platform. Full — full — full. Yes, but the guard's van is fortunately empty. What a boon! We enter at the head of a 'rush,' and make for the window to catch the air. In come trooping a great variety of human nature. We have the selfish benedict, who is rather disposed to chuckle at his foresight in having left the 'wife and chicks' at home. We have also the good natured fellow with two babies and a perambulator, with wife also, and quite a following of the fairer sex. Then there is the 'spooney' swain, excessively solicitous for the comfort of the loved one, whilst Darby and Joan take everything very quietly, so long as *he* can blow a cloud and *she* can save the prevender from being mutilated in the crush. When the 'van' is packed about as close as herrings in a barrel the whistle sounds, and then 'to the woods away.' But it gets tiresome. The air is very 'close,' and the stoppage and starting of the train produce an oscillating motion, rendering it somewhat difficult for us to 'keep our pins.'

We come at last to Wood-street, and here a large number of passengers alight, so that we will leave the 'break,' and try to find a more comfortable location. After this we arrive at our destination, where we meet a large number of visitors, some making for the

The Chingford Riggs' Retreat was actually in Woodford in Brook Road. It burned down in the mid-1930s and the site is now a caravan park.

Forest in this direction; others in that; whilst a good many pitch on the first green and shady spot, and make a terrible onslaught upon their stores of sustentation. We too 'refresh,' and strike the Forest to the right of Chingford village. The footpath takes us up hills overlooking pleasant landscapes and through fields of smiling corn all ready for the sickle. Presently we strike into the grateful shades of Hawk Wood, beneath which we ramble, and cast kindly glances at the merry little family picnics which are hidden here and there in quiet corners. But we wander further afield, and find fewer and still fewer of the many

thousands who have left the great hive for the Forest woodlands. Beneath this spreading oak we rest, and under the soothing influences all around us we converse on such topics as naturally suggest themselves. After awhile we proceed on our rambles, and passing Sewardstone Bury plunge into the depths of the Forest, where presently we are shut out from every human sound. Here the botanist and the entomologist may luxuriate; many of these spots are seldom visited; nature therefore flourishes, and invites the investigations of the curious. But we do not stay to botanize. Pushing on we reach the open

Butler's Retreat, on the other hand, can still be seen. Opened in 1891 in a barn previously used as a shelter in bad weather, it remains open for business in summer months although the licence was given up by the Butler family in 1971.

The Jubilee Retreat in Bury Road — named after Queen Victoria's Golden Jubilee in 1887 — had a colourful history. In the First World War it was a billet for Canadian airmen stationed at Chingford and in the late '20s was in use as a riding stable. The retreat was requisitioned by the government in 1940 as a centre for French refugees and was visited by Charles de Gaulle, and from 1941 was used by the Ministry of Aircraft Production. After the war the premises was converted into flats for the accommodation of Forest staff, but of the original pavilion today there is no trace.

near Fairmead Lodge, where there are several quiet parties, and where the whole scene is one of great natural beauty. In the woods at the back of the Lodge, where we approach one of the high roads through the Forest, we find the woodlands skirted by vehicles of every description. Landaus, phaetons, waggonettes, brakes, carts, and vans of all kinds have been pressed into the service of the excursionists, who are reposing in family groups, or rambling in the Forest, or gathering the dry twigs with a view to boiling the kettle. In some places a fair white cloth is spread over the grass, and very tempting look the edibles and drinkables displayed. We are getting a little tired perhaps, and there is many a generous heart there would gladly refresh the passing rambler, but the conventionalities of life intervene, and we are rather glad to hear a loud buzz beyond the trees on the further side, for that denotes a spot where the hungry and thirsty may be entertained. But we do not like it. There is a great crowd, with a sprinkling of the rougher element. John Barleycorn, too has been at work, and the effects are painfully visible. Howling barbarians torture donkies, and blasphemous Bohemians are endeavouring to persuade or cajole the unwary. These are the darker shadows of the scene, and here for the first time in our rambles we find a detachment of the 'Force.' We recognise the necessity for their presence, and we do not linger. Into the Forest again, and beneath the overhanging branches we rest us for awhile. We listen to the twitter of the birds; we gaze up into the azure sky; we note the gentle breeze playing

PHONE SILVERTHORN 1052

JUBILEE RETREAT CHINGFORD, ESSEX

ACCOMMODATION: 3,000 UNDER COVER

SCHOOL EXCURSIONS & SUMMER OUTINGS

with the glorious foliage. A sense of calm, and peace, and intense enjoyment, steals over us, and we yield ourselves to its kindly influence. Still, we have miles before us, and it is therefore necessary to break the spell. A short walk brings us into the 'thicks' of Fairmead Bottom. But thick as it is, ever and anon the merry laugh of the children shows that we are again in the region of family picnics. In this spot, where we wonder how a road could be found for the passage of the party, there are

all the concomitants of the evening meal. A blazing fire is crackling beneath the tea kettle. Cups and saucers are spread, and wholesome looking loaves, and cakes, and biscuits are lying about, so that we feel almost as though we were intruding as we come upon the group. But we pursue our way steadily until, emerging from the 'thicks,' we hear the sound of many visitors gathered amidst the glades of Queen Elizabeth. Hundreds and hundreds of persons are scattered about, whilst there is a

Fairmead Lodge itself (see also frontispiece) was one of the first catering establishments in the Forest area, being open as early as 1853 as both a guest house and for Sunday School parties. In fact it was the location chosen to entertain several hundred members of the Common Council of the Corporation of the City of London and their guests when they made their formal inspection of the Forest in October 1875. After the Conservators took over responsibility for the preservation of the Forest the historic house, which had once been the home of poet William Sotheby, was demolished around 1913, the rubble carted away and the site levelled. Today the driveway can still be discerned in Fairmead Bottom.

John Riggs opened his second retreat, a magnificent building able to cater for over 3,000 children at one sitting, at High Beach in 1881. It was run by his son William until the Great War when it was taken over by the War Office to be used as a training centre for the Army. However it had been relinquished by 1916 when a fire began in Sawyers Retreat next door which rapidly spread to both buildings. Despite the gallant efforts of two fire brigades, being mainly of wood construction within two hours both buildings were just smoking ruins.

perfect saturnalia of forestal 'amusements.' Cocoa-nuts may be 'shied' at, bowled at, pitched at, or Aunt Sally may be mutilated; and the chorus is varied by the shrill tones of a woman who calls out for a whole battalion of 'bottle-breakers.' There are also many other sights and sounds, 'too numerous to mention;' but we ascend the old oaken staircase of the Lodge, obtain a cup of tea, and then quietly saunter across the fields to the station. Here we are again closely packed for the return journey, and saving that there is a 'row' or two at the intermediate stations, where a rush is made for carriages already over-full, home is reached without any mishap. Here of course we will leave the reader. He will doubtless feel a little bit weary, but that is no more than may

When William Riggs returned from the Front, he purchased the Roserville Retreat a short distance away which he managed from 1919 until 1926. The property passed through several hands until sold with the adjoining house to Mr Fred Speakman in 1959. He made the old restaurant hall available as a classroom for schoolchildren visiting the Forest on nature studies until he retired in 1971. It still stands today.

The building was located on Wellington Hill on the site now partly occupied by the Youth Hostel.

Riggs opened his third retreat at Theydon Bois on Coppice Row adjacent to Theydon Plain in 1882 and put his son Thomas in charge. It was sold to Edwin Yates in 1916, becoming known thereafter as Yates' Retreat. After providing so much pleasure for so many people for so many years, in 1940 its end came violently in the dead of night as described in the chapter on Theydon Bois. Long-time Theydon resident Jack Farmer remembers on the site as it is today.

be expected after a walk through the Forest from Chingford to Sewardstone, from thence to High Beech, and back again by way of Fairmead Bottom and the glades of Queen Elizabeth. Our next journey we will make to 'fresh woods and pastures new,' for this fine old Forest is not to be explored in a day, nor is it to be described in the limits of a column of the *Express*.

Hackney Express and Shoreditch Observer,
August 12, 1876

On the morning of Wednesday last the 16th inst. important proceedings were carried out in the Forest district under the directions of the Epping Forest Preservation Society, which resulted in a vast amount of fencing being removed from enclosed portions of the Forest. At an early hour about eighty persons started from Poplar to the Forest, being conveyed in four private omnibuses, each drawn by four grey horses, the procession being led by Mr. George Burney (of the firm of Burney and Bellamy, tank makers, of Millwall, Poplar) and other gentlemen in a carriage and pair. The party, on destruction bent, proceeded to that part of the Forest at Wanstead, near the Green Man Inn, and immediately commenced operations by destroying about 1,600 yards of fencing surrounding a large field in the oc-cupation of Mr. Thomas Skinnerton, who rents it from Mr. Berwick, of Clay-street, Walthamstow. This wholesale clearance of the fences was carried out in the presence of the police — who were under the immediate orders of Mr. Inspector Anderson — by Mr. George Burney, the chairman of the Epping Forest Preservation Society. In reply to the inquiries of Inspector Anderson, Mr. Burney stated that he was a commoner of Loughton, and accepted all responsibility for the proceedings they were then inaugurating. This stretch of fencing disposed of, the party proceeded on to Buckhurst-hill, where they devoted their attentions to a fence owned by Nathaniel Powell, Esq., J.P., a considerable length of which speedily disappeared. Crossing to the other side of the road, the destruction of the fence, owned by Mr. Gellatly, of Loughton, was commenced, but owing to its great length, it was not levelled to the ground until 1.30 p.m. Mr. Burney then ordered his men to adjourn to the Crown public-house, at Loughton, for refreshment, and on the way there a gate leading into the nursery of Mr. Paul, (of Waltham Cross) was removed, the fence remaining untouched. Having refreshed the inner man they again bestirred themselves and commenced to destroy all the fences on the right of the road between Smart's-lane, Loughton, and the Woodford New-road. These fences are owned by Mr. Abbott, of Worship-street, Finsbury. Again on the wing, the fell destroyers next reached the Robin Hood public-house, near High Beech, in the immediate vicinity of which they utterly demolished a large portion of fencing put up by the landlord, Mr. Chilton. It was now about half-past four o'clock, and the shades of evening began rapidly to darken the landscape, so it was determined to start for London, and the

Where could one take 700-odd children today for an outing and give them all high tea in one building? The Poor Children's Outing Fund recorded just such an adventure (supervised by 56 adults) in August 1923. The Transport Workers' Children's Outing Society brought upwards of 25,000 children to Theydon in 1937 when for 9d they could have 'Bread and Butter, Fruit Cake and Lemon Cake, Jam Sandwich, Watercress and good Tea'. A 'Sausage Roll, Large Bath Bun and glass of Still Lemonade' cost 5d.

Coppice Row, Theydon Bois.

No sooner had William Rigg opened up at Theydon in 1882 than competition arrived in the form of George Drossett who erected a retreat fifty yards up the road on the opposite side. It was sold to Bill Gray about ten years later and it, too, came to grief in World War II.

To the Editor

SIR,—I was much pleased by the recent insertion in your paper of an article, congratulating those who have taken a prominent part in the salvation of Epping Forest, on the glorious termination of their labours. I also perfectly agree with the hint given, and followed up by a letter in a subsequent issue, as to the propriety of acknowledging in some public fashion the eminent services rendered by such public benefactors. This matter I hope will not be allowed to drop, or ever to droop. The names of Lt.-Col. Palmer — the last of the old verderers — Mr. J. T. Bedford, the St. George of the Common Council of the City of London — and last, though not least, the name of Mr. W. G. Smith, honorary secretary of the 'Forest Fund,' who for years past has by indefatigable exertion in connection with that committee, contributed in no small degree to the happy end of the Forest agitation, — should never be forgotten. . . .

I am, Sir, yours truly,

JOHN E. EAST GRAY, Capt.,
Author of 'Save the Forest,' &c.
Upton, Essex, 4th September, 1878

P.S. — May I be allowed to add, in praise of her Most Gracious Majesty, that when I had the honour of presenting my verses on the Forest to the Queen in 1868 — through the kindness of the Duchess of Wellington, then Mistress of the Robes — I received a letter from Her Majesty expressive of the deep interest she felt in that which stood so intimately connected with the benefit of so many of her loyal subjects; and this has been proved by the readiness with which the Queen has relinquished her own rights in the Forest for the public weal. Surely we have a right to cry, 'God Save the Queen!'

Hackney Express and Shoreditch Observer,
September 7, 1878

cortege rapidly proceeded homeward, evidently well satisfied with their day's work. The proceedings throughout passed off quietly, no oppositon being offered; nor was there any disorder, although at one time a large number of spectators was assembled. The party were thoroughly equipped with axes, spades, saws, ropes, and other tools, and it was surprising to see with what celerity the obnoxious fences disappeared before the efforts of the stalwart arms engaged in their destruction. A marked feature of the affair

was the good humour which prevailed during the day, the operators being fully impressed with the idea that they were performing a public service.

Inspector Anderson, who attended the proceedings from the beginning, was joined shortly after three o'clock by Mr. Superintendent Green and another Inspector. It is estimated that upwards of four miles of fencing were levelled.

Walthamstow Guardian, January 19, 1878

Mr. J. T. Bedford said it was now nearly nine years since he first conceived the idea of the Corporation preserving Epping Forest. He came down and saw a board stuck up bearing the words, 'Trespassers will be prosecuted with the utmost rigour of the law.' He immediately got over the fence and sat under a tree, and wondered who were the greatest trespassers — he or those who had put up the notice. [Hear, hear.] He went home and consulted Mr. Scott, the City Chamberlain, and they agreed that if the Corporation would sacrifice a revenue they were receiving of £9,000 or £10,000, the preservation of Epping Forest for the people might be accomplished. They went back to the time of Henry II, and found records by which the citizens of London

The Ragged School Union was formed in 1844 with the purpose of providing outings into the country for parties of East End children. Their retreat was located in Loughton on Staples Road and became the Shaftesbury Retreat when the Union amalgamated with Lord Shaftesbury's Society. Today the name lives on in the new estate which occupies the spot.

were confirmed in their rights of hunting in Epping Forest. He brought the matter before the Corporation in May 1871, and a Committee was appointed with only one instruction — Go in and win. He thought they would get over the matter for £100,000, but it would cost about a quarter of a million, and never was money spent in a better and nobler cause. [Cheers.] Mr. Bedford, then, in humorous terms, referred to legal and other difficulties which were encountered, and said that the case took three years in preparing, and twenty-one days in hearing. At last the day of judgement came; and the Master of the Rolls delivered the magnificent judgment which they all knew pretty well by heart. Then they naturally thought the thing was at an end; but a Parliamentary Commission was appointed, and it took them three years to prepare their scheme. The result of that three years' deliberation was a scheme which did not suit anybody, and that was put on one side; but thanks to the Government of the day, and to Sir H. J. Selwyn-Ibbetson of all men, the Epping Forest Act, 1878, was passed. He had a full reward for all his labours on last Whit-Monday, when he came down and saw 300,000 or 400,000 people innocently enjoying themselves.

House of Commons, June 18, 1880

On Saturday, on the invitation of the Corporation of London, the Duke and Duchess of Connaught went to Epping Forest to plant some trees in commemoration of the recent appointment of the Duke by the Queen as the Ranger of the Forest. . . . On arriving at Chingford carriages were in waiting to convey the party to a pretty part of the forest known as Hawkwood, about half a mile

There were two retreats at Buckhurst Hill. Guy's Retreat, also known as the Forest Lodge Tea Gardens, stood just to the north of the Roebuck. The original timber buildings were replaced in 1926, the new construction including a plant for the manufacture of ice cream. In 1948 part was occupied by the Loughton Labour Exchange and the building was converted into flats in the mid-1950s.

distant from the station, where spacious marquées had been erected. With a silver spade, handed to her Royal Highness by the Lord Mayor, the Duchess of Connaught planted the first of the memorial trees, which were of Normandy pine. Then the Duke of Connaught planted another, the Lady Mayoress a third, and the Lord Mayor the last. At the conclusion of this brief ceremony,

bouquets were handed by children to the Duchess, Lady Elphinstone, and the Lady Mayoress. Their Royal Highnesses next visited Queen Elizabeth's Lodge, and thence proceeded to the Forest Hotel, at Chingford, were they were entertained at luncheon by the Corporation, the Lord Mayor presiding.

The Times, October 18, 1880

The Forest Retreat in Queens Road catered for visitors to Lord's Bushes onto which it faced. It was in operation by the 1880s and could seat 500 at one go, being advertised as 'an ideal spot for a Sunday School Treat' and where 'Skipping Ropes lent free of charge'. It was operated by John Riggs from 1903,

taking his name, but when Bert Voysey took it over in 1908 it became known also as Princes Retreat. It closed in 1917 but it saw a brief lease of life in the 1930s as a rendezvous for the then-popular cycling clubs. Today a tenuous link with the past is provided by the playground which lies in front of the site.

THE ROYAL VISIT TO EPPING FOREST

We are requested to state that on the occasion of Her Majesty the Queen visiting Epping Forest tomorrow (Saturday), wheeled vehicles will be allowed to stand on the Forest along the Queen's route, provided that a clear space of not less than 30 feet in width, on either side of the road, be left for spectators on foot, and that the positions be occupied by the vehicles before two o'clock p.m.

It is arranged that the Royal train shall be provided by the Great Western Railway Company, and that it shall leave Windsor at 3.13 p.m. to-morrow (Saturday), travelling by way of the North London system on to the Cambridge line, and thence on the Walthamstow line, via Lea Bridge, reaching Chingford Station at 4.13. This well-arranged and convenient station is being decorated for the occasion under the orders of Mr. James Robertson, Chief Superintendent of the Company, and stands for the accommodation of 3,000 persons are being erected in the station yard, partly by the railway company, and partly by the Corporation of the City of London. A triumphal arch spans the entrance, and is in a forward state of completion. It will represent a castle keep, with square embattled towers on either side, a trophy of banners surmounting the arch. The main exit and booking-offices will be formed into a Royal reception room, draped and decked with flowers, and a new booking-office, ornamentally designed in keeping with the surroundings, has been temporarily built. The whole of the station will be devoted to the convenience of the Royal party and the spectators, and this spot, besides being the principal point of arrival for invited guests, and the general public, will be one of the chief points of interest in the day's ceremonial. As there are five lines running into the station, and as many exits, with a Bank holiday experience of 25,000 passengers each way per diem, there is hope that it will be equal to the emergency, relieved, as it will be to some extent, by the stations of Loughton and Buckhurst-hill on the opposite side of the Forest, and actually nearer than Chingford to

the culminating scene of the day's programme. Her Majesty will be received by the Lord Mayor and Corporation, and by a guard of honour of the Essex Artillery Volunteers, a detachment of whom will be stationed with their guns on the green sward, and will fire a Royal salute of 21 rounds. A procession will then be formed, in which the Queen will be conducted through the Forest, making a halt at Queen Elizabeth's Hunting Lodge on the hill, which her Majesty is expected to visit. This building has been renovated recently, and now bears little resemblance to the ancient and weather-beaten structure known to excursionists.

The procession will proceed by the new Ranger's-road, opened by the Duke of Connaught last year, the vicinity of which presents a significant sight in the fallen fences which hereabout lie just now scattered, marking the lines of enclosures which, in the

language of the forthcoming Royal proclamation, are henceforth to be 'free to the people for ever.' We know not whether this memorable appearance of a Queen of England on the spot so long associated with the name of her illustrious predecessor has had the effect of hastening the process of demolition; but certain it is that the work has recently been pushed on with increased vigour. Indeed, even within the last few days many fences have come down, conveying to the eye a pleasant sense of increased freedom. To the left of the road a view is obtained of the Connaught Lake, a handsome sheet of water some seven acres in extent, of recent formation, but already a favourite resort for boating parties. On reaching the New Epping-road, the procession will shortly diverge to the left and pass by way of Fairmead Bottom to High Beech, and the King's Oak. Here is erected a vast marquee and amphitheatre, in

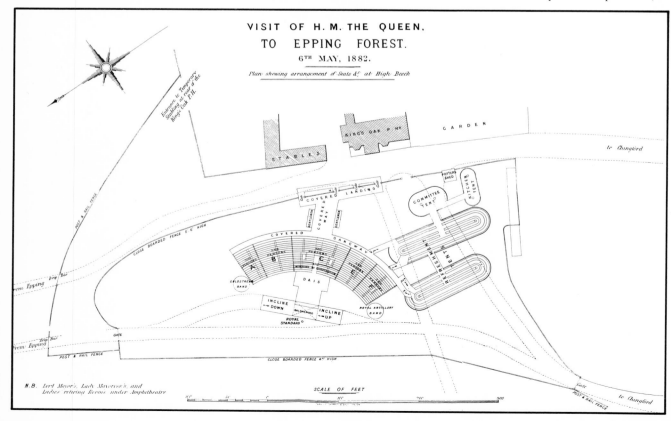

VISIT OF H. M. THE QUEEN,
TO EPPING FOREST.
6TH MAY, 1882.

Plan showing arrangement of Seats &c at High Beech

SCALE OF FEET

N.B. *Lord Mayor's, Lady Mayoress's, and Ladies' retiring Rooms under Amphitheatre*

52

VISIT OF

Her Majesty Queen Victoria

TO EPPING FOREST,

SATURDAY, MAY 6TH, 1882.

The Right Hon. JOHN WHITTAKER ELLIS, Lord Mayor.

REGINALD HANSON, ESQ., M.A. ALDERMAN ⎫ Sheriffs.
WILLIAM ANDERSON OGG, ESQ. ⎭

THE CORPORATION OF LONDON request the honour of the Company

of...

No............

NOT TRANSFERABLE.

Whinfield Hora,

Chairman.

QUEEN'S VISIT TO EPPING FOREST

which will be assembled the Peers and Commons, and other distinguished guests to the number of about 3,000. Bouquets will be presented to the Queen by the Lady Mayoress, and Miss Buxton, the daughter of Sir Thomas and Lady Victoria Buxton. The address of the Corporation will next be read by the Recorder (Sir Thomas Chambers), and handed to her Majesty by the Lord Mayor. Her Majesty will then, through the Home Secretary and the ranger, announce that the forest is devoted to the use and enjoyment of the public for all time. The announcement will be communicated to the public by a salvo of artillery, and by the playing of the bands on duty on the occasion. The Lord Mayor will then present to her Majesty a few of the gentlemen principally connected with the day's proceedings, and the Lady Mayoress will hand to the Queen a beautiful volume of photographs of the principal points of interest in the forest. It is

proposed to re-name Beech Wood, through which the Royal carriage will pass, as Queen Victoria's Wood.

The Royal train will leave Chingford for Windsor about 5.30. This being the first visit of her Majesty to their neighbourhood the inhabitants on the Essex side of London are much pleased and excited by the coming event, and a general holiday on Saturday is expected. Colonel Henderson has arranged for an extra body of 1,500 police to be present, and enterprising caterers are establishing themselves to provide for the wants of the many thousands of persons who will be assembled. The day's proceedings will be a fitting testimony to the triumph of the Corporation of the City of London, in their successful efforts to preserve this extensive tract of beautiful woodland.

Walthamstow Guardian, May 6, 1882

The ancient Royal Chace or hunting ground of Epping, with its sylvan scenes and pleasant greenwood recesses for the holiday enjoyment of Londoners, being henceforth legally preserved and freely dedicated to public use, was visited last Saturday afternoon by her Majesty the Queen, and by the Duke of Connaught, Ranger of the Forest, meeting there the Lord Mayor and City Corporation, to declare this final confirmation of a great boon to the people.

The weather on Saturday afternoon was bright and warm; and many thousands of people went out to Epping Forest by the two lines of railway — one to Chingford, on the western side, the other line to Loughton, beyond Woodford and Buckhurst-hill, eastward of High Beech, the place where the ceremony was to be performed. The day was, to a great extent, observed as a general holiday in the East of London. The Queen, with Princess Beatrice, attended by the Dowager Duchess of Athole, Sir H. Ponsonby, and the General Lynedoch Gardiner, travelled from Windsor by special train, on the Great Western Railway, changing at Acton to the Kew and Hampstead Junction line, and so on to the North London Railway, and thence at Victoria Park to the Chingford line. On arriving at Chingford, about four o'clock, the Queen was met by Princess Louise (Marchioness of Lorne) and the Duke and Duchess of Connaught. Her Majesty was there formally received by the Lord Mayor (Mr. Whittaker Ellis), Mr. H. J. Rebow (High Sheriff of Essex), Mr. Alderman Hanson and Mr. Anderson Ogg (Sheriffs of London), Mr. Deputy Hora (the Chairman of the Committee), and Sir Thomas Nelson (the acting Remembrancer). The Forest Sub-Reception Committee were also awaiting her Majesty's arrival.

A procession was then formed, which left Chingford station amid the booming of a Royal salute, the playing of the National Anthem by the bands of the Royal Artillery and the 3rd Middlesex Artillery, and the cheering of the people. Opposite the Royal

This triumphal arch was erected to span the entrance to Chingford railway station where Her Majesty arrived to begin her historic visit to the Forest. The wooden archway was retained as a form of monument to record the occasion but by the end of the century it was so dilapidated that it had to be demolished in August 1901.

Forest Hotel, the balconies of which were filled with spectators, the scene was very animated, and flags and banners streamed and hats and handkerchiefs waved on every side. At the junction of the roads a little farther on were stationed the children of the Woodford Schools, of Mrs. Gladstone's Home, the Merchant Seaman's Orphan Asylum, the Loughton Schools, the Buckhurst and Chigwell Schools, and the Princess Louise's Home. All along the route to High Beech her Majesty's reception was of a highly enthusiastic character.

The procession was headed by the mounted police, the members of the Epping Forest Sub-Reception Committee, the chairman of the Epping Forest Committee, the verderers of Epping Forest, the Under-Sheriffs of London and Middlesex, the officers of the Corporation of London, the Sheriffs of London and Middlesex, the Aldermen of the City of London (on the committee), the Lady Mayoress, and the High Sheriff of Essex. Guards of honour of the 1st Battalion Warwickshire Regiment and of the Essex Artillery Volunteers were stationed at Chingford Station. A salute was fired in the neighbourhood of Hawk's Wood on her Majesty's arrival. The Queen, accompanied by Princess Louise (Marchioness of Lorne), Princess Beatrice, and the Duchess of Connaught, occupied the first carriage. In the second carriage were the Dowager Duchess of Athole (Lady-in-Waiting to the Queen), Lady Adela Larking (in attendance on the Duchess of Connaught), Lady Eleanor Heneage (Lady-in-Waiting upon Princess Louise), and Lord Sandhurst (Lord-in-Waiting). The Duke of Connaught and Strathearn, K.G., Ranger of Epping Forest, rode by the side of her Majesty's carriage. The Right Hon. the Lord Mayor, General the Right Hon. Sir H. Ponsonby, Lieutenant-General H. Lynedoch Gardiner, Sir Maurice FitzGerald (Knight of Kerry), and Major-General the Hon. Sir H. Clifford followed her Majesty's carriage on horseback. An escort, under the command of Captain Lord Arthur Somerset and Lieutenant Selwyn (Royal Horse Guards), was in attendance.

On her Majesty's arrival at High Beech the Royal Standard was hoisted, and her Majesty was received by a Guard of Honour of the Essex Artillery Volunteers, and a salute was fired by a battery of the Hon. Artillery Company. The H Company of the 1st Herts. Volunteers was stationed on the route. The London Rifle Brigade, the 3rd Essex Rifle Volunteers, and the Leyton Volunteer Fire Brigade lined the route of the procession. Miss Victoria Buxton had the honour of presenting a bouquet to her Majesty. An address from the Corporation of London was read by the Recorder, welcoming her to the forest, and testifying to the deep interest which the Sovereign had taken in the movement which resulted in that day's ceremonial. Her Majesty, in reply, said:— 'I thank you sincerely for your loyal and dutiful address, and it gives me the greatest satisfaction to dedicate this beautiful forest for the enjoyment of my people. I thank you for your continued solicitude for my welfare.' The Lord Mayor then, in her Majesty's name, 'declared this beautiful forest open and dedicated to the delectation of the public for all time,' an announcement which was received with loud cheering, the bands playing the National Anthem, and the Artillery firing a Royal salute.

The Sheriffs of London and Middlesex, Mr. Deputy Hora, the mover, and Mr. Wheeler, the seconder of the address, were then presented to the Queen by the Lord Mayor. The Lord Lieutenant of Essex, the High Sheriff of Essex, Mr. John Thomas Bedford, and Sir Thomas Nelson (the City Solicitor) were also presented to her Majesty. The Queen then went to a part of the forest, where a fine specimen of the scarlet oak (Quercus coccinea) was planted in her Majesty's name, under the direction of Messrs. William Paul and Son, of Waltham Cross. Before the royal procession returned to Chingford, the Lady Mayoress had the honour of presenting to the Queen a volume of photographs of the most

interesting scenery of the forest. Lord Carlingford, Lord Lieutenant of Essex, received the Queen at the station. The Earl and Countess Granville, Sir William Harcourt, Home Secretary, Sir Richard Cross, and other persons of note were among the company. Her Majesty left Chingford at half-past five, and arrived at Windsor shortly before seven o'clock, amid the same tokens of loyal affection as on the outward journey. For thousands of people who remained in the forest there was provided at dusk a grand display of fireworks by Messrs. C. T. Brock and Co., at the rear of the Royal Forest Hotel, the grounds of which were also illuminated.

The Illustrated London News, May 13, 1882

At quarter to 3 left with Beatrice for Epping Forest, which we reached at 4. Great crowds all along the railroad and a very great one on getting out. Arthur, Louischen, Louise, and the Lord Mayor met us. Volunteers and troops were out, and everything extremely well arranged. A great stand, full of people, and a very pretty arch had been erected. Arthur rode next to my carriage, and Louise, Beatrice, and Louischen drove with me. The Lord Mayor and my two Equerries rode behind the carriage. Drove through enormous crowds, who lined the whole way, nearly 3 miles to High Beach, where an Address was received, and read, and I declared the Park open. The sight was very brilliant. There was a temporary building in which the Lord Mayor had entertained 10,000 people at luncheon. He hurriedly dismounted, and put on his robes, before presenting the Address, which was read by the Recorder, and I read a short answer, which caused great cheering. An album with views of this fine and picturesque Park, reminding one of Burnham Beeches and Richmond Park, was presented to me, and a little girl, daughter of Sir Fowell and Victoria Buxton (herself my god-daughter), was held up to the carriage, to give me a bouquet . . . Returned the same way. The enthusiasm was very great, and many quite poor people were out. The Park has been given to the poor of the East End, as a sort of recreation ground. Nothing but loyal expressions and kind faces did I hear and see; it was most gratifying.

*The Letters of Queen Victoria,
edited by George Buckle*

In an age when photography was in its infancy the quality of the photograph on pages 54 and 55 (the original of which is preserved at the Guildhall) is remarkable. The photo-engraving process had only been invented the previous year and in the magazines of the period the woodcut still remained the only credible form of pictorial illustration. This is how The Illustrated London News depicted the event in their issue of May 13, 1882. *Opposite and below:* Passing the Queen Elizabeth Hunting Lodge.

The costs incurred in the prolonged struggle to secure this vast tract of land from further encroachment were, no doubt, heavy: the aggregate of the purchase money, compensation for rights of lopping, the price of Wanstead Park, and legal expenses, amounting to some £256,275 [equivalent to some £8 million at 1985 prices]. But in exchange for this outlay a domain of rare beauty has been secured to ever-growing London, and generations yet unborn are likely to be grateful for the boon that has been conferred upon them; so that the almost romantic story of its rescue ought not readily to be forgotten by those who enjoy its cool shades and sylvan recesses.

Greater London, Edward Walford, 1883

It is in its varied aspects that the greatest refreshment is to be found for the eye and the brain, weary of dead walls and the turmoil of streets. The general opinion, so unmistakably evinced, that the Forest shall remain forest and not be civilised into a park, is but the expression of a true instinct. May the people of London for all time continue to draw full draughts at this source, and to profit by the companionship and teaching of nature.

Epping Forest, Edward North Buxton, 1884

After threading your way through the thorn bushes and brambles that cover Fairmead, as you rise the hill towards High Beech, you come upon the only really big oak tree growing at the present moment in the forest. The trunk of this tree, in its largest part, measures thirty-three feet in circumference and shows no symptoms of decay. At some time or other it has been disfigured by lopping at about 14 or 15 feet from the ground, but, although several limbs have been removed, it is still a fine-topped tree, spreading its arms all around, and is yet in its prime. On the highest ground in all the forest is High Beech, where a stump of from 18 to 20 inches high represents all that remains of the King's Oak. Forty years ago that stump stood six feet, but it has been carried away bit by bit to make into snuff boxes. The popular tradition is that the tree took its name from King Harold, who founded the monastery at Waltham; it is quite certain that Waltham Forest existed before the Norman Conquest. . . . Not a quarter of a mile distant, in the green path of the High Wood, stands the Stanley Oak, reputed to be the oldest tree in the forest. . . . What a spot for a picnic!

Baily's Magazine, circa 1885

To commemorate the occasion Queen Victoria commanded that two things be done: a tree be planted in her name, and that Beech Wood, on the southern slope of High Beech Hill be named henceforth Queen Victoria's Wood. The first deed was accomplished using this spade, photographed for us specially in the Royal Collection and reproduced by gracious permission of Her Majesty The Queen. The Quercus Velutina was planted not far from the King's Oak — even in 1882 only a stump. Unfortunately the Queen's tree died shortly afterwards and had to be replaced.

It would seem that the second of the Queen's requests was never carried to fruition. The renamed wood does not appear on any maps and the Conservators have said that they have no knowledge of an area of the Forest called Queen Victoria's Wood. (Come on Ordnance Survey — better late than never!) At least the Queen's Black Oak is thriving although completely unmarked by any commemorative plaque. (Come on Conservators, where's your sense of history?)

ADDITION TO EPPING FOREST.— The completion of the purchase of the lower portion of Higham Park, Woodford, was made by the Corporation of London, on the 10th February, 1891, and thus a pretty tract of 30 acres, 2 roods, 39 perches in extent, comprising Woodland, Lake, and a portion of the Ching Brook, was secured as an open space. This forms a pleasing addition to the narrow bridle path called the 'Sale,' which was the only rural link connecting the forest near Hale End, with the 'Lops' near Chingford Hatch, and it is hoped that the Duke of Connaught as Ranger of the Forest, will, early in the summer, formally dedicate the new portion to the use of the public.

Wanstead Parish Magazine, May 1891

The greatest indignation is expressed in the

various towns around Epping Forest on account of the reckless manner in which the trees are being felled. Every day waggon loads of magnificent trees are being carted away but it is difficult to trace their exact purchaser. At any rate the sale should have realized a very large sum of money. It is the intention of the inhabitants to immediately call public meetings to protest against the wholesale destruction of the timber, it being claimed that to turn the Forest into a mere park was never the intention or wish of the public. A visit to the Forest has verified in full detail, says the Central News, all the statements made, and it is quite clear that unless energetic action be taken to stay the hand of the destroyer, in a few weeks Epping Forest will be a thing of the past.

Pall Mall Gazette, April 12, 1894

Four thousand eight hundred and six trees (not 30,000) have been felled in the season 1893-4 in Epping Forest, Wanstead and Higham Parks (an area of about ten square miles), the greater part of these being small pollards, 6in. in diameter, and very many dead or decayed. When the cost of cutting and drawing has been paid, little or no profit remains, and last year the sum of £3,600 was placed by the Corporation to the Epping Forest Fund to meet annual expenditure. So far from Monk Wood being a desolate waste, I venture to say that in the course of a very short time the public will not be able to discern where the trees have been felled. I am pleased to say that the whole matter of the thinning and tree felling will engage the attention of experts in a few days. I have promised that no further cutting shall take place until the experts have reported.

Mr James Salmon, Epping Forest Committee,
April 1894

The Epping Forest devastators have only cut down four thousand eight hundred and six trees within twelve months. How much of the charmingly wild undergrowth has been hacked up and carried off, not even the devastators themselves could tell. When some hulking fellow fires the Forest he is punished — if he is caught. He deserves punishment. But those who are destroying the Forest with axe and saw ought to be blamed as well as those who would destroy it by fire. Visitors to Wanstead Park this summer will find that devastators have been busy there, as well as in the Forest. They have, amongst other things, sawn down the strange old tree which stretched over the path and dipped into the ornamental waters. Thousands of people made long journeys to see that tree. Artists photographed it. Visitors had come to feel a kind of affection for it. No doubt those who have had it removed can give a hundred and fifty reasons why they have hacked it down, but its admirers will be strongly inclined to believe that if the people who have this business in hand had only been as anxious to preserve it, as they are to 'improve' the park, it would be there still. If it had been an in-

No sooner had the Forest been saved than a new controversy began in the press concerning tree felling. These sketches appeared in the Daily Graphic on April 14, 1894, showing work under way at Monk's Wood.

fectious hospital it could probably have remained. Wanstead is said to have stuck such an hospital, horribly ugly and staringly prominent, at the very park gates, and though there has been protest after protest from the public, there it sticks still. This is the way public bodies persist in acting — they can spoil fast enough beauties the public wants, and can stick under the public eye and nose, objects that are certainly hideous and may easily become dangerous.

Essex Times, April 21, 1894

The Lord Mayor of London, accompanied by the Sheriffs, visited Epping Forest yesterday formally to open the recent addition to Highams Park, which is part of the Forest, and an extension of the Chingford golf course, which is also within the woodland area. In

1891 Highams Park, 30 acres in extent, was acquired by purchase. When the Ministry of Transport recently decided to carry the section of the North Circular Road from Grove-road to Becontree-avenue through the Forest they secured an option on an equivalent area of land adjoining Highams Park for exchange for the forest land proposed to be taken. Ultimately the Ministry found it possible to abandon their proposal to carry the road through the Forest and to complete their scheme by simply widening certain existing roads, which involved a much smaller encroachment on the Forest. In addition to the land given by the Ministry in exchange for this encroachment, the Corporation purchased the remaining 4½ acres on which the Ministry had an option. Thus there had been a total addition of 7½ acres to Highams Park.

The extension of the Chingford golf course

A study in tranquility in Highams Park — added to the Forest by purchases in 1876, 1891 and 1928. (See also page 203.)

The gates into the Forest — still within living memory to one writer in the Express and Independent in 1936 but now faded from view. This is the original Forest Gate as depicted by an artist in 1851 — it stood in what is now Woodgrange Road, in front of the Eagle and Child rebuilt around 1896.

had become necessary owing to the difficulties of play caused by the increasing number of visitors to the Forest in the summer months. when nine holes had to be closed. Eight new holes have now been added, and this will allow of play over 18 holes at all seasons. This new section of the course has been carved out of virgin forest. . . .

Press report, October 1, 1928

How many local residents remember all of the various gates which at one time gave access from the roads on to the forest areas?

There was one at the end of Harrow-road, Leytonstone (then Wigram's-lane) near Nevill's Bakery. A lame old man called 'Crutchy' used to open it at one period for traffic to go through.

A second gate stood at the forest end of Cannhall-road, a third near the Eagle and Child at Forest Gate, a fourth at the end of Davies-lane, Leytonstone. The road is named after Captain Davies who lived at what is now 'The Home of the Good Shepherd'.

There was a fifth gate near the Friend's Meeting House off Bush-road, Leytonstone, with a bridle path to the Green Man, and a sixth gate at the Cemetery bridge, at Little Ilford, before the Cemetery was laid out and when the farm there was 'Windmill's Farm'. A seventh gate stood at Tinker's Bridge at Manor Park near the Reformatory.

Express and Independent, June 13, 1936

Dec 12. Removal of remains of 3 German airmen from wreckage of Bomber nr Wake Arms and buried in 1 coffin at Chingford Mt Cemetery Dec 14, 1940. Motor Hearse. Undertaker and Bearers. Cemetery fees as paid £2. Gefreiter Anton Dornauer. Unteroff. Egidius Leipold. Unteroff. Max Jappsen.

Poulton & Sons, Undertakers, Epping.

On the evening of Sunday, December 8, 1940, a Junkers Ju 88A-1 from 6/LG1 took off from the German-occupied airfield at Orléans/Bricy, 50 miles south of Paris. At the controls of aircraft serial L1+KP was Unter-offizier Max Jappsen, his crew consisted of Feldwebel Egidius Leipold (Observer) and air gunners Gefreiter Anton Dornauer and Franz Weber.

The aircraft, travelling on a north-westerly heading, set course for England at 5,000 metres. As it approached the eastern outskirts of London, a well-placed burst of anti-aircraft fire from the Chigwell Rise battery (one of the first using radar-predicted guns) scored a hit and the aircraft descended in a northerly direction. Passing over Loughton, the under gunner fired a burst at a searchlight unit which was located in the grounds of Loughton Girls' School. Over Epping Forest the tail detached falling to earth in Warlies Park at Upshire. Complete loss of control followed, the Junkers smashing into the forest ten yards south of Lodge Road, some 200 yards from the A11, the shock-wave being felt in Upshire and

War comes to the Forest. December 8, 1940 — a Junkers Ju 88 comes to grief near the Wake Arms. There were no survivors. Once the surface wreckage had been cleared the site was left — just another incident in the turmoil of war.

Thirty-six years later a unique excavation takes place in the depths of the Forest. The crater had been used as a rubbish dump; after the dustbins and old bicycles had been removed, came pieces of aeroplane. This is one of the parachutes.

Evidence of the presence of unexploded bombs — a steel bomb fin.

Captain Spencer Henry, who defused the first bomb, watches as the steamed-out explosive harmlessly burns away beside Lodge Road.

Theydon Bois, both a mile either side of the crash. Burning fuel was spread over a wide area, the Loughton fire brigade, under the direction of Chief Fire Officer Ernest Rule, fighting for several hours to contain the blaze.

At first light on Monday a terrible scene of death and destruction became apparent, with the remains of the dismembered crewmen scattering the area, and the trees to the north of Lodge Road festooned with debris. Personnel from RAF North Weald arrived to clear up the mess and remove the surface wreckage. By Wednesday the local undertaker, Poulton & Sons from Epping, had been called in to remove what human remains had been found and these were buried in a single coffin on December 14 at Chingford Mount Cemetery. When the RAF team finally departed they fenced off, with picket posts and wire, the ten foot-deep crater made by the impact of the 12½-ton bomber.

After the war, the Conservators of Epping Forest used craters left by exploding bombs for the burial of refuse and the Ju 88 crater, quite near the Wake Arms public house, was used as a convenient tip for bulk litter.

Over the following years, vegetation grew around the site, and thirty years later no one would have realised the drama that had taken place nearly forty years before. That is, not until Tony Graves of the London Air Museum heard of the incident and obtained unique permission to dig in Epping Forest.

The excavation was planned for Saturday, July 10, 1976. Although the first objects recovered were only rusty dustbins and old iron, the petrol smell of a crash site was soon unmistakable as the excavator dug deeper. The first pieces of wreckage came to light about six-feet down, the hole being expanded to twelve feet deep and about fifteen feet long. It seemed that the group was mainly intent on recovering the twin Jumo 211 engines and many small items were left unnoticed. We later found we had one of the crew's harness straps which had snapped in the crash and also an MG 15 ammunition drum which had exploded in the fire.

Over the ensuing weeks, historical organisations in the area openly voiced their criticisms on the intrusion in what they considered was a piece of local history. Nor were the Epping Forest authorities happy about the state in which the area was left. Then, in January 1979, a member of the group contacted 590 Explosive Ordnance Disposal (EOD) Headquarters at Rochester in Kent saying that he had reason to believe a bomb still existed on the site.

A 15-man team under Captain Spencer Henry of 590 Squadron, Territorial Army Reserve (TAVR), arrived to set up camp in the forest on Friday, April 20, 1979. Early Sunday morning, using a JCB digger, parts of the aircraft were uncovered and, later that day, a piece of twisted metal sheeting was recognised as a bomb fin of German design. The paint was still visible showing the tell-tale 40mm yellow identification stripe denoting a thin-walled German HE bomb. With this piece of positive evidence, the team dug with renewed effort and late Sunday night a large object was detected at a depth of thirteen feet by Sergeant Bernard Cullum on the 4015 locator. Further excavation uncovered the nose portion of a German 500kg bomb at 4.00 p.m. on Monday afternoon. EOD HQ was immediately informed and the Regular Army Duty BDO, Major Barry Birch (OC of 49 EOD Squadron, RE), was called to the site.

By 9.00 p.m. all security precautions had been taken, the nearby A11 closed for half-a-mile in each direction, and the windows of the nearest house opened. Floodlights lit the excavation as Major Birch decided to allow Captain Henry to remove the fuse and perform his first live fuse extraction. By 11.00 p.m. the nerve-racking operation, carried out in pouring rain, had been completed.

The next stage was to trepann the bomb, the technical term for connecting up a special rotary cutting tool which makes a 3½-inch hole in the bomb casing without producing any heat. For this operation the bomb is winched from the excavation and set up on boards covering a shallow pit some fifty yards away. When holes have been cut in the bomb casing, a steamer is connected to the bomb. This device, something like a large kettle, produces piped steam which melts the cast explosive (in this case Amatol) which runs out and solidifies on hessian lining the pit. Steaming the bomb continued throughout the night. Next morning the first operation was to blow up the fuse pocket, and at 9.00 a.m. a tremendous bang and a cloud of black smoke was a graphic illustration of the power of the picric acid charge. Then the steamed-out explosive was ignited and a dense column of black smoke rose above the trees.

On Thursday, Sapper Hughie Marshall, the JCB operator, struck another bomb and this time it was agreed that a section commander in 591 Squadron, Captain Mark Klewin, should handle the immunisation.

After the road was opened, the search continued for a possible two further bombs which could have been on board. However although trenches were dug to a depth of fifteen feet all over the area, nothing further was located. Nevertheless the area could still not be certified as safe and a further operation was carried out in September 1979 in which bore holes were sunk all over the site to a depth of thirty feet. By lowering a bomb locator down the shafts, readings could then be taken below ground and plotted on a map to give a complete picture of the metal objects existing. No further bombs were detected and, after reinstating the area, the army departed . . . the three-year saga was at an end . . . leaving car-borne courting couples to dream their dreams in peace.

After the Battle Magazine No. 27, 1980

The Terriers left literally no stone unturned in their search.

The beechwoods south of the road and west of the Ditches Ride, demonstrate the 'false high forest' that can be developed by thinning old coppice. Each tree is, in fact, the last remaining shoot or two from the coppice stool, the remains of the whole being apparent at the bases of almost all the trees.

Near the Wake Arms, on the northern part of Dulsmead Hollow, the woodland has been almost untouched since the time that pollarding ceased. The grouping of the pollards shows that the original growth was coppiced, and the coppice shoots later pollarded.

Here (as in most of the beechwoods, where there is a dense, high leaf canopy in summer) there is no undergrowth, but in autumn the carpet of newly fallen leaves and patches of characteristic silvergreen moss is very attractive. The several clearings, in which the felled material has been left lying on the ground, were made in 1951 as part of a policy to test the capacity for natural regeneration which these areas might possess, and to make them more congenial in amenity. The material was left lying to afford protection to whatever growth established itself.

The area well illustrates the drift of wind-blown leaf mould, deep in places and elsewhere blown bare, the two extremes in which beech seedlings cannot establish themselves.

Epping Forest, Alfred Qvist, 1971

The Fairmead Oak, one of Epping's proudest possessions, was destroyed by fire on Sunday. The famous tree, I am told, has been dead for 30 years or more and has been carefully preserved. Concrete has been used in its trunk and its heavy branches have been propped up. There are no records as to the age of the Fairmead Oak but it is undoubtedly the oldest and most famous in the Forest. King Henry VIII is said to have started the Royal Hunts from it.

The West Essex Gazette, September 30, 1955

The increasing demand for water about Buckhurst Hill, Woodford and Loughton induced the Engineer of the East London Water Works Company, in 1876, to press for the establishment of an intermediate station at Forest Road, Walthamstow. A site for such a station had already been acquired from Viscount Maynard in 1855 and had been freed by Her Majesty's Commissioner of Woods from all rights of Forest then possessed by the Crown.

After some debate a contract was placed in July 1876 for the construction of a small covered reservoir to contain 1½ million gallons with machinery for repumping the water from the reservoir to a water tower on Buckhurst Hill. The reservoir was completed in September 1877 and the engine was started two months later.

The forest suffered from war in other ways. Just south of Woodridden Hill at the Wake Arms the explosion of a V2 rocket blew out an almost perfect circle of trees — still clearly defined after forty years.

When the Fairmead Oak *above* burned down in 1955, did title for being the King of the Forest pass to the Pulpit Oak at Buckhurst Hill?

Construction of the new reservoir on or rather under Forest land took place at the same time that the A406 was diverted to straighten out 'Waterworks Corner'. The aerial picture *above* was taken in June 1967; that *below* in March 1985.

In 1881, on Seaton's advice, the company decided to construct a second reservoir at the station, of the same capacity. The work was carried out by direct labour under his direction until his death in April 1882.

In 1894 W. B. Bryan advised the East London directors to enlarge the reservoir capacity again and in April 1895 the tender of Messrs. Kirk and Randall was accepted for the construction of a 7 million gallon reservoir which was completed in the following year.

In 1939, with the intention of increasing the reservoir capacity at the station, land on the west side of the works was bought from the trustees of the Walthamstow Spade Husbandry Society, but the rules laid down by the Society required that the allotments should not be underlet, that they should be cultivated by the spade and that they should not be worked on Sundays!

In 1963 the Metropolitan Water Board authorised the construction, at a cost of more than £8 millions, of a large new filtration and pumping station at Coppermills. It was realised at the time that in order to make prudent provision for the continuity of the

supply in the large area served from Woodford, it would be necessary to increase considerably the service reservoir capacity there.

Immediately to the west of the reservoir was the piece of land used for allotment purposes. It was at one time thought that the first part of a new reservoir might be built on this, on completion of which the old reservoir could be taken out of service and reconstructed. If necessary, a third section could subsequently be built on the site, immediately adjacent to that occupied by the suction tanks. The allotment site was not ideal, however, for it would provide accommodation for only about 13 million gallons, considerably less than the total requirement, and, because of its shape, construction would be relatively uneconomic.

About this time it became known that the Ministry of Transport were preparing a scheme for the construction of an extensive system of new roads in the vicinity which, if carried out, would seriously affect the amenities of Epping Forest by virtually stopping up access to the Forest from north to south. The only effective way through would be across the Board's land — the allotments

— referred to above. Discussions therefore took place between officers of the Ministry, the Corporation of London, who are the Conservators of the Forest, and the Board, the outcome of which was a proposal that facilities should be provided for building a new reservoir on Forest land to the north of the works site, and that the allotment site should be added to the Forest area and thrown open to the public.

The adoption of this plan would bring with it some advantages to the Board, notably the fact that by building on the Forest site the full reservoir capacity could be provided in one unit and the whole operation could be carried out more quickly and with a minimum of interference with normal working of the station. Some additional mainlaying would, however, be involved as also the disposal of a considerable quantity of spoil. From the public's point of view, the proposal would add some 4½ acres to Forest land, because, on completion, the surface of the new reservoir, grassed over and made accessible, would not be lost.

Metropolitan Water Board, April 1970

Wanstead-Woodford Borough Council is to oppose the City of London (Various Powers) Bill which includes legislation proposing the abolition of the Epping Forest grazing rights and the subsequent tethering of forest cattle.

The official decision to oppose the Bill — although the Council has always made it clear throughout the long cattle controversy that it was opposed on principle to any variation or abolition of ancient rights under the Epping Forest Act — came at last week's meeting of the Local Government Committee.

Chigwell Times, December 8, 1961

A House of Commons Select Committee has turned down the City of London proposal to restrict Commoners rights in Epping Forest by requiring grazing cattle to be tethered.

The tethering proposal, part of the City of London (Various Powers) Bill, was introduced on grounds that the cattle constituted a danger to road safety and damaged public and private property.

Petitioners against the Bill were Wanstead-Woodford Council, the Council for the Preservation of Rural England and the Commons, Open Spaces and Footpaths Preservation Society.

After a three-day hearing, the Select Committee ruled that the tethering proposal should be deleted. They approved the Bill with

What we see in these pictures is a 1,000 years of history, yet as urbanisation has spread its creeping tentacles across the Forest parishes, so has come the periodic call to banish the free range cattle. *Above:* **Wanstead Flats.** *Below:* **Woodford Row.**

amendments to go to the House for report and the third reading.

There has been considerable local controversy over the cattle in recent months. Many local people have complained that the creatures regularly dine off their bushes and herbaceous borders. Their heated feelings are countered by the cattle-lovers who point out that householders should fix adequate fencing round their homes and not leave gates open — and accept the cattle as part of the local scene.

Express & Independent, June 1, 1962

Those who have the right to graze animals on the Forest are termed Commoners. They are owners and/or occupiers of a half-acre of land or more, free of buildings, which lies in one of the Forest parishes — Epping, Theydon Bois, Loughton, Waltham Holy Cross (including Waltham Abbey and Sewardstone), Chingford, Chigwell, Woodford, Walthamstow, Leyton (including Low Leyton), Wanstead, Little Ilford and West Ham — and which has not been specially disqualified by the Act.

Only cattle and horses are now enlarged on the Forest, although the Act provides also for turning out sheep and pigs. The presence of

these animals on the Forest has been the most important factor in the continuation of the open grassland areas in that form. The disappearance, under urban development, of all the farms in the southern Forest parishes coupled with the periodic changes in farming practices, has caused considerable fluctuation in the number of grazing animals on the Forest. In 1912, the total number of animals was as many as 972; during the last war, about 600; in the 1950's, about 140; and in 1970, the highest number turned out on any one day was 543.

It must be remembered that the use of the Forest for this purpose is probably its oldest use (and was certainly the basis of the case fought and won by the Corporation of London, by which the Forest was saved for the enjoyment of the public at large). When, later, highways came to be established, they were established only by passage over common land, which position remains unchanged today. The highways are invariably common land as much as is the Forest lying on one side or the other; where a highway forms a link between two portions of Forest land, the animals have a perfect right to proceed along it.

Epping Forest, Alfred Qvist, 1971

When Queen Victoria came back to Chingford Plain last Saturday around 8,000 people were there to greet her. They swarmed behind her carriage to find fun, spectacle and amusement. And, best of all it was free. If anyone thought the idea of a look-alike Queen Victoria was corny the crowds who lined Station road to watch her procession didn't. Nor did the kids who got lost on purpose so they could go to the organisers tent and meet her.

The decision to celebrate Her Majesty's dedication of Epping Forest to the nation on its centenary was a popular one. Every club and association with an interest in the forest was there to spread the word among an enthusiastic public.

Even the uncertain weather was kind, except for a brief flurry of rain at tea-time, strong enough to send the less hardened scurrying for cover.

The entertainments followed each other with hardly a hitch. Everything from gymkhana to gymnastics drew enthusiastic crowds and, in the case of the mass jog, some keen participation. For the kids there was plenty of queuing for the bouncy castle, always a great favourite, the swings and roundabout. And the rapt attention of the wall of youngsters round the junior motorbike track was something to behold. The scouts barbecue ran out of meat yet more queues formed for the baked potatoes and the W.R.V.S. did stirling work with tea and cakes.

Everyone seemed patient and good humoured and keen to enter into the spirit of the occasion. The organisers, who themselves deserve great praise for their willingness and efficiency, were particularly impressed by the number of people who took the trouble to dress up in Victorian costume.

And they gave special thanks to the Waltham Abbey Army Cadets and 27th Chingford Venture Scouts whose communications and security efforts throughout the weekend oiled the wheels and relieved many a worry.

The police too, were kind and efficient both with the little girl, big eyed and excited, who wanted to tell her story to a bobby, and with the fracas in the beer tent that never had time to get out of control.

But it was the people who made the day. The people who planned and worked and took part in every bit of it from the pipe band on the Green at lunchtime to the fireworks after dark.

Yellow Advertiser, May 14, 1982

A hundred years ago it was the helter-skelter and galloping horse; in 1982 it was the bouncy castle and motorbikes. One wonders what the children will be enjoying at the bicentenary in 2082!

At least we had our Queen Victoria — Mrs Vera Bonner — a local amateur actress pictured here for posterity by Dick Cramp.

65

Deer

In the days when all Essex was a forest the red deer was its supreme beast. They were still being hunted in the nineteenth century, one stag being killed in October 1827 at Plaistow. This magnificent herd was pictured by Dick Cramp in Scotland.

If any freeman shall chase away a Dere, or a wild beast out of the Forest, whether the same be done by chaunce, or of a set purpose, so that thereby the wild beaste is forced by swift running to lyll out the tong, or to breathe with his tong out of his mouth, he shall paie to the King ten shillings amends for the same offence; but if he be a seruile person, then he shall double the same recompence; but if he be a bondman, then shall he lose his skinne.

Carta de Foresta, 1217

Next once a year into Essex a hunting they
   go;
To see 'em pass along, O, 'tis a pretty show,
Through Cheapside and Fenchurch Street,
   and so to Aldgate Pump,
Each man with spurs in horse's sides, and
   his back-sword 'cross his rump,
My Lord Mayor takes a staff in hand to beat
   the bushes o'er,
I must confess it was hard work he ne'er
   had done before,
A creature bounceth from the bush, which
   made them all to laugh,
My Lord he cried, 'A hare! a hare!' but it
   proved an Essex calf.

Pills to Purge Melancholy,
Tom D'Urfey, 1719

Hunting the deer was a royal prerogative, but from time to time the forest officials, the knights templars, foreign dignitaries and such ecclesiastics as the Abbot of Waltham and the Abbess of Barking, were permitted to hunt. For this a special royal warrant was granted, and a warrantable stag or buck would be selected by the keepers who kept an eye on the herds. Also, from time to time, again by royal favour, deer were selected as gifts of venison for various people. These were called fee deer. The favour was withdrawn at times when the number of deer fell below a certain level. Every time a deer was killed during a hunt, or even found dead from wounds, the keeper in whose beat it was found was instructed to sound the 'morte' (death) by blowing on his horn. This warned the neighbourhood of the

event. The following record of such an incident, quoted by Fisher, appeared at the Essex Swainmote at Buckhurst Hill in 1495: 'The kepe fande a sowyr dede in Chyngeforde hawe, the iiij day of Auguste, and the kepe bleu for the woodwards, and no mane woed anseure.' Presumably there had been some dirty work afoot! 'Sowyr' probably stands for the modern fourth-year fallow buck called a sore.

The hunting season, or grease time (French: *graisse*) varied from one animal to the next. One edict gave the following:

Hart and buck (male, red and fallow) from

the Feast of St John the Baptist (6 July) to Holyrood Day (25 September). Hind and doe (female, red and fallow) from Holyrood to Candlemas (14 February).

Fox from Christmas to Ladyday.

Hare from Michaelmas to Midsummerday.

Boar from Christmas to Candlemas.

Any conservationist will agree that, if a species is to survive and flourish, then the habitat to which it is adapted is as important, if not more so, than the species itself. With deer in Britain it is the wooded countryside

Although most of the remaining wild red deer were rounded up and taken to Windsor Great Park in the early 1800s, two were released experimentally in Epping Forest about 1880 but proved troublesome and had to be killed. However occasional sightings of red deer have been reported in surrounding areas as recently as 1964 at Roxwell, 1965 at Great Yeldham, 1971 at Navestock, and 1975 at Saffron Walden. In 1976 a red deer stag was reported being seen at Theydon Bois and in Wanstead Park: in January 1977 possibly the same animal was killed in an accident on the A11 near the Wake Arms. This 1885 engraving depicts Hawks Wood, Chingford.

which is best to their liking and, provided they can freely roam undisturbed among the bushes and trees, they will do so. The Norman huntsman was well aware of this, and so took a firm control on the land by making the laws to protect his animals, also by prohibiting any illegal enclosure which would hinder them. Even so, this practice went on, and from time to time was deplored by the sovereign. . . . In those days hunting was paramount on forest land. Later on, as this interest waned, more and more land was taken over and enclosed, partly to increase the Crown's revenue by means of taxes and rentals, and also to make way for farmland and housing. Ironically, this went contrary to the very purpose for which a forest was created, to the 'great famyshinge and destruction of our said Deare'. For nearly 600 years the sovereigns and their retinues

slopes overlooking Fairmead Bottom just below High Beech, where until recently there stood a fine old oak tree which could be seen from the main London-Epping new road. Every Easter Monday the citizens of London, in particular its cockneys, met by the old Fairmead oak.

Epping Forest, Alfred Leutscher, 1974

Saturday Evening some Gentlemen having been to dine seven or eight Miles out of Town on Epping Forest, and being induced to stay later than ordinary on account of the Clearness of the Evening; they were alarmed on their Return home, with the Cry of a Pack of Hounds, between the Eagle at Snaresbrook and Wansted; which was preceded by a Herd of Deer crossing the Road and the Hounds

ment prepared for her at the Reindeer, before which the stag was turned out. It ran for about two hours, and was afterwards lost.

Press report, 1813

From time immemorial, the festival of Easter has been considered as the opening of the season for the rural sports of the Cockneys, and by way of commencement, the anniversary of the far-famed stag-hunt in Epping Forest was celebrated on Monday last — a day which produced a rich harvest of glory and of gain to those 'lords of generous steeds,' vulgarly yclept stable-keepers. From Temple-bar to Shoreditch — from Islington to the Tower — 'an 'orse,' could not be procured for love or money. The consequence was, that thousands went to hunt on the top of a stage-

A picture with a long-forgotten story. Found by his son in the back of a picture once owned by the late Edward John Pestel, **former police constable at Woodford, who once lived in the North Lodge of the Knighton estate.**

hunted the woods of Waltham Forest with horse and hound, longbow and crossbow, and made merry at the abbey centres of Barking and Waltham. To quote one old rhyme:

> The second Charles of England
> Rode forth one Christmastide
> to hunt a gallant stag of ten
> of Chingford woods the pride.

At all events hunting of the Forest deer among the civilian population became an established custom. In contrast to the stately splendour of the colourful royal hunts and the excellent seats of the experienced members of the retinue, the civic dignitaries in more sombre dress must at times have appeared ludicrous on, or rather off, their unaccustomed places in the saddle. It seems that the attempt of the City fathers to emulate their superiors in the days of Elizabeth caused some ridicule at court. . . .

The origin of the so-called Epping Hunt of the eighteenth and nineteenth centuries is believed to be a continuation of the much older Easter Chase, which used to be held in the various chases around London. The Epping Hunt, a more localised affair, met on the

following, who immediately penetrated into the thickest part of the Forest, which the Gentlemen did not chuse to do, as they were not sure of good Footing for their Horses, and it was late in the Evening. — It is supposed the Hounds had broken loose from some Gentlemen in the Neighbourhood, and had fallen in with the Deer in ranging round the Forest.

Press report, 1765

An uncommonly numerous assemblage of genteel company attended the Epping Easter Hunt this year. Those in carriages were chiefly of the first classes of Nobility, and Gentry, and the horsemen in general capitally mounted. Mr. Pole-Wellesley of Wanstead House, having his stag establishment in this district, he has become the patron of the Easter Hunt, and sent a deer to be turned out before the company. He was present on his famous chestnut horse. His Lady, Miss Tylney Long Pole-Wellesley, was there also — she came in an open carriage drawn by four greys, and two postillions with outriders, etc., and with her company took station in an apart-

coach. The bridges groaned with the countless crowds of jolly souls, who, whether on foot or on horseback, in a carriage or a cart, hied along, glowing with ardour, to witness a spectacle, which may with propriety be styled 'the image of war.' Soon after twelve o'clock; the extensive sloping plain beyond the turn-pike-gate at the top of Woodford-hill was covered with a motley multitude — one might believe that every man, and woman too, in all Essex, had become a Nimrod for the day. The agricultural gentry shone conspicuous, by the ruddiness of their complexion, the appropriate richness of their costume, and the elegance of their charges, champing the bit in impatience for the chace. At one o'clock the victim of the day was announced. It was a bounden doe, taken in the forest on Thursday week. . . . The huntsman's horn having given the direful note of preparation, the men shouted, and the deer being freed; bounded from the cart, gambolled for a moment, and then moved with unequalled speed across the plain. She first bent her course northward, but afterwards turned eastward, and in a quarter of an hour got into the thick of the forest. Out of about seven hundred horsemen,

The Epping Hunt. The Easter Monday hunt would be considered barbaric by today's standards as a stag was captured only to be released specifically for the occasion, usually near the Roebuck, Buckhurst Hill.

not more than twenty pursued her the distance of a mile. Even in that space there were divers deep and dangerous falls; and it was ludicrous to behold some arch wags, who had previously proceeded onwards in anticipation of that result, bestride the empty saddle, and press on in the chace, mocking the fallen Nimrods. The crowd on the field, with about forty private carriages, and triple that number of 'one 'orse chas,' soon dispersed. Some regaled themselves at the ordinary at Rounding's, while others trudged to their respective homes, to recount the feats of the day. Those who remained to partake of Mr. Rounding's hospitality, were not backward in carving out fresh accounts for the evening and following day.— Pony and Donkey races, as the most elegant, took the lead. Three miserable ponies were accordingly produced to run for a silver-cup, about six o'clock in the evening. After one heat, however, the darkness of the night and the equality of the competitors, made it impossible to decide the contest, nor was it worth the trouble, it having been ascertained that there was no prize. One donkey, by walking over the course (for he could not run) took away a large Cheshire cheese for his reward.

Press report. April 1823

. . . The huntsmen of the east were all abroad by nine o'clock, trotting, fair and softly, down the road, on great nine-hand sky scrapers, nimble daisy-cutting nags, flowing-tailed chargers . . . some in job-coaches at two guineas a-day; some in three-bodied non-descripts, some in gigs, some in cabs, some in drags . . . while some on no stages at all, footed the road, smothered by dust . . .

At that far-famed spot, the brow above Fairmead Bottom, by 12 o'clock, there were not less than 3,000 merry lieges then and there assembled. The greensward was covered with ever moving crowds on foot, and the pollard oaks, which skirt the meadow on either side, were filled with men and boys.

But where the deuce is the stag all this while? One o'clock and no stag. Two o'clock and no stag . . . Precisely at half past two o'clock the stag-cart was seen coming over the hill by the Bald Faced Stag. Hundreds of horsemen and gig-men rushed gallantly forward to meet and escort it to the top of Fairmead Bottom, amid such whooping and hallooing as made all the forest echo again.

For a moment, all was deep, silent, breath-less anxiety; and the doors of the cart were

thrown open, and out popped a strapping four-year-old red buck, fat as a porker, with a chaplet of flowers round his neck, a girth of divers coloured ribbons, and a long blue and pink streamer depending from the summit of his branching horns.

He was received, on his alighting, with a shout that seemed to shake heaven's concave, . . . Presently, he caught a glimpse of the hounds and the huntsmen, waiting for him at the bottom, and in an instant off he bounded sideways through the rank, knocking down and trampling all who crowded the path he chose to take, and dashing at once into the cover, he was out of sight before a man could say 'Jack Robinson'.

Then might be seen gentlemen running about without their horses, and horses galloping about without their gentlemen; and hats out of number brushed off their owner's heads by the rude branches of the trees; and everybody asking which way the stag was gone, and nobody knowing anything about him . . . yet nothing at all to be seen, though more than enough to be heard; for every man, and every woman too, made as loud a noise as possible.

Meanwhile the stag, followed by the keepers

and about six couple of hounds, took away through the covers towards Woodford . . . he there turned back, sweeping down the bottom for a mile or two, and away up the enclosures towards Chingford, where he was caught, nobody knows how, for everybody returned to town, except those who stopped to regale afresh, and recount the glorious perils of the day.

Every-day Book, Hone, 1826

The Epping Hunt was as ludicrous as usual, and Greenwich Fair afforded its customary sports, and was as thronged as on any former occasion.

Press report, 1830

LAMBETH-STREET

DEER STEALING.—Two ill-looking fellows were brought before Mr. Walker and Mr. Hardwick on the charge of having in their possession two deer skins without being able to give a satisfactory account of themselves. The constable of Woodford, who apprehended them, stated that he was on the look-out for

Although this is a contemporary illustration, it seems that the BBC had clinched the contract to cover the event!

In the early 1800s Tommy Rounding was leader of the hunt in his capacity as chief huntsman to William Pole-Tylney-Long-Wellesley of Wanstead Hall.

some burglars, when he encountered the prisoners with a bundle, which he took the liberty of searching. The bundle was opened in the presence of the magistrates. It contained the skins of two male deers and a pair of heavy-nailed shoes. The skins appeared as if they had been recently taken off the carcase. One of the keepers of the forest at Wanstead had no doubt the skins were from the deer in the forest under his care. Mr. Sperring, the steward of the forest, stated, that shots had lately been heard in the forest, but the keepers had not been able to trace the authors of them. The prisoners in their defence alleged their having received the skins as a present from a person residing at Woodford, who went by the name of Prancer. They met the man by accident, and had never seen him before. He told them they were goat skins, and they took them for the purpose of making drum-heads with. The prisoners said they belonged to a travelling caravan which went about exhibiting performances (the nature of their performances did not transpire). The heavy-nailed shoes were claimed by the younger prisoner as the shoes in which he 'performed.' The magistrates remanded the prisoners until Wednesday, when it was hoped the constable might be able to secure the attendance of the third party accused. Both prisoners offered to give bail for their appearance, but it was refused.

Press report, 1831

'Where Ignorance is Bliss 'Tis Folly to be Wise.'— Happiness is certainly combined with a thick head, otherwise so many thick heads and strange frontispieces would not have exhibited on Monday upon the Epping-road. There was an abundance, nay, a superabundance of go-carts, that would not go, donkey-carts, dog-carts, and indeed every description of definable and undefinable conveyance. Numbers of Jews were mounted upon ponies of such a size that it was impossible, at a distance, to distinguish whether the sons of Israel were upon black dogs or brown horses. Wild Irish youths, sweet promise of a coming 'fine pisintry,' turned their never-ending Somersets during the whole line of road, from Shoreditch Church to Fair Mead Bottom. The day was most propitious for the hopes of those fledings of mankind who glory in white cords and a *nunter*, and fondly dream of *wenson*, and promise themselves *rich licks* of current jelly on Easter Mondays. At two o'clock or thereabouts, a four-year old buck was bundled out of the cart very much against his inclination; and in less than one half minute thereafter he ran great risk of being smothered in the crowd of gallant sportsmen who poured in upon him in the most handsome manner imaginable. At last off he trotted, followed close at heels by one couple and a half of hounds, and about eight hundred gallant sportsmen of every Whitechapel degree, each scampering helter-skelter, pell-mell, and, according to the proverb, leaving his sable majesty to take the hindmost. In two minutes one couple of the hounds were lost in the wood, while the remainder of the *pack* (one) kept in full cry, but whether the cry was caused by his being upon the scent, or from the lashes he received from his gallant followers, we are uncertain. What became of the buck nobody knows. However, a stag was started, a fox seen, and the hunt ended in the death of a BUCK rabbit; after which the gallant cockney-landers reached Tom Rounding's whittling depot, somewhat out of humour, but pretty considerably in appetite.

Press report, 1837

We have received the following precious *morceau* from a young gentleman, whose name, out of pity to himself, we kindly suppress, merely stating that he is one of the blooming '*assistants*' at the drapery establishment of *Rogers and Hitchcock*, in St. Paul's-churchyard. Poor young man, we sincerely hope he did not hurt himself in the effort; here it is:-

'DEAR EDITOR, — An having' a bit of a knack at poetry, as my Eliza says, send these loins, wrote 'em myself, and sung 'em at Tom Rounding's after the hunt.
          'Yours, ever, T— G—.'

Some loves to ride in a von oss shay,
    Ven there's neither cloud nor shower;
But an oss for me, on Easter day,
    To ride on an hunting tower (tour).
Yoix, yoix! so, oh! aint it sweet to go,
    Vile ve reg'ler knackers lags,
And vile ve *vistles* the tally-ho!
    To ride afore the stags!
        Chorous of vistling.

Oh! the vild var hoop of a 'Lumber troop',
    Might the henemy afront;
But give to me — if you wants a spree —
    The joys of an Easter hunt.
Then the wenson fine, with sparkling wine,
    Right off we gaily toss;
Oh! I feels quite up, as I drains this cup,
    To my noble hunting hoss.
        Grand chorous of vistling.

Anon, 1838

At the same time he was landlord of the Horse and Well (formerly the Horse and Groom) at Woodford Wells, seen here in 1905 and 1985.

Robert Cruikshank.

THE EPPING HUNT.

THE EPPING HUNT.— The Cockney sport of the Epping Hunt on Easter Monday is almost extinct. For years past it has been gradually declining; and the 'hunt' of Monday last will probably be the last we shall have to record. It was a miserable affair altogether; there was not a single hackney-coach, nor pony-chaise, nor safety-cab on the ground. London stayed at home, and even the dustmen refused to bring out their cattle. It was quite melancholy to look upon the hill from whence thousands used to survey the animated scene. It was bare and deserted. The very stag, ashamed of his company hid himself in the mazes of the forest in a few minutes after he was started, and the dogs sneaked back to kennel because they had nothing to do. The road was no longer the moving picture which sportsmen remember in former times. There were no runaway horses — no dismounted riders — no broken necks — no pleasure whatsoever. A few of the country folk who live about the forest alone came to enjoy the sport — they had it all to themselves; and sadly recompensed they were for all their pains.

Press report, April 1839

THE EPPING HUNT.— On Tuesday, Mr. Thomas Rounding, of the Woodford Wells, under the direction of Mr. Sherring, agent to Mr. Long Wellesley, and agreeably to ancient custom, succeeded, after a run with the dogs, of two hours and forty minutes, in taking a fine four year old buck, to be hunted on Monday next.

Press report, April 10, 1841

No official City hunts were held after 1807, and in that year the office of Master of the City Hounds, known as Mr Common Hunt — a probable abbreviation of the Commonalty's Huntsman — was abolished; a note to that effect appeared in *The Times*. Shortly afterwards the last of the wild Epping Forest deer was hunted by the well-known 'Tommy' Rounding, the chief huntsman of the Lord Warden, the Hon Wellesley Pole, of Wanstead. On 20 October 1827, after a good run, the stag was killed at West Ham. After that the Easter Day meeting, in which a carted stag was used, became a rowdy scene on Fairmead, as described by Tom Hood, in 'red coats, green coats, blue coats and black coats,

sporting coats, sweeps with no coats', all arriving 'in coach and chaise, whisky and cart, gig and waggon, hunter and hack, horse and ass . . .' A huge crowd would gather and spread itself across the plain, consisting of 'baronets, butchers, dandies, huntsmen and snobocracy . . .' The wretched stag, covered in ribbons, was brought across by cart from Buckhurst Hill to Fairmead and released. In terror it leaped away through the crowds, or it calmly made a bee-line for its home paddock behind the 'Bald Faced Stag'. The result was that few even saw it.

Epping Forest, Alfred Leutscher, 1974

We return now to Epping Forest as we find it to-day. Some of its natural charms we have already noticed. But few are aware how rapidly the waste and spoliation of the past are being repaired. Here are some of the most interesting instances. Within less than ten years the Forest area has been extended by reclamations until its three thousand acres have grown to six thousand. The fallow deer, which were well-nigh extinct (the red deer completely died out in 1827), have now increased until they number a full hundred.

The Leisure Hour, Henry Walker, 1883

I call them unique, as, though the same deer are found in some parts of Scotland, I believe these to be the only representatives in England of the ancient deer. The herds of tame fallow deer which are preserved in so many parks throughout England differ completely from the forest breed. The former are chiefly descended from ancestors imported from various parts of Europe, and for reasons that peculiarities are preserved and transmitted, we find in these herds every shade of colour from white to dun and black. The Epping Forest deer, on the contrary, show no such variations. They are all of a uniform dark brown, which appears to be black except when one is in very close proximity.

Epping Forest, Edward North Buxton, 1884

The Forest's animal life is protected against sportsmen; the only hunting allowed here being after such game as blackberries and bluebells, a sport carried on so keenly in spring that primroses begin to be rare. Now that a gun cannot be heard in the Forest, it shelters a great variety of birds, which learn to be bold in showing themselves to unarmed strangers, as well as shy creatures, like the badger, reintroduced after almost complete

The sanctuary at Theydon Bois *(above)* obviated the necessity for deer shelters *(below)* which were once a normal addition to the Forest scene.

extermination. Such had nearly been the fate of the deer, both fallow and roe, that a generation ago were believed to be practically extinct, but have been nursed back into life, here and there stirring the central thickets. Poachers also are not extinct, but now become dealt with in the commonplace procedure of petty sessions. It is said that a good many years ago a brood of prairie wolves was caught in the Forest, having perhaps been turned out in mistake for fox cubs. Foxes and hares are not free from occasional beating up by the hounds; but other animals, rabbits and so on, are left to struggle for existence.

Essex, A. R. Hope-Moncrieff, 1926

The Fallow Deer, which belong to a section of the *Genus Cervus*, are now the only deer remaining. It is many years since the Red deer roamed this Forest, the last of them having been transferred to Windsor Park, as they were found to do enormous damage to property and crops on the Forest borders, it being remembered that the Forest is entirely unenclosed. The Roe Deer are also extinct; the last two, of great age, were, I believe, killed about 1920. At the present time there are about 200 Fallow Deer in the Forest.

Rambles in Epping Forest,
F. H. Headley, 1948

The white stag of Epping Forest is dead. The body of the animal that defied all attempts by the forest authorities to kill it, was found by two young girls.

The stag had always been surrounded by mystery. Some people doubted if it even existed.

Now, in death, the stag has posed an even bigger mystery — who riddled its leg with shotgun pellets? The City of London Corporation, who administer Epping Forest, and once gave a 'Kill on sight' order, say it was not them.

When the white stag first appeared about four years ago, the forest authorities decided to kill it so that the purity of the ancient herd of black fallow deer would not be corrupted. But the order sparked off a nationwide protest and the hunt was called off.

The stag was left in peace, but last week the nine-year-old girls, Gaye Chisenhale-Marsh and her friend Hazel Turner were riding in Epping Forest, near Woodridden Hill, Wake

Arms, Epping, when they saw it lying near a fence on the edge of Sir Thomas Buxton's estate. It was dead and one hind leg was almost severed from the body.

Express & Independent, November 4, 1960

Epping Forest has harboured deer for many centuries and the herd of black fallow deer has been its principal animal feature. Opinions as to the origin of the herd are divided, but, although uninclosed, it was sufficiently a permanent feature for ownership to have been vested in the Conservators by the Epping Forest Act. . . .

In 1878 the herd, through heavy poaching, had become almost extinct, being down to 12 does and 1 buck. Under the protection of the Conservators, numbers improved to a maximum of about 270 in 1902. During the last two decades there has been a rapid decline in the number within the Forest, the cause of which decline is twofold, yet related.

The almost intimate contact with urban conditions into which their habitat and they themselves were brought, in no way tempered the wild condition of the animals. It is a long time since the deer deserted the relatively urban southern Forest Expanses and confined themselves to the rural northern woodlands.

In the most recent decades urban expansion and the changed pattern in which the Forest has come to be used, has resulted in at least a trickle of visitors always progressing, in one direction or another, through the woodland areas. However peaceably they pursue their walks, they and particularly their dogs which all too frequently have chased deer, sometimes pulling them down, exercise a disturbing influence on the animals, who are thus harried, however unwittingly by the public, from one part to another. The two effects have been, firstly, a considerable number of deaths through accidents on the highways by which the woodlands are much divided; and, secondly, most recently, the almost complete desertion of the Forest woodlands in favour of the relatively quieter private woodlands in the locality.

Recognizing the trend of events, the Conservators assured the perpetuation of the Forest strain of fallow deer, by presenting a few to Whipsnade Zoo and also by establishing a sanctuary of 109 acres on the edge of the Forest, stocked likewise by a few deer and a buck from the Whipsnade group. In both cases the animals have bred most successfully.

Epping Forest, Alfred Qvist, 1971

At a time when there is probably more talk than ever before about the need to conserve our flora and fauna, it is pleasant to be able to report that the Essex countryside has never been so well off for deer as it is today. Wild deer are now common over much of north and west Essex, whereas at the turn of the century they were restricted to Epping Forest and adjoining estates. Four species are present today whereas only one, the fallow, was present 50 years ago. The main part of the Essex Deer Survey was carried out, fortuitously, just in time to enable the spread of muntjac and red deer in the county to be dated with some accuracy. Unfortunately, much of the spread of fallow probably took place or was well under way by the time the Survey started. Deer have become more widespread in Essex despite the great increase in urban development and mobility of the population that has occurred this century. In fact, deer are living in extraordinary close proximity to towns. Both wild fallow and muntjac are frequently seen, and breed, in Latton Park and Mark Bushes situated adjacent to Harlow New Town with its 80,000 inhabitants. Appreciable numbers of wild

fallow deer may be seen from houses on the edge of Harold Hill and Harold Wood, situated within the boundary of Greater London. By contrast, the fallow deer in Epping Forest have declined greatly over the last couple of decades, the animals having moved largely to adjoining estates. This decline has been attributed by Qvist (1971), probably correctly, to increased human disturbance and an increased number of animals killed in road traffic accidents. Regular surveys of wild fallow on an estate near Brentwood since 1968 support the idea that excessive human disturbance may cause a decline in the deer population.

The preponderance of deer in north and west Essex is readily explained. Firstly, the only way that deer can spread into Essex is from the west and north: the industrialised Lea Valley to the south-west, the river Thames in the south, the Coast to the east and the Stour valley in the north-east provide effective, if not insuperable, barriers. Muntjac, roe and red deer have all spread into Essex from adjoining counties by these routes. Secondly, all the deer parks which have given rise to populations of fallow deer, except St.

Osyth Priory Park, are situated in north and west Essex. Thirdly, much of east and south Essex is unsuitable for deer, either because of extensive industrial development such as occurs on Thameside or because of the exposed marshland. The main London-Colchester road and railway, which run diagonally south-west to north-east through the county, also appear to provide some kind of barrier because, despite the presence of apparently suitable woodland, deer are rarely found south of this line. Deer originating from those in Weald Park are widespread to the north and west of Brentwood but few are seen across the road and railway, in the extensive woodlands to the south of the town.

The general impression obtained during the past year is that all four species of deer are still spreading through the country. There have been recent, but as yet unconfirmed, reports of roe deer being seen on the northern Essex-Hertfordshire borders. The resident red deer population in north-west Essex has recently (1976) spread towards Braintree and muntjac are still being reported from new localities. We can probably look forward to an even more widespread distribution of deer in Essex in the future.

Deer of Essex, D. I. Chapman, 1977

Every year forest deer have to die. The culling or killing is done by the Epping Forest Conservators for two purposes: to keep down the numbers that the sanctuary at Theydon Bois can support; and to make sure, under statutory legislation, that the herd is kept free from impure deer. The sanctuary was bought by the Corporation of London in 1960 from the Buxton family when the herd of black fallow deer was threatened with extinction. At one time the numbers in the herd dipped to 30.

At the moment the herd is 100 strong, but, says a spokesman for the Conservators, the optimum level the sanctuary can support is 50. 'This is not to say we will kill 50 deer,' he said. 'Mortality and the birth rate play a major part.'

The deer, black fallow, do interbreed with other types, and the conservators want to keep the herd, the 100-acre sanctuary pure. So impure examples, as well as the weak and old are culled to keep the herd to its optimum level.

West Essex Gazette, October 8, 1976

More than 40 Epping Forest deer are to be killed to bring the total in the deer sanctuary down to 80. A recent count showed 115 deer in the sanctuary, plus another eight in the forest — well above the usual maximum number.

Local people have reported seeing one herd of 15 and another of 30 in the forest, but this has not been confirmed by forest keepers.

West Essex Gazette, November 6, 1978

Two societies for animals yesterday condemned gangs of poachers who are killing hundreds of wild deer to satisfy Britains's newly acquired taste for venison.

The highly organised professionals are said to be killing up to 300 deer a week. They hunt at night and use snares, shotguns, crossbows and dogs. The gangs make big money by selling the meat to hotel and restaurant owners eager to include venison on their menus.

Mr John Foll, director of the Deer Society, said major poaching areas were Dorset, Epping Forest, parts of Hampshire, the Midlands and South Wales. His society had the names and addresses of all known poachers on computer record. Red deer taken illegally could fetch between £70 and £200.

The Daily Telegraph, February 25, 1985

Headlines in the local press late in 1976 highlighted the seeming paradox of killing deer in a sanctuary. 'Indeed the sanctuary must be the least safe place in the world should you be an old or excess-to-requirements deer', wrote one Chigwell resident. Pleas were made for the excess deer to be released and allowed to roam free in the Forest. The Conservators answer was that the likely result would be death of the animals at the hands of poachers or the motor car. In spite of poachers activities at Galley Hill, and the average of seven deer killed in road accidents each year, the nature lover can still find deer wild in Epping Forest today. Persistence and patience are the watchwords: this recent picture by Dick Cramp proves the point.

Ancient Camps

Old battle ground by time's sun greyed and browned,
What conflicts spell your history, what bloodstains rust your ground?
The talking wind has levelled your mound in a steady sweep;
And left only ghosts to show where lost traditions sleep.

Ambresbury Banks 1985 with acknowledgment

This entrenchment is now entirely over-grown with old oaks and hornbeams. It was formerly in the very heart of the Forest, and no road near it, till the present turnpike road from London to Epping was made almost within the memory of man, which now runs within a hundred yards of it; but the intrenchment cannot be perceived from thence by reason of the wood that covers it. It is of an irregular figure, rather longest from east to west, and on a gentle declivity to the south-east. It contains near twelve acres, and is surrounded by a ditch and a high bank much worn down by time, though where there are angles they are very bold and high. There are no regular openings, like gateways or entrances, only two places where the bank has been cut through, and the ditch filled up very lately in order to make a straight road from Debden Green to Epping market.

Letter from Mr Lethieullier, Camden's Britannica, 1789

On the south-east side of Copped Hall Park, there are traces of an ancient camp, described (as it appeared at that time) in a letter from Mr. Letheuillir to Mr. Gough, from which the following account is extracted:— 'This entrenchment is now entirely overgrown with old oaks and hornbeams. It was formerly in the very heart of the forest, and no road near it, till the present turnpike-road from London to Epping was made, almost in the memory of man, which now runs within a hundred yards of it; but the entrenchment cannot be perceived from thence, by reason of the wood which covers it. It is of an irregular figure, rather longest from east to west, and on a gentle declivity to the south-east. It contains nearly twelve acres, and is surrounded by a ditch, and a high bank much worn down by time, though, where there are angles, they are very bold and high. There are no regular openings, like gateways or entrances, only two places where the bank has been cut through, and the ditch filled up very lately, in order to make a straight road from Debden Green to Epping market. The boundary between the parishes of Waltham

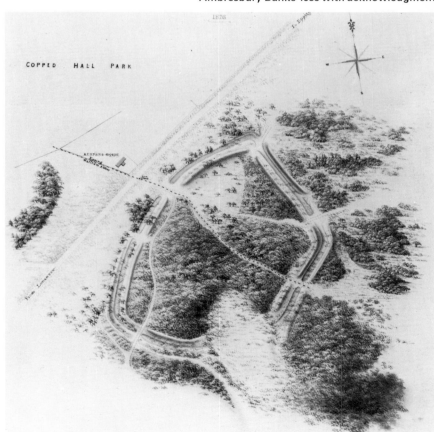

Ambresbury Banks was surveyed by William Doyley in June 1876. Edward North Buxton, the author and naturalist extraordinaire of Knighton, commented at the time that the remarkable state of preservation after more than a thousand years owed much to the fact that the camps were in the heart of the Forest and thus immune from the levelling action of agriculture.

73

Ambresbury Banks, being more easily accessible than Loughton Camp, was a popular Victorian venue for picnics. This is one firm's outing in 1900.

and Epping runs exactly through the middle of this entrenchment, whether carried so casually by the first setters-out of these boundaries, or on purpose, as it was then a remarkable spot of ground, I leave to better judgments to conjecture. As I can find no reason to attribute this entrenchment either to the Romans, Saxons, or Danes, I cannot help concluding it to have been a British Oppidum; and perhaps it had some relation to other remains of that people which are discoverable in our forest.

The History and Topography of the County of Essex, 1831

THE RIDDLE OF AMBRESBURY BANKS

The Britons mustered in arms at least 100,000 — some historians state their force at 250,000 — far outnumbering the Romans, who had, however, on their side the advantage of experience and skill in the art of war; and Boadicea, retiring at their approach, established herself in an entrenched camp in the forest, where, a short distance from Epping, near Copped Hall, and now known as Ambresbury Banks, the remains of her stronghold may still be traced.

Here she decided on awaiting the Roman foe. Some writers have assumed that the last struggle took place at Islington; others at Messing; but Morant and others, whose authority is decisive say: 'The famous battle between Suetonius and Boadicea was fought somewhere between Epping and Waltham, near which a fine camp remains.

Here, then, the opposing forces were drawn up. The Britons, like the Russians at Alma, had brought the ladies to see the fight and witness their triumph.

Their wives and children were taken in wagons to the field and ranged in a line along the rear of the battle — to become its victims, and to swell the slaughter of those they loved.

The skilful Romans had chosen ground accessible at only one point, with a forest at

the back. Having provoked the enemy to the assault, here they remained till the Britons had exhausted themselves, and expended their darts in an attempt to force the narrow pass; then assuming the form of a wedge their infantry bore down on them like an avalanche, while their horsemen with their spears swept the field.

The Britons were routed; and hemmed in by the rows of wagons behind, the warriors, their wives and children fell in one indiscriminate slaughter. The Romans lost only 400, but 80,000 of the Britons were left upon the forest turf.

How little does the quiet traveller from Epping to Waltham, or Loughton, think that a scene of blood like this has passed upon the very spot he is crossing.

People's History of Essex, Coller, 1861

PICNIC AT EPPING FOREST

This afternoon a forest picnic party will be held at Ambresbury Banks (the site of Queen Boadicea's camp), on the high road to Epping. Sir Antonio Brady, Verderer; Mr. A. Johnston, M.P.; Lieut.-Colonel Palmer; Mr. Deputy Stapleton; with ladies and other gentlemen who have taken a prominent part in resisting encroachments on the forest, will be present. The band of the 5th Essex Rifle Volunteers will perform a selection of music from three o'clock.

Globe, August 9, 1873

At the Field Meeting held on July 3rd, 1880, the President suggested that the scientific exploration of the two ancient earth-works, known as Ambresbury Banks and the Loughton Camp, would be a fitting and worthy task for the Club to undertake. The suggestion was warmly received by the mem-

bers present. On October 30th, 1880, permission to make the necessary excavations was granted to the Club by the Epping Forest Committee of the Corporation of London.

On the morning of May 30th the contractor and workmen were duly on the ground, together with our directors General Pitt-Rivers and Mr. D'Oyley, and several members of the Committee. A part of the rampart in the left-hand side entering the Camp from Epping Road had been staked out, but it was found that excavations there would necessitate the removal of at least one large tree; and a site to the right of the entrance free from trees of any size was finally chosen. The ground was speedily staked-out by the Surveyor, the bushes cleared away, and the turf peeled off. Then commenced the careful work which demanded the close attention of the explorers for eight or nine days. The earth was systematically dug out in 'spits' by the workmen and thrown into the barrows or cart, where each spadeful underwent a rigorous examination by the several members of the Committee on 'search duty'. It was found impossible to use the sieve in consequence of the clayey and agglutinative nature of much of the soil, and small geological hammers and extemporised spades were soon busily employed in turning over and over the *débris* of the ancient rampart. But some of the searchers found that their hands were really the best instruments in such close work, and several of the 'finds' were the result of persevering digital exercises. Throughout, the workmen were very careful and watchful, faithfully carrying out the directions given to them. . . . We were soon able to distinguish the 'old surface-line' or original undisturbed soil of the Forest, the exact limits of which it was so necessary to define. The artificial character of the soil composing the rampart was often very noticeable, the successive layers of deposited earth being readily distinguished. . . .

Although the occupation of watching the gradual and systematic removal of the rampart was oft times felt to be somewhat monotonous and tedious, yet the weather during the greater part of the time was so balmy, and the fresh spring woods so cheerful and pleasant, that the members on duty felt themselves amply repaid for their enforced sojournings in the 'house of the forest,' with its pillared arches, shadowy aisles, and arabesques of leaves and flowers. In the early mornings, especially, as we rode down from Loughton at five o'clock to meet the workmen at the Camp, the quiet beauties of the 'merry green woods' sank deeply into our minds; the sweet blossoming hawthorns bordering the Epping Road, snowy white when newly petalled, but flushing with a lovely pink as the myriads of tiny roses hastened to decay, were surely never seen in greater glory. Friends from time to time strolled over to watch our proceedings, and to share our primitive meals at the Wake Arms . . .

Journal entry, Essex Field Club, 1882

It was on a bright summer's day in 1872 that I took a ticket to Loughton for a ramble in the Forest, which thereabouts is exceptionally attractive. After crossing a streamlet, I ascended a prominent and elevated hill commanding a prospect of remarkable beauty and extent. As I wandered on, my attention was diverted from the natural charms of this lovely spot, by what past experience suggested might be an ancient moat or ditch. A few minutes examination produced the conviction that here was one of those renowned earthworks of which examples are scattered all over the country. After only a provisional investigation, and a mental resolve to make enquiry, other explorations were made, and the supposed earthwork was left, but not forgotten. . . . During three years I could obtain no further clue, so in 1875 I decided upon seeking for the Loughton entrenchment again. I went, therefore, and this time sought the place from the Epping New Road, or from the west. I did not know the precise position, and it was only with difficulty I discovered it; in fact, not until I had mentally abandoned my task, and concluded that the camp must have been a phantom after all. It was no phantom, however, and I traced the lines of the embankment and trench for a considerable distance. This was all I could do on my second visit, except that I took note of the exact locality. Since then I have been several times, and have traced the entire circumference, and obtained other details.

Personal account by Mr. B. Harris Cowper

Further examination, and a careful survey made in 1876 by Mr. D'Oyley, confirmed Mr. Cowper's first impressions, and to these gentlemen belong the credit of discovering and defining one of the most interesting antiquities of the kind in the neighbourhood of London. The camp is situated in the depths of the Forest, about a mile north-west of the village of Loughton, and about two miles south-west of Ambresbury Banks. It is marked on the new official map, but the dimensions there laid down are very misleading — in reality Loughton Camp is about 800 yards in circumference, and contains between eleven and twelve acres, the two Forest camps (Ambresbury and Loughton) being almost exactly of the same size. . . . The whole site is covered with forest, and a large number of very ancient holly trees grow in and around the camp. . . . The ramparts have suffered greatly from denudation, digging for foxes, sand &c. and in one place in particular, on the western side, the bank and trench have been completely destroyed, and the soil apparently literally tumbled down the face of the hill. Near this spot also, a considerable portion of the western glacis has been removed by the

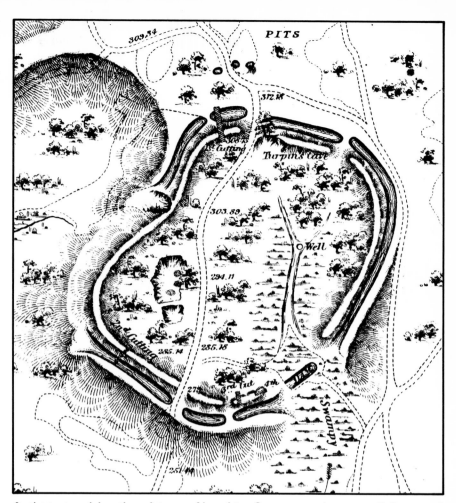

As the text explains, the existence of Loughton Camp was unknown until discovered by Mr Harris Cowper in 1872 who has received little credit or attention in recent years for his tremendous historical revelation. What tales the camp could tell if only its secrets could be unlocked. An attempt to do just that took place in 1882 when the Essex Field Club excavated the banks in three places — indicated on this drawing. It is interesting to note the addition of the words 'Turpin's Cave' as there are at least two other locations in Epping Forest which vie for this dubious privilege.

Forest 'improvers', to make room for their 'Green-ride'! . . .

The Club having resolved to continue the investigation of the Forest earthworks . . . the work was begun on May 29th, and was continued day by day until June 14th . . .

The mode of working . . . consisted in cutting sections through the rampart and ditch in order to expose the 'old surface line' . . . each spadeful of earth was sifted on its removal and carefully examined for relics, the position of each object as it was found being entered on a working section of the cutting.

Journal entry, Essex Field Club, 1882

Ambresbury Banks was built high on the forest ridge and if the trees had been cleared from the whole area it would have commanded a magnificent view southwards across the Thames to Kent and north-west almost to the Chiltern Hills — an excellent site for a hill-top fort.

To build the camp the area would first have been cleared of trees and the line of the walls would have been marked out in the clearing — perhaps the shape can best be described as a rounded square enclosing approximately 12 acres. The people would then have used bone and wooden tools to dig a ditch about 10 feet (3 metres) deep, piling up the soil in a bank 10 feet (3 metres) high on the inside. This high wall would have been reinforced with any large stones found in the clearing and could have been topped by a palisade made from the

felled trees. When you see the walls now, nearly 2,000 years after the camp was abandoned, it is easy to imagine how impressive they must have been when first constructed. There was only one entrance to the camp, guarded by two sets of large gates and here the earth was left undisturbed. Excavations have shown that the other gaps in the walls are the result of the banks being pushed back down into the ditch at a later period in history. They also indicate that there was some reconstruction work on the walls and it seems that the site was in use for 400-500 years, until after the Roman invasion. The excavations turned up very little evidence of regular human occupation and it seems clear that the camp was not used as permanent living quarters. Neither was there anything to confirm the legend of Queen Boadicea making her last stand against the Romans here. In fact it seems highly unlikely that she ever came near Ambresbury Banks. . . .

Loughton Camp is a similar construction to Ambresbury Banks, although it has not been so well investigated. It still lies hidden in the Forest, off the beaten track, north-west of Loughton. It can be found in the south-western corner of the junction of the Green Ride and the Clay Road at Sandpit Plain, although the area is riddled with sand and gravel pits and the walls are not so easy to identify as those of Ambresbury Banks.

Epping Forest through the Ages,
Georgina Green, 1982

In the eighteenth century highwaymen infested the roads around London attacking and robbing travellers at will. In 1763 Sir John Fielding, Chief Magistrate at Bow Street, attempted to introduce a small night horse patrol to guard the roads leading into the capital but it had to be disbanded the following year for lack of funds. Not until 1805 was the idea revived with the formation of the Bow Street Horse Patrol from 54 former cavalry troopers. With their uniform of blue and waistcoats of red, the 'Robin Redbreasts' were the direct forerunners of today's Metropolitan Police Mounted Branch.

Crime

The evil reputation of Epping Forest is of ancient date, and all through our social records stories of its terrors crop up. The Anglo-Roman travellers had not more dread of its coverts and thickets than had those who lived in its neighbourhood after the Peace of 1698, when, as Macaulay notes, a large number of discharged soldiers turned robbers, and were so daring and numerous, that for some time cavalry every evening patrolled the roads leading into it.

Walks in Epping Forest, Percy Lindley, 1886

Another time, Tom Gray [executed at Tyburn, March 10, 1713] and two other highwaymen meeting with one Mr. W—, a goldsmith living in Covent Garden, as he was riding to Epping, they robbed him and cut the girths of his stallion. The horse no sooner smelled the mares of these rogues but he was for covering them, being scurvy troublesome for all their whipping and slashing him, so that the mares leaped over some pales and the stone-horse after them, into the yard of Mr. W—'s, friends, who knowing his horse very well, and perceiving it without either bridle or saddle, secured the men until they knew what was become of him. Two or three hours afterwards, the aforesaid person coming also to the same house and telling his friends how these fellows had robbed him, they had them before a magistrate who committed them to Chelmsford gaol. But they did not tarry long there, for in less than a week they all three broke out, with a great many other felons along with them.

Captain Alexander Smith, 1926

On Wednesday last in the Afternoon the Bury Stage Coach was robbed upon Epping Forest near Epping Town, by one Highwayman on Foot, booted and spurr'd (having left his Horse hard by as best suiting his Conveniency at that time and Place) who afterwards made his Escape, when he had collected among the Passengers about four Pounds.

Press report, 1727

On Saturday night last about Seven o'clock five Rogues enter'd the House of the Widow Shelly, at Loughton in Essex, having Pistols &c and threaten'd to murder the old Lady, if she did not tell them where her money lay, which she obstinately refusing for some time, threaten'd to lay her across the Fire if she did not instantly tell them, which she would not do, but her Son being in the Room, and threaten'd to be murder'd, cry'd out, he would tell them if they would not murder his mother, and did. Whereupon they went upstairs and took near 100 l. a Silver Tankard, and other Plate, and all manner of Household Goods. They afterwards went into the Cellar, and drank several bottles of Ale and Wine, and broil'd some Meat, ate the Relics of a Fillet of Veal. &c. While they were doing this, two of their gang went into Mr Turkle's, a farmer's, who rents one end of the Widow's House, and robbed him of above 20 l. and then they all went off, taking two of the Farmer's horses to carry off their Luggage, the Horses were found on Sunday Morning in Old Street, they staid about Three Hours in the House.

London Evening Post, February 6, 1735

A few Days ago, a Servant to the Woodford Coachman driving a Chaise and Pair empty, over Epping Forest, was attacked by some Ruffians, who cut his Throat almost from Ear to Ear. 'Tis suppos'd they were disturb'd, having left about 32s. in his Pocket. He made a shift to crawl to Woodford to a Surgeon's, who sewed up the Wound, and 'tis thought he will recover.

About the same time a Higgler was found on the Forest in his Cart, with his Brains beat out, and the Horses standing still at a Gate.

Press report, 1739

Wednesday Night, about Six o'Clock, Mr. Hawes, Collector of the Customs for the Port of Boston in Lincolnshire, was stopped by a single Highwayman between the Green-Man on Epping Forest and Stratford, who attacked him in a very genteel Manner, telling him that he should be contented with his giving him what he thought proper, but on his Refusal he should be obliged to use rougher Methods, on which Mr. Hawes gave him a few Shillings in his Hat, with which he rode off; but before he got to Stratford he was again attacked by three Footpads, who pulled him off his Horse, and took from him his Watch and Five Guineas, his Whip, Hat and Wig, and then left him to make the best of his Way.

Press report, 1750

On Sunday morning, about Nine o'Clock, Mr. Braithwaite, a Weaver in Brick-Lane, Spital Fields, was attack'd in a Post-Chaise by a single Highwayman, between the Eagle on Epping-Forest and Woodford, who presented a Pistol to him, threatening to shoot him if he did not deliver his Money, but promising at the same Time, if he comply'd, he should receive no Hurt; accordingly Mr. Braithwaite

Widow Shelly of Loughton is tortured over her fire by members of the Gregory gang who terrorised the area in the 1730s.

The robbery of Mr Hawes the customs man 'between the Green Man and Stratford'.

gave him his Purse, containing about Seven Pounds, upon which he rode off with a Companion (who was on Horseback, and stood still during the Robbery, at about 200 Yards Distance) thro' the Woods towards Hale-End. He is a genteel young Fellow, about twenty, well mounted on a Bay Gelding, with a Star on his Forehead, dress'd in a Silver-laced Hat, brown Wig, a light Drab Coat, with a Hanger by his Side; and is very much pitted with the Small-Pox. It is remarkable, that Mr. Braithwaite pull'd out a Silver Watch and offer'd it; but he replied, Sir, keep it, I keep no Company with Tale-bearers.

Press report, 1750

This Morning two young Fellows were taken up, and committed, being accused of the Murder of Mr. Cary, the Higgler, near Epping. They are said to be 'Prentices to a Wine-Cooper of this City; and we hear there are several belonging to this infernal gang.

Press report, 1752

Saturday Morning Mr. Justice Bateman was robbed on Epping Forest in his own Coach by a single Highwayman, who very civilly demanded his Money, and afterwards rode off towards Wanstead.

Press report, 1753

Last Monday Morning about seven o'Clock, Mr. Starks, a Hop Factor in the Borough, was attacked by two Highwaymen well mounted, near the Eagle on Epping Forest, who demanded his Money, but Mr. Starks with the butt End of his Whip struck the Pistol out of the Fellow's Hand, which the other observing rode off, and his Companion was taken and carried to Chelmsford Gaol.

Press report, 1753

Where Mr Starks fought off his assailants in 1753 — the Spread Eagle, as it was then, dates from the late seventeenth century. *Right:* **Some 200 years on.**

Although we have no way of knowing exactly what the road between 'the Eagle on Epping-Forest and Woodford' looked like in 1750, we can still let our imagination take us back . . . to a time before lorries and cars . . . before metalled roads . . . before stately mansions . . . before . . .

'Stand and deliver!' Highway robbery was rife over the whole of the Epping Forest area and few were so bold as to venture into its depths alone. Contemporary prints can give us some idea of the time although the 'rigidity' of the art of the period makes them look somewhat unreal.

Still very much a reality is the old hanging tree at Buckhurst Hill. Before the road was moved, the oak stood alongside the London to Epping road (next to the lodge to Knighton — page 227). Today it is in the back garden of Mr and Mrs Edward Anderson's house, No. 654 High Road.

The same Day two Highwaymen, both dressed in blue-grey Coats, with Cockades in their Hats, and Hangers by their sides, well mounted, stopt Sir Roger Brampton in his Chariot on Epping-Forest, when they presented their Pistols, and robbed him of seven guineas, and then rode off, wishing him a good Journey, with a great deal of Ceremony.

Press report, 1753

On Sunday Evening two shabby-looking Fellows committed several Robberies in Epping Forest.

Press report, 1754

Last Monday Evening, between Five and Six o'Clock, as a Master Carpenter in Maddox-Street, Hanover-Square, was returning out of Essex, he was stopt, between the seven and eight Mile Stone on this Side of Woodford-Bridge, by a single Highwayman, well mounted on a brown Mare or Horse, with a black swish Tail, who demanded his Money, and the Highwayman taking off his Hat to receive it, the Carpenter struck at him with the thick End of his Whip, but missed his Head, and hit him across the Shoulders; upon that the Highwayman fired a Pistol at him, which shot through his Hat close to his Head, and then, both their horses rearing up, the Highwayman took out another Pistol, and asked him if he'd yield; but the Carpenter replying he would die before he would be robbed, the Highwayman said, You are an obstinate Dog, I shall be sorry if I have hurt you, but damn you, if you follow me one Step, I will turn and shoot you dead; and rode off towards Woodford-Bridge. The Highwayman wore his own Hair, had on a blue Surtout Coat, and is about five Feet nine Inches high.

Press report, 1755

Last Saturday Morning, about Four o'Clock, one John Munfer, a Higgler, was stopped upon Epping-Forest by two Footpads,

who obliged him to unload his cart, by oversetting it; when they rummaged it (as they called it) for a Turkey which they said had Money in its Body: but finding his Cargo to consist principally of Pork, Butter, and Pigs (and no Turkey), they only took a Pig, two Pounds of Butter, and Eighteen-pence in Money, and bidding the Higgler Goodmorrow, ran into a Thicket, and were seen no more. One was very stout, the other a little Fellow, both with loose Rug-Coats.

Press report, 1755

On Tuesday Evening as two Gentlemen on Horseback were coming to town, they were attacked by a single Highwayman upon Epping-Forest, and on his demanding their Money, one of the Gentlemen readily complied; but while he was delivering the same, the other Gentleman took an Opportunity of striking the Highwayman on the Head with his Whip; upon which the Highwayman attempted to shoot him, but the Pistol missing Fire, and a Farmer on Horseback appearing in Sight, the Highwayman rode full Speed into the Wood, and got clear off.

Press report, 1757

General Post Office, March 21, 1757

Whereas the Post-boy bringing the Norwich Mail from Epping to this office was, this Morning about Four o'Clock attacked and robbed on the road by the Obelisk or High Stone, near Leytonstone in the County of Essex by a single Highwayman on Horseback who presented a pistol to the Post-boy at the time ordering him to deliver the Mail otherwise he would blow his Brains out, which obliged the Post-boy to unstrap the Mail and deliver it to the Highwayman who took the whole Norwich Mail before him upon his horse, and rode away with it full speed towards Epping.

Press report, March 1757

General Post Office,
March 21st, 1757

Whereas the Post Boy, bringing the Norwich Mail from Epping to this office, was this morning about four o'clock attacked and robbed on the road by the Obelisk or High Stone, near Leytonstone, in the County of Essex, by a single highwayman, on horseback, who presented a pistol to the boy, at the same time ordering him to deliver him the mail, otherwise he would blow his brains out, which obliged the Post Boy to unstrap the mail and deliver it to the highwayman, who took the whole Norwich Mail before him upon his horse and rode away at full speed towards Epping. . . . The man who committed this robbery is described to be a middle sized man who had a white or very light coloured riding coat with a plain hat. He rode a brown or dark coloured little horse with a swish tail. This is therefore to give notice that whoever shall apprehend or convict or cause to be apprehended and convicted the person who committed this robbery will be entitled to a reward of £200, over and above the reward given by Act of Parliament for Apprehending of Highwaymen; or if any person or persons, whether the accomplice of the said robber or knowing thereof, shall make discovery whereby the person who committed the same may be apprehended and brought to justice, such discoverer or discoverers will, upon conviction of the party, be entitled to the same reward of £200 and also have His Majesty's most gracious pardon.

By command of the Postmaster General.

George Shelvocke,

Secretary.

Announcement, London Chronicle, 1757

Friday morning, Matthew Snatt, a Baker, was brought to the Bar at the Assizes held at Chelmsford, in Essex, to be tried for robbing the Norwich Mail on the 21st March last, and would not, for a considerable time, plead to the Indictment, until Lord Chief Justice

Mansfield, who sat on the Bench, was obliged to give Orders to the Gaol-Keeper to take him away, and let him be pressed gradually with Weights til he agreed to plead, otherwise in that Manner to Press him to Death (which is the Punishment the Law appoints for those that will not plead) but upon the above Order being given, he pleaded Not Guilty, and put himself upon his Trial. The Fact being fully proved against him, he was found Guilty, having nothing material to say in his Defence. After his Execution his Body will be hung in Chains at Laytonstone, where he committed the Robbery.

Press report, April 1757

Last Saturday morning about three o'clock, Mr. William Collett, of Loughton, Higgler, was stopped and robbed by two footpads, as he was coming to London, between the Bald Faced Stag and Woodford-wells, Epping Forest, on Stony-rock-hill, over-against where Snatt hangs in chains for robbing the Norwich mail. They were both lusty men, but it is hoped the keepers on the forest will not suffer them to harbour there long.

Press report, 1757

On Tuesday Mr. Piper, a Farmer, on his Return for Loughton in Essex, was attacked near Woodford Bridge by a single Highwayman, who robbed him of his Money, and shot him in the Shoulder, on account of his making Resistance.

Press report, 1757

Last night, about six o'clock, as a young lady was going home in a post-chaise to Woodford Bridge, she was stopt by three high-waymen near her own house, and robbed of what money, &c. she had about her. Her father-in-law, Mr. Dangerfield, being behind, and soon expected, the family sent a servant to acquaint him with what had happened; and on receiving the news he set out from Strat-ford, where he was, and was stopt near the same place by the same men, who carried him into the wood just by, where they robbed him, and cut off the pockets of his coat, breeches, &c. and he went home almost in a naked condition.

Press report, 1758

Saturday Capt. Cockburn, Commissioner and Comptroller of the Navy, was robbed by two highwaymen, near his own house, at Wood-riding, upon Epping-forest. Mr. Clay, of Golden-hall, was robbed about half an hour

The Highstone figures in many accounts of robberies in days gone by — one of the most 'famous' being the theft of the Norwich Mail. Matthew Snatt was brought to trial at Chelmsford; after his execution his body was hung in chains near the location of his crime as a deterrent to others.

All that remains of the original Highstone is the base believed to be late Roman in origin, the obelisk dating from the 1700s. This was the spot where Leyton was created a Municipal Borough on October 2, 1926.

after, going down Buckhurst-hill, by the same highwaymen, who that afternoon had their horses shod at Loughton, from whence they rode off for London.

Press report, 1758

Last Friday two higglers, returning from London to Epping, were stopped by two foot-pads beyond the Eagle at Snaresbrook; who robbed one of them of a thirty-six-shilling-piece, and fired a pistol at the other: the ball went through his right arm, which he has since lost the use of.

Press report, 1758

Robberies are every Day and Night com-mitted on Epping Forest, by so desperate a Gang, that though they are known to the Inhabitants, they are fearful of apprehending them.

Press report, 1761

. . . a gentleman and lady upon Epping Forest, near Snaresbrook, of a silver watch and upwards of six guineas and some silver.

Press report, 1763

On Sunday Morning last, as the Stage Waggoner belonging to Mr. Thomas Cock-sedge of this Town, was coming over Epping-Forest, he was stopped by a Footpad, who, on his making some Resistance, fired at him; the Ball entering his Cloaths, wounded him in the Breast, but he is thought to be in no Danger.

Press report, 1764

Wednesday Evening Mr. John Parker, Brush-Maker in Southwark, was stopped by a single Highwayman a little beyond the Bald-faced Stag on Epping Forest, and robbed of a Silver Watch and eleven Shillings.

Press report, 1764

Early on Friday the drivers of seven hay and straw waggons and other carriages were stopped by a gang of villains between Wood-ford and Loughton, in Essex, who robbed them of small sums in silver and halfpence, and stripped the other of his coat, waistcoat, hat, and watch, amounting together in value to about 9l.

Press report, 1788

79

Of the old Forest inns, none had a more romantic history than the old Green Man at Leytonstone, a favourite meeting place in the eighteenth century. The innkeeper was in the confidence of the highwaymen and gave them cover. One bedroom of this famous old house held an enormous chest in which three or four men could conceal themselves. Underneath the chest was a trap-door, through which the fugitives escaped to a room below. In the floor of the lower room there was another trap-door, opening into a cave, with a passage leading to freedom in the dense undergrowth of the Forest. Old pistols and other weapons were found from time to time in or about the old inn.

The Forest was now the terror of all honest citizens. In August 1695 our great English philosopher John Locke, writing to Edward Clarke from Oates his house at High Laver that 'There were several people robed [robbed] in Eping Forest the same morning we passed it. We heard of it at The Green Man and our Ladys hearts went pit-a-pat.'

Epping Forest, William Addison, 1945

On Tuesday evening about seven o'clock, as the Rev. Mr. Williams was coming to town in a post-chaise from Epping, he was stopped at Woodford, by two highwaymen, who robbed him of his gold watch and purse, containing ten guineas and a half. — They were young men, masked, and were exceedingly well mounted.

Press report, 1790

On Thursday, about four o'clock in the afternoon, as Samuel Dupont, Esq. and his lady were returning to their house in Broadstreet, from Woodford, they were stopped at the six mile-stone, near Snaresbrook, by two highwaymen; exceedingly well mounted, with masks over their faces, and armed with pistols, who took from them their gold watches, purses, &c which together contained about twenty-five guineas and some silver. They behaved very politely, and said it was real distress that induced them to take such a step.

Press report, 1790

Friday, three ladies were stopped in a carriage near Woodford Wells, by two highwaymen, who robbed them. The two men were immediately pursued, and separated. One of them was taken near Battle-bridge by a gentleman, who first knocked him off his horse. He was conveyed to Justice Spiller's, in Shoreditch. On him were found three purses, a loaded pistol, and a mask. The ladies not being present, he was committed for re-examination. — The other highwayman was also taken, and conveyed to Justice Blackborow's, in Clerkenwell. On him a purse, a loaded pistol, and a mask were also found. He was likewise committed for further examination.

Press report, 1790

The old Green Man at Leytonstone was a known refuge of highwaymen as the landlord Richard Bayes is reputed to have been in league with the criminal fraternity of the period. It was near here that Dick Turpin robbed Joseph Major on April 30, 1737 'some forty yards from the inn' stealing from him his racehorse Whitestockings, a knife, horse whip and seven or eight pounds in gold and silver.

The pond beside the inn would have existed in Turpin's day — a convenient watering hole in an age of horse transport. It remained to be seen until after the Second World War when it was filled in and landscaped into a public garden affording a modicum of peace away from the raceway of the nearby Green Man roundabout.

On Tuesday, about eleven o'clock at noon, as Sir William Plomer, Knt. and Alderman, was taking an airing in his carriage on Epping Forest, with a young Lady and Gentleman, they were stopped near the six mile-stone at Snaresbrook, by a single highwayman, who robbed them of a metal watch, and about fourteen guineas in gold and silver.

Press report, 1793

On Monday evening last, a chaise, in which were two Gentlemen, coming over Epping Forest, was robbed of a trunk of very considerable value, with which they got clear off. In it were contained sixty guineas, thirty-five half guineas, and sixteen seven-shilling pieces, in gold; eight pounds in silver, in Bank-notes, twenty-five of 1l each, twenty-three of 2l each, and three of 5l each; together with a very large quantity of gilt articles, such as patterns of watch chains, seals, rings, necklaces, earrings, &c. on cards.

Press report, 1802

On the east side of High Beech Hill, in the thick of the forest, is an excavation, almost hidden from sight by the overhanging trees and brushwood, which had become locally known as 'Dick Turpin's Cave,' from a tradition that it was one of the lurking-places of that notorious highwayman. This part of the forest was anything but safe for wayfarers, unless well armed, down to the end of the last century, deer-stealing being of common occurrence here.

Greater London, Edward Walford, 1883

One of the most famous landmarks to be seen in the area earlier this century was Dick Turpin's cave at High Beach — the one he reputedly used in May 1737 when he fled from London.

Fresh evidence came to light recently regarding the Roman camp, with the discovery of a Roman well below the Bell Inn, Epping.

It is believed to be one of ten situated along the A.11, running right through the camp.

The notorious highwayman, Dick Turpin, is said to have used this well as a hide-out when his other retreat at High Beech became too 'hot'. After one series of robberies he took refuge in the small hole under the cellar while his pursuers passed close by on the main road.

When Turpin was later caught and hanged, the well at the 17th century drovers' inn fell into disuse and was eventually forgotten.

The highwayman's haunt was re-discovered by workmen during reconstruction work at the inn.

Commented mine host, Mr. Leslie Barker: 'We tried emptying our well in the cellar by spending a whole night pumping it dry. But unfortunately the very next morning it was full of water again.'

Dick Turpin, it seems, found a damp and uncomfortable way of evading the long arm of the law.

The Woodford Times, August 19, 1960

It seems quite extraordinary the way a piece of history, even if it be coloured with legend, can be swept aside and all but forgotten in a few short years.

Like the memory, the inscription is slowly fading on Dick's father's grave in Wanstead Churchyard: Thomas died April 20, 1719.

Mrs. Stephens, an elderly widow woman, who kept a Chandler's shop within 200 yards of the Castle Inn at Woodford, was found murdered this morning. The murder must have been committed late on Saturday night the 5th instant. Her skull was dreadfully fractured, and her throat cut; her pockets emptied, a quantity of money taken from the till, and her watch missing. A man of the name of W. Cornwell, who had been employed as an ostler at Woodford, was taken into custody on the 16th, in consequence of his having given the watch to a publican as satisfaction for a debt. On being taken into custody he acknowledged that it had been in his possession, that he found it on Sunday morning, after the murder, at four o'clock, close to the pond near the Castle-inn, where he went to get water for his horses. He confessed that he had been at Mrs. Stephens' shop on Saturday, the evening of the murder, and had seen her in her shop about nine o'clock, previous to her shutters being put up. Several other suspicious circumstances being brought to light before the Magistrates, the prisoner was fully committed for trial.

Press report, June 7, 1813

William Cornwell, a horsekeeper, was indicted for the murder of Martha Stevens, at Woodford, on the 5th day of June last. . . .

Lord Ellenborough summed up the case [at Chelmsford] with great minuteness, after which the Jury, without any hesitation, found the prisoner Guilty. — His Lordship, in a most solemn and impressive manner, immediately pronounced the awful sentence of the law, that he was to be hanged and his body dissected. The prisoner received it almost with a brutal carelessness and exclaimed, 'Thank you, my Lord.' It is said, that in his way back to the gaol, and when he arrived there, he behaved in a like manner. His whole demeanour during the trial shewed no marks of feeling, but he seemed very attentive to the evidence.

Press report, August 6, 1813

Execution of William Cornwall. — The Judge having complied with the request of the Magistrates, the prisoner was brought from Chelmsford to Woodford in the gaol caravan, by half-past nine o'clock on Monday morning. The necessary preparations for the execution having been previously made, the High Sheriff, with the Magistrates and Civil Power, were in attendance at an early hour; and upwards of 3000 of the inhabitants of Woodford and neighbouring parishes were collected on the occasion. — The prisoner attended divine service at Chelmsford on Sunday last, and although he has continued to exhibit the same outward appearance of hardihood, his assumed fortitude seemed at that time to be much shaken, and he was near fainting in the church; but upon being removed into the air, he resumed his former manner. He afterwards expressed his disinclination at being shut up alone in his cell. The keeper of the gaol had very properly secured him since conviction with a straight waistcoat, and when the usual prison diet was offered the prisoner, he refused it, saying he was not dry or hungry enough to eat dry bread, or drink water. Upon his arrival at Woodford, he was immediately placed in a private room with the Rev. Mr. Kebbel; and notwithstanding the zealous endeavours of that Gentleman, he not only declined making any confession, but also steadfastly refused to join in prayer, confining himself to the same expression he had constantly used prior to his conviction — 'That he had nothing to say, but was innocent of the crime for which he was going to suffer.' These were also the last words he uttered under the gallows; and at five minutes before eleven he was launched into eternity. The body, after hanging the usual time, was delivered into the hands of the proper parties for dissection, agreeably to the sentence. The surrounding multitude conducted themselves with becoming attention and propriety.

Press report, 1813

On Thursday night, between 11 and 12 o'clock at night, as Mr. Flower, the son of Sir Charles Flower, was going to his father's country house on horseback, at Woodford, when he got near the George Inn, at Woodford, he was attacked by a single footpad, armed with a pistol, who ordered him to stop and deliver his money, or he would shoot him; Mr. Flower, trusting to the fleetness of his horse, spurred him, but he had proceeded but a few paces, when two more robbers rushed from the hedge and discharged a pistol at him, providentially the contents missed Mr. Flower, but entered the horse; the animal then stood, Mr. Flower jumped off, and the instant he alighted, he received a violent blow, which he supposed to be from the butt end of a pistol, in consequence of which he fell and lay senseless for a considerable time, he supposes about a quarter of an hour. When he came to himself, he found all his pockets emptied, his horse and the robbers gone; he with considerable difficulty reached his father's house, which was about a mile off, being very unwell from the effects of the blow, which he still feels. The robbers had the appearance of soldiers.

Press report, 1814

Daring Footpad Robbery. — On Wednesday morning, about half past ten o'clock, as a Gentleman was travelling in his single-horse chaise, near the 14-mile stone on the Epping road, three men suddenly rushed upon the chaise, seized the horse, and demanded the Gentleman's money. Astonished at the unexpected attack, the sun then shining bright, he asked them if they were serious, to which they replied with horrid oaths and threats; two of them then produced two common pistols, and one a horse-pistol, and swore they would shoot him if he did not instantly deliver them his money. He complied, and gave them four £1 Bank notes. This did not satisfy them, and they demanded his watch; this also he gave them, and which, together with the gold chain and seals, were worth £40: They then ran across Epping Forest. The Gentleman was within two miles of his own house, and got a number of men to go in pursuit of them; they were traced for a considerable distance by the marks of their feet, but the trace was however at length lost, they were all Irishmen, from their accent.

Press report, 1817

Novel Mode of Smuggling. — A few mornings since, a hearse, drawn by four black horses, and followed by a carriage resembling that of a private gentleman, arrived at the White Hart inn, Woodford, where ten horses were instantly put to both vehicles, and, with-

By the 1820s there were five inns at Woodford. The George, in former days called Horns Inn, dates from the early eighteenth century and therefore the present pub is the same building near where the son of Sir Charles Flower was attacked and beaten in 1814.

'When he got near the George Inn . . .'

out the loss of a moment, they drove off. The circumstance of the post-horses being ordered the night before to be in readiness, and drawn out into the street to await the arrival of the vehicle, as well as the great anxiety of the drivers to get off expeditiously, excited some surprise. It has, however, since been stated that the hearse and carriage were laden with upwards of £7,000 worth of smuggled silks, which, by this ingenious mode, were conveyed with perfect safety from London to Norwich. The constables and Excise officers at Woodford, and several towns through which the booty passed, have, since they heard of the fact, been ready to bite their nails for letting so valuable a prize escape.

Press report, 1831

Another of Woodford's inns stood not far away — the White Hart — a post house with an early nineteenth century frontage — the one we see today. Here, in the road outside, a daring and audacious robbery took place in 1831.

'Few indeed were those who dared to venture after dusk along the

Parts of this wood . . . lying in the deeper and dark hollows are singularly suggestive of their past history, when they formed the home and hiding places of reckless outcasts, upon whose lives a price had been set, and against whom every man's hand was raised, as theirs was against every man. From these deep thickets they stole when night fell on the Forest to slay the deer, or snare the smaller game, to cut and carry away the timber, or rob and slay some lonely traveller. Now and then they would break into the quiet home of a too conscientious and active gamekeeper, to revenge in torture and death some comrade's capture and execution. The terror of the country round, few indeed were those who dared venture after dusk along the New Road between London and Epping, unless they were either exceptionally bold men, heavily armed, or strongly escorted; and there was a time when even cavalry troops were employed constantly to guard the roads, now so secure and peaceful. This state of things was not put an end to until about the middle of the last century, when the estate, having long before passed into the hands of an old Yorkshire family named Conyers, Mr. John Conyers cut down the thickets, made paths through the wood, drove out the robbers and poachers, and, by erecting cottages and converting waste portions of the park or forest into cultivated land, succeeded in making the violent depredators honest, civilized and peaceable labourers upon his own estate: a worthy man, and one to be honourably remembered here in Essex.

Walks in Epping Forest, Percy Lindley, 1886

Apart from the charcoal burners few people actually lived within the area of the trees, preferring the safety of the villages. However, after the Civil War the Forest gave sanctuary to a number of discharged soldiers turned outlaws, particularly a gang called the Waltham Blacks who blackened their faces when out robbing travellers or poaching the king's deer. To protect unwary travellers clearings were made along the road sides, and these can still be seen beside some of the Forest roads as areas of newer trees and scrub, with the line of the older pollarded trees beyond — Goldings Hill is a good example of this.

Epping Forest through the Ages,
Georgina Green, 1982

On Thursday last Mr Underwood, a woolstapler, of Lavenham, in Suffolk, on his way to town, stopped at Sudbury, when a man of genteel appearance came up to him, and asked where he was bound to. He replied: 'To London'. The other then desired to bear him company, as he was a stranger to the road; they dined together at Braintree, and lay at Chelmsford. The next morning they set out together, and when they came to Epping Forest, the stranger said: 'Sir, here we must part, but first you must deliver your money'; and robbed him of ten guineas and a bank note; and, before Mr Underwood could get to town to stop the payment of the note, the fellow had got cash for it.

Loughton Gazette, November 21, 1903

MOTOR HIGHWAYMEN
A.A.'s Advice to Drivers

In view of the increasing attempts at highway robbery by motor bandits, the following statement by the A.A. will be of interest to all motorists.

It cannot be emphasised too strongly that motorists, in their own interests, should take no notice of signals made to them by anyone who is not in police uniform or has some clear identification such as that of an Automobile Association road patrol.

Mr. Stenson Cook, Secretary of the Automobile Association, who repeated this advice to a Press representative, says: 'It lays us open to criticism on the grounds of discourtesy, but today we feel that there is no other advice to give the motorist who is accosted by a stranger on a lonely part of the road.

'Even where people are reasonably satisfied that it is a genuine call for help that is being made on them, they can easily meet the situation by informing the next garage or the next A.A. patrol they meet.

'It is possible that many of these highwaymen have been driven out of London and from their normal pursuits of smash and grab raids by the efficiency of the Scotland Yard Flying Squad.'

It is equally clear from the views expressed by ex-Chief Constable Wensley, of Scotland Yard, that the outrages of the last few days follow a logical trend, and are not merely an isolated epidemic.

'The ingenious criminal,' he said 'has begun to realise that if he can carry on his raids with success in congested areas, such as London, there must be a much wider and safer field for operation on lonely roads.

'The motor car has come to his aid, and he uses it as an illegal weapon exactly as his predecessor used a jemmy.

'If his predecessor were found at night with such an implement, he was liable to penal servitude, and that is the only way to treat a man caught in illegal possession of a car. It should, of course, disqualify him for ever from holding a driving licence.'

The Woodford Times, August 19, 1932

May 1933: Altercation at the junction of the Southend and Chigwell Roads.

New Road between London and Epping.' Percy Lindley writing in 1886.

Epping New Road Bandits

Leslie Owen Wood, 19, labourer, and Victor Clarence Holmes, 17, clerk, on bail, were indicted for stealing a car of William G. Percival, at Chelmsford on August 26th . . .

A description was circulated, and at 9.30 p.m. P-s Carpenter saw the vehicle being driven by Holmes, who was accompanied by Wood, through Epping. The sergeant stopped Mr. Harold Vickers, who was riding a motor cycle, got on the pillion, and overtook the car. Called on to stop, prisoners did so, but when he reached the car it went off again. Remounting the pillion, the sergeant continued the chase. The motorcycle pulled alongside the car, and the sergeant drew his truncheon, but the car swerved into the motor cycle, and both the sergeant and Vickers were thrown off and injured. The officer pluckily continued the chase in a car, and the Austin car was found abandoned in Epping Forest. Later prisoners were arrested at Coulsdon, where they both lived.

The Woodford Times, October 14, 1932

A remarkable story of an alleged plan to rob Barclays Bank in Queens Road, Buckhurst Hill, was related at Stratford Police Court on Friday, when a Woodford man appeared in the dock.

Accused alleged that he was involved with three others in a scheme to raid the bank after business hours, tie up the clerk, take the strong-room keys from him, and then clear off with the proceeds. Revolvers and jemmies, as well as rope, figured in the statement which the accused is alleged to have made to the police, and he was remanded.

Two of the three other men have since been arrested and charged at Stratford.

The Woodford Times, April 14, 1933

SHOTS AT WOODFORD BANDITS ATTEMPTED COFFEE STALL RAID

The crack of a revolver, the whine of bullets, the screech of a police whistle, and a motor car racing down a road with a man clinging on, half in, half out, were the ingredients of a drama enacted in South Woodford in the early hours of Monday evening.

The scene was the coffee stall at the junction of the Southend and Chigwell Roads, owned by Mr. E. R. North.

Mr. North locked the stall up securely at 12.55 a.m. on Monday, and went home. Although he lives very close by, he had his car with him and he drove home, and it is this fact, he thinks, which gave the raiders an impression that he lived a considerable distance away.

'I had just put the car in my garage and locked up,' he told our representative, 'when my two dogs, Trixie and Peter, set up a furious barking.

'I drew my wife's attention to this, feeling that it meant trouble, and I at once got the car out again and went back to the stall at a fast pace, my wife being with me.

'Arriving there, I jumped out of the car before it had actually stopped, and found a dark-blue or black 16 h.p. Austin saloon car drawn up at the side of the stall, while at the back I found a man with a jemmy actually in the back door.

'I immediately pulled out my revolver and called "hands up". I blew my police whistle, but, owing to my wife, who cried "Don't shoot them," I refrained from firing.

'The man dashed to the car — there was the driver already at the wheel — and they then drove off furiously.

'The man I found at the back of the stall was unable to get into the car properly, and as it drove off at a fast pace he was hanging on, half in and half out of the car.

'As the car went off I fired three shots at it, but cannot say whether I hit it.'

The police very promptly answered the summons, but by the time they could arrive the raiders had disappeared.

We understand that no arrest has so far been made.

The Woodford Times, May 26, 1933

Lawlessness is again exemplified in two local instances — a daring burglary at Wanstead in which the thieves were hardened enough to take the risk of being surprised by any one of ten people in the house they chose to rob, and a robbery with violence under the cover of falling darkness in Epping Forest.

They are part of a general wave of crimes of the more daring and violent kind from which London in particular is now suffering.

But the Forest incident has a more local significance as well, for the Forest is unhappily a standing temptation to the law breaker of two kinds — the thief who is ready to use violence if necessary, and the sexual pervert, both of whom find cover there, and relative safety from detection.

In this matter the police are hard pressed, for even in normal times they would find it impossible to patrol either the Forest or our streets sufficiently for would-be criminals to be deterred. Instead they have to rely upon certitude of detection and arrest, and to achieve the maximum efficiency in that, they are compelled to seek the help of the general public.

Ted's cafe was demolished with the coming of the motorway in 1975.

West Essex Gazette, March 5, 1948

The Woodford 'goal' stood beside the High Road in front of Elmhurst. It ended its days as a bathroom and was demolished in 1928.

The constable's place of business was the watch house which stood somewhere near the church and the cage. Although officially he was supposed to have spent a fair part of his time there, it seems that it was often completely neglected. In 1723 the constable was told to turn out the woman and her daughter who 'have at present possessed themselves of it', and to buy a strong lock with two keys for the door. In 1799 it must again have been in a poor state, for it was then decided to rebuild it at an estimated cost of £99, which was to provide two rooms, one with a strong door and the other with a grate for the constable's comfort.

Neither do the stocks seem to have been in continual use at Woodford. In 1653 the manorial jury presented the lady of the manor to provide a pair of stocks and whipping post. Although new stocks were made, by 1673 they were said to be in disrepair; as they are not mentioned again for well over a century it is more than likely that they remained in that state. In 1822 the vestry resolved to provide a pair of stocks as near the watch house as possible.

Woodford Essex 1600-1836, E. J. Erith, 1950

Another unsolved murder in my files occurred in Epping Forest one November evening in 1952. Kenneth Dolden, an RAF man on release leave, had parked his car in a glade and was sitting in the back seat with his fiancée, Jacynth Bland, when the door was wrenched open by a man wearing a grey cloth cap pulled down over his eyes and with a muffler or handkerchief masking the lower half of his face. 'Get out,' ordered Dolden. The man leaned forward and fired three shots into Dolden's body. Miss Bland said later that the shots seemed muffled and she thought the gun might have had a silencer. Dolden managed to stagger out of the car, but immediately fell. Miss Bland ran to the road to call for help. Seeing another car parked, she gasped out her story to the driver and his woman passenger, and they all drove to the nearest police telephone box.

The police told Miss Bland to wait for them at the box, and the other woman stayed with her. The driver of the car said he would go back to the glade to try to help the shot man, but he was not there when the police arrived and he was never seen again. His passenger told the police he had picked her up that evening and had said his name was Bill. There was no reason to suspect him of being involved in the crime, and presumably he did not want someone else, such as his wife, to know that he had picked up a girl and taken her to the forest.

Dolden had died of the wounds in his chest and abdomen. The chest injury was plainly a contact wound, and the other two shots had been fired from the closest possible quarters short of actual contact. Beyond doubt his murderer had shot to kill.

Dolden was still breathing when he reached hospital, and in brief spells of consciousness

When Sir Robert Peel created his 'peelers' (later 'bobbies') in 1829, the responsibility for the detection and apprehension of criminals was changed immeasurably. From the days of the wayside gallows, village stocks and the 'lock-up' came the organised Metropolitan Police, initially only in central London but in 1839 extended to include Waltham Holy Cross, Loughton and Chigwell. The police station beside Chingford Green was built in 1887.

It was superseded by a new £900,000 sub-divisional building in 1975-77.

At Woodford the new replacement was erected in 1968 on a new site on the High Road some 300 yards further south.

he gasped out a dying statement to the detectives at his bedside:

'Hit on head . . . three shots fired at close range. . . . Man had mask on. . . . I have no idea who he was. He had cap on. . . . I tried to kick him . . . wearing overcoat. No idea how old. I had been there about half an hour. . . . Handkerchief round nose. . . . I think whoever it was was after car. There was no other car anywhere near when I drove into trees.'

Theft of the car seemed an unlikely reason for the murder, but the police never found a better one. Nothing in the lives of Dolden or of his fiancée suggested a more personal motive, and no clue to the murderer's identity was found. From his point of view it was, in fact, a perfect, if senseless, crime.

Forty Years of Murder,
Professor Keith Simpson, 1978

The number of assaults and sexual crimes against women in Epping Forest has risen steadily since the war and now as a preventative measure two mounted policemen will patrol the forest during the coming summer.

Chigwell Times, June 9, 1961

London's biggest-ever manhunt — after a fusillade of shots had brought death to two police officers and serious wounds to a third — ended in high drama in a phone box in Lake House Road, Wanstead, on Saturday night.

Scores of policemen in more than a dozen cars — officers in uniform and in plain clothes, some of them armed — converged on the telephone box, situated on the verge of Wanstead Flats. As the cars screamed to a

The Bonnie and Clyde era comes to Wanstead — drama at Lake House road.

halt their occupants leapt out to form a cordon round the box.

Two unarmed policemen from a patrol car approached the box. As they did so, a shot rang out and a man slumped against the door and fell on the footpath. Suffering from a wound beneath the heart, the man was rushed by ambulance to Whipps Cross Hospital, Leytonstone. An emergency operation was carried out to remove a bullet from his chest.

Scotland Yard have announced that the man is John Hall also known as Jan Helmwig. A picture of 30-year-old John Hall had been televised by the B.B.C. earlier in the day as that of a man whom the police wished to question in connection with the death of two police officers at Stratford on Saturday afternoon.

The time was about 1.30 p.m. A few

minutes beforehand a man had called at West Ham Police Station to answer routine questions. Suddenly, it is alleged, he produced a Luger pistol and was chased from the building. Sergeant Hutchins and P.c. Cox ran after him and Inspector Pawsey joined the chase in a police car. In Tennyson Road the sergeant and constable were close to a man when he turned. Shots were heard and both the pursuers collapsed. Also in Tennyson Road Inspector Pawsey jumped from his car but he had barely done so than other shots rang out and the officer fell, mortally wounded in the chest.

Every available policeman was called upon to take part in the hunt for the gunman. For hours they searched the districts round about.

Around 8 p.m. a dozen cars tore from West Ham Police Station, where high-up officers

Wanstead 'cop-shop' — the only original police station in our area — erected in 1885-86 at a cost of £2,366 11s. 10d.

Loughton received its new police headquarters in 1963.

were directing the man-hunt, and chased at high speed to Lake House Road, Wanstead, to take part in a closing chapter in the day's dramatic events.

The police chase was alerted following a telephone call to a newspaper. Scotland Yard were informed. Orders flashed to police cars and patrols and within a few minutes the kiosk was surrounded. The occupant, shot in the chest, slumped against the door as patrol officers approached the phone box.

All traffic along Lake House Road and nearby roads was held up as the drama reached its climax.

The Woodford Times, June 9, 1961

The staff of a South Woodford bank were terrorised by a masked gang wielding guns and a baseball bat in a £10,000 robbery, it was alleged at Stratford on Tuesday.

Redbridge Recorder, October 14, 1965

The massive police hunt for Harry Roberts, the man wanted for questioning about the police murders [of three policemen in Braybrooke Street, Shepherd's Bush, on Friday, August 12], continued in the Epping Forest area all day yesterday (Thursday). By noon the search had moved near Epping, and the man was reported seen in Theydon Bois and Theydon Mount. Police — there were 500 of them — were certain the wanted man was in the area.

The hunt, one of the largest ever in the forest, was started at 8.30 p.m. on Wednesday afer the murder squad had received a reliable tip-off that Roberts was sleeping rough in the forest. He is known to have kitted himself out with camping equipment. At 10 o'clock Chief Superintendent G. Evans of 'J' Division called off the hunt, but all roads were patrolled through the night.

Yesterday the hunt moved towards Epping, and four schoolboys phoned the police after they heard someone 'moving furniture around' in the Epping Foresters Cricket Club pavilion. . . . Within minutes scores of police had raced to the spot. Eventually they got into the pavilion, but Roberts, if he had been there, had gone.

West Essex Gazette, August 19, 1966

An intruder hiding in a public house lavatory shot dead a barman at point blank range after he had been disturbed by a pet dog. . . . The man, armed with a pump-action shotgun, smashed a leaded window to get out of the Rising Sun public house in Woodford New Road, when he found interior doors locked and bolted.

A raider of a similar description carried out a £1,500 armed raid on the pub last month.

The dog, a black labrador called 'Chips', was badly wounded by a second blast and died later.

Mr Dennis O'Neil, 53, the barman, went into the lavatory after closing time on Sunday when the dog began to bark. As he opened the door he was shot through the heart.

The gunman, wearing a leather jacket, tried the doors of the saloon and public bars but found they had been locked. He smashed a leaded window and ran across Woodford New Road into Epping Forest.

The Daily Telegraph, July 1978

A man whose body was dumped from a car at a lonely spot used by courting couples was identified today as the landlord of an East End pub. His body was dumped late last night from a car on Wanstead Flats. He had cuts to his face and hands and extensive bruising. Police say the dead man had been stabbed.

Evening Standard, November 28, 1979

A massive murder hunt started on Wednesday afternoon after the naked body of an unidentified man was found lying face down in a ditch at Church Road High Beech. The man, aged 40 to 45, was stabbed 'a number of times' in the upper part of his body. He was wearing only black swimming trunks.

Immediately police sealed off the area. Road blocks were set up half a mile each side of the Suntrap Nature Study Centre, opposite which the body was found. Only residents with identification were allowed to pass. The police were using the study centre as a murder headquarters.

Investigations continued under Detective Superintendent A. Wickstead and police began an inch-by-inch search of nearby forest land for the murder weapon. The immediate search area was roped off and a polythene sheet covered the spot where the body was discovered. A post mortem was carried out at

Murder most foul at the Rising Sun — built 1846, enlarged 1850, modernised 1960s.

St. Margaret's Hospital, Epping. Pathologist Dr. Ivy Tuck visited the scene of the crime before the body was removed.

The Independent, May 23, 1969

The old Claybury station was closed on January 12, 1976.

willingly and he drove to Epping Forest with the girl in the back seat 'chatting away quite happily.'

He walked into the forest for about a quarter of a mile with the girl. They walked to

Evans was jailed for life, with a recommendation from the judge that he should serve at least 30 years.

The Daily Telegraph, December 18, 1984

An alarming catalogue of complacency allowed Colin Evans, son of a former Essex County cricketer, to become the most sadistic child killer since the notorious moors murderers Ian Brady and Myra Hyndley.

The scandal of events leading up to Marie Payne's daylight abduction and death at the hands of a known pervert are bound to lead to demands for a full public inquiry. . . .

He invited her to go for a ride. She got in

a fallen tree trunk where he started to touch her. . . .

Evans pleaded guilty to the murder of Marie in March, 1983, and also to three charges of child stealing involving two incidents on the same day in May of this year.

It was his desperate attempts in May to abduct other children that led to his capture and the discovery of Marie's body in a shallow grave in Epping Forest. . . .

The changing face of law enforcement in Epping Forest: 'Bobbies on bicycles two by two'. Now its 'copper choppers' for the Metropolitan Police Air Support Unit based at the police training centre at Lippits Hill, Loughton with Bell 222 helicopters. In 1982 the Unit flew 2,000 hours and gave direct assistance to ground patrols more than 5,000 times resulting in over 700 arrests.

The Epping station comes under the jurisdiction of Essex Police. The building was rebuilt on the same site in 1938.

Roads

A glimpse of a bygone age. The old medieval Stump Road running through Wintry Wood must still look much as it did when highwaymen lurked in the Forest awaiting the unwary traveller. *Previous pages:* Epping New Road, circa 1916.

The chief responsibility for the upkeep of roads had been placed originally on individual parishes by an Act of 1555. Nevertheless, the lack of proper knowledge about road maintenance, coupled with increasing traffic along the main roads as waggons and carriages and carts began to be used more widely in the 16th and 17th centuries, together with the movement of herds and animals and flocks of sheep and poultry, meant that the road system was not adequate. In the 18th century travel was therefore both expensive and uncomfortable, and often the quickest and safest way to travel long distances was by coastal vessel.

Turnpike Trusts were organised to improve the system of main roads in England and, apart from a preliminary attempt in 1663 when the County Justices of Hertfordshire, Cambridgeshire and Huntingdon were empowered to put up gates to exact tolls for road upkeep, the first Act of Parliament setting up such a trust was passed in 1706. Eventually more than 1,100 trusts existed, caring for over 23,000 miles of road.

The Great Essex Road became a turnpike road in 1724 when the Middlesex and Essex Trust took over the responsibility for maintaining it as far as Shenfield, together with the branch road from Stratford through Leytonstone to the High Stone and then the two further branches to Woodford Bridge and Woodford Wells. This latter is now called the A11, which continues through Epping and Bishop's Stortford to Stump Cross on the Cambridgeshire border.

The Lea Bridge Turnpike and the Wragg Stage Coaches, W. G. S. Tonkin, 1974

The 'road net', if it can be called that, in the seventeenth century in south-west Essex with the main road to the north crossing over the Roding at Passingford Bridge. This map is dated 1733 but it appears to be a copy of the survey conducted by the Royal Cartographers, John Ogilby and William Morgan in 1678 for King Charles II.

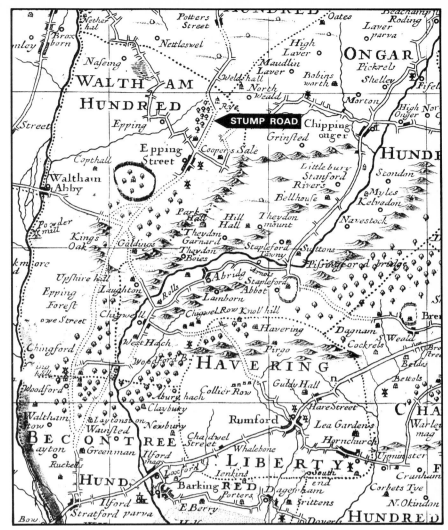

Projecting the Coopersale Road to Thornwood, from the air the course of the Stump Road is just discernible.

To the traveller of old crossing the River Roding, running more or less from north to south on the eastern side of the Forest, proved a constant problem. Woodford Bridge (see pages 6 and

7) was the first possibility; Chigwell Bridge *(above)* the second, with Passingford Bridge *(bottom)* the third and most easterly (see map page 93).

An Act for the better repairing and amending the Highways, from the North End of *Thornwood Common*, to *Woodford* in the County of *Essex*.

Whereas the Highways or Road between the Parish of *Harlow* and *Woodford* in the County of *Essex*, by reason of the great and many Loads which are weekly drawn through the same, are become so ruinous and in decay, that the ordinary Course appointed by the Laws and Statutes of this realm is not sufficient for making the same passable, neither are the Inhabitants of the several and respective Parishes, in which the said Road doth lie, of Ability to repair the same, without some other Provision of Monies to be raised toward putting the same into good and sufficient Repair, there being no Materials to be got fit for doing thereof, but at great Distance from the said Road: For Remedy whereof, and to the Intent that the said Highways may be forthwith effectually repaired and amended, and kept in good Repair, may it please your Majesty that it may be enacted.

Act of Parliament, 1707

Up at Epping at this time they grew tired of removing the stumps along the old stump road through Wintry Wood (the old route from Harlow to London went south-east to Hobbs Cross) when royal vehicles passed that way. The stumps were to protect this made road from damage by carts and wagons.

Pepys visited Saffron Walden on February 27, 1659, with a friend. He ' . . . took horses and straight to Saffron Walden, where at the White Hart we set up our horses, and took the master of the house to shew us Audley End'. On the following day they returned to London via Epping Forest (then known as Waltham Forest), where most of the route was good ' . . . but only in one path which we kept as if we were riding through a kennel all the way'.

Bridges capable of taking coach traffic

Toll houses on the Epping road. North of the town one was located close by the Blacksmith's Arms at Thornwood.

Above and bottom: **The southern toll gate stood close by the turning to Ivy Chimneys — the toll house was Belle Vue House, which has since had an upper floor added.** *Right:* **The nearby 'Forest Gate' Inn perpetuates the memory.**

across streams or smaller rivers were not all that common, and most places off the main routes had either a ford or a small wooden footbridge with a water-splash for traffic at one side. As regards the former, the fact is recorded in the name of Woodford, while at Harlow one of the latter combination was in existence at one time. . . .

At Epping Gate even in 1848 there were still some twenty-two coaches passing through. This was as nothing, however, compared with the scores of post-chaises, private carriages, gigs, wagons and carts.

One also expected to meet a few hundred head of cattle, sheep and pigs, besides geese and turkeys being driven on foot to market at London or elsewhere. Curiously enough, the hazard of cattle on the road is still to be met with today occasionally in the vicinity of parts of Epping Forest.

Essex Coaching Days, J. Elsden Tuffs

The Epping and Ongar Trust was set up by an Act of 1786 to maintain the road from Woodford to Harlow, and this Act enlarged the terms and powers of two previous ones. The first meeting of the trustees was held on May 2, 1769, at Epping Place, a large eighteenth-century red-brick house which still stands by the main road at the southern end of the town.

The trustees were responsible for collecting tolls from road users in order to maintain and

The toll gate at the London end of the forest road was located outside the old Bald Faced Stag at Buckhurst Hill — also referred to as the Bald Stag in some accounts. The inn dates back to the early eighteenth century being rebuilt in brick sometime before 1770. It was then a notable haunt of the criminal fraternity, and the notorious Jeffryes' murder is reputed to have been schemed in the bar in 1752. It was a prominent landmark on the road to Epping but when the new turnpike was completed in 1834 by-passing Loughton, a new toll house was built a few hundred yards to the south at the beginning of the new road. In 1936 a fire destroyed three-quarters of the old Stag, the present building, constructed in 1938, retaining only the bars and billiards room of the original inn.

improve the conditions of the road. Regular users could compound their tolls for an agreed sum. In order to collect tolls, in 1769 there were gates and tollhouses at Thornwood (by Duck Lane) and at the southern end of Epping town, near Epping Place. This second gate was moved to a position by the Ivy Chimneys turning, and in 1783, in order to stop drovers avoiding payment by crossing Bell Common, an additional side gate was placed on the side turning. This is now marked by the nearby Forest Gate inn. A third tollhouse and gate was erected in 1794 near the Bald Faced Stag, Buckhurst Hill.

Besides maintaining the road, the trustees carried out improvements. One of the earliest of these (in the 1770s) was the widening and embanking of the road leading out of Epping up the hill towards Harlow. Two others were to hill gradients. The first was Golding's Hill, Loughton, where an entirely new stretch of road was constructed in 1771-5 parallel to the old one, and the gradient made less severe by cutting down the top by sixteen feet and raising the lower part on an embankment. Both roads still exist side by side, with old

The completion of the Epping 'New Road' in 1834 by the Epping and Ongar Highway Trust stimulated an increase of traffic on the new through route bypassing Loughton and in the early nineteenth century some 25 coaches a day were passing through Epping. The Trust financed the construction and upkeep of the roads in its charge by the payment of tolls. The old toll house, its position moved from the Bald Faced Stag, re-mained at the fork of the two roads until 1930 (but see page 226). The junction layout was altered in 1975 and the apex cut back to allow for a right-turn lane. The old horse trough, the property of the Drinking Fountain and Cattle Trough Association, had disappeared by 1964 although by right any troughs not used for the original purpose of watering horses must be returned to the Association — not used to plant flowers!

cottages along the lower one. A similar improvement was made in 1781-4 to Buckhurst Hill. The road here was also straightened and the old road still takes a round-about curve past the Roebuck inn. Both works took a long time; Golding's because the original contractor defaulted, and Buckhurst because unexpected difficulties raised costs.

W. G. S. Tonkin, Essex Countryside,
May 1965

The principal settlement along the Newmarket road as it runs through Essex is Epping, which owes at least half its growth to the needs of travellers. In 1605 Epping had

Two major alterations were made to the Woodford to Epping road in the days when the community relied a hundred per cent on horse-drawn transport. At Loughton, in order to ease the strain on the horses pulling heavily laden carts up the steep and tortuous Golding's Hill (modern usage seems to drop the apostrophe), a new raised section of road was constructed parallel to the old.

Today, over two hundred years after the work was carried out, the old 'lower' road still runs beside the new — a remarkable piece of yesterday preserved today.

not one innkeeper among its ten victuallers. Six years later it had four. Soon after 1607, when James took Theobalds from Robert Cecil, first Earl of Salisbury, in order to shorten the journey to Newmarket, a road was cut through the forest to Epping, starting at the point on the old Waltham to Theydon road where the Wake Arms stands now. The whole of the northward road across the east of the country was either made or greatly improved at this time, though the principal highway from London to Newmarket and Cambridge continued to be on the other side of the River Lea.

The Newmarket road through Epping and Harlow is now one of the busiest in the country, but its popularity was slow in developing. After a moment's reflection the reason becomes obvious. It passes through Epping Forest, which long continued to be the haunt of highwaymen and other disturbers of

the peace. The effect of this fear of passing through the forest is to be seen in the lay-out of Harlow, the oldest town along this Essex stretch of the Newmarket road. It is built across and not along the present highway, which makes it clear that its trade came, not from those who had travelled from Epping, but from the people of Dunmow and the Roothings, who passed through on their way towards Hoddesdon and Ware. It is also evident that those who came in from London by Hoddesdon and wished to turn north at Harlow used a different way from the one we take now. . . . The original Epping was the present Epping Upland, which was fed by the road from Ongar and Coopersale into Hertfordshire by way of either Roydon or Waltham Abbey. It passed near Gaynes Park, in Theydon Garnon parish. . . . After crossing the main road, this older way runs down to Eppingbury, then up the hill to the old church and Chambers manor house. . . .

In 1611, or soon after that date, a road was made from Loughton to Wake Arms, and when completed it altered Loughton as thoroughly as the continuing stretch altered Epping. Loughton was swung up from the Chigwell side just as Epping was swung up from the Roydon side, and eventually a new road from London into East Anglia developed, which was to alter the whole lay-out of west Essex.

Essex Heyday, William Addison, 1949

Yesterday a Coach coming from Bishop-Stortford was overturned on Epping Forest, whereby two Persons and a Child were very much hurt.

Press report, 1764

To the Public

WHEREAS the Length of the Stage between London and Epping hath been found very disagreeable to Travellers, by being too much for the Horses to perform, and hath for that Reason been greatly complained of: In order to remedy this Inconvenience, Gentlemen, Ladies, and others, may, at Woodford Wells, be supplied with neat Post-Chaises and able Horses, (either in Pairs or Four) with careful Drivers, at 9d. and 15d. per Mile, by their most obedient, humble Servants,
WILLIAM BIGGS, and Co.

Press report, 1765

Ten years later in 1781 work began to straighten the bend at the top of the hill on the southern side of Loughton. The old and new roads can also still be seen and compared today.

The diversion left the Roebuck inn out on a limb, so to speak, but it received a new lease of life in 1853 when it became the new meeting place for the Epping Hunt. In Tom Rounding's day this had begun from the Bald Faced Stag but the Easter Monday meeting degenerated into an excuse for drunken revelry. The night before, the tame stag, stabled at the Bald Stag, would be decorated wth ribbons and flowers and be led round the local taverns before eventually being released on Fairmead Bottom the following morning before a crowd of thousands, with upwards of 500 horsemen ready mounted to chase the beast. When, as sometimes happened, it simply retraced its footsteps back to its pen, the rowdyism was only equalled by that which attended a kill. When the landlord of the Bald Faced Stag got fed up with the spectacle and banned the hunt from meeting at his inn, it moved a few hundred yards to the Roebuck. There it stayed for some thirty years until the Epping Forest Committee clamped down on the event declaring in their opinion that it was 'nothing better than a sham and a means of massing together the very roughest class in the neighbourhood of the various public houses'.

The Lea Bridge Road in 1827 was a gravel road on a clay subsoil, varying from 8 to 24 inches thick in the centre to 5½ to 9 inches at the sides. Equipment in use comprised four watercarts, eight water pumps, four wheelbarrows, one sieve, seven shovels, five pickaxes, fourteen scrapers, one rake, one toolhouse, a clock, two articles of furniture in the tollhouse, two lamp posts, six lamp irons, and five sundry small articles!

James McAdam (1786-1852), the famous road engineer, was appointed General Surveyor to the Metropolis Roads Commission, and later to many others including the Epping and Ongar Trust in 1830. His first report, issued from the Commission's offices in Whitehall Place, is dated 25th March, 1827, in which the Lea Bridge Road is described as follows: 'Its general form is upon the most approved principles: the material chiefly used on this road is small loamy gravel. The part near Lea Bridge has been lately repaired with broken flints, and is in a very good state: better means have been adopted for draining this road than any other round the metropolis. For three miles there are deep ditches on either side, with proper openings under the footpaths to allow the water to pass off. The surface is in good weather smooth and even, but owing to the gravel with which it is repaired, it draws heavily in wet weather: it will be desirable to extend the use of flints on this road in lieu of gravel, by which considerable improvement of surface will be effected. This road is watered, and the footpaths are repaired by the Commission, but it is neither watched nor lighted by the Commission'.

Also in the report was a very important paragraph: 'A new line from this Road beyond Whip's Cross has been surveyed through that part of Epping Forest forming a junction with the Epping Road, near the Castle Inn, being a distance of two miles. By this proposed alteration, a saving of five furlongs of distance would be obtained; the quick and awkward turning at Snaresbrook and the long continued pull, so distressing for draught horses, from Snaresbrook to Woodford, would also be avoided'.

This 'new line' is what is now called the Woodford New Road from its junction with Snaresbrook Road to Woodford Green and the commissioners obtained powers to construct it under an Act of 1829. In his report for 1830 (22nd April), the General Surveyor said, 'As this Road was through the Forest, and no consent of individual proprietors was requisite to be previously obtained, the Commissioners commenced it soon after the passing of this Act, at the expense of a small weekly sum, which has been regularly applied since that time; and they now have the satisfaction to say

The Woodford New Road photographed by Francis Emler shortly after the turn of the century. All Woodford's main roads were resurfaced with granite in 1900-5, this stretch being completed in 1901.

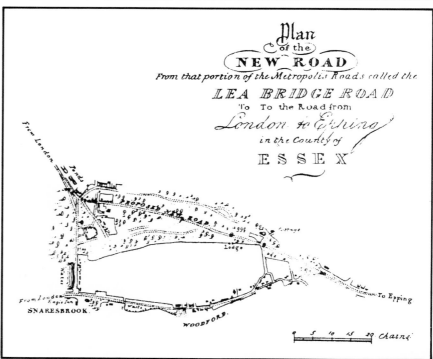

Public transport on the Lea Bridge Road had its beginnings with Francis Wragg and his horse-drawn coaches. Until the new road to Woodford was built, the route ran down alongside the Eagle Pond to the Woodford Road. When the Woodford New Road was built in 1829-30 (costing then about £1,200), a saving of five furlongs was achieved as well as eliminating the sharp turn at Snaresbrook and the long pull 'so distressing for draught horses' to Woodford. However it was rumoured that the main reason for the new road was that King George IV wanted to shorten his journey to Newmarket races!

Wragg had gone out of business by 1870 and in 1889 the Lea Bridge, Leyton and Walthamstow Tramways Company was running horse trams to the Rising Sun. The then-revolutionary electric tramway was introduced by the Leyton Urban District Council as far as the Napier Arms in 1905, converting to trolley buses in 1936-7. Diesel buses were introduced in 1959-60.

that the Road is almost completed, and at a cost that will scarcely exceed £1,200. So great an improvement in the neighbourhood of the Metropolis was, perhaps, never before effected for so small a sum'. In fact, on 26th March, 1829, McAdam had reported that neighbouring parishes would supply gravel on advantageous terms and labour by men on parish relief, so the Board authorised work to begin — this before the Royal Assent to the Act on 19th June, 1829! It would seem from the Commission's records that the New Road was opened either in May or June, 1830.

It was now the regular practice to have the Lea Bridge Road repaired with material from two sources — towards the Bridge flints and gravel were brought along the River Lea, while the other end was supplied with gravel from the Forest. One wonders how many of the dips and hollows in the gravel deposits of Epping Forest were originally diggings for the turnpikes! McAdam reported that experience proved that the best method was to apply thin coats of material which the traffic would compress and so add to the suface. Consequently there was no need for animals to have to drag carriages through a deep mass of loose materials. In 1835 the first supplies of Kentish Ragstone were used on the surface of the New Road and in 1836 a certain amount of kerbstone and flagging for footpaths was laid by arrangement with the local parishes.

In 1857 toll receipts were reported down because of the decrease in traffic due to the opening in the previous year of the Woodford

During 1927-30 the North Circular Road was extended from Edmonton through Walthamstow via the Crooked Billet and Forest Road to meet the Woodford New Road at the waterworks. In 1970-71 the North Circular was diverted north of 'Waterworks Corner' to a new roundabout at the top of Grove Road which itself was demolished by the approach to the motorway. (See also pages 63 and 119.)

Railway (the line from Leyton through Leytonstone to Loughton, now the Central Underground). The Clapton toll gate was removed as well and in its place at the entrance to Lea Bridge Road the Hackney Board of Works erected an obelisk with lamps. On 29th October, 1857, a great flood of the River Lea occurred and the road was heavily damaged between the river and the railway.

The Wanstead Orphan Asylum Committee enclosed the Eagle Pond in 1859 and the commissioners had to move their water pump to the road side. It was in the same year that the summer was long and dry so that the wells for watering the road surface dried up. In the 1860s, omnibus traffic and manure traffic continued to increase so that more and more flints and gravel had to be used to repair the road. Drains were laid along the south side of the road in place of the open ditches but even so, a severe storm in 1861 caused the Eagle Pond to overflow and a portion of the road was swept away. The annual reports refer to the continued building of new estates along the road and consequently a great increase in toll evasion, because, of course, traffic could travel on the New Road and along the Lea Bridge Road as far as Markhouse Road without coming to a toll gate.

The work of the Metropolis Roads Commission was ended on 1st July, 1872, by the General Turnpike Acts Continuance Act of 1871. At its end it controlled the Brentford, Uxbridge, Harrow, Kilburn, Stamford Hill and Green Lanes, and Lea Bridge Roads, and in its last report (1872) the Lea Bridge Road was reported 'much worn by the carriage of materials for the buildings on the Manor Estate at Sybourn's Corner'. On 11th, 12th and 13th July, 1872, auctions were held for the sale of turnpike houses, gates, bars, and stores. All toll houses were removed, and the roads became a charge on the local parish rates.

The Lea Bridge Road and the New Road were transferred to the control of the Hackney, Leyton and Walthamstow Highway Boards. The Board for Walthamstow had been set up on 14th November, 1862, under 5 and 6 Wm. IV, c.50 'for the Repair of the Highways' and among the members were Francis Wragg, Ebenezer Clarke, and John Budd. These three were local business men — Wragg the coach and carriage master, Clarke the printer, and Budd the merchant of Wood Street. William Houghton was appointed clerk at £25 a year with Samuel Ward as assistant surveyor at 25/- per week (increased

Snaresbrook Road — route of the final part of the original Lea Bridge Turnpike of 1757 from Clapton which terminated 'near the house known by the sign of The Eagle at Snaresbrook'.

to 28/- in 1863). The Walthamstow Board assumed responsibility for the Woodford New Road in 1872 and in July bought two pumps and two water carts from the Metropolis Roads Commission for £19. The first reference to work on the New Road is in the minutes of the meeting for 26th September, 1872, when the assistant surveyor requested instructions to repair 'that portion of the New Road in this parish lately given up by the Metropolis Roads Commission'.

The last committee meeting was held on 12th August, 1873, when the Walthamstow Vestry was replaced by the Walthamstow Local Board. A similar change took place in Leyton, and the Lea Bridge Road continued under local control until it became a county road under the Local Government Act of 1888. In 1883 a horse tram line was laid from Lea Bridge to Whipps Cross but it was an abortive attempt at public transport. In 1889 a successful tramway was opened and extended to the Rising Sun, and three years later across Lea Bridge to Clapton. In 1906 the tramway was electrified by the Leyton U.D.C., while the previous year the Walthamstow U.D.C. had laid an electric tramway along the New Road to the Napier Arms. Motor buses (1908) plied along the road, and later trolleybuses replaced the trams. Floods continued to plague the Lea Bridge Road until the last major one in 1946-7, but since then flood prevention schemes have proved effective.

With road improvements, including the roundabouts at Clapton, at Whipps Cross, at the Waterworks, and at Woodford Green, and the double track layout at Snaresbrook Road, the Lea Bridge and New Roads today carry a huge volume of traffic. But apart from the course of the road, the only visible link left from the beginning of the turnpike in 1757 is The Eagle at Snaresbrook.

The Lea Bridge Turnpike and the Wragg Stage Coaches. W. G. S. Tonkin. 1974

First day of the fishing season, June 1985.

In 1600 there were virtually only three roads of any importance in Woodford: the 'lower road' from Stratford over Woodford Bridge to Chigwell and Ongar; the 'upper road' from Stratford through Woodford Row to Buckhurst Hill and Loughton; and Sakes (now Snakes) Lane connecting the two. Of these the first was then the most important from the point of view of the King's people at large, for it was the old main road from London to Epping, Ongar and the centre of Essex. Since it only crossed the outskirts of the parish it was the one most subject to neglect by the local inhabitants. On the other hand it was the one with which the general public was most concerned as to its condition. For these reasons it was, of the three roads, the only one frequently mentioned at Quarter Sessions. The state of the other two roads was, for the most part, only a matter of concern to the parishioners. The upper road was the main artery through the more populated part of the parish, while Sakes Lane connected that part of the parish with the hamlet of Woodford Bridge.

'The Cross Roads' Woodford. The new road to Woodford joined the existing highway from Snaresbrook beside the old pump — another victim of change since these pictures were taken — the tranquil scene *above* in the latter days of the First World War. The house to the right of the first lady bicyclist in the picture *below* is The Roses demolished in 1946.

Woodford on a misty November morning. In 1972 the junction was altered to stop the two streams of traffic crossing each other by the building of a filter roundabout — a delightful scene in springtime with its carpet of miniature daffodils. The horse chestnuts — an integral part of the Woodford scene — were planted at the turn of the century when the species, originally from Eastern Europe, was popular for lining roads. However because of the danger from the fall of the spiky fruits, and the heavy deposit of leaves making wet roads treacherous, chestnuts are not now considered the ideal tree for the roadside. They are also not very long-lived and we must therefore expect their replacement in the not too distant future.

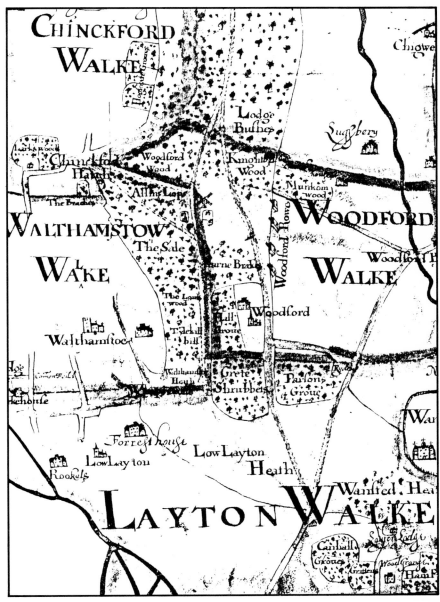

Snakes Lane is probably the oldest road in Woodford. In 1235 Maud in the Lane gave her name to a tenement called Lanes, later Sakes after the family of that name. It joined the ford at Woodford 'Bridge' to the 'High Road', then no more than a track through the forest. Later the name was corrupted to Snakes. The picture on the left dates from 1904 and shows the recently-constructed Ray Lodge County Junior and Primary School which catered for 1,000 pupils.

The expenses of the surveyors in terms of money cannot be properly assessed, for the repair of the highways was, in theory, carried out by the parishioners themselves, who were statutorily compelled to provide the necessary labour and cartage. The only expense involved was in the supply of materials, mostly in the form of gravel, and it was usually possible to obtain even this free of charge. In practice many property owners preferred to commute their 'statute duties', leaving it to the surveyors to obtain the labour and carts out of the money thus provided. If it was found impossible to repair the roads satisfactorily by statute labour and cartage alone, it was permissible to levy a rate to make up the deficiency, but only after Quarter Sessions, or, after 1691, the Special Highway Sessions, had investigated the case and given its order.

To compel the parishioners to perform their statutory tasks on the highways was not always an easy matter. In 1629 the Woodford surveyors returned a presentment to Quarter Sessions of those 'that refuse to work according to the statute'. Seven parishioners who ought to have provided 'teams', that is, men, horses and carts, had failed to do so on a total of twenty-four days, and thirty-six others had failed to supply labour on a total of 162 days. Small wonder that the roads of the past were not all they might have been. In 1630 the surveyors, George Thorowgood gent. and William Todd yeoman, were presented before Quarter Sessions for their failure to make a return of defaulters, and for their own failure to provide teams. Mr. Thorowgood was also charged with employing a great part of the statute labour for his own purposes instead of on the highways. To these presentments another parishioner, John Hayes, bore testimony, but he himself was presented nine years later for not sending his team to the surveyors of Barking where he also had property. By 1651 matters seem to have improved somewhat and the surveyors for that year were able to report that the gentry were generally doing their duty, although the cottagers and labourers had done 'little or nothing for themselves'.

Should a parish fail to keep its through roads in repair much annoyance was caused to travellers, often culminating in an indictment against the parishioners as a body. Such a charge was laid in 1694 when the vestry instructed the constables on next going to

This map dates from 1634.

Sessions to 'take care' of the matter and 'manage it with as little charge as they can'. It seems that the vestry was unduly optimistic in hoping that the affair could be so easily settled, for a month later we find it employing a solicitor, Mr. Goldeston of Ilford, who was apparently more successful in disposing of the indictment. In 1696 a clue is given as to who was the chief informer against the parish; a committee was then appointed to attend on Sir Edward Smith 'who has presented the lower road for a number of years past & so put the parish to a considerable expense'. As he frequently travelled over this road on his journeys between London and his residence, Hill Hall at Theydon Mount, he had obvious reason to be irritated by the delays and discomforts caused by the bad state of the road.

Love Lane, which has now disappeared . . . ran close to, and parallel with, the High Road from George Lane to Woodford Green. In 1768 it was decided to erect cross posts or swing gates at either end to keep out cattle. In 1803 Peter Mallard Esq. was given leave to raise 42 yards of this path adjoining his premises at Salwey Hill, and to drive a light chaise or carriage over it to his house. Salwey Hill takes its name from an earlier resident in the same house; in 1768 Mr. Salwey agreed to put up posts at his own expense on the hill.

Dodds Lane disappeared in 1828, when Mr. Mellish was given permission to inclose it into his estate. It lay very close to the present road called Churchfields.

Several ponds in the parish were a continual source of danger, especially at night, unless properly railed off. In 1768 the road at Hall Pond near the church was so treated, both to stop pedestrians walking into the pond in the dark and to keep horses from the footpath. The footpaths, if they constituted a right of way, were also the responsibility of the surveyors, who often neglected this part of their work. In 1816 repeated complaints were made about the bad state of the footpaths and watercourses generally. The surveyors were ordered 'to use more than ordinary vigilance' in this matter and this notice was drawn up for service on offenders against the public ways: 'Take notice that if you or any of you, Throw, lay or deposit any dirt, soil, soap suds, or any other filth or dirt, in the watercourses or on the footpath or Road, opposite or next to the cottage, or dwelling house, you or any of you now Occupy; or do at any time Obstruct the said Public way or footpath with Barrows, Carts, or in any other Manner Whatsoever; You, or all of you who may so offend, will be indicted at the General Quarter Sessions at Chelmsford in the said County, next after the committal of such offences and you will farther take notice to keep the said footpath and Watercourses in as far as the same may

Like the derivation of so many of our road and place names, Salway Hill achieved its title from a gentleman of the same name who resided nearby in the 1760s. The Cricketers was originally an ordinary house and was rebuilt in its present style in 1927.

extend in front of your dwelling House free from all and every Obstruction or Nuisance Whatsoever according to the Statute therein made and provided'.

Of several other footpaths mentioned only Warner's Walk is named. In 1809 the owner of Harts, the Rev. (later Sir) Samuel Clarke Jervoise, applied to inclose this path, which ran along the west boundary of his estate, and

to divert it to a parallel line nearer the High Road. To this the vestry agreed provided he extended the path from its northern end to the Turnpike, and enclosed the whole with rails and a row of horse chestnut trees, to the satisfaction of the surveyor. This extension joined the road near the spot where the 'Travellers' Friend' now stands.

In 1832 the surveyor was ordered to inspect

Windmill Lane led to the Walthamstow Mill which once stood at the top of Oak Hill near the present Napier Arms. It became known as Bunce's Lane in the nineteenth century after Dr John

Bunce who lived at The Roses in 1850. When the house was demolished, blocks of flats bearing the same name were erected on the site in 1947 and 1977.

the gates in the bridle path 'leading across the Meads from the old mills' and to report to vestry if he considered new gates were needed. Later he replied that he considered that the parish ought not to repair them as they were not its responsibility. This bridleway was probably that leading from the lower road to the bottom end of Horn Lane; it was in existence in 1772 and was probably in use even earlier.

The material for repairing the roads came entirely from local gravel pits, which were not always easy to find in convenient places. In 1732 it was reported that there was a gravel pit of great service to the parish open in the lower road, but as it 'must of necessity be filled up in the winter with water', it constituted something of a danger. By 1774 it appears that no suitable gravel pit could be found in Woodford for repairing the lower road and the surveyors resorted to pits in Chigwell. The surveyor sent a man to dig there and paid £3 4s. 6d. for the privilege, but the Chigwell

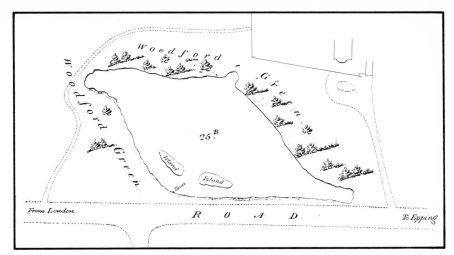

The necessity of supplying large quantities of gravel for road making has left us a legacy of ponds in the Epping Forest area, usually located right alongside the carriageway as is the case with the Sluice Pond on the west side of Woodford High Road. In 1733 '25B' was leased for 99 years by Miss Tylney Long of Wanstead Hall to a Mrs Sly at an annual rent of £2. In latter days its name changed according to those of the local residents, being called Johnston's, Cook's and Warner's Pond in its time. As it was situated on the more recent Firs Estate, it was only natural that this name was also attached to it.

authorities refused to allow the gravel he had dug to be taken away. The vestry told the surveyor to go to Chigwell to ascertain the reason for this refusal, and to quote the Highway Act, which empowered him to take gravel from any neighbouring waste or, with the approval of the Justices, even from private grounds.

Woodford Essex 1600-1836, E. J. Erith, 1950

When in 1744 no suitable gravel pit could be found in Woodford, the authorities looked further afield. This area on 'Lower Road' near Snakes Lane was leased by Miss Tylney Long to James Hannot Esq. in 1762 for 999 years at a 'peppercorn' rent. The gravel pit or pond no longer exists as such but we wonder who now has title until 2761!

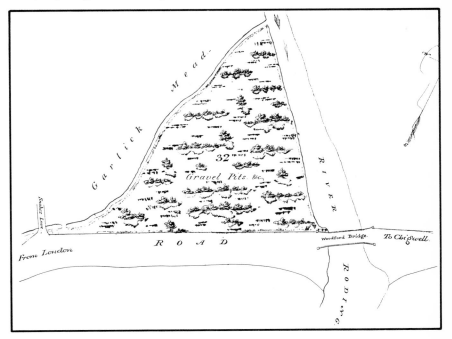

32 *James Hannot Esq.*
    Michaelmas: 1762
    For years 999
    Expires ..... 2761.

each face. Perhaps the strongest argument against the markers being of wood was the fact that in 1810 a mason was ordered to recut them.

All the milestones of the Epping and Ongar Trust were altered in 1822 by David Nash, an Epping stone mason, as they were 'not . . . agreeable to the directions in the new act'. There was a further change in 1837 when the new road had been built across Epping Forest: it was ordered by the trustees that 'the Mile Stones on the Epping Road be painted and lettered and figured correctly and that the Mile Stones on the Ongar Road be so placed as to correspond with and be a Continuation of those on the Epping Road so as to describe the correct Distance or Number of Miles from London and that they be lettered and figured accordingly'. It follows from this that even if the stones themselves within the district of this Trust are original the present inscriptions are at least the third reading. On many surviving stones, not only from the Epping and Ongar Trust, the faint or illegible incisions in the sides no longer facing the road indicate that the stones have at some point been taken out, recut, and positioned anew with the altered lettering.

Essex and the Industrial Revolution,
John Booker, 1974

Analysis of surviving records indicates that milestones were moved or re-inscribed when necessary to reflect changed conditions. Later as finger-post and then sign-boards replaced the old stones, they fell prey to neglect, souvenir hunters and road-widening schemes and few originals can be found today. This one stands at the Wake Arms re-inscribed London 13 miles.

Mileposts or milestones had a far greater significance to the horseman of old not equipped with a speedometer or distance recorder. The Highstone near the Green Man was probably the most well known in the area (see also page 79), this picture being taken of it in its original position before it was set back when the junction was re-aligned. Its well-worn inscription gives the distance to Epping as XI miles; Epping to Ongar through Woodford Bridge, Chigwell and Abridge as XV miles, and that to Hyde Park Corner (the traditional spot from which all measurements from London are still based by the Royal Automobile Club) as what appears to be 10 miles. However on the Ordnance Survey of 1862 the distance to London from the stone is given as 6 miles — historical accounts, viz the Press reports of 1790 and 1793 on page 80, using it as a convenient source of reference.

It is wrong to think of the milestone as a marker of antiquarian interest beside a modern road. In an age of no large scale local maps, dependent on county atlases which were, as they had to be, geared to the general rather than the particular, the milestone was a truthful point of reference — the only gratuitous information (apart from direction posts) which the traveller could expect. . . .

The records of the Epping and Ongar Trust show that the milestones on the Woodford to Harlow section were ordered to be new-faced in 1776. According to Winstone, the mile markers on the Epping to Writtle, or 'New' road, which the Trust took over in 1787, were to be of oak, 5 ft high, 11 in. wide, angular, and with letters and figures on each side denoting the distances from Epping and Chelmsford respectively. Winstone's source cannot be verified as the relevant page in the minute book has deteriorated with damp; enough of the entry remains, however, to show that the mile markers were to be 'of the best hea . . . ' according to the text. Presumably this might have been heart oak but it does make Winstone's statement suspect, particularly as later documentary references to the same markers are always in terms of milestones rather than anything specifically wooden. A stone of 5 ft. would not have been too high because at least 2 ft. was under the ground; and 11 in. was not necessarily too narrow because if the stone was triangular in section this would also have been the width of

The road to Ongar at the thirteen-mile post at Abridge. Here Gertrude and Bert Brighty opened the Copper Kettle cafe, better known as 'Old Mother Brighty's', in 1915. Both keen cyclists, it became a renowned wayside halt. Mrs Brighty died in 1935 but it remained in the family until the 1970s when it became the Roding Restaurant.

When the 'penny-farthing' bicycle was developed by James Starley of the Coventry Sewing Machine Company in the 1870s, it heralded a new era in personal transportation. The high front-wheeled bicycle lasted for twenty years until the invention of the 'safety bicycle' by H. J. Lawson Esq. in 1874, and the introduction of pneumatic tyres in 1888 by John Dunlop, ended the popularity of the 'ordinary'. Woodford Meet District Cyclists' Association began in 1898 and met every year up to 1914. *Above:* South Woodford 1906. *Below:* Penny-farthings on the Green.

A melancholy and distressing accident occurred on Saturday, on the journey of the Cornwallis coach to London, in passing Epping Forest. A respectable tradesman of Bury was conveying two boys, who had been in the country during the holidays, to town, and fearing a change in the weather, put the youngest (about seven years of age) who had not great coat, in the inside of the coach, himself remaining with the other on the top. It is supposed that the boy must have been leaning against the door and that it flew open; for being soon missed, his body was taken up lifeless, and dreadfully mangled, from the wheel having passed over it.

Suffolk Herald, 1827

In describing Epping Forest from a cyclist's point of view, the writer necessarily confines himself to the roads available for bicycling and tricycling, although it will be understood that the cyclist is not restricted in his enjoyment of the Forest beauties, but can at any time leave his machine and wander away into the pathless woods as freely as the railway or horse traveller. Of main-roads, one only that can properly be so-called traverses the Forest. This starts from *Aldgate*, and by way of *Stratford* and *Leytonstone* enters the Forest proper at *Woodford Wells*, going straight through the heart of the forest to *Epping*, continuing thence to *Cambridge*. At *Woodford Wells* this road divides, the more easterly side of the loop going through *Loughton* and rejoining the direct road at the *Wake Arms*. Of the two, the latter is the preferable, being of a better surface, although

109

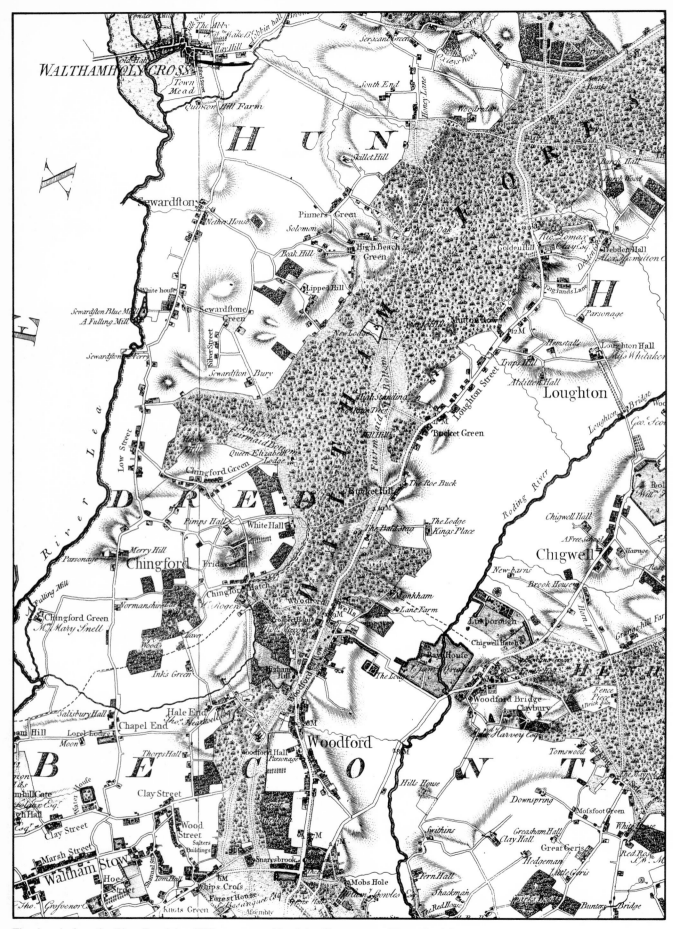

The days before the 'New Roads' — 1777 as surveyed by John Chapman and Peter André.

The Epping New Road — 'usually in a bad state of repair and much cut up by traffic in summer and autumn'.

more hilly, the former being usually in a bad state of repair, and much cut up by the traffic in summer and autumn. This can be said, in a modified sense, of nearly all the roads in the district. As a rule, they are describable as 'very fair, to good,' gravel and flint being the usual materials composing their surfaces; but the traffic during the dry season makes them very dusty. With the exception of the loop-road above described, the highways in the Forest are very serpentine, seldom going direct from one place to another, so that in thoroughly exploring their sinuosities the cyclist will frequently have to retraverse the ground, which usually slopes gently, in frequently varied undulations, without any very formidable hills to climb, *Chingford Old Church Hill* being almost the only ascent which a cyclist of average development cannot surmount, although *Lippitt's Hill, Strawberry Hill* and *Piercing Hill* are also very stiff. The usual maps of the district are perplexing, imperfect, and incomplete, making in some cases no distinction between rideable roads, footpaths, and more beaten tracks. Finger-posts are comparatively few, many being erected in the public-house interest to direct the traveller by devious ways to the doors of sundry houses of refreshment; and the milestones on the few direct roads can only be depended upon when there is no doubt about their reference to the exact route which is being followed. The two Great Eastern Railway branches touching the Forest — one to *Chingford Station*, the other to *Loughton*

How would Percy Lindley have described the same road today!

and *Ongar* — are bridged south of *Hagger Lane* and *Snaresbrook* Stations respectively; but north of those points there are frequent level crossings, in passing over which the cyclist usually has to exercise both patience and caution: patience to wait for the gates being opened by the tardy officials, and caution lest the irregularly-levelled metals should upset the balance of his bicycle or the spoke-threading of his tricycle.

Walks in Epping Forest, Percy Lindley, 1886

EPPING AND ONGAR
TURNPIKE TOLLS

TO BE LET

NOTICE IS HEREBY GIVEN, that the TOLLS arising at the several Toll Gates upon the Turnpike Road leading from Harlow Bush Common, in the parish of Harlow, to Woodford, in the county of Essex, and the Road from Epping to Writtle, in the same county, called or known by the names of the Bald Stag Gate, the Epping Gate, the Thornwood Gate, the Road Street Gate, the High Ongar Gate, the Norton Heath Gate, and the Duck-Lane Gate, the last-named being a Side Gate to both Roads, will be LET BY AUCTION, for One Year, to commence the 11th day of October next, at Twelve o'Clock at Noon, to the best Bidder, at the House of Richard Stokes, called Epping Place, at Epping aforesaid, on MONDAY, the 26th day of August next, between the hours of Twelve o'Clock at Noon and Three in the Afternoon of the same day, subject to such Conditions as shall be then and there produced and in the manner directed by the Act, passed in the Third Year of the Reign of his late Majesty King George the Fourth, for regulating Turnpike Roads, which Tolls are now let for One Year, ending the 11th day of October next, at the sum of £2,470, the Lessee paying the expenses of collecting them, and will be put up at that sum; whoever happens to be the best Bidder, must, at the same time, pay one Month in advance of the Rent at which such Tolls may be Let, and give Security, with sufficient Sureties to the satisfaction of the Trustees, of the said Turnpike Roads, for Payment of the rest of the Money, in advance Monthly, or in such proportions as shall be directed.—Dated 19th July, 1833.

JOHN WINDUS,
Clerk to the Trustees

Press notice, 1833

After Robert McAdam had completed the Woodford New Road, the surveyor turned his attentions to the last major project undertaken by the Epping and Ongar Highway Trust: the construction of the Epping New Road. From 1830-34 gangs toiled to clear a swathe through the forest on a line laid out by McAdam on the high ground some 300 feet above sea level to the west of the old road. A series of embankments and cuttings were intended to give a gradient-free journey and avoid the steep haul in and out of the Loughton valley. One reminder which can still be seen today of all that manual toil 150 years ago is Wake Valley Pond — the result of the excavation of clay for the road which then acted as a dam for the stream which runs through the valley. This picture was taken around 1916. James McAdam was knighted in 1834 on completion of the road and died on June 30, 1852.

The new road met the old at the Wake Arms where the original road passed behind the inn — on the right in the illustration *above*. This curve was eliminated and the road diverted in front. Whereas the milestone at Golding's Hill read 13 miles to London, the straight line of the new route reduced the distance from London to Epping by one mile: thus the marker at the Wake Arms became a similar distance and had to be altered (see page 108).

The Wake Arms was a popular staging post on the road to Epping. This photograph was taken in the days before the reconstruction and resurfacing of the road and the addition of roundabouts in 1936. On the right is the Fox and Hounds with the garage in the centre.

DRUNKENNESS. — *Robert Gosheron*, 22, of Anchor Lane, Bermondsey, licensed victualler, was charged by Police-constable Miller, 241 N, with being drunk while in charge of a horse and trap in the Woodford Road. — Fined 10s. and costs, or seven days.

Walthamstow, Leyton and Chingford Guardian, July 27, 1878

SERIOUS ACCIDENT IN WOODFORD NEW ROAD

Considering the very crowded state of the roads on Bank holiday, the day in this district was fairly free from accidents. One very serious accident, however, occurred on the Woodford New-road. Robert Miller, aged 50, of South Woodford, was knocked down and run over near the waterworks, about half-past nine at night, the people in charge of the trap driving away in the most cowardly manner. Martin was conveyed to his home and attended by Dr. Turtle, who found him to be suffering from fractured ribs and internal injuries.

Joseph Goodhall of Goswell-road, fell from a cart in Woodford New-road and received a nasty cut on the head. The wound was skilfully bandaged by Supt. Wells, of the Barking St. John's Ambulance Society, and the sufferer was then able to proceed home.

Several straying children were taken to the Lea-bridge police station, but they were all handed over to their respective parents.

Walthamstow, Leyton and Chingford Guardian, May 18, 1894

From 1908 the Fox and Hounds was managed by Charlie and Ada Herbert and this view shows a typical Sunday afternoon in the days before people knew of World War. The garage is on the left with Herbert's Tea Gardens between it and the pub. Charlie died in 1923 but his son Horace remembers that in those days the Wake Arms was 'an outpost beyond civilisation, without any main services' and in a unique location: the district of Upshire; the parish of Waltham Holy Cross with a Theydon Bois telephone number and an Epping postal address!

In recent years the Wake Arms suffered increasingly from its 'motorbike' image and became very run down although the owners, Grand Metropolitan, stated that they had plans to demolish and rebuild. However, it finally closed in 1982 and the removal of the roof to avoid paying rates completed the picture of dereliction. Now owned by the Host Group which has received permission to rebuild as a combined pub and restaurant. The Fox and Hounds was demolished in March 1966.

113

Jim Bartlett alongside the sign advertising his garage. Bill Froud stands on the left, Horace Herbert with Pat the dog

beside Jim's Citroën and 'Tubby' the AA man on the right. The building itself was part of the tea rooms.

Three months in 1931. With many new inventions — a recent example being the hang-glider — legislation always lags behind until the situation gets out of hand and urgent action is deemed vital. So it was in the early days of the motor car; at first anyone could buy one and anyone could drive one with no training or experience being necessary. In 1903 a blanket 20 mph speed limit was imposed, no doubt a sensible idea with the mixture of 'horseless carriages' and horses then on the roads. However, as the motor car was developed for mass production after the First World War, and as the popularity of private motoring increased dramatically, so did the death toll. One could not pick up a newspaper in the thirties and not read of accidents and loss of life on the roads, the Epping Forest area being no exception. The old 20 mph limit was ignored by everyone including bus companies which published timetables which

could only be achieved by exceeding the speed limit! A Royal Commission appointed to study the rising number of accidents reported in 1929 that the 20 mph limit should be scrapped as it was so blatantly broken that it brought the law into disrepute. The law was repealed in 1930 and replaced by heavier penalties for dangerous driving. However it was insurance underwriters at Lloyds that suggested to a House of Commons Select Committee that an official driving test was long overdue, yet when it was introduced on June 1, 1935, a concession exempted those already driving from taking it! A 30 mph limit in built-up areas (covering one quarter of Britain's roads) was introduced the same year. Both measures were successful in stemming the increasing mayhem on the roads and, despite a five-fold increase in traffic since 1935, the same number of casualties was not reached again until 1955.

ANOTHER EPPING NEW ROAD FATALITY

Shortly after 7 o'clock last night another fatality occurred on the Epping New Road, resulting in the death of Robert Hughes, of 23, Strone Road, Manor Park.

Hughes, who was a dirt track rider, had been practising at High Beech, but had had an accident, and was being towed home when, at the junction of Fairmead Road and Epping New Road, Loughton, he for some reason lost control of his machine and fell on to the roadway, a passing Rolls-Royce, driven by Capt. Bridge, of London, S.W., going over him. Hughes was killed instantaneously.

The Woodford Times, September 21, 1928

MOTOR CYCLIST'S FRACTURED SKULL

On Wednesday night a serious crash occurred on the Woodford New Road, when two motor cyclists and a pedestrian became involved with one another. The pedestrian was William Read, of no fixed abode, better known as 'Peggy,' one of the best-known characters in the Epping Forest district.

It appears that he was pushing his familiar hand barrow along the Woodford New Road, when the two motor cyclists and he came into collision. The motor cyclists were T. A. Keyes, of 38, Elms Avenue, Muswell Hill, and John Birmingham, of 184, Vicarage Road, Leyton, and Miss Ivy Bateman of Hackney, was riding on the pillion of Keyes's bike.

Keyes and Miss Bateman were taken to the Jubilee Hospital and detained, the former with a fractured base of the skull and the latter with leg and hand injuries and severe shock, while 'Peggy' was taken to Whipps Cross and detained with injury to his one sound leg.

The Woodford Times, July 10, 1931

Late on Thursday night of last week a collision occurred on the High Road, Woodford Wells, near Whitehall Road, between a car (which did not stop) and a motor cycle owned and ridden by A. G. Dunkley, of 140, Risley Avenue, Tottenham. Miss Violet Spratt, of Bethnal Green, who was riding on the pillion, was taken to the Jubilee Hospital and detained with concussion.

The Woodford Times, July 10, 1931

Last night a serious accident occurred near Johnston Pond, Woodford Green, in which two motor cycles and an Austin car were involved. The driver of one of the motor cycles, Mr. Jeffries, of Tottenham, was taken to the Jubilee Hospital and detained in a very critical condition. Miss Forsyth, of Highbury, a pillion rider on one of the machines, was detained with a severely lacerated leg.

The Woodford Times, July 10, 1931

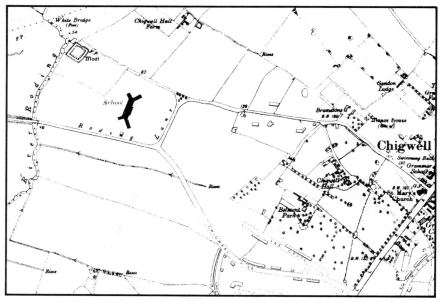

One must also appreciate that narrow winding roads, which followed the same course as ancient cart tracks around every obstacle, were hardly suitable for the motoring era. A good example is Roding Lane which originally dog-legged its way to Chigwell — by the end of the First World War Chigwell Rise (also known as Chigwell New Road) had been laid down to straighten out the nasty bend.

In 1908 the Roding burst its banks, inundating the valley, yet the road on its raised embankment remained passable.

This morning a serious accident, involving an R.O.P. petrol lorry, an Acme coach, and an Austin car, occurred at the junction of Rangers Road and Epping New Road. The Austin driver sustained a broken arm and leg.

The Woodford Times, July 10, 1931

Late last night a very bad accident occurred near Bedford Road, Woodford. Mrs. Topsy Rowland, aged 70 years, and her daughter, Miss Edith Rowland, of 'Eversleigh,' Derby Road, were knocked down by a motor car. Shortly after admission to Jubilee Hospital, Mrs. Rowland died from a fracture of the base of the skull, and her daughter was detained with shock.

The Woodford Times, July 10, 1931

The same oak has survived almost unchanged for eighty years. The picture was taken in the winter of 1983 when a temporary fence surrounded the site of the old refuse tip.

FIRE BRIGADE'S EIGHT HOURS' WORK

Epping New Road Closed

PAPER LORRY DESTROYED

Traffic on the Epping New Road was completely suspended on Wednesday night owing to an outbreak of fire on a five-ton lorry near the Robin Hood.

The lorry was laden with waste paper and burned fiercely. The Loughton Fire Brigade attended, and fought the flames for nearly eight hours before they got the flames under control, and then that only happened when the lorry and its contents had been completely destroyed. The heat was intense, and owing to the comparative narrowness of the road, all traffic had to be diverted while the Brigade were at work.

The Woodford Times, December 11, 1931

SERIOUS ACCIDENT AT WOODFORD

Car and Steam Wagon Collide

Several accidents are reported in our district, the most serious of which occurred last Friday morning at about 8.30 a.m. A saloon motor car, driven by Herbert Thomas Hodge, of High Street, Much Hadham, with Mrs. Longden Thurgood, aged 30, of The Links, Much Hadham, as passenger, was proceeding towards London. On approaching Woodford Wells the driver ran into a bank of fog, and, it is said, he pulled out to overtake a 'bus proceeding in the same direction. At the same time, however, a steam wagon, driven by Reginald Frederick Collins, of 7, Tidbury Street, Battersea, proceeding towards Loughton, also drew out to pass a stationary 'bus. The two vehicles met head on, and the car was wrecked.

The Woodford Times, December 25, 1931

SERIOUS MOTOR SMASH

OCCUPANTS SERIOUSLY INJURED

A car which was being driven down Goldings Hill, Loughton, on Sunday afternoon, crashed into a post at the junction of the hill and Lower Road, turned three somersaults and landed on what was left of its four wheels. The body was torn from the chassis and flung several yards away.

By a miracle, the driver, Mr. Alfred Jenkins, of 45, Chandos Road, Stratford, and his two companions, Mr. George Lockwood, of 145, Norman Road, Leytonstone, and Mr. George Webb, of 47, Chandos Road, were not killed.

The Woodford Times, September 1, 1933

By 1930 massive road building schemes were under way, serving not only the motorised tourist but also helping to alleviate increasing unemployment. When the North Circular Road reached Woodford (see page 102) Grove Road became the link with the Southend Arterial Road completed in 1932.

TRAFFIC ROUNDABOUT FOR WOODFORD?

Suggested Remedy for Dangerous Crossing

A traffic 'roundabout' is a possibility for Woodford, provided the Ministry sanctions the expense.

In the opinion of the Essex County Surveyor, statistics showing the number of accidents which have recently occurred at the junction of the Chigwell and Southend Roads render it vitally necessary that something should be done without delay.

When the road was constructed the crossing was scheduled as suitable for a 'roundabout' traffic system. . . .

The County Surveyor declares that traffic is daily increasing on both the roads affected, and the Ministry say that twenty-eight collisions occurred at the junction during the year ended June 30th, 1932.

A flashing beacon has been in operation at the junction for the past five years, but this is insufficient for weekend traffic, when a policeman is usually on point duty.

The Woodford Times, July 14, 1933

Below: Halcyon days . . . before anyone thought up the idea of arterial roads or motorways. The annotations refer to the dates that particular granite-surfaced roads in the area were repaired just after the beginning of the twentieth century.

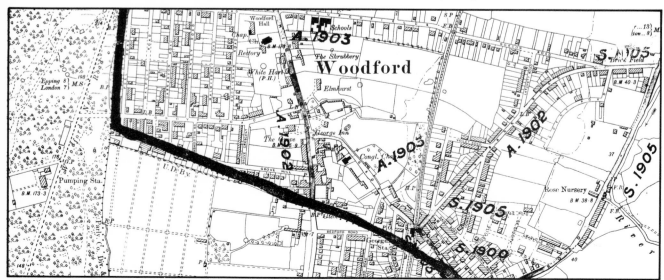

Grove Road, being an ordinary residential street, was never suitable for its new rôle. Attempts were made in the late 1950s to improve the junction but it could only be a partial solution. These views show the changing face of Gates Corner. *Above:* March 25, 1966 showing the widened 'throat' of Grove Road and *below*, on March 5, 1985, the dramatic transition to the combined ten-lane Southend Road and M11 motorway scything across South Woodford.

Woodford Avenue, known originally as the Ilford Arterial Road, was one of the results of the Greater London arterial roads programme drawn up during the First World War. A single carriageway was completed in the 1920s — this view is impossible to match today because of the development of the Clayhall Park estate on the intervening open fields.

People at Chigwell are today pointing to a desolate-looking farmstead called Hill Farm between Chigwell and Woodford as the site of the L.C.C.'s next housing estate.

At present some of the meadows serve as football pitches.

The farm was bought by the L.C.C. nearly two years ago. It consists of about 100 acres, and the Council has secured the option of purchasing a further 150 acres in the neighbourhood.

Disturbed by the prospect of another London invasion, Essex County Council has just appointed Professor S. D. Adshead, the town planning expert, to investigate the proposal and to prepare a report on the probable social and other consequences to the County of Essex of the development of a cottage colony at Chigwell.

A prominent resident of Chigwell said to an *Evening News* correspondent today: 'As the farm is on the River Roding and is partly waterlogged, it seems a queer place to choose for a housing estate.

'There is no factory within six miles and the nearest station is 1½ miles distant. There are many acres of Crown land between Chigwell and Ilford served by good roads that would be much more suitable for housing schemes.'

Mr. H. R. Selley, M.P., Chairman of the L.C.C. Housing Committee, expressed surprise at the Essex County Council's action.

'Essex people need not be alarmed,' he said. 'We have had an estate at Chigwell for some time, but we shall certainly do nothing at Chigwell during the coming year, and we may not build a housing colony there at all.

'We have secured certain estates outside the County of London for housing, if necessary, but the new subsidy arrangements may make a difference to our programme.'

Evening News, March 14, 1933

Below: Roding Lane, running from Woodford Bridge to Wanstead, met the new road at Hill Farm — hence the name Hill Farm Estate on the signboard. This picture was taken as the area was being developed — just look at it now!

Likewise the Eastern Avenue was an important link in the London to Southend road. Its construction in the 1920s meant the loss of George Lane, Wanstead. The George Hotel, although barely visible in the picture *below*, provides the link.

The Robin Hood crossroads was a notorious accident black spot — indeed the whole of the Epping New Road has claimed countless lives — one of the most tragic in recent years being that in October 1978 of a young soldier on leave going to see his family one Saturday evening when his motor bike collided with a lorry between Rangers Road and the Robin Hood. Today Gunner Nurse lies in High Beach churchyard — yet another victim of the 'Murder Mile'.

COUNTY OF ESSEX
ROAD TRAFFIC ACT, 1930

Prohibition of all Vehicles from using sections of the Epping New Road (A11) in the Urban District of Chigwell, Essex.

Notice is hereby given that by reason of works of repair and reconstruction being required on the undermentioned sections of road, the Essex County Council intend to make an Order under Section 47 of the Road Traffic Act, 1930, prohibiting all vehicles from using those sections of the Epping New Road (A11) Urban District of Chigwell, in the County of Essex, which are described below:
(1) That part of the said road between its southerly point of junction with the Cross Roads immediately south of the Robin Hood Public House and a point immediately north of its junction with Rangers Road (A1096), a distance of about 2,000 lineal yards.
(2) That part of the said road between a point immediately south of its junction with Warren Hill and a point immdiately north of the 'Warrenwood House' Public House, a distance of about 370 lineal yards. . . .

Public Announcement. March 13, 1936

The attention of Chigwell Council has been drawn to the alarming state of affairs that would develop if the High Road in Loughton and Buckhurst Hill had to bear the heavy stream of traffic during the reconstruction of the Epping New Road between the Wake Arms and the Buckhurst Hill-Woodford boundary.
The clerk said he had received a letter from Mr. Horace White, of High-road, Loughton, pointing out that the Essex County Council had advertised for tenders for the reconstruction of Epping New-road between the Wake Arms and the Buckhurst Hill-Woodford boundary. These tenders were in two categories. One was for re-making the road all at once, closing it completely while the work was in progress, and the other was for making half at a time. Mr. White said that if the road were completely closed an enormous amount of traffic would have to be diverted through Buckhurst Hill and Loughton. He urged that the Council should bring their utmost pressure to bear on both the Essex County Council and the Ministry of Transport against the closing of the road.

The Express and Independent,
March 14, 1936

This was the first roundabout to be built on the road during its reconstruction in 1936. The junction with the road to High Beach was moved to the south but the course of the old one can still be traced through the Forest.

Before and after. The M11 was the most important road development built through the Epping Forest area since McAdam's New Road. At its southern end its snaking tentacles serpentined their way alongside the River Roding to join up with the Eastern Avenue. Here a large gyratory roundabout was constructed in an effort to cope with the increased traffic the motorway was bound to engender but it proves inadequate to handle rush-hour conditions.

The A11 is an important trunk road serving traffic between London and East Anglia. At its southern end, it runs through built-up, populous areas and then following a north eastern and a northern route, passes through Epping Forest and several urban areas. In these urban areas the road, constructed many years ago, is poorly aligned, of narrow width with many buildings on each side. This road construction is not fit and, indeed, was not intended to carry the volume and type of traffic now using it. Sections of it are now carrying four times the volume of their safe carrying capacity. . . . I do not think that the construction of the motorway would . . . cause widespread damage to amenities or the visual scene. Phrases such as 'devastation of the countryside' or 'desecration of the landscape' go much too far in my opinion, in describing the effect of a motorway on the countryside. Having regard to the Royal Fine Art Commission and other important bodies associated with the Ministry in the landscaping and treatment of motorways and the embankments and structures thereof, it is clear that the result in this case will be of the highest order and by no means so damaging to the visual scene or amenities as some objectors tend to think.

Public Enquiry on the construction of the M11 motorway, Inspector's Report, November 14, 1969

The opening of the M11 sections from Redbridge to Harlow yesterday, Thursday, was all set to be a damp squib of an affair. After months of delays, and a furore of objections to the traffic pouring off the end of the motorway into Wanstead, the opening of the multi-million pound scheme was designed to go off with a whimper rather than a bang.

Described by the Department of Transport as 'a low key affair' the opening consisted of a mere moving of the barriers out of the way on the slip roads at about 11am. Not for the M11 a celebrity cutting the tape surrounded by approving local dignitaries. Wanstead awaited with apprehension an influx of heavy traffic both to and from the new road; the rest of the area is just waiting to see what will come of the promised decrease in through traffic on smaller roads.

Work started on the Redbridge to Loughton and Loughton to South Harlow sections of the motorway in October 1973, and was scheduled to take three years. When it became clear the contracts could not be completed on time a date was set for Spring 1977. It is now six months overdue and has cost the taxpayer a total of more than £20.67 million — from Redbridge to Loughton nearly £12 million and from Loughton to South Harlow nearly £9 million.

West Essex Gazette, April 15, 1977

Day-Trippers and sightseers visiting the M11 have been dangerously disobeying motorway regulations. They have been seen reversing, doing U-turns and pulling up on the hard shoulder to admire the view by police patrolling the new road.

'They have been doing all sorts of things you wouldn't believe,' said a spokesman from the Motorway Control Unit. 'I think this is something which will possibly pass as the

Of all the properties swept away by the motorway, the 'old mill by the stream' at Woodford was the most tragic. There had been a watermill on the Roding since earliest times and this illustration shows the mill and bridge some time before 1900.

In 1919 Bill Jacobs took over what was then the Mill Inn and opened up as a garage. He obtained the Wolseley dealership in 1934, his eldest son Richard joining him in 1937. Dick Jacobs eventually went on to become a well-known racing driver with the MG marque, taking a considerable part in the development of the Mk II TD. *Above:* The 'Mill' as it appeared in 1952 with the garage extension behind the old inn which became an office and service bays. *Below:* Four years later, modernised, with new showroom and real vintage vehicles at the traditional Roundabout traffic jam. Note the 'bubble car' on the right.

'The small photograph was taken on the day we were forced to close and shows me in front of an empty showroom with the neon signs removed. Not a happy day' — Richard Jacobs in a letter, February 13, 1985.

In March 1947 Frederick Gibberd was appointed to design one of the six 'new' towns to cater for the people of the East End of London made homeless by war. The site chosen was on farmland to the west of Harlow. The old A11 was completely unsuitable for the needs of a developing new town and Gibberd was given the projected route of the North Orbital Road to be built around London and also the line of the proposed new motor route from Cambridge to London. This was scheduled to run down the Lea Valley so Gibberd planned his town accordingly, with the industrial side located alongside the new 'motorway' to avoid heavy lorries interfering or crossing the housing areas. Lo and behold when the Ministry of Transport published their plans for the M11 in 1964, Gibberd discovered that it had now been moved to the opposite side of the town along the Roding valley, completely ruining his whole concept, then nearly twenty years in the making. As Sir Frederick commented later: 'It was like asking a man to plan a seaside town only to learn, too late, that the sea has been shifted to the other side!' The reason given: to save £15 million. The before and after photographs show the result.

novelty wears off. We have stopped some of them and taken details, which should put a stop to this sort of thing. People have got to realise that this is as much a motorway as the M1.'

West Essex Gazette, April 29, 1977

Following the opening of the M11 motorway, the A11 between Leytonstone and Stump Cross is to be renumbered the A104, B1393 and A1184.

Press report 1978

The opening of the M25, between the M11 and A10, will intensify existing forest traffic problems. By forcing some action it may prove a blessing even if heavily disguised and considerably delayed.

Traffic to the Waltham Cross entry at Honey Lane to the M25 will converge along minor forest roads around High Beech. Woodridden Hill running from Honey Lane to the Wakes Arms, on what is still to me the A11, will also bear heavy traffic.

The Conservators, opposing an entry so close to the forest, warned they would refuse any widening of the forest roads — a refusal which could be overcome only by an Act of Parliament.

Traffic destroys the precious tranquillity of the forest but there are other powerful objections as well. It is difficult to make a true unit of a strip ten miles long and never more than two miles wide. Roads divide anyway but roads heavy with traffic form a severe barrier, splitting the forest into island sites, destroying any sense of unity.

Epping Forest is probably the finest ancient woodland in the country. It harbours many endangered species including rare mosses and lichens, which are excessively sensitive to pollution. Traffic fumes drift into the heart of the forest and some species have already disappeared. More will surely follow if traffic increases.

Cattle now graze only in the summer months and deer are confined to their sanctuary. Both measures were taken as the animals, when at large, constituted a danger to themselves and to traffic, especially motorcycles. Happily the deer are returning, coming in from the surrounding estates. An ad-

One legacy on the positive side, reminiscent of the ponds bequeathed us by earlier roadmakers, was this lake between Buckhurst Hill and Chigwell produced by the extraction of gravel for the M11.

ditional reason for confining the deer was that disturbance — often unintentional — prevented them breeding. It would indeed be sad if increased traffic had the same effect and nullified their return.

The traffic problem can be tackled in two ways. In the short term the small forest roads can be closed to through traffic. This would restore some of the tranquillity to the forest and force us — for we are all sinners — back on to the main roads. Unfortunately Woodridden Hill has become a main road and the position there could deteriorate.

A north facing entry to the M11, adjacent to the existing entries in Loughton and traffic for the M25 could avoid the forest altogether by joining the M11 there and using the M11/M25 interchange. The Department of Transport is committed to a survey when traffic patterns have stabilised to determine if the additional entry is justified — the north facing slips in the current jargon. Relief from this seems years away. We must hope that no permanent damage occurs while we await a permanent solution.

Traffic is not the only problem. Even before it opened the M25 was generating develop-

ment demands. The Bell Hotel at Epping has increased its motel accommodation. Applications for a hotel in Epping and a supermarket in Buckhurst Hill have been submitted. At the junction of Woodridden Hill and the A11, the Wake Arms stands, a hideous eyesore — roofless to save paying rates. The owners, no doubt are waiting till increased demand justifies a more massive development.

But all is not gloom. The M25 runs in a tunnel beneath Bell Common at Epping. On its concrete roof the soil is being restored on a peat base. Next year village cricket will return to what is unkindly known as the £10 million cricket pitch. It should have started this year but the vast amount of peat required drained the supplies of the whole of Britain and could not be collected in time.

The real bonus, however, is the 14 acres near Ivy Chimneys being given by the Department of Transport to compensate for the land beneath which the tunnel runs. So the forest grows!

Robert Mitchell writing in Essex Countryside. July 1984

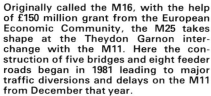

Originally called the M16, with the help of £150 million grant from the European Economic Community, the M25 takes shape at the Theydon Garnon interchange with the M11. Here the construction of five bridges and eight feeder roads began in 1981 leading to major traffic diversions and delays on the M11 from December that year.

Watched by Essex County Council Chairman Bob Daniels, the Secretary of State for Transport David Howell cuts the ceremonial ribbon on April 27, 1983 to open the M25 between the A127 and M11. The westbound section which crosses Epping Forest at Bell Common was not completed until some months later. With its roadside chain-link fencing, and being floodlit at night, the M25 has proved an almost impenetrable barrier to deer moving from open farmland in the north to the shelter of the Forest. By May 1985 the Conservatives reported that two animals had actually been killed on the road. *Below:* These few hundred yards of reinstated land on top of the tunnel give the only free access through the concrete curtain.

The Secretary of State for Transport, Mr. Nicholas Ridley, opened the M25 link between the M11, Theydon Garnon, and the A10, Waltham Cross, on Wednesday morning.

The opening, at the Bell Common Tunnel entrance, means that 73.5 miles of the 121.5 miles of motorway are now open. The whole M25 orbital route ringing London should be completed by late 1986.

The latest eight-mile section, including tunnels at Holmesdale, Waltham Cross, and Bell Common, Epping has cost about £120 million, and includes all the electronic aids to help keep what may become one of the busiest motorways in Europe on the move.

Predictions by the Department of Transport show that by the turn of the century up to 100,000 vehicles a day will be using the road, with up to 200,000 at the interchange with Heathrow Airport.

And by 1987 when the M25 is completely open, 50,000-60,000 vehicles a day are expected to use the section between Waltham Abbey and the M11 interchange.

The motorway will be lit throughout its length, and both tunnels have lights and automatic control systems constantly monitoring traffic, including 42 cameras linked to a police control point.

The new section is part of a crucial link between the A1 and the North, and the Dartford Tunnel and Channel ports.

Said the DoT spokesman: 'By the end of 1986, when the M25 is completed, it will provide an uninterrupted link of three and four dual-lane carriageway between the 18 major radial routes that link the capital with the English regions, Scotland and Wales.'

'It is perhaps the most important piece of transport history for London since the River Thames was opened to navigation.'

'Already the M25 is a key element in the strategy to develop the eastern side of London, particularly the docklands area.'

As well as the tunnels, which have sensors to detect fog and ice, the new section has 21 bridges, underpasses and culverts, 15 signs and signal gantries, and 3.6 miles of acoustic fences and earth banks.

Guardian & Gazette, January 27, 1984

Construction of a £125 million motorway across London to connect the M11 to the Blackwall Tunnel route under the Thames was authorised yesterday by Mrs. Chalker, Transport Minister.

It means a journey which can now take up to an hour on the congested roads of Stratford, Leyton and Wanstead will be cut to a mere four minutes.

There is already a motorway-standard road on either side of the Blackwall Tunnel, providing a fast route from south-east London but petering out north of the river.

The four-mile 'missing link' from Hackney to the M11 will cost about £13 million more than originally planned because the Government is to adopt changes recommended after a public inquiry.

It will be put into a 'cut-and-cover' tunnel beneath the Green Man roundabout which is the junction of the A11, A12 and A114 roads.

Epping Forest will be protected as a result. There will also be a deeper cutting at Leytonstone and an extended tunnel at George Green, Wanstead, both for environmental reasons.

The Daily Telegraph, October 11, 1985

Railways

Above: **George Lane Station pictured early this century.** *Below:* **In August 1935 the London Passenger Transport Board photographed all their stations on the Central London line as part of the modernisation scheme submitted to Parliament.**

In January 1909, I put on my new broad-brimmed boater with its green and white hat-band and set off from South Woodford for Loughton High School. . . .

We had to travel from George Lane (now South Woodford) station on the Great Eastern Railway. In the station yard one or two horse cabs (four wheelers) stood waiting to be hired by passengers with luggage. The drivers of these cabs (nicknamed 'Beaky' and 'Old Peter') were well known figures and knew when they would be wanted every evening to take their regular patrons home from the station. There were also one or two hansoms at George Lane station but they disappeared some time before the four wheelers were superseded by taxi cabs.

Inside the station only a short length of each platform was roofed over but on each side there was a General Waiting Room and a Ladies' Waiting Room where, in winter, fires were kept burning. This proved very convenient as the schools had very strict rules forbidding boys and girls to travel in the same compartments on trains, or to fraternise on railway platforms. So at George Lane the boys from Loughton, Chigwell and Bancroft's School used the big General Waiting Room, while the girls herded into the tiny Ladies' Room next door.

German raiders had a near miss on the station on the night of October 14, 1940 when two high-explosive bombs fell in George Lane. The censor authorised the release of this picture two weeks later.

The trains ran at irregular intervals and some of the morning trains were non-stop from Snaresbrook to Liverpool Street. In the evenings, on certain trains, Snaresbrook was the first stop. Nearly all Ongar, Epping and Loughton trains stopped at every station after Snaresbrook.

As we waited on the 'down side' of George Lane Station for the Loughton train, the opposite 'up' plaform was crowded with business-men, and school boys and girls. Some of the men, and the occasional Westminster boy, wore black silk hats and carried umbrellas and all wore dark suits, black boots, bowler hats in winter, and boaters in summer. Brown shoes and tweed jackets might be permissible at work on Saturday mornings but not on ordinary days.

At the station the porters knew all the regular travellers by sight and rarely asked to see their season tickets. Indeed there was an indignant protest made when the Railway Company ordered that tickets must be shown every day at the barriers.

As season ticket holders we used the second class compartments. These were upholstered in reddish brown velvet and had dark green roller blinds at the windows. The locks on the doors could be wedged from the inside by inserting a halfpenny against the catch — a very useful device for keeping out enemies! On very cold days large, flat, rusty tins filled with hot water were placed under the seats as footwarmers.

Third class carriages had no such luxuries. They were always at the front and back of the train and were called 'cattle trucks', because the partitions between the compartments only reached up to shoulder level, so that inside one could see over and indeed climb over the whole length of the coach. The seats were hard and were covered with shiny black imitation leather.

Porters were placed along the platforms to slam the doors shut. Each engine carried a large destination board and as a train came in, porters shouted its destination and the name of the station.

The guard had a green flag by day and an oil lamp by night, as well as a whistle, to give the engine driver the signal to start. There was the guard's van at the front and back of each train to carry luggage, dogs, bicycles and even favoured passengers.

At both stations between George Lane and Loughton there were level crossing gates opened and shut by porters, and passengers

Waiting for the 9.07 — then and now. Dresses went up in the twenties; hats came off in the fifties!

crossed the lines from one platform to the other when no train was in sight. One or two daring spirits crossed at George Lane and Woodford when a down train was standing in the station.

Memories of travelling from Woodford to Loughton, Margery M. Smith Transactions No. 1, Chigwell Local History Society, 1970

Londoners of all classes will be startled to learn, from a communication which appears in our columns this morning, that a large number of the metropolitan commons are once more in danger. The source of this danger is not this time the earth hunger of enclosing landlords, but the expanding ambition of railway directors and engineers.

The Daily News, December 20, 1880

SIR,— The public need be under no apprehension about the Great Eastern Railway absorbing 70 acres of Epping Forest. The extension of the railway to Chingford has brought such masses of people to that one spot that it is exceedingly desirable some of them should be taken further on to the highest and most beautiful part of the forest at High Beech, and this is what the railway company proposes to do. In consequence of Epping Forest running considerably to the west at Chingford the railway company are obliged to traverse it to get to High Beech. Seven acres is probably nearer the total quantity of the forest they will absorb instead of the 70 shown on their plans, which contain large powers of deviation. The proposed line is absolutely

In 1856 the end of the line for the Great Eastern was at Loughton. Fifty years after it opened, it was still one of the most profitable sections on the GER suburban system with one third of each train first class.

necessary for the full enjoyment by the London public of the forest. — I am, &c.,
T. J. NELSON

The Daily News, December 21, 1880

Lord CLAUD HAMILTON, in moving the second reading of the Great Eastern Railway (High Beech Extension) Bill, said that the projected railway, which extended from Chingford to High Beech, had the approval of the Conservators of Epping Forest. A small outlying arm of the forest would be intersected by the railway, for the construction of which it would be necessary to take nine acres of land. The line would, however, open up some of the most beautiful parts of the forest, which were now practically inaccessible. (Hear.) The bill

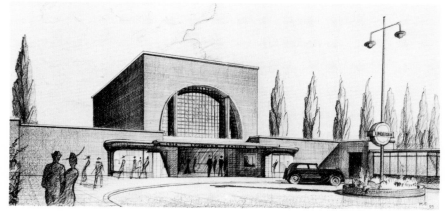

Of all the stations in the Epping Forest area, Loughton has seen the greatest change. This is the original artist's impression for the new station opened by the LNER in 1940. The map extracts from 1892 and 1963 show the re-siting of the new station some 500 feet to the north-east.

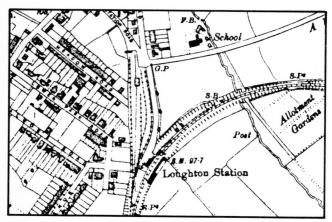

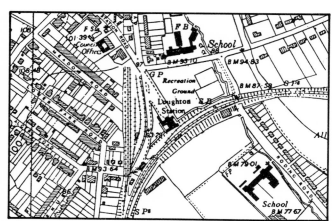

had met with strong opposition from several professors, a great many butterfly fanciers, and gentlemen who visited the forest in pursuit of the insect tribe — (laughter) — but in favour of the bill there were petitions signed by 16,000 persons, including 2,000 ministers, managers of Sunday-schools, superintendents of Band of Hope Unions, and other heads of educational and temperance associations, who represented an aggregate of something like 300,000 adults and children. If the House threw out the bill it would infringe the intention of the Act of Parliament, which dedicated the forest not merely to a few interested persons but to the poor of London. (Cries of 'Oh' and cheers.)

Mr. W. H. JAMES opposed the bill on a very important principle. Railway companies were always anxious to run through common lands which they would not have to pay for. There was no reason whatever why the Great Eastern Company should not attain the given point by running through land which they would have to pay for. A station could be built in the locality in question without destroying the forest, if the company chose to bear the expense. The House divided—

For the second reading	82
Against	230
	148

The announcement of the numbers was received with cheers. The bill was accordingly rejected and the amendment agreed to.

House of Commons, March 12, 1883

The Great Eastern Railway opened the extension of its Loughton branch to a terminus at Chipping Ongar in April 1865, and so completed the line which serves a considerable part of Epping Forest.

The terminus had been at Loughton for nearly nine years and the new extension began at a junction just short of this original terminus, which later became a goods yard.

Epping had had the prospect of a railway many years earlier, for in 1846 powers had been obtained by the Eastern Counties Railway to build a branch to the town; but as nothing came of the project these powers were allowed to lapse. Later on, however, further authorization was received for the line and it

This view is dated around 1905, the year electrification of the GER suburban services was first recommended by a Royal Commission. Nothing was done at all until the lines became part of the LNER and even then under the 1935 New Works Programme only conversion of the Loughton line was contemplated. That was achieved by November 21, 1948 and tube trains finally reached Epping on September 25, 1949.

was commenced from a junction with the Cambridge route of the Eastern Counties between Stratford and Leyton.

The branch was opened as far as Loughton in August 1856, with intermediate stations at Leyton (then known as Low Leyton), Leytonstone, Snaresbrook, George Lane, Woodford and Buckhurst Hill. Initially the weekday train service comprised eight trains from Fenchurch Street and one from Bishopsgate, and the journey time by the best service to Loughton was forty minutes. A similar service operated in the reverse direction. Single fares were 2/- first class from London to Loughton, 1/6 second class and 1/- third class.

In August 1859 the Epping Railway was incorporated for the purpose of establishing rail communication between Loughton, Epping and Chipping Ongar. The authorized capital was £100,000 in £10 shares, with powers to raise loans to the extent of £33,000.

Unfortunately the Eastern Counties Railway was unco-operative and opposed the passage of the Epping Railway Bill as well as a further Bill introduced by the latter company to extend its proposed railway from Chipping Ongar to Dunmow. Although parliamentary sanction was also obtained for this extension it was never built.

By an act of July 27, 1862, the Epping Railway was transferred to the newly formed Great Eastern Railway and the latter company inherited legal and parliamentary expenses to the tune of over £5,000, quite apart from

As electrification advanced the unfinished sections were still worked by steam, a Holden 2-4-2 tank engine working a push-pull service on the single track to Ongar until electrification was extended to the end of the line on November 18, 1957.

engineering expenses of £2,500. In addition there were a number of claims by landowners with whom contracts of sale had been entered into by the Epping Railway, which was not ready — or indeed able — to pay.

Under the Great Eastern the plans of the former Epping Railway gradually took shape, the line being built as single track. By early April 1865 it was ready for the Board of Trade Inspector's visit and he duly authorized its opening for passenger traffic.

The actual opening took place at short notice, therefore no preparations had been made for marking the occasion. However, an impromptu notice from the town crier of Chipping Ongar was the signal for some hastily arranged festivities, which naturally centred around the railway station.

The cadet corps of Dr. Clark's Grammar School was on the platform to fire a volley in greeting as the first train steamed into Ongar. There was a desperate rush for tickets, a certain Mr Low, of Stanford Rivers, succeeded in securing the first to be issued. During the day the 18th Essex R.V.C. band was in attendance at the station, and in the evening the numbers of spectators and passengers for excursion trips increased. Unfortunately, as the last train from Epping arrived at North Weald the locomotive was derailed and, although nobody was injured, the train was greatly delayed and many anxious faces were to be seen at Ongar station, for the train did not reach there until five o'clock next morning! This opening-day accident rather shook the confidence of some in the safety of the new line.

The Loughton line had been built at a time when funds were short, and consequently it followed the contour of the ground rather closely, resulting in many level crossings. Between Epping and North Weald a steep incline culminates in a summit level 340 feet above sea level, which was the highest point on the entire Great Eastern system (apart from the Elsenham and Thaxted Light Railway).

The track was later doubled beween Loughton and Epping and the gradual development of the inner suburbs and the opening of Liverpool Street station in 1874 and its extension twenty years later all brought further traffic — quite apart, of course, from the extensive excursion traffic carried to Epping Forest during the summer months.

K. A. Frost writing in
the Essex Countryside in February 1966

In 1905 a Royal Commission recommended electrification of the G.E.R. suburban services. Between 1893 and 1905 various electric, including tube railway, schemes were proposed for North and North-East London. The G.E.R. opposed most of these Bills. No electrification was started until the lines were part of the L.N.E.R., the conversion of the

Ongar — new end of the line and scene of the jubilant opening of the Epping Railway in April 1865.

Loughton line being carried out jointly with the London Passenger Transport Board (now London Transport Board) under the 1935 New Works Programme. In 1912, the Central London Railway was extended from Bank to Liverpool Street and renamed Central Line in 1937.

The Central Line tube was extended

through Bethnal Green to an enlarged sub-surface station at Mile End for cross-platform interchange with the District Line, and surfaced at Stratford, where new platforms provided easy interchange with the L.N.E.R. The line then went underground again, surfacing at Loughton Branch Junction and joined the original line approaching Leyton

On January 3, 1966 the Eastern Region's freight trains were finally withdrawn heralding the closure of the goods' yards at

Woodford, Loughton, Theydon Bois, Epping, Blake Hall and Ongar and the removal of the surplus track.

At Theydon Bois later brickwork harmonises with that of the original Great Eastern Railway.

Station. Beyond Leyton the L.N.E.R. line as far as Epping and the loop line from Woodford to Newbury Park were electrified and a new tube section constructed from the latter point to Leytonstone.

By September, 1939, the work was well advanced. It was resumed after the war and on December 4, 1946, the first section from Liverpool Street to Stratford was opened. On May 5, 1947, Central Line trains were extended to Leytonstone. Electrification reached Woodford on December 14, 1947, and the new tube section from Leytonstone to Newbury Park opened on the same day. Electrical operation was extended from Newbury Park to Hainault on May 31, 1948, while electrification of the loop line was completed on November 21, 1948, when a shuttle service began over the northern section from Hainault to Woodford. On the same date electrification to Loughton was completed. As electrification advanced, the unfinished sections were still worked by steam trains. Further retrenchment came on September 25, 1949, when tube trains reached Epping. For eight years a push-and-pull service consisting of early L.N.E.R. coaching stock and a Holden 2-4-2 tank engine worked the single-track Epping-Ongar section until tube trains took over on November 18, 1957.

Edward Treby, Railway Magazine,
September 1968

London Transport announced last night that a Bill is to be promoted in the forthcoming session of Parliament to secure the powers necessary for their share of the transport developments in London announced by the Chancellor of the Exchequer in the House of Commons on June 5. Mr Chamberlain outlined a scheme to encourage the early electrification and development of the suburban railway and Underground systems in the London Passenger Transport area. . . . The powers to be sought will include sanction for the eastern extension of the Central London Line to a point where it will connect with the Loughton and Grange Hill lines of the London and North Eastern Railway; the extension of the Highgate line northwards to East Finchley, where it will join the London and North Eastern Railway's Edgware-High Barnet lines; station improvements on the Underground system; and the provision of additional trolley-omnibus routes.

The Times, November 23, 1935

The Ministry of Transport has authorized Essex County Council to proceed with the removal of a number of level crossings on the Epping branch of the London and North Eastern Railway.

When war broke out a number of road schemes that would have been necessary by the removal of the level crossings were not put in hand. These included an alteration in Grove Green Road, Leytonstone, the widen-

ing of High Street, Wanstead, and the construction of pedestrian subways at Eagle Lane, Wanstead, and George Lane, Woodford, a footbridge in Marlborough Road, Woodford, and a viaduct at George Lane, Woodford, and a subway in Queen's Road, Buckhurst Hill.

The Times, April 26, 1940

The extension of the Central Line transpired to be one of the most complicated undertaken by London Transport in recent years. The driving of new tube tunnels east from Liverpool Street began just before the war. It was a task not without its difficulties as the tunnels had to traverse, or rather burrow through, marshy ground lying beneath several streams that formed part of the River Lea

In all there were five level crossings on the Central London Railway, renamed the Central Line in 1937, all of which had to be closed on electrification and traffic diverted. The usual solution was to build either an underpass as at Leytonstone or a bridge which was done at South Woodford, Woodford and Theydon Bois, seen *above* circa 1900 and *below* today with the flyover in the background.

system, and more marshy ground further on where they dipped under the River Roding, near the present Redbridge station. In these conditions the method employed to drive the tunnels at depth was to work in air compressed sufficiently to keep out the water, which meant that the miners and material had to enter and leave the working chambers via an airlock.

But where at one place the tubes rose to only a few feet below the surface, leaving insufficient coverage to prevent air leakage, the earth had to be consolidated by chemical means. And more difficult still at another site, near Stratford, where this process could not be used, the tube tunnels had to be built partly in sunken cofferdams, or watertight enclosures.

The tunnels were actually driven, but not furnished with track or equipment, when war came — and all work ceased. In London, many tube stations were used as deep night shelters for the public, but a stretch of the unfinished Central tube tunnels was put to different use as a munitions factory no less than five miles long! It was accomodated in the two and a half miles of twin tunnel lying between Leytonstone and Gants Hill, on the

way to the Loop Line mentioned earlier. It was equipped with machinery, and a light railway to carry the manufactured material, which included aircraft components, shell fuses and other munitions of war. In addition to the three unfinished station entrances to the factory, two other entry points were made, so that no worker had to walk more than 400 yards to his or her machine.

When war ceased, all five miles of the concrete false floor for the machines had to be moved down to the original track bed — a colossal job, pressed forward with other work to enable the line to open for public traffic in 1947.

H. F. Howson. Essex Countryside

The Central Line extension to Leytonstone was opened on Monday, May 5, 1947 and what a 'to-do' it was! That evening rush hour from Liverpool Street, intense as ever, found passengers for Leytonstone crowding down the escalators! By 5.30 p.m. Central Line's east-

bound platform was so choked that further passengers had to be dissuaded from descending. Within ten minutes, so efficient was London Transport, the flow was resumed. Out at Leytonstone the new Central Line trains ran into the main up and down platforms, while steam services to Loughton and Epping improvised as best they could on one solitary outer platform.

Of course, there was overcrowding, but operational problems existed, too. I wonder how many passengers were aware that one eight-coach suburban steam train emptied out at Leytonstone more passengers than two Central Line trains could take, put together?

Still, time passed, punctuality, etc., improved, and the Central Line settled down to its new-found task. Coal trains still ran to Epping at night, steam hauled as of yore.

The next advance came in December 1947 when Central Line services were extended to Woodford. Soon LPTB trains there were running every four minutes during peak hours. At the same time new tube stations

What a delightful snowy scene in 1900 outside Snaresbrook station — fit for a Christmas card indeed!

These views give a good idea of the engineering works involved in altering the Wanstead High Street bridge.

Car parking had always been a problem at Snaresbrook, the station yard being small and restricted at the top of the sloping ramp. This picture was taken in 1935. It was therefore the first station on the line to lose the facility of its goods' yard which was closed, the track lifted, and converted into a car park in September 1949.

LNER at Woodford, steam trains puffing at the platform, horse-droppings on the road . . . and houses on the Monkhams Estate at £1,150. Those were the days!

opened at Wanstead, Redbridge and Gants Hill, completing the Central Line link with the LNER at Newbury Park. Now the way was clear to withdraw steam services between Woodford, Fairlop and Ilford. This was done to facilitate extension to Hainault, and many will recall the fleet of special buses, marked 'Railway Service — Woodford — All Stations' which deputised for a while.

Meanwhile, at Ilford station a large crowd turned out, close to midnight, to see the last steam train off to Woodford. The locomotive's smokebox bore a large Union Jack, detonators exploded under her wheels, and her whistle was blown almost continuously. Then, in came the last train from Woodford, and the stationmaster declared the line closed by breaking a bottle of 'champagne' over the engine.

A fortnight later similar scenes took place when the last steam trains ran between Leytonstone and Woodford. More detonators exploded, and the Union Jack was joined by a laurel wreath. On it was the inscription — 'Leytonstone-Woodford, 1856-1947. LNER. GER'. A few hours later the first tube trains went into operation, almost unnoticed.

T. Middlemass. Essex Countryside

This particular engine LNER 7785 was built in 1904 and not withdrawn from service until 1955. The picture shows the scene on June 11, 1938.

The Victorian station buildings have served us well and are an everyday reminder of the age of steam. However at Chigwell Lane since 1945 the landscape had been transformed with the building of the Debden Estate by the London County Council. A change of name was deemed appropriate and the station was rebuilt more in keeping with its modern surroundings.

An extension of the Underground system over the British Railways (Eastern Region) line from Loughton to Chigwell Lane, Theydon Bois, and Epping will be open to the public on September 25. It is five miles long, and will mean that most sections of Epping Forest will be served by the tube.

This is the latest of eight extensions which have been made to the Central Line since 1946, and which have added a total of 34 miles to the Underground system. The line will have 250 trains daily, with a six-minute rush-hour service as far as Chigwell Lane, which is to be renamed 'Debden' after the L.C.C. estate near by. There will be 130 trains daily, with a 12-minute rush-hour service, over the remainder of the line to Epping. Travellers from Epping will reach the Bank by Central tube in 43 minutes and Oxford Circus in 52 minutes.

Underground drivers are now walking up and down the track to familiarize themselves with every inch of it before the first train runs.

Beyond Epping the service to Ongar will continue to be operated by steam trains.

The Times, September 15, 1949

Rectory Lane will never be the same again.

The posters of the period are a poignant reminder of days gone by. 'British Agent', starring Leslie Howard and Kay Francis began its run at the Majestic on Monday, August 19, 1935, while Stanley Baldwin had the leading rôle in the National Government formed on June 3. *Above and right:* The station was opened on August 22, 1856. *Below:* The goods' station located at Queen's Road, Buckhurst Hill, was constructed in 1859 and closed on January 6, 1964.

The new London Transport Underground extension from Loughton to Epping on the Central Line was opened to the public yesterday.

Permanent-way, signals and electrical workers spent the night putting the final touches to the new line, and the first tube train, driven from Loughton to Epping by Mr F. G. Maxwell, operating manager of the London Transport railway network, left punctually at 7.01 a.m.

The new extension has involved the electrification of the Eastern Region steam line from Loughton to Epping and has added three more stations and five more miles to the Central Line. The extension has put Epping Forest on the tube map and will serve a population of 15,000 people and 10,000 more when the new L.C.C. housing estate at Debden is completed.

The Times, September 26, 1949

Work on electrifying the six-mile section of the Central Line beyond Epping to North

From 1903 the Loughton line was served by a new loop, the Woodford and Ilford Branch. An intermediate station called Roding Valley and opened in 1937 was inserted between Woodford and Chigwell to serve the southern part of Buckhurst Hill. This section of track was electrified in 1948 and the section between Newbury Park and Ilford abandoned.

As Queen's Road never ran further than the old brickfields a few hundred yards to the east of the line, the loss of the level crossing was not a major problem bearing in mind the existence of the Palmerston Road-Roding Lane bridge. The goods' station building still stands alongside the sealed crossing, the yard now a car park.

Weald, Blake Hall, and Ongar will begin early in 1957, London Transport announced yesterday. It will take between 12 and 18 months to complete and will cost £100,000.

This section of the line is at present operated by a steam shuttle service. After electrification, the shuttle will be run with two-car trains of normal tube type, at the same frequency as the present service. London Transport say that the number of passengers at present using the line beyond Epping would not justify the running of full-length trains through from Central London. If the traffic grows as expected, the question of through trains will be reviewed.

The Times, November 1956

Ultimately, of course, the Central Line reached Ongar. Since then disputes over frequency of service, and inevitably, fares, have sharpened into debate as to who should bear the cost of maintaining the line. . . .

Nowadays, so many folk run cars it is easy to join the present clamour for cuts in public spending . . .

T. Middlemass, Essex Countryside

An underground link was driven from Leytonstone to Newbury Park with new stations at Wanstead, Redbridge and Gants Hill.

Concurrent with electrification, the fine old GER station at Leytonstone was demolished and rebuilt.

Snaresbrook and Whipps Cross

The long association of orphanages with the Snaresbrook-Wanstead area first commenced with the purchase of 28 acres (together with Eagle Pond) from Wellesley-Pole for £2,400.

The Infant Orphan charity was instituted in Hackney by Dr Andrew Reed in 1827 with the object to 'board, clothe, nurse and educate poor orphan children, or the children of confirmed lunatics'. Children were able to remain until reaching an age of 14 or 15 with 60 orphans being admitted by election each year. The foundation stone was laid at the beautiful setting on July 24, 1841 by Prince Albert, and two years later the building, costing £24,963, was completed and opened formally by Queen Victoria's uncle, Leopold, King of the Belgians. In 1874 the enclosure of former Forest land was deemed illegal but a settlement was reached by the exchange of Eagle Pond for rent free tenure while the property was used for charitable purposes. The society added 'Royal' to its title in 1918 and became the Royal Wanstead School in 1938. Mounting costs forced it to close in 1971 whereupon it became an educational trust being financed from the income obtained from the Home Office which leased the site for conversion to a Crown Court. Although it is a Grade II listed building, additions have not followed the traditional Elizabethan style of Sir Gilbert Scott's and George Moffat's original design.

some eight acres in extent, which has been secured for public enjoyment, in the shape of angling and boating in summer, and for skating in winter. As late as the beginning of the present century herds of deer roved freely about the forest glades in this locality, whilst the large pond was a favourite haunt for waders and other species of wild fowl. But

The Merchant Seamen's Orphan Asylum was originally established in 1817 at St George's-in-the-East at Wapping but by 1859 it had outgrown its facilities and a new seven-acre site was purchased from Lord Mornington of Wanstead Hall for £1,686 19s. 6d. Here, beside the road to Chigwell, G. C. Clarke's Venetian Gothic building was erected in 1861-62, the foundation stone being laid by the Prince Consort on June 28, 1861. Within forty years the original stone had deteriorated to such an extent that it was replaced by a new one (top right) unveiled by the Treasurer and Chairman, Edward S. Norris, on July 13, 1900.

This delightful village [Snaresbrook], on the confines of Epping Forest, is not far distant from the river Rodon (sic), about a mile and a half from Woodford, and seven from London. It contains several capital houses, the residences of gentlemen's families; these surround a fine expanse of water, embellished with clumps of trees and beautiful rural scenery. The neighbourhood, naturally pleasant and healthful, is highly improved by art, and has been selected as a suitable situation for numerous elegant seats and country villas. The road passes along the borders of the lake, and the Eagle Inn is a favourite resting-place for parties of pleasure, who, during the summer season, are constantly passing this way into Essex.

The History and Topography of the County of Essex, March 1831

Whip's Cross is at the extreme southern angle of the parish, and forms the entrance to the forest at the point where the roadway crosses through to the Eagle at Snaresbrook. It is supposed that Whip's Cross was so named from having been in former times the starting point from which persons who were found stealing wood or deer from the forest were whipped at the cart-tail through Wood Street to Stoker's Corner. No doubt this whipping process was of frequent occurrence in former times: that is, if the thieves did not escape with their booty scot free.

The forest at this point opens out in the form of a fan, crossed by two good roads, that to the right leading to Leytonstone and Wanstead 'Flats', and the other direct on to the Eagle at Snaresbrook, on the Woodford Road. If, before the preservation of the forest was taken in hand by the Corporation of London, the 'rights' of the commoners extended to gravel and sand-digging, they seem to have exercised those rights to the utmost extent in this part of the forest, causing the

destruction of a large number of fine trees, principally oaks, and the formation of numerous cavities, which become ponds in rainy seasons.

The three principal features of Snaresbrook are the Eagle Inn, the Infant Orphan Asylum, and the large lake, known as the Eagle Pond, that fronts both of them — a sheet of water

The chapel, inaugurated by the Prince and Princess of Wales, was added in 1882. In 1919 the building was sold for £23,000 becoming the Convent of the Good Shepherd and a home for girls in need of care or correction and readjustment of morals, some 200 girls being employed in the laundry and on needlework.

In 1937 the Essex County Council purchased the site, intending to demolish it to build a new hospital. However plans were shelved on the outbreak of war and the building converted to an Emergency Medical Hospital.

Just a mile to the south-west lay Forest House, the residence of Lord Goring, Earl of Norwich, who gave it the name Goring House during his tenure in the seventeenth century. In 1834 the Poor Law Amendment Act was passed and parishes formed 'Unions' to erect and administer workhouses and infirmaries for the chronic sick, the homeless and the destitute. The West Ham Union workhouse was located at Langthorne, Leyton, and Forest House was purchased in 1889 as an annexe for some 300 aged men. Within the grounds an infirmary *(below)* was built in 1900-03 with 672 beds in twenty-four wards housed in four blocks. The demand for workhouse places lessened with the introduction of the Old Age Pension and Insurance Acts and Forest House was offered to the War Office in 1915 for war wounded. This was not taken up until October 1917 when a War Hospital opened catering for 180 acute and 160 convalescent patients in the annexe and all of 'A' and part of 'B' Block in the infirmary.

with the gradual encroachment which has been made on the forest in the way of 'enclosures', Snaresbrook has become almost severed from it, whilst rows of 'genteel' cottages and smart villas have of late years sprung up, forming a strong contrast to the few old-fashioned houses of the wealthy citizen of which the hamlet at one time mainly consisted.

Greater London, Wilfred Walford, 1883

In 1917 the name of the infirmary was changed to Whipps Cross Hospital and administration passed to West Ham Borough Council in 1930. Forest House then became an old people's home, being closed in 1962. The 1960s was the decade of official vandalism and, having been replaced by the Samuel Boyce Lodge, Lord Goring's mansion dating from 1683 was unceremoniously pulled down.

BLOCK B

BLOCK A

SITE OF LAKE

SITE OF FOREST HOUSE

After a nurse was drowned in the lake in 1949, it was filled in and is now the site of a car park.

Yesterday morning as some Gentlemen were hunting near Epping-forest, they startled a hare, which took into a little wood near Snaresbrook; as soon as they had entered, on a sudden the hounds stopt: When the horse-men came up, they found the dogs stood under a tree, on which hung the body of a man well dressed; he was immediately cut down, but it is supposed that he had been dead two days; his watch and money were found in his pockets, and two letters, by which it was discovered that he was an inhabitant of Whitecross-street. One of the letters was from his landlord, demanding the payment of rent; and the other from another person demanding the payment of a sum of money.

Press report, 1774

Monday a battle was fought for fifty guineas, between one Ryan and Dunn, near the Green-man, on Epping Forest. After a contest of near three-quarters of an hour, it was ceded on the part of Dunn, in consequence of his having received a foul blow from his antagonist. It was left to the decision of the standers-by to determine betwixt them; who unanimously declared that the wager was not fairly won.

Another battle was fought on the same spot between a collier and a sailor of Gosport, for twenty guineas. The latter had received a challenge from the former, and came from Gosport on purpose to contend with him. After a conflict of half an hour, the challenger got a good drubbing.

Press report, 1786

FOOT RACE.— A sporting match took place on Monday morning, at Snaresbrook, Epping Forest, between Lieut. Hopkins and — Conyngham, a Yorkshire pedestrian, who was matched thirty guineas to twenty. The distance was four miles, over a mile of turf, and the winner was backed to do the four miles in twenty-two minutes. The pedestrian started with light drawers on only. It was as fine a race as ever was seen. Both were together at the last mile, and struggled hard; but Conyngham headed his adversary in the last hundred yards, and won cleverly.

Press report, 1822

CLARKE v TIME.— On Monday last, at the early hour of six o'clock a.m., a select few assembled near the Rising Sun, New-road, Woodford, a veteran pedestrian, well-known in the days of the 'Old Cope' as 'Charley Clarke the Barber,' having matched himself to walk seven miles within the hour, for £10. At a few minutes past seven he toed the scratch, attended by a friend, and shortly after started

Although technically in Walthamstow, Forest School, as its name implies located within the Forest, lies between Whipps Cross and Snaresbrook. Having recently celebrated its 150th anniversary, the school has seen dramatic change since the first 'modern' building was erected in the wake of a flying bomb hit on the Junior School in August 1944. Originally opened as a proprietary grammar school, it became a public school in 1947. The addition of a girls' school in 1981 recorded another milestone, in educational advancement, let alone 'molecular' architectural design!

in his usual fair and manly style, walking each mile in the undermentioned times:- First mile 7 min 32sec, second 16min 5sec, third 24min 25sec, fourth 33min 46sec, fifth 42min 25sec, sixth 51min 45sec, and the last in 59min 58sec; thus winning by two seconds only.

Press report, 1866

Last evening Dr Ambrose held an inquest at the Mortuary, Wanstead, on the body of a woman, unknown, who was found in the Eagle Pond, Snaresbrook, shortly after noon on Tuesday. The evidence showed that Mr A. Granshaw, head barman at the Bakers' Arms, Lea Bridge-road, was walking past the Eagle Pond, accompanied by a spaniel dog

Gowan Lea on the other hand had failed to survive the pressures on private schools. Opened in 1902 by the Misses Gowlett and Freeman, from whose surnames the name was coined, it merged with the nearby Wanstead College (on the site of the present Hermitage Court flats) when that school closed in 1933. In 1970 Gowan Lea itself shut its doors for the last time and, like most of the spacious properties on Wood-ford Road, succumbed to the developer and his faceless flats.

belonging to Mr. Robinson, the manager of the hotel. While he was throwing stones into the pond for the dog, his attention was called by a friend named Knight to a parcel lying near the farther bank. He observed that perhaps it was the body of some child that had been thrown in, and with a view to drawing the dog's attention to it, they threw stones as near to it as they could. The spaniel soon sighted the bundle and at once seized it and swam with it a considerable distance. The burden was so heavy that the plucky little animal twice sank from exhaustion before it finally reached the bank. It was then discovered that the bundle was the body of a woman. Mr. Granshaw at once communicated with the police at the Wanstead police station, and the doctor who was called said the body had probably been in the water some 10 hours. The police stated that the body had not been identified. It was that of a woman of about 55, respectably dressed. Only a few trifling articles and a halfpenny were found upon her. Dr Ambrose expressed admiration at the courageous conduct of the spaniel, which is only a small animal and a great pet of Mr. Robinson's.

Walthamstow, Leyton and Chingford Guardian. February 1, 1901

17/18 August, 1915 (Night)

Target: London.
Enemy forces: Navy Zeppelins L10 (Oblt-z-S F. Wenke); L11 (Oblt-z-S H. von Buttlar); L13 (Kptlt H. Mathy), returned early; L14 (Kptlt A. Bocker), returned early.
Results: 10 killed, 48 injured, £30,750 damage.
Defence sorties: Six.

The German Naval Airship Service persevered in its attempt to achieve a major raid on London, and this time one Zeppelin did reach the north-eastern outskirts. Mathy's L13 was again turned back by engine trouble, and the new L14 spent three hours circling off

the Norfolk coast before her crew gave up hope of rectifying two ailing engines.

L11 came in over Herne Bay at 21.30 hr, flew south to bomb Ashford and nearby villages then departed, again over Herne Bay, at 23.45 hr. Von Buttlar filed a glowing account of his attack on 'Woolwich'.

Wenke, in L10, one of the ablest airship navigators, crossed the coast north of Bawdsey at 20.55 hr, flew a direct course to London and bombed the Walthamstow-Leyton-Wanstead area at 22.30-22.45 hr, causing heavy damage and some casualties. A puzzling discrepancy in an otherwise good operational performance was his claim to have attacked central London, six miles to the south.

The Air Defence of Britain 1914-1918. Christopher Cole and E. F. Cheesman, 1984

Horse power 1900-1985. The fountain has survived the ravages of time throughout both war and peace. Originally it was protected by a ring of stone bollards, now the traffic is kept away by an alteration in the line of the pavement.

The year — 1920, the place — Whipps Cross, Walthamstow, the extreme southern edge. Compared with the present, the area was quieter, with less movement in the sweet-smelling air. The clip-clop of horses' hoofs could be heard in the near distance and the occasional snort or whinny as they pull the heavy wagons up the incline from the direction of Bakers Arms.

The driver is not sitting bolt upright with the reins in his hands — he is asleep. This is the one advantage that mode of transport had over the motor vehicle of today; the faithful

horse would head home unerringly. A Silver Cloud Rolls Royce cannot emulate that.

I am nearly eight years old and have just finished my roller-coaster run up and down the scores of small hills surrounding the Hollow Pond. The boatman has an inverted boat which he is making pond worthy on trestles. A low singing noise can be faintly heard. An LCC tram swooshes past at 45 to 55 mph. The almost straight run of one and a quarter miles from the Green Man on a special tarmac track was a delight to those tram drivers; if a passenger had the temerity to ring the bell en route, the driver was almost annoyed and considered himself done out of something.

At Whipps Cross a brass band would entertain us every Sunday morning. As a boy, these musicians struck me as an evil crowd because they sat on beer crates. Later some sage companion of mine explained that all wind-blown instruments required moist lips which mitigated their behaviour in my eyes. The playing was heavenly, proving that the large beer intake did no harm.

The Hollow Pond really came into its own when hard frozen in a cold winter. The faces of everyone, old and young, became ruddy and the universal tyrant, poverty, was momentarily forgotten. The only chap looking glum was the boatman but, happiness being infectious, he soon forgot his financial demise and joined in the fun.

I remember the smell of roast chestnuts, and the toffee apple vendors, and skates for hire. There was never a dull moment and we were quite sorry to have the thaw when it eventually came.

Five hundred yards from the Hollow was a smaller natural pond going east which we called the 'Batho'. In the warmer months we used to swim there and being free, it was well patronised particularly in the early mornings. I recall a chap minus both legs who swam like

The Hollow Ponds — another legacy of the demand for gravel for road building, have changed little in eighty years — only the boats have shrunk in size!

a fish, dived like an Olympic competitor and generally showed us all how it should be done. I certainly couldn't match him even with my full compliment of limbs.

Come Saturday and Sunday there was always something going on at Whipps. There were itinerant entertainers galore; one chap used to imitate Houdini, swathing himself in chains, then making a pretext of an impossible extrication. Another would manage to attract about a dozen people around him, then make a meal of razor blades, lamp glass and other hardware. He would then demonstrate that the 'meal' really had been eaten by widening his mouth for all to see. What a way to earn a living!

*H. W. Tunstall writing
in the Essex Countryside*

The Hollow Ponds Bathing Pool, which has been for many years, in spite of its mud, the Mecca for many local swimming enthusiasts, has been completely transformed during the past few months, thanks to the concerted action of the Leyton and Walthamstow Borough Councils; and the Lord Mayor of London, Sir Maurice Jenks, will perform the opening ceremony on Saturday, May 7th.

The scheme, which has been carried out at a cost of £6,000, was done between the Leyton and Walthamstow Councils. There are four large dressing rooms, two for ladies and two for gentlemen, decorated in a pleasing buff colour that will absorb the sunlight and obviate the uncomfortable glare so often associated with the exteriors of light colour.

The pavement which surrounds the pool has been designed with a similar regard for the practical. The colours are buff and red. The pool itself is irregularly oval in shape, the sides being made of concrete. At the entrance end the water is seven feet deep, and a large circular basin is provided for diving, which can be carried out from a height of twenty feet. There is a straight stretch of one hundred yards where races can be held. At the shallow end the water is only two feet six inches deep, and a paddling pool, one foot deep, is available for the children.

The capacity of the pool will be a thousand bathers a day, but it is only anticipated that

Shovelpower. In an effort to alleviate the local unemployment problem, in 1905 a swimming pool was dug on Forest land beside the Hollow Ponds. It was merely a natural lake filled by underground springs and it soon became muddy and unhygienic. In 1923 the Leyton and Walthamstow councils agreed to further works being carried out by the unemployed and over the next eight years the pool was lined with concrete, the surround paved and changing facilities provided. It opened in a blaze of publicity in 1932 only to suffer the same problems and be closed a year later.

IMPEREX.
For keeping water **in** or **out** under **any** conditions.

GREAT BRITAINS LARGEST
SWIMMING POOL.
Capacity:- 1,300,000 gallons

A. P. HOWELL, M.I.C.E.
BORO ENGINEER AND SURVEYOR,
LEYTON CORPORATION

The reinforced concrete floor and retaining walls are waterproofed throughout with **IMPEREX**, rapid hardening and waterproofing liquid.

six or seven hundred will attend each day in good weather.

Thousands of tons of gravel have been excavated for the bed of the pool, and a great deal of mud has been removed from the bottom in the process of levelling and cleansing. A miniature railway was constructed to convey the gravel to the required places in the bed, and to reinforce the banking and the surrounds. The whole of the work has been carried out by some sixty men.

The pool is filled by natural springs of drinkable water, which flow into the pool from the surrounding gravel to the extent of about 24,000 gallons a day. Consequently the water is perpetually fresh, the old water draining out into the Hollow Ponds nearby. The pool will be drained and cleaned each year.

The Woodford Times, Friday, April 29, 1932

Literally thousands of people found their way to the swimming pool at Whipps Cross — the new 'Lido' constructed at a cost of £7,000 by the Leyton and Walthamstow Borough Councils jointly — the opening of which was the Lord Mayor's last official function.

The water gleamed fitfully in the sunshine, and the two sounds most heard were the band and the droning of an aeroplane. But there was much to attract the eye while awaiting the arrival of the Lord Mayor. The surroundings of the pool are buff coloured, and the dressing rooms, with their pillars, looked quite impressive standing out as they do against the background of the banks and the shrubs.

The Lord Mayor, accompanied by the Lady Mayoress, was received by the Mayor of Leyton and guided to the specially erected dais, where a microphone for relaying the speeches had been installed.

The Chairman then announced a surprise item. The first two swimmers, he said, would be the Mayor of Leyton and the Deputy Mayor, Councillor Thorn.

After changing into bathing costumes, Alderman Shimmin and Councillor Thorn plunged in and swam for a short while.

On Sunday the Lido was visited by hundreds of spectators, and the few hardy bathers had a large and interested audience. Unfortunately, the previous day's spick-and-span appearance had completely disappeared, for young hooligans, who had presumably evaded the police at the opening ceremony and afterwards, had caused great damage to the banks surrounding the pool. Shrubs and bushes had the appearance of being wilfully trampled down, and soil from the banks covered the paving surrounding the water, completely altering its cheerful aspect.

The Woodford Times, May 13, 1932

Major work was then undertaken to convert it into a modern chlorinated swimming pool and the Whipps Cross Lido opened in 1937. However the viability of open air swimming depends so much in this country on the vagaries of the British summer. There will be many who will say that the weather is not what it used to be but then perhaps people are not as hardy as they were! Possibly the demands of other leisure activities have equally affected the passion for outdoor swimming. Be that as it may, with the growth of the trees around the pool, by afternoon the sunbathing areas increasingly fell into shadow. Parental concern over access to the Lido through the Forest must also have played its part in reducing attendances to under 20,000 per annum by 1981. The Lido never reopened after September 4, 1982 and the pool had been filled in and the land reinstated by December 1983.

Leyton's Lido, the open air bathing pool which was constructed early last year at Whipps Cross, is once again closed, and the 'Express' is informed that it will not be re-opened this season.

This decision will come as a great surprise to many people, for the Lido as it was familiarly known, was re-opened only on July 29th after being closed for some time for the purpose of emptying and cleaning.

During the Bank Holiday, however, and subsequently as a result of the heat wave, so many bathers attended that recently it was decided to take a sample of the water. This was examined and as a result of the examination the authorities declared that it was unfit for bathing purposes, and the pool was closed immediately.

Stratford Express, September 2, 1933

SITE OF THE LIDO BATHING POND

A double tragedy occurred on Monday morning while the sudden thunderstorm was at its height.

A large oak tree in the forest, just off Snaresbrook Road, near Forest School, was struck by lightning, and, by a freak of the storm, two men who were sheltering under another tree over fifty yards away were hit by the deflected flash. One, a youth of 17, who was on holiday from Scotland, was killed, and the other, an elderly man from Walthamstow, was severely injured. Yet a third man, Mr. Ewing Hunter, of Wanstead, was found dead in the forest on the other side of the road, about 400 to 500 yards away. . . .

Two forest keepers, Mr. F. Primett and Mr. J. Sawyer, had amazing escapes, for they were standing under a tree very close to the one which was struck, and only about fifty yards away from the men who were also struck.

The Woodford Times, June 23, 1933

Pilot Officer Atkinson, 71 Squadron, was killed whilst performing aerobatics over Woodford.

Operations Record Book, RAF North Weald

Curly-red haired Roger Atkinson killed October 15, 1941 only four days after joining 71 Squadron.

The Eagle Squadrons, Vern Haughland, 1979

War comes to Snaresbrook with a vengeance. It was the evening of Wednesday, October 16, 1940 that a high-explosive bomb fell in Snaresbrook Road blasting trees and severely damaging The Hermitage, former home of Lady Morrison whose custom it was to hold large charity fêtes in the grounds. Two people were killed in the explosion. After standing derelict, the mansion was demolished after the war and replaced with ubiquitous flats.

Spitfire Vb AD123, Pilot Officer Roger Hall Atkinson. Aerobatic practice No. 11 Group Fighter Command, over Woodford. Broke up in mid-air above cloud when climbing steeply. Pilot's boot caught under rudder pedal. Pilot baled out but ripcord not pulled. Main body of crash edge of Epping Forest, quarter of a mile to ENE of Rising Sun

On the afternoon of Saturday, August 31, 1940, Pilot Officer G. K. Gilroy took off from Hornchurch to intercept enemy raiders over the Thames. His Spitfire X4271 was hit about 6.20 p.m. and he baled out over Ilford. When he landed he was mistaken for a German and set upon by local people before being admitted to King George Hospital. His burning aircraft tumbled to earth crashing into No. 14 Hereford Road, the engine falling in the front garden of No. 12. The only casualty was a dog.

Hotel on Woodford New Road. Fell through trees at eighty degrees spinning to right. Engine fell out of fuselage and fell 50ft away upside down. Entire port main plane was attached to fuselage, both front and rear spar broken just inboard of outboard Browning gun. The starboard main plane entire leading edge missing. Spar broken five foot from root of main plane and fuselage. Missing parts of aircraft scattered over an area of one mile in diameter with the centre 1½ miles west of main crash.

Aircraft accident card.
Air Historical Branch, RAF

Officer Commanding remarks that order grounding pilot received after pilot had taken

off. Aileron instability and consequent structural failure of starboard wing. Adjutant knew pilot unfit for flying but Flight Commander not told. Did not appreciate his duties and responsibilities . . . as not taking immediate and definite effect to ensure pilot did not fly.

Air Ministry Court of Inquiry

ATKINSON, Pilot Officer (Pilot) Roger Hall, 102048, RAF (VR). 71 Squadron, 15 October, 1941. Age 20. Son of Lt-Col. Albert King Atkinson and Florence Hall Atkinson, of Chicago, Illinois, USA. Plot 21, Row A, Grave 10.

Commonwealth War Graves Commission
Brookwood Military Cemetery, Woking

The first flying bomb salvo of the war comprising ten bombs (five of which crashed almost immediately) was launched against the United Kingdom from France by Flakregiment 155(W) commanded by Oberst Max Wachtel on June 13, 1944. Just over a month later on July 19 one landed on the corner of Eagle Lane at Snaresbrook causing two fatalities and injuring eight others.

The history of Wanstead is indelibly entwined with its manor house which lay some 300 yards south-east of the parish church. In 1271 its value was only 1s. a year, and up until the fourteenth century it was probably of modest dimensions, but by 1499 it was of sufficient size to warrant use as a royal hunting lodge for the surrounding Forest. Both Henry VII and Henry VIII visited Wanstead Hall, as it was then called, but in 1549 the records speak of the house as being 'in great ruin'. It was rebuilt by Lord Rich who owned it from 1549 to 1567 and greatly enlarged by the Earl of Leicester.

Wanstead

We have great noise here of a new spa or spring of this nature found lately about Wanstead, in Essex, and much running there is to it daily by both lords and ladies and other great company, so that they have almost drawn it dry already; and if it should hold on, it would put down the waters of Tunbridge, for which for these three or four years have been much frequented, insomuch that they who have seen both say it is not inferior to the spa for good company, numbers of people, and other appurtenances.

Sir John Chamberlain, August 1619

The parish of Wansted is computed to be twenty miles in circumference, separated from Barking by the river Rodun. The village is on the borders of Waltham Forest, on a hill commanding a view of the city of London, and its environs; the hills of Kent, the river Thames, and a wide extent of a highly cultivated and beautiful country. . . .

The grant of this manor by Alfric to the church of Westminster, was confirmed by Edward the confessor; but before the end of that monarch's reign it became, probably by exchange, the property of the church of St. Paul, and was afterwards appropriated to the bishop of London; under whom, at the time of the Domesday survey, it was holden by Ralph Fitz-Brien. It afterwards passed through various possessors to Sir John Heron, whose son, Sir Giles Heron, being attainted, his estates were seized by the crown, and this manor was granted, by Edward VI to Robert Lord Rich, who made it his country residence, and is supposed to have rebuilt the manor-house, then called Naked Hall Hawe. His son sold it to Robert, Earl of Leicester, who enlarged and greatly improved the mansion, and in May, 1578, entertained Queen Elizabeth in it for several days: here also, the same year, in September, he solemnised his marriage with the Countess of Essex. On the Earl's decease, in 1588, Wansted, with other lands in the adjoining parishes, became the property of the Countess, his widow, who afterwards married Sir Christopher Blount, and, by some family conveyances, this manor became vested in Charles Blount, Earl of Devonshire, on whose death, without lawful issue, in the year 1606, it appears to have escheated to the Crown. The following autumn, James I spent some time here, after his return from a western progress. It was afterwards the property of George, Marquis of Buckingham; of whom, in 1619, it was purchased by Sir Henry Mildmay, and his wife Anne. Their descendant, Sir William Mildmay, and others, conveyed it to Sir Josiah Child, whose son Sir Richard, afterwards created Earl Tilney, erected Wansted House in the year 1715, near the site of the ancient mansion.

The History and Topography of the County of Essex, March 1831

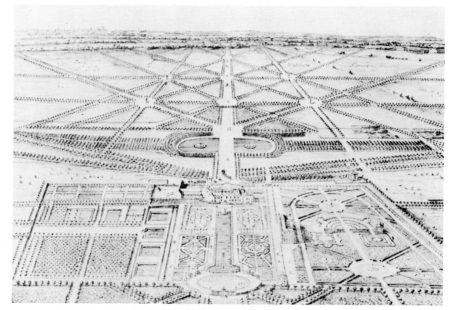

Sir Josiah was not particularly interested in the house and made no important alterations to it. However he lavished vast sums on the park, laying out the magnificent grounds which must certainly have rivalled Hampton Court. According to Daniel Defoe 'innumerable rows of trees . . . avenues and vistas, to the house, all leading up to the place where the old house stood, as to a centre'. John Evelyn (see page 14) commented in his diary in 1683 especially on the new fishponds and walnut plantations. This is the view in 1715 looking west towards London. St Paul's can be seen on the skyline.

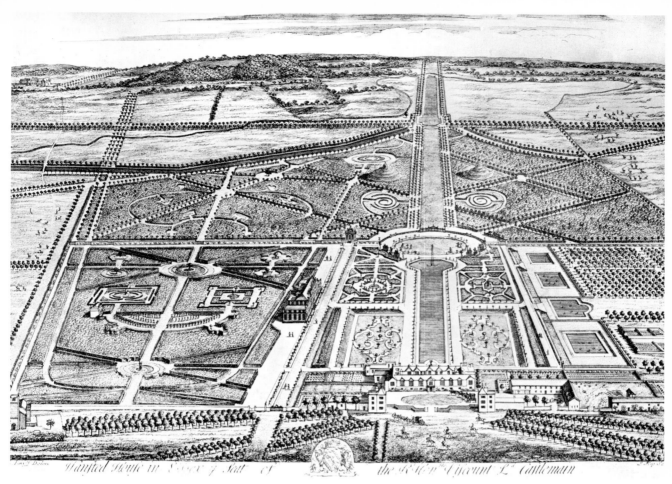

Wanstead House in Essex, Seat of the Right Honble Viscount Lord Castlemain

This aspect depicts the view to the east towards the River Roding, canalised as part of the architecture of the park. Wanstead Church can be seen in the lower left with the orangery more or less in the centre. The circular area beyond the fountain is the bowling green.

Our aerial shot, taken at the same low oblique angle, shows a little more of the area in order to put the house and grounds in perspective with the surrounding built-up areas. Wanstead Church is the reference point. The Basin in the foreground had been enlarged from a smaller lake by 1735.

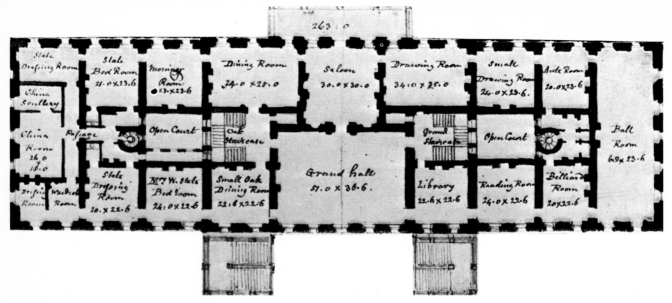

The coming of Sir Josiah, for he was made a baronet in 1668, marked the dawn of a renaissance at Wanstead. By 1683 the old-fashioned house, which Pepys complained 'being not full of people looks flatly,' was the centre of a large and flourishing estate, its owner going to 'prodigious cost in planting walnut trees . . . and making fish ponds many miles in circuit.. . .''

Of these gardens, these must have been made between the creation of the Castlemaine Viscountcy in 1715, and the destruction of the old house in the same year; the gardens depicted may therefore be regarded as the work of Sir Josiah Child.

The main axis, running approximately east and west, is already clearly defined, showing the parterre and canal with the *jet d'eau*, the circular bowling-green and palizado, later to be swept away in favour of plain lawn. West of the house, to either side of the Leightonstone drive, the park is planted with avenues in *quincunx* formations, with statues at the *rond-points*.

The gardens proper lay to the east of the house. The parterre was probably the work of George London, certainly much in his style.

Sir Josiah's half-brother, Richard, succeeded to the title in 1704 and he commissioned Colen Campbell, one of the foremost architects of the day, dedicated to the Palladian style and the author of 'Britannicus Vetruvius'. The magnificent building he designed was 260 feet wide and 75 feet deep clad in white Portland stone. The west front had a grand Corinthian portico as its central feature with perron staircases descending on each side to the forecourt.

To the south were situated the kitchen gardens, and opposite them the greenhouse, banqueting house, and another *quincunx*, centring upon an urn. Beyond the formal lay-out winds the River Roding, already regimented into canals, but greatly to be elaborated by the first Earl.

It is significant that the new gardens should have preceded the new house, for in the days of Child, 'when Nature was universally subdued by Art' the lay-out of house and grounds looked outward. . . .

. . . It was not, however, until his [Sir Josiah Child's] second son, Richard, had succeeded to title and property that the House was really to come into its own. For some reason Richard had been a Tory, but in 1715, the year of the Jacobite rebellion, he prudently joined the Whigs. This convenient change in his political convictions occasioned his elevation to the peerage, first as Viscount Castlemaine, and later as Earl Tylney — a title taken from the large Hampshire estates inherited from his mother-in-law of that name.

In the same year old Wanstead House was taken down, and Colen Campbell invited to submit designs for a mansion proportionate to the newly enhanced honour of the family. The house then built was one of the finest achievements of English Palladian architecture, and, since it was destroyed in its prime, and knew not the spoiling hand of generations, provided, in its fabric, as in its surroundings, a perfect example of a Whig lord's residence.

It was composed of a central block, raised by one storey above its lateral wings, which contained the great saloon to the east, and to the west the hall, gained by twin stairways

The old Hall was demolished and the new House erected between 1715 and 1722 — one of the greatest mansions of the time.

beneath the pillars of a Corinthian colonnade. The garden front was enriched, in 1747, by the great Ionic columns of the Duke of Chandos's ill-fated palace of Cannons. From each side of the central block ran two suites of apartments, linked at either extremity by the chapel and ballroom. 'Nothing,' writes Gilpin, 'can exceed their convenience. They communicate into one grand suite, yet each, by the addition of a backstair, becomes a separate apartment.' It is difficult to say whether we are better pleased with the grandeur and elegance without, or with the simplicity and contrivance within'.

Campbell also intended quadrant colonnades with terminal office wings to embrace a noble forecourt upon the entrance front, but, although it is evident that they were seriously intended (for they were included in anticipation by many artists who depicted the house), it appears that they were never built.

In 1722 the house, without the wings, was standing, with the gardens much as Sir Josiah Child had left them. By 1735, however, these too had been brought up to date, and the place had for some time been attracting visitors.

Recent years have seen the opening of many private houses and gardens to the public; but it is often forgotten that this merely represents a return to one of the original purposes of a mansion — to act as a show place. The whole structure and layout of a palace such as Wanstead was a typical feature of the Grand Style in which the Whigs imitated their Roman prototypes, whether in their imperialism, their oratory, or their domestic architecture. Publicity was one of the means by which they maintained their position; privacy was an innovation of their more exclusive descendants.

The gardens of Wanstead, thanks to their proximity to London, rapidly became a show place, and as early as 1724 Defoe recorded that 'it has become the general diversion of the citizens to go out and see them.' Forty years later Royalty were to follow the popular example, and Walpole mentions Wanstead and Oatlands as among the first houses visited by the new King and Queen.

In the meantime, however, changes were taking place in the grounds, which attracted the attention of Le Rouge, who included plates of them in his *Jardins Anglo-Chinois*. The title is significant, for the rigid formality of the Dutch and Italian garden had given place to the artificial asymmetry (or *sharawaggi*), supposedly borrowed from the Chinese.

The chief difference was the removal of the formal east parterre, and the substitution of the vast lawn and terrace. Bowling-green, banqueting house and palizado were swept away, and the avenue follows the gentle descent down to the River Roding. To either side the radiating alleys and spiral mazes were replaced by serpentine walks that open unexpectedly into glades and amphitheatres;

The ballroom at the southern end was hung with tapestries said to have been saved from the old house and to have dated from the Earl of Leicester's time. There were paintings by Holbein, Raphael, Rembrandt and van Dyck and the room itself was the setting for William Hogarth's 1729 painting 'Assembly at Wanstead House', now in the Philadelphia Museum of Art.

only the two mounts, features of the first lay-out, remained.

Beyond the confines of the garden, just over a hundred acres in all, considerable elaborations were made in the waterworks. To the south, large new ornamental waters appeared, one of them containing an island, apparently representing England, Scotland and Wales, while to the north-east a labyrinth of canals were cut from the river, with here a sham fortification, and there a Roman ruin, and a little later a 'curious grotto . . . en-crusted with pebbles, shells and stalactites, crystals and looking glasses,' said to have cost £2,000 independent of the costly materials.

This was the addition of the second Earl, whom Walpole described as the most generous creature in the world, for it was his lavish custom to make gifts of furniture to his guests. Walpole, whose views upon gardening, as on most matters of taste, were somewhat in advance of his time, found the grounds at Wanstead wretched and managed to avoid accepting any furniture, 'compounding', as he puts it, 'to bring away only a haunch of venison'. His opinion on formalism largely foreshadows that prevalent to-day: the new Wanstead gardens, though substituting tortuous asymmetry for the 'tiresome and returning uniformity' of the previous scheme, still made no terms with the surrounding country, and the great house stood, chaste and elegant indeed, but bearing no trace in its design of that local quality that makes a building at once harmonise with its surroundings. Far from being a part of the landscape, it rose naked and shameless from its artificial setting.

Upon the death of the second Earl, the property passed to his nephew, Sir James Tylney Long of Draycott. He enjoyed his inheritance for ten years, during which time he rebuilt the church and made some sim-plifications in the grounds. The exact extent of his alterations is a matter for conjecture. The only evidence is to be obtained from the present conditions of the park. It can probably be safely assumed that no money was spent on the place after Sir James's decease.

At his death, in 1794, Wanstead had reached the height of its perfection. The rigid outlines of the former lay-outs were softened, in some places by deliberate plantation, everywhere by the natural growth of the trees; for by then, in place of the serried ranks of lime and walnut, the united plumage of an ancient wood extended wide its undulating canopy. Nature, in fact, had already begun to reassume the land, and had laid her mantle over the house, clothing its nakedness and assimilating it into the countryside, a countryside already recognisable as the England we know to-day.

And thus it was to remain; for upon Sir James's death the property passed to his young daughter, Catherine, a ward in Chancery. During her minority the house was let to the Prince de Condé, father of the luckless Duc d'Enghien, and other French refugees. During this time, the future Louis XVIII, housed by Lord Buckingham at Gosfield, was a frequent visitor.

In 1812, however, Catherine, who was one of the richest and most courted heiresses in the country, not unnaturally married, the object of her connubial aspirations being a certain William Pole Wellesley, grandson to the Earl of Mornington, and nephew of the future Duke of Wellington. Their marriage was solemnised on March 14 at St. James's, Piccadilly. The bride was dressed in white satin and Brussels lace valued at 700 guineas, and a fortune in jewellery. She also brought her husband an estate of some eighty thousand a year. Wellesley brought nothing but his already formidable debts — and he forgot the ring.

Bitterly was she to regret this match, for her bridegroom, who was as reckless as he was unprincipled, neglected and ill-treated her, and adopted a devil-may-care attitude towards her property, as the result of which she was to see, within ten years of her wed-ding, her entire estate squandered, and her beautiful house levelled to the ground, its proud columns prostrate in the dust. After the fall of Wanstead, her husband found it necessary to quit the country in order to avoid his still numerous creditors, leaving his poor wife to die, at the age of thirty-five, of a broken heart. Her body was taken to Draycott, the funeral *cortège* being joined at Chippenham by the Duke of Wellington, who rode to pay his last respects to the wife of his disreputable nephew.

The Gardens of Wanstead House.
Country Life. July 1950

It is constructed according to the best rules in the Corinthian order, and the front entirely of Portland stone. The portico in the centre is supported by pillars of the Corinthian order, and under it is the landing place that leads to the great hall, where there are a vast variety of ornaments and paintings by the best masters in Italy. The dining-room is on the left of the hall, being twenty-four feet square, and adjoining to it is the drawing-room, of the same size. On the right of the hall is another dining-room, twenty-five feet square, and a drawing-room thirty by twenty-five. On the chimney-piece of the drawing-room is the representation of an eagle taking up a snake, elegantly cut in white marble; and from this room is an entrance to the bed-chamber, from which is a passage into the ball-room, which is seventy-five by twenty-seven feet, and con-nects the whole front line of apartments.

Complete English Traveller. 1771

Towards the end of his life, after rebuilding the House, Sir Richard Child, Viscount Castlemaine since 1718 and the first Earl Tylney from 1733 (he changed his name to Tylney in 1834), appears to have turned his attentions to the park. This short canal and parterre were replaced by a terrace and a lawn and the orangery demolished. The orangery or conservatory was a splendid building in its own right having fifteen bays and six statues on top of the parapet.

ESSEX ASSIZES

THE KING
v.
WELLESLEY POLE
TILNEY LONG WELLESLEY

This was an indictment which has excited considerable interest in the county, as it was to try the right of the public to a right of way through Wanstead Park, from which the defendant, who has lately married the heiress to the Long Estates, has attempted to exclude them. Mr. Sergeant Best ably opened the case, and named the Noble Persons who had been possessors of Wanstead Park, none of whom he said had ever disputed the right of the public to pass through it. — He then called a number of most respectable witnesses, thirty-two of whom were in attendance, and they incontestibly proving that the road had been used as long as they remembered, for almost every purpose, the Judge interposed, and said enough had been proved to shew it was a public road. After Mr. Serjeant Shepherd had addressed the jury for the defendant, and called some witnesses, who could not shake the testimony of those for the plaintiff, the jury returned a verdict for plaintiff; the park will therefore be re-opened to the public at large. Mr. W. P. Long also failed in an action to oust his tenant G. Wright, Esq. from his extensive farm of Rochford Hall, in this county; a Special Jury, after a long trial, returned a verdict in favour of Mr. Wright.

Press report, March 21, 1813

The trial between the inhabitants of Wan-stead and W. P. Long, Esq, came on at Chelmsford on Friday, upwards of sixty witnesses were in attendance to prove a road through Wanstead Park, which was fully established, and a verdict given accordingly. The park, which has been closed up since the marriage of Miss Long with Mr. Pole, will now be opened to the public at large.

Press report, 1813

On Wednesday, Mr. Long Wellesley gave a grand fete to his uncle, the Duke of Wellington, at Wanstead House. The Prince Regent, the Duke of York, the Prussian Princes Frederick William and Henry, left town about six o'clock, to be present at the dinner. In the evening there was a grand ball, which was attended by upwards of one thousand distinguished fashionables.

Press report, July 3, 1814

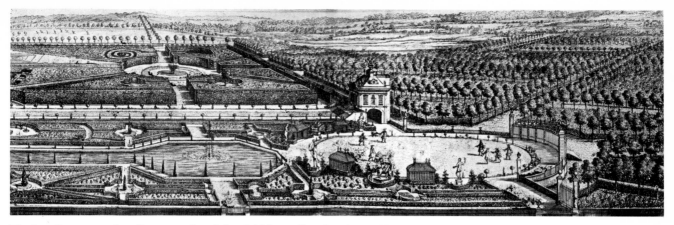

The bowling green also disappeared and the rigid formality of the Italian garden softened, its edges becoming mellowed with the maturing of the surrounding trees. The plan below dates from 1735, the year after he adopted his wife's name when she inherited the large estates of her family, and makes an interesting comparison with a modern aerial shot.

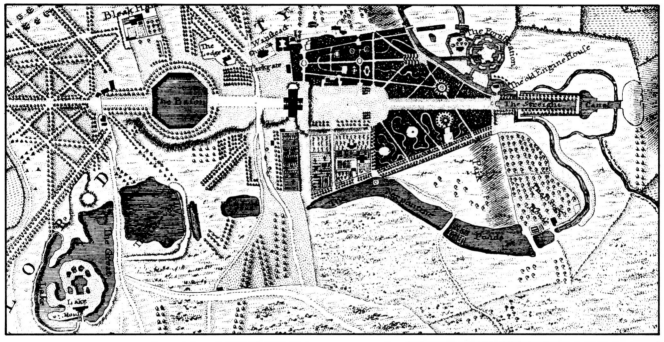

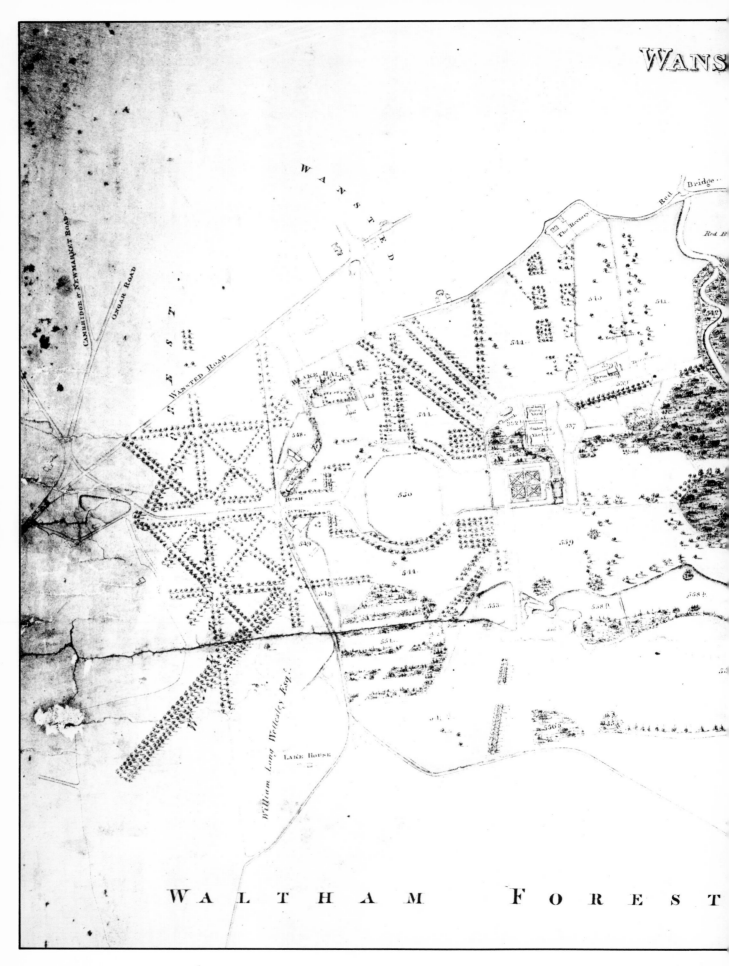

ESSEX
WANSTEAD HOUSE

VALUABLE COLLECTION of FINE PAINTINGS, BRONZES, SCULPTURES in MARBLE, & CASTS from the ANTIQUE, splendid GOBELIN TAPESTRY, DAMASK and VELVET HANGINGS, &c.

MR. ROBINS, of Warwick-House, Regent-street, London, informs the Nobility, Gentry, and Connoisseurs in Fine Arts, that, by Order of the Trustees, he shall offer

FOR SALE BY AUCTION,
At the Mansion, Wanstead House,

On WEDNESDAY, the 19th of June, and two following days, at Eleven o'Clock,
The extensive Collection of valuable Pictures, Bronzes, Sculptures in Marble, Casts from the Antique, Superb Gobelin Tapestry, of matchless beauty.

Press announcement, 1822

WANSTEAD HOUSE
SPLENDID LIBRARY of VALUABLE and CHOICE BOOKS, BEAUTIFUL ENGRAVINGs, &c.

MR. ROBINS, of Warwick House, Regent-street, London, informs the Nobility, Gentry, and the Public, that, by Order of the Trustees, he shall offer

FOR SALE BY AUCTION,
On the Premises, Wanstead House,

On MONDAY, the 8th July, 1822, and Four following Days, at Eleven o'Clock,
The Valuable Collection of ANCIENT and MODERN BOOKS, elegantly bound, embracing many early Specimens of Typography, continued by every Work of celebrity to the present day; also abounding in the Graphic Art, with the most choice impressions from the Foreign and English Schools. . . .

Press announcement, 1822

GIPSIES.— An extraordinary occurrence took place on Monday last in Epping forest. A Gentleman of the Bank of England went with his wife and children to Wanstead House, and after the close of the day's sale, retired into the forest, about a mile and a half, to dine on the grass. After dinner, one of the children, a boy about five years of age, strayed away from the party, and his parents soon began to be apprehensive at his absence, which continued for three or four hours, notwithstanding the activity of some persons employed to search for him. The terrors of the parents became exceedingly great, but they were considerably relieved by the appearance of a gipsy man, who told them that their little boy was safe, but that he could not be restored to them except the sum of a sovereign was given to those who had him under their protection. The conditions were most gladly accepted, and, after a short delay, the gipsy returned with a troop of his people, amounting to between 30 and 40, bearing the child in the midst of them. The poor infant was in a state of complete stupefaction at the time, the gipsies having given to him some drink to reconcile him, it is supposed, to the change in his situation. The price of his liberation was paid without a murmur, and he was put into the arms of his mother, whose agitation had nearly bereft her of her senses.

Press report, July 1822

The magnificent State Bedstead which must have experienced many a royal romp went for the ridiculous price of £21. Most of the items must still exist somewhere today, possibly still in private hands, so we contacted every major museum in Britain to try to ascertain if they had any Wanstead House artifacts in their collections.

WANSTEAD HOUSE, ESSEX.

Magnificent Furniture,
COLLECTION OF FINE PAINTINGS AND SCULPTURE,
MASSIVE SILVER & GILT PLATE,
SPLENDID LIBRARY OF CHOICE BOOKS.
THE VALUABLE
CELLARS OF FINE-FLAVOURED OLD WINES, ALES, &c. &c.

A CATALOGUE
OF THE MAGNIFICENT AND COSTLY
FURNITURE
OF THE PRINCELY MANSION,
WANSTEAD HOUSE,
CONSISTING OF GRAND

COSTLY STATE BEDSTEADS, WITH RICH VELVET, SILK, DAMASK, AND OTHER FURNITURES; WINDOW CURTAINS AND HANGINGS; EXCELLENT BEDDING;
Splendid Suites of Drawing and Ball Room Curtains of Genoa Velvet, Damasks, and Silks, trimmed with Gold Lace;
COUCHES, SOFAS, AND CHAIRS, TO CORRESPOND; BEAUTIFUL AXMINSTER CARPETS;
BRILLIANT PLATES OF GLASS; SET OF ORIENTAL EBONY CHAIRS AND SOFAS; SCREENS AND CABINETS;
RARE OLD CHINA, AND RICH CUT GLASS;
A Variety of Parisian and Buhl Cabinets and Bookcases; magnificent Library Tables; Cabinet Articles of every Description; elegant Clocks; superb Chandeliers; full-sized Billiard Table;
SPLENDID SERVICES OF MASSIVE RICH CHASED AND GILT SILVER PLATE,
ABOUT 22,000 OUNCES,
IN USEFUL AND ORNAMENTAL ARTICLES;
Valuable Agate-Handle Knives and Forks; exquisite Carvings in Ivory, superbly mounted; magnificent Plateau, &c.
A VALUABLE
COLLECTION OF FINE PAINTINGS AND SCULPTURE,
BY ITALIAN, FLEMISH, AND ENGLISH MASTERS;
Bronzes, Casts from the Antique, splendid Gobelin Tapestry, Damask and Velvet Hangings, &c.
Library of Ancient and Modern Books,
Elegantly Bound, embracing many early Specimens of Typography, continued by every Work of Celebrity to the present Day; also abounding in the GRAPHIC ART, with the most choice Impressions from the Foreign and English Schools.
The choice fine-flavoured OLD WINES, in Wood and Bottle;
CAPITAL HOME-BREWED ALE;
Fixtures; Two Fire Engines; Brewing and Dairy Utensils; Garden Lights and Tools; Green House Plants; Pleasure Boats, Punts, capital Harness; and a Variety of other Articles,
The whole forming an Assemblage of the most valuable Property ever offered to the Public:
WHICH, BY ORDER OF THE TRUSTEES, WILL BE
SOLD BY AUCTION,
BY MR. ROBINS,
(OF WARWICK HOUSE, REGENT STREET,)
ON THE PREMISES, WANSTEAD HOUSE,
On MONDAY, 10th JUNE, 1822, and 31 following Days,
SATURDAYS AND SUNDAYS EXCEPTED, AT ELEVEN O'CLOCK.

To be viewed on WEDNESDAY, the 22nd of MAY, and every Day till the Time of Sale (Sunday excepted) by Catalogues, at Five Shillings each Part, to admit Three Persons, which will be delivered at WANSTEAD HOUSE; at Messrs. ROBSON, LIGHTFOOT, and ROBSON's Office, Castle Street, Leicester Square; at Messrs. BRUNDRETT, SPINKS, and REDDISH's, Temple; and at Mr. ROBINS's Office, Regent Street.

Printed by J. BRETTELL, *Rupert Street, Haymarket.*

The sale of the century was held in 1822 when creditors to the estate forced the auction of first the contents to be followed the next year by the House itself. The plan on the previous pages shows the estate at the time of liquidation.

28

LOT 4.

A SUPERB MAHOGANY FRAME DOUBLE SCREWED LOFTY
STATE BEDSTEAD,
With handsome panelled Head Board, and massive square Dome Canopy over, with broad moulded Cornice,
Plumes of Feathers and other Ornaments,
COVERED WITH BROWN MORINE, DECORATED WITH
CRIMSON VELVET, AND ELEGANT MORINE FURNITURE,
WITH DEEP BANNER
DRAPERY TASTEFULLY DISPLAYED,
Trimmed with Parisian Fringe, and bordered with crimson Velvet Roset Ornaments, twisted Ropes, Tassels, &c.
AND STATE FRAME, COVERED EN SUITE FOR THE BEDSTEAD,
5-Feet-6 wide by 13-Feet-6 high.

The Devonshire Collection at Chatsworth was the only one to reply positively with a photograph of this beautiful library table giving us just a glimpse at the opulence of the interior furnishings. It went under the hammer on the twelfth day's sale as Lot 26 and sold for £92 8s. 0d. Then it stood in the Great Hall of the House; now it can be seen in the Sculpture Gallery at the home of the Duke and Duchess of Devonshire.

Wanstead-house was sold by auction, on the premises, on Monday last, for £10,000; one of the conditions of sale binds the purchaser to clear every thing away, even to the foundation, by Lady-day, 1825. The biddings commenced at £1000, and advanced by thousands till they reached £8,000, when they dwindled to an advance of £100 each bidding, till they reached the sum at which the building was sold. The purchasers are Messrs. Stannard and Athow, of Norwich, in conjunction with three others of their townsmen. The auctioneer announced to the company, by their request, that they intended to sell the whole in lots, large or small, to suit buyers, and they absolutely sold a pair of marble chimney-pieces for 300 guineas, before they left the room. Thus is sacrificed, on the shrine of extravagance and gambling, a mansion, which cost in its erection more than £360,000, and which has no equal in the county of Essex.

Press report, 1823

WANSTEAD HOUSE

THE MATERIALS of this magnificent and extensive Building are now SELLING by PRIVATE CONTRACT; and persons may be accommodated with every description of BUILDING MATERIAL, (from the Cottage to the Palace,) on the most reasonable terms, upon application to Mr. JOSEPH STANNARD, on the Premises.

Press report, 1823

WANSTED HOUSE.— The materials of this princely mansion are now dispersing, and although a considerable time must necessarily elapse before it shall be cleared away, still such is the great variety of applicants, that it will ere long be reduced to a wreck, and like the 'fabric of a vision,' there will be nothing left to trace even its base. Whilst some lament the cause of this event, and heave a sign for

---

LOT 26.

A MAGNIFICENT SQUARE

Library Table,

Top lined with costly Russia Leather, and broad stamped Border, Brass moulded Edge, with rich chased or-moulu Shells at the corners, on a superb massive Oak Frame, sumptuously carved and gilt, with Grecian scroll panelled Truss Supports, on solid square moulded-edge Plinths and Casters, with Neptune's Head Ornaments in the centre, supported on each side by elegant large scroll Wings, the Ends decorated with Festoons of Oak Leaves and Acorns, Raffle Leaf and Shell Ornaments, massive Mouldings round the Frame, &c. and handsome Crimson-ground Chints Case, lined White Calico, 9 Feet long by 6 Feet wide, and 3 Feet high

---

fallen greatness, there are those who contemplate the scene with much more cheering prospects; and none have greater cause to adopt the latter, than those gentlemen who so judiciously contracted for this large mass of the best materials, and the chastest workmanship. The sale has now been open to individuals little more than fourteen days, during which period some of the more choice articles have been disposed of. Lord Tankerville, and the Rev. Savill Ogle, of Newcastle, have hitherto been the largest purchasers, particularly for the marble

chimney-pieces, four of which have been sold for £426. Nearly £2000 has already been realized, whilst the interior remains but little disturbed, and the exterior not touched. Still the prices asked are spoken of as extremely moderate; the wainscot floors are sold for about £5 per square; wainscot doors, with locks and joints, 2s. to 2s. 6d. per foot. The sale during the present summer is expected to be confined to the fittings-up of the interior. However lamentable it may be to the lovers of the arts to be informed of the circumstance, it is no less a fact, that the historical paintings

161

What an indictment the destruction of the House is upon the Victorians. Was there no one who had £10,000 to invest in a palace which had cost nearly 400 times that sum? The Press reports give us an inkling of how people felt at the time but with stately mansions then in plentiful supply, there were no thoughts of preservation. Long-Wellesley was a wastrel; he had to be made to pay his debts and his creditors demanded that not one stone should be left upon another.

upon the ceilings so much admired for their designs and the execution of them, being painted upon plaster, are rendered useless, as being irremovable; they must in the general wreck, return to the dust with that brittle composition which they now so magnificently embellish. The speculators who purchased the lot, are fortunate in selecting from among them, Mr. Stannard, an eminent surveyor and builder from Norwich, who constantly resides at the house; the pleasing manners and abilities of this gentleman, will not fail to assist in adding much to the profit of himself and his co-partners.

Press report, 1823

The greater part of the creditors of Mr. Long Wellesley, whose demands were under the sum of 200*l.*, have recently been paid in full; and those whose demands were above that amount, and who signed the Trust Deed, have already received 10s. in the pound; and will shortly receive the remainder. Mr. Long Wellesley is expected in England about the end of September or October next. Mrs. Wellesley and the three children are now at Draycot, where Mr. W. will then join them.

Devizes Gazette, 1823

The celebrated ebony chairs and sofa, once the boasted *gems* of Queen Elizabeth, and which are so particularly alluded to by Horace Walpole in one of his letters, for their singular beauty and antique character, after experiencing various transfers and vicissitudes of fortune, came into the possession of the late Lord Tilney. They were next purchased at the sale at Wanstead House, by Graham, of Waterloo-place, by whom they have recently been sold to Lord Macdonald, of the Isles. We hope his Lordship intends to deposit them in his ancient and venerable mansion in Scotland, and to secure their preservation by his successors as a family heir-loom.

Press report, 1823

The fashionable world is much occupied at present with the melancholy circumstances which attended the death of Mrs Wellesley Long Pole, who expired last week at Richmond. We have received several commendations relative to the causes of her illness, and the state of her family, but they are of too private and delicate a nature to be alluded to in a public journal.

Press report, September 1825

Nonetheless it must have been a very profitable deal for Stannards who sold the whole house piece by piece. This obelisk, which stands in the field next to The Warren on the Epping New Road between Buckhurst Hill and Loughton, is the only known fragment we can now attribute to Wanstead House, one of the twelve seen in the print *(top)*. Wellesley-Pole was a nephew of the Duke of Wellington and General Grosvenor, who lived at The Warren at the time and served the Iron Duke at Waterloo, erected it in memory of the charger he rode during the battle.

WANSTEAD HOUSE, ESSEX

SECOND SALE

And which will comprise the Grand Corinthian Portico, fine Statuary Marble, Marble Chimney Pieces, and Effects.

MR. W. W. SIMPSON
(OF 24, BUCKLERSBURY,)
Will have the Honour of offering for

SALE BY PUBLIC AUCTION

By Order of the Proprietor, on the Premises, on TUESDAY, JUNE 29, and Two following Days, in Lots, for the convenience of Purchasers — each day's Sale to commence at Twelve o'clock,

A CONSIDERABLE PART of the valuable BUILDING MATERIALS of the above costly and magnificent Mansion; comprising a truly-designed
CORINTHIAN STONE PORTICO,
Which consists of eight Corinthian columns, 3 feet 3 inches diameter, with superb capitals, supporting a grand pediment, with finely-carved modellans, and other beautiful enrichments, and which, for architectural magnificence and elegance, which combines a peculiar chasteness of design, this colonnade cannot be surpassed, and it would be much indeed to be deplored should this unrivalled portico not be perpetuated as a national specimen of architectural beauty and taste, in some one of the public or private structures now in progress throughout this kingdom.
The EAST FRONT consists of Six Corinthian Pilasters, with superior carved capitals, surmounted by a grand pediment, enriched with basso relievo; also beautiful window architraves, with pediment head and trusses. The interior fittings consist of very fine stone and wood frontispieces, a circular-headed frontispiece, with exquisite carved figures; superbly carved and enriched statuary; marble and stone chimney pieces; eight beautiful Ionic columns; fine Grecian vases; many thousand feet of paneling, dado and wainscoating; wainscot and other six panelled doors, door jambs, architraves, base and surbase mouldings; a quantity of fine carved and gilt stone architraves, stout sashes and frames, and beautiful Venetian windows; a quantity of stone blocks, good sound bricks, oak and fir timber (in various scantlings), and other useful building materials.

Press Announcement, June 1824

Poor Catherine Tylney Long. She inherited the manor of Wanstead on the death of her infant brother, Sir James Long, Bt., in 1805. Lady Catherine then became probably the richest woman in England with an annual income of £80,000. She married William Wellesley-Pole in 1812 and within ten years he had squandered her fortune and brought her to financial ruin. She separated from him in 1819, her health suffered, her mother died in 1823, and she passed away destitute on September 16, 1825. They took her back to the family seat at Draycot, Wiltshire, for burial and there laid her to rest in the family vault in the little chapel of St James. Draycot House was auctioned in 1919 by Earl Cowley, purchased by a local builder, Ted Bent, who pulled it down in 1950 and used the stone to build a new house on the site.

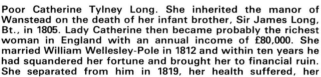

Monday last in Chancery with consent of W. Wellesley, a receiver was appointed to his estates . . .

Mercury. 1826

An application was made in the Court of Chancery for an injunction by the trustees of the estate for the benefit of Mr Long Wellesley's children to prevent that gentleman from cutting down in the park 2,000 trees which had been marked and advertised for sale on the 9th instant. It was argued that Mr Wellesley had already sold much timber, without the consent of the Trustees . . .

Press report, 1828

Not a vestige of Wanstead House once the pride of Essex remains, nor a single stone 'to prate of its whereabouts'. There are now only wanting the remaining lofty trees to be felled, the whole of the ornamental waters to be drawn off, and the grotto to be demolished, to render its once delightful park a scene of sad and melancholy desolation. The seat of hospitality and social enjoyment has vanished, and nothing is left to perpetuate its splendour. The admiration and partiality of the neighbouring peasantry designated the place one of the wonders of the world, but not a fragment is now seen, to remind us of its former magnificence and importance.

Press report, 1835

At the sale of the contents of the mansion the family portraits were reserved; but even these subsequently shared a similar fate, for they, too, were sold in 1851, at the auction-rooms of Messrs. Christie and Manson, 'in consequence of the non-payment of expenses for warehousing-room'. Their dispersion was the last event in the history of Wanstead House, which once had vied with Canons in its glories, and now came to share the same fate.

Greater London, Edward Walpole, 1883

A spendthrift, a profligate, and a gambler in his youth, he became a debauchee in his manhood . . . Redeemed by no single virtue, adorned by no single grace, his life has gone out even without a flicker of repentance.

Obituary for the Hon. William Pole-Tylney-Long-Wellesley, Morning Chronicle, 1857.

What else still remains? Well the stable block was saved and can now be seen as the Club House for Wanstead Golf Club whose course now rambles through the park, Earl Cowley having sold part of the land to Wanstead Sports Ground Ltd in 1920. Unfortunately the architects and planners of another age appear equally disrespectful of antiquity even though this is a Grade II listed building.

In the latter part of the eighteenth century, Wanstead House still displayed all the splendour which the Childs, the Tylneys, and the Longs, had lavished upon a palace fit for the abode of gentle and royal blood. Little did I dream that in one quarter of a century I should see its proud columns prostrate in the dust, its decorations annihilated, its pictures and sculptures dispersed by the magic of the hammer; at one period simply a deserted mansion, at another a refuge for exiled princes; then for a brief space polluted by riot and profligacy; and ultimately its lawns and gardens swept away, its stately groves and avenues remorselessly destroyed, and myself present at the sad catastrophe. Such, however, were its short and painful annals; and, except the grotto, not one stone now remains upon another. The palace, destined to stand for ages, and on which time had made no inroads, was removed, with the approbation of the Lord Chancellor, when little more than a hundred winters had passed over it: when its features were just mellowed, its woods and plantations in full luxuriance, and all around it smiling in perfection. Wanstead House was the most attractive object (of its kind) near London, and a national ornament. I was familiar, with every little bower and secluded avenue; I knew where its blossoms were fairest and the fruits choicest; could thread the mazes of its delightful foliage and exotic gardens, its limpid waters, and its verdant lawns, all which I have visited at dawn and at sunset, in midday and at night.

Provincial Excursions, 1843

As we look upon the mansionless park — for all that remains is the steward's house — the overgrown walks, and once almost Elysian pleasure grounds now let out for pasturage, we cannot but sigh over this sad page of patrician history.

People's History of Essex, Coller, 1866

On Tuesday last, the beautiful grounds of Wanstead Park were formally opened to the public. The Epping Forest Committee left Fenchurch-street Station shortly after three o'clock, and were met at Snaresbrook by a number of carriages, and conveyed to the park through a private road owned by Lord Cowley. Shortly after passing the Wanstead Parish Church, the members of the committee alighted and at once proceeded to the Temple, a place used partly as a committee room, and partly as a house for the keepers. After a short stay there, the members proceeded on a tour of inspection of the extensive grounds, a labour which occupied some hours. It may be recalled to mind that the Corporation have secured this park of 184 acres by an exchange of 50 acres of land scattered about, and the payment of £8,000 to Lord Cowley.

Press report, August 5, 1882

The City's association with Wanstead Park began in the middle of the nineteenth century. In 1851, Viscount Wellesley, the eldest son of the profligate Long-Wellesley (who after his Wanstead days inherited the earldom of Mornington) regained the property from the mortgagees and shortly afterwards attempted to enclose thirty-four acres of waste at Aldersbrook. By this time enclosures of forest land had reached alarming proportions and within a few years were to lead to the action that eventually saved Epping Forest. It was at Wanstead that the rescue began. In 1854 the Commissioners of Sewers for the City of London bought most of Aldersbrook Farm for a cemetery. This purchase gave the City Corporation commoner status, and when in

Destined to stand for ages but demolished within a century.

1871 Earl Cowley (cousin and heir of the Viscount Wellesley who had already enclosed land at Aldersbrook) enclosed twenty acres, the Commissioners of Sewers brought an action against him. At the end of three years of litigation, judgement was given for the Commissioners, which meant that Wanstead Flats had been saved and the way had been cleared for the consequential action that finally led to the saving of the entire Forest by the Epping Forest Act of 1878.

Earl Cowley acquired the thirty-four acres enclosed in 1851 in exchange for the lakes and woodlands of Wanstead Park, together with £8,000 in cash. The extent of the acquisition by the Corporation was said to be one hundred and eighty-four acres of ornamental grounds, with thirty acres of water. To be more accurate, the present inclosure totals one hundred and forty acres, of which about seventy acres are woodland, thirty-eight acres grassland and the remainder water and islands. When the Park was formally opened by Mr Deputy Hora, Chairman of the Epping Forest Committee, on 1st August 1882, it was widely recognised how much this happy conclusion to the long drawn-out litigation was due to the untiring labours of Mr John T. Bedford. By a strange irony it might also be said to be due to the unprincipled conduct of Long-Wellesley, who, as the City of London's counsel said, by the reckless sale of the Stewardships of his Manors and of the Court of Attachments had brought about the collapse of the system by which the Forest had been preserved since Norman times.

Wanstead Park, William Addison, 1973

Dear Wanstead Park! what joys are thine,
  How many a shady nook,
Where I may at my ease recline,
  Or saunter with a book.

The cuckoo shouts his loud clear note
  And waits his mate's reply;
The throstle swells her speckled throat
  With songs that pierce the sky.

Across the glade a rabbit runs,
  His scut raised high in air,
He thinks he hears the keeper's guns,
  And hies him to his lair.

Bold robin pipes his cheerful strain,
  His notes rise higher and higher,
Alas! he hears a rival's song
  His bosom flames with fire.

The blackbird trills a roundelay,
  O lovely gush of sound!
Which through the quivering summer's day
  Fills all the air around.

The linnet flits from tree to tree,
  While twittering songs of love,
And hush! there steals across the lea
  The cooing of the dove.

The insects hum in mazy round,
  The leaves are whispering too;
A brown rat glides along the ground,
  And disappears from view.

High overhead the solemn crow
  Wheels in his homeward flight,
Then settles on some tree's top bough
  As gently falls the night.

Dear Wanstead Park what joys are thine
  Through all the changeful year,
Thy beauties to this heart of mine,
  Are dear and yet more dear!

Among thy glades the children play,
  Light-hearted, happy, free,
'Till Nature flings her mantle grey
  O'er bird, and flower, and tree.

Long may I know those pleasant glades,
  Long may my heart rejoice
To wander neath thy leafy shades
  Entranced by nature's voice!

"That voice which never did betray
  The heart whose love is true"
So sang sweet Wordsworth in his day;
  Dear Wanstead Park — Adieu!   *Anon*

SITE OF WANSTEAD HOUSE

THE SHOE-BLACK BRIGADE.— On Wednesday Mr. Alderman and Mrs. Finnis gave their annual treat, at their seat at Wanstead, to the boys constituting the Shoe-black Brigade of the metropolis. The juvenile brigade marched to the station at Fenchurch-street, with flags flying and drums beating. They entered the grounds of Mr. Alderman Finnis in an equally joyous and triumphant manner, and, after amusing themselves in various ways, they sat down, to the number of 275, to a most ample dinner. Dinner being over, Mr. Alderman Finnis briefly addressed his youthful guests amidst cheers of the heartiest kind, and was followed by Mr. Justice Halliburton. Mr. Payne, Deputy Judge, and who has for so many years taken a deep interest in this and all other philanthropic movements, then addressed the 'boys' at considerable length and with much humour. The learned gentleman concluded with some lines, being the 1215th poetical address he has delivered, when speaking at public meetings held for religious and philanthropic purposes. The boys then resumed their playful exercise in the grounds, and in due time sat down to tea. Shortly before eight they left the grounds and returned to the station, where a special train was provided for them, after spending a most delightful day. An ample and excellent banquet was provided for the grown-up friends of Mr. Alderman and Mrs. Finnis, nearly two hundred in number.

Press report, 1858

Park Gates, home of Alderman Sir Thomas Finnis, Lord Mayor of London in 1856-57, stood alongside the entrance to the park. It was demolished in the early part of this century for the building of the Blake Hall Estate. The original piers of the carriageway to the House are now listed Grade II*, the star indicating that the item is classified one stage above a simple Grade II. (See also page 15.) The balls atop the piers were added when the right-hand pillar was repaired by the local borough council.

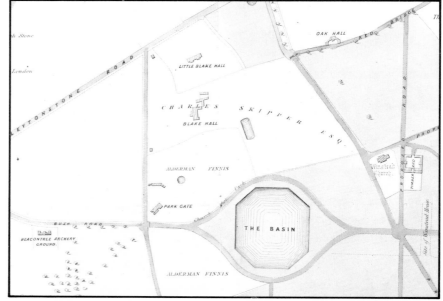

The parish of Wanstead, including the hamlet of Snaresbrook, covers an area of some 2,000 acres, and contains a population of about 9,500, having doubled itself since 1871. This number, however, includes the inmates of the Infant Orphan Asylum. The village lies to the right of the Chigwell Road, between it and the river Roding. It is about half a mile south-eastward from Snaresbrook station on the Ongar branch of the Great Eastern Railway, and seven miles from Whitechapel or Shoreditch churches. Wanstead Park stretches away on the east: the long level waste known as Wanstead Flats, some 800 acres in extent, lies beyond the village on the south, and Leytonstone bounds it on the west.

The name of Wanstead seems to be derived . . . 'from the Saxon words *wan* and *stede*, signifying the white place, or mansion'.

Wanstead Flats are about 400 acres in extent, and their area was formerly overgrown with furze, heath, and a few scattered trees; but of late years its appearance has been considerably changed by the formation of brick-fields, etc. Early in the present century George III held a review of 10,000 troops on Wanstead Flats, and in 1874 the open portion was secured by the Government for the purposes of military drill and exercise. For very many years this locality was a familiar haunt of the gipsy tribe, and of others who follow the wandering life of that fraternity, their caravans and tents being scarcely ever absent from the borders of the Flats.

Greater London, Edward Walford, 1883

The dead body of an infant was discovered on Friday afternoon in Wanstead Park. In one of the closets near the old grotto, Mrs. Pounds, of Sebert-road, Forest Gate, saw what appeared to be the feet of a baby. Shocked by the sight she hastened to inform Robert Puffett, the park-keeper. Puffet at once went and found the dead body of a female child, apparently about a month old, lying in the receptacle. The body was wrapped in a blue-striped white diaper. The head and face were wrapped round with two binders of calico, which covered up the nose and mouth. The child had on a white calico shirt with the figures 711 marked in black ink. There were no marks of violence upon the body. — A post-mortem examination was afterwards made, and Dr. Collins stated that death was due to bronchitis. — An inquest was opened by Mr. C. C. Lewis at the Eagle Hotel, Snaresbrook, on Monday evening, and evidence of the finding of the body having been given, the inquiry was adjourned.

Walthamstow, Leyton and Chingford Guardian, June 1, 1894

Bleak or Blake Hall was served by two sweeping drives, giving access either from Bushwood or the London road. It had been built around 1690 by Sir Joseph Martin, its red brick and stone facings being a local landmark. The Duke of Connaught stayed here when official business in connection with the Epping Forest Committee brought him to the district. (See for example page 51.) It was demolished in 1909 preparatory to the development of the area.

The house stood here in the foreground, straddling Felstead Road.

Little Blake Hall stood on the site of 'Jalna' — No. 2 Seagry Road — and evidence of the old estate is still apparent to an observant visitor who perhaps can pick out the odd very mature chestnut or fir tree adorning a garden of the much younger houses to be found in the area of Seagry and Draycott Roads.

The Warren — its name perpetuated in the Drive of that name which now crosses the grounds — was formerly the agent's house to the Tylney estate. This delightful study was taken in 1912. Twenty years later it was demolished yet part of the old wall to the grounds still survives in a garden opposite Raynes Road.

The original parish church was partly in red brick bearing possibly traces of Carolingian influence and it had been covered with stucco.

As the life centring around the manor increased, so the enlargement and renovation of the church no doubt became a necessity. Anyway, this was done early in the sixteenth century, probably by Sir John Heron, the then lord of the manor. The assumption is that another aisle was added and the square tower erected.

It was in this enlarged building that Queen Elizabeth is said to have worshipped during her frequent visits to Wanstead as Robert Dudley's guest; and here too, on June 20, 1624, Archbishop Usher preached before James I.

By about 1770, when there were approximately 120 houses in Wanstead and a population of 670, it was thought that a more spacious church was becoming a necessity.

Wanstead Parish Church,
Winnifred Eastment.

Wanstead in Essex July 13. The first stone of the new church building here was laid with great solemnity by Sir James Tylney Lord, Bart., assisted by the rector, churchwardens, trustees and principal participants of the parish. After the ceremony was performed, the gentlemen and ladies who were numerous, were elegantly entertained with a cold collation at Tylney-house.

Press report, 1787

. . . It was resolved, at the instance of Dr. Glasse, the present rector, to pull it down, and build a new church on a larger scale, nearly adjoining to the old site. The first stone of the present structure was laid on the 13th of July, 1787, and it was finished and consecrated in 1790. The building is of brick, cased with Portland stone, and having a portico of the Doric order: at the west end is a cupola, supported by eight Ionic columns. The inside is extremely neat and elegant, without any unnecessary embellishment: it consists of a chancel, nave, and two aisles, separated by columns of the Corinthian order. The pavement (which is remarkable for its beauty and neatness) is of stone, brought from Painswick, in Gloucestershire. In the chancel is a beautiful window of stained glass, by Eginton, of Birmingham, representing our Saviour bearing the cross, from the picture at Magdalen College, Oxford. In the east window of the north aisle are the royal arms; in the south aisle, those of the late Sir J. T. Long, Bart.

The History and Topography of the County
of Essex, March 1831

WHEREAS on Wednesday Night, or Thursday Night last, the Parish Church of WANSTEAD, in the County of ESSEX, was feloniously broke open, and stolen therein the following Articles, viz. a Chocolate-colour Pulpit-cloth, two Communion Table Prayer-books, marked on the Covers, 'St. Mary, Wanstead; Toten, Churchwarden;' one large

Old Wanstead Church was enlarged circa 1715 from an earlier chapel erected by the lord of the manor around the end of the twelfth century. Queen Elizabeth worshipped here on her visits to Wanstead but today nothing remains except these overgrown flagstones in Wanstead Churchyard — sealing the tombs which lay beneath the centre aisle.

Under the influence of Sir James Tylney Long, and on land he provided from his park, a new Georgio-Italian building was designed by Thomas Hardwick to blend with the classical style of the new Wanstead House just a hundred yards away to the south. Its cost was £9,150, provided by public subscription and the sale of annuities which expired in 1862. The sale of vaults in the crypt also raised 100 guineas each. In 1790, after the consecration of the new church the rector, Dr Samuel Glasse, had the old church demolished, the break with the past being sealed by the melting down of the old Queen Anne communion plate, the only mitigating feature of his wanton act being that the same metal was to be used for the new set.

and two small Prayer-books, bound in blue Morocco; and the Linings of three Pews, two blue and one green.

Whoever will give such information to Sir Sampson Wright, at the above Office, as may be the Means of apprehending and convicting the Offender or Offenders, shall receive FIVE GUINEAS Reward.

Press report, August 20, 1788

On Friday night some of those wretches called resurrection-men, made a daring attempt on Wanstead church-yard, and in part succeeded. They first got up the body of a child, recently interred, on the edge of the grave; they then commenced on the grave of the parish beadle, and had made some progress, when they were fortunately disturbed, and made their escape with the child only. These fellows are supposed to belong to the same gang that last year opened a grave in Chingford church-yard, from which they took a patent iron coffin, broke it to pieces, and carried away its unconscious tenant.

Press report, October 27, 1824

At Wanstead the prevalence of body-snatching led to the parish instituting an armed guard in 1830. At first the watchman used the vestry in the church until this sentry box was erected the following year in the churchyard. Dedicated to the memory of the Wilton family, it was designed after the style of the entrance to the Holy Sepulchre in Jerusalem. It still stands today.

The original rectory stood on or near this site in South (or Parsons, but now Redbridge) Lane but it was rebuilt about 1830. In 1924 it was sold to Essex County Council which demolished it to build Wanstead County High School.

'The Hermit of Bushwood,' Henry Plodden, the out-of-work carpenter, who lived for over a month in the hollow of the King Oak, in that part of Wanstead Flats known as Bushwood, is there no more. He was moved on at last by the authorities yesterday, and he folded up his sacks and tarpaulin and stole away as silently as Longfellow's Arabs. All that remains now of his dwelling place is the great oak, with its gaunt branches black against the December sky, and the bare, naked hollow, scooped by Nature out of the tree trunk.

Henry Plodden was seventy-four years old, and without home, money, or food, he came upon the King Oak in Bushwood and saw that it would make a desirable residence. The knotted roots formed ridges round the tree to keep the rain out; the hollow was as comfortable as the back of an armchair, and could be made as soft with the dexterous use of sacking and newspapers. Then, for a roof, he took more sacking, and supported it by sticks, and when night-time came Henry Plodden shut himself in, and slept in the ghostly silence of the wood, with only the birds and creatures of the undergrowth for company. In the morning people brought him food, and some gave him pennies, and during the day many sightseers from Leytonstone, Forest Gate, and the neighbouring suburbs threaded through the muddy roads to look upon the man who dwelt in a tree-trunk. Henry Plodden was comfortable and warm; that was all he wanted to be.

Press report, 1905

Arthur Hands, the well known Wanstead photographer, took this picture around 1912 when local firemen set up this ladder arch at the entrance to St Mary's Avenue (originally just called Church Road) to welcome King George V on a visit soon after he came to the throne. Beside the road lies one of John Evelyn's tree-lined carriageway drives — probably the best preserved to be seen today.

By the Church we come up into the loosely-spread village of Wanstead, running into Snaresbrook, which I take to be a suburb of some means, having counted a dozen cabs outside the station at the hour when the City disgorges its victims; but its roomy gardened mansions are being pressed on by smaller and closer built houses. What a year or so ago was the last London street on this side, keeps alive the name of Oak Hall, that in 'Long-Tylney-Wellesley-Long-Pole's' day was headquarters of another profuse adventurer, 'George MacGregor, Cacique of Poyais,' whose story has been told in *Bonnie Scotland*.

Essex, A. R. Hope-Moncrieff, 1926

How are the mighty fallen! Could Wanstead really ever have looked like this? We are reliably informed by Bill Hands that this picture, taken in 1895 by his father Arthur, shows the present Leicester Road — the track alongside the fence! Spot the retouched out sign board — advertising plots on the Grove Estate?

The Grove Estate was centered on the land occupied by Wanstead Grove, said to have been built about 1690 by Sir Francis Dashwood. The sixty-acre, well-timbered estate was purchased by Humphrey Bowles in 1759 for a sum of around £10,000. He died in 1784 being succeeded by his son George, a notable benefactor and future High Sheriff of Essex. On his death in 1817 the property passed to his niece, Anne Rushout, who soon decided the building was too dilapidated and should be rebuilt. This, whether by good fortune or otherwise, coincided with the demolition of Wanstead House and it would have been surprising if some materials from the big house down the road were not used in the reconstruction of The Grove. The new house cost Miss Rushout £10,000, immediately pushing the mansion to premier position in the Wanstead property stakes. Anne's tenure lasted over thirty years until it passed on her death back to the male line of the Bowles family. However the upkeep was completely beyond the resources of the new owner and it was sold for £9,250 — a sad reflection on the days before inflation when property was a poor investment!

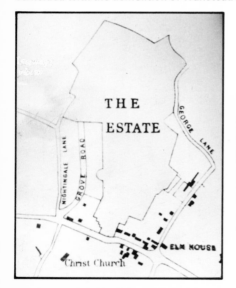

In 1885 Wanstead Grove was put up for auction and the land sold for building. The house which stood here at the junction of Grove Park and The Avenue was demolished in 1889.

The lake was filled in but the Temple, a classical stone summerhouse, was spared and it now forms a fine centrepiece in the garden of the house which has taken the same name in The Avenue.

George Draper, 32, a hawker, of Cropley Street, Hoxton, was charged with obtaining money by false pretences by crying false news. — Mr. Frank Jackson, a draper, of 15, High Street, Wanstead, said that on Monday evening he was in his shop when he heard a cry of 'Shocking discovery in Wanstead.' He went out and saw the prisoner selling the *Star*. Witness bought one, the accused charging him a penny for it, and when he looked at the paper he could find no report as to any discovery at Wanstead. — Mr. Manby, of 47, Mornington Road, Wanstead, said that the prisoner was calling out, 'Shocking tragedy of a young gentleman at Wanstead.' Witness bought a paper, and all he found was a paragraph relating to a Wanstead resident who had been found dead at Cranham, near Upminster. — Mr. H. Hubbard (the Clerk): Wasn't that shocking enough for you? — No, it was not. (Laughter.) — The Prisoner: I said 'A tragedy of a Wanstead gentleman, not 'at' Wanstead. — Mr. W. P. Griggs (examining the paper): Why, here's a shooting affair at Woodford. Isn't that worth anything? — Constable Hammer, 260J, said that he heard the prisoner calling 'Tragedy on Wanstead Flats' — Mr. W. P. Griggs: Did you buy a paper? — The officer: I procured one. He would not take my money. (Laughter.) I asked him why he was charging a penny for his papers, and he said it was not worth while coming to Wanstead for less. — Mr. Hubbard: He was very nice to you. He did not obtain any money fraudulently from you? — No. — The prisoner denied that he cried any false news. There had been a tragedy, he said, but he did not call out 'at' Wanstead. — Mr. W. P. Griggs said there might be a doubt as to the actual words called by the prisoner, and he would be discharged. — William Downey, 38, a labourer, of Clerkenwell, who was similarly charged, said he was only calling 'Shocking discovery of a Wanstead man.' — Mr. W. P. Griggs said that the Bench were of opinion that the accused was trying to take people in, and he was sailing very near the wind. However, he would be discharged, although

he would not get off so easily if he was brought before the Court again.

Walthamstow, Leyton and Chingford Guardian, February 7, 1913

More sacrilege. The oldest property in Wanstead, Grove Cottage on the corner of George (now Nutter) Lane and Leicester Road, dating from the early 1600s, swept away as recently as 1957.

Hitler also did his best — this is The Shrubberies in Grove Park — hit on the night of September 8, 1940.

Home of the Nutter family — the Applegarth — dating from around 1710, now one of Wanstead's most historic buildings.

'Mob's Hole, a tumbledown cottage at the bottom of Nightingale Lane, taken by my father in 1918.' Photograph from Mrs Joyce Green of North Weald.

The strange way in which local place names can arise and then, in course of time, disappear from popular usage and from the maps, is commented upon. . . . Wanstead can claim an example of this disappearance of formerly well-known names. It is Mob's Hole, which, though it may still be familiar to the minds of some older residents, does not appear on modern maps and is rarely mentioned today. Yet it is marked quite clearly on a map published in 1777.

The name Mob's Hole was used to describe generally the small area which lies at the bottom of Nightingale-lane, Wanstead. In the midst of it lay the small green, now fenced in, surrounded by a group of little cottages.

Not many people will know what the word Mob, or Mobb, as it was sometimes spelled, really signifies. It was a seventeenth century term, now obsolete, for a pickpocket.

Mob's Hole's chief claim to fame — although many who know its name are not aware of it — is that a certain lady with commercial instincts once kept what we should term a roadhouse there in the eighteenth century. Her name was Butterfield — Lady Butterfield she called herself, although from all accounts it was a dignity of name only, and a self-styled one at that.

Out to Lady Butterfield's hospitable house and gardens at Mob's Hole, Wanstead, would come riding the young gallants of the 1700s, with their more adventuresome lady friends. For it must be remembered that Wanstead lay a good distance from London town, and the

road was an uncertain one through a countryside infested with footpads and other dangerous gentlemen.

However, the more daring of the young bloods did frequent Lady Butterfield's pleasure gardens at Wanstead quite regularly, mostly riding out on horseback for a joyous

carousal when they arrived at Wanstead Village's 'roadhouse.'

Lady Butterfield was nothing if not modern. In other words she was an early and enlightened believer in the old adage 'It pays to advertise'. She added to this well-known tag the words, 'In newspapers,' as do all sensible modern business people, and proceeded to bring her 'roadhouse' to the notice of all and sundry through the medium of the Press. Here is an advertisement she inserted in *The Post Man*, a London paper, June 24-27, 1710:

'To all Gentlemen and Ladies.
If Rare Good Young Beans and Pease can
    Tempt Ye,
Pray pass not by my Hall with Bellies Empty;
For King Good Usage everyone can tell;
My Lady Butterfield does al excel;
At Wanstead Town, a Mile of the Green Man
Come if you care and stay away if you can.'

Here is another of her advertisements, this time from a paper of 1717:

'This is to give notice to all my honoured masters and their ladies, and the rest of my loving friends, that my Lady Butterfield gives a challenge to ride a horse, to leap a horse, or run on foot, or halloo, with any woman in England, seven years younger, but not a day older, because I would not under value myself, being 74 years of age. My feast will be the last Wednesday of this month, April, when there will be good entertainment for that day, and all the year after, at Wanstead, in Essex.'

Express and Independent, June 13, 1936

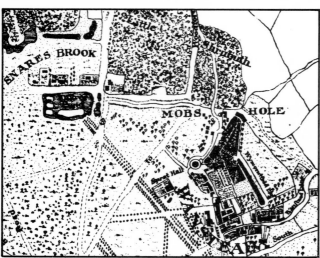

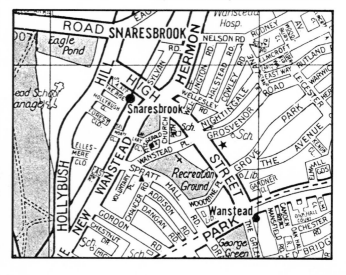

The changing face of Wanstead. The George and Dragon, established circa 1716, and Admiral Sir William Penn's home, Elm Hall.

The new George built in 1906. The 'Cherry Pie' stone (see page 33) was saved and replaced in the side wall in George Lane.

George Green. The knarled and twisted remnants of some of Sir Josiah's trees: five in 1920 . . . three in 1984 . . .

A new Picture Palace, to be known, as the Wanstead Empire, has just been erected at the motor-bus terminus, Wanstead, adjoining the George Hotel. The hall is built on the latest approved principle, and is a much more commodious structure than the outward appearance would suggest, as will be gathered from the fact that it has seating accommodation for 600 people.

It has been covered with plush-covered tip-up chairs, of very comfortable design, and the convenience of patrons has been further studied by allowing plenty of room between each row of seats, and in the gangways.

Another feature that will also be appreciated, especially on a wet day, is the commodious vestibule, which will accommodate 200 people, so that there should be no necessity, when there is a crowd, for some people to be kept waiting out in the rain while others are getting their tickets.

It is proposed to run the theatre on high-class lines, and with a view to keeping it select the prices of admission have been fixed at 4d., 6d. and 1s. First-class films will be shown, and an excellent orchestra will provide music.

A powerful electrical plant has been in-stalled and, in fact, everything has been done to make it a thoroughly up-to-date cinema. Mr. Geo. W. Kerry, of Leytonstone, has been appointed manager, and judging from the excellent programme arranged, he is leaving no stone unturned to make the undertaking a success.

The Woodford Times, 1913

So the old Wanstead Kinema, opened in 1913 as 'The Wanstead Empire,' is to become a bowling alley.

Long-standing residents, particularly those who were once regular patrons — and perhaps even did a little courting in the double seats — may feel a twinge of regret at its passing. But at the same time their regrets may be warmed by the thought that the premises which have entertained so many local people will continue to do so — with a new look and a new form of amusement. For ten-pin bowling is a family sport that is gathering an ever increasing number of devotees in this country.

One of the former owners of the Wanstead Kinema was Mr. Frank Warman, a local builder, who bought the premises in 1919.

Mr. Warman died in 1951, but Mrs. Beatrice Warman, his wife, now in her seventies, still lives at Station Approach, Snaresbrook.

And this week she recalled the days when she and her husband owned and operated the Kinema (then the Wanstead Empire). Mr. and Mrs. Warman retained the Kinema until 1928, and over the years made many changes and alterations to the building itself.

'When we had the run of the place it seemed to go well, but after we left it changed hands many times,' said Mrs. Warman.

In those days the charges for admission were 1s. 3d., 1s., 8d. and 5d. 'We always got good-class people to our shows and some people would come from as far as Abridge,' said Mrs. Warman.

Chigwell Times, January 13, 1961

A hundred years ago the old village baker's shop once stood next to the George and Dragon, alongside the village lock-up and the George café. In 1913 a small moving picture hall was built behind the shops to cater for the new phenomenon of silent films.

Further along the High Street on the east side lies The Mall — a group of five early eighteenth century houses. The Mall House stands on the left in the picture *above* with Stone Hall next to it,

Mount Pleasant on the right, and then Manor House and Sheridan House. Of these only the Manor House *(below)* survives intact today as the West Essex Conservative Club.

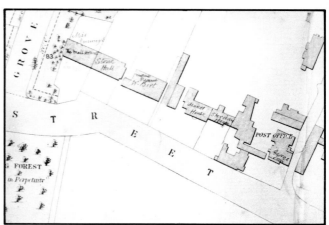

All were of great artistic and historical merit, Stone Hall being included in 'The Monuments of Central and South-west Essex'. Thus lovers of old Wanstead were not a little aghast when permission was given for a row of nondescript shops to be erected in the front gardens. As Winnifred Eastment,

renowned local historian, commented: 'It is beyond comprehension that the local authority did not ensure permanent preservation of these architectural gems by acquiring them the moment they came on the market'. This picture tells the story with the remains of Mount Pleasant behind.

The view from afar — from Church Green with The Mall House peeping through the trees.

Woodbine Place alongside Church Green now in the centre of the Wanstead Village Conservation Area introduced in 1970.

The High Street 1894. Memories of days long gone — the Old Tuck Shop.

The Clock House, the former home of Captain, later Lord Kindersley of National Savings fame, in the High Street was one of the last of the big old mansions to be pulled down. Now replaced by Clock House Parade.

'Masons' Corner' 1907-1985 RIP. The famous bicycle shop which gave its name to the junction closed in July 1985.

Before we leave Wanstead mention must be made of the Swiss Cottage, a picturesque timber building dating from around 1850 which stood in the corner of the garden of Lake House. When the Lake House Estate was built earlier this century the chalet remained tucked away in Bushwood. In 1962 the Metropolitan Police selected the site, including No. 26 Belgrave Road, for a multi-storey accommodation block for police cadets from Hendon Police College. As the police do not have to submit to local planning permission, the development went ahead in spite of protests from local residents; the 100-year-old wooden chalet effectively steam-rollered by the Government into oblivion. The aerial picture on page 13 shows the location.

Wanstead tailpiece — both happy and sad. The 'Flats' have been the location of a remarkable contrast of events. From George III (1760-1820) reviewing his troops paraded for inspection, through the mass meetings of the enclosure campaign in the 1870s, to the transit camp for troops being concentrated for the D-Day invasion. The military presence in June 1944 was in addition to the permanent gun site near Herongate Road. On August 15 a flying bomb crashed there, killing three servicemen and injuring two, bringing the Flats well and truly into the front line. Another was killed and three more injured when a V2 landed nearby on October 9. The US Signal Corps sent their own man down to take these pictures.

I returned to my office after an incident near the Wanstead Golf Course and settled into a chair for a snooze. I had been asleep for about an hour when I was awakened by the roar of an approaching V1 and moved to a corner of the room away from the window. The bomb passed over and, almost immediately, the engine cut out and I had the feeling of being suspended in space as I waited for the explosion. It came, a resounding b o o m, after the usual ten second pause and not very far off. I put on my dusty old cap and buttoned up my tunic as I waited for the call from the Area Control.

'V1 explosion in Blake Hall Crescent, Wanstead, sir. Your car has been ordered.'

Oh God; here we go again. What frightful scenes should we encounter this time? We had become accustomed to rows of shattered houses and shops and the back street factory with a dozen girls entombed; to the heart-rending cries of the bereaved and to children screaming for their parents; to the torn and hideously mangled bodies to be recovered from debris; and to the little corner shop, a heap of ruins, with customers slashed by flying glass, laying amid bundles of firewood and tins of corned beef.

I asked my driver if she knew where we were going. Yes, she knew, and we were there in a few minutes. All the trees in the vicinity had been defoliated by the explosion and the

pungent smell of chlorophyll mingled with the musty odour of mortar and other dusts. Only the stench of blood was missing, something, at least, to be thankful for. A number of houses had been demolished and women and children were being removed from the debris.

As we toiled, several V1s roared across the sky and there came a chorus of 'Seig Heil! Seig Heil! from hundreds of German throats in the P.O.W. camp, a few hundred yards along the road. How I prayed for one of them to come down smack in the centre of that compound but my prayer went unanswered and the bombs flew on, to crash in Poplar or Stepney or points west.

The houses in Blake Hall Crescent lay in a

A second rocket exploded harmlessly on the Flats on November 1. The hutted camp used to house homeless after the war was demolished together with the other wartime installations and the area reinstated by 1964.

The happier side — Bank Holidays on the Flats. Both pictures show the Whitsun fair: *above* **in 1929 and** *below* **in 1985.**

hollow which restricted the area of blast. Casualties, relatively, were light and we were able to clear up rather more quickly than usual and make our way home. There was no knowing where or when the next buzz-bomb would dive.

The P.O.W. camp came near to disaster about a week later, when a flying bomb crashed on the anti-aircraft rocket installation on the opposite side of Woodford Road,

killing a number of gunners and A.T.S. girls. The blast set fire to dry grass on the site and it was by a narrow margin only that the N.F.S. stopped the fire before it reached the magazines, crude corrugated-iron sheds, with openings screened with hessian curtains protecting the rockets laid out on racks.

It was a close shave.

The London Blitz, Cyril Demarne, 1980

A young boy found an unexploded hand grenade on Wanstead Flats last Thursday. Firemen were on hand attending a grass fire near the junction of Lakehouse Road and Dames Road.

The child was exploring the charred area when he found the grenade, which had no pin.

Police say the grenade was dated 1911 and that the spot where it was found was a former prisoner of war camp. Roads were blocked off for more than an hour.

Woodford Guardian, September 1976

Woodford

Previous pages: Lincoln House was built around the 1860s on the western side of the High Road at South Woodford. The entrance with its pillars and lamps can be seen mid-way along the brick wall in the picture *above* taken by Woodford's renowned photographic chronicler, Francis George Emler, in 1901. *Right:* Occupied by the well respected Bianchi family, after her husband died, Mrs Bianchi moved out to a smaller property (8 Chelmsford Road) while her son Antonio took the house over. He left in 1921 to go to Broomhill Road and thereafter Lincoln House remained empty save for a caretaker. It was only used occasionally for committee meetings at election times and, although the house had survived the cutting of Grove Road (see pages 118-119), it was demolished in 1931 to make way for the Lincoln House Estate. *Below:* This in turn suffered from the building of the new ten-lane viaduct in the mid-1970s yet one building has managed to survive to make a convenient point of similarity. (Francis Emler died on November 29, 1928 in Whipps Cross Hospital after a long illness and was buried at Chingford Mount Cemetery. His work lives on.)

The George Hotel with Bayfords, the sadlers, next door. The row of houses was demolished prior to the building of the 'super cinema to seat 2,000 persons' which opened in 1935.

About the year 1629, and the eighty-fourth of his age, George Herbert was seized with a sharp quotidian ague, and thought to remove it by change of air, to which end he went to Woodford in Essex, led out thither more chiefly to enjoy the company of his beloved brother Sir Henry Herbert and other friends then of that family. In his house he remained about twelve months, and there became his own physician.

Izaack Walton, 1593-1683

Afternoon Dances
At Majestic Ballroom

In addition to the usual Saturday dances, the management of the Majestic Ballroom, South Woodford, announce that a series of afternoon dances will in future be held every Thursday from 3.0 to 7 p.m. The popular Romany Serenaders Band will provide the music.

Express and Independent, November 23, 1940

The Grove, also called Grove Hall or Woodford Grove, on the opposite side of the road could trace its origins back to the seventeenth century. Sir Peter Eaton built Grove Hall in 1701 and the impressive front gates bore his coat of arms. When he died in 1729 the estate passed to his son Peter and when he died in 1769 to a cousin. The house was rented to various tenants between 1777 and 1854 when the property found a new owner, Mr Washington Single. It was he who converted the building into two separate dwellings: Grove Hall and The Grove. Between the wars the property remained empty although the London North Eastern Railway company took over part during the Second World War. The years of neglect had taken their toll and in a dilapidated condition, it was finally demolished in 1958 and by 1963 the site had been redeveloped with the construction of an office block for Fenchurch Insurance.

Facing Grove Hall on the eastern side standing in its own secluded grounds lay Grove Lodge (618 on map) dating from 1835. The London General Omnibus Company wanted to purchase and demolish it in the 1920s to build a bus garage but instead it was taken over by the County of London Electric

Supply Company. In 1924 Electric Parade was built in its front garden and, although still owned by the London Electricity Board, it fell into decay and came close to demolition before being listed as a Grade II building of special historical interest in June 1976. It can be found hidden away behind the shops.

To all constables and officers. Marie Stanhop, Thomas and Richard, hir sonnes, Elizabeth, Alice and Phillippa hir daughters were openly whipped at Woodford in the countie of Essex, the 7th Day of June, 1661, for wandering Rogues according to Law, and are assigned to passes forthwith from Parish to Parish by the officers thereof, the next direct way to Norringham neere the Bishopricke of Durham, where they confesse they were borne and dwelled last, and they are limited to be at Norringham afore-said within five weekes now next ensueing at their perille, given under the handes of the Minister, Churchwarden and Constables of ye said Parish of Woodford.

Parish Records, Woodford, 1661

NAPIER ARMS TAVERN, WOODFORD

PIGEON AND STARLING SHOOTING. At Mr R. Patrick's, on Thursday next, Aug 15, a grand day's sport will take place for a fine fat calf, by 26 members, at 10s each, 5 pigeons each, from 5 traps, handicapped, double guns, the use of both barrels, 1¼oz of shot. Afterwards a gold watch will be shot for by 20 members, at 10s each, seven starlings, on the same conditions as the above. S. Hammond, of 31, Kent-street, Borough, has received orders to attend with 40 dozen of his dashing blue rock pigeons, and 20 dozen of swift starlings, for all comers. The sports will commence at 1 sharp.

Press report, 1728

On Sunday Morning died at Woodford in Essex, Mr. Webb, formerly an eminent Colourman in Wapping, but having acquir'd a plentiful Fortune, retir'd from Business, that he might enjoy the Pleasures of a contemplative Life.

Press report, 1743

On Thursday was married at Woodford in Essex, Mr. Robert Foster, an eminent Shipbuilder, in Partnership with his Father, at Shadwell Dock (a young Gentleman in the highest Esteem among all his Friends and Acquaintance) to Miss Ridge, of Woodford; a young Lady endowed with all those Qualifications that can possibly render the Marriage State happy, with it Fortune of 10,000 l.

Press report, 1755

Last week three persons were bit by a mad cat at Woodford in Essex. They were sent to be dipped in sea water.

Press report, 1760

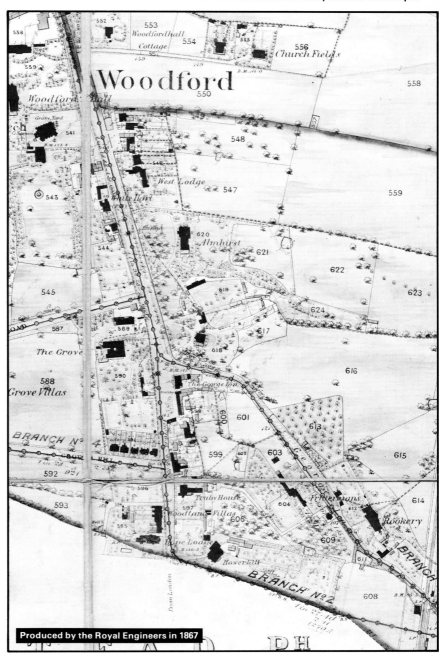

Produced by the Royal Engineers in 1867

189

Above: **A few hundred yards to the south stood Glebelands (called Bowerhill on the map on page 189), the estate straddling the Wanstead-Woodford parish boundary. In 1853 it was purchased by Robert Barclay of Knotts Green, Leyton, and his daughter Ann and her husband Henry Fowler settled there. The house was enlarged shortly afterwards by the addition of the wing on the right. The people of Woodford owed much to the Fowler family. His second son, Gurney Fowler, served on the Woodford Urban District Council at the turn of the century, the very time that improvements to the Council's roads were deemed a necessity. As the various methods of resurfacing were then only at the experimental stage, Gurney Fowler had a stretch of Woodford High Road resurfaced at his own expense in order that the Council might judge its suitability before embarking on a major scheme. On his death, Glebelands was sold and demolished about 1920 for building the estate which now takes its name.** *Right:* **The line of Glebelands Avenue just missed the coach house which was retained as a private dwelling. However** for years after the Second World War it lay derelict *(below left)* with the grounds overgrown. In 1976 it became a listed building and work to restore and convert it into the Glebelands Rest Home was completed in October 1982 *(below right).*

Just to the north lay Truby House with its magnificent cedar tree, the property first being occupied by Thomas Maitland under a lease from the Earl of Mornington dated 1775. During later years it became a school and Richard Truby, the then-owner who gave it his name, added the wing on the right about 1820 for the accommodation of his scholars. With the great expansion of Woodford which began in the late 1920s, the Woodford Council scheduled it under their Town Planning Scheme as being a suitable site for shops. With the urbanisation of the area (some 2,000 dwellings being added just before the new decade began), the Council wanted to build 'parades' of shops — the 1930 version of the shopping centre — along the main roads to avoid haphazard side development and to build up the commercial side as most people in those days travelled to Leyton and Walthamstow to do their shopping. In 1931 the property was sold; the cedar tree was chopped down in December and the foundations of Woodford Parade rose from the ashes in the early months of 1932.

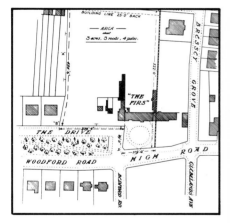

Below: **Development nearby — The Firs demolished to build Malford Court.**

191

Another family whose name is closely bound up in the history of Woodford is that of the Godfreys. Their Rookery estate lay on the east side of the High Road, Michael Godfrey, the first Deputy Governor of the Bank of England, inheriting the property when his father (also Michael) died in 1689. When he was killed at Namur in 1695 his brother Peter, another director of the Bank, took over. On Peter's death in 1724 it passed to his third son (Peter) who left the estate to his brother Thomas in 1769. It was he that had the tall Corinthian column erected on the family vault in St Mary's Churchyard in 1771. In 1804 the family sold the property to another London banker, George Smith, but not long afterwards he had resold it to John Hanson. He demolished the old house but retained the kitchens which he converted into cottages complete with grandiose crenellations — Woodford's very own castle (top). However the coming of the railway in 1856 ruined the

estate as the line cut the grounds in two and completely spoiled its seclusion (see map page 189). The property then passed through several hands before being sub-divided into building plots in 1870 for housing. A network of roads named after flowers — Maybank, Daisy, Violet, Cowslip, Primrose — was laid down, the old Rookery demolished, and a new house (above) erected about 1878. This later became the location of Woodford College, its headmaster, the Reverend G. A. Sweatman, former curate at St Mary's, living in one wing which had been converted into a separate house called Ellerby. Right: After the school moved to Grove Road (to the building which later became the Grove Hotel lost during the motorway development), the house fell into decay, the roof caved in, and by the 1920s was fit only for demolition. The Gas Light and Coke Company acquired the site which they redeveloped in 1930 into new offices and showrooms.

An exercise in preservation. With the growing awareness of the necessity to preserve our past, in 1971 the Town and Country Planning Act set out the requirements for the compilation of registers of all buildings of special historic or architectural interest. Generally speaking all buildings constructed before 1700 were automatically listed; most buildings between 1700 and 1840, and selected outstanding buildings erected between 1841 and 1939. Nos. 32 to 44 High Road date from the early eighteenth century and were listed Grade II in April 1973.

Although the buildings were demolished in 1980, exceptional lengths were gone to in order to preserve the façade intact, including the reaffixing of the plaque which proclaims 'Established in the Reign of George II' (1727-60). Although this was not an original fitment as proved by the contemporary picture, it nevertheless adds a nice touch of antiquity. The restoration earned a Civic Trust commendation in 1983.

Facing the Rookery estate on the south side of George Lane lay Frithmans, a property comprising two distinct buildings, the later part constructed around 1770. In the 1840s it was a school run by Elizabeth Arundale, one of her pupils being William Morris. In 1851 the widow of Dr Stephen Mackenzie moved in with her eight children (a ninth was on its way) following the tragic death of her husband earlier that year who had been thrown from his gig at Leytonstone. Mrs Mackenzie mitigated her financial predicament by running the school and one of her sons went on to become the noted Royal physician, Dr Morrell Mackenzie. At other stages in its history Frithmans became 'Federation House', a refuge for Belgians fleeing from the disorders in their country, and 'The Crêche' during its tenure by Sylvia Pankhurst for her work with refugee children.

Portions of the northern end of the estate had been released to the Congregationalists for the erection of their Early English-style church in 1886. This became the South Woodford United

Reformed Church in 1972 on amalgamation with the Presbyterians but, with dwindling congregations, the church was finally closed and demolished in March 1983.

South Woodford United Reform Church, which has stood on the triangle in George Lane since 1886, is to close after services on Sunday, October 17.

The church found itself faced with the 'impossible' task of needing to raise more than £60,000 to put the buildings in good order.

Minister Leslie Fidgen explained: 'The membership is ageing; folk have moved away or died and to encourage newcomers to attend a vast building when numbers are small, is not a realistic proposition these days. Also, unfortunately increased vandalism of the buildings has created an almost impossible situation for the present membership to cope with.'

Special closing services of thanksgiving will be held on Sunday, October 17. Mr. Fidgen said the sale of the site will be used to extend the work of the United Reform Church elsewhere.

Guardian and Gazette. October 1982

Frithmans itself was demolished in two stages, the newer part first around 1926 with the old section going in 1931. The last owner was Mr F. P. Mills who had opened the South Woodford Cinema beside the church and he took the opportunity to enlarge and modernise in 1932 as the new Plaza.

William Morris was born at Elm House, Clay Hill, on 24th March 1834. When he was six, the family moved to Woodford Hall, a spacious Georgian mansion, which stood in fifty acres of park along the London to Epping road. The estate included about a hundred acres of farmland between the hall and the river Roding; only a fence separated the park from the Forest. Woodford Church was alongside, the churchyard being reached from the hall grounds by a private doorway. The old village pound and stocks stood on the green opposite. 'When we lived at Woodford,' Morris wrote to his daughter, fifty years later, 'there were stocks there on a little bit of wayside green in the middle of the village: beside them stood the cage, a small shanty some twelve feet square, and as it was built of brown brick roofed with blue slate, I suppose it had been quite recently in use, since its style was not earlier than the days of fat George. I remember I used to look at these two threats of law and order with considerable terror, and decidedly preferred to walk on the other side of the road; but I never heard of anybody being locked up in the cage or laid by the heels in the stocks. . . .'

At nine he was sent to a preparatory school in Walthamstow, kept by the Misses Arundale, and rode the two miles from his home to school on his pony. A year or two later the school was moved to George Lane, Woodford. Morris remained there until his father's death in 1847.

Epping Forest, William Addison, 1945

Although Sir Richard Child retained the manor of Woodford, he sold the hall and most of the remaining demesne lands to Christopher Crow, so that by 1838 only about eighty acres in Woodford remained as part of the Wanstead estate. Crow sold the hall to William Hunt in 1727, after obtaining a private Act of Parliament. The hall remained in the family until about 1801 when it was bought by John Maitland. In 1777 the hall, with fifty-six acres lying behind and a further ninety-two acres, had been leased to John Goddard, a Rotterdam merchant, whose widow died there in 1814. By 1820 Maitland himself had taken up residence. He inherited the manor of Loughton in 1825 and died at Woodford Hall in 1831. His son William Whitaker Maitland succeeded him and leased the hall first to William Cox, then, in 1840, to William Morris, father of William Morris the poet and craftsman. The Morris family remained there until 1848. In 1869 the Woodford Hall estate was sold to the British Land Company for building development. The house was used until 1900 as Mrs. Gladstone's convalescent home and part of it still remains to be seen today behind the parish church Memorial Hall which was built in front of the site in 1902.

The Victoria History of the County of Essex, Volume VI, 1973

A parade of shops was erected on the land made available by the demolition of the house and thus the aspect of George Lane was fixed for the following forty years. In 1978 the Plaza finally succumbed to the inroads television had made on the cinema and history turned full circle with the redevelopment of the Frithmans site once again to cater for the changes in shopping habits of the 1980s. Even the drinking fountain, provided by Miss E L. Fowler (of Glebelands) in 1899 'for the benefit of humans and animals' and hailed as being of 'attractive design and a pleasing amenity to the district' has disappeared.

Woodford Hall lying next to St Margaret's had been acquired by Sir Richard Child (of Wanstead House fame) in 1710 when he purchased the manor and incorporated it into the Wanstead estate. After Sir Richard sold the Hall it later passed to the Maitland family of Loughton (see page 318). Its most notable tenant was William Morris who attended the Arundale School in George Lane.

Little of historical value was sacrosanct to the Victorians and the bulk of the Hall was demolished in 1900. A small part of one wing remains in Buckingham Road converted into a private house called Chapel le Frith.

The church, dedicated to St. Margaret, was erected in 1817, on the site of the former ancient building, at an expense of nearly £9,000, defrayed partly by subscription, and partly by rates. It is situated on the lowest part of the village, on the west side of the London road, and is an elegant edifice, in the ancient style of English architecture, with a square embattled tower; the nave separated from the aisles by six pointed arches, carried up to the roof, which is of open wood-work, supported by eight pillars, and surmounted in the centre by an octangular lantern tower. The east window is of stained glass, divided into three compartments, containing figures of our Saviour, the four Evangelists, and St. Peter and St. Paul.

The History and Topography of the County of Essex, March 1831

Fire investigated: Detectives were investigating last night the cause of a fire which badly damaged St. Mary's Church, Salway Hill, Woodford. More than 50 firemen fought the blaze which was discovered by the Rev. Robert Birchnell, the rector, shortly before the evening service. It damaged most of the roof of the seventeenth-century church.

The Times, February 10, 1969

For centuries man has dreamed of a time machine to take him into the future or past. West Essex Archaeological Group have a very simple time machine for taking them into the past — they call it a shovel.

This week their digging has taken them back to before 1693 in the heart of South Woodford, at the parish church. Members are using the tragedy of the fire which gutted St. Mary's Church in the High Road 18 months ago as a chance to find out more about the medieval church which preceded it.

They are busily digging in the nave arcade and have already worked down to find the 1693 floor level. Below this main floor level they have found traces of another floor dating from when the aisle was built, about 1600. There are several earlier chalk floors beneath this.

On their way back through time they uncovered the foundations of the now burnt-out 19th century church, and a brick vault built in 1816.

In the vault were five coffins, three of lead and two of wood, dating from the 18th century.

The Independent, August 7, 1970

The new church was rededicated in June 1972. Only about 60 burial sites are now marked.

The fire of 1969 which left only the four walls and tower of the parish church standing gave the West Essex Archaeologists Group a unique opportunity to investigate the earlier structural history of St. Mary's (formerly St. Margaret's). During the work of rebuilding the church, the graveyard was landscaped necessitating the removal of 240 headstones and tombs. The Godfrey monument was retained. (See also page 34.)

196

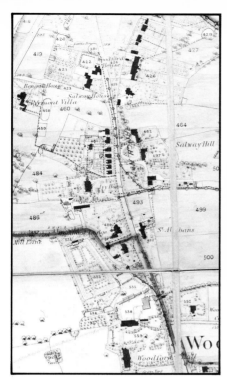

On the east side of Salway Hill lay Salway Lodge, both of which took the name from Richard Salway, banker and merchant, who lived there in the eighteenth century. The property passed through several hands, notably Sir Peter Mallard, JP, in 1832; Joseph Dent, the publisher, in 1910, and Mr. J. Lusty, the soup manufacturer, in the 1920s. It saw service in both world wars, becoming, it is believed, No. 39 Squadron headquarters (part of No. 49 Wing, Royal Flying Corps) during the First and occupied by the Royal Air Force in the Second.

The coach house in the hollow had once been the quarters for one of Sir John Fielding's horse patrols (see page 76): in fact with the police station right on his doorstep, Sir Peter often held court from his front window!

MORE NEW HOUSES
PLANS APPROVED BY WOODFORD COUNCIL

At last Tuesday's meeting of the Woodford Council, among the Building Committee recommendations was one for 52 new houses in Arlington Road and Marlborough Avenue on the Salway Hill Estate, and another for a shop and flats on Salway Hill. Other building applications approved had reference to one house in Park Avenue, four houses in Mayfair Gardens, and two houses in Monkhams Avenue, and various alterations and additions.

The Woodford Times, January 23, 1931

After the war all was demolished and replaced by the flats of the same name.

The vast majority of old Woodford has now been lost — one moment it was there, the next it was gone. All these old timbered buildings stood within a few hundred yards of each other on the High Road at South Woodford right up until the 1950s. It was not as if people were uncaring — only that the scales fell from their eyes too late. Is it significant that in each case the culprit has been the motor car?

The parish of Woodford contains within its bounds some 2,150 acres. It is a village of scattered mansions, nearly all standing in their own grounds. It comprises no regular High Street, and scarcely a row of shops. In 1821 the population was 2,700, which number had increased in 1871 to 4,600, and this again during the next ten years to upwards of 7,100. Woodford has two stations on the Epping and Ongar branch of the Great Eastern Railway, about a mile apart: one at George Lane, for Church End; and the other further eastward, in Snake's Lane, for Woodford Green and Woodford Bridge.

Greater London, Edward Walford, 1883

In its Jubilee Year I send the Borough of Wanstead and Woodford my heartfelt congratulations on a quarter-of-a-century of solid achievement. The past twenty-five years have seen some of the most stirring events in the history of our famous land, and the changes around us have been striking both on a great and a lesser scale.

Here in Essex, in our local scene, our population has grown so much, that what was only one thinly-populated constituency is now represented in Parliament by no less than three Members. The Borough of Wanstead and Woodford and its administrators can look back with satisfaction over a quarter-of-a-century of advance.

We have all been through much together, and I am honoured to have represented you in Parliament for so long. You have all shown a kindness and a support to my wife and myself through the years of war and peace that have been a joy, a comfort and a source of strength. We are both very proud to be Freemen of this great Borough. Long may it prosper in peace and happiness.

Sir Winston Churchill,
Silver Jubilee Message, September, 1962

However all is not lost. When Alf and Charlie Jessop had their carriage works on the spot where Gates service garage now stands, Mr Wilberforce Garman had his dental practice in Homeleigh next door. Then it was No. 111 but now it is No. 140.

A late eighteenth century Grade II building, when Gates purchased it for office development they were obliged to preserve the building which has largely been reconstructed inside while retaining a similar exterior appearance.

Hurst House, also known as the Naked Beauty, has long been a landmark overlooking the Green. It dates from around 1714 having been built by a brewer Henry Raine.

On Friday a disastrous fire caused irreparable damage to Hurst House, one of Woodford's oldest buildings. The house was built in 1714, and many of the rooms are pine panelled, and there is a fine carved oak staircase and marble flagstoned hall.

At 9.10 on Friday morning the owner occupier, Mr. S. A. Scoffin, together with Mrs. Scoffin and their small son, left the house by car. A few minutes before 10 o'clock the domestic staff were roused by the continuous ringing of an electric bell in the kitchen, the indicator pointing to bedroom No. 1. They ran upstairs, only to find that the nursery and part of bedroom No. 1 were in flames.

The old pine panelling burned with amazing rapidity. The fire brigade immediately arrived and did everything in their power, but the whole top floor was in an incredibly short space of time a mass of flames, and the whole of the bedrooms on the first floor were soon involved. The flames spread to the top storey of the house, the first floor and top storey being almost gutted and the contents reduced to a mass of charred wood. A valuable oil painting on the staircase was destroyed, and great damage was caused by the enormous amount of water . . .

Stratford Express, November 28, 1936

From 1819-28 it was a school under the name of Woodford House It underwent alterations during the tenure of Edward Rider Cook in 1881 but had become dilapidated by 1929 when purchased by Mr S. A. Scoffin. He spent much time and money on restoring it to its original grandeur only to have the house gutted by fire in November 1936. It became a Grade II* listed building in 1954 and has recently been renovated by Mr and Mrs F. R. M. Williams.

Another notable preservation: Brian Watson's reconstruction of Thomas Kendon's butcher's shop in Johnson Road in 1977.

Woodford includes the four districts of Old Woodford (or Church End, as it is popularly called), Woodford Green, Woodford Wells, and Woodford Bridge. Of these, the three first lie, in the order above named, along the high road from London to Epping. They are all remarkable for the broad belts or tracts of open woodland which skirt the road on either side, compelling the houses for the most part to retreat gracefully from the dusty highway.

Greater London, Edward Walford, 1883

JOHNSTON'S POND

Sir,— H. Gordon Kaye's letter greatly interested me. I well remember my father telling me Johnston's Pond was a gift and should not be filled in or enclosed. The water was free to all-comers, and in his young days was the chief source of supply to Woodford Wells. I believe part of the old platform still remains near the path from where the water was dipped. There were good fish in the pond; I have caught some good carp and roach there. I wonder how many still retain common rights? It would be interesting to know.

A. Read Wilkinson
The Woodford Times, February 26, 1940

WOODFORD AND ITS GREENS

Sir,— I was very interested in your recent leading article on the above subject, and I am sure that all residents of Woodford should be very grateful to the Council for the efforts they are making to preserve the freshness of our various greens. Ugly tracks are quickly made by thoughtless people. There are plenty of properly constructed paths, and the time saved by cutting across the grass from one to another surely must be infinitesimal, and not worth the ensuing damage. This week I am

The 'Men's Club' pond in front of the old Wesleyian chapel, converted for non-secular purposes in 1904. Also known as the Potato Pond, it received a thorough springclean in 1983 by unemployed youth working on community projects under the Manpower Services Commission.

glad to see that the terribly ugly patch by the Men's Club Pond is being dug over, presumably with a view to the sowing of grass seed. I was more than sorry to see, however, people making their way across this patch in spite of the restraining hurdles. I have no doubt that this was force of habit, and perhaps they will remember in future. I am

sure we do not want our lovely Green enclosed with posts and rails like the open spaces in the inner suburbs are.

I am, Sir,
Yours faithfully,
COLONEL H. JOLLY, T.D., D.L.

The Woodford Times, January 23, 1931

On the western side of Woodford's Greens lay the manor of Higham Bensted, part of the parish of Walthamstow, an area noted for its fine countryside. Its boundary with Woodford, perpetuated in those of the present day London Boroughs of Waltham Forest and Redbridge, ran almost through the manor house of Higham Hall. With the expansion of housing in Walthamstow which gained momentum in the 1870s, open land was at a premium and within twenty years encroachments were being made on the estate as parcels were sold off for redevelopment. In 1891 thirty acres, including the Fish Pond, were purchased for £6,000 from Mr Courtenay Warner and added to Epping Forest as Highams Park. The last occupant of the house was Dr Jacobs, Bishop of St Albans who left in 1914. During the First World War the building was used as a temporary hospital and in 1919 purchased by Essex County Council to become Woodford County High School for Girls.

In 1768 Anthony Bacon built a new brick and stone manor-house designed by William Newton (1735-90) at Higham Bushes on the Woodford boundary. It was at first called Higham Hill, but later Higham House, Higham Hall, or Highams. The five-bay central block had two storeys and a semi-basement, fully exposed by the falling ground on the west side, and was flanked by single-storey wings, each terminating in a pedimented feature. The three central bays on the east front were divided by giant pilasters and surmounted by a pediment; the entrance doorway was approached by a double flight of steps. In 1785-90 William Hornby removed the pediment to add a balustraded third storey and a central cupola. Thus Humphry Repton, commissioned by John Harman in 1793-4 to improve the property, criticized the house as 'extravagantly lofty'. To reduce the apparent height of the west front he designed the present continuous iron balcony to the ground floor rooms, supported on stucco arches forming an arcade in front of the basement windows. The lake created by Repton is now part of Highams Park.

In the 19th century, perhaps when Edward Warner acquired the property in 1849, two extra bays were added at the south end of the west front with a matching extension of Repton's balcony. The addition contained a new drawing room and had full-height bow windows facing south. Probably at the same time the ground level at the centre of the east front was raised, the entrance steps were removed, a porch was added, and the basement windows in the flanking wings were altered. At an earlier period the roof cupola had been replaced by a wider lantern.

Victoria History of the County of Essex,
Volume VI, 1973

WOODFORD'S STATELY AVENUE

There will be general regret felt in the district that it has been considered necessary in the interests of public safety to remove seven of the beautiful Italian poplars from the north end of the Avenue facing Broomhill Road, Woodford Green, which adds so much to the beauty of this part of Woodford. It will be remembered that a year or two ago several gaps were made in the Avenue during a very high wind, and there was much discussion at the time as to what could be done to prevent the remaining trees from sharing a similar fate. Nothing, however, has been done.

Early this week great surprise and consternation was caused when the Forest Authorities, acting on representations from the Woodford Urban District Council, sent a gang of woodcutters to cut down the trees. So expeditiously did they work, that by Wednesday evening the seven remaining trees nearest Broomhill Road, between Snakes Lane and the Terrace, were levelled to the ground. There were originally nine trees here, but two were blown down in the last heavy gale.

We understand that it is not proposed to take down any of the other trees in the Avenue, and that those that have been removed would not have been touched but for the danger to passing traffic along the road in the event of the trees or some of the heavy limbs blowing down in a gale.

The Woodford Times, February 10, 1933

SIR, As you are aware, a vast majority of local residents and, I should imagine, many others are shocked and horrified by the decision to destroy our beautiful avenue of poplars . . . the usual reason for cutting down beautiful trees is given — they are dangerous.

Of course they are. So are scores of other things like electric appliances, domestic fires, kitchen steps, ladders, boilers and roofing tiles, not to mention cars and aeroplanes.

No doubt some are more dangerous than others, but nobody would think of suggesting that they should be done away with because of a million to one chance that somebody might get hurt.

We who live in this particular part and are constantly walking through the avenue are the people most likely to suffer injury from falling trees or branches, but I think I can safely say that about 99 per cent of us — if not all of us — would rather run this remote risk than lose our lovely trees.

We should like to be satisfied that the decision was supported by more than one outside and really capable opinion — not only the opinion of people whose job it is to cut down trees.

I should have thought that with skilful forestry it ought to be possible to minimise any immediate danger by judicious lopping or other means, and if absolutely necessary a few trees at a time might be felled and replaced by planting, this process being spread over a number of years.

And has the possibility of transplanting at least a proportion of mature trees been considered?

Of course, so far as the present generation are concerned, replanting the whole avenue with young trees is only of the remotest interest, as it would be many years before anything approaching the beauty of the fine old poplars could be obtained.

And now we have this ridiculous wire fence to clamber through every time we walk across the Green.

I wonder how much it cost? My little dog is the only one who appreciates it; he seems to regard it as especially set up for him.

Yours faithfully,
R. NORMAN

The Independent, October 7, 1966

It is sometimes quite amazing the way history repeats itself, the echoes of the 1930s being repeated a generation later.

Originally planted in 1880, odd specimens had had to be felled over the years when they became a danger to life and limb. A number were cut down in 1951 and, after the decision had been taken to completely replant The Avenue, the first three trees were removed on September 26, 1966. It was originally planned to complete the job in January 1967 but the bad weather of that winter delayed the job until the Spring, when the remaining 79 trees were felled.

They were replaced with alternate plantings of planes and black poplars on a slightly changed alignment.

WOODFORD'S NEW PUBLIC HALL

Woodford now possesses a public hall of which it has every reason to be proud, and one which represents the last word in up-to-date refinement and efficiency. We refer, of course, to the new Wilfrid Lawson Hall, which was formally opened on Saturday last. Many were the congratulatory remarks heard among those who were present on that occasion, a report of which appears elsewhere in these columns.

A few particulars concerning the new hall may not be out of place at this juncture. It was on June 8th last that the work of reconstructing the old hall was put in hand by the contractors, Messrs W. M. Brand, of Stamford Hill, the completion of the new hall being scheduled for the first week in October. Friday last saw the building sufficiently complete for the Woodford Wells Amateur Dramatic Society to give its first performance of the season there — a highly creditable achievement, when it is remembered that unexpected and well-nigh insuperable difficulties were encountered and had to be overcome.

It can with confidence be affirmed that there is no hall within a radius of some miles which can compare with it for its all-round usefulness, comprehensive equipment and pleasant style. Every possible requirement seems to have been anticipated, and there is

no doubt that skilled workmanship, the most up-to-date appliances and best-procurable materials all play their part in the construction of this very attractive hall.

The total seating accommodation, with comfortable, tip-up regulation seats, is 307-230 in the body of the hall and 77 in the airy gallery. Further seating can be provided if necessary. The aisles are roomy, and this space is not encroached upon by unsightly heating apparatus. Radiators recessed artistically in the walls on either side supply steady warmth, and an adequate ventilation system has been installed.

Overhead the rooms of the hotel have been renovated, and the added length of the hall enabled an additional three rooms to be provided. Throughout hot and cold water is installed and hot-water radiators fitted. There is also a new bathroom on this floor, fitted with every labour-saving device, including heated towel rail. An efficient emergency exit leads down to the hotel yard, by means of a strongly constructed iron staircase.

We understand that the total cost of the work exceeds £6,000, and there is no doubt that every penny has been spent to the very best advantage.

A word of congratulations is due to the directors of the Wilfrid Lawson Hotel, Limited, for their courageous enterprise, and to the architect, Mr. R. W. Lone, A.R.B.A., P.A.S.I., M.R.San.I., who has accomplished wonders considering the limitations which the site imposed.

The Woodford Times, October 14, 1932

Two controversies on either side of the Green: trees in the 1960s and a building in the 1970s. The Wilfrid Lawson Temperance Hotel (see also page 35) which had been constructed for a sum of around £6,000 in 1883, had outlived its 'dry' image by the 1930s when it became Woodford's public meeting place. It was badly damaged by a mine in 1941 and in 1950 was sold to the National Health Service which converted it into a training centre for nurses. It served in this role from 1951 until the North East Metropolitan Hospital Board sold it at public auction in March 1972 for £93,000. Two years later it was demolished and, amid much speculation over malpractice, the site was not redeveloped until 1980.

Yesterday saw the seal set on the creation of the eleventh Borough within the administrative County of Essex. The amalgamated urban districts of Wanstead & Woodford have been invested with the civic dignity and powers of a municipal Borough, its Chief Citizen is the Charter Mayor, its Chief Executive Official is the Charter Town Clerk, and next month will bring the election of the members of the first Corporation, and the consequent appointment of aldermen.

Scenes of enthusiasm throughout the day marked the visit of His Royal Highness the Duke of Gloucester, K.G., K.T., bearer of the Charter of Incorporation. Last week-end there was regret and consternation when it was announced from Scotland that the Duchess, who was with the King and Queen at Balmoral, had had to cancel some engagements owing to indisposition. On Wednesday, however, came the glad tidings that she had recovered and would accompany the Duke to Woodford. then came the disappointing news that she was unable to be present.

The bells of the Woodford parish church began to chime a full peal. To their joyful tones leading figures in the county and district set forth from the Town Hall. . . .

At the boundary the Royal visitor was received by the Lord Lieutenant, who presented to him the dignitaries accompanying him.

The procession then re-formed, with the Duke and his Equerry at the rear, for the return to the Town Hall, and the ceremony of the presentation of the Charter.

The arrival of the Royal party at the dais for the ceremony of presentation was heralded by a fanfare by trumpeters of the Life Guards. Then came the offering of the official welcome to Wanstead and Woodford by the Charter Mayor.

'The need for public open spaces, so urgent a problem in many towns to-day, is here met by the beautiful stretches of forest land. 730 acres of which lie within your boundary. I understand also that the Council have provided for the public benefit some 50 acres of pleasure grounds and open spaces, which, with your other natural advantages, should ensure that Wanstead and Woodford will ever retain the attraction which has always made it so justly popular as a place of residence. . . . '

When the Duke of Gloucester left for the Ashton Playing Fields ceremony, there was another peal of bells from the parish church, and hearty cheering from the crowds of people, to whom the ceremony of the presentation of the Charter had been transmitted by means of loud-speakers.

The route to the Playing Fields was via High-road, Woodford, Woodford Green, Johnstone-road and Snakes-lane. All the way there were spectators to give a warm greeting to the Duke.

The main gates of the Ashton Playing Fields, created to provide an entrance to golden hours of happiness for youngsters from the humblest parts of London and nearby, were opened by the Duke of Gloucester with a golden key. With a similar key he opened the Pavilion which is to be used as a child welfare clinic and adult education school, and each ceremony was the occasion of an excited scene almost unprecedented in Woodford.

Made from wrought iron, the gates are emblazoned with the figures of two youths, one of whom plays tennis while the other handles a cricket bat, and they are a fitting symbol of the athletic prowess which will be made possible by the provision of the fields. The Pavilion is built on the best modern lines, and is a fitting place for what will be a new social experiment in Woodford.

Two trees to commemorate the occasion were planted in front of the Pavilion, the first by the Duke of Gloucester, and the second by Mr. Ramsay MacDonald, P.C., M.P.

Press report. October 14, 1937

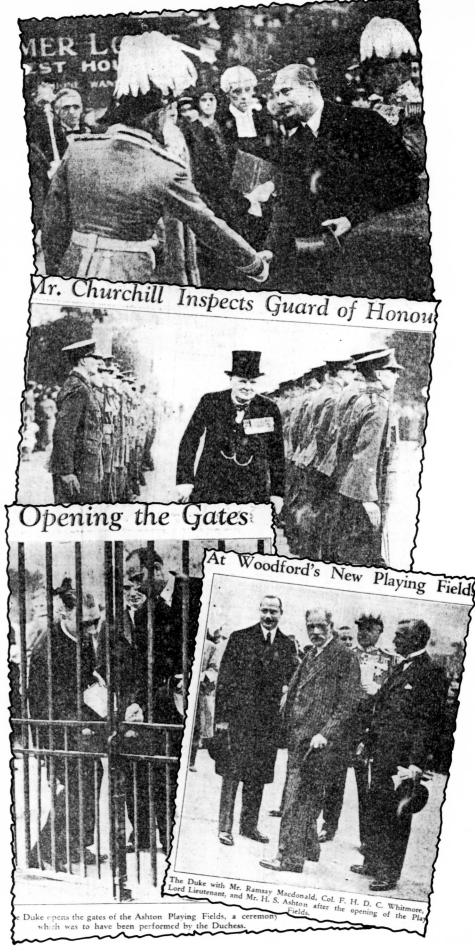

Mr. Churchill Inspects Guard of Honour

Opening the Gates

At Woodford's New Playing Fields

The Duke with Mr. Ramsay Macdonald, Col. F. H. D. C. Whitmore, Lord Lieutenant, and Mr. H. S. Ashton after the opening of the Playing Fields.

The Duke opens the gates of the Ashton Playing Fields, a ceremony which was to have been performed by the Duchess.

When His Majesty the King on Saturday visited Woodford Green to inspect a mass parade of Local Defence Volunteers — more popularly known as Parashots — he was challenged by a V.C. member of the L.D.V.s and asked to produce his identity card. Other members of the Royal party were similarly challenged.

His Majesty arrived at the Napier Arms, Woodford Green, shortly before three o'clock. There he was met by Platoon Commander Bramham and two motor-cyclist orderlies, who preceded the Royal party down Oak Hill and along Cottenham Road.

One dispatch rider was sent forward to inform the Lord Lieutenant of Essex, (Col. H. Whitmore, C.B., C.M.G., D.S.O.) at the White House of the arrival of the King in the grounds.

His Majesty was received at the entrance to the grounds by Lieutenant General Sir B. N. Sergison-Brooke, (G.O.C. London Command), the Commander London Area, L.D.V., and the local Zone Commander L.D.V.

The Royal party, proceeding along the drive, was stopped and challenged at a road block. Here amid the beautiful forest surroundings, armed L.D.V. guards were alert and ready.

Woodford prepares for war. Improvised sandbagged pillboxes were later replaced by concrete strongpoints built to a standard style by council employees or civilian contractors. This emplacement lies in the fork of the Woodford New Road and High Road on the Green. The spire is that of the Congregational Church, a casualty in 1944.

His Majesty, called upon to prove his identity, produced his identity card for inspection by Mr. Harold Kenny, V.C., attached to the Chingford section of the L.D.V.

The King entered the strong point at this spot and chatted for a few moments to Mr. Kenny. Asking him for details of the gallant exploit for which he was awarded the Victoria Cross, His Majesty recalled that as the Duke of York, he met Mr. Kenny at the Hackney Empire at a concert during the last war.

Having been allowed to pass the road block, the Royal party drove on to the White House, where the Lord Lieutenant was awaiting the King. . . .

The King and his party then walked through the rose garden to the High School grounds, where normal L.D.V. training and instruction were in progress. His Majesty showed keen interest in these activities, watching intently instruction with Bren and Lewis guns, musketry training, signalling, map reading, and ju-jitsu — at which the L.D.V.s exhibited a readiness and skill that boded ill for any parachutist. He saw the observer corps, factory guards, and a recruit squad in training. . . .

Paraded before the King when he took his place at the saluting base in the stand on the Rugby Ground were over two thousand L.D.V.s, serried ranks of men who have eagerly responded to the War Minister's call for volunteers to defend their country and their families against possible invaders, men of all ages, of all classes, men of one spirit and one loyalty. Theirs is a spare-time job. They are devoting most of their leisure time to it, at work on the job and in training themselves to do it to the utmost of their capacity. Their enthusiasm is enormous, their earnestness as great as their readiness to perfect themselves at their job. . . .

The parade having been reported 'present and correct' by the Zone Commander to the King, the Royal Salute was followed by the March Past — an impressive sight which will live long in the memories of those who took part and those who saw it.

Express and Independent, July 27, 1940

King George VI reviews the first parade of Local Defence Volunteers, forerunners of the Home Guard, at the football ground.

207

... Grove House was traditionally said to have been a hunting seat of the Earl of Essex — of Robert Devereux, I suppose, the favourite of Queen Elizabeth.

A portion of the north wall of this mansion still, I am informed, remaining bears a shield, sculptured in stone, and charged with the inscription I.L.B. 1580. These initials, together with the arms of the Companies of Merchant-Adventurers and Grocers, which will be subsequently noticed, seem to show it was rather built for the country villa of a wealthy citizen. It had, among several others, three apartments, one distinguished by the traditional or perhaps fanciful appellation of the ballroom: another by that of the banqueting room: a third, from its wainscoted walls, the oaken chamber. The ballroom was a long gallery. On that part of the walls of this room, which united at an angle with the ceiling, were, in twelve compartments, as many subjects of rural life painted in fresco. Six of these paintings remained tolerably perfect; while the others exhibited only a few traces of their former existence, or were obliterated by a coat of whitewash, with which the whole in modern days had been covered, owing to the following remarkable circumstances. The old mansion had been occupied as a school, and the master had made this spacious gallery the dormitory of his scholars. When the children went to bed by twilight in the long summer evenings, the figures on the walls so disturbed their infant imaginations that they could not settle themselves to repose. The pedagogue was no antiquary, and the phantoms were exorcised by the plasterer's brush. In the course of subsequent years the crazy mansion was left empty and abandoned, the whitewash peeled from the walls, and the shadows in German fresco again made their appearance. What remained perfect of these limnings has been preserved by a young lady of taste.

Gentleman's Magazine, May 1833

Of all the damage inflicted on Woodford during the war, the most serious, from the historical standpoint, was the total destruction of Essex House [formerly Grove House, Woodford] by flying bombs in 1944. This ancient building, standing in Broomhill Road, a short distance from the western end of Snakes Lane, was much restored and altered, but had many claims to the attention of those historically interested, for incorporated in its fabric were portions, components and relics of older buildings, as well as memorials of former owners or residents. These features, dating from the

In 1580 John Lambert, a London grocer, built Grove House on the east side of the Green (see map page 197). It was famous for its frescoes but these were obliterated by Richard Truby before he moved his school to Truby House (see page 191) in 1811.

In 1832 all but the one wing was demolished and Essex House rose on the foundations of the old cellars. The new building continued the tradition of education with the formation of the Essex House School which only came to an end in 1914 when the German principals were obliged to return to the Fatherland. It was then sold to John Wyles of Wanstead who converted the property into four separate dwellings. The original Grove House wing stands on the left.

The road on which it stood became known as Broomhill Lane, later, probably when it was made up, it became Broomhill Road. Here beside Essex House on the corner of Snakes Lane was built Eagle House, in latter days the location of the Woodford Nursing Association.

On the south side of the Grove/Essex House site lay the Congregational Church built in 1837. A flying bomb exploded between the church and Essex House on June 26, 1944, severely damaging both buildings and killing Mr William Day, his wife, and their son Victor who were sitting in his lorry outside the church. Three days later a second VI completed the destruction and all three buildings had to be demolished after the war.

sixteenth century onwards, made the house a link with past Woodford and carried down to the present day memories of a place differing entirely from the one we know.

Essex House, L. Robinson, 1946

Wrecked by Flying Bombs in June, 1944, the Woodford Green Congregational Church has remained derelict ever since and is now likely to be demolished according to information obtained this week to the effect that the church is not to be rebuilt, the church membership being now merged in the Woodford Union Church.

The Woodford Times, August 9, 1946

Sir Winston Churchill has every hope that he will continue as member for the Woodford Division. This was the indication of his future he gave to more than 500 of his constituents when he opened the new Sir James Hawkey Hall in Broomhill-road, Woodford Green, on Saturday afternoon.

Crowds gathered outside the hall to welcome Sir Winston as his car drew up behind the Mayor's car. Ald. Mrs. E. F. M. Hollis handed him the key to the hall. Turning to the crowd, Sir Winston waved the key above his head before approaching the front door.

Inside, Mrs. Hollis, wearing the Mayoral robes, welcomed Sir Winston on the spacious stage of the new hall. She said that representatives of many organisations within the borough had been invited to the opening. 'Before we reached this stage,' she said, 'we had our disappointments, with differences of opinion with Ministries, so much so that the original plan of making this site a shopping centre was discarded.'

Of Sir James Hawkey, she said the name was synonymous in the borough with local government. 'We who served under his leadership knew something of his time and talent which have gone into the civic work of this borough,' she said.

Of Sir Winston, Mrs. Hollis said: 'We are proud of the fact that our member for Parliament is Prime Minister — but we are even more proud of the fact that our member is Sir Winston Churchill.'

Then Sir Winston slowly crossed the stage to unveil the plaque he personally had presented to the hall.

The Guardian, April 1, 1955

June 1977 and the Queen's Silver Jubilee provides an opportunity to recreate a cricket match of old. Woodford Green Cricket Club is the second oldest in the country, willow hitting leather on the Green for the first time in 1735.

Above: **This picture was taken by Aerofilms in June 1931 and indicates the development of the area between the Green and the railway line by that date. It gives us a good insight as to the reason why certain of our roads follow the pattern that they do — the cul-de-sac of Mayfair Gardens has been neatly designed to fill the available field! The new Broadmead Road crossed Charteris Road but stopped short of the railway line — the contract for the bridge was not issued until 1939. Beyond it in the fields lies Milkwell Farm. *Below:* Swallowed up in the sprawl of March 1985.**

Objections to the making up of Charteris Road were now considered.

Mr. Simpson said that for many years Charteris Road had been a quiet road. Then several houses were erected. The Council now wished to make the road up and carry out work that had been satisfactorily done by the clerk to the Chingford Council. There were 15 house owners in the road, and of these 12 objected. These 12 owned a frontage of 1,057 feet. Eleven owners objected together, and the other was Mr. James T. Lane, of 91, Snakes Lane, whose frontage was 540 feet, and who had no use for Charteris Road, as his entrance was in Snakes Lane. The cost per foot of frontage was 33s. The other 11 owners strongly objected to bearing any part of the cost.

Mr. Ward said that the estimated cost of the making up of the road was £2,214 9s. There was a very old sewer there, and a new one had been made.

Mr. Leonard Moller, of 60, Ingatestone Road, Woodford, stated that Charteris Road was used by the general public. He thought it would be a disadvantage to make it up. It had been used a great deal more since the sewer had been put there.

Mr. Fuller asked the Bench to decide whether it was a private road or not.

Mr. Simpson objected on the grounds that he had not received a month's notice of this objection.

This case was also adjourned until October 10th.

Council report, September 14, 1928

Under the system of Regional administration which in war-time was to divide the whole country into twelve regions, Wanstead and Woodford, Barking, Chigwell, Chingford, Dagenham, Ilford, Leyton, Waltham Holy Cross and Walthamstow together formed Group 7 of the London Region. As an essential part of the scheme, each Local Authority was to have its own Control Centre, suitably protected from bomb-blast, Wanstead and Woodford chose as the site for its Control Centre the garden at the rear of 13, Broomhill Road. Here, unseen by passers-by, Council workmen began, towards the end of August, 1938, the seemingly impossible task of constructing a blast-proof Report and Control Centre which should be ready for use in fourteen days.

First, the ground was dug to a depth of 4ft. 6ins. in order to allow two Nissen huts to be sunk for half their height. The Nissen huts were erected end to end, with a gap between them providing space for a protected entance way and for lavatories.

The huts, in sections, arrived on the fifth day. The suppliers' erector reported at 6 p.m., dead beat, but was persuaded to give half an hour's instruction on the method of erecting the curved sheets. When he came back at 8 o'clock next morning he was astonished to find one hut in position and almost half of the other erected.

When fixed, the huts were covered with reinforced concrete to a thickness of 18 inches, on which was piled earth 3 feet deep. Later, an annexe at the rear provided three rooms for rest or for other use.

When war broke out, little had to be done to equip the Centre for its work, considerable improvements having been made from time to time. Staff for maintaining continuous day and night duty consisted of 60 men and women.

It Happened Here. Stanley Tiquet, May 1947

Ten terraced houses in Horn-lane, Woodford, and a single house are to be demolished eventually to make way for the approach roads to the Broadmead-road Bridge.

West Essex Gazette, March 5, 1948

The 1960s saw a far reaching transformation on the Green. With the electrification of the railway line, and the closure of the Snakes Lane level crossing in 1948, Broadmead Road had become the major east-west route between the upper and lower roads. After passing The Terrace *(above)* the road ran in front of Little Horn Lane and No. 13 Broomhill Road *(below)* before turning left down Fairfield Road.

By 1964 traffic was such that this awkward 'chicane' had to be eliminated. Little Horn Lane was lost with its terrace houses and cobbler's shop as was the old wartime control centre — now more or less beneath the westbound carriageway!

In the days of oil lamps and open grates, fire was an ever-present hazard, especially in the many timber buildings. In 1920 the fire station was located in the grounds of the Council office. Sixty-five years later the fire brigade remains on the same site although the Willows has been demolished. The training tower was renewed in 1983.

Early on Saturday morning se'nnight, the inhabitants of Woodford were alarmed by an immense body of smoke issuing from the forest, which was instantly succeeded by flames. On arriving at the spot (about 300 yards north of the Wells) it appeared that some persons on their way to Holly Bush Fair had kindled a fire for the purpose of enjoying a rural breakfast, and had imprudently left the live embers, which communicated to the trees, and threatened destruction to the whole forest. Mr. W. Rounding, who first discovered it, collected the neighbouring villagers, and having procured several water carts and garden engines, after several hours' exertion, succeeded in extinguishing the fire.

Press report, 1815

The indignation excited in the neighbourhood by the conflagration which destroyed the fine old mansion of Bellevue-house is far from subsided. The insurance-offices, which are heavy sufferers, are by no means satisfied with the explanation given of the origin of the fire. Orders have been given to dig up the ruins and search them with the most rigid care, to see if traces can be found of the various descriptions of furniture, and of the children's clothes, trinkets, and books, all which are said to have perished in the flames. An examination of witnesses took place on Tuesday, at the Phoenix-office, in Lombard-street. There has likewise been an examination of witnesses at the White Hart Inn, Woodford-bridge. Mr. Radley, blacksmith, and landlord of the White Hart Inn, said he was first on the premises after the discovery of the fire. It was between three and four o'clock in the morning of the 18th inst. The house was on fire at all parts. He found Mr. Balls lying on the lawn behind the house, apparently in a fit. A young woman (afterwards ascertained to be the housemaid) was with him. The first thing done was to place him in a chair. He had often observed the house before. It seemed deficient of furniture. Several of the rooms were unfurnished. The school consisted of eight scholars, and was kept by Miss Kendall, who, in February last married Mr. Balls.

Press report, October 1836

FIRE AT WOODFORD, ESSEX.— Yesterday morning at an early hour, the cry of 'Fire!' was raised by the mounted horse-patrol. Immediately a great number of the inhabitants turned out, and on proceeding towards Woodford-bridge discovered the fire to be raging in the interior of Woodford Ray House, the seat of Thomas Lewis, Esq., situated on an eminence on the eastern bank of the river Olne. The Woodford parochial engine was soon brought to the spot, and got to work from the river, and played admirably. By five o'clock the fire had increased, and it was not till that moment that a messenger was sent to London for assistance. He reached the Wellclose-square station at a quarter to six o'clock, and the Jeffery-square station at six. The engines of that establishment were instantly dispatched with a strong muster of the brigade-men, under the direction of the foreman of that establishment, Crookland. They travelled at a great speed, but by the time they reached Woodford, which was within 35 minutes after their departure, the conflagration was at its height, and the mansion enveloped in flames from its basement to the roof. The attention of those engaged at the engines was directed to the outhouses, consisting of dairy, scullery, coach and cart houses, and stables, which were situated adjacent. The Wellclose-square engine was brought into operation immediately, and the brigade, by their well-known experience, succeeded in preserving these out-buildings with but slight damage. At a little after seven o'clock the walls of the mansion fell inwards with a heavy crash, and after that time the flames gradually sunk; but the ruins during the whole of yesterday emitted dense volumes of smoke. It is said that the whole of the property is insured in the Royal Exchange Insurance-office, and to its full value. Upwards of twenty-five workmen are sufferers: they had been at work in repairing the mansion, and left all their tools and instruments, which were entirely consumed.

Press report, 1838

At a late hour on Wednesday night last an extensive fire broke out in the village of Woodford, in Essex, which consumed the whole of the extensive buildings attached to the White Hart Inn. The property consumed comprises the extensive stabling, granary, tap (adjoining the inn), a cottage, and several small outbuildings.

Press report, 1844

The earliest list of residents in Woodford was drawn up in 1235 and one name, Benet Mascall, is associated with Marshalls, a tenement on the Green near the end of Snakes Lane which at that time ran on a more northerly line. An adjoining tenement was that of Richard Hert and it was here in 1617 that Sir Humphrey Handforth, Master of the Wardrobe to James I, built a house called Harts. This illustration was reproduced in Gentlemen's Magazine in July 1789. One of Harts most notable residents was Richard Warner, the writer and botanist, who developed the garden during the eighteenth century. Two hundred years later evidence of his handywork remains — this is the second largest plane tree in the country.

The relationship between overcrowded conditions and tuberculosis was referred to by several speakers on Saturday afternoon, when His Worship the Mayor of East Ham, Alderman G. H. Manser, J.P., opened the new tuberculosis pavilion at the Corporation's sanatorium at The Harts, Woodford Green.

'All too frequently,' said Councillor F. H. Edwards, the Vice-Chairman of the Public Health Committee, 'do many of our patients who are treated here go back to their over-crowded homes at East Ham, where the good that has been done here is gradually undone again later on. We have got to do something to prevent tuberculosis as well as to cure it.'

Dr. Benton, the ex-Medical Officer of Health to the Borough, who presided, referred to tuberculosis as 'the white scourge.' He pleaded, as he had done for the past twenty years, for the isolation and segregation of 'T.B.' cases in order to prevent its spreading. The treatment of this disease, he claimed, should be a national cost.

The Woodford Times, November 3, 1933

The axe has fallen on Harts Hospital, Woodford Green, and Lugano Nursing Home, Buckhurst Hill, and now it hangs over Jubilee and Forest Hospitals in Woodford Green and Buckhurst Hill.

On Monday owners Waltham Forest Health Authority agreed proposals to close Harts and Lugano and, in private session, decided to start talks on the possible permanent closures of Jubilee in November 1984 and Forest in September 1985.

At the meeting, packed with protestors, the Lugano closure was the first to be agreed, by an eight vote to six margin. The Harts decision followed with the same majority.

Waltham Forest Health Authority, which runs geriatric and some acute services in the 'Wanstead and Woodford strip', hopes that it will save £100,000 a year by closing 26 geriatric beds in Lugano and up to £800,000 a year by closing Harts' 78 geriatric and chest care beds.

With this and the possible Forest and Jubilee closures the Authority hopes to meet target cuts of £1.7 million by 1986.

Before Harts Hospital is offered for public sale, Waltham Forest Health Authority will consult with other health authorities on an alternative use for the building.

Redbridge Guardian, September 30, 1983

The first house was demolished in 1815 and a new mansion erected the following year in the Regency style, the first occupier being a Mr Mellish. Shortly thereafter Brice Pearse, owner of the Monkhams Estate bordering Harts, diverted the course of Snakes Lane to consolidate his own property. James Spicer, founder of the paper merchants, Spicers Ltd, still in being today, purchased the estate in 1858. At the close of the First World War it was owned by William Brown but after he died it came on the market and was purchased by the County Borough of East Ham in 1919. Much against the protests of local people it was converted and opened as a tuberculosis sanatorium but, such is the way of the world, that there was equal protest in 1983 when it closed! As has been indicated with regard to the Metropolitan Police development at Bushwood (page 181), the Government and public utilities, including hospitals, are above the law when it comes to planning permission. Whereas the ordinary citizen or company has to seek consent before erecting, extending or demolishing a building, no such restraints are put upon the Crown. Even if buildings are listed they can be altered or knocked down without any formal consent being necessary. Now that Harts is closed one must assume that the hospital authorities will be debating its fate. The fabric is already deteriorating but there is no way that the local authority can force the Board to maintain it. It will require constant vigilance to ensure that a back door demolition job or a sale of part for building development does not take place.

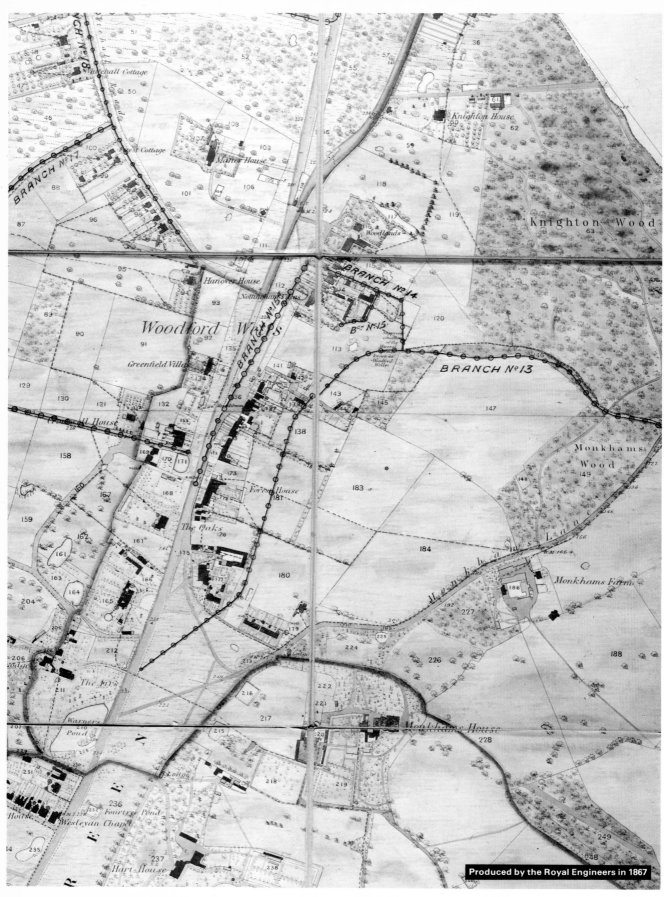

Produced by the Royal Engineers in 1867

The two major estates of Monkhams and Knighton as they were in 1867. Bancroft's School has yet to be built. From 1820 the Manor House was the site of Woodford's workhouse but was built anew by Richard Hallett in 1863. The last occupant was a well known city merchant of the time, Thomas Read, but when he died in 1884 the property was purchased by the Drapers' Company who were on the look-out for a suitable site to move their school from East London.

Up-to-date catering accommodation has undoubtedly been a long-felt want in Woodford Wells. Particularly in the summer months has this been the case, when, with the present-day transport facilities, large numbers of people have come out from London and its environs to the tracts of forest extending from Woodford to the neighbourhood of Epping itself. While many of these visitors go farther afield than Woodford, there is a considerable number who find pleasurable relaxation in the immediate neighbourhood of Woodford Wells, to whom adequate catering facilities in that district will prove an inestimable boon.

To meet the needs of these folk, and of residents also, who may be glad to avail themselves of such provision from time to time, Mr. F. Leach, of Woodford Green, is opening an up-to-date catering establishment at Barclay Hall.

The Woodford Times, March 13, 1931

A few doors along at Nos. 71-73 lay Barclay Hall opened in 1931; thirty years later came the Calypso coffee bar, beloved of the younger folk with its reputation for 'froffy cofe'. Closed for many years, no doubt the building holds a twinge of nostalgia for readers both young and old.

Above: **The Travellers Friend, Woodford Wells, achieved the unofficial name of 'The Spivs' from its reputation as a meeting place for the sharper elements from the metropolis.** *Bottom:* **A Sunday lunchtime jar for local vintage car enthusiasts makes a fine comparison. Splendid Charlsworth-bodied Alvis drophead on the left.**

It is the 50th anniversary of a monument Sylvia Pankhurst had set up near Mornington Road, Woodford Green, to commemorate British Bombing on the North West frontiers of India *(sic)*, which she condemned.

She had lived at three different places in the Woodford area. Yet, in 1982, on the 100th anniversary of her birth, there was not a murmur of her existence in Redbridge. The date went unnoticed.

Renewed efforts are being made to MPs to push for a plaque in the area commemorating the years she spent in Woodford. . . .

A Sylvia Pankhurst Memorial Walk and a peace picnic were arranged by Gill Mac-Donald, Malcolm Apps and Sylvia Ayling with about 100 people from Redbridge and Waltham Forest going past the sites of the Pankhursts' Woodford homes. Sylvia's son Richard Pankhurst and his family also joined them.

They walked past Woolworths in George Lane, South Woodford, once the site of an estate, Frithmans, where the suffragette lived. There she had a creche for under-privileged children from London's East End. They went past the site of the now demolished number 3 Charteris Road and to the site of a small cafe she owned called Rose Cottage, near the monument . . .

Her daughter-in-law, Rita Pankhurst, addressed local people gathered around Sylvia's memorial. . . .

From living under the same roof as her for four years, Rita said: 'I learned the meaning of dedication; hard and continuous work on behalf of others; readiness to suffer unpopularity, ridicule and harassment for her principles. With all she was a gentle soul who inspired affection in all who worked with her.

The name Pankhurst will forever be associated with the suffragette movement whose 40-year campaign achieved its aim of votes for women in 1928 — the year its leading light, Emmeline Pankhurst, died. Her Women's Social and Political Union resorted to extreme measures to achieve its end and riots, window breaking, assault, and complicity in the bombing of Lloyd George's house, led to her being imprisoned many times. Her eldest daughter Christabel directed a campaign of arson from Paris where she had gone to avoid arrest for conspiracy. Mrs Pankhurst called a truce in 1914 on the outbreak of war and formed her organisation into one of national service. Her youngest daughter Sylvia was an ardent pacifist and she founded the Workers' Dreadnought in 1914 and carried out 13 hunger strikes before being imprisoned in 1920. She lived in three places in Woodford: Frithmans (see page 194), No. 3 Charteris Road now demolished, and Rose Cottage *below* which lay on the west side of the High Road at Woodford Wells *(above)*.

'She died in 1960, just too early to see how women have got organised all over the world. In Ethiopia there is a fine memorial at her grave. In Britain, having so often opposed the Establishment, she has never been officially honoured.'

Guardian & Gazette, June 1, 1984

When Mussolini attacked Ethiopia on October 2, 1935 it heralded a new viciousness in the conduct of war, and Sylvia was moved to erect on October 20 her Anti-Abyssinian memorial in front of Rose Cottage as a protest against aerial bombing. The memorial survives today — in fact it is a listed monument — and it enables us to pinpoint the site of Rose Cottage with precision.

Having occasion to pass through Woodford late on Saturday night, I was surprised on reaching that part of the High Road across which some years ago stretched the old toll-gate, to find a brightly-lighted stall standing half hidden among the trees and bushes of the forest. A blazing fire was burning at the side, over which was suspended a large boiler, while three dusky forms were flitting about, now in the glare of the light, and now among the shadows of the trees, busily preparing something for their stand. Upon a closer inspection I discovered that the stall was a coffee-stall and the dusky forms were those of the proprietor and his assistants who were actively engaged in cutting up bread and butter and cake, and preparing tins of hot coffee. Being the only person within sight or hearing, and considering the lateness of the hour (12 o'clock p.m.) and the unfrequented spot upon which the stall stood, I might well be pardoned for wondering for whom this midnight repast was being prepared. Judging from the huge piles of bread and butter and the abundant supply of hot coffee, it was obvious that the coffee-stall keeper was expecting no small nor chance body of customers, and arguing from the class of provisions and the accompanying surroundings, I concluded that the caterer calculated his consumers, whoever they might be, would possess voracious rather than dainty appetites. Leaving the place where I had been standing, I walked up to the stall and politely enquired of the proprietor the cause of such studied preparations.

The stall-keeper, a most respectable, civil, and obliging man, in answer to my question informed me that he was preparing for blackberriers. 'Blackberriers!' said I, 'but surely you don't get enough of those individuals down to recompense you and your assistants for a night's labour'? 'Well,' said my informant, 'I am only here three Saturday nights just at the height of the season, and you would hardly credit it, sir, but between one and two o'clock in the morning I have had as many as from two to three hundred blackberry boys round my stall at a time. Most of them come down from London in gangs, and after regaling themselves at my stall, they stretch themselves down under bushes, or on fallen trees, where they take a short nap until either the cold or the first peep of daylight awakens them, when the business of picking the blackberries begins. Indeed, some are so anxious to be the first 'in the field' that they are busily at work before daylight picking the fruit by the aid of lanterns.'

The Times, September 30, 1887

The late-eighteenth century rambling mansion of the Oaks at Woodford Wells was the seat of the Duchess of Newcastle, Henrietta Pelham-Clinton. When the Roman Catholic parish of Woodford was created in 1894, the Church of St Thomas of Canterbury was erected at her expense the following year abutting the southern face of her house. She also funded the building of a Franciscan friary on the other side of the church.

The Duchess died in 1913 and in 1920 her home became the Convent of the Poor Clares. The site to the south of the Friary was developed in 1964 with the building of St Paul's Roman Catholic School but in the 1970s two separate fires wiped out the Convent and Ivy Lodge next to the Friary. The church survived unscathed in both incidents. The aerial comparisons date from the late 1960s and 1985.

Of a rough gravelly hill, and there
Lay a small valley nowise fair
Beneath them, clear at first of all
But brake, til 'midst the rushes tall
Down to the bottom alders grew,
Crabbed and rough; and, winding through
The clayey mounds a brook there was
Oozy and foul, half choked with grass.

William Morris. 1834-96

Before the Poor Law Act of 1597 the relief of the poor had been financed mainly by a system of voluntary contribution, to which a certain amount of compulsion had been added by certain statutes towards the end of the sixteenth century. The Act of 1597 compelled overseers to levy a rate and to distrain on property for arrears. At Woodford the amount of rates varied, as would be expected, in much the same proportion as expenses. . . . In 1680 the overseers' rate was 4d. in the £ (which raised £34 11s. 0d.) and the constables' 1d. Added together their two rates gradually increased until the end of the century and in

In 1135 we know that the forest at Munckenhill was held by the Abbot of Stratford Langthorne and remained in religious hands until the Dissolution of the Monasteries. Apart from the woodland, 'Munkom House' was devolved with the estate when Edward VI passed it into secular hands. In 1640 there were two separate sites for Munkom House and one corresponds with that of the farm which lay at the right-angle bend formed where Monkhams Lane turned left to cut through the Forest. This picture was taken in 1931 when open fields lay between it and the railway line, the farm then being run by 'Mae' Watts, a keen naturalist and photographer.

1699 amounted to 8¼d. in the £. The overseers' rate first reached 1s. in 1707 and then remained fairly stable for about forty years. In the second half of the eighteenth century it rose rapidly reaching a peak of 9s. in 1801. After the revaluation of 1804 the rate was brought down to 3s. 9d. but then again increased, reaching a maximum of 7s. in 1817 and 1834, representing about 16s. on the old assessment. It is a measure of the economics effected by the Poor Law Reform Act of 1834, that by the time that the new system was fully operative it was only necessary to call for a rate of 3s. 6d.

Woodford Essex 1600-1836, E. J. Erith, 1950

GORED BY A BULL
WOODFORD MAN'S TERRIBLE DEATH

The Coroner, Dr. A. Ambrose, investigated at the Wilfrid Lawson Hotel on Wednesday afternoon the death of Mr. Ernest William Harrington, aged 53, a horseman, of 141, Monkhams Lane, Woodford Green, which occurred in the Jubilee Hospital on Sunday following his having been attacked and gored by a bull on Friday.

Samuel Edward Earey, a farm labourer, of 143, Monkhams Lane, said that on Friday afternoon he was helping to get the bull back into its box with deceased. Witness had hold of the rope which was attached to the ring in

It was demolished in 1936 during the development of the Monkhams estate and Farm Way cut through the site.

the bull's nose, and deceased was on the other side of the bull with a fork. 'As I was turning to go into the shed,' said witness, 'the bull turned on deceased, who was pinned between the posts and the gate. The bull gored him in the stomach. I pulled all I could to get him off, and I had the rope quite tight. As Clarke came up towards the gate the bull turned

Close by lay the timber-framed house of Little Monkhams, probably dating from the late sixteenth or early seventeenth century. The picture on the left was taken in 1901, the house being greatly altered in 1920.

round and brought deceased from the gate to the ground and left him there. I pulled again, and as I pulled he made for me.' Witness added that he had been at the farm for nine

years, and had never known this particular bull to be fierce before.

The Woodford Times, May 20, 1932

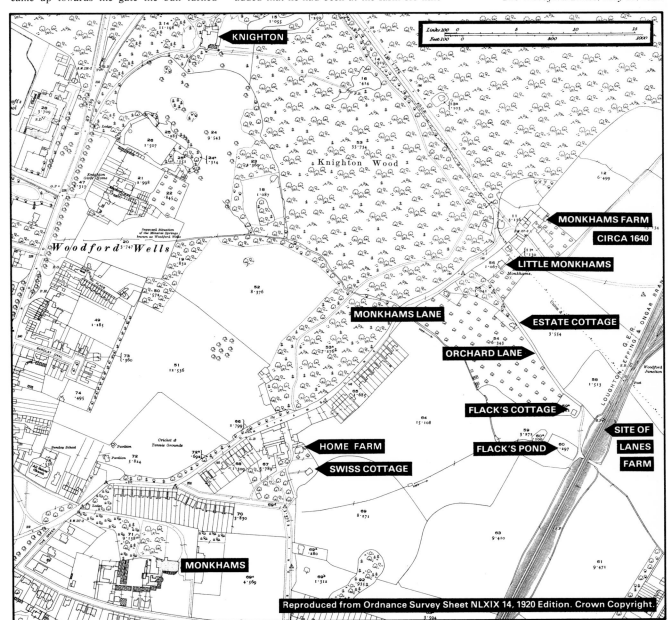

Left: **Just beside Little Monkhams, Orchard Lane ran down to Lanes Farm, the site of the second Munkom House. Unfortunately no pictures of the farm exist as it was swept away when the railway was pushed through in 1856 although the** farmhouse itself survived until 1892. However this picture shows Orchard Lane as it was in 1931 with the Estate Cottage on the left. *Right:* **At the end of Orchard Lane, up this cart track, lay Flack's Cottage.**

At the Stratford Police Court on Wednesday the Justices heard the objections to the Council's apportionments in regard to the proposed making-up of Kings Avenue and Queens Avenue.

Outlining the Council's case, Mr. John A. Simpson, LL.B., the Clerk, said that the part of Kings Avenue (which he took first) near the Broadway was already made up, but the road was being progressively developed, and there was only about 80 feet at the end of the road that was either not already built on or under construction. There was only one feature that was out of the ordinary as compared with the average road. The land at the side sloped considerably, and it was necessary to put in a land drain to take the water from the road to avoid flooding by surface water. That made a difference of about 11d. per foot on the cost of the whole road.

Five owners objected because they considered the cost excessive as compared with other roads done by the Council. The estimated cost of this road was 23s. 7.4d. per foot over the whole frontage. The apportionments had been based on frontages, and the objectors claimed that the amount was excessive. Mr. Roper, for instance, said that other roads had been made up at a lower cost, and that 18s. 6d. per foot was enough. Another objector said that building materials, etc., were down in cost, and 20s. per foot would be sufficient to charge. In reply to this, Mr. Simpson pointed out that Monkhams Drive was made up in 1927 at a cost of 18s. 9¾d. per foot. That road was only a tarred gravel surface, whereas Kings Avenue was to be tarred granite. This job was with the same contractors. The only reason, in his opinion, why they accepted that job, said Mr. Simpson, was probably because they wanted a job to keep their men at work, because in the same year they had the work for part of Kings Avenue, for which they charged 22s. 3¾d. per foot. That figure, in fact, said Mr. Simpson, was about the same as for other roads for the past few years.

It had been said, added Mr. Simpson, that Woodville Road had cost only 18s. 11d. per foot, but that was because of the fact that no kerbing was necessary, and kerbing meant 4s. 4d. per foot. Maybank Avenue cost 19s. 6d. per foot, but there again no kerbing was required. In 1930 Glebelands Avenue was made up at a cost of 17s. 4½d, but that low price per foot was due to the fact that the road had both kerbing and channelling, which otherwise would have cost another 8s. 4d. per foot.

The Woodford Times, November 6, 1931

Behind Flack's Cottage, although difficult to distinguish in the picture at the top of the page, lay the railway embankment This had a tunnel built beneath it to give access from the end of Orchard Lane to the dust heaps in the brick diggings down by the Roding. In front of the tunnel, in a steep depression, lay Flack's Pond.

Just look at that depression today! The tunnel, long since filled in, lay at the bottom of the back gardens of Nos. 150 and 152 King's Avenue while Flack's Cottage stood on the site of No. 164 on the left. The pond was drained in 1935 so that King's Avenue could be extended to meet Farm Way.

Above and bottom: **The second Monkhams farm, Home Farm (see map page 219), mid-way along Monkhams Lane survived until the estate was developed in the 1930s. The farm cottages bordering the road remain to this day — they date from 1899.**

Below: **Behind the farm buildings stood the Swiss Cottage — the agent's house for the Monkhams estate photographed here when Stephen Harper was the bailiff. It too survives today, although drastically remodelled as No. 9 Princes Avenue.**

The big house was built in 1738 by Thomas North. When Brice Pearse owned the estate, he had the line of Snakes Lane altered — the old road then being incorporated into the grounds as a convenient path to the station.

THE WAR IN SOUTH AFRICA

Notwithstanding the heavy rain of the morning of Monday, the invitations which Mr. and Mrs. A. F. Hills gave to the relatives of soldiers at the war living in the Beacontree Division was largely responded to, and from the time of departure for Monkhams until the hour of leaving no rain fell. The Walthamstow party were conveyed in six brakes from Hoe-street Bridge, and included four or five wounded soldiers, who are now convalescent.

The entire party, which numbered about 400, were received by Mrs. Hills on the lawn, and invited on entering to a concert in the large hall of the house, where 'Tom Bowling', also 'Obedient to the Call', with its refrain of 'Cheer, Boys, Cheer', were sung, and the organ and violins discoursed patriotic music, by which all were moved — some to tears. Until tea, which was provided in a large marquee, the beautiful greenhouses and the vast grounds of Monkham's were enjoyed.

The Woodford Brass Band played on the lawn, and an hour later there were bountiful provisions in the marquee, where the soldiers, wives, and mothers, were all seated. Mr. Howard moved a vote of thanks to Lady Lencha Warner, as president of the Becontree Division of the Soldiers' and Sailors' Families' Association, and to Mr. and Mrs. Hills and, needless to say, the resolution was passed with cheers and loud hurrahs, which the women seemed as well able to ring out as it would have been had the tent been filled with the soldiers themselves, instead of the 'girls they left behind them.'

After this little ceremony the guests were passed to another marquee, where an entertainment, which was intensely humorous, kept the whole party full of merriment until it was time to return to the brakes and railway station.

Walthamstow, Leyton and Chingford Guardian, June 19, 1900

Another notable owner was Henry Ford Barclay who lived and died at the house, 1864-1892. He generously allowed the gardens to be used for numerous functions and gave the land on which All Saints Church was built in 1874. The entrance ran through the front garden of No. 7 The Green!

THE IMPORTANT AND VERY VALUABLE
Freehold
RESIDENTIAL AND BUILDING ESTATE
distinguished as
'Monkhams'

Situate in the Parish of Woodford, adjoining the Railway Station (from whence the City is reached in about 25 minutes), and extending to Woodford Green; whilst Post and Telegraph Office, Church of England, Roman Catholic and Nonconformist Churches, Shops, &c., are all within a few minutes' walk. It comprises an attractive old-fashioned substantially-built and commodious Mansion, built on two Floors, occupying a happily chosen and elevated position, enjoying a Southern aspect, and commanding delightful and extensive Views across its undulating Park Lands, and a richly wooded expanse of country beyond.

It is approached from Woodford Green by a beautifully Timbered and Shrubbed Carriage Drive, guarded by a Capital Entrance Lodge, which contains Four Rooms and a Bath Room, whilst from a Private Path across the Estate the Station is reached in about 5 minutes.

The property lies most compactly, and specially appeals to any Gentleman wishing to reside amidst beautiful rural surroundings and good society, and yet within very easy access of the City. On the other hand, owing to its Great Prospective Value for Building Purposes, and its Proximity to the Station and General Configuration, it equally claims the attention of Societies, Syndicates and Investors generally for Very Profitable Development, as a whole, or in parts without interfering with the present Residential amenities.

ON THE GROUND FLOOR
A marble paved Entrance Porch leads to Vestibule with oak parquetry floor and oak panelled dado, which in turn leads to Outer Hall, fitted in similar manner, and giving access to the

GRAND SALOON HALL
Measuring about 40 ft. by 21 ft., lighted from Roof. This Apartment is fitted with oak parquetry floor, open tiled fireplace, marble curb and richly carved mantelpiece. The walls are beautifully panelled in oak with deep frieze in *alto relievo*, and the ceiling is tastefully decorated and coved. From this Hall ascends the

IMPOSING PRINCIPAL STAIRCASE
With heavily carved oak panels and Gallery Landing in character. On this Staircase is a fine two-manual organ, by "C. Martin" of Oxford, worked by electric power.

CHEERFUL LIBRARY
Measuring about 23 ft. by 18 ft., fitted with brass mounted slow combustion stove, tiled hearth and marble and slate surround, oak

When Monkhams was purchased by James Twentyman in 1903 it was for one purpose only: to sell off plots for housing development, a process which continued over the next forty years. The house itself with its magnificent saloon *(below left)* and dining room *(right)* was demolished two years after Twentyman's death in 1928.

parquetry border, and very handsome mahogany fitment of bookshelves, cupboards, overmantel and window seat.

CHARMING MORNING ROOM
Measuring about 26ft. 6 in. by 18 ft. 9 in., fitted with brass mounted slow combustion stove, tiled hearth and marble curb, tiled and carved oak mantel, oak parquetry border, oak panelled dado, and range of carved oak bookcases and cupboard as fitted one side.
These three Rooms all communicate with each other and with the Saloon Hall, and afford a complete circulation for Receptions or Balls.

STATELY DINING ROOM
Measuring about 39 ft. 6 in. into bay by 22 ft., having door into Serving Room, and fitted with large open register stove, tiled hearth, black marble curb, and richly carved and decorated marble mantelpiece, oak parquetry floor, walnut panelled dado, with carved walnut pilasters, and beautifully panelled and decorated ceiling.

THE MANSION
Is lighted throughout by electricity generated on the Premises and is heated throughout by hot air. Company's Water is laid on. The Drainage, which is on modern principles and connected with the main sewer, is believed to be all that can be desired.
The Interior of the Mansion is exceptionally well fitted and decorated, and the Property generally has been brought up to its present high state of perfection by a most lavish expenditure of money, combined with great artistic taste.

At a convenient remove from the Mansion, and with separate Entrance from the road, is the

CAPITAL STABLING
Arranged round an enclosed and paved Yard, and surmounted by a Clock. It comprises ten Stalls and five Loose Boxes; large Coach House for eight Carriages, smaller Coach House, Trap House, Harness Room, Loft, four Rooms for Grooms; a Suite of three Bed Rooms, Bath Room and two Living Rooms for married Coachmen; Dog Kennel, Smithy, &c. Brick built Engine House and Battery Store for Electric Light.

Auction Catalogue, Messrs. Trollope,
June 24, 1903

The mystery of underground tunnels found under old tennis courts on a building site in Tudor Close, Woodford Green, has been solved. For the tunnels — as predicted by consultant engineer Grahame Rudkins, of Brentwood — are the remains of an ornamental fountain. Arnold Hills, the second owner of the early 19th century 21-bedroom palatial mansion Monkhams House and also rich owner of the Thames Ironworks, had the fountain constructed as part of an Italian garden. . . . The builders [of the new estate] now face a bill of several thousand pounds for employing consultant engineers to fill in the tunnels and make foundations safe.

West Essex Gazette, December 9, 1976

THE GREAT STORM

The terrific storm which raged for several hours on Wednesday night brought its trail of floods in Woodford and surrounding districts as in other places.

Following a day of most oppressive sultriness, the thunder began to mutter in the distance at about 6 o'clock, and less than an hour later it burst in all its fury over Woodford. For something like half an hour it raged 'dry,' and almost everyone, knowing the danger of a 'dry' thunderstorm, was wishing it would rain, when, suddenly it seemed as if the very heavens themselves opened. Even the oldest Woodfordians can scarcely remember such rain as then fell for fully an hour without intermission.

In a few minutes the roads became raging torrents, and for a time most traffic was brought to a standstill. The best of sewers would have been totally inadequate to deal with the water that came down, and roads which are not normally susceptible to flooding suffered almost as badly as any.

The High Road, Woodford Green, was almost covered, there being not more than a foot or two in width on the crown of the road that was free, while Snakes Lane became a veritable cascade.

At the Broadway, a picture of which appears here, traffic was brought practically to a standstill, there being only three cars which

'The beautiful parklands which surround the Mansion slope away in gentle undulations to the south, are intersected by charming Woodland Walks and richly studded with Forest Timber and Ornamental Trees. The grounds are delightfully studded with . . . a profusion of choice shrubs, Terrace Walks, Sloping Lawns, a lovely Italian Garden with Pergola, a quaint Dutch Garden, Herbaceous Borders and Rhododendron Clumps. There are pretty clumps of Woodlands, a most productive Orchard, and at the bottom of the Park is a large Ornamental Lake with Boat House and well stocked with fish.' Monkhams auction catalogue.

braved the flood at its worst to carry marooned railway passengers across the flooded area to the comparative dryness of the regions beyond. The water here was well over a foot deep.

Early on in the storm the gates at the Eagle Lane level crossing jammed, and all traffic had to be diverted via Hermon Hill and George Lane. Then, to make matters even worse, a water main burst at the junction of George Lane and the Chigwell Road, causing an upheaval in the roadway. This stopped all traffic there, and all the 'buses had then to be diverted via Poulteney Road and thence into George Lane. This upheaval by the way, was not repaired until quite late yesterday (Thursday).

Two manholes burst in the Chigwell Road opposite Oxford Terrace, completely blocking the road, which was flooded to a depth of between two and three feet, while all the houses there were inundated.

Salway Hill suffered badly, for in addition to the storm water rushing down the Hill, it also rushed down Empress Avenue, while, in addition, the old river behind St. Aubyn's School overflowed. The combined waters met at the corner, and the cottages there were flooded out with the furniture floating about. The cottages themselves to all intents and purposes might for the time being have been in the middle of a lake.

At Woodford Green the same story was to be told. The lower hall at the Men's Club was flooded to a depth of six inches, while the baths, which are some four or five feet above the level of the lower hall were half filled with water forced up from the sewers. We learn that yesterday morning, after the water had been drained out, there were a number of young frogs disporting themselves on the floor. At least, that is what we are told!

The Woodford Times, August 7, 1931

The 'lake' eighty years later, scene also of the great deluge in 1931.

INTERESTING VIEW OF KNIGHTON IN 1862

The above picture is reproduced from a photograph taken 70 years ago and presented to the editor by the late Mr. Basil Hooper some few years before his death. There are probably few persons still living in the district who can remember when Woodford Wells looked like this. But for the information of those whose memories will not carry them so far back, we will point out a few features of interest to be noted:

It will be observed that the picturesque lodge at the southern entrance to the Knighton Estate, opposite Bancroft's School, with which most people are now familiar, had not then been built.

Another point worthy of notice is that the present main road to Buckhurst Hill had not been made when this photograph was taken. The private carriageway to Knighton was originally the High Road to Buckhurst Hill. Some years later the present road was cut through the forest and joined up with the original road near Knighton Villas.

In order that this new road might be constructed, it was necessary to pull down the old Toll Gate and cottage from the site it occupies in the photograph, and re-erect it about 40 yards nearer to Buckhurst Hill, where it remained until a year or so ago, when it was removed to enable road improvements to be made at that spot. Very few will remember the old Turnpike in the position in which it appears in the photograph.

On the left of the picture will be seen the toll collector's hut, which then stood at the corner of Whitehall Road. At the time the photograph was taken, and for some years after, the traveller could not get beyond Woodford Wells either in the direction of Chingford or Buckhurst Hill without paying toll, unless, as sometimes happened, a driver slipped through by a ruse.

Still further to the left of the picture will be seen a carriageway across the green. This led to the carriage drive of Manor House, for many years the residence of one Thomas Read. The Manor House disappeared about 40 years ago, and Bancroft's School was erected on the site.

It will be noticed that the point from which the photograph was taken was then common land, but has since been enclosed, and now forms part of the front garden of Hanover House, while further to the right other houses have been built. We believe the enclosure took place during the residence at Hanover House of the late Mr. Diedrich Swinge, a wealthy sugar refiner, who came to live there about 60 years ago. Note the footpaths running across the common, forming a short cut between the High Road and Whitehall Road.

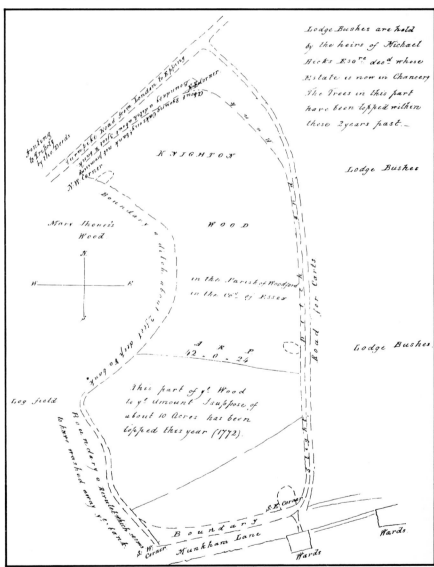

'The Ground is for the most part uneven and is almost covered with Beech, Hornbeam and Oak pollards which are about a foot diameter 3 feet from the Ground. Part of the Wood (seemingly about 10 Acres) has been lopped this year (1772) the rest is nearly of an equal growth and I suppose will be lopped very soon.' Part of the annotation to this plan of Knighton Wood which had obviously been enclosed before 1772 and the trees cut or lopped for timber. By the nineteenth century it was owned by the Pearse family as part of the Monkhams estate but was sold to Richard Hallett (later of the Manor House — see page 214) who built Knighton House in the Forest. In 1863 the estate was sold to E. N. Buxton Esq.

Only if one is as influential as Mr Edward North Buxton — Chairman of the London School Board, Justice of the Peace, Verderer, and champion of the movement to preserve Epping Forest — can one take over a main road as the drive to one's house! After the road was moved in **1866**, the old lodge called the Bell House was superfluous and a new South Lodge was built at the beginning of the new drive. At the same time, of course, the toll house had to be moved. (See also page 97)

Knighton Mansion can be seen near the centre of the top of the picture, and the houses on the left in the distance are Knighton Villas. The white house in the corner adjoining the Knighton Estate was the residence of the late John Hooper, a much-respected citizen of that time, and father of the late John Desmond Hooper, for many years Surveyor to the Woodford Local Board, and of the late Basil Hooper, who died at Woodford a few years ago. The house has disappeared and others have taken its place.

The Woodford Times, August 21, 1931

The purchase of about 40 acres of the Knighton Estate at Woodford, Essex, has been completed this week by the City of London Corporation. The land will be administered for the use of the public as part of Epping Forest, although separated from the Forest by two main roads and houses. A charming woodland and two lakes are included in the land acquired.

The Knighton Estate, where the late Mr. Edward North Buxton resided for over 50 years, consisted of about 100 acres, partly in Woodford and partly in Buckhurst Hill urban districts. When the estate came into the market some months ago a public meeting

The new southern entrance to the estate beside the South Lodge, as it was *left* during Knighton's heyday and *right* in August 1984 — the year the oak tree died. This is the only thatched house in Woodford, up for sale in July 1984 at £75,000.

was held at Woodford with the object of saving the whole or part of it from the builders and preserving it as a memorial to Mr. Buxton. Woodford Urban Distict Council contributed £5,000 towards the purchase of the woodland area, and the City Corporation found the balance on the condition that the spot should become, for public purposes, an addition to Epping Forest, in which Mr. Buxton took a keen interest.

Money could not be raised publicly to buy the remaining 60 acres of the estate, which was sold on Tuesday to an Essex land and estate development firm.

The Woodford Times, June 28, 1930

On Wednesday morning an Inquiry was held at the offices of the Woodford Council by the Ministry of Health to hear the Council's objections to the lay-out proposed on the Knighton Estate by the Southend-on-Sea Estates, Ltd.

Our representative attended, but was informed that the Inquiry was to be private, and that Press representatives would not be admitted.

While waiting to learn whether the Press would be admitted or not, our representative interviewed one of the officials of the Southend-on-Sea Estates, Ltd., and elicited the following information regarding the proposed lay-out of the estate. The builders proposed to line the streets on either side with a narrow strip of land planted with shrubs, which would have the effect of forming a small screen for the houses.

The Council at their meeting on April 21st, as reported at the time, turned this plan down for the reason that they considered it would be too expensive to maintain.

The Woodford Times, May 8, 1931

The old Loughton Road became the drive to Knighton House — demolished in 1935.

Sir, — In common with many other of the older inhabitants of the neighbourhood, I have been much interested in the articles and photographs of Old Woodford which have appeared in your paper in recent months.

Many of the old places I remember as a small child — my family having come here in 1868. The pictures and information of the old Toll House are specially interesting to me, and I join with 'A Woodfordian' in hoping that the old 'Bell House' can be saved as a relic of the Woodford of long ago.

Yours faithfully,
ARTHUR C. DORLING

THE EDITOR'S REPLY

We are very grateful for the many expressions of appreciation received of the articles and pictures of Old Woodford, and for the kindly assistance of our readers in helping to keep this series going.

We fully endorse our correspondents' hope that the Old Bell House may be preserved as a relic of the Woodford of long ago. We have been making enquiries, which we had hoped would have enabled us to make a definite statement on the matter in this issue, but owing to our going to press two days earlier than usual in consequence of the Christmas Holidays, we shall have to postpone making an announcement until next week, as the information promised us is not yet to hand.

The Woodford Times, December 25, 1931

No longer used the Bell House fell into disrepair and was pulled down in 1934.

It stood in the back garden of No. 652 High Road, exactly where Bryan Perry built his pond in 1970!

Although situated in Buckhurst Hill, the Village Hospital is part and parcel of the history of the Jubilee. Financed by public subscription on the initiative of Dr C. H. Livingstone and opened around 1869, the hospital in Knighton Lane was the only one then serving the district. Now it is the private residence of Edgar and Pat Brame.

Woodford was *en fets* yesterday (Thursday) on the occasion of the visit of T.R.H. the Duke and Duchess of Connaught and Strathearn to open the Woodford Jubilee Hospital.

As the hour for the ceremony approached large numbers of people congregated along the route from Knighton to the High Street with the object of obtaining a sight of the illustrious visitors. The ranks of the sightseers were swollen by the children of the elementary schools at Woodford and Buckhurst Hill, who were granted a holiday in honour of the event. The children of St. John's schools, Buckhurst Hill, were prettily grouped under a large oak on the borders of the parish in Whitehall Road. As their Royal Highnesses passed, the girls curtseyed and waved Union Jacks, and the Duke and Duchess responded with gracious bows. On the Green and all along the beflagged route to the marquee, which was to be the scene of the formal proceedings, prettily dressed children and ladies attired in the becoming costumes of the season gave a lively charm to the scene; while the inevitable vendor of penny 'Royal wavers', etc., and an occasional 'cool summer drinks' man, whose long-suffering visages and plaintive cries spoke eloquently that they realized that they had somehow got among the wrong crowd, moved wearily along the line. Enthusiastic photographic artists were busily engaged in taking snapshots to serve as souvenirs. The largest crowd had, of course, assembled in the vicinity of the hospital, where the sloping ground afforded all an admirable opportunity of viewing the greater part of the proceedings. At intervals the chimes from the old Parish Church were borne in liquid melody on the swinging breeze . . .

The Woodford Times, June 2, 1899

June 1, 1899 and the Duke and Duchess of Connaught pass down in front of The Terrace (see page 211) to Broomhill Walk for the opening of the new Jubilee Hospital. Prince Arthur was Queen Victoria's third, and favourite, son and she bestowed on him the title of Duke of Connaught and Strathearn in 1874. He married Louise, daughter of Prince Frederick Charles of Prussia in 1879. He served in the Army becoming Field-Marshal in 1902. The Duchess died in 1917, the Duke in 1942.

The final nail has been hammered into Jubilee Hospital's coffin.

Health Minister Kenneth Clarke drove it home last week, when he rubber stamped plans to close the hospital.

Announcing the closure in a letter to Patrick Jenkin and other local MPs, Mr. Clarke said he had agreed the closure because it was part of a sensible re-organisation of local services. He gave three reasons:

'Firstly, because I believe that Jubilee Hospital is no longer suited to the provision of acute medical care.

'Secondly, because I believe the finally agreed plans for re-providing services elsewhere are adequate.

'Thirdly, because the proposal is in line with the district's overall strategy of making better use of all its health care resources.'

Guardian & Gazette, July 19, 1985

Sir James Hawkey, J.P., chairman of the Wanstead and Woodford Council, was one of the busiest men in the district on Coronation Day, when he went from place to place visiting the scenes of the Coronation celebrations.

Street teas were the most important celebrations from the children's point of view and they were held in every conceivable place.

In the gaily-decorated Iron Room at Holy Trinity Church over sixty children sat down to a tea and entertainment organised by the mothers of the district.

Wanstead people allowed nothing to interfere with their Coronation celebrations. Teas were held in places varying from a garage to a tarpaulin shelter, the children enjoying tea under these novel conditions probably more than they would have done in the open.

As the afternoon wore on, it became obvious that the teas at least would have to be held under cover, and hasty preparations were made to ensure that the boys and girls — and the grown-ups too — should not be cheated of their participation in the great event.

A typical case was that of the residents of Voluntary-place, who showed great ingenuity and enterprise in converting a garage belonging to Mr. S. Godly into a 'banquet hall'.

Scarcely a street in Wanstead was without a liberal display of flags and bunting, and the High-street probably deserves 'first prize' as a result chiefly of the enterprise of the local shopkeepers.

Express and Independent, May 15, 1937

Another Royal visit, this time by the then-Queen Mother, took place in **1938** when Queen Mary paid her first visit to Woodford, to the student's hostel which bears her name. The picture shows the entrance lodge to Elmhurst which had been purchased in **1925**; demolished with the building of the Southend arterial road.

The Queen planted this tree which stands opposite Lynden Hall, and not far from the new multi-storey Halls of Residence which were built in **1969**.

Queen Mary paid her first visit to Woodford on Saturday afternoon when she opened Lynden Hall, the new hall of residence for women students of Queen Mary College (University of London). The occasion was in the nature of a visit by Her Majesty, but a large crowd assembled at the entrance to the new building in High-road, South Woodford and enthusiastically cheered on her arrival and departure.

Along the route taken by Her Majesty through Leytonstone and Wanstead, many assembled at the road-side and saw her go slowly by.

At the appointed hour — three o'clock — the Royal car entered the drive, pulling up in front of Lynden Hall, where Her Majesty was welcomed by the Mayor of Wanstead and Woodford (Sir James Hawkey, J.P.) and extended a great reception by the many students who were lined up, wearing caps and gowns. . . . Her Majesty was actually in the building for about twenty minutes, and on coming out proceeded with the ceremony of planting a hornbeam tree in the front lawn, to commemorate her visit.

Express and Independent, May 21, 1938

'Royal' occasion almost forty years later — the Silver Jubilee of our present Queen, celebrated by street parties and festivities all over the area. These children put on their display in Mill Lane. The old cottage was renovated two years later.

229

The 'tower of Babel' of the Chigwell and Woodford Bridge Gas Company which raised such a furore when it first reared above the open fields of Milkwell Farm in 1928.

THE WOODFORD BRIDGE GASOMETER

Councillor Miller, at the conclusion of the business on the agenda, rose to voice the criticism of Woodford Bridge in particular and of the rest of Woodford in general regarding the gasometer at the bottom of Snakes Lane. The feeling in Woodford Bridge about it was very very bitter, and amongst many epithets cast about it was 'the modern Tower of Babel.' As far as his recollection of Biblical knowledge went many languages were spoken during the construction of the Tower of Babel, and there were many sets of language being used about this one, most of it very bad. It was a terrible eyesore and a monstrosity.

Woodford Council Meeting, June 19, 1928

One of the ironies of history. Babbling towers of a different kind erected on the fields of Milkwell Farm in 1968 dwarfed the gasometer into insignificance until it was dismantled in September 1985.

Since the Middle Ages the fields bordering the Roding had been a source of clay for brick-making. It was while he was British Minister in Venice that Sir James Wright first became interested in the manufacture of artificial slate having seen the process in operation in Italy. After he purchased Ray House (on the left in the picture *above*) in 1770, he built this factory in the grounds and the business carried on an extensive export trade with the West Indies. The house burned down in 1838 — the newspaper report is reproduced on page 212. The factory was demolished soon after Sir James's death in 1804.

This is to give Notice,

THAT the Makers of Pantiles being much multiply'd of late, the Price of Pantiles is now fallen to Four Shillings and Six-pence per hundred, at the Kilns near Woodford Bridge in Essex, where any Person may now be furnish'd with good Marketable Ware at that Price, and deliver'd to any Part of the Town at one Shilling per Hundred Carriage.

Press report, 1739

Woodford Bridge, a village in the parish of Woodford, nine miles from London, on the road to Ongar, situated on a fine eminence, forming a very picturesque appearance. Near the bridge is a neat pump of excellent water, brought hither in 1776 at a great expense by the proprietor of the estate for the accommodation of the poor inhabitants; and not far from this is a manufactory of artificial stone.

The Ambulator, 1793

The last brickfield, that of W. & C. French, lasted until 1964. When it closed it ended an era which had lasted nearly five hundred years.

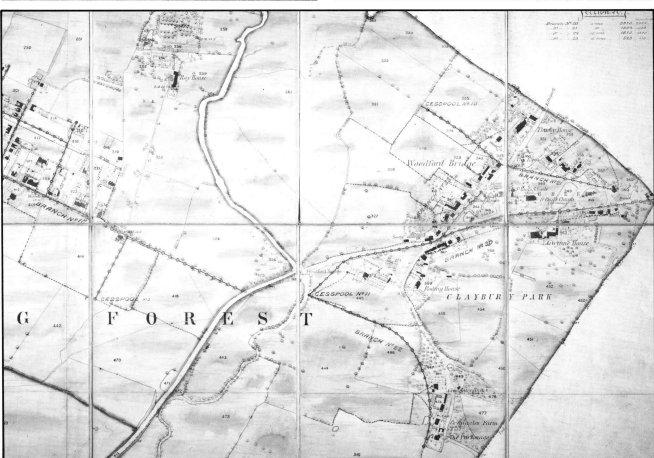

STOLEN or Strayed, from the White-Hart Inn, Woodford-Bridge, Essex, on Friday, the 21st of October last,

A Black Mare, with a bald Face, white hind Legs clipped close, and Sprig Tail, about fourteen Hands three inches high.

Whoever will bring the said Mare to John Smith, of Woodford-Bridge aforesaid, or give Information how she may be had again, shall receive One Guinea Reward; and if stolen, whoever will give Information as above, and of the Person or Persons who stole the said Mare, so that he, she or they, that stole her, or either of them, may be duly convicted thereof, shall, upon Conviction of the Offender or Offenders, receive a Reward of Three Guineas to be paid by the said John Smith.

Press announcement, 1768

Has anybody seen a black and white mare . . . or Sir James Wright's little dog . . .?

A SMALL TARRIER BITCH LOST last Week, near Woodford Bridge, Essex, of a Fawn Colour; answers to the Name of VENOM.

Whoever will bring her to Lord Le Despencer, in Hanover-square, shall have Half a Guinea Reward.

Had on a Brass Collar, with the Name 'Sir James Wright, Bart. Teignmouth House, Devon.

Press advertisement, 1789

An ancient ford, where Woodford bridge is now situated, was the occasion of the name of the parish, which is wholly included in the forest. It is three miles in extent from east to west; and two miles from north to south. The village, enclosing a green, is distinguished by the purity of its air, and the beautiful and extensive prospects in various directions.

The History and Topography of the County of Essex, March 1831

The White Hart in Woodford Bridge is referred to in many contemporary reports but the building we see today was built about 1900, the picture *above* being taken in 1908 by the late Mr W. L. F. Wastell, a leading member of the Woodford Photographic Society and President of the Royal Photographic Society in 1922/3. The ancient row of cottages on the left have been a part of the scene for over two hundred years.

Derelict cottages which have been a local eyesore for years are to be given a new lease of life. Brock Builders, which bought the properties from Barnardo's three years ago, started work on renovating the dilapidated cottages in Chigwell Road, Woodford Bridge, last week.

And for local residents, who say they have watched the buildings literally fall down after several years of neglect, it is not a moment too soon. Their complaints about the buildings have, up until now, fallen on deaf ears, they claim.

Publican Kenneth Joyce, who runs the White Hart pub opposite the cottages, says the restoration notice was put up by Brock Builders over a year ago. 'It's disgraceful. The buildings have just been left to fall down. They are an eyesore,' he said.

And many of the boards preventing people from entering the cottages have been pulled down by children, making the property very unsafe, he added.

Owned by the Dr Barnardo organisation since the early part of this century, by 1980 the cottages, listed Grade II, were derelict and their plight was highlighted in our previous publication 'Woodford — Then and Now'. Notice was served on Barnardos to ensure that they did not deteriorate any further but before work was begun, they were sold to Russell, French and Brock Limited. This company has a reputation for restoring historic buildings and plans were drawn up and submitted for their complete refurbishment.

'Lots of people moan about it when they come into the pub -- we are all wondering what is being done about them,' he said.

The news has also been welcomed by Opticians James Scott, sole occupants in the row. It is the only building still in use which has not gone to rack and ruin, but with tarpaulin covering the roof to keep out the rain and chronic damp, it too needs renovating.

Said receptionist Mrs Eileen Smith: 'This shop has been here for donkeys years as an opticians but we shall be glad to move as the building is in such a terrible state.'

But they will not be moving far — just to the other end of the row once rebuilding has finished there.

As a Grade 2 listed building the 17th and 18th century cottages must retain much of their original character and any change that might affect their outward appearance needs special planning consent. This, say Brock's, has led to the considerable delay before work began this month.

Work is expected to take a year, weather permitting. The buildings are to be converted into eight cottages and the opticians.

Guardian and Gazette,
January 25, 1985

Thomas Barnardo, the medical missionary from Dublin, began his work in East London, devoting his attentions to the rescue of destitute children, and he founded the national homes which bear his name in 1866. Although he died in 1905 his work was carried on and in 1910 William Paget purchased Gwynne House, then empty, for the organisation. During the next twenty years accommodation blocks were built for boys in the grounds, the girls' Village Home being located at Barkingside. With the increasing tendency towards fostering, Barnardo's relinquished the site during the 1970s.

The estate was tastefully redeveloped in the early 1980s and Gwynne House was converted into the Prince Regent restaurant.

Roding House, which used to stand in Roding Lane North, was taken over by the Homes before the Second World War as a reception building. Now replaced by Hood House.

One of the most interesting properties in the Woodford Bridge area was Great Gales Hall, of which every room except the billiard room was oak panelled, and which was also closely associated with the farm of the same name. It was still standing in 1932 when this picture was taken specially for the Woodford Times' series of historical articles on old Woodford which ran in the paper during 1931-33 although the farm itself had been demolished in 1927. The newspaper articles provide a rich source of contemporary material at a time when the area was turning rapidly from a village into a suburb and many of the large old properties were falling foul of the age of unrestricted house building. Great Gales Hall was also the venue for the local ghost story which appears to be fairly well authenticated. According to the 'Times, the story runs that between about 1865-1870, while the house was in the occupation of the Boltons, one year, when the family, with the exception of one son and two servants, had gone away for a holiday, on the day of their departure and shortly after they had left, the bells began to ring without any apparent cause. These bells were of the old-fashioned wire type, with the bells suspended on springs in a row outside the kitchen door. One of the servants ran out to see what was the matter, without discovering any reason, and alarmed, went back to the other servant, and together they further investigaged, but still without any result. Meanwhile the bells continued ringing with increasing din. Thoroughly alarmed the two women sought outside assistance, and a gardener and the sexton of the church came along, but the cause of the ringing baffled them also. All day long the ringing continued, and it was still in full swing on the son's return home that night. Further search of a most minute character was unproductive and finally, in order that sleep should not be disturbed, the bells were taken off, but even then the springs from which they were suspended continued violently vibrating, and so continued for days. No explanation was ever forthcoming, but in the neighbourhood it was freely attributed to supernatural agency. In the end the house was purchased by the Woodford Land Company for development. This is where the entrance to the drive lay with the Hall behind Nos. 48-62.

At a meeting of the Local Government Committee held in London on Tuesday, it was agreed, on the suggestion of Mrs. Chisholm, that in connection with the amalgamation of Wanstead and Woodford, the former place should be divided into four wards. It was pointed out that there were already four wards at Woodford.

In view of the expression of opinion by the Ministry of Health against double names, the committee recommended that the names of the amalgamated urban districts of Wanstead and Woodford, the amalgamated district of Loughton, Buckhurst Hill, and Chigwell, and the amalgamated urban districts of Waltham Holy Cross and Chingford should be 'The Snaresbrook Urban District,' 'The Chigwell Urban District,' and 'The Waltham Abbey Urban District,' respectively.

Mrs. Chisholm thought it would be a pity to drop the name of Wanstead, which dated from the time of William the Conqueror. She moved that they should call it Wanstead and Woodford. The reason she suggested that

Thurlby House, a Grade II listing from the latter part of the 1700s, was also used by Barnardos between the wars. A small cemetery was consecrated in the grounds in 1927 which still survives; the house is now used as a public library.

Wanstead should be placed first was that it was the older name, came first alphabetically, and had a higher rateable value.

Mr. A. M. Mathews said that Wanstead might have a higher rateable value now, but Woodford was growing rapidly.

The amendment was carried.

An amendment that the amalgamated districts of Waltham Holy Cross and Chingford should be called Chingford and Waltham Abbey was also carried.

The proposal as to the Chigwell name was carried.

The Woodford Times, October 16, 1931

How few people there seemed to be in Woodford, and how many dogs! . . . The suberb is sliced by main roads, and the cars and long-distance buses speeding to Southend and Newmarket leave only a distant hum in hundreds of empty side-roads. In Bethnal Green people are vigorously at home in the streets, their public face much the same as their private. In Woodford people seem to be quieter and more reserved in public, somehow endorsing Mumford's description of suburbs as the apotheosis of 'a collective attempt to lead a private life'. . . .

The contrast is all the more striking because Woodford and Bethnal Green both belong to East London. Although Woodford is officially in Essex, there is no visible boundary between it and London. Buildings stretch almost all the way from Bethnal Green through Leyton to Woodford, and now even farther out to the belt of new Council estates.

This unity is more than geographical. The

One of the most picturesque spots in the Woodford area — unchanged for over 80 years. The Crown and Crooked Billet has existed since the 1700s — only the fowl of yesterday have given way to the mongrels of today.

suburbs grew out from the city, where most of their inhabitants came from. The population of Woodford has been rising rapidly all this century, most sharply of all in the boom years of private building immediately before the war — the annual rate of increase was 1,600 in the 'thirties, as compared with 660 in the 'twenties and 810 between 1946 and 1951. A few of the additional people have come from rural Essex and East Anglia. Many of the countrymen came off the land to be gardeners, the country-women to be servants in the big houses around Epping Forest.

These people of 'good farming stock', as one of them put it, met in Woodford; the far greater flood coming in the other direction from the city. Fifteen per cent of the people living in Woodford (as represented by our general sample) were born in the East End, 26% in the inner Essex boroughs of Leyton, East Ham, West Ham and Walthamstow, and 20% elsewhere in Greater London. The rest, apart from the 12% born in Woodford itself, came from the provinces, where more younger people originated than older — 29% of the 414 people in their thirties and forties were born outside Greater London, against 18% of the 90 people aged 70 or over. But people from the inner London districts are still the core of suburban society. Often they have arrived by stages, they or their parents moving, as children or after marriage, from Bethnal Green or Poplar to Walthamstow or Forest Gate, and then on to Woodford. Their starting point is impressed on them all the same.

Family and Class in a London Suburb,
Peter Willmott & Michael Young, 1960

REDBRIDGE

This new administrative area comprises the areas of Ilford and Wanstead and Woodford, part of the borough of Dagenham and part of the urban district of Chigwell, and was established as a London borough by charter dated March 10, 1964. . . .

The London borough of Redbridge is principally residential in character, with an estimated population of 248,550 and an area of 13,983 acres, . . . Most of the attractions and interesting features of Redbridge are such as one might expect in any up-to-date progressive community . . . and many acres of Epping Forest lie within the borough.

The County Handbook, 1965

Sir, May I ask your publication of this letter inviting the expressions of opinion of the residents and owners of property in Maybank Road re the question of Motor Buses now running through this hitherto quiet thoroughfare. It is the fact that living in this road has become painful and intolerable by reason of this nuisance. It can be proved that the nuisance is injurious both to health and property and besides this, there is the cost of the maintenance of this thoroughfare. Although the buses have been running about ten days only, it has been found necessary already to make repairs to the road. Is this not a situation which might be taken up by the Ratepayer's Association? I should be glad to assist both personally and financially to any likely action which might be taken up by the residents in a body to approach our Council or to the authorities who have the power to divert this traffic. Why could not the buses be compelled to keep to the main road instead of using a market place and bye roads, the Maybank Road not having been made for the vehicular traffic of the land under notice?
Yours faithfully,
H. H. ELLISON
Eden House, Maybank Road, S. Woodford

The Woodford Times, January 23, 1914

The first motor buses: January 12, 1914 outside the Crown and Crooked Billet.

The quaint old Fox and Hounds and the blacksmith's next door lasted until 1965.

So impressed are local residents with the magnificent exploits of the R.A.F. that, not content with giving every available piece of aluminium for the making of Spitfires, they are now undertaking to pay for their construction. Spitfire Funds have been launched in Leyton, Wanstead and Woodford, Chingford, Epping, Chigwell and Walthamstow, and in all cases contributions have been received before the scheme has been officially launched.

Express and Independent, August 24, 1940

Placards about the borough show the latest figure required for the Spitfire Fund. Many have commented on the posters which have been displayed throughout the Borough for some months urging support for the Spitfire fund.

Now that the sum aimed at has been collected I think the one responsible for the writing of the posters should have a word of thanks. On making enquiries I found that Mr. R. L. Fowkes of the A.F.S. executed the work and congratulate him on the poster's attractiveness.

The Woodford Times, December 1941

The Spitfire presented to the R.A.F. by the borough of Wanstead and Woodford has seen much action with a Polish Squadron in fighter sweeps over France. On one occasion the machine, piloted by a Polish airman, shot down a F.W.190, while the Spitfire was escorting bombers.

Councillor D. L. Forbes has recently heard from the Public Relations Officer at the Ministry of Aircraft Production, who writes:

'The Spitfire presented to the Royal Air Force by the people of Wanstead and Woodford has been flown by a Polish pilot. The Squadron to which this aircraft was attached has a fine history and a record number of enemy aircraft shot down to its credit. During the Battle of Britain the Squadron was particularly active and the successes of its pilots soon made it the champion Polish Squadron in Fighter Command.'

'*Borough of Wanstead and Woodford*, during an engagement in which two German planes were destroyed, accounted for one of them. On this occasion the Squadron took off to escort bombers over France. Visibility was good and in bright sunshine the Spitfires crossed the coast on their way to the target. Little interference from hostile aircraft was experienced by the pilots and the bombing proved most successful. Setting course again the Squadron turned for home, but the Germans were waiting for them and dived down on them suddenly from cloud cover. During the combat which followed little

damage was suffered by the Allied aircraft but two of the German aircraft were claimed by the fighter pilots as destroyed.'

'The dogfight involving *Wanstead and Woodford* occurred in defence of one of our bombers which was being attacked by an F.W.190. The German fighter, though firmly held off by the gunners, was making repeated attacks on the bomber. The Spitfire pilot following on the tail of the German, fired a short burst, and the F.W. broke off the

National defence. Having raised £5,107 in the Spitfire fund, Wanstead and Woodford's name was given to Spitfire VB P8789 which was allocated to the strength of No. 118 Squadron on September 15, 1941. (The official amount necessary to be collected for sponsorship of an aircraft was £5,000 per engine, i.e. a Lancaster would cost £20,000.) However this aircraft was lost on June 1, 1942 whereupon the name was switched to AA882, this being the Spitfire flown by the Poles of No. 303 Squadron. One ingnominious incident, not publicised at the time, was when Flying Officer E. Horbaczewski landed it with the undercarriage retracted at Hibaldstow in Lincolnshire. It survived the war and was struck off charge in August 1945 and scrapped. What a pity the Borough were not minded to preserve it; then it could have been purchased from the Air Ministry for £100; today the value is over £250,000!

assault. A few seconds later, the fuselage seemed to catch fire and the aircraft dived out of control towards the ground.'

'Boulogne, Lille, Calais, Dunkirk, and many other places have become familiar to the pilot who flies this aircraft and the people of Wanstead and Woodford may be sure that their Spitfire is playing a great part in Fighter Command's offensive against the Luftwaffe.'

Express and Independent, August 29, 1942

Local defence. If the mains dried up water for fire fighters was initially to be obtained from the Roding, nearby ponds and swimming baths. In addition hundreds of 40-gallon drums were positioned at strategic places along the roads, and 95 static water tanks were built throughout the Borough to give an emergency water supply for the local and Auxiliary Fire Service. This one stood on the Green near All Saints Church — lettering by Reg Fowkes!

Above: **On the night of October 9, 1940 Tudor Close, Monkhams Drive and Worcester Crescent were blasted by a stick of bombs** which straddled the Monkhams estate. One bomb landed in the front garden of No. 14 Tudor Close.

Who was it that said that lightning never strikes the same place twice? Five weeks later on November 16 a land mine floated down over exactly the same spot, to explode just before midnight between No. 14 and No. 58 Monkhams Avenue. This time the damage was more severe — these censored pictures never having been published before now.

Wartime emergency. Early in 1941 the Ministry of Food was planning the introduction of facilities to cater for the feeding of large numbers of people at nominal prices. Winston Churchill minuted the Minister in March 1941: 'I hope the term "Communal Feeding Centres" is not going to be adopted. It is an odious expression, suggestive of Communism and the workhouse. I suggest you call them "British Restaurants".

Everybody associates the word "restaurant" with a good meal, and they may as well have the name if they cannot get anything else.' The Borough's first restaurant was opened at the Memorial Hall (above) in September 1941, a second in Wanstead High Street in September 1943. By March 31, 1947, when they closed, the Woodford restaurant had served 613,194 meals and that at Wanstead 263,232.

MRS. CHURCHILL TO OPEN BRITISH RESTAURANT

Mrs. Winston Churchill is to open Wanstead and Woodford's first British Restaurant at the Memorial Hall, South Woodford, next Friday, September 12. The Memorial Hall is undergoing a complete transformation. The hall is being redecorated in cream and green and this colour scheme will also be used on the crockery, on the small tables — which are covered with inlaid lino, pleasing to the eye and easy to keep clean — and in other directions throughout the Restaurant. Not the least striking feature of the newly decorated hall is the borough coat of arms which occupies a prominent position on the stage, forming a colourful, back-ground.

Woodford Times, September 5, 1941

The war wounds of Wanstead and Woodford are disappearing, but they are too deep set for speedy total healing. The levelled site, wide and deep, patterned by weed-grown paths leading to houses that were; the gap in a row of shops where a trader's name still looks up from the pavement which his vanished shop once fronted; the illusory facade masking the shell of a building open to the sky — these are typical of what to each of us has become part of a scene made familiar by Time.

There were other marks that scarred less heavily the face of the Borough — scars, perforce self-inflicted: the gashes torn on Green and sidewalk in order that there might be shelter for the public, shelter for Wardens, from the weapons of the air.

Public shelters, Wardens' Posts exist no longer, though the signs of their having been will not for a long time be wholly effaced. And new houses are replacing those demolished.

But each empty site that remains, each filled-in excavation, holds for many a memory — a memory recaptured with a strange sense of a distant past — of those five years when the people of Wanstead and Woodford, with high courage or with quiet fortitude, endured much. To some the memory may be one of sadness and of suffering; to some of happenings that seem today fantastic, even humorous; to others who pass the spot where 'our Post' once stood, or look across at a building that played its part in the scheme of Civil Defence, the memory will be of the fellowship of good companions, members of a team who worked 'as neighbours, among neighbours, for neighbours.'

It Happened Here, Stanley Tiquet, May 1947

On October 7, 1943 a raider approached the junction of the Southend Road and High Road releasing a stick of three high-explosive bombs. One fell behind the parade of shops on the High Road and another in the grounds of Elmhurst, then occupied by the military, demolishing a Nissen hut. The original Evening News caption of 'Bomb damage in Woodford, 3 killed 20 injured' became, on its return from the Press Censorship bureau, 'Bomb damage in London area, some casualties a few fatal'. In fact it is believed that there were seven fatalities and allegations were raised about a serious delay in the arrival of Civil Defence ambulances and personnel and that one ambulance had run out of petrol on the way. (Records show that the incident occurred at 22.05 and the ambulance was not dispatched until 22.26. As a result the Ministry of Home Defence was pressed into holding an inquiry into the incident.)

Just one incident . . . in one street . . . in one town . . . on just one night . . . but who remembers it today?

Woodford police are maintaining a 24-hour guard on the borough's new statue of Sir Winston Churchill, unveiled at Salway Hill, Woodford Green on Saturday afternoon [October 31] by Field Marshal Viscount Montgomery in the presence of Sir Winston and Lady Churchill. Purpose of the guard, it was stated this week, is as a precautionary measure against practical jokers. 'We do not anticipate any trouble,' said a Council spokesman this week, 'but it was thought the presence of the police would deter anyone from playing any pranks.' The statue, which has attracted the interest of hundreds of passers-by since Saturday's historic occasion, is to have a police guard 'until further notice'.

The afternoon of the ceremony, originally postponed from October 3 because of the General Election, dawned fine but cool. Police closed Salway Hill to traffic and by early afternoon a crowd began to collect, later swelling to between four and five thousand people, round the roped enclosure which surrounded the draped statue and a small, covered dais from which the speeches were to be made.

The band of the Royal Corps of Signals and the guard of honour provided by Wanstead-Woodford's adopted regiment, the 45th (Essex) Signal Regiment, T.A., resplendent in ceremonial 'blues', formed up on the road — and silence fell as the crowd waited for the arrival of the distinguished visitors. Several small boys secured lofty vantage points in the trees in front of 'The Roses' flats.

First to arrive was Sir Stuart Mallinson C.B.E., D.S.O., M.C., D.L., J.P., representing the trustees of the statue committee, accompanied by the sculptor, Mr. David McFall, Members of Wanstead-Woodford Borough Council, the aldermen in their robes of office, and other invited representatives took their places in the enclosure reserved for them. The Mayor and Mayoress, Councillor and Mrs. G. C. E. Dixon, after being received by Alderman R. A. Dalton, chairman of the statue sub-

committee, waited beside the dais to welcome Sir Winston and Lady Churchill, a burst of cheering greeting the arrival of Sir Winston's car.

The last car drew up with Field Marshal Viscount Montgomery and the Lord Lieutenant, Sir John Ruggles-Brise, and as the band played the general salute the guard of honour presented arms with a precision that reflected weeks of training for the occasion. After inspecting the guard Lord Montgomery took up his position on the dais with the principal guests and Councillor Dixon introduced the ceremony.

The purpose of the occasion, he said, was to do honour to Sir Winston and to commemorate the faithful, outstanding and unique service he had rendered in the House of Commons for 35 years as representative of the borough. The statue, said the Mayor, had been paid for by public subscription. It had

now been presented by the trustees to the Borough Council to hold in trust for the people of Wanstead-Woodford.

Asked to carry out the unveiling ceremony, Lord Montgomery first paid tribute to the guard of honour and expressed pleasure 'at seeing several men who were with me in the Eighth Army'.

Then, turning to Sir Winston, he said: "It may seem to us today almost an impertinence to act as though we should ever need a reminder of Sir Winston's appearance or his achievements. This famous man to whom this statue is designed is still most happily with us, enjoying in dignity and quiet the evening of his splendid life. But that, alas, will not always be so. Future generations will not only need but will desire to know what he looked like, and it is most fitting that you in Woodford have decided to supply the answer. He did so much for the world but you helped him to take his place in the House of Commons when he was without a seat and without a party. He has received your unfailing loyalty for more than a quarter of a century. Woodford was his political Alamein. . . .

After watching the drape flutter away, the Field Marshal looked carefully at the statue for a moment, then gravely saluted the two Sir Winston Churchills, first the statue and then the smiling figure on the dais.

Moving to the microphone Sir Winston declared: 'I am deeply obliged to my old friend and comrade for the very kind things he has said. When I consider the war years of his own brilliant achievements and his own long career of devoted service to this country I reflect that of him it may well be said: 'I have built a monument more lasting than bronze.'

'I am most grateful to the people of Wanstead-Woodford for the signal honour you now do me. You have sustained and supported me throughout the 35 years I have had the privilege of representing you in Parliament.'

Express and Independent, November 6, 1959

There are few residences so near London that have the seclusion and charm of the White House. Built originally in the latter part of the nineteenth century by Lady Henry Somerset, it was intended as a rest and holiday centre for East Eand workers. Lady Henry Somerset did not remain very long, however, and after a few years the property was leased to the Bishop of St. Alban's and later other owners, and subsequently was purchased from Lord Somers, her son, one-time Governor of Victoria and Chief Scout after Lord Baden Powell, by Sir Stuart Mallinson, who acquired the property in 1926.

The house now retains a delightful atmosphere of a home that is cherished. Off the entrance hall is a fascinating room built originally by Lady Henry Somerset as a Chapel, and its essential characteristics remain. It is panelled with timber from the Ypres area which matches a fine old Flemish mantelpiece.

The grounds comprise nearly thirty acres, much of which is beautiful woodland. The terrace is dominated by a grand old oak tree over five hundred years old. The house, planned by C. F. Voysey, was built with the tree as a central point.

The grounds have been used by many organisations, such as Churches, Welfare, Invalid Children's Aid, Red Cross, Scouts and numerous youth, sports and military units.

The people who have enjoyed the amenities of the White House are representative of all nationalities and interests.

The late King George VI made the first review of the Local Defence Volunteers (later the Home Guard) in July, 1940, more recently in happier times, Sir Stuart bowled the Duke of Edinburgh 'first ball' on the practice wicket.

Sporting personalities include such famous names as Harold Abrahams, Douglas Lowe, D. Drysdale, G. P. S. Macpherson, W. W. Wakefield, Dorothy Round, Jack Hobbs, Pelham Warner, G. O. Allen, Herbert Chapman and stars of the Association Football World.

Sir Winston and Lady Churchill have been frequent visitors and made the White House their base for election campaigns in 1950 and 1951. Switchboards, Secretaries and all the paraphernalia of a twentieth century politician took root in the White House at these times.

Lord Montgomery of Alamein has made more than one visit, and so have other Service Chiefs over the years.

The Lord Lieutenant of Essex, Chairman of the Essex County Council, The Lord Mayor of London, Lord Aberdare, Lord Mackintosh, Lord Simon, Lord Wakehurst, Lady Barnett, Lady Baden Powell, Sir John Barbirolli, The Hon. Arthur Villiers, Sir Basil Henriques, James Gun, The Bishop of Lichfield, The Bishop of Chelmsford, Sir Alan Cobham, Gypsy Smith, and so the list goes on. . . .

Throughout the past twenty-eight years at all times, Sir Stuart and Lady Mallinson have always given a special welcome to our friends from America. Mrs. Lewis Douglas, Mrs. Gifford, Mrs. Aldrich — wives of the last three American Ambassadors to the Court of St. James — and many Service personnel have enjoyed much time in the house and grounds.

The Commonwealth has had its share of visitors as have many other nations, and it may truly be said that Sir Stuart and Lady Mallinson have practiced goodwill and fellowship that can do nothing but enhance the eternal quest for better relationship throughout the world.

Anon.

The last act. The final tree was planted by Sir Winston Churchill's biographer, historian Michael Gilbert. Almost as if it heralded the end, within days Sir Stuart — the grand old man of Woodford — 92 years old, had died.

In May 1953 Field-Marshal Viscount Montgomery of Alamein planted the first tree for Sir Stuart Mallinson at his house beside Highams on Woodford High Road. Thus began the White House arboretum which eventually spanned five Prime Ministers, one Viceroy of India, two Governor Generals of Australia, one Governor General of Canada, one Governor General of New Zealand, twelve Knights of the Order of the Garter and Prelate, two Knights of the Order of the Thistle, two Admirals of the Fleet, four Field-Marshals, two Marshals of the Royal Air Force, five Supreme Commanders Allied Powers Europe, three Deputy Supreme Commanders and one astronaut.

Sir Winston Churchill's eye would have twinkled above that stern expression if he had been at The White House, Woodford Green last week. The picturesque residence of Sir Stuart Mallinson in Woodford Green was the scene of the final tree-planting ceremony.

The honour of following 130 great names in history — including Earl Mountbatten, Poet Laureate Sir John Betjeman, Astronaut Frank Boorman and record-breaking athlete Dr Roger Bannister — was this time bestowed on Winnie's historian, Martin Gilbert.

The author of *Winston Churchill — The Wilderness Years* planted the last tree in the famous Arboretum in a place specially reserved for him between trees planted by Sir Evelyn Wrench, founder of the English Speaking Union, and Sir Harry Brittain, founder of the Pilgrims of the USA and Britain.

Mr Gilbert's honour was the final place in the jigsaw of woodland which has greeted a wealth of great leaders and personalities. They included, of course, the remarkable politician and leader Sir Winston. Said Sir Stuart: 'One of the greatest times was when Sir Winston put his hand on my shoulder in October 1951 and said he was leaving the White House to meet the King, to form a new government.'

Historian and professor of English at Merton College Oxford, Mr Gilbert has been the former Prime Minister's official biographer for 13 years, following the death of predecessor Randolph Churchill.

He said: 'Ten years before the war, Sir Winston returned home to find one of his most splendid trees had been cut down. And he remarked: 'I am opposed to two things — tyranny and arborecide.'

Mr Gilbert's plaque is overlooked by a variety of trees given root by the former Prime Minister of Australia, Sir Robert Menzies, our ex-PM Edward Heath, MP Shirley Williams, Master of the Rolls Lord Denning and musician Yehudi Menuhin.

There's also a special corner set aside commemorating American presidents. Names like Woodrow Wilson, Calvin Coolidge, Herbert Hoover, Franklin Roosevelt, Dwight Eisenhower and Lyndon Johnson are emblazoned across the Presidents' Grove. Sir Stuart, now 93, said the relationship between Britain and the USA was invaluable.

The ceremony was attended by former Lord Lieutenant of Essex Sir John Ruggles-Brise, Major Nigel Capel-Cure, an ex-Vice Lieutenant of Essex, Mr Alex Hart, agent-general of British Columbia, Mr Philip Arnold of the US Embassy, Mrs Patricia Noble of Epping Forest Trust, Mr Jack Fuller, Waltham Forest College Principal, and Mr Peter Webster, managing director of the Mallinson Group, Australia, and Mrs Ann Mallinson.

Room has run out for any more trees behind the Mallinson home. But, as Churchill might have said, the 131 honoured few will be remembered by so many.

Guardian & Gazette, October 1981

A fire swept through the White House last Thursday night causing £½ million worth of damage to the historic Woodford Green landmark. The impressive house was a visiting place for the world statesmen while owned by the late 'grand old man of Woodford,' Sir Stuart Mallinson. He left the property to the community.

Fifty firemen from stations far afield started fighting the blaze just before 10pm. They took several hours to control the blaze. The roof caved in and the first floor was severely damaged.

Fire fighting efforts were hampered as the house is several hundred yards from the nearest hydrant. Extra hoses were rushed there. . . . Experts were still sifting wreckage this week to discover the cause, Arson is not ruled out. . . .

Redbridge Guardian, December 9, 1983

The White House in Woodford Green, gutted by fire in December, is to re-open as a home for the elderly. Owned by Waltham Forest borough, and one of the most distinctive period buildings in the area, it was extensively damaged in the blaze caused by careless disposal of cigarettes or matches.

After considerable debate in which the future of the historic building was in jeopardy, councillors on the social services committee finally opted last week for a plan to use it as a short term centre for the elderly. The renovation and conversion is expected to cost about £350,000, but is still subject to confirmation by the resources committee. When completed it would accomodate up to 20 people. . . .

Guardian & Gazette, June 1, 1984

Two years later his house burned down putting a tragic full stop to an era which had lasted fifty years.

243

244

Buckhurst Hill

Roads to Buckhurst Hill. As can be seen by comparing the picture *above* with that on the previous page, the signpost by the toll house was changed at some stage from 'Buckhurst Hill and Loughton' to 'Loughton and Epping'.

There's Buckett's Hill, a place of furze and
  clouds.
Which evening in a golden blaze enshrouds.

John Clare, 1793-1864

Last night died Mrs. Stephens, who many Years kept the Bald-faced Stag on Epping-Forest. Her Death was occasioned by her being over-heated last Sunday and Monday in cooking for Company.

Press report, 1753

This Morning Mr. Richard Rock, L.M. was married at Woodford in Essex, to Miss Thompson, of the Park, Southwark, a very agreeable young Lady of Eighteen. After the Ceremony the new-married Couple repaired to the Bald-faced Stag, where an elegant Entertainment was provided.

Press report, 1753

[Buckhurst Hill] was formed into an ecclesiastical district out of the parish of Chigwell in 1838, since which time the number of its inhabitants has very largely increased. In 1871 it amounted to 2,500, being nearly three times as many as it was ten years previously, whilst according to the census returns for 1881 it has now reached about 4,000. At the foot of the hill, further eastward, is a railway-station on the Epping and Ongar branch of the Great Eastern Railway, around which are clustered several small cottages and 'villa residences.' From the top of the hill some beautiful views are obtained over the surrounding country, including the high ground on the opposite side of the valley of the Roding; whilst a pleasant and picturesque piece of the forest ground lies along the old Cambridge road to the left, between Woodford Wells and Loughton.

Great London, Edward Walford, 1883

It is no mean pleasure to be able to bring home pictorial records of our foreign tours, home excursions, or summer-day outings in the shape of photographs. And no great labour is involved, or experience demanded for its enjoyment, the art having been of late years so wonderfully simplified.

Camera and lens, focussing-cloth, tripod or camera-stand, dark slide, dry plates, bath and bottles, all together will occupy but little space in your travelling-trunk . . . and a very serviceable set may be obtained for from two to five guineas, including everything required for a beginner, viz., the camera with its lens and focussing-screen, the camera-stand, the dark slide, plates, chemicals, dishes, developing lamp, etc.

A good camera is a very beautiful piece of highly-finished cabinet-work. For outdoor work the form of camera most in favour is that which has a leather body folding together after the fashion of a concertina, technically known as bellows-bodied. This renders it lighter than it would otherwise be, and a camera for the tourist. . . . Dry Plates range in size from $4\frac{1}{4}$ by $3\frac{1}{4}$ inches through a dozen degrees up to 15 by 12 inches, the prices changing with the sizes proportionately — the smallest ranging from 1s. to 1s. 9d. per dozen, and the largest from 18s. to £1 8s. . . .

And now, turning to work, let us plunge into the forest depths of Epping, where pictures of great beauty and in great variety are awaiting transference to our sensitive dry plates. . . .

Exposure. — You next come from under the dark cloth and throw it aside, remove or raise the focussing-screen, and substitute for it the dark slide. And now comes the amateur's severest test. . . .

Walks in Epping Forest,
Percy Lindley, 1886

W. L. F. Wastell of Malmesbury Road, South Woodford, who took both pictures, was out and about taking photographs in the early years of this century. Photography in those days was an exciting if elaborate adventure. Although dry glass plates had superseded 'wet' plates in the 1870s, one still had to have a darkroom on hand to change the light-sensitive plates in the cumbersome cameras of the day — hence the mobile set-up in this picture.

On 1st October, 1933, the Councils of the Urban Districts of Buckhurst Hill and Loughton, and the Rural Parish of Chigwell, were abolished to make way for the newly-constituted Urban District Council of Chigwell, and the former Urban Districts and Rural Parish became, respectively, the Buckhurst Hill, Chigwell, and Loughton Wards of the amalgamated area. Loughton Ward has been divided into two to form Loughton (North) Ward and Loughton (South) Ward. The three districts of Buckhurst Hill, Chigwell and Loughton have a great deal in common and the amalgamation was initiated and supported by the residents.

Buckhurst Hill, Chigwell and Loughton
Official Guide, 1954/5

The vestiges of an old pack-horse road may still be traced through Lord's Bushes, along Squirrels Lane, and so across the water meadows to the foot-bridge over the Roding; thence past the site of Luxborough House, to Chigwell Hatch. There is not a prettier walk from Buckhurst Hill, and in the early summer, before the grass is cut, the number of flowers in these damp alluvial meadows is astonishing. The clumps of Comfrey, Meadow-sweet, Golden Bedstraw, and the curious Yellow Rattle, are sure to attract the notice of the rambler; while somewhat later the river banks are charmingly decorated with Purple Loosestrife, Skullcap and the Willow herbs. The Roding is noted as being a flower-decked stream, and from the bridge at the Cascade a wealth of Arrowhead, Water Plantain and Yellow Iris may be seen any fine day in July, and even glimpses of the Kingfisher and Water Vole may be caught if you are very quiet, and very lucky.

Buckhurst Hill Illustrated,
John W. Phelp, c.1897

Buckhurst Hill's most historic carriageway. This stretch of Monkhams Lane was, when this picture was taken on April 18, 1919 by Arthur Crow, FRIBA, a normal road and, indeed, right up to the 1960s it was a legal right of way for carts and motors. Today this is not the case and now it is only designated as a footpath, barriers having been erected at each end to deny access to vehicles. All except fifty yards now falls within the jurisdiction of Epping Forest District Council.

While the 92 acres of Lord's Bushes had been secured for the public in the Act of 1878, the adjoining Knighton Woods, originally part of Munkoms, remained enclosed as part of the Knighton Estate until 1930. The estate cottage lay at the southern end of Monkhams Lane but when the fences came down no doubt it too was demolished.

TRAMWAY TRIALS IN LORD'S BUSHES

In order to test the system, a strip of land has been obtained in Epping Forest at Buckhurst Hill, where a piece of tramway road, 1,710ft long, has been laid. The line is on an incline for nearly its whole length, the steepest gradient being 1 in 18¾, and the average 1 in 22¾. Up and down the line and round these curves a number of runs were made, both with full and empty carriages, at good speeds, and with perfect success. Considering the saturated state of the land on which the line is laid, the train ran with remarkable steadiness, giving a good earnest of what it will do on a sound piece of road. The time occupied in the run was exactly 60 seconds, or at a rate of 30 miles an hour, starting and stopping included.

The Graphic, January 18, 1873

A visitor to Buckhurst Hill in the winter of 1872/73 might have been just lucky enough to witness one of the most bizarre events ever to take place in the town — the trial run of a steam tram through a sylvan glade in Lord's Bushes. An experimental line some 600 yards long was laid down in December of '72 by the newly-formed Lisbon Steam Tramways Company on a roughly NW to SE alignment from a point near the keeper's lodge on Knighton Lane down to the entrance of the old Monkhams Farm. The Company considered that this area of Epping Forest came nearest to simulating conditions in Portugal where they hoped to open the tramway.

The track consisted of a single rail, flanked on either side at a distance of 20 inches with longitudinal timber sleepers. Only the bogie wheels of the locomotive ran on the centre rail — the flangeless driving wheels, which had a tread of 1ft. 2ins, ran on the timber baulks which were 9 ins wide.

Only one locomotive was tested at Buckhurst Hill, No. 2, christened 'Cintra'. It was built, as were all the others, by Sharp, Stewart & Co. Ltd., of Manchester and cost about £1,500. It hauled one 2nd and one 3rd class carriage, each seating 18 persons, and one goods van. Passengers entered from the sides and were seated back to back, an arrangement similar to that employed on the 'knifeboard' horse buses running in London at the time. Up and down the line and round the curves puffed little 'Cintra', its carriages full of excited local school children, the proceedings being watched by Company officials and the intrigued local station-master, John Newman. Several good runs were made on gradients as steep as 1 in 20 and

At the top end of the lane lay North Lodge, one of the three gatehouses serving the estate. It still survives.

at times speeds of 20 mph were attained. It was not expected, though, that the average speed in service in Portugal would exceed about 12 mph.

Victorian Buckhurst Hill, C. Johnson, 1980

The unmetalled lane was the location for what must be one of the most unique events to take place in Epping Forest, although why the company chose Buckhurst Hill to simulate Portugal is not recorded.

Although today we may look on the Forest at Buckhurst Hill as one entity, the character of the former estate is still apparent — its more open aspect and leafy walks, its rhododendron clumps . . . and its man-made additions to the lake.

Knighton was for upwards of 60 years the home of the late Mr. Edward North Buxton, who was in the forefront of all movements for the preservation and improvement of Epping Forest. When Mr. Buxton bought the bulk of the Estate in 1863, it had quite unique residential advantages in its nearness to London and its proximity to the Forest; these advantages are present to an even greater degree today. London has been brought nearer by its outward growth and by increased and accelerated travelling facilities, and the Forest remains, as it will remain, unchanged and uncurtailed, a fitting memorial to the men who won it for the perpetual enjoyment of the people.

There can be few residences for the City Man which combine in so remarkable a degree the advantages of Town and Country. If these factors are advantageous to the single owner of a residential Estate of this character, they are no less advantageous to the hundreds of smaller proprietors who would settle there if the Estate were developed on well considered lines. With its natural undulations, its wealth of Forest trees and shrubs, its ready-made gardens and parklands, its nearness to the Railway (Buckhurst Hill and Woodford Stations are within a mile of the property and the journey to the City by train takes under half an hour), to Churches, Shops, Omnibus routes and exceptional educational and sporting facilities, the property presents unusual attractions to estate developers. Add to these its long frontages to important roads, and its proximity to the Forest, and it will be understood why the claim may be made that Knighton is one of the finest building estates that has ever been offered in the Epping Forest districts. . . .

Knighton Auction Catalogue, June 24, 1930

The Duke of Connaught, who is Chief Ranger of Epping Forest, yesterday opened to the public Knighton Wood, Buckhurst Hill, the 37 acres of woodland which has been acquired as an addition to the forest.

Knighton was for over 60 years the seat of the Buxton family, and the late Mr. Edward North Buxton, who was for many years Verderer of the Forest, had a great deal to do with the preservation of its amenities. The cost of the woodland opened yesterday, which was part of the estate, was 10,000 guineas, found in equal shares by the Woodford Council and the City Corporation.

The woodland narrowly escaped serious damage by fire about half an hour after the Duke had returned to London. A large hay stack caught fire in a field separated from the woodland only by a narrow lane, across which the flames were blown by a strong wind. The Woodford fire brigade and a downpour of rain saved the woodlands from damage.

Press report, July 22, 1930

Knighton Estate is without exaggeration the choicest site in one of the most delectable residential areas near London. Adjoining Knighton Wood, a sheer joy, it combines the advantages of a country home with the amenities of town.

Here Messrs. Gale & Betts, Ltd., whose aim it is to give clients *every* satisfaction, holding that a satisfied customer is an investment bound to show a return in some way, are erecting houses ranging from £1,000 to £2,250. All are freehold, and are detached or semi-detached. There are no road charges, and clients are given the choice of fireplace, decorations, colour of bathroom, design of leaded lights, and every endeavour is made to satisfy all personal requirements.

No man rushes wildly into the expenditure of a thousand pounds or more, unless he happens to be a millionaire, and even millionaires, I am told, are not as rash as we might believe. This purchase of a house is a serious business. There is so much to consider: one's family, health, business, retirement, and, as one will have property to bequeath — one's descendants. It is essential, therefore, that one's house shall be well and strongly built, in healthy surroundings unlikely to be spoilt by the spread of towns, accessible to one's place of business, and yet sufficiently rural to give rest and peace.

Without exaggeration, one can claim quite safely that the Knighton Estate, Woodford, fulfils all these conditions. With regard to the houses themselves, the very reputation of Messrs. Gale & Betts is sufficient assurance of sound workmanship and first-class materials, and one visit to the houses will convince one that here is something quite out of the ordinary, both in attractiveness of design and quality. Every conceivable labour-saving device and other modern improvements are included, so essential in these days of servant problems.

Wonderful as these houses are, the one feature which immediately impresses itself on the mind is their truly magnificent, one might say unequalled, position, actually facing Knighton Wood, without doubt the most delectable stretch of that amazingly beautiful Epping Forest, and to be surrounded by this forest ensures the complete rural atmosphere of one's home for ever.

Gale & Betts Limited, Sales Guide

Original caption: 'Epping Forest, Lord's Bushes, 18th April 1919'.

When originally envisaged, St John's was to be a chapel of ease to St Mary the Virgin at Chigwell and it was consecrated as such in 1837. However, when Buckhurst Hill became a separate ecclesiastical district the following year, and established as a separate parish in 1867, a series of enlargements was carried out to cater for the expanding congregation.

Interesting because well located within the Forest District, the Parish of Buckhurst Hill cannot fail to be attractive, by reason of the many pleasant spots around it; and it is well adapted for a place of residence, by virtue of its natural beauty, and the interesting social life maintained by the inhabitants and carried on within their homes, and in its public buildings. . . .

Buckhurst Hill Illustrated,
John W. Phelp, c.1897

We regret to announce the death of Mr. Cyril Digby Buxton, second son of Mr. E. N. Buxton, J.P., which occurred early on Tuesday morning under most painful circumstances at Knighton, Woodford, the residence of his father. The deceased gentleman had only just recovered from an attack of influenza, which was followed by a disordered liver, and this appeared to cause depression. After being absent from Knighton with his father for a few days, Mr. Buxton returned home on Monday afternoon, and later in the evening dined with some friends of the family residing in the neighbourhood. He was back again about a quarter to ten, and on the lodge-keeper's wife opening the gate for him he wished her good night as usual, and soon after entering the house retired to his bedroom. Some time after this he told a nurse who occupied an adjoining room that he was going downstairs, and as he did not return she followed him, and was horrified to find him lying in a room with his head shattered by gunshot, the weapon being by his side. Assistance was at once summoned, but life was found to be extinct, and death must have been instantaneous. The sad affair has cast a gloom over the neighbourhood.

Essex County Chronicle, May 13, 1892

Probably the most illustrious visitor to the church was the American President Theodore Roosevelt who attended morning service in May 1910.

For many years the history of Buckhurst Hill was bound up with the Buxtons. The family graves (including that of Cyril who committed suicide at Knighton in 1892) lie in the shadow of St John's where the new tower was a gift of Edward North Buxton in 1879. The clock had previously been given by the family in 1872. This portrait of Edward North now hangs in the boardroom of Truman's Brewery, formerly Truman, Hanbury and Buxton, in Brick Lane — built partly on the site of No. 29 Hanbury Street where Jack the Ripper killed his second victim in 1888. (Painting by Sir Hubert von Herkomer.)

The Buckhurst Hill church which has undergone the most dramatic change, both in faith and outward appearance, is the 'King's Place' church. It was originally built in 1887 to replace a small iron church which had been erected on the site by Congregational seceders who had broken away from their parent body to follow the teachings of their minister, the Reverend W. Dorling. He aspired to the doctrine of 'larger hope' for sinners whereas a part of his congregation preferred to believe in that of eternal punishment. Many of those who contributed to the cost of building the new church were the same people who had subscribed in 1866 to the original building at the top of Palmerston Road. Reverend Dorling was appointed Pastor of the new church for life, and he led his breakaways for the next 35 years until his retirement in 1906. His personality was such that the building was referred to as 'Mr Dorling's church' and when he went, so did the building — sold to become the Palmerston Road Baptist Church whose congregation met in the original iron building next door. By the 1960s the 1887 building had become dilapidated and out-dated and it was demolished to build a new church which was opened on March 12, 1966. The old corrugated iron building still survives.

Fifty years ago, on June 20, 1912, the Forest Hospital, one of the most up-to-date in the country at the time — was opened 'before a large and representative company' by Colonel Mark Lockwood, C.V.O., MP.

The hospital, costing £4,250, was built from public subscription and £250 was still needed when the hospital was opened. The money was collected a few weeks later.

Many local people, some of them former staff at the hospital, others patients in earlier days, remember its history well.

Buckhurst Hill's oldest resident, 95-year-old Mr Charles Linder, of St Just's, Powell Road, who has lived next to the Forest Hospital since it was built, remembered what the site was like before the hospital was founded:

'There was a thick wood — Pluckett's Wood — where many people would pick bluebells,' said Mr. Linder. 'When the hospital was opened a large crowd of people dressed in academic robes attended, including the first doctors the hospital had — Doctors B. F. Pendred, Butler Harris, C. R. Dykes, Norman and P. W. Moore.'

Mr. Linder recalled that the idea of the new hospital came from these doctors, who had previously attended the Village Hospital, in Hospital Lane — now Knighton Lane — Buckhurst Hill. The doctors arranged a public meeting in 1909, and the next year a site was obtained from Colonel Rous. By 1911 building was started, and the then Lord Mayor of London, Sir T. Vezey Strong, came to Buckhurst Hill to lay the foundation stone.

Sir Frank Foster, C.B.E. was the man who supervised the building of the hospital, which was designed by well-known local architects Tooley and Foster.

'Of course, the hospital was not nearly as big as it is now,' explained Sir Frank. 'The building then was confined to what is now the main entrance block.'

One person our reporter talked to remembered the hospital well as the place where she spent the 'happiest days of my nursing career.'

She is Mrs. L. C. Burnell, of 96 Queens Road, Buckhurst Hill.

As we have seen (page 228) the Village Hospital opened in 1869 was the first formal establishment for medical treatment in the district although two rooms rented in 1866 on the High Road at Buckhurst Hill in charge of an elderly domestic servant without medical training could be claimed as a forerunner. The Buckhurst Hill Medical Provident Society, founded in 1873, opened the Medical Provident Home in 1889 in a converted house and shop in Queen's Road. There were two five-bedded wards, a day room and another which served as an operating theatre. Barclays Bank now occupies the same premises.

'I'll never forget the time when I first came to the hospital as a nurse in 1919,' remarked Mrs. Burnell. 'On leaving the station, I walked across a field, passing a pond, which was in the dip below the hospital — now the junction of Amberley Road and The Meadway. I continued up the steep hill to what looked like a large house. In those days the hospital was isolated from the community.

'I was taken aback,' remembered Mrs. Burnell, 'When I saw the place where I was to sleep. All the nurses had to sleep in what would now be used as a linen cupboard. You can imagine how much sleep we had.

'Despite our cramped quarters, there was a very friendly atmosphere. There was Miss

With the increase in the local population after the turn of the century, and occasioned by the recently-introduced compulsory medical inspection for school children, an appeal for funds was launched in 1911 for the building of a brand new hospital. Opened in June 1912 at a cost of £4,250, in its first year the hospital records 69 operations, many of them serious. An X-Ray unit was installed in 1919 as 'a thanks-giving for the Victory of our Arms', and a further extension was completed in 1928, partly to cater for the dramatic increase in road casualties (see chapter on Roads).

Arnott, the staff nurse; Nurses White and Epps, probation nurses; Sister Hall, sister-in-charge; Miss Slater, and Matron and myself, on the resident staff.

'In those days the men's private ward was near the entrance downstairs, and cost the patients six guineas a week. The women's private ward was upstairs and was a little cheaper, costing five guineas. The balcony ward — a semi-private ward, which had three beds — cost about three pounds. This later became a children's ward.

Another nurse at the hospital in its early days was Mrs F. Adams of 36, Starling Close, Buckhurst Hill. Mrs. Adams remembers the Matron Miss Marianne Slater.

'She was a great disciplinarian, but she never asked us to do anything she wouldn't do herself,' said Mrs. Adams. 'I remember her reputation with the police at that time. Whenever they heard Miss Slater's voice they would run from the casualty ward, where they helped undress the drunks. Miss Slater believed that only the nurses should look after the drunks. The police attended because there were no male nurses at the time.

Miss Eve Mackeson, of 45, Church Hill, Loughton, was Matron for six months when Miss Slater had a serious accident.

She remembers the Forest Hospital as a very busy hospital, admitting most of the acutely ill patients and all the accidents. This was because St. Margaret's Hospital — which now takes these cases — was then the Epping Poor Law Institution.

Miss Mackeson recalled the hospital's once inadequate telephone exchange.

'It rarely functioned at night as there was no night staff and the porter went to bed.

'There were no local ambulances either, so patients were brought to the hospital by car, or by an evil looking hand-pushed litter with a hood. Sometimes the men who pulled the almost medieval contraption were so exhausted that we often had to revive them with cups of strong tea.'

Miss Mackeson added that the nurses had to 'turn their hands to almost anything,' from assisting in the theatre 'stitching-up' casualties, taking emergency X-rays and

The Forest had one sister, two trained and two probationer nurses and two domestic staff to cater for the 21 possible patients. This picture was taken in 1912.

doing physiotherapy, to stoking the boilers in an emergency and operating the electric-light engine at night after a busy day, as there was no main electricity at that time.

In 1920 the hospital was cleared of patients to permit builders to erect the Balcony Ward — now the British Legion Ward. The hospital returned to normal in three months and the new ward was opened by the Lord Mayor of London.

The next extension came in 1930, when the

Marquis and Marchioness of Carisbrooke opened the operating theatre and private ward section, which had been donated by Mrs. G. Bell, of Sewardstonebury.

The Queen Mother, then the Duchess of York, was to open the extension. But at the last minute she was unable to attend as the birth of Princess Margaret was imminent.

In 1934, a new X-ray room was built.

It was not until July 5, 1956 that a new out-patients building was opened by Lady Churchill, and two years later another operating theatre extension was opened by Sir Graham Rowlandson, Chairman of the North East Metropolitan Regional Hospital Board.

In March, 1960, a clinic was built for the General Ward, and later in the year a clinical room for the private wards and an extension to the men's ward were added.

In 1961 an extension was built for the porters and maintenance staff, and in November Loughton Round Table formed the Forest Hospital League of Friends.

Since 1950, the hospital has been a training hospital for enrolled nurses. Thirty nurses have been trained and passed the Enrolled Nurses' examination at Forest Hospital.

Press report, June 1962

Local residents, angry at the proposed closure of Forest Hospital, Buckhurst Hill, are planning to hold a forum on the matter

Buckhurst Hill Residents' Society is to circularise its members to sound out opinion and gauge the strength of any support it might get in pursuing the matter further.

A spokesman for the society said there is a lot of strong feeling locally about Forest Hospital's future and anger at the possible loss of yet another small hospital.

Many people feel that the hospital belongs to the people of Buckhurst Hill and not to the NHS because it was built and presented to the area many years ago.

Guardian & Gazette, July 19, 1985

Today the hospital operates almost under a continual sentence of death, its demise having been mooted for several years in spite of local petitions against closure.

The Roebuck stands on the old road, skirting the brow of the hill, affording visitors very charming views of the Forest towards Loughton, and from the garden in the rear over the valley of the Roding to Ongar Park Woods and Abridge. The old house has been recently improved and turned into a modern hotel, but the name at least must be very ancient, as the roe-deer certainly disappeared from the Forest before the end of the 16th century. In 1884 this graceful animal was re-established in its former home by the liberality of Mr. E. N. Buxton, one of the Verderers, and a glimpse of the small herd may often now be caught by the quiet rambler through the Monks and Theydon Woods.

Buckhurst Hill Illustrated,
John W. Phelp, c.1897

Gorse bushes opposite the Roebuck Hotel, Buckhurst Hill, which have for many years presented a picturesque view from the road-way, caught fire shortly after 11 a.m. on Saturday last, and were practically destroyed. The Buckhurst Hill Fire Brigade was summoned, but did not attend, and the flames were eventually subdued by onlookers. The cause of the outbreak is not known.

The Woodford Times, May 8, 1931

The Roebuck photographed by W. L. F. Wastell around 1900. The inn dated back to at least 1770 although according to the Victoria History of the County of Essex the building of those days stood slightly north of the current one.

This picture was taken in the late nineteenth century shortly before its rebuilding to enlarge it into the modern 'Old' Roebuck.

On the other side of Warren Hill lies the old Reindeer Inn, parts of the building dating back to the sixteenth century. It was built originally as Little Standing, an observation tower from which spectators would gather to watch the progress of the hunt. (Great Standing is now Queen Elizabeth's Hunting Lodge.) In the 1700s it was extended to form an inn, a licence dated May 1, 1747 authorising 'William Simmons of the Warren House in Fair Mead Bottom to use the occupation of an Ale-House Keeper in his house, the Sign of the Rayne Deer'. It achieved a reputation with its Sunday visitors from London for serving an excellent rabbit pie but in the early nineteenth century it was converted into a private house. After the death of the first owner it was purchased by General (Later Field-Marshal) Thomas Grosvenor who erected the monument or grave marker in the field below the house (see page 162). Today The Warren, a Grade II* listed building, is the headquarters of the Conservators of Epping Forest.

Rein Deer, Epping Forest, Eleven Miles from London, with immediate posession.— By Mr. Adams, at the Auction Mart, near the Bank of England, on Thursday, the 2nd of September, at Twelve, by order of the Executrix of the late Mr. John Allen.

The Valuable Lease and Goodwill of the old-established Inn, the Rein Deer, now in full trade, so justly celebrated for its beautiful situation, and frequented by families of great respectability. The premises are in the completest order, have been improved at a considerable expence, are conveniently arranged for the accommodation of numerous or select parties, an inclosed yard surrounded by stabling, coach houses, barns, granary, and other out-buildings; pleasure ground, three kitchen gardens most abundantly stocked and cropped; a field and three hoppets of pasture land adjoining. Nearly surrounding the premises, is a productive Rabbit Warren, the whole about Ten Acres, be the same more or less. The premises have an extensive and very valuable right of pasturage for the breeding and grazing of cattle, are tithe free, and held for an un-expired term of about 22 years, at a very small rent.

May be viewed, and printed particulars had at the Black Boy, Chelmsford; White Hart, Romford; Epping Place; Angel, Ilford; Half Moon, Hertford; Saracen's Head, Ware; Bull, Hoddesdon; Falcon, Waltham Cross; of Mr. Rounding, Woodford; John Jessop, Esq. Waltham Abbey; on the premises; at the Auction Mart; and of Mr. Adams, No. 122, the corner of John-street, Minories.

Press report, 1813

Today the old inn has been upstaged by the rather more modern building on the A11 although even that changed its name during the three-year period spent researching this book: from the Reindeer to the Colorado Exchange!

Another illustration of the changing face of the local hostelries. The Warren Wood House stands nearby, the adjacent hill becoming the Forest's traditional winter sports centre when snow falls.

The Loughton section of the Chigwell Fire Brigade accomplished a really excellent piece of work in the early hours of Sunday, when they were called to deal with a fierce outbreak of fire at the 'Bald Faced Stag', Buckhurst Hill.

Although the hotel was severely damaged, the fact that it was not completely burned to the ground is due to the splendid efforts of the Brigade.

The alarm was given by two maids in the employ of Mr. Justice Crossman, of Buckhurst Hill House, and the inmates of the blazing hotel just managed to escape with their lives.

It was soon after 3.30 on Sunday morning that the two maids were alarmed by the sound of crackling and, looking out, they noticed that the hotel — which adjoins the grounds of Buckhurst Hill House — was blazing furiously.

From horse to horseless carriage yet the pub itself lives on.

The alarm for the Bald Faced Stag fire was raised by staff at Buckhurst Hill House, the home of Sir Stafford Crossman of the Mann, Crossman & Paulin brewing company and a judge of the High Court of Justice, Chancery Division. He was also father of Richard Crossman, MP. Dick Crossman, who later achieved a place in history with the publication of his diaries, was born at the house. On the day war was declared, the

Auxiliary Fire Service moved in and began sandbagging the property (left) but when Judge Crossman arrived home from Kenya he turned the volunteer firemen out into the stables. Accommodation was later found for them in the Water Board premises opposite. Built in 1869, Buckhurst Hill House was converted into flats in the 1950s and the stable entrance lost with the construction of new houses (right) in Knighton Lane.

The Bald Faced Stag — probably more a reference to a white blazed animal rather than literally bald — is one of Buckhurst Hill's most famous legacies. This picture was taken at the beginning of the century — some thirty-odd years before the disastrous fire after which its appearance was considerably transformed (see page 96). In those days most inns provided hay in baskets for browsing steeds while their owners were inside quaffing their ale, and William Ketts, who occupied the Stag stables, was no exception. The unusual view *(right)* shows the rear with the skittle alley — another feature of many inns at the time, since upstaged by bar billiards and, latterly, invaders from space!

The alarm was given and the manager, Mr. L. Stock, and his wife, were able to make a hurried exit in their night attire. They saved their young baby and were also able to rouse the cook, who was sleeping on the top floor.

The door of the bedroom in which Mr. and Mrs. Stock and their baby were sleeping, was burned off its hinges.

The Fire Brigade were called by the police by telephone and, as so often is the case, the call reached the wrong brigade in the first instance.

The telephone was on the Buckhurst Exchange, and the call was put through to the Woodford Fire Station.

Superintendent Norwood transferred the call to the Loughton Fire Station at once, but there was inevitable delay through this occurrence.

However, the new Dennis tender was away from the station within two minutes of the call, and less than three minutes later the new Dennis pump was also on the way with a full crew.

When the Brigade arrived on the scene the rear and side of the building were blazing furiously, but the firemen tackled the flames expeditiously and efficiently.

Quickly an excited crowd of onlookers gathered outside in their night attire and watched the efforts of Chief Officer Poulter and his men to get the blaze under control. This they succeeded in doing after about one and a half hours' strenuous work, and all credit is due to them for saving the bars, billiard room, and the front of the house from serious damage.

The Woodford Times, May 22, 1936

After the extension of the railway to Loughton, development of the Buckhurst Hill area was rapid. Between 1851 and 1871 the number of houses had increased nearly 250 per cent, acres of farmland being destroyed and parts of the Forest enclosed. In the latter case, once Forest land had been built over, the provisions of the Epping Forest Act, whereby any illegally enclosed land had to be returned, was void. In the jargon of today, one could really describe Buckhurst Hill as being a 'green field development' and a nineteenth century version of the 'new town'.

Central to that development was its 'High Street' — Queen's Road — which still retains much of its Victorian atmosphere, and Buckhurst Hill has avoided the excesses of the supermarket phenomenon . . . at least, that is, up to 1986. It goes without saying that it is shopkeepers which characterise an area and Metson's had traded in Queen's Road as long as anyone could remember — there had always been an outfitters at No. 48. The picture on the left of Leonard Metson dates from 1908; in July 1983 it was a sad day indeed to see the closing down sale on his son's retirement.

THE PROGRAMME
—at a Glance

1.0	Old Folks Lunch.
1.0	Carnival Marshals on the Top Green.
1.30	Carnival Procession, via Queens Road, Victoria Road, and Stradbroke Grove.
2.30	Carnival Parades in Celebrations Field for judging.
3.0	Coronation Beauty Queen Contest—Circus Tent.

THROUGHOUT THE AFTERNOON AND EVENING

REFRESHMENT LOUNGE & TEA GARDENS
Fully Licensed · Popular Prices
Under the personal supervision of Stanley G. Saunders

JACK HYMAN presents his **TWO ORCHESTRAS**
THE SWING BAND AND SWEET MUSIC
(by arrangement with Brough Dagnan) Pianos by Saville

3.0	Car Rally—Starting from Bald Faced Stag.
3.15	Children's Sports.
5.0	Grand Circus—First Performance.
5.30	Soot and Flour Fight—Chingford Rugby Club v. Queens United Football Club.
7.0	Distribution of Children's Prizes.
7.0	Darts Championship Final—Refreshment Garden.
7.30	Fire Brigade Display.
7.30	Children's Dances.

8.0 THE KING'S SPEECH
Arrangements will be made to relay His Majesty's Broadcast to the Empire in the Refreshment Gardens and in the Circus. You are requested to be in your seats **EARLY.**

8.0	Grand Circus—Second Performance.
10.30	Torchlight Procession—Stradbroke Grove, Roding Lane, Corner of Alfred Road and Back.
10.30 to Midnight.	Jack Hymans **TWO** Orchestras together.
11.0	Display of Fireworks.
11.30	Coronation Bonfire.
12.0	*God Save the King*

THE CARNIVAL

Elephants & Horses entered by Rosaire.
The Highway Code entered by Boys School, Princes Road.

CLASS I. Tradesmen's Decorated Vehicles.

1	A. Warren	6	Harrisons Stores	11	L. S. Parks.
2	A. C. Willis.	7	A. H. Murray	12	W. C. French.
3	S. Jefford.	8	A. H. Murray	13	W. C. French.
4	Lucton's Laundry	9	R. H. Piggott	14	Gas Light and
5	Harrisons Stores	10	R. J. Richards		Coke Co.

15 County of London Electricity Co.

CLASS II. Tradesmen's Decorated Horse Drawn Vehicles.

1.	W. & C. French	3.	United Dairies, Ltd.
2.	W. & C. French	4.	United Dairies, Ltd.

CLASS III. Tradesmen's Decorated Bicycle.
1. A. Warren.

CLASS IV. Decorated Private Cars.

1.	R. G. Borkett.	3.	H. W. A. Woollard.
2.	R. G. Borkett.	4.	A. Eburn.

CLASS V. Decorated Motor Cycles.
1. W. Green.

CLASS VI. Decorated Cycles.

1 A. North.	6 D. Barker.	11 J. Digby.
2 B. North.	7 O. Osborne.	12 P. Mann.
3 R. Glasscock.	8 A. Sparks	13 E. Reed.
4 E. Rowe.	9 J. Gingell.	14 M. Reed.
5 B. Hatley.	10 G. Andrews.	

CLASS VII. Decorated Prams and Mailcarts.
1. A. Warren   2 S. Mann.

CLASS VIII. Fancy Dress. Ladies and Gents.
1. L. L. Lake—Persian Lady   3. K. Lusher—Cinderella.
2. A. J. Morris—Local News   4. E. Crouchman—Prince.

CLASS IX. Tableaux. (A short story runs through Class IX.)

After the Great War came the Armistice and rejoicing. Two lovers meet at Penzance and following their wedding complete with a gold coach, they buy a little house. Of course, they know the soundness of the U.S.A. With their children at school, they take a trip across the Atlantic and realise how much progress travel has made since the days of the galley ship, more than ever they proudly realise how much it means to be a part of the great British Empire.

1. War Scene ... Buckhurst Hill British Legion.
2. Staff of Life ... A. H. Murray.

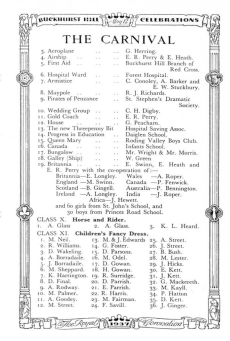

THE CARNIVAL

3.	Aeroplane	..	G. Herring.
4.	Airship	..	E. R. Perry & E. Heath.
5.	First Aid	..	Buckhurst Hill Branch of Red Cross.
6.	Hospital Ward	..	Forest Hospital.
7.	Armistice	..	C. Conoley, A. Barker and E. W. Stuckbury.
8.	Maypole	..	R. J. Richards.
9.	Pirates of Penzance	..	St. Stephen's Dramatic Society.
10.	Wedding Group	..	C. H. Digby.
11.	Gold Coach	..	E. R. Perry.
12.	House	..	G. Peacham.
13.	The new Threepenny Bit	..	Hospital Saving Assoc.
14.	Progress in Education	..	Daiglen School.
15.	Queen Mary	..	Roding Valley Boys Club.
16.	Canada	..	Infants School.
17.	Bungalow	..	Mr. Wright & Mr. Morris.
18.	Galley (Ship)	..	W. Green
19.	Britannia	..	E. Swinn, E. Heath and

E. R. Perry with the co-operation of:—
Britannia—E. Longley.   Wales —A. Roper.
England —M. Swinn.   Canada —P. Fenwick.
Scotland—B. Gingell.   Australia—P. Bennington.
Ireland —A. Longley.   India —J. Roper.
Africa—J. Hewett,
and 60 girls from St. John's School, and
30 boys from Princes Road School.

CLASS X. Horse and Rider.

1.	A. Glass	2.	A. Glass.	3.	K. L. Heard.

CLASS XI. Children's Fancy Dress.

1. M. Neil.	13. M. & J. Edwards	25. A. Street.
2. R. Williams.	14. G. Foster.	26. J. Street.
3. D. Wakeling.	15. D. Parsons.	27. B. Bush.
4. A. Borradaile.	16. M. Odel.	28. M. Lester.
5. J. Borradaile.	17. D. Gowan.	29. J. Hicks.
6. M. Sheppard.	18. H. Gowan.	30. K. Kett.
7. K. Harrington.	19. R. Surridge.	31. J. Kett.
8. D. Final.	20. D. Parrish.	32. G. Mackereth.
9. A. Rodway.	21. E. Parrish.	33. M. Kayll.
10. M. Palmer.	22. R. Harris.	34. P. Hatton
11. A. Goodey.	23. M. Fairman.	35. D. Kett.
12. M. Street.	24. F. Savill.	36. J. Ginger.

The people of Buckhurst Hill feel rightly proud to associate themselves with those millions of loyal subjects throughout the Empire who offer their heartfelt congratulations to Their Most Gracious Majesties King George VI and Queen Elizabeth.

Upon this day of great National rejoicing our hearts are united by a common joy. Among the people of our village, the significance of this day will never be forgotten. It will live on in our memories and in our hearts long after the pomp and pageantry of the occasion have taken their place in that silent past which is history And from the bottom of our hearts, the true spirit of this day shall constantly reverberate in the sincere expression of undying loyalty, and the unswerving allegiance to our King and country that have ever made us part of a great nation.

Many among us are fortunate in being able to cast back our minds to Coronations of dearly remembered kings, who in their day also led our country and its people with such whole-hearted devotion. To all of us, it falls now to lift up our hearts once more, to rejoice at the Coronation of His Most Gracious Majesty King George VI, and we do so, perhaps more than ever before, in these complex times, with new hope and with the full confidence that he will shepherd our Nation and our Empire, united, to fresh fields of glory.

Souvenir Programme, Coronation Day,
May 12, 1937

The Coronation Carnival proceeding down Queen's Road, photographed from an upstairs window of Metson's.

259

Queen's Road had been constructed in 1856-57 and its upkeep taken over by the parish ten years later. Not so with Prince's Road *(above)* built at the same time, which was not accepted by parish authorities until 1870. Even then they had to wait until 1897 before Buckhurst Hill Urban District Council installed kerbing and a tarmacadam top dressing. Note the old Chigwell Board School on the right, constituted in 1872 and becoming Buckhurst Hill County Primary School in 1950.

1880

21st September. Yesterday afternoon the Warden's son, William Butler, who was absent in the morning and who had neglected to pay his last week's fee, came in with 3d instead of 6d, and was sent home for the remainder by order of the Fees Committee. In some cases where the parents are known to be honest, I allow a few days grace, but these people have given an immense amount of trouble with their fees at various times, and a few months back after getting several weeks in arrear, they denied the existence of the debt altogether. Since that time if they have been allowed credit for a week they have invariably sent only 3d the following Monday instead of the double amount.

1872

17th August. The boys have been much more troublesome lately than usual which I believe to be caused by the intense heat of the room. The rays of the sun pouring down from the roof, the sawdust rising in fine powder and the smell from the perspiring children render the place the reverse of healthy or pleasant. I seldom leave the room in the afternoon without a severe throbbing headache and Mr. Byner continually complains of the same when his division has been in the schoolroom.

31st August. The sawdust rises in such large quantities that in a few days the ink becomes quite thick and has to be changed.

1873

22nd March. Mr. Heyward still fails to maintain anything approaching good order in the 4th class, the boys seem to ignore him altogether.

29th March. At the last meeting of the Managers the inability of Mr. Heyward having been carefully considered he was advised to seek another situation that they might be saved the unpleasant duty of dismissing him. The opinion of the Meeting was that his failure resulted not from the want of will but from the lack of physical strength.

8th November. There appears to be quite a smoking mania amongst the boys — some of them smell so strongly of tobacco that it is quite unpleasant to approach them. In going through the woods on Wednesday I caught five of the 1st class lads some smoking and the others eating peppermint drops to take off the smell. I have spoken to the boys on the subject and have threatened to inform the parents of any of them whom I may discover doing so in future.

1874

31st January. The night school is exceedingly troublesome. Some evenings the lads stand about the road howling and making dreadful noises to the great annoyance of the neighbours both before and till long after school. So bad has been their conduct that I have been compelled to complain to the police In school they appear more intent upon fun than learning.

25th July. The boys have scarcely settled down to work again, in the months of June, July and August large numbers of low classed excursionists visit the woods and it is desirable to keep the boys as much as possible from the immorality which prevails among many of these, — drunkenness, swearing and all sorts of vice appearing to be their sole enjoyment.

22nd August. Mr. Chelnick lives at Snaresbrook and brings a little lunch with him and I found that he was in the habit of going to a Public House for beer and as none of these are of a very high class near the school, and as I believe that such a practice would have a bad effect on the boys, I expostulated with him on the matter and offered either to let him have a glass out of our cask or give orders that his beer may be brought to the school. I was compelled to mention the matter as I was aware that on one occasion he went to the same house twice in the dinner hour.

12th September. William Basden swallowed a pin on Thursday. I am continually warning lads against putting things in their mouths, eyes, ears and nostrils but the little boys are so forgetful and the monitors so useless that accidents of these descriptions often occur. I sent the lad into the house and made him eat as much hard dry bread as possible and I am pleased to say that he suffered no apparent ill effects of his stupidity.

26th September. On Tuesday Wakelin thrust a piece of slate pencil into his ear actually pushing it out of the reach of his fingers with another piece of pencil until it was so

deep down that I was quite unable to extract it, the end being only just visable, so I sent him to my own medical man, Mr. Cory, who after much difficulty succeeded in getting it out. It appeared on investigating the matter that amongst the boys there is a habit of pretending to perform a conjuring trick which consists in making credulous little boys believe that a piece of pencil, a pea etc., can be passed through one ear and come out at the other, or out of the mouth. This silly lad emulating what the others had only pretended to do only succeeded in jamming the pencil into his ear.

26th September, Henry Masters returned to the school on Thursday afternoon besmothered with horse dung, and complained that G. Long was often in the habit of annoying him in this way on his return from school. The lad was in such a horrible state and smelled so badly that even after he had been well washed we were obliged to saturate his clothes with scent to overcome the stench.

5th December. The evening school was in such an uproar on the occasion of the Board meeting that the members went into the room and spoke to the lads urging them to be attentive. But even in the midst of one of the gentlemen speaking some of them got up and left the room, returning after an adjournment to the neighbouring beer house.

1875
13th November. The monitors receive instruction at my house on Saturday mornings from 8 till 12 o'clock.

20th November. I regret to record that all the monitors were guilty of smoking in the classroom on Wednesday.

1876
15th January. In consequence of the unpunctuality of the teachers I have been obliged to direct that they shall enter the time of their arrival each attendance.

1877
16th March. Received a summons this

These fascinating extracts from the old Prince's Road School records were kindly supplied by Lawrence Carr, headmaster from 1946-73. Buckhurst Hill County Primary School closed in 1976 and a fire (no doubt started by G. Long) sealed its fate.

afternoon from a police constable for punishing G. Long on Friday last. I was simply astounded as I had had no previous intimation whatever as to what was going on. The punishment was not in the least severe, and was not given in any heat or temper on my part. Some weeks ago, seeing several marks in the class reading books, I gave warning that I should consider it my duty to punish any boy proved to be guilty of such an offence. On Friday last, teacher M. Foster caught the boy Long deliberately marking the pictures in a filthy manner. The boy was brought to me and received the punishment promised. It consisted of 6 strokes on the lower part of the body and was inflicted before the whole school and teachers. The boy certainly did not make much fuss about the punishment, for he went to his place and almost immediately began to annoy his teacher. He was present in the afternoon, was playing about on Saturday and was out in the street on Sunday. On Monday he went to Stratford and has been at school every time since.

In every teacher's opinion, he is a thoroughly bad boy — in fact the worst in this school, for some long time it has been felt that his influence here has been bad. He has been punished by my predecessors for stealing, swearing and rude behaviour to teachers. He has only been early 9 times out of 99 attendances and has for years been a source of annoyance to every teacher in the school. He spoils almost everything he uses in the shape of School property and I felt last Friday that I should not have done my duty to my Managers, my school or myself had I passed unnoticed such a gross offence.

1878
20th May. All the Teachers and Monitors were unable to repeat their verses this morning at lesson time, and were ordered to remain after school until they were known.

27th May. Teachers' Home Lessons very indifferently done they had to remain in the evening and complete them.

One needs little imagination to appreciate the significance of Palmerston Road, constructed three years after his death in 1868.

Victorian development in Roding Lane — Bridge Terrace now replaced by Buckhurst Court flats for the elderly.

Our picture this week is of 'Luctons,' High Road, Buckhurst Hill, a house — since demolished — which was associated with the name of the famous highwayman, Dick Turpin.

'Luctons' was one of the oldest residences in Buckhurst Hill, and was originally a small white cottage standing on the common. It was built in the early part of the 17th century. Mr. Nathanael Powell bought the property in 1855, and added to it at two different periods. The larger portion was added about the year 1860.

After Mr. Powell's death in 1906, the estate, which, with its adjoining fields, covered about 20 acres, was sold to Mr. Wm. Lee, who had the house pulled down and proceeded to develop it. The estate is now fully built over, but the majority of the houses have been built during the last 12 years or so. Many of the fine old trees on the estate were cut down, but some of them were saved by being brought into the lane by a special arrangement of the footpaths.

Mr. Powell was born in 1813 at Shore Place, Hackney, and in 1834 became a partner in the firm of Messrs. James Powell & Sons, The Glassworks, Whitefriars, London. He was made a Magistrate of the County of Essex in 1860, and subsequently Deputy-Lieutenant and Alderman of the County. For many years he was Chairman of the old Chigwell School Board. On his marriage with his cousin, Miss Agnes Powell, daughter of Mr. and Mrs. David Powell, of Bence House (now Newnham House), Loughton, he lived in London, and in 1846 he removed to Walthamstow. Subsequently for a short time he lived at Bence House, Loughton, before settling at 'Luctons.' His father-in-law, Mr. David Powell, was killed by lightning in one of the fields at Bence House, in May 1832, and his mother-in-law died in 1852.

Mr. and Mrs. Nathanael Powell had thirteen children, only nine of whom grew up — two sons and seven daughters. The elder of the two sons, Harry, went into his father's business, while Edmund took Holy Orders, and afterwards became Bishop of Mashonaland. Of the nine children to grow up, only two survive, the Misses Sophia and Beatrice Powell, who are now living at 'Southfleet,' Buckhurst Hill, a house built in the grounds of 'Luctons' by the late Nathanael Powell shortly before his death.

The Powell family have been prominently associated with the Church and its work at Buckhurst Hill ever since St. John's was built. It is interesting to recall that Mrs. David Powell was the prime mover in getting St. John's Church erected in 1832.

The Woodford Times, December 9, 1932

William Lee purchased the estate around 1906 and promptly pulled down the house to provide plots for building. Luctons itself lay right here: partly in the road and partly on the site of No. 25 Luctons Avenue. Today the Powell family tomb can be found in St John's Churchyard, Nathanael being a cousin of Baden-Powell (see page 364).

How many of the older residents of Buckhurst Hill remember this pool? It lay within the grounds of St Just, Powell Road, and Mr Leslie Linder allowed youngsters, the Scouts and so on, to use it frequently.

The following year when again visiting Hill Top, I was allowed to take away some of the code-written sheets in order to study them at my leisure, I hoped that I could find a clue which would eventually lead to their translation, but the next few years passed without any definite results, and all attempts to break down the code failed. By Easter 1958 I was beginning to think somewhat sadly that these code-written sheets would remain a mystery for ever.

On the evening of Easter Monday, 1958, I remember thinking to myself, I will have one *last* attempt at solving this code-writing, more to pass the time than with any anticipation of success. I selected a sheet at random, and then, quite by chance, noticed a line near the bottom of the page which contained the Roman numerals *XVI* and the year *1793*. Was this a clue — could something of consequence have happened to a Pope bearing the numerals XVI, or to King Louis XVI in the year 1793? I consulted a Dictionary of Dates without success, and then, almost by chance, looked up Louis XVI in the Index to the Children's Encyclopaedia, where I read 'Louis XVI, French King: born Versailles 1754; guillotined Paris 1793'. Here at last was a possible clue!

Leslie Linder and his sister Enid were the most enthusiastic 'students' of Peter Rabbit . . . of Johnny Town-Mouse . . . of Jemima Puddle-Duck . . . of Squirrel Nutkin . . . Here at St Just he wrote his 'History of the writings of Beatrix Potter' and here he achieved the renowned breakthrough to crack her shorthand-coded journal. Enid Linder illustrated her brother's work with remarkable 'then and now' comparisons such as the one *below* of the cross-roads at Sawtrey — the real life setting for the frontispiece for 'The Tale of Piggling Bland' published in 1913.

It so happened that this particular line of code-writing contained a word in which the second cipher-symbol was the letter *x*, and, while there was no justification for assuming this to represent an *x*, it immediately suggested the word *executed* as the equivalent of *guillotined*. Fortunately Beatrix Potter had left the letter *x* unchanged, and the clue was therefore valid. In actual fact the word turned out to be *execution*, and the likelihood of this word was confirmed by noticing that it appeared to contain nine cipher-symbols, of which the first and third were the same.

With the help of these assumed symbols, other words were deciphered, and by midnight on that memorable Easter Monday practically the whole of Beatrix Potter's code-alphabet had been solved, and one of the early sheets of code-writing partly translated. If this particular sheet had not been an early example, written in bold copperplate style, it is doubtful whether I would ever have discovered the basic symbols of her code-alphabet.

In 1981, when Mr and Mrs Peter Ashton purchased the house which had stood empty after the death of Mr Linder, they found the swimming pool crumbling and beyond repair with no alternative but to fill it in.

The Journal of Beatrix Potter, translated from her code-writing by Leslie Linder. 1966

When Langfords came under the hammer at 2.30 p.m. on September 22, 1927 the last vestige of another of the old manors was lost. The manor of King's Place or Potells or Langfords dated back to the reign of Edward III when his son obtained 92 acres of land from the Lord of Chigwell Hall. Having passed through many owners during the next 450 years, in 1853 it was sold to the National Freehold Land Society who broke it up for building development.

'Potteles' or 'Langfords', an ancient palace or lodge, now 'King's Place Farm.' A purchase was made by the Crown in this parish (Chigwell) as early as 1350; and another of house and lands by King Edward IV, of Robert Langford in 1477. Afterwards it came into the possession of the Duke of Clarence. On his decease it came to the Crown. In 1512 King Henry VIII granted the keeping of his palace called 'Potteles' to the care of Sir John Risley; at his decease it was granted to William Comptom and his heirs. Lord Compton obtained a renewed grant of it from Queen Elizabeth in 1596 in the names of Spence and Atkinson; since that time it has passed through a number of families.

History of Essex, Elizabeth Ogborne, 1814

Unfortunately, nothing remains of the house at Waltham to which the triumphant lover conducted Anne after his progress with her through the country. Its historic interest would be great, for here it was that Cranmer gave his famous opinion with regard to Henry's divorce from Queen Catherine. Neither are there any traces of the hunting-place called Poteles, or Longford Palace, which stood at the bottom of where Palmerston Road, Buckhurst Hill, is now, a spot which Anne must have frequently visited while staying with the king at Waltham.

Frequent excursions were made by the pair into the forest — Anne mounted on a magnificent palfrey, the cynosure of all eyes, the king delighted as a schoolboy to exhibit his skill as a marksman for her applause. In his eagerness, one day, he shot the tame doe of an old woman resident in the forest, but discovering his mistake, he generously compensated her with seven shillings and sixpence.

London's Forest, P. J. S. Percival, 1909

Centuries ago 'The White House' or 'Langfords', now occupied by Mr C. B. Bond, standing in the middle of the parish, was a royal hunting-box, and from this King's Avenue derives its name.

There is no traceable account when the old building was pulled down. In the year 1773 a farmhouse occupied the spot, known as 'King's Place Farm', this was a few years ago converted into a beautiful villa residence, and retaining the royal name of 'Langford Place'.

Directory of Woodford, John James, 1896

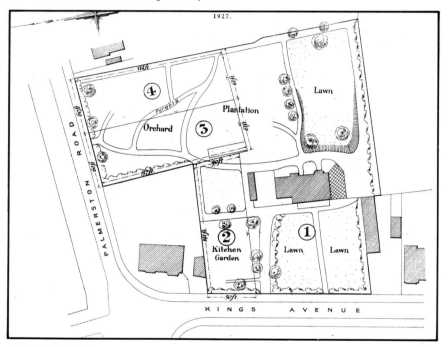

Today the name has been retained for the new road and estate which has been built on the site and gardens of Langfords.

From March to May 1950, the late Ernie Rule, well-known Loughtonian and long-time member of the Fire Brigade, set out to record in detail the 27 public footpaths in the area, some of which were being infringed by enclosures of a modern age, or lost through neglect or lack of use. Footpath No. 10 runs from Forest Edge, Buckhurst Hill to High Road, Chigwell.

Footpath No. 10

Forest Edge Buckhurst Hill to High Road Chigwell.

Guide post on East side of Forest Edge Buckhurst Hill between Nos. 16 and 18 reads: Public Footpath No. 10. To Cascades, Luxborough Lane and High Road Chigwell.

Turn to east from Forest Edge between properties Nos. 16 and 18, to fenced way that leads to footbridge over Railway (structure of concrete and steel built to replace gated level crossing 1949) and Albert Road. Cross road to sign post and fenced way. (Note, entrance has been obstructed with posts to prevent cattle passing, one post only left.) Follow fenced way to Northern end of Chestnut Close (Tarmac Path), cross close and follow fenced way to Cascade Road and Cascade Close. Allotments on left on North side, to guide post on West side of Cascade Close (one arm of Guide Post Missing). Follow road to right hand for 20 yds, cross over road, and pathway then leads south between properties Nos. 2 and 3 Cascade Close. Then over cartway through allotment grounds, fenced on both sides, to grassland, with the River Roding on left hand side. Footpath No. 10 and 13 meet at entry to Railway Bridge over River Roding. Pass under

Railway Bridge, western arch to iron footbridge over river. Cross over iron footbridge to well defined footway between hedges with Railway on left to Luxborough Lane. Follow lane to junction of Lane with Chigwell High Road, by Great West Hatch Hospital. Guide post at junction by fence of Great West Hatch.

Unpublished manuscript, Ernie Rule, March 1950

Chigwell

To many the name of Chigwell is synonymous with Charles Dickens. In 1841 his novel Barnaby Rudge was published and as soon as it appeared there was speculation by its readers as to the location of the 'Maypole' inn. To the people of Chigwell, it was obvious that the author had based his description of the building 'with more gable ends than a lazy man would care to count . . . ' on the King's Head in Chigwell Road although there were three inns actually called the Maypole in the area at the 'time' depicted in the book (1775) — at Chigwell Row, Barkingside and Collier Row. Mrs N. Powell, a friend and neighbour of Mr and Mrs Dickens at Tavistock House, intrigued to know the truth, asked Dickens outright. 'The fact is I patched it,' he replied. 'The place in my mind was Chigwell Row but I moved the "King's Head" inn to the site of the real Maypole as more suitable for my story.' A simple straightforward explanation of an author using a little poetic licence.

Chigwell, my dear fellow, is the greatest place in the world. Name your day for going. Such a delicious old inn opposite the church-yard, such a lovely ride, such beautiful forest scenery, such an out-of-the-way rural place, such a sexton!

Charles Dickens, 1812-1870

In the year 1775 there stood upon the borders of Epping Forest, at a distance of about twelve miles from London — measuring from the Standard in Cornhill, or rather, from the spot on or near to which the Standard used to be in days of yore — a house of public entertainment called the Maypole; which fact was demonstrated to all such travellers as could neither read nor write (and sixty years ago a vast number, both of travellers and stay-at-homes, were in this condition) by the emblem reared on the roadside over against the house, which, if not of those goodly proportions that maypoles were wont to present in olden times, was a fair young ash, thirty feet in height, and straight as any arrow that ever English yeoman drew.

The Maypole — by which term from henceforth is meant the house, and not its sign — the Maypole was an old building, with more gable ends than a lazy man would care to count on a sunny day; huge zig zag chimneys, out of which it seemed as though even smoke could not choose but come in more than naturally fantastic shapes, imparted to it in its tortuous progress; and vast stables, gloomy, ruinous, and empty. The place was said to have been built in the days of King Henry VIII; and there was a legend, not only that Queen Elizabeth had slept there one night while upon a hunting excursion, to wit, in a certain oak-panelled room with a deep bay-window, but that next morning, while standing on a mounting-block before the door with one foot in the stirrup, the virgin monarch had then and there boxed and cuffed an unlucky page for some neglect of duty. The matter-of-fact and doubtful folks, of whom there were a few among the Maypole customers — as, unluckily, there always are in every little community — were inclined to look upon this tradition as rather apocryphal; but

whenever the landlord of that ancient hostelry appealed to the mounting-block itself as evidence, and triumphantly pointed out that there it stood in the same place to that very day, the doubters never failed to be put down by a large majority, and all true believers exulted as in a victory.

Whether these, and many other stories of the like nature, were true or untrue, the Maypole was really an old house, a very old house, perhaps as old as it claimed to be, and

perhaps older, which will sometimes happen with houses of an uncertain, as with ladies of a certain, age. Its windows were old diamond-pane lattices, its floors were sunken and uneven, its ceilings blackened by the hand of time, and heavy with massive beams. Over the doorway was an ancient porch, quaintly and grotesquely carved; and here on summer evenings the more favoured customers smoked and drank — aye, and sang many a good song, too, sometimes — reposing on two grim-looking high-backed settles, which, like the twin dragons of some fairy tale, guarded the entrance to the mansion.

In the chimneys of the disused rooms, swallows had built their nests for many a long year, and from earliest spring to latest autumn whole colonies of sparrows chirped and twittered in the eaves. There was more pigeons about the dreary stable yard and outbuildings than anybody but the landlord could reckon up. The wheeling and circling flights of runts, fantails, tumblers, and pouters, were perhaps not quite consistent with the grave and sober character of the building, but the monotonous cooing, which never ceased to be raised by some among them all day long, suited it exactly, and seemed to lull it to rest. With its overhanging storeys, drowsy little panes of glass, and front bulging out and projecting over the pathway, the old house looked as if it were nodding in its sleep. Indeed it needed no very great stretch of fancy to detect in it other resemblances to humanity. The bricks of which it was built had originally been a deep dark red, but had grown yellow and discoloured like an old man's skin; the sturdy timbers had decayed like teeth; and here and there the ivy, like a warm garment to comfort it in its age, wrapped its green leaves closely round the time-worn walls.

It was a hale and hearty age though, still: and in the summer or autumn evenings, when the glow of the setting sun fell upon the oak and chestnut trees of the adjacent forest, the old house, partaking of its lustre, seemed their fit companion, and to have many good years of life in him yet.

Charles Dickens, Barnaby Rudge, 1841

This conversation was not publicised until 1912 and even then it was not widely known. Thus the controversy of 'Chigwell or Chigwell Row' bubbled away merrily, Dickensian addicts visiting both places to see whether from the front of Dickens's 'Maypole' the sun could be seen as it 'begun to peep above the forest trees', as described in Chapter XXXI, realising that this was not possible at the King's Head which faced west, whereas it could be done at the Maypole on the cross-roads at Chigwell Row. Even then the latter building was certainly of the wrong period. In 1927 one commentator, Mr. A. T. Wintersgill, in an address to the Leyton branch of the Dickensian Society, explained that 'today all the outbuildings [of the old inn] are gone, and half the pond only is left, the other half having been filled in to enlarge the "yard" attached to the present inn. The brick nucleus of the old inn is now converted into two dwelling houses . . . Immediately in front of the old inn is a small wood of recent growth which very effectively hides the old inn from people who pass along the high road.'

This was all very well, and adherents to the 'King's Head' school of thought could still go there and muse on past events in the 'Chester Room', that is until Mr W. Chapman Walker researched the history of the King's Head for the Managing Director of Messrs. Mann, Crossman & Paulin, the owners, which was published in a booklet for patrons in the 1930s. His findings provoked another bombshell; when Charles Dickens visited Chigwell with his friend Forster the present King's Head was not an inn! The real King's Head of the period was in fact on the south side of the building, a fact borne out in this old photograph. The building on the left (the present King's Head) was then a boarding school called The White House.

Sadly both the old King's Head and the original Maypole have both been demolished. *Above:* The former was lost with the provision of a run-in to the car park sometime before 1930; the latter in 1970 for a building plot *(below)*.

Sir, — It will be a relief to the minds of all Dickens-lovers to know that The Maypole of John Willet is still intact. Rumour exaggerates so much and so fast that there may now be many who imagine that they will never again have the satisfaction of entering the fine old Jacobean hostelry that figures so conspicuously in the pages of *Barnaby Rudge*.

Except for a few small panes of glass already made good, slight damage to a modern chimney stack, and the falling of a very narrow strip of plaster the structure is undamaged. The bomb that fell in the churchyard opposite was a small one and its effects on the inn were much reduced by the old brick wall that runs along the roadside. Windows on the north, south, and west sides of the church have been blown in or out, but these were mainly filled with plain leaded glass. One of the yews has lost a few branches, boarding has been torn off the picturesque wooden belfry (already made good), and the south porch will require to be retiled.

Altogether a delightful village, so much loved by Charles Dickens, has escaped with comparatively slight damage, and if Providence is kind, it may emerge from the war with very few scars.

Yours obediently,
GORDON HOME
Foxbury, Hambledon, Surrey.

The Times, April 12, 1941

Chigwell's Maypole Cottage — believed to be the original Maypole Inn mentioned by Charles Dickens in *Barnaby Rudge* — is to be demolished. The future of the cottage, behind the Maypole Inn, Lambourne Road, has been in the balance for many months.

Last week at an auction at the Bald Hind Hotel, Chigwell, a Loughton building and developing firm purchased the cottage for £23,500.

Scot-Rown, of Church Hill, said this week 'Work will start on the cottage in about two months. The building will be pulled down to make way for 10 luxury houses, each with three bedrooms.

West Essex Gazette, August 7, 1970

Chigwell's parish church of St Mary can date its history back to the twelfth century although the present building owes much to Sir Arthur Blomfield's reconstruction plans of 1886. Over the centuries the building had been altered or extended many times but by the 1850s the accommodation was insufficient for the growing population in the days of almost universal church-going. The first plan in 1853 was to add a south aisle but as this would have meant demolishing the original Norman fabric, the plan was abandoned. Nothing was done until Sir Arthur proposed that the old north aisle be demolished to build a new, larger nave, whereupon the old nave would become the south aisle. *Right:* Before and *below* today.

Chigwell is the most southern part of this Hundred. In records the name is written Cingwell; which was undoubtedly formed from the two Saxon words; Cing, and Pelle, that is King's Well. For the Saxons use C instead of K. which they pronounce strong like it. The name was occasioned by a Well in Chigwell-Row behind the wind-mill, among the trees, whose water has a purging quality; and the late Dr. Frewin used to speak in its favour. That celebrated Physician was born in Chigwell-Row, in an old mansion house, now pulled down, once belonging to the Pelling family, and afterwards to the Frewins. Here the Doctor's mother died, and he used to visit the place every two or three years till his decease. Near this well, there is a Hole, or hollow place wherein is a Water of the same nature, perhaps proceeding from the other. In Havering Liberty, there is also another purging Water, in a Well near Bone, or rather Bourn Bridge, under which runs a small stream of common water.

The name of this parish is otherwise written in records Cingheuuella, Cinguehella, Chiwellia, Chickwell, Gykewell. . . .

The History and Antiquities of the County of Essex, Reverend Philip Morant, 1763-1768

The timelessness of Chigwell is singularly refreshing. Here Conservation is spelt with a capital C, and preservation has been aided by restrictions on private building.

The history of St Mary's is bound up with that of Chigwell School. The Reverend Samuel Harsnett was vicar of Chigwell from 1597 to 1605 and also became master at Pembroke College, Cambridge. Although his controversial activities constantly brought him into conflict with his contemporaries — at one time he was accused of over fifty offences from laziness with his accounts to giving permission for the publication of seditious books and Popery — as far as Chigwell was concerned he made up for it by building and endowing the school. This was at the time when Harsnett had surmounted his unpopularity, possibly through being favoured by James I, and had risen through the bishoprics of Chichester and Norwich to become Archbishop of York.

. . . Caused to be erected two fair and large School Houses in the Parish of Chigwell in the said County of Essex; to the end, intent and purpose that the children and youth of the said Parish and other adjoining Parishes from Time to Time for ever hereafter be in one of the said Schools instructed and taught to Read, Write, Cypher, and Cast Accounts, and to learn their Accidence; and in the other School House to be instructed and taught the Latin and Greek tongues.

Foundation of Chigwell School, Indenture, April 13, 1629

Chigwell's uniqueness has largely come about by its isolation amid farmland, preserved as part of London's 'Green Belt'. This was created by the London County Council in 1935 after it was realised that over 8,500 acres of open land suitable for recreation had been lost over the previous five years. It was seen that the 'lost paradises of London' would go at the rate of a thousand acres a year unless something was done to stem the tide. That something was the provision of £2 million by the LCC over the next three years to make grants of up to fifty per cent of the cost of buying up land, the remainder to be made up by the local authority. Thus the battle to preserve the Forest itself was paralleled by action fifty years later to preserve the open spaces — an act of foresight we all now enjoy.

The property — Grange Court, Chigwell — described in these Particulars, is one which is difficult to adequately describe in a particulars prepared for the purpose of an Auction Sale. It is a good example of an early Georgian residence, standing back from the road, and, as is a feature frequently found in residences of this type, it is entered from the north, with the main front and principal rooms planned along the whole of the southern side.

A chief point to be noted by those contemplating the purchase of a house of this character, is its perfect state of condition, in which it has been maintained throughout, both inside and outside. The residence is in perfect decorative repair, the domestic quarters are ample for all requirements, though not cumbersome. There is ample stabling for the horse-lover, four separate coach houses or garages, and living accommodation for two married employees, each being provided with bathroom accommodation. To turn to the gardens and grounds, they are complete, there being fine glasshouses in perfect order as regards structure, heating, and the trees and vines therein. The lawns are beautifully studded with fine cedars. There are rose gardens, herbaceous borders, sunk gardens, a perfect kitchen and fruit garden, being entirely walled round, and a young orchard, the remainder of the property being paddocks.

Notes on the sale of Grange Court on Thursday July 28, 1927

Boarders from the school also now occupy Grange Court on the opposite side of the road, a Grade II* late eighteenth century mansion extensively remodelled in 1774. During the Second World War it was used by the Army, notably the Hampshire Regiment and Scots Guards who carried out exercises in the surrounding fields. Well aware of the penchant of young boys for collecting souvenirs, the CO of the Hampshires came to the school to lecture the boys not to touch unexploded grenades and their like that they might find.

In 1948 the Old Chigwellians purchased Grange Court as a memorial to those boys who had given their lives during the Second World War. It became the Prep department of the Junior School until 1976 when purpose-built accommodation was provided in the grounds of the school itself whereupon Grange Court was converted into senior boarders' dormitories like that of the old gardener's cottage *(below)*. In 1927 the estate comprised 14 acres; today the majority of the area has been developed for housing.

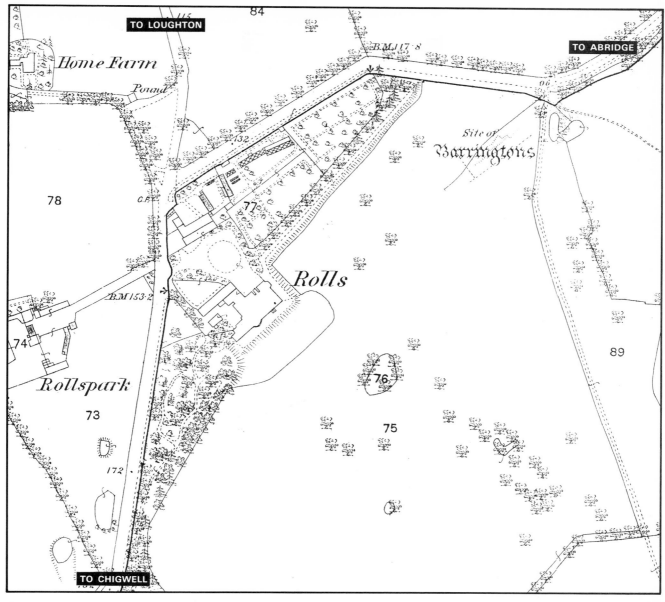

One of the most interesting changes, historically, in Chigwell concerns the road to Abridge. In 1700 William Harvey purchased the Barrington's Manor of Little Chigwell, the seat of which was Rolls House which then lay on the western side of the road.

He died in 1731 but his son, also William, instituted proceedings to alter the course of the road and so enable the estate to be consolidated to the east. This move was carried out shortly afterwards, the dog-leg bend around the high brick wall at 'Rolls Park Corner' existing to this day.

At the time of the Norman Conquest the Manor of Chigwell was held by Earl Harold, but in 1066 it was given to Ralph de Limesi of Wolverly, Warwickshire. The first site of the manor house, complete with moat, was directly alongside the Roding near the White Bridge *(above)* rebuilt in concrete in 1960.

According to a survey taken in the reign of James I, the number of acres in the parish at that time was 4,027, which included 1,500 acres of Epping and Hainault Forests. The present area of the parish, including Buckhurst Hill, is a little over 4,500 acres. The population a quarter of a century ago was 2,600. In 1871 this number had nearly doubled itself; and according to the census returns for 1881 it has now reached 5,400. A fair is held here annually in September. The parish is thickly studded with good mansions, mostly the residences of City merchants; and there are also several fine old halls and manor-houses, where in bygone times dwelt the lords of the soil.

Greater London, Edward Walford 1883

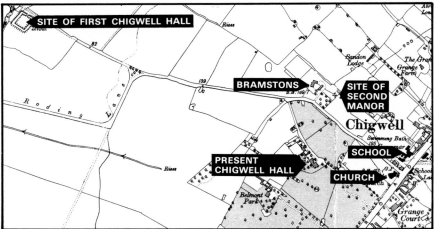

The river site had become deserted by the middle of the seventeenth century when a new manor house was built on higher ground about 300 yards behind the school. The site lay in the grounds of the more modern Bramstons *(below)* which was built by Lydall Savill in 1908.

Another 'Manor House' was built by Sir Henry (Harry) Hicks who held the manorial rights from 1723 to 1755. He chose a position close to Woodford Bridge, and originally called the house Bowling Green. Today it is a Roman Catholic Convent.

SITE OF FIRST MANOR HOUSE

The personnel at the R.A.F. Station Chigwell will all have left by the middle of this month. And they are all glad to be going.

'It's just a field with a couple of huts,' explained Corporal Technician W. K. Marshall on Tuesday, 'Everyone seems to be miserable and we have nothing to do except load lorries and pack equipment. It costs a fortune if you want any entertainment — Chigwell is miles from anywhere.'

Chigwell Times, December 1, 1961

The three-year-old mystery surrounding the ownership of the vacant Chigwell R.A.F. camp was finally solved this week. Savill's Trustees, holders of property throughout the Chigwell area, admitted that they are the original owners of the land.

Thus ends the speculation which began in 1962, when the R.A.F. moved out of Chigwell and the question of the camp site's future was raised.

The 88-acre site is under the jurisdiction of the Ministry of Defence, who are obliged to offer the land to the original owners — despite the persistent interest of Chigwell Council.

Chigwell councillors have been increasingly curious about the identity of their competitors for the land. The R.A.F. and the Ministry of Defence have remained silent.

But this week at the City headquarters of Savill's, Mr. John Savill told the Gazette, 'Savill Trustees are definitely the original owners of the land, and as such we are interested in purchasing it.

What would Savill's do with the land if they acquired it again?

'Well, we shall have to make inquiries about that to find out what can be done with it,' said Mr. Savill, who is one of eight partners in the firm. 'After all, it is an expanse of concrete at the moment.'

West Essex Gazette, January 14, 1966

With the crisis in Europe escalating, in May 1938 the Royal Air Force opened RAF Chigwell as a recruiting centre for No. 909 Balloon Unit. It was intended that the Chigwell Rise station should be an active part of the London defensive system and the construction work virtually obliterated the site of the first manor house. By August, No. 4 Balloon Command were in residence and No. 948 Balloon Squadron became operational shortly after the outbreak of war the following year. The RAF retained the base after the war, it being used for several different signals and radar support units. It finally closed on December 1, 1958, being retained on a care and maintenance basis until a disbandment holding party moved in on March 5, 1962 to reduce the station to inactive status for parenting by RAF North Weald and, later, RAF Debden. The future of the camp remained in limbo until the RAF finally gave up the site in December 1968.

The death of the camp on the left is mirrored by the birth of the motorway on the right.

The other notable manor in Chigwell is that of Little Chigwell, more commonly known by the name of the family which held the tenancy from the twelfth to the sixteenth century — the Barringtons. With their tenure having spanned 450 years, Thomas Barrington, who sold the estate to Thomas Wiseman of Great Waltham in 1563, must have had not a little to answer for in breaking with the family's traditional seat. Indeed, it brought the new owner little pleasure for he died the same year! In 1926 the manorial rights were purchased by the well-known Chigwell landowning family of Savills although the freehold in the estate and its manor house, Rolls House, remained with the then-owner, the Reverend Rossendale Lloyd, brother of Lieutenant-General Sir Francis Lloyd, until he died in 1940 whereupon it was inherited by his son Andrew.

Above: The L-shaped mansion itself was a mixture of seventeenth and eighteenth century wings, and it was requisitioned by the Army in World War II. Unfortunately the military do not have a good reputation for taking care of other people's property and a fire caused by a bomb which severely damaged the roof didn't help. When handed back after the war it was merely a shell and most of it was demolished in the 1950s. This picture was taken at the time by Bert Steel, of the Chigwell, Chigwell Row and District Historical Society. *Below:* The property is now divided into five portions: the main part Bretts; the Orangery, the Stables, the nursery and cottage (closed in July 1985), and the bailiff's 'cottage' (see also page 273).

There had been a fall of fire bombs in the vicinity of Manor Road, Chigwell. Several houses were alight and fire pumps were at work when I arrived; I was reconnoitring the area when there came a fall of marker flares in fields about half a mile to the north of the built up area. At once, two fire pumps set off in the direction of the flares.

'Stop,' I yelled to the officer of the leading pump. 'Where are you going?'

'To black out those flares,' he replied.

'Leave them to burn,' I told him. 'Let them drop their load on the fields.' So the appliances returned to the job in hand, the crews glancing somewhat apprehensively in the direction of the white glare, anticipating a deluge of high explosives. But there was no further bombing in the area, that night.

Somehow, the Nazi lines had become crossed. Surely, the aim was to follow the markers with bombs? But the bombs arrived first and the markers, far off target, came later. In any event, Chigwell, a dormitory suburb on the eastern outskirts of London, hardly presented a strategic target worthy of bombing.

The London Blitz, Cyril Demarne, 1980

While on the subject of the Second World War, the Prince of Wales stands as the supreme horror in Chigwell's war diary, and the whole Epping Forest area. April 19 was a disastrous night throughout Essex and of the total of 262 fatalities, 35 occurred in this little pub in Manor Road. Although the incident was reported in the press at the time, the name and location were withheld by the censor, it being described as an 'hotel'.

Heavy casualties occurred in Saturday night's raids on the London area — one of the most vicious attacks made on London by waves of raiders which dropped scores of flares and fire bombs and many large calibre high explosive bombs.

Material damage was extensive, especially in residential areas.

Among the buildings hit were a police court, a cinema, a dance hall, a hotel, and a mansion on the outskirts of London.

The hotel which was struck received a direct hit from a heavy bomb and was completely wrecked. There were many people in the hotel at the time and loss of life was severe.

A darts match was in progress when the explosion occurred.

The Woodford Times, April 25, 1941

Charrington's Prince of Wales at Chigwell has risen phoenix-like from the foundations of the old public house which was built in 1932 and destroyed by a land mine nine years later. It was opened on Wednesday by Mr. H. A. Chisenhale-Marsh, a director of Charrington and Co., Ltd.

To conform to War Damage Commission requirements, the new house is built to the shape of the previous building, but the half-timbering has disappeared. Warm multi-coloured hand-made bricks have been used with 'antique' tiles on the roof, while the upper storey is finished with Tyrolean rendering. This combination blends extremely well with surrounding properties.

One of the features of the old Prince of Wales was the fine chimney stacks and great care has been taken to make sure that the new stacks are as impressive as the old.

The car park, which before was very small, will now accommodate 50 cars.

Chigwell Times December 6, 1963

That night it was cloudy and German aircrews reported that they could only see through gaps in the clouds. The normal balloon barrage was encountered flying at 1500-2000 metres as was accurate anti-aircraft fire. The RAF sent up night-fighters to intercept the 504-strong force as it approached London. The main bomb load comprised normal SC bombs ranging from 250kg-1,000kg. Its aircraft were guided by Knickebein — the German radio-navigational aid — but London's dockland was the actual target and it was a chance in a million that the Prince of Wales received a direct hit. It was a terrible sight which greeted rescue workers with dismembered bodies and parts of bodies being festooned all around. People say it took over a week to clear up and even then many of the victims could not be identified . . . besides regulars, just casual customers who suddenly one night failed to come home. They were buried together in this corner of Chigwell churchyard. Is the overgrown state of the grave a symbol of how much we care? Even the pub changed its name to Sloanes in December 1983.

On the night of Saturday April 19, 1941, about 60 people were enjoying a drink at the Prince of Wales pub, Manor Road, Chigwell. Minutes later 35 of them were dead and the rest badly injured. The cause of this disaster was a German parachute mine landing on the roof of the pub.

Immediately Chigwell Council went into action to arrange the funeral of the victims. Some made private arrangements but 20 were buried in a communal grave at St. Mary's Church, Chigwell. Now, to mark the 30th anniversary of the Prince of Wales disaster, Chigwell Council are to give a facelift to the grave. They are planning to pave over the grave and provide flower beds at each corner. Said a council spokesman: 'After the disaster we undertook to maintain the grave. Cutting the grass has become a bit of a problem so we have decided that it would be best to pave it over'.

The Independent, April 1971

July 12, 1951. Accompanied by the Prime Minister, the future Queen is presented with a bouquet by Master David Rickets Allen, grandson of the Clerk of the Trustees of the London Parochial Charities who acquired the site for the centre way back in 1938. Contributions were made available from the King George V Jubilee Trust, the King's Camp Fund and the Ministry of Education to create a comprehensive camping and recreation centre for the people of Greater London.

A large camping and sports centre which is now being built in Essex, at a cost of £250,000, is intended to be one of the show pieces at the Festival of Britain in 1951. The centre is intended to be used by young people and families who cannot afford holidays by the sea, and it has facilities for all popular games and many social recreations.

The project, which is another of the generous schemes of the London Parochial Charities, was deferred by the outbreak of war after land had been acquired at Grange Farm, Chigwell, Essex. A few temporary structures were put up, enabling the ground to be used as a camp site, but now that it is hoped to have the scheme completed in time for the festival permanent building is going on at speed.

At the international camp of the World Assembly of Youth, Her Royal Highness signed the visitors' book and there met people from 24 different countries who were staying at the centre.

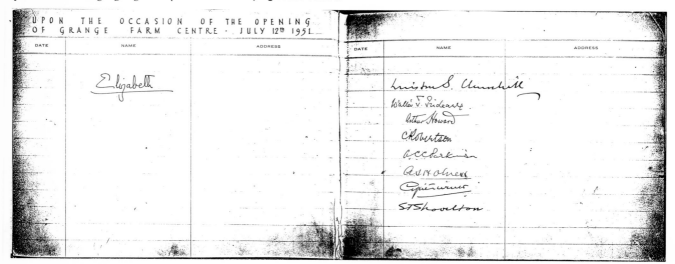

The centre is planned primarily for boys and girls and it will be open to parties from youth organizations all over England, although anyone will be able to obtain admission to the grounds for a small charge. Because of its location, it will be especially valuable to the youth of east London.

The layout is spread over 107 acres and the dormitory area includes a hutted camp and a site for tents which will be particularly useful to scouts and guides. The hutted camp will house about 400 and in the canvas camp there will be room for another 200. The grounds can accommodate several thousand day visitors.

An assembly hall, which will be open to local residents during the winter, is sited close to the camp entrance, where there is also a control office. Beyond Grange Farm, which will be used as the warden's house, there will be tennis courts, a bowling green, the main football and cricket pitches with running track, a swimming pool, sun garden, miniature golf course, and a children's playground. A Rugby football ground, secondary football pitches, and the canvas camp are placed farther to the north-west.

The Times, 1950

Cheering crowds packed into the grounds of Grange Farm Centre on Thursday afternoon and lined the streets outside to witness an occasion which will go down as one of the most memorable in the history of Chigwell — the visit of H.R.H. Princess Elizabeth accompanied by the Rt. Hon. Winston Churchill, to open the centre.

Thousands of excited people crowded into the grounds of the centre — designed to cater for the recreational needs of over-populated London — and lined the roads as the Princess arrived in her sleek black car with the Royal Ensign flying.

As the car swept round to the permanent building of the site, the people surged forward to wave and to secure a vantage point for the opening ceremony.

The Princess and Mr. Churchill were received by the Lord Lieutenant of Essex (Colonel Sir Francis Whitmore), after which the Trustees of the London Parochial Charities were presented.

Dr. W. T. Prideaux, chairman of the Trustees, then conducted the Princess and Mr. Churchill to a specially prepared dais in front of the camp centre.

As the Princess, wearing a becoming black and white striped tie silk coat, over a grey and white spotted gown, and white accessories, appeared, deafening applause greeted her.

First speaker was Dr. Prideaux, who extended a welcome to the Princess on behalf of the trustees of the Council and the management.

Amid more applause, Princess Elizabeth rose to speak, saying that she was very glad to declare the centre open.

Her Royal Highness recalled that two years ago her husband, the Duke of Edinburgh, visited the centre to see the development of the open space in which he was so deeply concerned.

Mr. Churchill called for cheers for the Princess to which everyone responded to acclamation.

After the opening ceremony the Princess toured the grounds; the crowd followed her in a pressing mob.

Chigwell Times, July 13, 1951

At a short ceremony at Grange Farm Sports Centre to mark the 'take-over' by Chigwell Urban District Council for administrative purposes, Mr. Norman Crafford, Chairman of the Urban District Council, said: 'Grange Farm is like a disease. It runs in the veins of the people, and we shall be glad to run the centre in much the same way that it has been run for many years.'

The aspirations of a brave new world seeking to lift itself out of the dark years of the 1940s — a sporting centre created for tomorrow's youth of Europe. A visitor from yesterday's generation to the Grange Farm of today would be ashamed.

In reply, Sir Donald Allen, chairman of the management said: 'I am sure that the council will look after the centre, and in doing so I hope they will look after the helpers here, for they don't ask for much.'

After the short ceremony, Sir Donald told a reporter: 'I bought the centre in 1937 'when it was a derelict farm and decided that a sports and camping centre would be an ideal place for both sexes, young and old to come into contact with each other.'

Mr. H. Collett, warden of the sports centre, commented: 'The council are determined to keep Grange Farm going in much the same way, keeping to the same principles. The promises of improvement are very encouraging.'

Express and Independent, April 9,1965

Grange Farm Leisure Centre — due to close in the Spring — has already made its way into the annals of local history. . . . but in recent years various factors have contributed to Grange Farm's decline, including the falling strength of the pound abroad, a general drop in tourism and changes in holiday trends.

Since 1974 the centre has lost almost £½ million and been described by the district council as 'a burden on the ratepayer'. It has even been estimated that Grange Farm would probably lose a further £100,000 if it were to stay open this year.

Accordingly the district council recently decided that the site must close on March 31,

and stop providing caravanning and camping facilities for visitors from all over the world.

Negotiations are now going on with the Charity Commission to see whether or not the site can be sold.

If it is sold, the district council plans to try to recoup its losses, and put the rest of the money towards charity.

Guardian & Gazette, January 14, 1983

Chigwell's Grange Farm could become an exciting, bright new leisure and educational centre serving the whole of London, by next spring.

This is the ambitious plan from Forest Projects Ltd, which hopes to turn the dilapidated area into a unique centre for recreation, sport, social events and new permanent jobs for local people . . . with part of the land a giant nature reserve containing rare breeds of animals and wildfowl.

Also planned are adventure playgrounds, museums, picnic areas, a lecture theatre, restaurant, and sports facilities for children and handicapped people.

Said chairman of Forest Projects Richard Hoskins: 'We want an initial five-year lease. During this time we would open up the site which will give the trustees and public the chance to see what we are doing. We are confident we will have earned the right to stay on.'

Guardian & Gazette, October 11, 1985

279

The changing face of Chigwell pubs. The modernisation of the King William IV, nestling behind the trees on the left in the picture of Chigwell Road *(above)*, is unusual in that the old inn was left in situ while a completely new building was erected on an adjacent plot. The new King William IV was open in March 1983, the original empty at the time of writing.

The Bald Hind — serving ale since 1770 when it was known as the Bald Faced Hind.

The Jolly Wheelers, whose bar is severed by the boundary with Woodford Bridge, dates from 1778.

Luxury flats, with prices starting from £13,750 for a two-bedroomed apartment and extending up to £30,000 for a penthouse, are being offered at The Bowls, Vicarage Lane, Chigwell, by a small local builder, T. A. Clark (Holding) Ltd., in delightful green belt surroundings. There are panoramic views to the south across the Thames valley to the Kentish hills beyond, to the west round to London, and to the north over green belt land to parts of Epping Forest.

An unusual aspect of this superb development is that the present phase allows for a variety of combinations of bedrooms and dressing rooms, with a top limit of six bedrooms and three bathrooms. A purchaser can, in consultation with the developers, make any arrangement he may require, and that goes for the internal decoration as well. Only a small amount of equipment is standard and cannot be altered except for colour. A noticeable feature of all the flats is that there are no wasted areas. Every foot of space has been sensibly and economically used. Noise transmittance has been virtually eliminated by the use of an acoustic blanket in the floor construction, and a condition of the lease is that purchasers lay fitted carpets to all areas except kitchens, bathrooms and cloakrooms.

The present block consists of twelve flats and two penthouses (one of which has already been sold, the purchaser spending a further £9,000 on decoration and furniture). Fifty-two flats from previous phases have already been sold, and the developers are convinced that the new ones will be snapped up.

From the purchaser's point of view almost every convenience has been considered — fully automatic gas-fired warm-air central heating with thermostatic control in each individual flat, heated airing cupboard, constant hot water by immersion heater, an automatic system of water-softening equipment, waste disposal sink units, to mention only a few of the outstanding installations.

Incidentally, the purchaser is responsible only for the interior decoration and upkeep of his flat. A managing agent administers the site and its buildings, repairs and redecorates the exterior, cleans and lights the entrances and stairways, and looks after the lifts and the approaches to the buildings. The purchaser has little to worry about except to look after his own flat.

These luxury flats are the obvious answer for those people who want spacious, comfortable homes without the bother of maintenance.

Essex Countryside, April 1969

From country house to condominium — The Bowls at the junction of Vicarage Lane, Manor Road and Lambourne Road.

In the archives of the Hospital there is a wonderful book prepared by Humphry Repton, the landscape gardener, who in that year of 1791 came down at the request of the owner of Claybury Hall to compile a book of suggestions for the improvement of the grounds. His delightful sketches show the layout which he found when he arrived and that which he proposed by way of amendment.

Our Georgian visitor would, however, see more extensive alterations than those envisaged by Repton. A Hospital which accommodates over 2,000 patients and 200 resident staff is more like a small town than a Hospital, and Claybury Hall is now only a small part of the network of buildings which form the home of such a large number of people. An interesting thing about the development of Claybury is that when the Commissioners in Lunacy made their 49th report in 1895 they referred to Claybury Hall in the following terms: 'There is also a mansion on the Estate which has been adapted for the reception of fifty male patients' and Claybury Hall is still used for about that number of patients despite the passage of 60 years.

There are some more interesting things to be gleaned from those old reports: for instance, the report of 1887 which deals with the purchase of the Hall and its grounds tells us that it cost £36,000, and further that it commanded 'an extensive and southerly view', although in those days the southerly aspect was over open fields, and now it is over the roofs of Woodford Green and Ilford.

Even in those days the health service found it difficult to deal with the demands made upon it: in 1892 the Commissioners reported the difficulty of finding accommodation anywhere for London patients and they said that although after a year the Claybury Asylum would be completed and more accommodation would be available, there would still be left 'boarded out' a sufficient number of patients to fill 'another Asylum of considerable capacity.' When the cost of the building amounting to £484,000 is added to the purchase price it will be seen that the total cost of Claybury was well over the half-million mark — a large sum of money for those days — but one wonders what the cost of purchase and building would be at the present time!

Originally the Claybury Hall estate was held by Barking Abbey and today it physically lies within Ilford. Nevertheless the link forged with Chigwell came in 1786 when it was sold to James Hatch of Chigwell Hall who had purchased that manor for £30,000 in 1764. Thereafter Claybury descended with the Chigwell estate until 1887 when it was sold to the justices of the County of Middlesex who wanted a site to build a lunatic asylum.

Building contracts have often been the downfall of those who undertook them; the first firm of contractors which was engaged on the work of building Claybury Hospital went into liquidation — probably as a result of having attempted far too much — and gave a great deal of trouble to the Architect, Mr. G. T. Hine, because work stopped in December leaving the walls in a state which meant that rain and frost could do untold damage. Poor Mr. Hine had to make the best shift he could to get the exposed portions cemented over to prevent this damage, but it is obvious that he was a man of resource, and a warm tribute to his ability and energy was paid by the Building Committee. Mr. Hine retaliated in good measure by thanking the Committee for their 'very kind and ever ready support and assistance'.

The familiar contour of the Claybury water-tower and chimney on their tree-girt hill has become so much a part of the local scene that it is hard to believe that there was a time when it was not there; harder still to believe, not only that the Commissioners exhausted all the possible sites in Middlesex (whose Asylum it originally was), but that before picking on Claybury they actually signed a contract for the purchase of land at Theydon Bois. How different our skyline would have been had their lawyers not been able to get them out of what proved, on consideration, to be an unworkable site.

Once the site had been fixed, and the first

The Local Government Act enacted the following year transferred the responsibilities for all asylums to county councils and, accordingly, London County Council took over the management and completion of the building which was opened in 1893.

STABLE BLOCK

HALL

HOSPITAL

Privilege without responsibility? We have already commented on the privileged position in which hospital boards find themselves when it comes to preserving listed buildings; briefly there are no powers or penalties to force them so to do. So far, the dereliction of the stable block (listed Grade II) has escaped the public limelight. Built in 1785, it was accepted by the Department of the Environment as being of historic importance in 1974 but was abandoned after it was damaged by fire. Since 1979 it has been quietly falling down, which most probably suits the purposes of the authorities, who will no doubt in due course announce that 'its demolition is now necessary because the building is unsafe'.

difficulties overcome, work went on smoothly enough, and by 1889, when the new London County Council took over responsibility for the Hospital, there was only the super-structure to be completed at the trifling cost of £337,945! From then to the opening day was another four years — a long time perhaps for one building — but it must be remembered that this one building is in fact the size of a small town, with a total population of nearly 3,000.

Claybury Hospital Management Committee, 1958

The rundown of services at doomed Claybury Hospital should be gradual, says Redbridge Community Health Council.

Consultations should take place from ward to ward in preparation for the closure, members agreed at last Thursday's meeting.

There are 850 patients in the hospital who will be gradually moved into the community over the next 10 years. One hospital block on the site at Woodford Bridge has already been closed. Other vacant buildings will be boarded up as more patients are transferred from the hospital into the community.

West Essex Gazette, October 25, 1985

Today the Claybury Hall that James Hatch purchased no longer stands. It was a large gabled building but he demolished it five years later and had rebuilt a new hall on the same site by 1791. This is the mansion which survives to this day within the grounds of the hospital and is used for district administrative offices.

The sister village of Chigwell Row has also withstood the test of time . . . skirts it seems have not!

I pass the vicar's white abode,
And pondering take the upward road,
 By busy thoughts o'erladen,
To where the pride of Chigwell Row
Still lives — a handsome widow now,
 As erst a lovely maiden.

Here hills and dales and distant Thames,
And forest glens, green proof proclaims,
 Of Nature's lavish bounty,
And dub thee, lofty region still,
Surrey's tall foe, the Richmond Hill
 Of this our Eastern County.

Diverging from the road, the sod
I tread which once, a boy, I trod,
 With pace not quite so nimble.
But where's the Maypole next the lane,
Who dared to banish from the plain
 That wreath-encircled symbol?

Abridge, her tank and waterfall,
The path beneath Sir Eliab's wall
 I once again am stepping,
Beyond that round we rarely stirred;
Loughton we saw — but only heard
 Of Ongar and of Epping.

James Smith, 1775-1839

A FOREST FETE
NEAR CHIGWELL ROW

On Saturday, a grand fete, in the gipsy style, was given by several ladies of the neighbourhood of Chigwell, at the foot of Hog Hill, in the centre of the forest of Hainault, which formed one of the most pleasant sights we have lately witnessed. The party, near forty in number, assembled about three o'clock, the ladies dressed in a most elegant manner, when they sat down to a cold collation, during which several popular and beautiful airs were performed, in a superior manner, on the French Horn, by Giovanni Pussi, a first-rate performer on that instrument, accompanied by the piano-forte.

The party, after repast, then rose and commenced dancing with 'Voulez vous dansez', which was followed by several other favourite dances and quadrilles (for which a select band was engaged) under a grove of trees, encircled by garlands. Upon the whole it was one of the most enchanting scenes imaginable. The company did not separate until the evening was far advanced.

*Chelmsford Chronicle,
September 3, 1819*

A battle was fought on Tuesday, between Tom Sweeney and Ned Savage, for £5. aside, near the May Pole, on the skirts of Epping Forest. This affair made so little noise, and the spot itself was so very secluded, that their Worships the Magistrates for the County of Essex received no hint of what was going on. No interference took place, therefore, on their part; but, owing to the smallness of the stakes, and perhaps owing to the recollection of the various disasters attending the last fight in that direction, between Harry Jones and Barney Aaron, a very limited muster of metropolitan amateurs graced the present exhibition. After a severe struggle, in the 28th round, Sweeney went in, and hit Savage several body blows, right and left. Savage staggered and fell — not to get up again; his seconds tried to get him on his legs, but, finding the experiment impracticable, they were obliged to give in for him.

Press report, 1828

The Grove, Chigwell Row, traditionally the home of Sir Francis Drake, was sold last month.

The Local Review, December 1912

George Shillibeer. What does the name convey to you? Probably nothing — unless it makes you want to smile at its queerness. Yet every time you travel in a 'bus you ought to breathe a little prayer of gratitude to the fates that raise up Shillibeers. For it was a gentleman of that name who built and ran the first 'bus London ever saw. What is more, he lived for several years in Essex, at Grove House, Chigwell Row.

Shillibeer, to begin at the beginning, was born in 1797 in Tottenham Court-road, and joined the Navy at an early age. He served on the 'San Josef' and the 'Royal George', but quitted when he had attained the rank of midshipman and went to learn the trade of coach building from a firm in Long Acre.

Young Shillibeer proved an adept at this business and soon had enough money to leave for Paris and set up in business on his own.

Here in Paris it was, apparently, that the word 'omnibus' began to be popularly used in the way in which we know it today. It is, of course, the dative plural of the Latin word 'omnis' and means 'for all'. It had been used first of all by a coach proprietor in Nantes, who named his vehicle, 'L'Omnibus.'

Shillibeer, who was steadily gaining experience in building all types of public and private vehicles, was, in 1825, given an order to construct two new and improved types of omnibuses by M. Lafitte who, besides being a banker, was an omnibus proprietor in the French capital. It was whilst he was building these two 'buses that Shillibeer was struck with the idea of providing London with the same means of transport, and, no sooner had he finished the Paris order than he set out for London, determined to put 'buses on the streets there.

Previously London's public conveyances had been run on the ordinary stage-coach principle, except that they made short journeys. On the whole these short stage coaches were unpopular — many of them catered for parcels, which got in the way of passengers, the fares were excessive, no one ever knew when the next coach would run and the coachmen were invariably rude to the passengers.

Paris already had the 'omnibus' system — vehicles on which a flat rate of five sous was charged for a journey. London was to follow suit, thanks to George Shillibeer.

On Saturday, July 4, 1829, the first omnibus made its appearance in an English street. It was a long-bodied affair with the word 'Omnibus' painted on the sides, and it travelled from the 'Yorkshire Stingo' at Paddington via what are now Marylebone, Euston and Pentonville-roads — they were then New-road — and City-road to the Bank of England.

Express and Independent, June 13, 1936

Fire swept and completely gutted the 400-year-old Grove Country Club at Chigwell Row during the early hours of Monday morning. Guests had miraculous escapes, and were taken to houses in Grove Lane in their night-clothes, but Mr. Harold Ranyell was rushed to King George Hospital with a broken pelvis after leaping more than 40 feet to safety.

Three others, including the proprietor and his wife, Mr. and Mrs. Henry Garwood, jumped 30 feet from windows to escape the inferno.

The fire is thought to have broken out in the lounge, two hours after the last of the guests had gone to bed.

'Junior' a black mongrel dog belonging to Mr. and Mrs. Winston Waite, of 'Abbots Court', Grove Lane woke the household with his barking at 3.30 on Monday morning. 'He was crazed with fear', said Mrs. Winifred Waite. 'He could hear the roar of the fire and smell the smoke as the club is only at the bottom of our back garden. My husband rushed downstairs to call the fire brigade just

When Chigwell Row became a separate parish in 1867 its own church — All Saints — was consecrated but the tower we see today was not added until 1903.

as Mr. Garwood was hammering on our door for help.

The whole place was an inferno, terrifying. At first only the lounge appeared to be alight and then the entire house went up. At times the flames were leaping a good 60 feet into the air.

Mr. Harold Ranyell was encouraged by neighbours to jump when he appeared at a window 40 feet up against a background of flames. He jumped, bounced on a veranda and fell a further 20 feet. He and Mr. Garwood were taken to hospital, where they were said on Wednesday to be comfortable.

The Woodford Times, February 21, 1964

George Shillibeer's house came to a sad end in February 1964.

Around and about in Chigwell. This is Miller's Lane.

Gravel Lane, almost unchanged in 80 years.

Lambourne Road: modest development since 1903.

Stop the clock in Hainault Road where time, if not the seasons, has almost stood still.

Luxborough Lane, the ancient way to Luxborough Hall, the other main manor in Chigwell just south of Chigwell Hall to which it was attached in the sixteenth century. In 1716 the estate was heavily in debt and had to be sold — to Robert Knight of the South Sea Company. When the bubble burst in 1720 Luxborough passed into the hands of trustees although Knight attempted to buy it back in 1744. It had reverted to being part of the Chigwell Hall estate by 1800 when our friend James Hatch (see pages 282-283), who must have had a penchant for demolishing buildings, knocked down the Hall. This had originally been constructed sometime in the sixteenth century and rebuilt in 1716-20. It was never replaced and today nothing remains to mark the site of the former mansion on the playing field beside the river.

Loughton

The town of Loughton lies to the east of Epping Forest and west of the Roding, adjoining Chigwell; it is 12 miles from London. The ancient parish of Loughton became an urban district in 1900 and in 1933 was united with the Urban District of Buckhurst Hill and Chigwell civil parish to form the Chigwell Urban District. The area of the ancient parish was approximately that of the present Loughton (North) and Loughton (South) Wards of the urban district, taken together, and in 1931 comprised 3,961 acres. For ecclesiastical purposes the ancient parish was divided in 1887 by the creation of the new parish of St. Mary, in the south of the town.

The best approach to Loughton is from the north, by the road through Epping Forest from the 'Wake Arms'. The forest has always formed an important part of the landscape of Loughton. Over 1,300 acres of the forest were within the ancient parish and were preserved by the Epping Forest Acts of 1871-80. The road leaves the forest about a mile south of the 'Wake Arms', at Goldings Hill and runs south down hill, becoming Church Hill and then

Lower Road, the old road into Loughton from the north before its reconstruction to ease the strain on the poor horses negotiating the steep pull (see page 98), still lies alongside Golding's Hill. This area of the town is almost a world of its own and is referred to by many of its older residents as 'our end'.

High Road and continuing to Buckhurst Hill and London. For many centuries this road, 2 miles long, was the main focus of settlement in the parish. South-east of Goldings Hill is the new Loughton: the large housing estate of Debden, built since 1945 by the London County Council. The estate takes its name from the ancient manor of Debden, which lay at its northern end, around Debden Hall and Debden Green. Debden Green itself does not form part of the estate. It is a pleasant little hamlet of about eight houses, mostly of the 19th century and later, grouped about the ancient green. Loughton Hall, on the site of another ancient manor, is now in the centre of the Debden estate, a mile south of Debden Green. Beside the hall is the little church of St. Nicholas (a chapel of ease to St. John, Loughton) which stands on the site of the original parish church. The Roding forms the

boundary of the parish in this direction. There is an ancient crossing at Loughton Bridge a mile south-east of Loughton Hall. The railway from London via Stratford and Woodford, now part of the Central London Line, enters Loughton from the south. After passing though Loughton station it makes a wide arc east and north to Theydon Bois and Epping. Debden (formerly Chigwell Lane) station is ½ mile south-east of Loughton Hall. Rectory Lane, an old path which has become the main road through the new estate, runs from Church Hill south-west to Debden station and Loughton Bridge. Alderton Hall, which like Debden Hall and Loughton Hall was the centre of an ancient manor, is at the south-west edge of the new estate.

Victoria History of the County of Essex,
Volume IV, 1956

Rudyard Kipling, the last of the Victorian romantics, had a brief liaison with Loughton. Born in India in 1865, he was separated from his parents when only six years old, being placed in the care of a relative at Southsea, and his unhappy childhood is reflected in several of his poems. This was where he stayed, the farmhouse on Golding's Hill opposite the pond, now replaced with a Forest keepers' house.

The Forest has been a place of healing for many tired minds. . . . Rudyard Kipling came into the Forest as a boy, following a nervous breakdown. He had been at Southsea for six years, living in an establishment that passed as a school for children whose parents were in India. The husband of the school-mistress was a naval captain. Kipling and he went walks together, and were on excellent terms. The wife was of a different kind. She was a fanatical evangelical, obsessed by visions of hell and revelling in torment. The children entrusted to her care were beaten and cowed. If Kipling had not had relations in England his life might have been blighted at the start by this excessively god-fearing woman. But each year another house was open to him for one blessed month. It was the home of his uncle and aunt, Sir Edward and Lady Burne-Jones, with whom love and happiness abounded, and the fires of hell were shut out. There he met also an honorary uncle, William Morris, whom the children called 'Uncle Topsy'.

The frightened boy came to imagine he saw terrible things that were not there. When his eyes were examined he was found to be half blind. Miseries crowded upon each other till at last his mother came over from India. When she went into his room to kiss him good night, he shot up his arm automatically to ward off the expected blow. Mrs. Kipling, of course, took him away at once.

It was in this state that Rudyard Kipling came to Loughton, where he made his home with a farmer on Golding's Hill, and ran wild in the Forest for several months. At Loughton he found everything he needed. The farmer's wife was kind and motherly; her niece, Patty — who lived in Loughton till she died at a great age quite recently — the postman, and the farm-boys were all his friends directly, and the place of the captain in his life was taken by a gipsy named Saville, who told the boys tales of his skill in selling horses. The farmer was less friendly than the others when he discovered that young Kipling had taught one of the cows to stand and be milked in the field.

Jacob Epstein has had a cottage in Loughton for more than twenty years. It was in a shed in his garden overlooking Monk Wood that 'Rima' was carved during the winter of 1924-25. During the following year 'The Visitation' was modelled in the same

place, and Epstein said how much he would have liked this figure with the folded hands, so expressive of humility, to remain standing on a knoll above the trees, looking across the Forest that had been so much in his mind while he worked. In 1933 he painted nearly a hundred water-colours of the Forest.

Any week-end you may see Epstein wandering in the Forest, humming to himself, and not suspect you are in the presence of such genius as his unless his measuring and appraising eyes chance to meet yours. There cannot be other such eyes in England. You will find yourself warmed by the radiance of a smile of rare sweetness and simplicity. Instinctively you will respond. You will feel quickened and excited, and then suddenly almost frightened by the searching intensity of the eyes that have penetrated and dissected you.

Epping Forest, William Addison, 1945

Members of Chigwell Council and Chigwell Art Society attended the unveiling on Friday of a plaque to commemorate that sculptor Sir Jacob Epstein lived and worked for some years at 'Deerhurst,' Baldwins-hill, Loughton.

Sir Jacob lived in the house from 1933 until 1950 and his associations with Epping Forest, which the house overlooks, dated from the 1920's.

He left 'Deerhurst' in 1950 to live in Hyde Park Gate.

Sir Jacob Epstein: born in New York City 1880; died London in 1959.

West Essex Gazette, July 9, 1965

Loughton in the 1700s consisted of dwellings almost entirely located along 'Loughton Street' — the present High Road embracing Church Hill and Golding's Hill — (see map page 110). Even by the late nineteenth century there had been little development elsewhere, the road still being bordered by fields for much of its length.

The old forge has withstood the test of time. Advertising design on the other hand has seen remarkable changes: from the smithy of yesterday to the manufacture of water softeners today!

W. ARNILL,
Veterinary Shoeing Forge
Horses Shod on the Latest Science. LOUGHTON, ESSEX.
SMITHS WORK IN GENERAL.

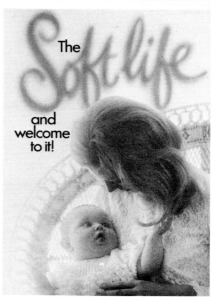

The Softlife and welcome to it!

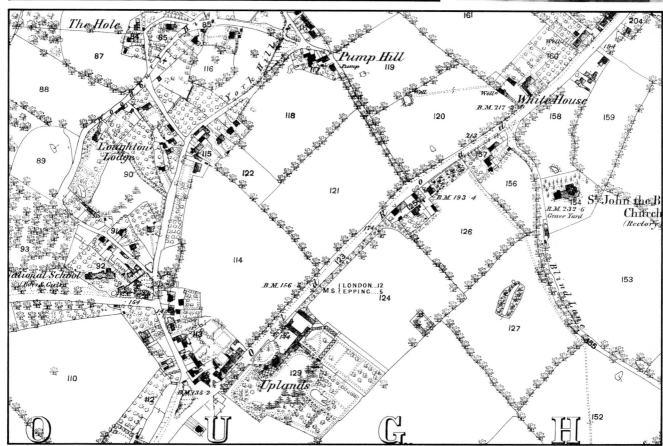

The King's Head, first recorded in 1736, gave Church Hill its alternative name of King's Head Hill. At one time a lock-up for **miscreants was located on the green in front of the inn — hence the original name of Cage Green.**

Loughton is, indeed, changed but cricket has been played opposite the King's Head for nearly a hundred years and the outside of the inn is virtually the same as it was at the turn of the century.

Two years ago, however, the interior was completely modernised and where, once, all was delightfully cluttered and Victorian there is now plain wood panelling and an original wallpaper pattern that would have horrified the great William Morris.

The King's Head has, for a long time, had a close connection with Loughton Cricket Club. Bill Garrett, an Essex County cricketer who was landlord for nearly forty years, played for the club and, before the new pavilion on the ground was built, the inn was the place where the matches were discussed until late into the evening.

In those days a quart jug of beer cost 1s. 4d. and in the hot summers of old when, apparently, it never rained, the quantity consumed was awe-inspiring.

The King's Head was then more a club than an inn and Mrs. Amy Garrett used to preside over a table loaded with bread and beef dripping sandwiches which were offered free to all-comers. In the depth of winter labourers would come to the inn from off the fields and warm themselves with huge bowls of her excellent soup.

There is a remarkable photograph taken about a hundred years ago which shows a mortuary by the side of the old inn. On the Green a picnic is in progress and, while the ladies look starchly demure in their wide white aprons, their escorts proudly stand around with their bowler hats at the correct angle. The photograph originally belonged to Mass. Jenkins, who was potman at the inn from 1902-1915.

Two years ago the major reconstruction of the interior of the King's Head was completed and the inn now consists of the York and Lopping Bars and a restaurant.

The camera has been a wonderful medium for saving for posterity pictures of buildings and scenes of the past. Unfortunately, however, all too often these old photographs are destroyed and what would have been an interesting historical record is lost.

Thanks to a wonderful collection in the possession of Alec Diggens, who was for many years a builder in the town, many invaluable pictures of Old Loughton have been preserved. In the Lopping Bar I was privileged to see these wonderful photographs, all fully documented.

The unpaved roads, used only by an occasional horse and cart, and the splendid old houses gave me a nostalgic feeling and there was something sad in seeing quiet leafy lanes which today are busy thoroughfares.

The King's Head is one of the most popular meeting places in Loughton and many of the regular customers have used the inn for a large number of years.

The Loughton Gazette, March 31, 1967

The old building was demolished in 1901 and its replacement opened in 1906. Today this is called King's Head Green.

Cricket Field Cottage lay on the opposite side of the road. At one time it is believed to have housed a constable and his family — a convenient spot to oversee his charges in their cage. The cricket club was established in 1879.

'To members of the parish of Loughton who died on active service in the Great War 1914-1919.' The war memorial was unveiled by Lord Lambourne, Lord Lieutenant of Essex (formerly Colonel Mark Lockwood), on June 24, 1920.

Fifty-six years on. Sunday, November 14, 1976 — the Loughton branch of the British Legion parade at the annual Service of Remembrance.

For over ten hours members of the Chigwell Fire Brigade were fighting a spectacular blaze that threatened to destroy the large premises of Messrs. Goulds, in High Road, Loughton.

The fire was discovered on Wednesday evening, and the alarm was sent through to the Fire Brigade at 7.46 p.m. Within a few minutes the full brigade attended, and found a large granary at the rear well ablaze. Flames many feet high leapt from the wood and corrugated buildings, and there was grave danger of the whole premises becoming involved.

Superintendent Poulter and Chief Officer Eaton, who both attended the fire, saw the best way of preventing the flames spreading was to isolate and play on the adjoining premises. They did this, and finally, dog-tired, with their faces begrimed, but with their work accomplished, the firemen were able to pronounce the buildings out of danger.

They had worked all night, until nearly six o'clock, playing jets from two hydrants, and it was a splendid piece of work.

The granary was filled with baled straw and the damage amounts to many hundreds of pounds. Attracted by the glare in the sky and the bell of the fire engine as it hurried through the High-road, there was a large crowd watching the blaze, and they had full value for their money.

The Loughton Gazette. February 6. 1937

Anti-supermarketeers watched as a piece of old Loughton bit the dust on Sunday afternoon. The Presto supermarket developers had moved in on the Albion Granaries site in the High Road.

It was a sad moment as the 100-year-old clock above the Brown's sign was lifted to the ground.

Local councillor Richard Brady, the driving force behind plans to have the future of the site rediscussed by the council, said: 'I think it's a great pity that a bit of old Loughton is going.'

LRA complained that demolition was not due to start until Monday.

But this was refuted by a council spokesman. He said notice was served by the developers on the council on Friday afternoon. And the council sent down building inspectors on the first working day afterwards — in this case Monday.

'This is the normal thing we do under any development,' said the spokesman.

Tonight (Friday) Epping Forest Council's development committee is meeting at the Loughton offices to deliberate on the supermarket plans.

This is in response to a motion from Mr. Brady carried unanimously at the last council

The Gould dynasty. For virtually a hundred years the Gould family were at the commercial heart of Loughton. Since back as far as the 1780s, when Chalkley Gould leased the 358-acre Alderton Hall Farm, the family have been associated with farming in the area. His son John concluded a lease of Home Farm at Chigwell from Sir John Eliot Harvey of Rolls Park in 1818 and John's son Chalkley took Border's Farm in 1844. However, the real founder of the firm was John's other son, George Gould, who set up as a corn merchant at Trap's Hill Farm in 1856. The Albion Granaries in Loughton High Road were originally purchased by Goulds in 1868 but sold and later repurchased in 1885. George had retired in 1879 but under the guidance of his two sons, George Sydney and John Herbert, the business continued to flourish. This was the age of the horse, and Gould's local trade was supplemented by the development of the London side of the business based at Bow Bridge Wharf. Shops were opened in Buckhurst Hill and Woodford and the Loughton granary was rebuilt in 1886 *(above)* at a cost of £7,032. From corn and forage the business expanded into other enterprises: dairying, haulage, contracting, grocery retailing, and even furniture removal and storage, with outlets stretching from Stratford to Harlow. Moreton Mill was purchased in 1912, and the 1,000-ton silo built at Bow in 1932 but the old horse trade was dying and efforts had to be made to create new business. By now the firm was managed by the grandsons of the founder, Alfred and Cyril, and when great-grandson Peter Gould joined the firm in 1949, it marked the beginning of the fourth generation.

meeting that the development committee be instructed to rethink the supermarket's planning permission originally given in October 1979. The committee was also instructed to consider costs and the consequences of revoking planning permission. LRA will be demonstrating at the meeting.

The first item on the agenda will be to close the meeting to the press and public.

A lawyer and planning expert representing LRA will, however, be allowed in to address councillors before being asked to leave.

West Essex Gazette. June 5. 1981

Today all has gone: the old mill . . . the silo . . . the granary . . . and Goulds itself. Split into Goulds and C. and A. Gould in 1939, the former closed in 1949 and the latter was taken over by Spillers in 1966. Most recent to be demolished, the Albion Granary, latterly occupied by Browns Engineering, torn down amidst local furore in 1981. As a sop to the conservationists, the planners made a point of including the old clock purchased by George Gould in 1886.

Brook Cottage, home for many years of Mr. H. W. Lewer who deplored the passing of old Loughton . . . and that was before the war! Today it is difficult to reconcile the present Woolworth's store with the same spot.

A new store was born in Loughton High Road on Friday.

It was a moment shared by the shopping public and the people who had built it, a moment of achievement and acclaim, with a touch of sincerity and solemnity.

'In opening this store I would like to couple a prayer for peace in our children's time, that they may enjoy its facilities.'

So said actor Kenneth More on the stroke of 11 a.m. — and the London Co-operative Society's shining new supermarket was open to the public.

Excitement ran high along Loughton High Street on Friday morning. It was an excitement to be found on both sides of the huge plate glass windows. For it infected the local housewives as they peeped in at the bright lights and the shining displays — and also the staff of over 60, eagerly 'on parade' for the first customers.

Outside a queue began as early as 10 a.m. As the minutes ticked by the waiting crowd grew and grew until it was several hundred strong, stretching from both sides of the wide glass doors to fill the entire forecourt of the store.

And a very orderly crowd it was until the arrival of the car. A sight of the jaunty, smiling figure of Kenneth More, deep red carnation in the buttonhole of his dark blue suit, brought a cheer and a surge forward to the store entrance.

At the door, Mr. More was greeted by Mr. Colin Barker, assistant chief officer for L.C.S., and there, between two pillars, was the symbol of the occasion, a tape of the Co-op's rainbow ribbon. Mr. More was handed a pair of scissors by Miss Pat Schooling, of the Co-op's Public Relations section. Snip — the ribbon fluttered to the ground, and in came the shopping public to throng the spacious aisles for a spree among the bargains.

*Express and Independent,
November 30, 1962*

Shoppers were stunned this week at news that Loughton's giant Co-op supermarket will shut — once the second biggest supermarket in Britain — it will close on September 3 and leave a big question mark over the future of the High Road.

Will another supermarket chain move into the prime site allocated by Epping Forest Council for 'shopping purposes only?'

Or will newcomers Presto be left with a monopoly as the centre's only large foodstore?

Rumours are rife that the advent of Presto at the end of last year has played a large part in the Co-op's decision to quit 'caring and sharing' with local residents.

West Essex Gazette, August 12, 1983

A six-shop development to be housed in the shell of the former Co-op supermarket in Loughton High Road is in the pipeline.

Centric Securities Ltd, based in London,

has made a planning application to Epping Forest District Council for alterations and conversion to the supermarket at 196-200 High Road, Loughton to form six units.

The company, which bought the site for an undisclosed sum, told the Gazette it hoped to let the shops and had been approached by a number of traders interested in the scheme.

The firm's director, Richard Midda, said the six shops could include a food store, men's clothing, ladies' clothing, a shoe shop and chemist.

'We think the area would benefit from a scheme like this,' said Mr. Midda. 'It will improve that little pitch in Loughton tremendously as there will be a cross-section of traders based on site.

'Our architects have come up with a pretty scheme and we do plan on spending a lot of money on it.'

Said Mr. Midda: 'The High Road needs these little shops rather than the supermarket. In fact, I think the town is crying out for it — it is dead there at the moment.'

West Essex Gazette, December 23, 1983

Looking at 'then' and 'now' photographs can be like taking a trip on H. G. Wells' time machine. We can start in 1900 and then push the lever forward to travel to 1985 but if we avoid stopping in the two decades from 1962-1983, the supermarket passes us by. Opened in a blaze of glory — killed by the cut and thrust of high street warfare.

A big step towards a brighter Loughton was made on Tuesday afternoon when, in the presence of a large and representative gathering, Miss Evelyn Laye opened the Loughton Cinema, the first picture theatre to be erected in the district.

It is unnecessary to describe the external appearance of the Cinema, for it is now practically completed, and all who have passed have expressed admiration at the skill both of the architect and builder, and really graces what in future will be one of the chief shopping centres of the district.

Internally the building is replete with everything tending to the comfort and artistic sense of patrons. The walls are of a dainty and delicate tint which appear to great advantage under the electric lamps, the lights from which are diffused through large and handsome shades. There is nothing gaudy but every appurtenance and appointment has been chosen with the greatest taste.

The screen is clearly seen from all parts of the house, and immediately in front a large space has been lowered and railed off from the auditorium for the accommodation of the orchestra. This will comprise six ladies who will be under the direction of Mrs. Winifred Bennett, L.R.A.M. There will also be a panatropa.

When the audience were seated awaiting the arrival of Miss Laye, the orchestra, under the direction of Miss Bennett, delighted with selections which were awarded loud applause.

As the heroine of *Blue Eyes* made her way down the gangway to face the audience she was given a very hearty welcome, which she smilingly acknowledged.

Miss Laye said it gave her great pleasure to be there, and when she was in her West End theatre at night she would think of them in their charming picture theatre. She spoke of the first film in which she appeared, *The Lovely Lady*, and said how horrified she was to find that she had a squint, and that one side of her face was bigger than the other (laughter). She had very great pleaure in declaring that charming picture house open (applause).

Mr. C. Jacobs said it was his pleasing duty to extend welcome and thanks to Miss Evelyn Laye, one of the most charming actresses of the day, whose success in *Blue Eyes* at Dalys Theatre was known to them all. It was a good omen that one so successful should open Loughton's first cinema, and he hoped that a similar success would meet the efforts that had resulted in the erection of that building. He congratulated Mr. and Mrs. March upon their enterprise in filling one of the few wants of Loughton, and providing its residents with

ACTION! 'O'Banions' torpedos hit the Capone headquarters in the 48-hundred block of West 22nd Street, Cicero — the machine-gunning of the Hawthorne Hotel in Chicago on September 20, 1926.'CUT. Reminiscent of a scene from one of the many Hollywood gangster movies which played at the Loughton Cinema, seen on the right, this hardly looks like the High Street we know today.

that up-to-date picture theatre. He felt, and he was sure there were others who felt likewise, that there was a want in that district for such a place of amusement. The district had grown, and was growing, and now they had their own cinema, with no need to go to George Lane or Epping as they had to do in the past.

Mrs. March, after briefly returning thanks, said she was going to ask Miss Laye to go to the operating room and throw the first film on the screen.

This Miss Laye did, after which, having been photographed, she left for London, and as her car was driving away the sky overcast and a deluge of rain descended.

But this did not matter to the audience inside the hall, for comfortably seated they were treated to a fine programme of films, which included the *Further Adventures of the Flag Lieutenant*, and the pictures were made the more enjoyable by the music which accompanied their showing.

West Essex Gazette, October 13, 1928

From Evelyn Laye to Dorothy Perkins. Saturday, May 25, 1963: a sad day indeed for

Loughton High-road has lost its little bit of Hollywood.

The Century Cinema's neon sign flickered out, its silver screen finally darkened on Saturday night — and its curtains closed on thirty-five years of celluloid laughter, thrills and romance.

There were no curtain speeches . . . Granada wanted their cinema to die without fuss.

The staff of 25 — projectionists, usherettes, ice-cream girls, cashiers — accepted transfers elsewhere or got a 'golden handshake' according to their period of service.

On Monday technical staff arrived to tear the equipment, seats and gilt fittings out of the dream-factory, leaving it a shell ready for demolition.

The only display card in the foyer, 'Sorry! We're closed,' reminded the cinema's faithful old-age pensioner patrons not to take their seats as usual.

As projectors whirred on Saturday for the 7.10 p.m. showing of *The Cool Mikado*, a 61-year-old Loughton man took his last look at the cinema in action.

The man, Mr. Alfred Sparrow, of 2, Brooklyn-court, was first manager of the Century when the young star Evelyn Laye opened it in 1928.

Of the cinema's closing, Mr. Sparrow, who was manager for 12 years till 1940, said simply, 'It's the trend these days, isn't it?'

A look inside proved his point. Less than 40 people were in the 600-seater Century on Saturday night.

Needing two-thirds capacity every night to show a profit, the cinema had not been a business proposition to Granada for some years.

Not enough of the over-twenties came. Seats filled only for the million-dollar, star-studded epics and the low-budget Sunday horror films. The Century never sank to the level of keeping alive by showing nudist films.

Unavoidable though it may have been, the going of the Century will leave a gap in Loughton High-road — a gap which could not be filled by the shops due to be erected there by a London firm of developers.

West Essex Gazette, May 31, 1963

Blows the bakers was at 166 High Road, later occupied by Goodalls. The old police station (see also page 88) can be seen on the left.

A man died and another was slightly injured yesterday (Thursday) morning when part of a 14-foot sewer trench near the police station in Loughton High-road, caved in on them.

The men — employees of Linney and McLaughlin, a Barnet firm of contractors — had gone down the trench to inspect it for depth.

Mr. H. A. Silver, of Staines, Middlesex, was operating an excavator by the trench when the two men climbed into it.

'I heard a scream and the whole lot collapsed on them,' he said.

Mr. Silver shouted for aid and within minutes dozens of police officers and firemen rushed to the scene.

Shopkeepers and passers-by crowded around the barrier which surrounded the trench, as police and workmen fought to free the men from the clay.

A doctor went down to give pain-killng injections to the trapped men.

Fifteen minutes later — at 10.45 a.m. — rescuers helped a young, dark-haired youth out of the trench.

He was led to a waiting ambulance wiping clay from his face and arms.

As the ambulance drove off to St. Margaret's Hospital, Epping, Father Alphonse Knapp, priest at St. Edmund's Roman Catholic Church, Loughton, arrived.

He took off his coat and clambered down into the trench to administer the last rites to the dead man.

Later Father Knapp said, 'I was passing when I heard that one of the men trapped under the clay was a Catholic.

'I went down to see him. He was dead.'

Just after noon an ambulance edged up to the mouth of the trench and the body was recovered.

Guardian & Gazette, February 4, 1966

If people will eat fruit in the street, why will they persist in littering the pavement with the refuse, thereby endangering the lives of unwary pedestrians? On 1 October Wm. Evans (30) was walking along the High-road, when he slipped on a banana skin, dislocating his shoulder. He was attended by Dr. A. Butler Harris.

The Loughton Gazette, October 8, 1904

cinema buffs in Loughton when the lights went up for the last time.

A post office was first established on the corner of Forest Road in 1840 in Joe Barton's, the tailor's, where his wife and daughter ran the newsagents and postal side in the front part of the shop. When Mr. Barton died in the 1880s, Agnes carried on until her death in 1902. The telegraph had been brought in to

the village in 1871 and the telephone followed in 1908. One of the poles bringing the wires up from the station can be seen against the wall — the bottom portion of each one having been painted white in 1896 after local people complained to the Council about walking into them in the dark!

Looking for all the world like Civil War Yankee troopers, Loughton's postmen line up some time around 1890 with the

postmistress and her two daughters. They are L-R: J. Hawkes, H. Bull, J. French, — Squires, — Godfrey and J. Hunt.

Around 1908 a new building was erected by Horace White, FRIBA, a few doors along. This lasted until the growth of

Loughton dictated a further expansion whereupon the present building was opened. Now occupied by Luzenac Talc Sales.

The village's many minarets . . . are a feature of most of the buildings designed by the late Mr. Edmond Egan, A.R.I.B.A. . . . The tiny example lent distinction to the waiting room of the late Dr. Berthon Pendred's house, although I doubt whether its presence meant much to us villagers as we waited apprehensively to face the Doctor's piercing blue eyes and unfold the sad story of our manifold ailments. The National Health Service was but a dream in those days but Loughton's poor never saw a doctor's bill!

Will Francies writing in the Express and Independent, August 25, 1961

Dad's Army would have been welcome in the old home that once housed Loughton's war operations.

The building that now plays a minor part in Loughton High Road, as Brown's Garage, used to be headquarters for the emergency services and general war control for the area.

At the start of the Second World War the local council took over the house and it became an ARP depot. The war centre, as it was known, was equipped with small fire pumps and all the services were co-ordinated by the personnel manning the station. In the tower they watched for fire bombs. If one was spotted, the authorities would be informed and the required emergency vehicle would be sent to the location.

The house was built by Irish architect Teddy Egan, who settled in Loughton around 1870. He set up home and a business as an architect and estate agent in the old house. Mr. Egan was also a master carpenter and incorporated seven types of gable into the house. Up to the last war, before the council took over the house, it existed as a home and surgery for Dr. Pendred.

Frank Brown bought the house from the Maitland trustees — Rev. Maitland was the former local squire at one time in Loughton in 1947. Mr. Brown was by now a well-known Loughton business-man, as he ran a garage in The Triangle (behind The Standard pub, in Loughton High Road).

During the war years the garage was turned into a production engineering works, making ammunition. The employees were wives of soldiers, young girls and boys before they were old enough to join the forces.

After the war the place reverted back to a garage and the High Road house took shape as the present-day car sales business. The business began to boom, dealing at first with second-hand cars. The site was rebuilt around about 1960, the separate buildings used by the ARP were demolished and a car sales area was established.

Guardian and Gazette, February 10, 1984

Opposite the 1931-vintage post office. What a beautiful shady spot. 'The Gardens' were a welcome break in the otherwise commercialised west side of the High Street until the infill development by the London Co-operative Society.

Another 'dated' comparison: Dr Pendred's surgery, appropriately still a doctor's of sorts. Four star petrol was 184p per gallon in August 1983.

This picture of the High Road was taken by Mr. A. Seeley of Richmond Hill around 1870-71 before even the building on the corner of Station Road was put up. The cab 8980 is being driven by Mr. Moore, an employee of Sadlers. The lady outside her shop has been identified as Miss White.

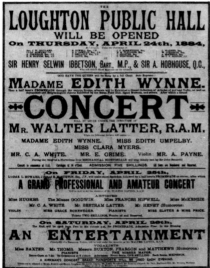

The building on the corner of Station Road was put up prior to the erection of Lopping Hall *(below left)*; completed 1883-84, in the incredibly short period of six months even by today's standards . . . and during the winter at that! *Below right:* The loppers immortalised in stone above the doorway. Originally the inscription read 'Public Hall' but that was erased and reinscribed 'Lopping Hall', yet the ghostly outline of the original wording can still be discerned beneath the new.

The proceedings commenced with the singing of the National Anthem, the solo of which was taken by Madame Edith Wynne, after which Col. Howard called upon Sir Henry Selwin-Ibbetson to address the meeting.

Sir Henry, in opening the hall, said that in the presence of one who had taken such an active part in the origin, if he might so call it, of the hall in which they were assembled, he hardly felt himself justified in taking the position which he had been asked to assume that night, viz., that of declaring the hall open. . . . He little thought, when he was present at the laying of the foundation stone of this building, that he should have been there that night to see what he had seen of the progress made in the creation of a hall of such utility as they now saw before them. In these days, when education was so much thought of, and they were all of them endeavouring to raise the standard of thought in their midst, halls of this kind, where men could meet together to discuss various subjects, to benefit by lectures, or to see such exhibitions as some of them had already seen in the rooms below, must do good, and must be deserving of whatever encouragement public men or private individuals could give them. He passed on to say that they had a building in the parish now which was serviceable not only for the daily recreation of those who had the right to belong to it, but for purposes which, if properly developed, might do much to improve and cultivate the better tastes of those around

302

them. He was sure no one who had seen the interesting results of the investigations of the Field Club in their neighbourhood, specimens of which were shown below, could fail to note that this building had done good in bringing to the notice of those who would not otherwise have had an opportunity of seeing them, specimens of the greatest interest. He passed on to say that they would be enabled to bring together everything to instruct those who lived in that neighbourhood, and he was sure that those who had already taken an interest in the hall would do their best to make it a means of further usefulness and instruction to the neighbourhood. It was because it would be a centre of intellectual and general usefulness that he had great pleasure in taking part in the proceedings that evening, and in declaring the hall open.

The Woodford Times, April 15, 1884

The Epping Forest Act, 1878, provided for the purchase by the Corporation of London of virtually all enclosed common lands, so that 5,500 acres could be made available for public access (subject to bye-laws).

In addition, the Act effectively abolished lopping rights, although a further Epping Forest Act passed in 1880 granted power to an arbitrator — Sir William Hobhouse was appointed to the post — to pay compensation as appropriate to those who had not previously sold their rights to Maitland.

Eventually, it was agreed that 280 householders should receive £3 11s each, a total of just under £1,000, and that a further sum of £6,982 10s should be paid as compensation and used in part for the erection of a reading and lecture room suitable also for parish meetings.

A maximum of £3,000 was set aside for the purchase of a site and construction of the building, the remainder to be held in trust to provide income for maintenance and the purchase of reading material. It was envisaged that further income would arise from the letting of the rooms.

Lopping Endowment Trustees were elected by the Loughton ratepayers, a process which continues to this day. The first six trustees were George Burney, John Free, Martin Harris, Claude Hilton, Samuel Lloyd Howard and Jonathan Maynard. Edmond Egan, ARIBA, was appointed as architect and his brother as builder.

After the laying of the foundation stone by the Lord Mayor of London in September 1883, building work quickly progressed, so that by April 1884 the Lopping Hall was ready for its official opening. Even John Whitaker Maitland, from whom the trustees had

The ornate drinking fountain which had been erected in 1870 was demolished by a bus in 1934. The replacement built in 1936 and which still stands today, albeit waterless, was designed along more simple lines.

acquired the site, was on hand, reportedly to comment that he hoped the hall would be used for educational purposes and temperance meetings.

There have been many trustees of the Loughton Lopping Endowment Fund since 1884 and there have been changes in the purposes for which the Lopping Hall has been used. In the 1930s, it was recalled by one of the present trustees, part of the building was in use as council offices.

Now much of the ground floor has been let (to two shops and a bank) which provides a steady income to help the fund to meet outgoings. Nevertheless, the Lopping Hall continues to function as the hub of social life in Loughton and most of the accommodation, under the auspices of a resident manager, is in almost daily use.

Even though the income derived from the various users of the Lopping Hall (which has a small hall downstairs, a large hall, the Willingale Room and a private licensed bar on the first floor and a green room/dressing room on the top floor) is considerable, it cannot on its

own meet the rising costs of maintaining an albeit soundly-constructed century-old building.

In 1982, £4,000 was spent on roof repairs alone. Other expenditure in recent years has included replacement by electrical equipment of the clock tower's original works which were donated by the Gould family of Loughton.

The people of Loughton seem certain to ensure that the Lopping Hall's 100th birthday will not pass unnoticed by the town. It was after all the ancestors of some of them who risked fines and imprisonment in their fight to maintain the ancient lopping rights, and whose efforts resulted in the award of substantial compensation for eventual surrender of those rights when Epping Forest was saved for the benefit of future generations.

Judging from the pleasure which the Lopping Hall gives to thousands of people each year, one has to conclude that the compensation money used to finance its construction was very wisely spent.

David Tyler, Essex Countryside, March 1984

The Hall is used for a wide variety of meetings and events including exhibitions. This display was put on during the war on behalf of our Norwegian allies and is interesting because it includes German equipment recovered from the Junkers 88 crash in December 1940 near the Wake Arms (pages 60-61) and a Browning machine gun from Flying Officer Pisarek's Hurricane (page 316).

'New' Station Road. Strictly teetotal and for males only, the Men's Club opposite the Hall was built in 1901 by Reverend W. Dawson who passed it into the hands of a body of trustees two years later.

A young Loughton lady once bitterly complained to us that whereas the youths and men of the village have a club of their own, the poor girls have no such facilities for enjoyment. 'Why should we be left out in the cold?' she exclaimed in accents trembling with real pathos. 'Why should we be utterly neglected? We do not wish to share your Bachelor Club, but why should we not also have a club?' From a woman's point of view, no doubt, there was some reason in her plaint, but we refrain from expressing any definite opinion; it might be dangerous. We have, however, often thought that Loughton Club might play an even more conspicuous part than it does in the social life of the village, and though the permanent installation within its precincts of the fair daughters of Eve would be as impracticable as it would be undesirable, we do maintain that now and then it might, with advantage, open its arms, so to speak, to embrace them. Very soon the smoking concerts will re-commence — at least, we hope so — but does it not seem rather selfish to keep all these pleasures to ourselves? Could we not have occasional ladies' nights? At all events, some such experiment is worth trying. The ladies go in and out of the Epping Institute, none daring to make them afraid.

The Loughton Gazette, October 8, 1904

The Loughton Fire Brigade was summoned to a motor car which, after backfiring, had burst into flames in Rectory Lane shortly before noon on Monday. Chief Officer Heath and a full complement of men responded to the call, and were on the spot very shortly after its receipt. The front part of the car was burnt but the firemen managed to save the body. It belonged to Miss Leech, daughter of Mr. A. W. Leech, J.P., of Goldings Hill. As the regular driver of the fire tender did not receive the call, Mr. Frank Giblett was asked to take his place, which he consented to do. He had to drive in his cap as none of the helmets of the firemen were big enough for him to wear.

The Loughton Gazette, December 13, 1926

Wooden buildings that housed the men and memories of Loughton Fire Station in the changing years since the last war, were unmercifully swept aside last week. On Friday I saw the last of these black shacks — restrooms, washrooms and messrooms — torn apart by workmen and bulldozed flat before the coup de grace . . . the 'funeral pyre'.

Fireman Les Moore recalled the early days. 'I started my service in Loughton. The buildings were put up at about the end of the war by the Auxiliary Fire Service's Brigade Constructional Workers. The old buildings have done good service,' he reminisced.

Les, sitting in the light and attractive new Fire Station in Old Station Road, looked out on to the scene of devastation at the rear.

On the opposite side of the road the old vehicle bay and offices were empty and closed, their future use uncertain. The new building houses men, machines, equipment, canteen, and various other rooms including a dormitory and rest-room.

The site of the old buildings will be used for drill practice, and includes a drill tower.

Express and Independent, March 13, 1964

Loughton firemen celebrated the official opening of their new Fire Station on Saturday with a spectacular demonstration of their skill.

The demonstration followed a short opening ceremony by Ald. G. E. Rose, chairman of Essex County Council's Fire Brigade Committee.

Giving a brief history of the fire service in the area, Ald. Rose said that the horse drawn engine was introduced in 1904.

Seven years later, in 1911, call bells were installed in firemen's houses. The old fire station, at present used as Council Offices in Old Station-road, was opened in 1935.

The new station is of a standard design with two bays. It has a two-storey administrative wing with a single-storey appliance room with electrically-operated overhead doors at the front and hand-operated overhead doors at the rear leading to the large drill yard.

It was built at a cost of more than £40,000, including demolition of the site's prefabricated buildings of the former fire station.

Express and Independent, August 14, 1964

Old Station Road. The Fire Station No. 62 was rebuilt in 1964.

Above: **Between the wars Tom Maddison was the licencee at the Holly Bush. His was a large family and his son took over. In this picture the yard leads through to Smarts Lane and the skittle alley behind the inn.**

Right: **How many Loughton residents remember the Johnson sisters Marjorie and Rene? Their parents tiny newsagents shop, No. 142, lay alongside the yard. This picture was taken around 1927 when the family lived at 30 Forest Road with Trigger the mongrel.**

In 1975-76 the Holly Bush was revamped and extended and the site of the little paper shop blanked off by the new brick wall on the right. The present day scene can also be compared with that at the top of page 302.

Acting under editorial instructions, I found myself, on the evening of Tuesday last, journeying to the town of Loughton, on the borders of Epping, with the object of being present at the ancient ceremony, to be performed for the last time, of cutting boughs from the trees in a certain portion of the forest when the clock from the church-tower should strike the hour of twelve.

My orders were brief, and not altogether devoid of a vague, uncertain element. I was to present myself at the Crown Inn at Loughton and inquire for Mr. Burney (a name not unknown as that of a steady and vigorous champion of the people's rights in the forest), who it was understood was to address the people.

Arrived at Loughton between nine and ten o'clock, and having followed not more than three wrong directions in a distance of a quarter of a mile, I found mine hostelry, which at the hour that I reached it was packed to overflowing with the male inhabitants of the place, noisy and excited, and armed with choppers, axes, bills, and reapers, and looking fitter for a marauding expedition than for the peaceable work of dismembering the forest trees.

Having made my way to the bar I inquired for Mr. Burney. 'Mr. Burney is not here.' 'Where is he?' 'Don't know.' 'But he was to hold a meeting here.' 'Was he? But he isn't going to.' This was cheering, and more particularly so when, upon further inquiry, it turned out that a mistake had occurred in the arrangements, that Mr. Burney had in consequence gone to Chingford, and might or might not be back at eleven o'clock, when the inn closed. 'P'raps you'd better wait.' Well, there being no alternative, perhaps I had.

The inn parlour offered an inviting retreat, with a blazing fire and a grateful odour of brandy punch. The guests of the parlour were some three or four of the keepers of the forest, 'much at their ease o'er pipe and mug,' who were waiting here till it was time to start for the scene of the ceremony. 'You see, sir, it's a dark night; there'll be many men we know, professional poachers, amongst the lot, and though we don't expect nothing, we think it safer to be about in case.' There are few pleasanter resting-places than the inner parlour of an old inn; and when one's companions have tales to tell of forest life and poaching adventures, and can sing, some of them, a good song, it is not necessary to say that an hour or two passes quickly and enjoyably enough.

With eleven o'clock came the order to turn out. Still our speaker had not arrived, and the

At this point in our story we must pause, as having reached the Crown inn we have come to one of the most historic places in Loughton, for it was from here that the people of the village set out on the very last lopping expedition on Tuesday, November 11, 1879. Little did the loppers know of the future significance that the eleventh hour of the eleventh day of the eleventh month would have for those of the next century. All they knew was that at 11.00 p.m. on that day, when the Crown closed, they would embark on one of the turning points in the Forest's history. Significantly Lopping Hall overlooks the forecourt in this early photograph.

men were preparing to make a start without him. For myself, I was all unprovided for, as regarded lodging for the night, there being 'no room in the inn', and small chance at such a late hour of finding sleeping accommodation elsewhere. Moreover there was no time to make arrangements, for the column was already on the march and trooping up through the dark, silent street with shouts and songs, in the direction of the forest. Abandoning therefore, of necessity, all notion of provision for the future, I gave myself up to the present, and accepting the guidance of a friendly keeper, made a start with the rest. We had scarcely started when we were overtaken by two covered carriages, in which were Mr. Burney, who had driven over from Chingford, Mr. Shaw-Lefevre, M.P., Mr. Burney, jun., and Mr. D'Oyley, jun., son of the superintendent of the forest.

Leaving Loughton behind, we went over a rough uneven road till trees along the edge of the forest came in sight. Then we began to mount upwards, and follow the deviations of a narrow pathway which gleamed white beneath our feet. The rain had softened the ground, and made it moist and boggy; and stumps of trees, shrubs, and bushes, magnified by the darkness of the night, rose up gaunt and terrifying. Treacherous pitfalls let down many of those to whom the road was unfamiliar; I believe I distinguished myself here beyond the rest.

In a few minutes — probably by day the way would have seemed absurdly short — we ceased climbing, and came to a flat spot of considerable area, on one portion of which had been erected a large shed (at a cost, I was told, of some 200*l*.), the structure of which, as well as could be then discerned, was pic-

Considerably 'Tudorised' by 1962, three years later it succumbed to the developer, completely nullifying the focal point of the 'village'.

turesque and solid. An iron railing enclosed it round. Over this the men jumped, and into the enclosure, in the centre of which the lanterns were set down, and a ring being formed two or three nimble-footed ones, laying aside their axes, grasped hands, and danced madly, to the accompaniment of a flute and a tin whistle. In a little while the excitement became catching; one after another entered the ring, men dancing with men, and breaking out into sudden snatches of wild song. It wanted now but a few minutes of midnight. Suddenly a light flamed out close by, and some three or four fellows were seen kindling a gigantic torch, formed of a log of wood with wool and tow well soaked in oil wrapped about it. The dancers left dancing, and all gathered round the blazing pile, which threw a vivid glare upon the scene but now involved in almost darkness. The trees, still clothed in leaf, stood out in strong relief, and cast great shadows behind them. Nooks and woody recesses were illumined, while the darkness of the distance looked yet more dark by contrast. It was an odd and an animated scene on which the flaring torch cast its glow.

The group around it was composed of boys and men of different ages, old grey-headed ones whose memories went back to the loppings of half a century ago, and young children who capered about the fire, and struck their sticks into it, and made the red sparks leap out on all sides. General attention was fastened on four men who, by their great height and strength of build, stood prominent in the group. These were the brothers Willingale, the heroes of the night, for it was owing to the firmness and bravery of their father, 'old Willingale,' at a time when the lord of the manor had almost succeeded in wresting the privilege from the people, that the right of lopping and topping was restored and preserved. 'Old Willingale' with two of his stalwart sons, suffered imprisonment for their audacity on behalf of themselves and the townspeople, and this was the reason why the name of Willingale was on every lip, and why the cry, 'Three cheers for the Willingales,' met with such a lusty response.

The minutes seemed to drag slowly as the time for the commencement of the work drew near, and some who lay stretched out before the blaze beguiled them by recounting the doings of similar occasions in the past. It was told how, one 11th of November, the lord of the manor, wishing to deprive the people of their rights, gave them a great supper, at which the liquor was circulated freely in the hope that under the influence the hours might pass unnoticed, and so by their own action the barter be lost to the townsmen: but how one of

the feasters kept a clear head, and running out on the stroke of twelve, cut a bough, and carried it in in triumph.

'Two minutes to twelve' shouted a voice in the rear of the crowd. In a moment the fire was abandoned, and all who had instruments selected a tree and took up their position beside it. Some scaled the trunk and climbed into the topmost boughs, their axes shining amongst the leaves. A sudden and complete silence fell on all. There was no noise but the whistling wind and the roaring fire. All ears were strained to catch the sound which was momentarily expected to issue from the clock tower. 'They've stopped the clock' whispered a voice; for this was a trick which had been attempted more than once in past years. But scarcely were the words out of the speaker's mouth when the clear ring of the bell broke upon the midnight air, and a hundred axes crashed amongst the trees. In a moment the ground was strewn with boughs, which fell thickly all around, and were gathered up and carried with shouting on the shoulders of the children. Branch after branch was lopped off and fell to the earth, and the axes of the four tall brothers were seen to be plied vigorously. For a few minutes the cutting continued, and then as if by common consent all stayed their

hands, and when the cheers and shouts which broke out again and again had subsided the speakers came forward to address the crowd.

The City Press, November 15, 1879

And now I think of the Crown Hotel as boyhood memory pictures it, dreaming in the sunshine, the ostler's bell summoning him to attend the traveller's horse, the whiles the traveller washes down the dust of travel with a pint of mine host's brown ale. No motor bus had then defiled our High Road with its noise and stench. Peace brooded — a blessed quiet prevailed at all times, accentuated by the lovely backcloth of Epping Forest glimpsed between the buildings. For centuries had Loughton dreamed away the summer days (outwardly anyway). The Epping New Road, driven straight throught the forest depths, years before, left Loughton as a calm backwater. But the first solid tyred open top red bus penetrated the calm and linked the road to The Crown with the world's greatest City in 1915, later, in 1920, to pass right through the still peaceful village en route to Epping. Time marches on, and who would be without the bus service today?

The two brothers Patmore, in the early days of their business association, occupied what is now the Gazette offices. That was in 1913, but brother Tom died tragically in 1920, leaving 'Ted,' as he is known to his many friends, to press on through the difficult years alone, but to win through to found the Company's present large motor service station.

The Gazette building stood alone, surrounded by the garden of Hardings, residence of the late Mr. Henry Lincoln, a man of strong Christian principles, materially expressed in his generous gift to the village of Lincoln Hall, for the furtherance of the Brotherhood movement, so near his heart, also in the building of the almshouses adjoining, known as the Lincoln Homes. Though shops and offices cover the old orchard, the house still stands.

Messrs Patmore's service station and the adjoining row of shops cover Mr. William Sadler, the jobmaster's yard, garden, and orchard. His house, now occupied by Messrs. Worthy, has been carefully renovated and retains its old-world charm in a pleasant setting. Loughton village has lost so much, and gained not at all in this respect. . . .

*Will Francies writing in the
West Essex Gazette, March 20, 1953*

Nostalgia: When commenting on the changes in Loughton, perhaps it is best left for Will Francies to have the final word. He was born in Smarts Lane in 1902; played in Loughton as a child, and has spent the majority of his life in its bosom. Over the years his writings have been a joy to all those who reminisce and remember those days never to return. Sadly he passed away in November 1985.

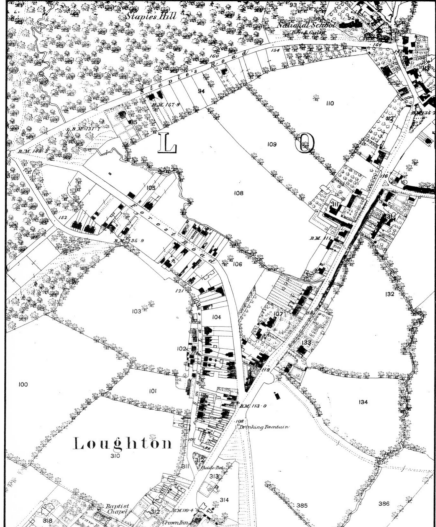

As the traditional meeting place for the cutting of the first boughs was on Staple's Hill, it is reasonable to assume that the route taken from the Crown on the last lop most probably ran down Forest Road.

One of the oldest families in Loughton are afraid of losing the home they have lived in for over 70 years.

Members of the Sadler family, a name that dates back to the last century, live in quaint old cottages at Smarts Lane, dangerously near the area due for demolition by Chigwell Council.

Two off-street car parks are planned by the council as well as considerable improvements to the corner of Smarts Lane and High Beech Road.

Already Nos. 1, 3 and 5 High Beech Road have been put under a demolition order. Considerable anger was provoked by the council's announcement that the corner building, Victor's Handy Man shop, would be pulled down.

Loughton Historical Society complained that the 'quaint' tower, a rare example of a 19th century local architect's work, was a valuable part of old Loughton.

Demolition on No. 5 High Beech Road, which overlooks the gardens of the four old cottages in Smarts Lane, began on Tuesday.

In a letter to the Loughton Historical Society, Chigwell Urban Surveyor Mr. Robert Edwards said the council wanted 'to acquire by negotiation any property that should come on the market between the corner and the premises of C. S. Foster & Sons.'

Mr. Albert Sadler, who has lived as a bachelor in one of the cottages for 55 years, said: 'This is about the only part of old Loughton left. If they try and buy up this house I shall fight it.'

His sister Queenie, living next door with her husband, Mr. Fred Atkins, said: 'I've lived here all my life. I don't want to move.'

Mr. Atkins added: 'We've heard nothing from the council. We know the council can force us to sell but we won't get worried until we hear from them.'

Express and Independent, May 8, 1970

The other possible route to Staple's Hill would have been via Smarts Lane on the right. In the old days the characteristic building on the corner of High Beach Road was Sandall's bakers: more recently it was Victor's handyman's shop.

'One generation passeth away, and another generation cometh: but the earth abideth for ever.' Ecclesiastes, Chapter I, Verse 4.

Yet another part of old Loughton's familiar scene disappeared this week when the horse-drawn milk float of Street's Dairies made a last delivery to customers.

For many years residents of Loughton have been accustomed to the sight of the blue painted float with Robin, a 23-year-old Welsh Cob, between the shafts.

Now he and his jovial master Mr Jack Street, in his traditional breeches, have made their last calls. On Sunday the United Dairies took over the rounds with modern electric vans.

Sitting in his Smarts Lane Depot on Tuesday Mr. Street said he had 'two great friends and colleagues' in Mr Bill Carter and Mr George Hockley who worked the rounds with him.

But since Bill's recent death Mr Street felt he could not carry on. George has decided to carry on milk delivery with the United Dairies.

As a boy Mr Street (64) began delivering milk on a bicycle in the Loughton area from his father's premises in Smarts Lane.

Guardian and Gazette, March 28, 1969

The end of an epoch. *Left:* **Jack Street with Tommy in 1935;** *right:* **in 1969 with Robin.**

The High Road (or Old Road as it was called at the time this picture was taken) where it leaves the village on the southern side. Albion Hill rises on the right up to Nursery Road. In the dip lies the Bull's Head Pond, so named after the old inn of the same name which survived at the top of The Crescent until the 1930s

The pond is also known simply as the 'Horse Pond' for obvious reasons or by some 'Buckhurst Hill Pond' although the open stretch of Forest between Buckhurst Hill and Loughton is a jealously-guarded barrier against ribbon development.

Prior to 1900 the expansion of Loughton had been negligible. In 1777 the population is recorded as 1,269 and this had only doubled a hundred years later. Even up to 1914 the increase, with its consequent pressure for more houses, had proceeded at a steady pace — from 4,730 in 1901 to 5,749 in 1921. However, building really began in earnest between the wars, and whole new roads sprang up: Priory, Brook and Brooklyn, Tycehurst, Spareleaze, Woodland, Habgood and Hillcrest to name but a few. Close to the latter lay Newnham House, beloved of Will Francies because its kindly owner, a wealthy merchant, gave parties for the local children at Christmas. Recollecting fifty years later he recalls 'only the shocking pranks we played with the extra large helpings of jelly ladled out from huge wash-basins, ungrateful little beasts that we were!' Newnham House went the way of so many of the large old properties whose upkeep demanded a staff so large that few could afford the cost that it entailed. Demolished in February 1962 and replaced by more manageable flats.

A plan to build a big new housing estate on Green Belt land between Loughton and Buckhurst Hill caused widespread anger and alarm this week.

The estate would occupy the valley known as North Farm, where W. & C. French, the contractors, at present have their industrialised housing plant.

Residents in Hillcrest Road, Summerfield Road, Spring Grove and Stradbroke Grove, Buckhurst Hill, heard of the plan on Friday.

An outline application has been lodged with Chigwell council for planning permission for a residential development of 51.25 acres and public open space of 44.45 acres at North Farm.

This would mean the extension of Spring Grove to join up with Stradbroke Drive and the extension of Summerfield Road to join the Spring Grove extension.

Houses would be developed up to the railway line leaving a Green Belt area next to Buckhurst Hill High Road.

But many of the residents had been assured by the council, when they purchased their houses, that the land would remain a Green Belt area.

Now Mr. Douglas Barton, of 47 Hillcrest Road, has sent a letter to all residents who will be affected, informing them of a meeting that will take place in the small hall in Lopping Hall tonight (Friday) at 8 p.m.

Mr. Barton told the Independent: 'The purpose of the meeting in principle is to oppose the development or any samples of development in that broad area.

North Farm has lain in 'no-man's-land', as it were, between Loughton and Buckhurst Hill ever since the sixteenth century. Timber-framed and roofed with hand-made red tiles, it was carefully restored in the 1920s and stands as one of Loughton's 54 Grade II listed buildings. The site around it has been extensively developed by W. & C. French to house their plant for prefabricating houses.

'It has been called to decide upon a concerted plan of action against the application.

'There is more than a sort of selfish point of view attached to this. The proposed development is on an area of Green Belt which ought to be preserved against all-comers.'

A spokesman for Messrs. French said that the application came from their Development Company and the only person who could comment was unavailable.

Chigwell Times, March 6, 1970

Lopping Hall was overflowing with angry residents from South Loughton on Friday evening, at the meeting to discuss the proposed development of the North Farm area by W. & C. French, the building contractors.

Friday's meeting brought together all the residents who will be directly affected by the development, namely those in Hillcrest Road, Summerfield Road, Spring Grove and Stradbroke Grove, Buckhurst Hill.

Many other people not directly involved also supported the meeting.

A number of objections to the scheme were voiced, the main one being that the land is Green Belt and should be preserved as such.

West Essex Gazette, March 13, 1970

Local residents have won their fight to keep a wedge of Green Belt between Buckhurst Hill and Loughton.

Environment Minister Peter Walker has rejected the appeal by W. & C. French against Chigwell Council's refusal to allow housing development on their land at North Farm.

He announced this week that he accepted the recommendation of Mr. S. W. Midwinter, who conducted the public inquiry in February.

Mr. Midwinter reported: 'I am of the opinion that the appeal site forms an important part of the Metropolitan Green Belt and I am not persuaded that there is sufficient reason in this case from the established policy of preventing general development here.'

W. & C. French, the Buckhurst Hill contractors, were appealing against three plans for the land being turned down.

They have a large commercial depot in the middle of the land, which the Inspector described as 'an unfortunate, non-conforming intrusion into the open land.'

Under French's development plans this would have gone, but the Inspector believed the Green Belt wedge was still of great value with the depot there.

Mr. Midwinter said: 'The land not only plays a part in preventing the spread of the

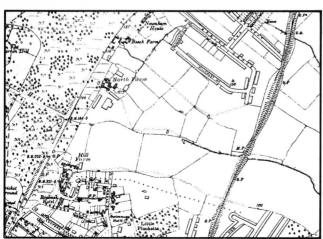 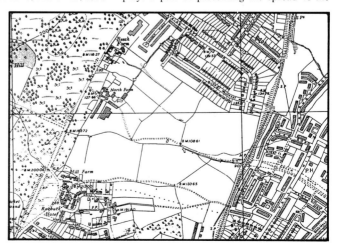

Nevertheless Loughton and Buckhurst Hill have become joined east of the railway in the Roding Road-Valley Hill District.

Someone once said that the price of freedom was eternal vigilance. Much the same consciousness is necessary today to protect what little has survived. Once lost it will never be regained.

built up area of London but it is also the major portion of the remaining, mainly open, gap between the adjoining communities of Loughton and Buckhurst Hill.

'Although these places have already been joined by recent council housing to the east, the areas west of the railway are separate and distinct and, in my opinion, there is virtue in their remaining so.

'I think the proposed development would result in the virtual merging of the two communities in spite of the fact that an area of open land would be preserved on the High Road frontage and, in one scheme, a band of open space about 100 yards wide would still separate the housing areas.

'The existing farmland has considerable amenity value and the safeguarding of this small but useful section of the approved Green Belt should, in my view, be upheld as a matter of principle.'

Mr. Midwinter said that although there was

a need for housing in the outer metropolitan area there was still remaining housing land in Chigwell without using North Farm.

The news of the inquiry result brought a joyous reaction from the Chigwell Urban District Green Belt Preservation Association — specially formed to fight the loss of Green Belt land.

Chairman Douglas Barton, of Hillcrest Road, Loughton, described the news as 'glad tidings indeed'. He said: 'It was greeted with joy by the members of the Association.'

West Essex Gazette, July 16, 1971

Building may go ahead on North Farm, Buckhurst Hill — but not in the form that sparked off so much controversy last year.

For Chigwell Council wants to use some of the land for its planned public hall.

A council spokesman said that only a 'small' part of the land would be taken up for the public hall.

The land the council plans to build on has been used for commercial use before, and does not encroach onto the Green Belt.

West Essex Gazette, March 17, 1972

The plan to build homes on part of North Farm, Loughton, which caused uproar among nearby residents last year, may be repeated.

The owners of North Farm, W. & C. French Ltd, have told Chigwell Council they are still hoping for planning permission for residential development of the whole of the site.

And because of the development plans the council's aim to build a public hall on a piece of the site, between Loughton and Buckhurst Hill, have been disrupted.

The company says it is not prepared to consider selling any of the land for a public hall.

As far as the council is concerned the matter will have to be considered over again. Discussions are back at stage one at committee level.

But thoughts are now circulating that the North Farm affair may be stirred up again.

It was French's plan to build on the Green Belt land that prompted massive opposition from local residents which finally led to a lengthy inquiry and final defeat for the proposed development.

This week W. & C. French would make no comment on the new proposal.

West Essex Gazette, April 21, 1972

The East Anglian Aero Club, the country's latest acquisition to its flying facilities, had its official send-off on Saturday with the opening of the Loughton aerodrome at Abridge. It is the nearest flying ground to London, and has been passed by the Air Ministry. The aerodrome, owned by Commercial Airways (Essex), Ltd., is about 90 acres in extent, and one of the principal objects of the Aero Club is to provide flying instruction by fully qualified pilots, and to give licensed airmen an opportunity to fly advanced types of aircraft. Gipsy Moth machines provide facilities for early training, and Rolls-engined Bristols for advanced flying. With a well-appointed club house, the club already has 35 members, all of whom are flying enthusiasts. . . .

The club and ground were opened on Saturday afternoon by Mr. J. C. Lockwood, M.P. The start was not auspicious from the point of view of the weather. Thunderstorms, with copious rain, were frequent, but with one exception the display that had been arranged was carried out.

Mr. Lockwood said he was sorry the attendance was not larger, but what they lacked in quantity they made up for in quality. . . .

A club of that sort did a great deal to encourage aviation. It was essential that the people of this country should become air-minded, and the club would be of great assistance in that direction. It would offer facilities for training pilots and for joy-flying. It was the nearest aerodrome to London, and he was told that one day it might be the chief airport in England. If that came to pass they would be proud of having been present at its initiation.

Believed to be the youngest pilot in England, John Lipton, an 11-year-old boy, gave a capital demonstration of his ability. Flying with Capt. Bannister [the chief instructor], he took control in mid-air and cleverly performed various evolutions. On landing, John told a reporter that he had flown well over 200 hours. His ambition is to reach the age of 17, so that he can take out an air-pilot's ticket.

The Woodford Times, June 23, 1933

A plane was stunting over the fields between Loughton and Theydon Bois. It spun, dived, and then looped the loop. It went into another loop, and owing to the terrific strain struts broke, half of the wing was broken clean off and the plane crashed to the ground, bursting into flames.

Now that we have travelled the High Street from top to bottom and ended with an aerial photograph, this may be the time for a short transgression to Loughton's aerodrome — at least that was what Stapleford Tawney was called when it opened in 1933. Its 180 acres had been purchased by Edward Hillman to expand his scheduled services to Paris which had commenced earlier that year from Marylands Aerodrome near Brentwood (now a golf course!). That year Hillman Airways went from strength to strength, services being inaugurated to Liverpool, the Isle of Man and Belfast within a few weeks of moving in. Tragically Ted Hillman died suddenly in January 1934 at the age of forty-five.

Two men in the machine were killed, their bodies being little more than charred remains when it was possible to extricate them.

They were Pilot Officer Arthur Thomas Campling, of the R.A.F., North Weald, and Mr. Peter Arison Scott, a medical student, aged 23, studying at the London Hospital, Mile End Road.

Metropolitan policemen, ambulance, and Chigwell Fire Brigade were quickly on the way to the accident, but they made a wide detour before they arrived.

Then they managed to get out one body, but the other was buried beneath the machine, and it was only after extra equipment had been brought that they were able to extricate the other body.

Cyclists, pedestrians and motorists groped their way across the swampy fields and ditches, and police had to throw a cordon around the blazing wreckage. Darkness fell rapidly, and many were hopelessly lost before they finally gained the road.

Call received at Loughton Fire Station approx. 7.44 p.m. but particulars given by caller placed site of fire in Chigwell sub-station area. Chigwell sub-station turned out to call and approached from Abridge Road. Loughton Fire Station notified, with further particulars. Chief Officer Eaton and one man proceeded to fire on First Aid Crash Tender, and ambulances left station 8.33 p.m.

West Essex Gazette, June 1936

Although Hillman Airways continued to expand after its founder's death, with Dragon Rapides like G-ADAH, which still survives today, flying four trips to Paris each day with three each to Ostend, Brussels and Antwerp and two to Belfast, by October 1935 the company was in financial difficulties to the tune of £28,000. A take over by Whitehall Securities Corporation led to Hillmans being amalgamated into that organisation's existing airlines — United Airways and Spartan Air Lines — to form British Airways Limited based at Heston.

Mrs Jim Mollison, better known under her maiden name of Amy Johnson, flew with Hillmans, getting experience on twin-engined aircraft. *Left:* Mr Allan Church (of Epping sausages fame) photographed her taxi-ing G-ACEV onto the apron. *Right:* Outside the terminal building, possibly with her aviation pioneering husband. She was tragically killed in 1941 over the Thames Estuary ferrying an aircraft to the RAF.

The first recorded use of the aerodrome by North Weald squadrons was in late March 1940 when Hurricanes of Nos. 56 and 151 Squadrons were flown over after the last operation of the day for an overnight stop in case of enemy night attacks on the parent station. Shortly after dawn the aircraft returned to North Weald to prepare for the day's operations.

This shuttle procedure continued for the next few weeks but the first squadron to be permanently based at Stapleford was No. 151 Squadron which moved in from Martlesham Heath on August 29, mounting several patrols the same day. On the first sortie, the squadron encountered fifty Bf 109s although without scoring. On a later patrol, Pilot Officer A. G. Wainwright flying a Hurricane was shot down by a Bf 109 but baled out and was admitted to Epping Hospital with fractured ribs.

The action on the 31st started early with a Luftwaffe raid on North Weald during which No. 151 Squadron shot down a confirmed Bf 109 from the fighter escort. On the second patrol a Do 17 was confirmed shot down near Hornchurch and the third patrol resulted in a Do 215 being brought down over the Thames.

After a somewhat short stay, the squadron was ordered to move on September 1, and taking over their aircraft were the pilots of No. 46 Squadron. The squadron's Operational Record Book gives an interesting description of their new base:

'The aerodrome was found to have a pronounced slope down towards the hangars, there were several ridges running across the 'drome and the surface was extremely rough. The aircraft were dispersed around the wood which ran along one edge of the landing field, crews and equipment were housed in hurricane and bell tents and a marquee. There were two corrugated iron huts and several trenches for protection from blast. A small stream running through the wood was used by the airmen for washing purposes.'

From now on the squadron was in daily contact with the Luftwaffe and on September 3 the squadron intercepted thirty Ju 88s escorted by fifty Bf 109s and Bf 110s attacking North Weald. In the ensuing battle four Hurricanes were shot down and Sergeant G. H. Edworthy reported as missing. Later three Hurricanes bounced what they thought were three Ju 88s flying in formation; tragically they proved to be three Blenheims from No. 25 Squadron returning to North Weald. Two were shot down and one pilot, Pilot Officer D. W. Hogg, killed.

The Battle of Britain, Then and Now, 1980

On September 3, 1940 I was in the upper section of a flour mill behind Ongar High Street when I heard the sound of aerial combat. I rushed to the loading bay overlooking the town and, peering into the sky, saw the unmistakable sight of an aircraft spinning viciously to earth. I naturally thought it was an enemy aircraft but, to my dismay, as the aircraft neared the ground I identified it as a Blenheim.

I can state that the tragedy would have probably been compounded had the Blenheim crashed in the centre of Ongar as it gave every indication of doing. At about 1,000 feet, however, Pilot Officer Hogg presumably initiated spin recovery and the Blenheim was in the process of pulling out when it crashed in a shallow dive between Ongar and Greensted. The other crew member, Sergeant Powell, meanwhile, had been descending by parachute and landed just behind Ongar High Street at Castle Farm.

There might conceivably still be people who would be glad to know that although Pilot Officer Hogg died he averted an even greater tragedy.

Letter from R. W. Wheelhouse, Coggeshall, January 12, 1983

The Royal Air Force took over the aerodrome in 1938 as a satellite for North Weald. Additional land was acquired for dispersed accommodation sites and a 2¼-mile concrete perimeter track constructed with six double aircraft blast pens. The aerodrome surface was painted with tar lines to simulate fields and camouflage it from the air. The perimeter track obliterated the old apron but part of the historic terminal still survives — but for how long? The facilities were used by the RAF during the war and Thorn who leased the buildings for many years afterwards kept them in good order; now they are derelict and abandoned but this one at least should be preserved. Its location can be seen on the picture at the top of the page opposite.

I took off for my first operational flight over England together with Paszko (Paszkowski — section leader) and Tolu (Lokuciewski). After a while I began to fear that the flight will be a fiasco, when suddenly I saw the bursts of artillery fire indicating that enemy aircraft were somewhere near. Paszko also noticed these signs, and to show that he was not only pious but also hot-blooded he did not lose any time but waggled his wings as a warning to get ready for the attack and turned sharply to starboard towards the enemy formation, attacking the end pair of Dorniers, one of which soon burst into flames. That left two of our 'planes and one Dornier and therefore nothing for me, but below us there was a fight in progress and I decided to join it. I soon had before me an aeroplane with a Swastika on its tail. With a height advantage there was no difficulty in making the attack. I had time to notice the flames issuing from the Me. 109 when I, myself, received a burst from behind and my Hurricane started to smoke heavily, going into a steep dive. I released the belts and slipped off the helmet whilst trying to get the 'plane away from houses and into the open spaces but the Hurricane was already past the vertical line and I found myself literally ejected from the cockpit. It was not until I landed that I noticed the loss of one shoe which probably caught against some lever in the cockpit.

Combat Report, Flying Officer Marian Pisarek. September 7, 1940

The late Wilf Nicoll with a piece of the exploded ammunition box.

The Hurricane, now in its death dive, headed towards Roding Road where it smashed inverted into the back lawn of No. 40, burying itself beneath the air raid bunker in which the Brockwell family were sheltering. With a roar the fuel tanks exploded and blazing high octane petrol cascaded into the shelter. A cheer went up all over Loughton from the watching villagers, oblivious that this was not a German machine crashing.

Constable Laurie Perigo was first on the scene, and was followed by Walter Bullen with a rescue team within two minutes. Fighting their way through the smoke, flames and exploding ammunition they strove to reach the shelter in the forlorn hope that someone could be saved. When they finally doused the flames, they found that one side of the shelter had collapsed, bringing down the roof. Mr. and Mrs. Brockwell had been killed instantly by the blast and Mrs. Gurden, further inside the shelter, had been burnt to death.

Meanwhile Flying Officer Pisarek was drifting serenely across the allotments towards Alderton Hill on his parachute. At No. 61, Mr. and Mrs. Tibble were excitedly watching the battle through binoculars. Next door, at the Red Lodge, Charles Cranwell, an ex-RNAS WWI veteran but now a private in the Home Guard, stood watching in the garden. When Mr. Tibble shouted that a pilot had baled out and was drifting their way, Charles Cranwell ran indoors for his Lee Enfield. Loading it with a five round clip he dashed outside just in time to see the pilot become entangled in a knarled old oak tree in the back garden.

Swinging himself from side to side the pilot released his harness and climbed to the ground to find himself looking down the wrong end of a rifle. Pisarek offered his identity card and then calmly took out a comb to neaten his hair.

Charles Cranwell had no sooner begun to realise that the pilot might not be a German after all when the garden became alive with police, soldiers and some hostile civilians. Being tall, blonde and not able to speak much English, it was presumed he was a German and he was promptly hustled to Loughton Police Station. There, after thorough questioning, his identity was established. Before he left the station, news arrived of the deaths in Roding Road. Flying Officer Pisarek was extremely distressed.

Thirty years passed and the incident was forgotten in Loughton until the facts were uncovered by another policeman — an enthusiastic amateur historian — Constable J622 Wilf Nicoll [who died in 1982]. Tracking down the various eye-witnesses and contacting the Polish Air Force Association led to parts of the Hurricane being put on display at the opening of the new Loughton Police Station (on the site of the old one) in 1971. PC Nicoll even went to see the new owners of No. 40 Roding Road but they were reluctant to discuss the crash or show him the garden.

There the matter rested until 1976, when Tony Graves and John Tickner, of the London Air Museum, read about the crash in a Polish Squadron history. By now No. 40 had changed hands and the new owners, Mr. and Mrs. Paul Pinagli, were very interested to learn what had happened years ago in their small, suburban back-garden.

At the time, the surface wreckage of the Hurricane had been taken to the local council yard in Old Station Road, Loughton, to await collection by the RAF. One wing was found several gardens away and two of the Browning machine guns were displayed throughout the war years at the local Lopping Hall. It was not known exactly what remained below the ground as even the remains of the air raid shelter had been removed after the crash.

Bravely, Mr. Pinagli gave permission for the London Air Museum team to move in and, on May 29, excavations began. Over the course of three Saturdays, using hand tools at

Ex-Home Guard Charles Cranwell (since deceased) points out the oak tree in the back garden of Red Lodge on Alderton Hill, to Wilf Nicoll, where he 'captured' Flying Officer Pisarek after his parachute landing.

first, the complete wreckage forward of the aerial was recovered. It was on the last Saturday, in the presence of members of the Polish Air Force Association, when the engine was to be lifted from the excavation, that the greatest find came to light. The black shoe which had been lost by Marian Pisarek as he left the aircraft, was found cased in mud and entangled in the wreckage.

Mr. Brockwell, his wife and mother were all buried in Loughton Cemetery. Marian Pisarek went on to fly 47 sorties with 303 Squadron during which time he shot down four enemy aircraft. On January 23, 1941, he was made commander of No. 315 'Deblin' Squadron. He was promoted to Wing Commander on April 18, 1942 and took command of the Northolt Wing. Just eleven days later, he took off on his last mission. Leading the wing on an operation over Desvres in northern France on April 29, they were attacked by a superior force of Me 109s and Fw 190s. Two pilots failed to return — one of which was Marian Pisarek. His body was never found; neither was the crash site and today no memorial or inscription remains to remember his passing.

After the Battle No. 13, 1976

Flying Officer Pisarek's shoe comes to light in a Loughton back garden — buried with much of his plane for thirty-six years. Now on display at the Tangmere Military Aviation Museum in Sussex.

Before we leave aviation, these views are offered as a graphic illustration of the expansion of Loughton since the picture *above* was taken in 1928. Looking north-east, Warren Hill is in the foreground with Nursery Road on the left.

The Domesday books, that remarkable administrative accomplishment completed for William the Conqueror by seven or eight panels of commissioners in 1086 covering the majority of England, lists six separate estates in being at Loughton. Alderton and Debden manors had been given to the abbey at Waltham on its foundation in 1060 and so they remained until the Dissolution in 1540, by which time they had been amalgamated with neighbouring estates into the manor of Loughton Hall.

There was probably a house very near the site of the present building as far back as 1522 when John Stonard, a familiar name locally, was granted a lease for 41 years of the manor of Loughton or Lucton, another well known name, by the monastery of Waltham. The house must have been built on quite a grand scale as Stonard's grandson, also named John, was able to entertain Queen Elizabeth there in 1578.

In 1601, Sir Robert Wroth, the then occupier, describes the house as having become 'Very ruinous and parte of it in such decaye that yf it be not repayred it will falle downe.' He mentioned his proposal to make alterations to the house in order to make it fit for entertaining the Queen again. . . .

The house at this time [1612] must have been a sumptuous edifice and was visited by many notable dignitaries such as Ben Jonson, James I and Princess Anne of Denmark.

The property was eventually acquired by John Maitland of Woodford Hall in 1825. He carried out extensive alterations both inside and out and the records show the house as it must have been shortly before the tragic fire which destroyed it in 1836.

The house faced south and a path led from a pair of fine iron gates, surmounted by the Wroth crest, to the roadway. This road (now Borders Lane) was diverted to its present course in 1879. The whole of the house was destroyed with the exception of one or two outbuildings and was left a ruin for some forty-three years. In 1879 the new hall was built virtually on the same site. Parts of the previous house which had escaped the fire were incorporated in the new building, including a staircase designed by Inigo Jones.

Britannia Quarterly. Winter 1975/76

My dearest Mother,

I shall now try to give you a more collected account than I have yet been able to do, although I have really destroyed two letters I had nearly finished, from them being so unsatisfactory.

On Saturday evening we had perceived two or three bits of burning soot come down the library chimney, and not feeling comfortable, I looked up the chimney, and William opened the window and went out of doors to see if he could distinguish any smoke or sparks from the chimney, but there was no appearance of anything.

Instead of putting wood on the fire as usual, we put a little bit of coal which I brought in my hand from the ante-room fireplace, and we sat the fire just out. Not a spark had fallen from the chimney during the last hour and William said he thought we might safely go to bed. Previously, he again opened the window, went out, and saw all safe, and I looked up the chimney.

On going to bed I named it to Bayley and begged her to go down again, which she did — every spark was out, nor was there smoke or smell of burning. Bayley also looked up the chimney, and then we all went to bed.

At five o'clock, College was awoke by the three bells of the ante-room, library and saloon that had been hung about a month previously by a bellringer over the pantry door, beginning to ring violently. He jumped up and ran to the library, but could not get through the ante-room. He came up to our room and called. We jumped up, and for the children and William to run down, see the state of things and send to Rolls (Lady Lonita Harvey's) for the engine as it is left in her offices. The engine soon arrived but was very ineffectual, but at Romford where they saw the fire, they immediately sent off for their engine. It acted very well.

When Mr. Cecil Lune (at Rolls) who married this Mary Harvey, heard the bell ring and engine required, he jumped up, ran to the top of the house and looked towards Loughton. He had previously ordered his house to be in readiness. For a few moments he thought we had been thus taken, but seeing a red column rising, he ran downstairs, jumped on his horse, galloped to Chigwell, sent off express for the engines from London and then galloped back to Loughton to see what use he could be of with his servant. His services were *invaluable*. Had he been a brother he could not have done more.

In the meantime we, at Loughton, after trying the ante-room door which it was impossible to enter, and satisfied as we must not lose a moment to do what could be done to save property. It was Sunday morning — no human creature but ourselves was awake. The Laundry Maid stayed with me and the others all went to be as useful as they could. The children were, in a few moments, carried in blankets to Gingell's, by which means they, the Gingells, with their farming men were awakened and came to our assistance.

The Laundry Maid and one of the other servants ran with me into the gallery to see what we could save. It was *darkness that*

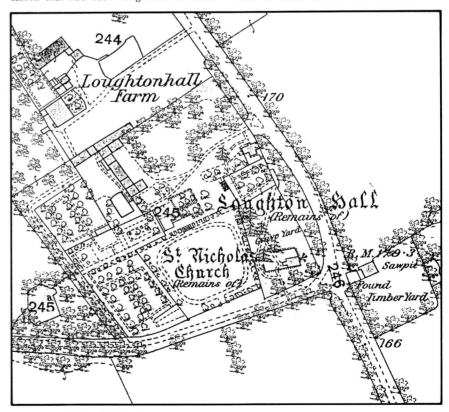

After the joining of the manors, Loughton descended (together with the advowson of the rectory) through John Stoner (1522), Thomas Darcy (1551), Mary Tudor (1553, two months before she became Queen), the Duchy of Lancaster (1558), Susan, daughter of John Stoner and her husband Robert Wroth (1579). It then stayed with the Wroth family through five generations until sold to an alderman of the City, William Whitaker, in 1745. The manor hall, with the parish church beside it, lay a mile east of the village not far from the bridge over the Roding. The avenue of trees which lined the road leading up from the river was cut down during the Napoleonic wars when a high price could be obtained for timber.

might be felt, — however, we got to the top. Though we had candles, they were useless — and tried to cut down the pictures and secured *all the Bronzes*, and a few, *but very few*, of the paintings, the harp and piano and four new Morocco easy chairs, with the ink stand and India screen, also the top of a cabinet which contained some valuables.

I shall never forget the sensation, and heard so dreadful a noise in the King's Room that I thought it was full of men shouting, and all around the house the same. It never occurred to me it was the floors of timbers giving away, and I put my hand on the catch to open it, but it was so hot I started back and could not turn the latch, and it was most providential as when we were leaving the gallery I had great difficulty in persuading the people then collecting to carry out the piano, and no entreaty could induce them to save the slab of marble, nor was the gallery entered after. The whole of the King's Room, Oak Room and Pink Room must have been in flames.

I ran downstairs as William had expressly forbidden any person whatever *to open window, shutter or door*, and not one, excepting the *front door* was opened until the last effort to throw the furniture out of the windows . . .

The lamps were lit in the Stone and Oak Hall for the convenience of getting out all that could be done, and there was never the least danger to any person employed.

Being *Sunday morning*, no creature was about or passing till Gingell's men came in, so we felt all dependant on our own and servant's exertions when the fire burst out, and indeed, from the first, we felt *nothing* could extinguish it.

William had also sent to Town for the engines, but when they arrived the whole was nearly destroyed. Parts of the walls are still standing, but must soon fall, and the appearance is truly desolate. The Library is still burning or smoking, but they are now removing the rubbish to see what books, if any, can be rescued. Every book, alas, is gone. The Library which was just completed and

The Reverend Maitland is somewhat of an enigma. On the one hand he enclosed 1,000 acres of the Forest, agreeing in 1864 to split the land with his tenants on a two-thirds — one-third basis, thus invoking bitter opposition from the villagers over their loss of the right to cut wood for fuel, yet on the other hand he was a 'faithful priest and zealous public servant'. The land he gained he sold for building plots and when he died in November 1909 he left an estate worth £126,000, an enormous sum, being the equivalent of around £3¾ million today.

perfect, the Study Library, and Mrs. Whitaker's which was in the Pink Room, Dick's work baskets and boxes, every paper I ever valued and all my recollections of early childhood are alike gone, and all the children's presents were locked up in my desk.

Can you give me the number of the five pound note you sent. If so, I can proven it, as it was in my desk. I cannot write more as I have not the time. I hope this account is more collected than the likes I wrote before which I was obliged to destroy. All are quite well, and had Mr. Hamilton been a parent his house and friendship could not have been greater. Henrietta and William Junr. are at Mrs. Walton's. As yet, we have no plans, but I object to Brighton.

Loughton Hall was insured for £3,000. The furniture at £2,150. The Beer Cellar has given way — the Wine Cellar's yet safe. At the Imperial Insurance Office they told William yesterday when he went up to see the Director, there was no blame — all that could be done had been done, and offered to give him a draft for the amount of the sum, as it was considered at the office, a total loss.

No accident happened but one man who fell from a ladder, his head was cut but not much worse. I cannot describe the affectionate kindness of all, high and low, far and near. Misfortunes bring to light many unknown friends.

Letter from Anne Maitland to her mother, December 14, 1836

The present Hall, now a farm-house, was constructed partly out of the materials of the ancient building. The great gates of the old Hall still remain, and are elaborate specimens of hand-wrought iron-work. . . .

Greater London, Edward Walford, 1883

In 1944 the Hall and 644 acres of land were sold to London County Council for the building of the Debden Estate, begun in 1945. During the war it was the home of several hundred servicemen and the Prime Minister, then Winston Churchill, was entertained there.

In 1949 London County Council handed Loughton Hall over to Essex County Council who made it into a community centre. Since then its vast range of activities meeting all types of leisure needs has made it one of the leading centres in Britain.

Britannia Quarterly, Winter 1975/76

Loughton Hall [the work of the architect William Eden Nesfield] has been adapted by Essex County Council primarily for the accommodation of the Debden Community Association, but it is also in use temporarily as an infants' school for 200 children. In addition a central kitchen, to supply 500 meals a day, was required to assist with the feeding of other permanent schools on the estate which had not yet got canteens. This kitchen, also at present shared with the Community Centre, will later revert to them for their own use. A small playground in the grounds also serves the Centre as a car park.

Lead thieves had stripped the box gutters, flashings and lead piping, and a very serious outbreak of dry rot had caused the total loss of a section of the roof, large sections of the upper floors (which had been temporarily shored) and the complete ground floor, with the exception of the hall and theatre. The external balconies and turned balustrading were beyond salvage. All windows and fittings had been badly damaged and, in many cases, destroyed by vandals.

The upper floors were replaced in timber by trimming the cut-away sections with R.S.Js. and splicing on joist extensions. The patched floors were later sanded, stained and polished. The box gutters at eaves level were repaired and lined with reinforced asphalt. The boiler house stack, which had heavy oversailing courses, was unstable and had to be reduced in height, while the remaining chimney heads were rebuilt in their original form.

A box gutter at second floor level had to be removed and was replaced by a rendered band figured to match the treatment in the rendered gables, and capped with a drip course of tiles. Balconies were replaced with asphalt flats and a low coping. The ground floors were filled up solid and finished with $\frac{1}{16}$ Accotiles. Lavatory cubicles are of light pressed steel construction, mainly of standard sizes but with some purpose-made sections.

A small new store was erected at the stage end of the hall for storage of portable stage and curtains and of the nesting steel chairs. The elaborate oak staircase was reconstructed to open up the circulation space in the entrance hall, and various partitions were removed to enlarge the general purposes room, the canteen and the kitchen. The painted pine panelled and moulded ceilings were saved and have now been restored to their original form.

The Builder, May 4, 1951

On Whitaker's death in 1752 the estate was inherited by his widow Anne, and when she died it passed in turn to their unmarried daughter, also named Anne. In her will of 1825 Miss Anne Whitaker left the manor to John Maitland of Woodford Hall. He only lived another six years and when he died his son, William Whitaker Maitland inherited. In 1836 a disastrous fire swept through the building, which remained a gutted shell until demolished and rebuilt in 1879 by the Reverend John Whitaker Maitland.

When the Hall was destroyed in the fire of 1836, the parish church of St Nicholas *(above)*, which stood alongside the house was even more out on a limb and it was decided that a new, larger replacement place of worship must be built nearer the High Road. This was St John's, built in Blind Lane (it subsequently became Church Lane) in 1846. To help raise the £6,500 necessary for the rebuilding, the old church, which dated possibly from the fourteenth century, was sold for demolition. The sum raised: a paltry £89! After St Nicholas was dismantled, for some reason the chancel was retained, converted into a mortuary chapel. This was demolished in 1877 and the present church that we see today *(above right)* built a few yards to the west. At the same time of course, the new Loughton Hall was going up on the foundations of the original building nearby. In 1947 the church was adapted as a chapel of ease for the new Debden estate then in course of construction by the London County Council.

The site of the old St Nicholas church can be pinpointed by the flagstones covering tombs which originally lay within the building.

Meanwhile William and Anne Maitland moved up to another property that they owned, Golden Hill House beside Golding's Hill. The original house had been built by Richard Clay, a London draper. *Left:* This picture shows the second Golding's Manor, the first having been pulled down about 1820. William Maitland lived in the house until he died in 1861 and by 1939 it was owned by Lord Stanmore. In September 1940 a land-mine drifted down over Loughton and gunners in the High Street manning a Bofors on the back of a lorry opened fire to try to explode the missile in the air. All that happened was that the blast from their gun blew in the doors of the Century Cinema, the mine continuing to float down towards Golding's Manor. It exploded on the roof, injuring Lord Stanmore's sister, the Hon. Mrs. Hamilton-Gordon, and causing severe damage. In 1948 the estate was sold and broken up for housing. The stable block remains, converted into Stanmores, while Golding's Manor Cottage has been built on the site of the house itself.

Debden, variously recorded in bygone days, in different chronicles, as Depden, Deepden, Depdon, Dependon, Dependana, Dependin, from Saxon words all of which mean 'a valley', is a small hamlet situated about mid-way between Loughton and Epping, a mile and a half south of the main road linking these two places and thirteen miles from London.

It is assumed that a manor house must always have existed either on the actual site

The other ancient manor of Loughton was at Debden Green, reached either via Clay's Lane or England's Lane *(above)*, **possibly named after the family of George England (1633). Formerly it was known as Rie Lane from William atte Rie who lived there in 1327.**

now occupied by the hall (mention is made of the 'erection' of the hall, and this is taken to mean the re-erection) on a site very near that of the present building. The original site is, however, more likely to have been that at

present occupied. The original manor house would not necessarily be mentioned, as although they were the seat of the lord of the manor, it was not the custom to make particular mention of the buildings themselves.

It is also a point of interest that the name Debden Hall is not of itself the name of the building, but that of the manor; history records that the manor has been written of as Debenhall, and also as Debden Hall, both names going back almost to the time of the Conqueror. It would seem from this that when the actual hall was built it received the name of the manor as it actually then existed, without the said name being in any way modified.

Siward Uld is recorded as holding the lands at the time of the Confessor. At the time of the great survey the lands belonged to one Ralph Peverel, the whole being eventually divided into six manors, of which it appears that Debden Hall or Debenhall was one.

William, grandson of the Ralph Peverel mentioned, succeeded to the estate of the hall (the division of the lands into six manors seems to have been prior to this, as is also the adoption of the name). He lost it, in common with all his other possessions, in 1153, when he was disinherited by Henry II and had to flee the country for the crime of poisoning Ralph, Earl of Chester.

In 1155 Henry gave it to his own son, John, Earl of Mortain, who on succeeding to the crown conferred the estate on Geoffrey Fitz-Piers, Earl of Essex, whose daughter Maud conveyed it by marriage to Henry de Rohun, Earl of Hereford. He was succeeded by his son Humphrey, the grandson of the same name, who died in 1298, and in turn by his great-grandson, Humphrey de Rohun, Earl of Hereford and Northampton, who died in 1372, having married Joan, daughter of Richard, Earl of Arundel, by whom there were two heirs, Eleanor, who married Thomas of Woodstock, Duke of Gloucester, sixth son of Edward III, and Mary, who married Henry, Earl of Derby, afterwards Henry IV. Lady Eleanor had one son and four daughters, of whom Anne, the eldest, became sole heir of her mother, succeeding to a partition of the Rohun estates with the other co-heir, who was Henry V. Hence the manor of Debden Hall became vested in the Crown as part of the Duchy of Lancaster and was part of the jointure of the queens of Henry V, Henry VI and Edward IV.

It was conveyed by grant (recorded value at the time being about £33/13/4) by Henry VIII to Thomas, Lord Audley, from whose only daughter it descended to her son, Thomas Howard de Waldon, Earl of Suffolk, in whose family it continued till 1660, when it was sold by James, Earl of Suffolk, to Thomas Grove, who in turn sold it to Sir Richard Browne, Bt.

The property had come under the hammer at Winchester House, Old Broad Street, on October 8, 1920. Nine years later it was destroyed by fire and the property was purchased by the Austin family who built the present hall on the site in 1930. When Mr. Austin died in 1936 the estate passed into the hands of trustees until January 1948 when purchased by Mr. T. W. Parker. *Below:* Now redeveloped — this is Ripley View.

The latter died in 1672 and was succeeded by his son, Sir Richard, who married Frances, sister of Sir Robert Atkins, who was at that time Chief Baron of Exchequer. Both Sir Richard and Lady Atkins died in 1685. It is recorded that one died first and the other died within a space of three days from a broken heart.

Sir Richard had sold the estate in 1680 (that is five years before he died) to John Edwards, whose son and heir, Henry, sold it with the manor of Deynes to Richard Chiswell in July 1715. This Richard Chiswell was the son of Richard Chiswell, merchant, of London.

Richard Chiswell the son erected (or re-erected) the mansion of Debden Hall itself in the year 1715. According to the records so far traced regarding the actual architecture itself, the south-east side was built in Grecian style, ornamented with massive pillars. This would seem to be the main side, or front, of the mansion.

S. R. Cotton, Essex Countryside

The news that Loughton's new international swimming pool at Traps Hill was to be opened to the public on Saturday morning really caused a splash. Such a big splash, in fact, that 150 local swimmers christened it in the first hour.

Two of the first in the deep end as the doors opened at 8 a.m. were 21-year-old Margaret Blatch, of the High Road, Loughton, and her friend, Rosemary Hipkin, of The Crescent, Loughton.

Many 'mums and dads', who had taken their children to the pool but who did not fancy the prospect of such an early morning dip were free to wander round and tour the rest of the premises.

The pool will be officially opened this Saturday by Councillor Richard Spurge, Chairman of Chigwell Urban District Council.

Justly proud of their new venture the council say: 'This indoor pool was designed in the knowledge that an open air pool, surrounded by outdoor sports facilities, sun terraces and cafe-restaurant already existed within the urban district. For this reason it was considered unnecessary to provide outdoor amenities at Traps Hill.

'The siting was determined by the fact that the council had already acquired the land for public purposes and that it was well situated in relation to the development in Loughton which forms a substantial part of this widespread urban district.'

Express and Independent, September 1, 1967

Linking the old and new Loughtons is Trap's Hill, in former days says Will Francies 'an eerie place on a dark winter's night when the sudden hoot of an owl, and the moan of the wind in the lofty elms would send the lone wanderer scurrying to the lonely old "Priors" atop the hill.' On the right the gardener's cottage at the entrance to the drive to Brooklyn.

Trap's Hill was strictly Gould territory. George had been established at Trap's Hill Farm from 1856 where his four children were born. In 1888 George had Brooklyn *(above)* built while his son, John Herbert, moved into the farm. The house — its name is perpetuated today in Brooklyn Court at the foot of the hill — stood on the site of the present swimming pool and library car park.

LOUGHTON

TQ 49 NW 1/34   14/2/72

TRAPS HILL, Nos. 51 and 53

GV   Grade II

House, C17, extensively altered in C19. Timber-framed and brick, stuccoed, slate roof. Near-square plan, C17, extended to NE and E in C19, and refronted to NW in C19. 2 storeys. Ground floor, 4-panel door and light over in shallow doorcase, early C19. One double-hung sash window of 12 lights, early C19, one bow of double-hung sash windows of 4-12-4 lights, early C19, one bay of 3 double-hung sash windows of 4 lights, late C19. First floor windows as on ground floor, with one double-hung sash window of 4 lights, late C19, over door. Parapet and 2 string courses. The roofs of the rear wings are of handmade red clay tiles. This building originally formed a 'Unit System' group with Priors (now No. 7 Rowans Way) the first identified in Essex, fully described and its ownership documented in K. L. Sandall: The Unit System in Essex, Archaeological Journal vol. 130, 1975, 195-201.

List of Buildings of Special Architectural or Historic Interest, Department of the Environment

A reprieve is in sight this week for Traps Hill House, for months a bone of contention between preservationists, who describe the building as one of the most interesting in Loughton, and the owner who calls it a monstrosity.

The house, part of which is thought to date back to the 16th century, has been threatened by the owner's plans to demolish it. As a listed building it is now protected from demolition, and renovation plans have been prepared.

Builder Mr Denis Brown of Scot-Rown Ltd., 10 Church Hill, Loughton, bought the property last year with plans to demolish and redevelop, but his application, like one previously submitted, was refused.

Another application to build nine houses there but leaving the building intact was granted, but as site development plans go forward a question mark has been hanging over the fate of Traps Hill House and adjacent Priory House.

Members of Essex Architectural Research Society visited the site on Sunday 'to carry out a survey with a view to publishing the facts at a later date' explained the society's chairman Mr Raymond Small of 28 Forest Road, Loughton.

The original building, described by EARS members as 'probably the finest timber frame house of its kind in the country,' has had several additions made over the centuries. An important peculiarity, they say, is that it has been two separate large dwellings in one building since the 18th century.

Meanwhile Mr Brown, frustrated by opposition to his plans and in the face of what he calls 'preservation madness,' decided that if he could not beat them he had better join them, and has now had renovation plans drawn up.

Mr Brown is outspoken on the subject of preservationists. 'Just because of the old section at the back they recommend that the whole thing should stay,' he said. 'I have made the most of a bad job but those two tatty buildings are 90 per cent abortion, rubbish and ugliness.'

Describing the new application White & Mileson partner Mr Drummond Clapp said: 'The plan is for renovation and modernisation of the building to bring it up to acceptable living standards with minimal interference to existing structures. I think it will probably be accepted.'

West Essex Gazette, December 1, 1972

Trap's Hill House lay alongside the farm of the same name and was acquired by Chalkley Gould in 1806. It was later occupied by his son George who in 1856 let it to his nephew. Isaac Chalkley, George's son, lived at the house practically all his life and when he died in 1907 the property was let.

In 1972 this was a battleground: conservationists versus the developer. Trap's Hill House on the left and 'lonely old Priors' on the right. No prize for guessing who won.

On the opposite, or northern, side of the road lay Rose Farm comprising 33 acres stretching right down to the High Road. About 1870 George Gould rented the farm for £85 per annum from Mr. Rohrweger of Uplands, and shortly afterwards the large farmyard was pulled down. Gould & Sons let the house and remaining buildings to a Mr. Miller, while the present cricket ground was established on fields beside the Church Hill in 1879. The Rev. J. W. Maitland then purchased the property, allowing Mr. Miller to remain as tenant until the latter purchased it outright. Other fields were sold off to Ketts & Co., to develop the Uplands estate. Rose Farm itself survives to this day, listed Grade II.

A plan by actor Jack Watling to demolish Alderton Hall, his early 17th century manor house in Alderton-hill, Loughton, has brought a strong protest from local historians.

Mr. Watling has sought Chigwell Council planning permission for the old timber framed and white weather-boarded house to be replaced with seven houses and garages.

Chigwell Council, which has received an objection to the plan from Chigwell Local History Society, is to make a decision after the views of the West Essex Area Planning Officer are known about the proposal.

Alderton Hall is included in a list of buildings of special architectural interest compiled by the Minister of Housing and Local Government.

With his actress wife, Pat Hicks, and their children, Mr. Watling moved from Buckhurst Hill to Alderton Hall nine years ago.

At first he rented the old manor house but later bought the property.

Guardian & Gazette, April 10, 1964

Actor Jack Watling will not be able to build on the estate which surrounds his home — picturesque Alderton Hall, Loughton.

The Minister of Housing and Local Government this week confirmed that the land is not for development.

And Alderton Hall itself — it stands in its own grounds at the top of Alderton Hill — cannot be pulled down.

The Ministry have confirmed a Building Preservation Order by Essex County Council that the house is of historic interest.

Express and Independent, July 20, 1966

A latter-day 'lord' of Alderton Hall attempted to have it demolished in 1964 only to be thwarted by the Minister of Housing and Local Government.

Over on Alderton Hill lay another Gould farm — Alderton Hall — whose 269 acres had been leased by Chalkley Gould about 1779 from Anne Whitaker (see page 318-19) at 15/- per acre. Chalkley renewed the lease in 1789 at 18/- per acre and his son John had it from 1831 to 1850 at 26/- per acre. John gave up farming the following year and held a farm sale on August 28, 1851.

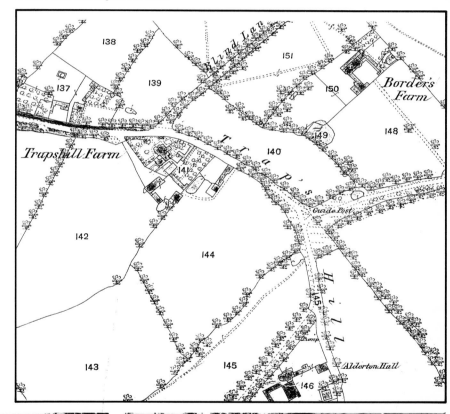

By far the largest Gould farm was Border's Farm leased from the Maitlands. It grew in size during the latter part of the nineteenth century as other parcels of land were added: from 96½ acres in 1859 to 359 acres in 1914. When the Padfield family bought Alderton Hall Farm in 1919, including Cowless Marsh and the Upper and Lower Marshes, Goulds noted in a memorandum that 'we had to give up all our marshland (which paid us best) after draining it and farming it for so many years'. To make up for the loss, in June 1921 Goulds Limited purchased the 375-acre Loughton Hall Farm for £14,250.

One might think that such pictures are a far cry from the Debden of today but in fact Border's Lane is little changed from the days that Goulds reigned supreme. The lad and lassie may have faded into obscurity but the bank where they sat probably seventy or more years ago is still there. The pond has been filled and a school now occupies the site of the farm. Originally St Nicholas County Primary School when opened in February 1948, it is now St Luke's Special School.

This comparison gives a good idea of the original width of Trap's Hill at the junction with the High Road. Brooklyn Court now on the left. The Methodist Church on the opposite side of the road was built in 1903.

The most sensational happening for many years in Loughton, was a fire at the Roman Catholic Church of St. Edmund of Canterbury, on Monday evening, which had a ghastly sequel. Shortly before 9 o'clock smoke was seen issuing from the building and the police and Fire Brigade were notified. Within four minutes the brigade, in command of Supt. T. Poulter and Chief Officer J. T. Heath, were at the scene of the outbreak. The firemen found the church a mass of flames, but after some little time they were able to subdue them. The building was then entered, and near the entrance door at the front was noticed a figure, which appeared to be one of the statues which ornamented the church. After a while, however, a P.c. saw that the supposed statue was wearing a pair of boots, and it was noticed that it was the body of a man, unrecognisably charred. The remains were removed to the Mortuary, and the next morning were identified as those of Alfred Springlett Noakes, of 26 Friern Road, East Dulwich. His record was an unenviable one, he having come out of prison the previous July, after serving a sentence of two years for breaking into a church.

The fire practically destroyed the whole interior of the building, the altar, however, was saved, and curiously enough the flames stopped by a safe which contained the consecrated Host. That the sacred elements were saved, was a source of great gratification to the priests and congregation.

The Loughton Gazette, September 29, 1934

To Loughton's growing Catholic community of 1,700, the 40-year-old parish of St. Edmund's became 'complete' on Saturday with the opening of the church's new £24,000 social hall.

About 60 parishioners and guests, including three local clergymen, attended the opening and blessing of the hall by the Bishop of Brentwood.

Speaking on behalf of the parishioners, Dr. St. John Murphy said that before St. Edmund's was built, Loughton Catholics had to travel to Woodford to worship.

In the mid-thirties, he said, St. Edmund's was burnt down but a year later a new church was opened on the same site.

After the war as the number of Catholics grew, mainly because of the Debden Estate, a new combined church and hall was built in Willingale-road.

Then in 1958, a new St. Edmund's was built in Traps-hill. 'We had an almost complete parish,' said the doctor, 'except for a hall, and today we are here to see that dream becoming reality.'

West Essex Gazette, January 6, 1967

One of the worst tragedy's to occur in Trap's Hill! — the incineration of the nearby Catholic Church of St Edmund's in September 1934. This first church, which had been built in 1926, was a corrugated iron structure and although the interior was badly charred with the shellac having caught alight, the building was restored the following year. The tiny church could only seat 100 (a later extension increased this by fifty per cent) but it continued to serve until the new St Edmund's was opened in July 1958.

The Debden estate is planned on a site to the east of the developed area of Loughton. The land slopes towards the River Roding and has interesting variations in contour. It is well wooded and the general aspect is southerly. A tree-lined country road traverses the estate, running north to south and this has been scheduled by the Ministry of Transport to be widened to a Class II road with industrial carriageways. It has been possible to preserve a large number of the existing trees by surrendering sufficient land to make one side of the old road with its line of trees into a central island of varying width.

Industrial sites have been reserved on the southern flank and will be separated from the housing areas by the railway line. Chigwell Lane Station is in a central position in relation to the estate, conveniently adjacent to both the housing and industrial areas.

The planning of the new estate was greatly influenced by the main physical features of the site, e.g., the existing roads, the undulating levels, the considerable number of good trees and the tree-lined stream traversing the southern area of the site from north to south. A water walk has been planned along the course of this stream with development on one side only of the flanking roads.

The principal shopping centre has been planned on one of the main estate roads near its junction with Chigwell Lane just north of the railway station. In the immediate vicinity sites have been set aside for other communal buildings, e.g. cinema, refreshment houses, etc. Two subsidiary shopping centres are planned on existing roads.

London County Council housing report, 1945

At the end of the Second World War, the London County Council were faced with an enormous housing problem, caused not only by the large numbers of houses destroyed, but also by the need to provide homes for the thousands of soldiers and civilians returning to their peacetime jobs. A plan was proposed by Professor Abercrombie for ten new satellite towns (only eight were actually built), with the LCC to build new 'cottage' estates in the country. The building of Debden began with these prefabs along Oakwood Hill. The site was redeveloped for light industry in the late 1970s.

The first development of the G.L.C. estate began early in 1947, with the erection of Emergency Factory Made Bungalows — prefabs — for short, these numbered 306. They were meant to have a life time of 10 years, but in 1957 the Ministry of Health granted an extention of a further 10 years. The prefabs are at the moment being gradually dismantled and at the southern end of Oakwood Hill site they have been completely removed and new houses and flats are being built. The Prefab Site is located along Oakwood Hill, between the underground railway and the River Roding. It is planned to replace all of the Prefabs and use the site as an extension to the G.L.C. Estate.

However, soon after the erection of the Prefabs, the foundations for the first permanent houses were laid over in the Broadway area of the estate in 1949. The building materials used in the permanent houses varied greatly, so that one can see the traditional brick buildings, the roofstone and the Cornish Stone Units. The houses vary in size and design, and the estate consists of two, three, four and five bedroom houses, some maisonettes, flats and bungalows for the elderly. The entire estate consists of 325 acres incorporating 4,335 dwellings. The estimated population in 1962 was just under 16,000 people and a recent survey revealed (1969) 19,000.

Debden Community Housing report, 1971

Clouds of doubt have cast a shadow over next year's holiday plans of many tenants living on Loughton's Oakwood-hill prefab estate.

The anxious tenants are not planting out new gardens or redecorating since hearing reports that their homes will be pulled down next year.

They have had so many false alarms during recent years that many have sought the advice of local organisations and officials.

Debden Tenants' Association has had so many appeals for information that it has written to G.L.C. district officer Mr. Kempsall for any details he has of any proposed development.

Others have approached local councillors for their advice and views on what they should do, and when in fact the 300 prefabs are being demolished.

On Wednesday a spokesman for Greater London Council said negotiations are still going on with Chigwell Council about the zoning of the area.

If the site is zoned for housing, new houses can be built on the prefab site.

Mr. William Reynolds, chairman of Chigwell Council's town planning committee, said that the last decision on this was taken about a year ago.

Then it was decided that the site should remain scheduled for industrial purposes.

West Essex Gazette, November 26, 1965

According to Scotsman Wilf Nicoll, police constable at Loughton and one of the first home-beat officers on the estate (the Debden police 'neighbourhood' office opened in November 1970), who always enjoyed a good story, when Rectory Lane was reconstructed by German PoW labour working simultaneously from either end, they deliberately misaligned the two ends of the road when they met near Pyrles Lane!

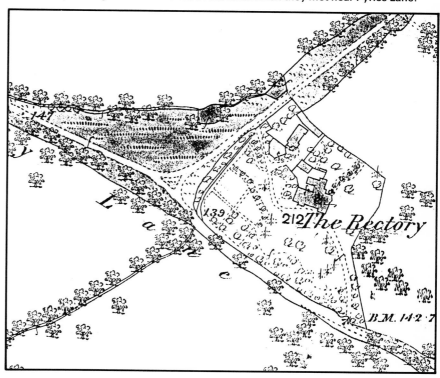

Nearby stood the old rectory. It had been damaged by a flying bomb and succumbed to the burgeoning estate. Demolished in 1953.

329

Staple's Road's schools. A National School was established in Loughton on the corner of Staple's Road and Woodbury Hill (see map page 293) in the early part of the nineteenth century. This building was enlarged to try to keep pace with the expanding population but, by 1887, the town had grown to the point at which the Government insisted that a school board be set up to deal with the problem. The Board decided to construct a new school for boys not far away on the southern side of Staple's Road and this opened in 1888 (above). In 1891 a new infants' building (on the right of the picture) was put up adjoining the boys' leaving only the girls in the original National School building.

When the Board decided to build a new girls' school, a site was chosen on the other side of the boys' building. These girls are enjoying a day out in the Forest with the headmistress. Miss A. K. True, sometime during the First World War.

After the new school was opened in 1911 the old girls' building — that of the original National School (left) — was no longer used for educational purposes and it was demolished in

1938-39. Ashley Grove flats (right) now stand on the site which amazingly still retains the old style, if not the actual original, wooden paling fence.

Loughton has always been a haven of private schools. As far back as 1833 there were two fee-paying boarding schools, one or two middle-class day schools and three or more dame schools. In 1878 there was a school for boys run by Mr. J. C. Holloway, ten years later it was known as Madras Hall 'for the sons of gentlemen', later Madras House School, before being relocated in 1890 in a purpose-built school *(above)* as St John's College. *Below:* Today the same school still in being as Loughton School for boys.

Above: Originally Loughton County High School for girls was opened in a house in York Hill in January 1906 with 29 pupils, the headmistress having one permanent member of staff and a visiting science master. In May 1908 the first part of the present building *(below)* in Alderton Hill was opened, temporary buildings being added in 1917. A swimming bath was installed in 1922 and a new assembly hall built in 1930. A new wing was built in two stages: 1923 and 1930. Today the school is also used for adult courses run by the Epping Forest district.

This beautiful part of old Loughton gives the lie to the 'flat Essex' theory, the gently sloping York-hill, as it passes the War Memorial, winding steeply upward to the high ridge which is Baldwins-hill.

Little here has changed since my boyhood. The 'new' Wheatsheaf public house, like its charming neighbour, The King's Head, was designed by Mr. Horace White, who was Loughton U.D.C.'s Surveyor for many years.

York-crescent is built on the site of a building I first recollect as St. Ethelburga's Home for Girls. I remember no more of these young ladies than the straw hats they wore as they marched to our church. Between the wars the home became York House Hotel, but I imagine lack of support led to its closure. I have often wondered how Loughton manages without an hotel!

Since 1886 the Chiswell family has dealt in antiques in the picturesque building opposite, once a farm-house. Forest-way branches steeply off on the left, its wooden cottages reminding us of the primitive forest village of not so long ago. Back to York-hill, to pass, on our upward journey, the pleasant little wooden house, Alma Cottage, which once was Barrett's School. Ever upward, past delightful King's Hill, reminiscent of a Devonshire lane, the whitewashed 18th century King's Cottage adding to the illusion. Beside this hill is a private burial ground, long since disused. The forgotten dead sleep on. Their removal would involve complicated and lengthy legal and ecclesiastical proceedings.

Now York-hill thrusts more boldly upward to the very threshold of that delightful and popular 'pub' — The Gardener's Arms, where, today, a grand-daughter of dear old 'Granny' Hughes (the pub's landlady, for many a year), will draw up your pint in the bar where Jacob Epstein quaffed his, in the company of gardeners, folk off 'the Hill' and from the village below.

Just here we are on the 'roof' of Loughton and can view the village spread out below, its jumble of roads and buildings appearing strangely unfamiliar, and, far, far beyond (given a clear day) see London's river as a silver thread on the horizon, the smoke plumes of vessels confirming the evidence of sharp eyes.

Will Francies writing in the Loughton Gazette, April 24, 1953

The area around York-hill was once the property of the Duchy of Lancaster, but it is most unlikely that there is any significance in this curious fact and the association undoubtedly post-dated the Wars of the Roses. This part of Epping Forest is one of the highest points in Essex and often when Loughton is shrouded in mist the Gardener's Arms basks in the sunshine.

Built on to the 16th century inn is an old tea room which was, at one time, dilapidated and plans were made for it to be demolished and the space used for a car park. That scheme fell through and the present tenant of the Gardener's Arms has, during the past three years, carried out a major reconstruction. The result of his efforts is an attractively furnished hall which last month was officially opened with a wine and cheese party in aid of Shortacres Old People's Home.

At the back of the hall is a balcony, known locally as Wigan Pier, from which during the war it was possible to have a horrifying view of London under fire. Today the heights of

Shooters-hill, across the river, can clearly be seen on a fine day.

The Gardener' Arms was once a free house and it was in 1933 that the property was bought by Manns Brewery. At that time, the inn was enlarged by the addition of the present saloon lounge.

Before coming to the Gardener's Arms Ronald Tyler, the tenant, and his wife Lillian were at the Ship Inn at Thurrock. Many of the bar fittings from that inn were brought by Ron to Loughton and this accounts for the nautical atmosphere in the bars. While he has been in residence he has also carried out a large number of changes to the interior of the inn.

There is a pleasing air of cleanliness in the bars, all the brasses gleam brightly and the tables in the lounge are either home-made or converted kilderkins.

From the Ship were transferred navigation lights, a masthead lamp, a splendid specimen of a ship's wheel, a couple of port-holes and a hand-operated semaphore lamp. Other unusual items in the bars include Algerian

The historic Lopping Tree — reputed to be the one from which a symbolic bough had once been cut to demonstrate the existence of the lopping rights. Children from nearby Staple's Road school used to call it the 'initiation tree' as all new entrants to the junior school were made to crawl though its hollow trunk. It lay on the green opposite the present glass company. In the background the white building is Alma Cottage, originally Loughton's first dame school.

The Gardener's Arms, now a listed building Grade II.

daggers and Siamese hand shields which rub shoulders incongruously with an ancient bottle-opener and a very old cow bell.

A street lamp illuminated by an oil burner recalls the far-off days before the introduction of gas and electricity. Perhaps the most fascinating exhibit is an object rather like a long wooden spoon. This is apparently an offertory box which was passed along the pews in a church. An old change till which saw service until a few years ago now looks rather forlorn in the corner. Although splendid in construction, it was slow in operation and out of place in this computerised age.

Ronald Tyler is very happy at the Gardener's Arms, which he describes as a 'good local.' He has many plans for the future and I am sure he would agree with the poet who wrote of 'A good plot, good friends, and full of expectations.'

West Essex Gazette, October 28, 1966

Things ain't what they used to be — but publicans Bob and Kit Worrell, of the Gardner's Arms, Loughton, have spent out almost £70,000 to bring back that old charm.

Since they took over the pub in York Hill a year ago, Bob and Kit have toured the auctions and antique shops for 'oldy worldy' tables and chairs to fit in with the decor.

Said 53-year-old Bob: 'It hadn't been touched for a number of years and it was in a hell of a state.

'The roof leaked, there were outside toilets and the kitchen was very small.'

They decided that the pub was in need of a face-lift to retain the building's character, so they contacted their brewery Watneys who gave them £40,000. Bob and Kit put up another £30,000 towards the project and then called in the builders.

Since December the building has been in turmoil with floorboards and roof tiles being replaced, construction work in the kitchen, and new indoor toilets.

But on Wednesday the waiting and the chaos proved worthwhile as Bob and Kit held a grand opening for the new premises.

From now on they hope to serve proper lunch-time and evening meals in their new restaurant, with their son Stephen doing most of the cooking, and the function hall which has not been used for years is being redecorated for the summer.

Guardian & Gazette, March 16, 1984

The changing face of Britain's pubs — as personified here at The Royal Oak. A unique institution, in the days of the horseman the inn performed a dual rôle: accommodation for the traveller on his wearysome journey and sustenance and shelter for his mount. *Left:* The Royal Oak, built in 1860, possessed four bed chambers, two coach houses and three stables. When this picture was taken in 1904 Conrad Young had held the licence for 28 years but that year he died and shortly afterwards the building was demolished. It stood in Smarts Lane, just beyond the junction with High Beach Road *(above right). Below:* The replacement put up at the other end of the site and re-orientated 180 degrees to face Forest Road.

It had to come, of course, but still it was horrible to learn that the brewers of Britain plan to spend more than £2,000 million over the next three years on a facelift for our pubs. This gross extravagance is designed to lure back those customers who have defected to wine bars or who prefer to drink from 'six packs' in front of their television sets.

Although, I suspect, the perfect pub has always been easier to find in Dickens or in sentimental pre-war films than in real life, most pub-lovers carry about with them an image of their ideal.

Like so many elements of our natural life, the pub has gone from bad to worse during the past 25 years or so. Is it destined to follow the half-crown into limbo?

*Jeremy Lewis writing in
The Daily Telegraph, July 22, 1985*

Another aspect of the British way of life which has changed in recent years is the demise of the corner shop — not that the Withers' General Store lay on a corner!

Closing down this week-end after serving the locality for 46 years is the Withers' general store in Forest-road, Loughton.

Miss Grace Withers, who lives there with her sister, Miss Ethel Withers, and has run the business since her father, Mr. Edward Withers, died just before the last war, told the Gazette this week she was retiring.

Her family had moved from Tottenham to take over the shop in Forest-road in September, 1917.

Said Miss Withers, 'We have had some very nice customers and we are very grateful.

'As we could not buy as cheaply as the big supermarkets that have come along, we have not been able to sell some things as cheaply as them, but many of our customers have remained loyal to us.'

The Loughton Gazette, July 1963

Centre left and right: **No. 74 Forest Road in 1917;** *above* **Miss Grace Withers back in her old shop in 1985, now a private house.**

T.R.H. The Prince & Princess Of Wales

LOUGHTON'S FAMOUS VISITORS

1908: Their Royal Highnesses The Prince and Princess of Wales, later King George V and Queen Mary.

1923: The Duke and Duchess of York, later King George VI and Queen Elizabeth.

1944: Mr. and Mrs. Winston Churchill on King's Green.

Loughton at war. Tragedy at Habgood Road, where the Bedden family were killed by a direct hit on their Anderson shelter in the garden of No. 38 on April 19, 1944.

Girls from a local factory crowded round Mrs. Churchill when she paid an informal visit to the National Savings selling centre in Loughton High Road on Wednesday afternoon to buy a Defence Bond. As she stepped from the car Mrs. Churchill was welcomed by Mr. F. S. Foster, J.P., C.C., who conducted her across the road to the selling centre. After signing the visitors book, Mrs. Churchill asked to be introduced to all the people present, the various members of the National Savings Committee, W.V.S., and Chigwell councillors, etc., and as Mr. Foster started introducing them a whole lot of factory girls arrived and forming themselves into a long queue each in turn went up and shook hands with Mrs. Churchill, and when Mrs. Churchill, with Miss Anstey, Controller of Chigwell W.V.S., stood for the photographer, one of the girls rushed up and putting her arm through Mrs. Churchill's, had her photo taken at the same time.

Mrs. Churchill made a little speech in which she expressed her pleasure at seeing the women looking so happy and so full of the courage and determination which the whole country felt.

Three cheers were given for Mrs. Churchill and all joined in.

The Loughton Gazette, June 17, 1944

Women at war. The De La Rue company took over two of the empty shops in Brooklyn Parade which had been completed just prior to the outbreak of war. Mrs. Churchill came to Loughton to visit Civil Defence organisations in the area.

Dogs at war. The Light Rescue team photographed with their canine helpers in the yard of the Council offices in Old Station Road. Peter is fourth from the left next to Irma and Storm. Controller for Group 7 of the London Region of Civil Defence (which covered the eleven local authorities in Metropolitan Essex with headquarters at the New Town Hall, Forest Road, Walthamstow) was Frank Foster (later Sir Frank) on the left of the picture opposite with Mrs. Churchill.

The Dickin Medal, donated by the People's Dispensary for Sick Animals, is engraved with the words 'For gallantry, we also serve'. The colours of the ribbon are green, brown, and pale blue to symbolize valour on sea, land and sky. The animals' V.C., it was only awarded for exceptional bravery. . . .

Another amateur rescue dog, whose heroic work also won him a Dickin Medal, was a little mongrel called Rip, the mascot of the A.R.P. at Poplar. Having been found homeless and starving after a heavy raid in 1940, Rip obviously thought it was his duty to rescue others and was soon sniffing out casualties trapped under buildings. How welcome to the victims must have been the first sounds of those scrabbling paws and shrill terrier yaps, and the first sight of the grinning Tommy Brock face with its merry friendly eyes.

Such were Rip's and Beauty's fame that towards the end of the war the authorities decided to train dogs officially to trace casualties. Out of fourteen dogs who were posted to work in London, five of them — Jet, Irma, Peter, Thorn and Rex — all won Dickin Medals. The dog's worst fear in life is fire, which is why Londoners owe such a debt to their rescue dogs, who battled through blazing, collapsing buildings, choked by smoke, and often repeatedly sick from gas leaks.

Animals in War, Jilly Cooper, 1983

Here in Woodford Bridge Road over 3,000 pets are buried in the PDSA animal cemetery. The earliest records date from 1935 and amongst them we found those for our brave war dogs. Peter, awarded the Dicken Medal in 1945 for outstanding bravery, originally came from Birmingham. He died in November 1952 and lies in grave 569, unfortunately unmarked. Mrs Beatrice Cooke, who lovingly looks after the cemetery, showed us the spot. Here also lies Storm, who starred in two pre-war films and who was buried without fuss, a ceremony or even a mourner in July 1948. She won the DM as did her daughter, Irma, who lies buried with her in grave 196. The cemetery, which closed in 1964 for lack of space, also includes other animal heroes: Punch, DM, who served in Palestine; Mary, DM, the pigeon mortally wounded carrying messages . . . Simon, DM, the cat from HMS Amethyst of Yangtse River fame.

Top dog. Peter was a search and rescue dog who had an impressive record in finding air-raid victims who had been buried alive in bombed buildings. If the victim was still alive the dog would lie down quietly on the spot, but if the person was dead he would dig furiously into the rubble. The dog kennels were located where Brown's new car sales are now, beside Dr Pendred's house (page 301).

Chingford

In the Domesday Survey the manor of Chingford St. Paul is described as comprising six hides, and containing '50 acres of meadow, pannage for 500 hogs, two fisheries, nine beasts, two sumpter-horses, 27 hogs, and 100 sheep;' and it is also added that there were 'always four slaves.' The extent of the manorial rights were encroached upon both by Peter de Valoines and Geoffrey de Magnaville; and in a survey of the manor taken in 1245, we find it reduced to five hides.

Greater London, Edward Walford, 1883

Liza rushed into the room, and called to her mother, who was still asleep:

'Mother! mother! I'm going to Chingford!'

Then tearing off her old dress she slipped into her gorgeous violet one; she kicked off her old ragged shoes and put on her new boots. She brushed her hair down and rapidly gave her fringe a twirl and a twist — it was luckily still moderately in curl from the previous Saturday — and putting on her black hat with all the feathers, she rushed along the street, and scrambling up the brake steps fell panting on Tom's lap.

The coachman cracked his whip, the trumpeter tootled his horn, and with a cry and a cheer from the occupants, the brake clattered down the road.

Liza of Lambeth, Somerset Maugham, 1897

From Woodford, Chingford Lane runs down past the northern extremity of Highams Park (see page 203) to Chingford Hatch.

Hale End lies at the southern end of the Park. This is, or rather was, the keeper's cottage — then and now.

Chingford Hatch where Epping Forest's very own waterway, the Ching, crosses the road. The brook takes the excess from Connaught Water but the streams that feed the lake rise in the Forest below High Beach. Originally called the Bourne, the small river eventually has its outfall in the Lea. The Dun Cow inn stands on the left.

A 40-year-old relic of the past has found a final resting place — alongside a Chingford pub.

On Sunday two cranes gently lowered 'Gwen', a 26-seater coach from the famous Brighton Belle Pullman train, into position for a final 'coupling' to a 'waiting room' which is being built as a small lobby for customers at the Horseless Carriage.

Over the next few weeks the carriage will be completely refurbished and converted into a restaurant with a self-contained kitchen and a specially dressed staff in keeping with fashion of the Belle's heyday.

A big crowd of spectators had already gathered when the carriage arrived on a special transporter from Harlow having travelled up from Brighton the previous day.

'Gwen', who has yet to be finally restored to brown-and-cream livery, will be an added dining attraction to the pub and not an extension of the present restaurant facilities.

Walthamstow Guardian, May 9, 1975

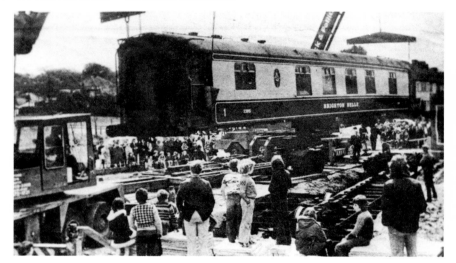

A chequered history for the pub at the bottom of Friday Hill. In 1834 William Peppercorn is listed as retailing pork and beer at the Hatch and his premises may well be the same as those which became the Dun Cow Hotel, first mentioned in 1851. By 1929 the old building *(top)* had been demolished, being replaced by The Manor Hotel, later renamed The Manor Arms. In 1965 Whitbreads sold the freehold to the London County Council, but leased back the property which they rebuilt and renamed the Horseless Carriage. The new pub was strikingly altered ten years later by the addition of one of the Pullmans from the Brighton Belle which was craned onto a short section of railway track laid on the forecourt. Used as an extension to the restaurant, it was removed in 1981 when the lease was transferred to Beefeater Steak Houses whereupon a new 'olde-worldy' extension was built on the spot and the name changed again to The Wheelwrights.

Chingford originally comprised of two manors: Chingford St Paul's in the north-western part of the parish and Chingford Earls in the south-east. The former, as its name implies, was held by the Dean and Chapter of St Paul's Cathedral for some 500 years, but by 1544 both manors had passed into the hands of King Henry VIII. He died three years later. In 1551 the young King Edward VI, then 14 years old, no doubt at the instigation of the scheming Duke of Northumberland, granted both the manors to Lord Darcy. However, the following year Darcy handed Chingford back to the King who passed the manor to his half-sister Princess Mary. Within a few months the young King had contracted tuberculosis and by May 1553, two months before his death, he drew up his will under Northumberland's influence to exclude both Mary and her sister Elizabeth, and instead put the Duke's daughter-in-law, Lady Jane, on the throne. As we know from our history books, Lady Jane Grey only ruled for nine days before Mary I became Queen. The following year she granted Chingford Manor to one of the widowed ladies of her bedchamber, Susan Tongue. Within four years Friday Hill House had become the new manor house, the name coming from a local family who lived in the area.

The legendary table which once graced the hall of Friday Hill House. In spite of an intensive search, its present whereabouts cannot be ascertained.

THE SIR-LOIN TABLE

There is now, or was lately, at Friday-hill House, in the parish of Chingford, the oak table upon which King Charles knighted the loin of beef. The house is in a large building, containing more than thirty rooms, and is in a dilapidated state, but has lately been repaired. Report has it that it was originally a hunting seat of Queen Elizabeth. The table is thick, and has a clumsy appearance: is made of English oak, and from the effects of time is a little decayed. Some of the knots of the wood have been lately taken out, and pieces of oak of the same age neatly let into it, and the top newly polished.

Press report, 1831

If the L.C.C. scheme succeeds, what is to become of Friday Hill House? Will this stately old English mansion be placed in the hands of the housebreakers or will it be converted into a recreation institute for the use of the people who will be housed in the cottage colony with reading rooms and libraries? The fate of this magnificent building with its characteristic Tudor lines should not be lightly decided upon.

Its present owner and occupant is Miss Boothby Heathcote, who was born there 83 years ago, and who has been identified with many charitable causes in Chingford since the days when it was an Essex village up to its present growth into a London suburb. Members of the Heathcote family have lived at Friday Hill in an ever-descending succession to Miss Heathcote since the childhood days of Queen Elizabeth, although the present house is the third to be erected on the site. The fate of the first mansion is obscure, but the second building was destroyed by fire about 100 years ago. The present mansion was built in 1839, and it is reputed to have been erected upon exactly similar lines to the house of Tudor times.

Centuries ago Friday Hill and Pimp Hall had many a Royal visitor, for hunting in Epping Forest was a popular Royal pastime in those days. In the fine panelled oak entrance hall to Friday Hill House stands a plain polished oak table on which it is stated:

'King James I, knighted the loin of beef. The quaint ceremony is claimed to have been performed at Pimp Hall, and the table bears the simple but illuminating inscription on a brass plate: "All lovers of roast beef will like to be informed that on this table the loin was knighted by King James I on his return from hunting in Epping Forest".'

From the early 1600s the manor has been held by the Boothby-Heathcote families. The Boothbys had tenure until 1774 when Robert left it to his half-sister Lydia, wife of John Heathcote. When the Reverend Robert Boothby-Heathcote, rector of Chingford, inherited the estate in 1838 he pulled down the old house (some reports state that it was destroyed by fire) and erected the present building to the design of Lewis Vulliamy. This drawing depicts the magnificent hall. Thereafter the manor descended with the Heathcotes until the death in 1940 of Louisa Heathcote, his last surviving child.

But that is not all. In the house is also preserved a panel from the Royal stage coach in which Queen Elizabeth drove to St. Paul's Cathedral to give thanks for the dispersion of the Armada. A blunderbus used by Dick Turpin hangs over the staircase, and the story is told that this ancient gun was discovered in Chingford Old Church where the famous highwayman once hid from his pursuers. It is said that he left the blunderbus behind when making a hurried escape from his own hiding place.

The house comprises 35 rooms, some of which are ornamented with exquisite oak carvings, charred in places during the fire of 100 years ago, from which they were saved. A magnificent piece of ornamental figure carving, reminiscent of the decorative work surrounding the altar in some English church, surmounts the fireplace near the main staircase. The house, with its lofty rooms, winding passageways, and complete absence of electric or gas fittings is one of the dignified old mansions of the kind which are fast disappearing in England. The handsome oil paintings, rare prints and delicately engraved metal work add lustre to its walls.

'I love everything that is old,' wrote Oliver Goldsmith. . . . They still use oil lamps at Friday Hill House.

Press report, February 21, 1936

Although the family owned around 600 acres in Chingford, much had been sold prior to the Second World War for building. The Friday Hill property was purchased by the London County Council who laid out a housing estate on it after the war. Today the house is used as Chingford Community Centre.

Friday Hill before and after development in the 1930s by Chingford Urban District Council, created a Borough in September 1938.

At the end of May last a completely new public house — the Sir Loin — was opened at Friday Hill, Chingford, Essex, by Mr. S. H. Combe, M.C., chairman of Messrs. Watney, Combe, Reid & Co. Ltd., London. It is situated in the middle of a new housing estate populated mostly by residents from Bethnal Green. The name of the house is unusual, but it is historic in the fact that on the opposite side of the road there was formerly a large country house known as 'Friday Hill House', used by King James I as a hunting lodge when he came to hunt in Epping Forest. The house was formerly the seat of the Heathcote family, and on a table in the front hall there was a brass plate on which was engraved 'All lovers of roast beef will like to be informed that on this table "the loin" was knighted by King James I on his return from hunting in Epping Forest'. At the opening ceremony Mr. Combe said it was thought appropriate that this episode should be perpetuated by naming the public house the Sir Loin.

Originally, on the present site was another large house known as 'Little Friday Hill House'. It was burnt down some hundred years ago and subsequently rebuilt. The London County Council bought the whole estate some years ago and the building was used as offices in connection with the new housing scheme. The licence for the new house was transferred from the Rising Sun at Lambeth, under the Licensing Planning Act, 1945, and Mr. Combe said he believed this was the first planning removal to a permanent building in the London area.

The Brewing Trade Review, July 1952

A major redevelopment programme is underway at the Sir Loin public house in Chingford.

It is the first time any structural alterations have been made since it opened on Friday Hill Estate in the early 1950s.

When they are completed later this year the governor, Neil Spanjar, hopes it will become one of the area's most attractive watering holes.

The main feature is the introduction of a children's room. This concept has become increasingly popular with breweries and provides comfortable and attractive places of safety where parents can leave their youngsters while enjoying a drink.

The alterations are planned in three phases. The first two are already started. Additional car-parking is being made possible by using part of the pub's extensive garden, with access from Normanton Park. This will give 30 extra bays. The present facilities will continue to be used, but made more attractive by landscaping.

Waltham Forest Gazette, January 25, 1985

The Barn, which still stands, saw many of Henry's revels, and one legend tells us that His Majesty, while standing in the Barn, heard the guns fire on Tower Green announcing the execution of Ann Boleyn, and straightaway left his revels to return to London where he married Jane Seymour next day.

The barn is 60 feet in length and has huge oak beams, some of which still hold their bark. They are pegged into the structure not nailed.

Pimp Hall was rebuilt in 1572 — and this date was impressed on the wall above the porch covered with plaster, but was not discovered until 1924 when the lease was held by Wallace Bolton. His family resided in the house from 1878 to September 1928 when they left on expiration of the lease from the Heathcotes of Friday Hill.

The house contained a secret passage and small room behind a chimney stack, which the builders found during the renovation in 1924. The room was six feet square and contained a lady's black stocking which fell to pieces when

---

SIRLOIN

King James the First of England
Rode forth one Christmastide
To hunt a gallant stag of ten,
Of Chingford Woods the pride.

The wind blew keen, the snow fell fast,
And made for earth a pall
As weary men and tired steeds
Returned to Friday Hall.

The blazing logs all on the dogs
Were pleasant to behold,
While grateful was the steaming feast
To hungry men and cold.

With right good will
All took their fill,
And soon all found relief,
While James his royal trencher filled
From one huge loin of beef.

'Odds fish', quoth James, 'a noble dish.
Ah, noble made by me.
By kingly right, I dub thee knight;
Sir Loin henceforward be.'

And never was a royal jest
Received with such acclaim;
And never knight than good Sir Loin
More worthy of the name.

Perpetuating a legend at the Sirloin, Friday Hill, although the original sign by John Turner which depicted James I was later changed to one bearing the likeness of Charles II! Little Friday Hill House was originally the residence of Miss Boothby-Heathcote's chauffeur and it was purchased by Watneys in 1952.

344

To the north of Friday Hill lay the manor of Pimps, also called Gowers and Buckerells after Sir John Gower and Stephen Buckerell, both early tenants. It was probably originally a free tenement held by the main manor and although it was occupied by several other families — the Rampstons, Hares, Barnsleys, Nodes, Gundrerys, Hammonds, Venours and Dents — it is with Reynold Pympe, who had it in the 1400s, that the name is more commonly associated.

brought into contact with the air. A further passage going past the chamber ended abruptly. Both passages led from a secret passage entered by a sliding panel in the bedroom over the dining room.

This room also boasted a rather weird happening on occasions. Despite the door at the top of the front stairs being locked and barred at night, sometimes the door would open and close and a ball of light would travel round the room, then disappear. An investigation showed that no outside light could be responsible because the level of the windows was lower than the roads nearby.

Other ghostly things happened to the residents at Pimp Hall. These things I have heard on the assurance of Mr. Frank Bolton, of Victoria-road, Chingford, whose father was the last tenant of the farm. In the bedroom over the dairy was a bloodstained floor, and according to local talk a murder had been committed in that room sometime during the farm's history. A grey cloaked lady in Victorian costume walked at night and many members of the Bolton family, including Mr. Frank Bolton, have seen her. Also strangers entertained for a night in the bedroom above the hall had come down to breakfast next

morning white-faced, and declaring that someone constantly breathed on their faces in the night.

On the lower floor of Pimp Hall Farm near the Dovecot a 'digging for tunnel' bid was carried out by Mr. Frank Bolton's two brothers in approximately 1925, while he stood by and watched.

His brothers dug behind the Dovecot down to about 20 feet. They found various solid walls and the bricked up entrance of a tunnel leading to Friday Hill House cellars, this having been bricked up by Edward Bolton, their grandfather, during the nineteenth century when it became too dangerous to be used.

The dovecot contained stabling for three horses under the hay loft, and both it and the barn are the only parts of the farm left standing.

The property was bought by London County Council for the start of the Friday Hill housing estate, the grounds of the farm covering approximately 20 acres of land. The house was left deserted, and began to rot and fall down, so the Council demolished it in the interests of safety after the Second World War.

The beautiful elm drive has mainly gone, but a few trees remain, and these together with the barn and the dovecot are the only reminders Chingford has of a farmhouse with a history.

Elizabeth Hayes

An historic empty barn in Chingford will be transformed into an agricultural and folk museum now that a £137,000 project has been given the green light.

Tithe Barn, at Pimp Hall, off King's Road, is a 16th century legacy which will be revamped and turned into a unique facility of great value to the area.

The project was proposed by the Community Programme Agency in Walthamstow, and will provide work for at least 24 people. The agency hopes that work will start on Monday.

The funding for the project comes mainly from the Manpower Services Commission, with a £20,000 'good faith' contribution from Waltham Forest.

The CPA has budgeted for a year. The money covers the cost of all materials and equipment and also wages of the plumbers, roofers, tilers and carpenters who will be employed on the project.

Pimp Hall farmhouse was a two-storey building, timber-framed and plastered, dating from the late 16th century.

It became derelict and was gradually demolished during 1936-9, but the timber-framed barn and dovecote survive — an echo of the 16th century way of life.

In 1978-9, money was spent restoring the dovecote because it was unstable. And now the CPA has selected Tithe Barn for a project of restoration also.

Project Director, Ron Harle said: 'At the moment the barn is just standing there with rubbish in it. But when we have finished it will once again look like a 16th century barn.

'It will be of great benefit to the community as it will attract a lot of attention nationwide, and will be a good place for students to visit.'

And Terry Robinson, Operations Manager, described the work of the CPA as 'restoring yesterday for tomorrow, bringing community benefit.'

The Community Programme Agency, in Hoe Street, is an MSC funded organisation which has been going for more than two years.

It takes long-term unemployed people and puts them back into work for a year, enhancing their prospects of future employment.

Yellow Advertiser, August 9, 1985

The main part of the sixteenth-century Pimp Hall farm was demolished 1936-39, leaving the barn, used until recently by Waltham Forest Council for storage, and the dovecote empty.

In case readers wonder why such a large building was provided to keep birds, in the Middle Ages doves were bred for the table and their droppings used to make gunpowder!

In the year of our Lord, 1950, during the hot spell of early June, I alighted from a 38 bus and sat down on a seat by the roadside at Chingford Green.

The church clock had just commenced striking the noonday hour, and I leaned back for a short rest before starting my walk towards the forest. Before the second stroke from the clock, something in my mind seemed to give way. Time had slipped back 55 years and found me gazing on a scene familiar to my boyhood days.

On the further side of the road was a tall, thick-set hedge, behind which was an old half-timbered farmhouse. At the left end of the hedge, and a little out of its alignment, stood the village smithy. The blacksmith, an old man of almost superhuman strength and

The 'new' church of St Peter and St Paul was dedicated in 1844. Designed by Lewis Vulliamy.

physique, was outside, shoeing a horse, and from inside the forge came the unmistakable sound of roaring bellows and a hammer beating out the shape of a horseshoe on the anvil.

In 1885 Jones Forge stood alongside Tile House Farm in Maddox Lane facing the Green. Now it's the site of this row of shops, the name of the road slowly falling into disuse as Station Road gained prominence after 1878.

My line of vision then turned to the right of the hedge, and I was looking at the quaint old-world inn, known as the Bull and Crown, with a little grocer's shop alongside. It was in the early days of the Chingford Urban District Council, and a well-known local itinerant trader, who went by the name of 'Toby,' was standing in his cart in front of the inn, addressing a small audience on the merits of two candidates for election — Messrs. Brown and Herring.

After describing in glowing terms the everlasting benefit it would be to the village community if these two gentlemen were returned, he concluded his oration with the words: 'Remember the names, gentlemen, and if you do forget, think of the supper awaiting you to-night — "brown bread and herrings." '

A remarkable man, a reincarnation of his namesake, 'Uncle Toby' in Laurence Sterne's *Tristam Shandy*. The words fell on my ears, as it were, from one long since departed. I made a half-turn and by my side sat a man in holy orders, our curate, the Rev. W. T. Dyne.

He asked me if I knew it was correct that Toby's son, William, had been awarded the Royal Humane Society's certificate for saving life, and I was able to assure him that such was a fact. He had rescued a boy from drowning in the River Lea, near Flanders Wier, and Police-sgt Traveller had interested himself in the case and recommended William for the honour.

A slight commotion of children's voices at the rear of the seat caused me to turn my head, and on the village green I saw a huge brown bear. The animal was secured by a chain, muzzled, and in charge of two men.

The bear was standing on its hind legs and performing grotesque movements in obedience to certain crude military words of command from one of the men. The children's hilarity was unbounded, but I knew that later on their delight would change to consternation when, after the men and bear had passed on to the next village, rumour would get abroad

that the bear had escaped and was roaming the countryside.

The church clock was now giving out the final resonant note, proclaiming mid-day. The striking mechanism had come to rest and, as one emerging from the darkness of a bygone age, I turned to speak to the curate, but he had vanished.

From a short distance away I heard a voice, in a pronounced Cockney accent, calling aloud: 'Bull and Crown. Here you are, sir; mind the step, lady'.

I opened my eyes and before me stood a 102 bus, and where, in my day-dreams, I had seen the thick-set hedge, I was looking on a row of shops, owned by the Enfield Co-operative Society.

Some stretch of imagination must be exercised to recognise the Chingford of to-day contrasted with village life in the last century,

Before the days of photography it was The Bull Head, the road being called Bull Lane. In 1901 the street was renamed King's Road in honour of Edward VII who was crowned that year. The present French château-type architecture dates from 1899.

but the old scenes, manners and traditions still linger as romantic recollections in the minds of its few remaining inhabitants.

The characters referred to or mentioned by name in this article are no longer living, with the exception of one, 'Young William.' He is now an old man, and his most cherished possession is a framed vellum certificate for saving life presented to him by the Royal Humane Society.

A Glimpse of Old Chingford, W. J. Maine

The various 'Greens' which are to be found in the Epping Forest area are just as much a part of the Forest proper as the woodland. Chingford Green, seen *above* in the 1890s, is a good example. When the Corporation of the City of London, acting as commoners in view of its ownership of the cemetery beside Wanstead Flats, fought the case against the enclosure of the Forest, there followed a period whereby the Corporation systematically purchased all the remaining Forest waste — those areas of uncultivated land of the eighteen Forest manors. The Act of 1878 restored illegally enclosed land which had not then been built upon but exempted enclosures made before August 14, 1851. Any other land within the area of the Forest as it was in 1641 was automatically included. The pond beside the lock-up facing King's Green was filled in in 1896.

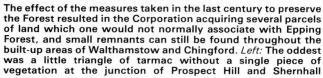

The effect of the measures taken in the last century to preserve the Forest resulted in the Corporation acquiring several parcels of land which one would not normally associate with Epping Forest, and small remnants can still be found throughout the built-up areas of Walthamstow and Chingford. *Left:* The oddest was a little triangle of tarmac without a single piece of vegetation at the junction of Prospect Hill and Shernhall Street. It remained part of the Forest until October 1955 when it was exchanged with the Borough for land elsewhere. *Right:* Most unusual today is probably the stretch of greensward which lies outside Walthamstow greyhound stadium, which together with a number of other odd pieces of roadside verge throughout Chingford are still classed as parts of Epping Forest.

Station Road has seen little outward change — only the fashions and methods of transport belie the passing of 80 years.

Chingford is a very scattered parish, and apparently the chief population has drifted away from its former centre, as the old church stands far away from the abodes of man, except one old farmhouse and the vicarage. Its site is high, for Essex at least. In 1871 the number of the inhabitants was about 1,250, but during the next decade it had increased to nearly 1,400. This increase may be partly accounted for by the fact that since 1874 Chingford has been in direct railway communication with London, the forest branch of the Great Eastern Railway having been in that year opened, with its terminus near the new church at Chingford Green. Here are located the largest number of houses forming the village; others are at Forest Side, about half a mile eastward, and others again form the hamlet of Chingford Hatch.

Greater London, Edward Walford, 1883

When Chingford Urban District Council was created on January 1, 1895, it was here in a rented shop at No. 34 Station Road that it set up its first 'Town Hall'.

Amazingly this sufficed for 32 years until 1927 when the Council approached the Government for permission to borrow £11,500 to construct a purpose-designed Town Hall, as befitted the expanding district, at this site *(left)* on The Ridgeway. It was opened by Brigadier-General R. B. Colvin, Lord-Lieutenant of Essex, on December 12, 1929.

When the Bishop of Chelmsford (the Right Rev. Dr. Wilson) spoke recently of the desirability of incumbents of parishes where P.o.W camps are situated providing for the spiritual welfare of their inmates, the Rev. J. E. Howell, the Catholic priest in Chingford, where there are 400 Germans behind barbed wire, had already been visiting the camp regularly for several months. The prisoners also are visited by their own Lutheran pastors.

The first newspaper correspondent to have been allowed by the authorities inside the camp, where he was given complete freedom to speak to the men, our reporter was impressed by their good behaviour and by the orderliness which was evident everywhere.

Veterans of the Russian front, Italy, the Africa Corps, North-West Europe and the Channel Isles, the prisoners, who for the past 18 months have been working on building sites in the district, have constructed an excellent little church.

Flanking the altar are two imitation stained-glass windows, surmounted by a reredos skilfully painted in bright blue, with a crucifix hanging centrally. The floor is concreted in squares of white and pink, and the Communion rail and pews are of stained wood. Electric chandeliers are suspended from the roof. The small wooden tower and belfry houses a single bell, tolled before the Sunday services. . . .

The Woodford Guardian, September 6, 1946

From 1855 onwards the Crown was disposing of its forest rights for £5 per acre and by the 1860s both Richard Hodgson and the Reverend Robert Heathcote had taken up and enclosed Chingford Plain. The land was ploughed up and cultivated but the Conservators reinstated the former arable land. In 1888 a public golf course was laid out on the Plain originally extending across Bury Road, but it was realigned in 1954/5 entirely on the western side of the road. An interruption occurred during the last war when an Army camp was built on the part of the course alongside Forest View to house crews for the nearby anti-aircraft battery.

Later in the war it was converted into a prisoner of war camp, the prisoners constructing this makeshift church, sited on the 1st fairway, just opposite the Loretto Convent occupied by Dominican Nuns during the war. Mother Teresa would play her piano with the window open to the delight of the prisoners who were employed on site preparation and house building in the Chingford and Chigwell areas. When the Germans left, the buildings provided temporary accommodation for children from St Paul's School, Woodford Wells before work began to reinstate the golf course in 1951. This was completed by March 1953, the unique camp church being demolished in the process, yet odd foundations, too difficult to remove, still survive.

A petition signed by 2,200 people was presented to Chingford Council this week urging them to save the local beauty spot, Pole Hill, for the public. The Council scheduled the area as an open space under the Town Planning Act. . . . Councillor Smith said before they scheduled the land there were two points to consider — would the Forest authorities accept the land, and also would the owner sell at a reasonable price? Under the Town Planning Act, land required for a park or recreation ground could not be acquired compulsorily. The owner of Pole Hill, Colonel Lawrence, was in India and would not be back before 1934, when he wanted to build a house there in addition to the one he already had.

Councillor Restall said the longer they were in dealing with the land, the more likelihood there was of it slipping away, because there was a possibility of houses being built on the verge of that lovely position.

Leytonstone Express & Independent, December 10, 1927

Councillor Miss M. L. Mathieson, J.P., presided at a special meeting of Chingford Council on Tuesday evening at the Council Offices, when it was decided to accept the offer of Colonel Lawrence and purchase the land at Pole Hill.

The Chairman reported on the interview of the Town Planning Committee with Mr. A. Crump, solicitor on behalf of his client Mr. T. E. Shaw (Colonel Lawrence) concerning the land at Pole Hill. The cost would be £4,450 and legal costs.

Councillor Stoneham asked the exact acreage of the land.

The Chairman: Between fifteen and sixteen acres.

The Chairman remarked that Mr. Shaw was offering the Council the land at the same price at which he bought it. It was a generous public-spirited offer and he was making no profit out of it. He bought it in the first place to save it.

Leytonstone Express & Independent, July 13, 1929

Chingford, Queen Boadicea's Obelisk on Pole Hill.

To the schoolboy of the inter-war years, no greater adventurous character had ever lived during the Great War than Colonel T. E. Lawrence. Hailed by the newspapers of the period as the Uncrowned King of Arabia, his exploits fired popular imagination and numerous books and articles described his battles with the Arab army against the Turks. His subsequent enlistment in the RAF in 1922 under an assumed name all added fuel to the legend. That the legend has its roots in Chingford is something of which we can justly be proud. Lawrence had been born in Tremadoc, Caernarvonshire, in 1888 and in 1896 the family moved to Oxford. While at Jesus College he met and became firm friends with Vyvyan Richards who in 1909 came to teach at Bancroft's School. Lawrence was a frequent visitor, at least as far as his foreign travels would permit, and would camp under canvas with Scouts and cadets on Pole Hill, overlooking Chingford Plain. When Richards proposed in 1912

that they construct a permanent hut on the hill, Lawrence was more than enthusiastic. 'Yes the Epping scheme', he wrote to Richards, 'a superb idea'. So attached to the place had he become that in September 1919, on the day he left the Army, Lawrence purchased some five acres of the hill: the whole 'upper field', enlarging over the following five years by further purchases. That first parcel lay just to the south-west of the Greenwich obelisk, *(above)* erected on the hill-top in 1824. Its purpose was to act as an azimuth mark for a new telescope being installed at Greenwich but it was abandoned in 1836. When the line of zero longitude was established by international agreement in 1884 it was found that the true course of the Greenwich meridian lay nineteen feet to the east of the obelisk. Because of its war-like spearhead, it came to be romantically linked with Queen Boadicea as marking the site of one of her battles!

Subject to approval of the plans, the Ministry of Health has given permission to Chingford Urban Council to spend £200 to provide a memorial on Pole Hill, Chingford, to Lawrence of Arabia, who owned the site for about 10 years after the war. The whole of the hill, about 14 acres, now belongs to the public and was added to Epping Forest lands three years ago.

Press report, 1932

As Conservators of Epping Forest the City of London Corporation is to be asked to change the name of Pole Hill, Chingford, to

Lawrence Hill, or to employ the name so that it shall perpetually commemorate the association of 'Lawrence of Arabia' with the mound. Alternatively, there is a suggestion that the name should not be altered, but that the Conservators' consent be requested for a tablet to be placed on the hillock to the memory of the late Col. Lawrence, or Aircraftsman Shaw, as he was generally known when he lived at Chingford. The base of Pole Hill is level with the Ridgeway, which approximately is level with the dome of St. Paul's Cathedral. From the top of the hill there are magnificent views. In the Great War Pole Hill was an anti-aircraft station, and

after the war Shaw lived there and acquired the freehold of the sixteen surrounding acres. About six years ago Chingford Urban Council opened negotiations with him, and he sold the hill to them for £4,450 and the hut for £350, the amounts in each case being exactly what he had paid for the property. When deciding not to make any profit out of the transaction he especially stipulated that the hill should become part of the Forest, and in due course the Council transferred the hill to the Conservators in exchange for pieces of Forest land.

Press report, 1935

In 1921 a grass fire completely destroyed Richards' hut but by the end of the following year a larger replacement had been erected with the help of boys from Bancroft's. This was the year that Lawrence enlisted in the RAF under the name of John Ross and he was already contemplating that the actual printing of his massive account of his Arabian adventures 'The Seven Pillars of Wisdom' would be carried out in the building on Pole Hill. However, in 1923, having been forced to leave the RAF because of publicity, he attempted to escape the attentions of the press by joining the Royal Tank Corps in Dorset, later returning to the RAF under the name of Shaw. In 1924 he took a cottage at Moreton, where he suffered his fatal motor-cycle accident in May 1935. When Vyvyan Richards left Bancrofts in 1922 to live in South Wales, the link with the Epping Forest area was severed. The 1st Highams Park Rover Scouts used his building but when Lawrence sold his land to the Conservators via Chingford Council in 1929, it fell prey to vandals, and was dismantled and re-erected at The Warren at Loughton about 50 years ago.

Although money was set aside for the purpose, sadly it appears that nothing came of the proposal to erect the memorial or rename Pole Hill. Instead the name 'Lawrence Hill' was given to a road near Mansfield Park in 1938 and 'Arabia Close' to a cul-de-sac near the Hill in 1965.

Camels over Chingford. During the First World War No. 56 Wing headquarters was located 'at Whitehall, Chingford' under No. 1 (Training) Group for the South-East Area. (No. 7 Balloon Wing, under Home Defence, actually had its HQ in the Royal Forest Hotel from December 1917 to June 1919.) The small grass aerodrome was located in the right-angle formed by Low Street (since 1934 Sewardstone Road) and Lea Valley Road, and bordered on its western perimeter by a tributary of the Lea.

Early in 1915 we moved to new quarters at Chingford . . . The one drawback, and I am not sure it really was a drawback, was the smallness of the airfield. It was even smaller than Brooklands and was surrounded by a reservoir, streams and swamps. Though it had its advantages, in that pupils were forced to learn how to land in a restricted area, I was nevertheless surprised that it had been chosen as an airfield. . . .

It was only a few days later that Ince, a young Canadian, stopped his prop while coming in to land in a J.N.4 Curtiss. Not wishing to call out a mechanic, as he was some distance from the sheds, he got out and swung the propellor himself — forgetting to close the throttle. For the first time, I imagine, in the history of the Curtiss engine, this one started straight away and revved up. After knocking Ince over, the machine then proceeded to take off on its own. Flying down the centre of the aerodrome about ten feet up, it made a gentle right-hand turn with exactly the correct amount of bank and flew over the brook. Then, as if prompted by some devilish whim, it suddenly turned straight for the armament store. The armament store was full of bombs and fuses, and the plane caught it fair and square in the middle. There were about 100 people on the aerodrome, and, when the plane hit the store, they flattened themselves on the ground with their hands over their ears like a pack of cards. But the machine was the only thing that exploded! . . .

One of the best photographs I still retain of this period is of Flight-Lieut. Norman W. C. Blackburn's crash at Chingford. This Blackburn, brother of the pioneer Blackburn, stalled at a good 1,000 feet, nose-dived and crashed into the bank of the reservoir with his tail in the air. His engine was buried 5 feet in the ground. Everyone ran out expecting to find a crumpled body in the wreckage, but, though the seats were concertinaed, there was no sign of a body. We thought he must have

been catapaulted into the reservoir and just as some of us were preparing to dive into the water a shout came from the road on the other side of the aerodrome. It was from Blackburn. Dripping with water and slime, he was calmly walking back after his 'ducking'.

That Chingford reservoir, like the sewage farm at Brooklands, could have told many a strange story. So often, in fact, did our pilots and their machines make its acquaintance, that we found it wise to keep a boat permanently moored there in readiness.

First Through the Clouds, F. W. Merriam

The aerodrome played an important training role for the Royal Naval Air Service with No. 155 Squadron (Bombers) and No. 138 Squadron (Fighters) at what was called in 1918 No. 207 Training Depot Station. It was a non-operational equipment depot from January-December 1919 and the newly-formed Royal Air Force used it as a Photographic Experimental and Design Section.

In 1893 a scheme for a chain of reservoirs to be constructed in the flood plain of the Lea was prepared by William Bryan, the engineer at the East London Water Works. Originally it was proposed to dam the complete river valley but this was considered too drastic and the modified scheme involved the building of reservoirs with earth ramparts, lined with concrete to prevent erosion. Work commenced on the first in 1908, King George V pressing the button to start the pumps to begin filling the reservoir from the Lea. The old river itself disappeared, its flow being channelled along aquaducts on either side.

Work on the second reservoir on the south side of Lea Valley Road, which would completely cover the old aerodrome and 334 acres of land, was not begun until 1935. During the excavation a Bronze Age coffin was uncovered and taken to the London Museum in Lancaster House but was unfortunately destroyed during the Blitz. The war also interrupted construction work and delays were experienced from landslides. Thus it was not until September 4, 1951 that Mr William Girling, chairman of the Metropolitan Water Board, inaugurated the reservoir which now bears his name.

The Metropolitan Water Board considered in private on Friday the arrangements to be made on the occasion of the opening by the King of the new Chingford reservoir, which is being constructed in the Lea Valley. It will hold over three thousand million gallons, the water surface being 416 acres in extent; the pumps will be capable of dealing with 180 million gallons of water each day; three and a quarter million tons of earth will be comprised in the embankments, and the cost of construction will be about £350,000

An estimate of £4,000 was approved in connection with the opening. A draft of the programme assumes that the King will proceed to and from the reservoir by road, and that the ceremony itself should take place at the northern end of the reservoir, where the power house and pumps are situate, and where the turning of the water into the reservoirs could most conveniently be performed.

His Majesty has intimated to the Metropolitan Water Board that he will be pleased to visit Chingford on March 15 to open the new reservoir. The King will be accompanied by the Queen, and the Royal route to the scene will include one of the principal East-end thoroughfares with probably an alternative route for the return journey.

Press report, February 1903

On Saturday, May 17, Their Majesties, the King and Queen drove through the City and East London to Chingford, where the King inaugurated the new reservoir of the Metropolitan Water Board.

Their Majesties received everywhere a most loyal greeting. At the City boundary they were received by the Lord Mayor and Sheriffs in state, and in the Eastern suburban districts the King was presented with and replied to seven addresses.

Press report, May 1913

A tunnel nearly 19 miles long carrying water from the Thames to the Metropolitan Water Board reservoirs in this area was inaugurated today by the chairman of the board, Mr. L. R. Webster. He pressed a button to start water pumping into a reservoir from the tunnel main in a shaft 70 feet below the ground.

The 8ft. 6in. tunnel has been driven in 10 years at an average depth of about 100ft. through the London clay at a cost of about £5m. It will bring unfiltered water from the river at Hampton, Middlesex, to the Lee Valley, where it will be purified to provide a domestic supply to east London.

For many years the water supply to east London had caused anxiety during periods of less than average rainfall because the demands from the densely populated and highly industrialized area had outstripped the resources available from the River Lea.

The Times, September 28, 1960

Lost forever under the waters: Flanders Wier on the Lea near Priory Avenue.

353

Chingford, Essex. — There is no harm in Frearson, the late London butcher, going to Waltham Abbey Market, on a Friday, but it would be more to his credit to return home like another tradesman in the evening, and not leave his half-starved horse tied to a gate for two hours together. Is this the reason why Miss P. has discontinued to receive his visits? If this young man does not mend his ways, we shall take him in hand. Sending his poor horse to Leicester for his friends to keep is very discreditable; he ought to have paid the man belonging to Deacon's waggon the 22s according to agreement.

There is no harm in bloated Hayton having a small tinker's shop, built in the front of his garden, and which he says is only for amusement, but it would be quite as well if he was not to talk so much of living retired, and of his independent circumstances. We hope to hear soon that he has paid all his old standing debts in Shoreditch, and how was it he left that spot? His language (when drunk) is most disgusting, and his manners are equally indecent. Reform this or we will compel you.

There is no harm in Goldacre (not Greenacre), landlord of the King's Head, doing all the busines he can, but why does he frequent the tap-room, and drink and play all manner of low games with the queer characters who frequent his house? If the police extended to this place, your license would be in danger. Be advised, Mr. G., stick to civility, and be more careful.

We have a lengthy list of worthies connected with this place, and as our limits will permit, our duty will be to give their real character.

We advise Mr. Baker, Fit Sam, Turkey Burriel, Boasting Tinker, and the steeple chase Butcher, to look out — "Breakers ahead."

Press announcement. 1840

The war memorial to men of Chingford who fell in the Great War has been erected on a piece of Forest land given by the Epping Forest Committee, and it commemorates the loss of 240 sons from the Forest district. It is in the form of a great Celtic cross, and is of unusual size and beauty. The work of a local designer, Mr. W. A. Lewis, it is composed of Cornish granite, and stands on a double-stepped pedestal. Within sight of the beautiful Chingford Church, it faces green and woodland which would be the special memories of the young men whose names are engraved on the sides of the stone. The inscription reads: 'In grateful remembrance of the men of Chingford who died in the service of their country in the Great War, 1914-1918. 'We are the dead . . . To you, from failing hands, we throw the torch; Be yours to hold it high.' The arrangements for the memorial were made by a committee, with Mr. Harry Jones as chairman and Mr. H. Bartlett as hon. sec.

The memorial was formally unveiled and dedicated on Saturday, in the presence of a great assembly, by Lord Lambourne, Lord-Lieutenant of Essex, and the Bishop of

Several famous names were in the RNAS at Chingford, amongst them the English dramatist Ben Travers and Ivor Novello. The actor cum film star and composer of 'Keep the Home Fires Burning' would often travel up the hill to the King's Head where he played the piano for servicemen, and he is also believed to have entertained troops at nearby Sewardstone Lodge, a military hospital during the Great War. Harold Owen, the brother of the poet Wilfred Owen, was also stationed there.

King's Head Hill naturally took its name from the inn which has stood at the top of the road since at least 1782. The building opposite originally housed Chingford's Post Office and before the Second War was the location of Pracy's sweetshop, beloved of schoolchildren, especially from St Egbert's College. St Egbert's, on The Ridgeway, was taken over during the war as a civil defence depot for the rescue service, stretcher parties, and later for crews from the ambulance service and mobile first aid posts.

The small piece of 'Forest' land facing the King's Head was made available for Chingford's War Memorial, unveiled on September 24, 1921 by Lord Lambourne who, as we have seen, had unveiled Loughton's memorial the previous year. The old police station can be seen on the right. (See also page 86.)

Chelmsford. The ceremony began with a procession from the Parish Church to the memorial, led by the band of the 7th Essex Regt. (T.F.). The procession was composed of clergy, the Memorial Committee, Chingford Urban Council, ex-Servicemen, firemen, special constables, Boy Scouts, and relatives and friends of the fallen. At the memorial the hymn, 'O God, our help in ages past', was sung. The Rector of Chingford, the Rev. A. M. Batty, prayed, and the Rev. H. J. Gamble, Congregational minister, read a passage of Scripture.

Following the unveiling, Lord Lambourne said it was a matter of great pleasure to those who loved their country that in nearly every town and village in Essex there was a memorial cross on the road or green. That was not only a memorial to those who had died, but it was an emblem of our Christian religion. These men would have died in vain had not God directed our efforts and given us the victory over our enemies. We remembered how in the darkest days of the war a great

religious feeling spread over the land — and we were saved. As these men had conquered the foreign enemy, so we had to conquer at home misery, suffering, poverty, and especially the want of religion in the land. If we asked God's help He would make this nation greater than any nation which ever lived.

The Bishop of Chelmsford, who dedicated the Cross, said that great array of names had a great lesson for them all. Looking at what was going on this country, it almost seemed as if these men were saying, 'We tried to save England, but you will not let us'. To-day the people were running amok and seemed to have lost the greater ideals which animated them during the war. There was a spirit of grabbing and grasping on the part of nearly every section of the community. The spirit for

which the Cross stood was the good of the community, and that should come home to everyone who looked at it. Alluding to the terrible unemployed problem, the Bishop said those who had fought for the country should be able to live in comfort and should not have the misery of unemployment at their door. He urged them to maintain the spirit and the ideals with which they fought the war. Let everyone take up the cross of doing something voluntarily for the common good and the glory of God.

The 'Last Post' was sounded by buglers, and the Bishop pronounced the Blessing. Floral tributes placed at the foot of the cross by relatives of the men formed a beautiful mass of flowers.

Walthamstow Guardian, September 30, 1921

So the Old Church became unsafe. It was decided to leave it as a 'picturesque ruin'. Men left the old love and turned to the new one on the Green. Picturesque the Old Church may have been; a ruin it certainly became. The eighty years following 1844 are a sad story in the history of this old House of God. The ivy rioted in profusion and smothered the building, crushing it like the tentacles of an octopus. (Dr Cox records that an ivy stem against the buttress on the north side was 33 inches from one side to the other. Of two stems on the Tudor Porch, one had a girth of 27 inches, and the other of 24 inches.) The 'Green Church', men came to call it — it was so covered with vegetation. The glass dropped out of the windows. Birds and bats flew in and out. Mr. Kemp resident in Clapton since 1869, told the writer in September, 1930 how he had been fond of walking to Chingford Old Church on a moonlit night and looking in through the paneless window at two balls of fire on the beam across the chancel. They were the eyes of an owl!

In 1880 the Parish Church on the Green was closed for two months for repairs and all services were held in the ruined Old Church. But marriages were not allowed. Evening services were held by Canon Russell in the ruins on the first Sunday in the months of June, July, August and September in the years 1884-89. Crowds came to them and seats had to be placed outside near the paneless windows for those who could not be accommodated within. It was a weird experience. Mr. Bruce Cook, Headmaster of the Church School 1889-1925, recalls it. The birds venting their suprise at the disturbance of their peace; the crowds passing up and down the Mount on their way to and from the Forest; folks returning to Tottenham, after a ramble, by the public path which ran through the churchyard; the sound of hymns and prayers floating out of the dank, smelly building through the glassless windows, will not easily be forgotten by those who took part. In 1889 the roof had to be shored up, and in 1890 the building was thought to be unsafe and the services were abandoned. They were the Swan Song of the Old Church. The silence of decay and death settled on the once holy place. In her dying throes she excited much pity. Her fine situation, her pathetic decay, touched chords in many hearts. From near

One of the most fascinating facets of the history of the village is that surrounding the old church. Standing on the prominence of The Mount, All Saints has been a feature of the Chingford scene since Norman times. The church which stands today was originally built about 1270 but it has been extensively altered and added to over the centuries. The tower was erected about 1400. Extensive repairs were necessary in the next century and the roof was replaced. In the seventeenth century the south wall of the aisle was raised and as a result the line of the sloping roof was broken, with a separate low-pitched roof covering the loftier aisle creating a vulnerable valley gutter in the hollow formed by the two roofs, where water and leaves could build up. Ivy was allowed to climb the walls and roof — hence its nickname 'the green church' — and subsidence made the building dangerous. By the 1840s its deterioration was so advanced that it was considered beyond repair, and it was decided to build a new church on the Green (see page 346).

and far they came to visit her. Artists, skilled and unskilled, drew and painted her. As many as seven have been seen at work at one time. Devotees of the new art of photography climbed the Mount with their cumbrous cameras. Periodicals and magazines continually reproduced pictures of the well-known ruin.

But the end was not yet. Like King Charles II, she was an unconscionable time a-dying. At last, in March 1904, the roof of the nave fell in, crushing in its fall the beautiful thirteenth-century arcade, and badly wrenching the chancel arch, and giving a further push to the Tudor porch. Messrs. Foster and Sons, of Loughton, were employed

Chingford old church has had many dedications over the years, but locals have usually referred to it as All Saints. After the new church had been built, the old increasingly fell into a picturesque ruin, much illustrated by artists and photographers, like the study on pages 338-339. In 1904, part of the roof collapsed, completing the scene of desolation.

'Old Church Road, a dusty highway leading up to the ruin on the Mount.' Cherrydown Farm on the left. Lewis & Company on the right catered for the cemetery facing the church established on the site of Mount Farm in 1884.

themselves a cosy gambling den in the old Tudor porch, a piece of panelling from the chancel forming the table which was supported by some of the old stones. Some of the heavy gravestones of the chancel floor had been smashed in the effort to raise them to get at the lead coffins beneath — fortunately without success. Many were frankly sceptical of the possibility of saving the Church. Not so the architect, Mr. C. C. Winmill, F.R.I.B.A. An Essex man by birth, he had made his first drawing as an articled clerk in 1886. It was Chingford Old Church. After forty-two years, he was now to return to his first work, to which he brought ripe experience, trained taste, careful attention to detail and an incurable enthusiasm. Miss L. G. Boothby-Heathcote, of Friday Hill, daughter of the Rector of 1844, eventually undertook the financial responsibility. The architect estimated £6,000, and it is a tribute to Mr. Winmill's care and efficiency, that, in spite of many unknown adverse circumstances, he had only exceeded his figure by £40 when he had completed his task.

The Story of Chingford Old Church,
Reverend C. B. H. Knight, 1932

With the cost of repairs generously underwritten by Miss Louisa Boothby-Heathcote, the remarkable reconstruction of All Saints took place between 1928-30.

to clear away the debris, but they cannot tell the writer what happened to the material so removed. No beams or rafters of the old roof were found in 1928, nor any of the old tiles, and very little of the stones of the pillars and arches of the arcade. Something was done to preserve the chancel. Its roof was retiled. Mural tablets were moved into this chancel. The three seventeenth-century ones of the Leigh family had been removed to the new Church when it was enlarged in 1903. All windows were bricked up. It was a ruin indeed.

When the work of reconstruction was taken in hand, the task was enough to daunt the most optimistic architect. The south wall was crumbling and was nearly two feet out of the perpendicular. The beautiful thirteenth-century arch in the south wall had recently collapsed and lay crushed under a pile of masonry. Cracks were everywhere. The chancel arch was dangerous. The space inside was an indescribable scene of desolation, weeds, shrubs, saplings. Children for years had made it a playground and boys found a tempting target in the open vizor above a mural tablet in the chancel. Men had made

A letter has been sent this week to the Ministry of Health by Chingford Antiquarian and Historical Society.

It urges that a decision on the Compulsory Purchase Order Chingford Council want applied to a piece of land in North Chingford — including Gomme's Farm — be delayed until new facts which have a direct bearing are presented by the Society to the Ministry.

A petition has been organized by the Antiquarian Society and will, it is estimated, bear the signatures of 2,000 local residents when completed.

Actual wording of the petition is: 'We, the undersigned, being residents and ratepayers of the Borough of Chingford, desire to make further protest to the Council against any property known as Gomme's Farm as being both habitable and of local historic interest.'

Over 40 petition sheets have been circulated and among those which have already been returned to the Society secretary is one bearing 70 signatures while other sheet-totals do not fall far behind.

Commented Mr. A. L. Martin, secretary of the Antiquarian Society: 'We consider the farm to be of great architectural value and of local historical interest. It is also in a good state of repair and lends much dignity to Old Church-road in which it stands.'

In the mid-1800s Chingford was farming country and at one time there were over forty farms in the area. On the road passing the old church there were six, this picture showing the land of Gorme's (or Gomme's) Farm on the left.

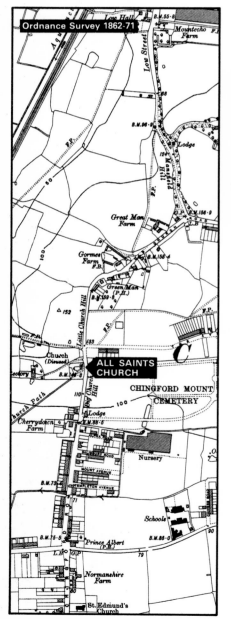

By 1949 Gorme's had shrunk to virtually just the farmhouse and garden and a Compulsory Purchase Order to take over the property was fought vigorously in 1951.

Asked why the petition had not been organized earlier Mr. Martin told a *Guardian* reporter that it was not known — except to Miss Margaret Edsall, of the Farm — that Gomme's Farm was included in the land for which the compulsory Purchase Order had been applied, until a short time before the inquiry was held.

The inquiry was held at the Town Hall on July 27th. Opposition was made by Miss Edsall, the Antiquarian Society, and Mr. James Soper, freeholder of the land.

Chingford Town Clerk (Mr. F. J. O'Dowd) reported that there were 1,632 families awaiting accommodation in Chingford and said the land was necesary to the development of adjacent ground already owned by the Council.

When asked what would be lost on his proposed housing schedules if Gomme's Farm was not included in the order the Borough Engineer, Mr. S. J. Helier, estimated three pairs of houses, two blocks of maisonettes, or two blocks of six flats.

Miss Margaret Edsall said: 'I feel it is very hard on me since my people went to Gomme's Farm 60 years ago and I was born there shortly after. I know no other home and do not really want to.'

The farm, over which controversy has been raging for several weeks, is a seventeenth-century half-timbered and plastered building which stands on the corner of Old Church-road and Lambourne-gardens.

All that remains to mark its passing — this mulberry tree which originally stood in the garden.

The petition, which is the result of many hours of arduous street canvassing by Society officials, is expected to be completed within the next few days

The Walthamstow Guardian, August 19, 1949

The decade before it had been a fight of a different sort . . . and this time it was the very district itself which was up for grabs. 'The Walthamstow Grab' was the main topic of conversation in 1931-33 when Chingford's larger neighbour attempted to take over a large slice of Chingford, Buckhurst Hill and Woodford. The Essex Review Order of 1934 confirmed the existing boundaries; in fact instead a small portion of Waltham Cross was merged with Chingford much to the annoyance of their people! The trams were one aspect which entered into the argument: extended from Walthamstow to Chingford *(above)* in 1905 it was reported that 'The trams of Walthamstow seem to please some people and annoy others'.

THE WALTHAMSTOW GRAB
MINISTRY'S DECISION

We understand that the Essex County Council have this week received the decision of the Minister of Health upon the County proposals relating to a certain number of districts in the County, including those in this immediate locality.

The Minister proposes to confirm without modification the proposals of the County for the amalgamation of Wanstead and Woodford, and the constitution of the new Chigwell Urban District, comprising the present Urban Districts of Buckhurst Hill and Loughton and the Parish of Chigwell.

With regard to the proposal of the Walthamstow Borough Council for the inclusion in the Borough of the Chingford Urban District and parts of the Urban Districts of Buckhurst Hill and Woodford, the Minister has come to the conclusion that a case has not been made out for including these areas in the Borough. . . .

The Woodford Times, March 10, 1933

The Prince Albert on the corner of New Road still exists but has now sunk out of sight below the supermarket! Opposite, the old tram terminus is still used by London Transport — from trolleys to Titans!

By 1922 there were still a dozen working farms under cultivation. Chingford's development as a dormitory suburb thereafter increased pressure on the remaining open spaces but the Borough held some 200 acres to be preserved for amenity purposes. Most important of these is Larkswood Park which includes 47 acres of the ancient Larks Wood — not itself today part of the 'official' Epping Forest but, nevertheless, historically just as much a remnant of the old Royal Forest of Essex. Around the Wood were grouped four farms: Larkswood Lodge Farm, Larks Farm, Larks Hall Farm and Inks Green Farm *(above)* which disappeared about 1960. Inks Green Road, which now joins Larkshall Road at this spot, was made up in 1949.

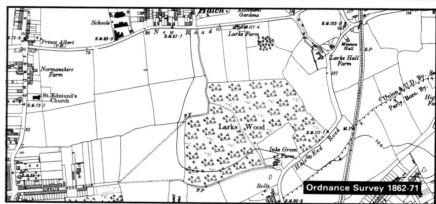

Ordnance Survey 1862-71

Larkswood swimming pool, constructed on the site of Larks Farm for a cost of £24,000 in 1935-36, is regarded as one of the finest open-air pools in Britain. Designed by Chingford's own Borough Engineer and Surveyor, Mr S. J. Hellier, he conceived the unique idea of building it in the shape of a cross with two shallow arms suitable for toddlers and non-swimmers and another, much deeper, equipped with a full range of diving boards. It was opened by Sir Kingsley Wood, Minister of Health on July 28, 1936.

Sir Kingsley Wood, the Minister of Health, on Tuesday opened the Larks Wood open-air swimming pool constructed by the Chingford Urban Council. He said that Britain was becoming more health minded, particularly the younger generation, who were rightly demanding more and better opportunities for leading a healthier life. Britain was now spending over £100,000,000 a year to maintain and improve the health conditions of the nation. For the provision of swimming baths local authorities had obtained sanction to loans of over £6,000,000 in the last 10 years, and the figure for the year 1935-36 reached nearly £1,000,000. With the great increase in the swimming habit, it was vital to have good standards and especially pure water.

The new swimming pool has cost £24,000, and represents one of the biggest schemes yet undertaken in the district. The pool has a water area of 2,700 square yards and holds 765,000 gallons, and is enclosed by a wide shrubbery. Shower baths are placed in pagoda recesses. A six-inch coping around the pool prevents grit and foreign material from entering the water, and another novelty is the teak footboard along the sides 3ft. below water level, which provide a comfortable 'rest' for swimmers. Sun-bathing areas, water chutes and similar equipment are installed, and provision is made for under-water lighting. The chloramine process and filtration has been adopted based on a six-hour turn-over.

Walthamstow Guardian, July 31, 1936

Plans to destroy Larks Hall Farm in Chingford — the only surviving farmhouse in the area — came under fierce attack this week.

The Leyton Society has taken up the fight for the farmhouse because, it claims, it is almost unique.

Chingford Historical Society wanted the farmhouse to be listed as a historical building but the Greater London Council and Department of the Environment have refused because 'it is not considered of sufficient interest.'

The farm, which lies in just over three acres of land, has been in the family of Miss Ann McCunn for several generations and Miss McCunn still lives in the house.

Walthamstow Guardian, October 31, 1975

Today (Friday) sees the opening of a brand new pub in Chingford, the Larkshall in Larkshall Road, Chingford.

The pub, built and adapted from historic Larkshall Farm, marks an important milestone for both local conservationists and Courage Eastern, the brewery which owns it.

For years the future of the farmhouse has been in doubt, and now after threats of demolition it has been saved.

The building dates back hundreds of years, and up until the 1970s was owned by the McCunn family. It then passed into the hands of the council, and while flatlets were built on the site, the historic building was left standing.

Then it was adapted for use by a housing association for one-parent families, but when this became impractical the building was left vacant.

And it was at this point that Courage, the brewers became interested.

Explained Mr Barry Fenton the area retail manager for Courage: 'Although Courage Ltd owns over 6,000 pubs, we have never had one in Chingford and this is an area we are very interested in.

'And the minute we saw it we knew it was exactly what we had been looking for. So we bought the farmhouse and the land surrounding it and immediately started work.'

Guardian & Gazette, August 20, 1982

Larks Hall Farm, or at least part of the farmhouse, is of late Tudor or early Stuart vintage although the roof was added in Victorian times as part of a restoration carried out in 1890. At that time the farm comprised some 11 acres but by 1946 this had shrunk to just one acre. Its future was in doubt for several years until August 1982 when it was taken over by Courage Brewery who reportedly spent £300,000 rebuilding and converting it into a public house.

Now just a memory. Unlike Larkswood, the Kingfisher, which was opened two years previously in Oak Hill by the lovely Miss Joyce Cooper, did not stand the test of time. Immensely popular before the war with the people of Highams Park and Woodford, perhaps it just suffered from the ability of people in the 1950s and 1960s to travel further afield in their own transport in search of competing pleasures. From 1964 it found a brief lease of life as a nightclub but its reputation was not improved by the publicity given it by a gangland shooting and it closed soon afterwards.

A glorious summer day was a fitting accompaniment to the opening yesterday of the deliciously inviting bathing pool at Oak Hill, Woodford Green, to be known as the Kingfishers' Pool.

It nestles snugly in an old world garden amid charming forest surroundings, and enjoys a privacy which many similar places lack.

It is barely four months since Forest Lodge was standing on the site now occupied by the swimming pool and club premies, yet in that comparatively short time a vast amount of work has been done and a most pleasing transformation effected, the house having been converted into commodious and well equipped club premises.

The idea of the Kingfishers' Pool originated with Mr. Bernard Sheppard, of Sheppard Bros., Woodford Green. He had just bought the Forest Lodge Estate at Oak Hill for the purpose of developing it as a small building estate. He realised, however, that by building a dozen houses there, the beautiful surroundings could only be enjoyed by the few, and he was desirous that its amenities should be available to the many. Having carefully surveyed the site he came to the conclusion that the setting lent itself to something that would be an asset to the district both from a social and sports point of view.

In order that the work might be finished in time it has been necessary during the latter part of the time to work day and night gangs.

The carrying out of the full scheme will involve an expenditure of approximately £20,000, the capital being provided entirely by the directors.

Every effort will be made to keep the club at a high standard, and it is hoped local residents will avail themselves fully of the facilities now provided for indulging in this health-giving sport and useful accomplishment of swimming, and also of sharing the amenities of the well equipped club.

We understand that nearly one thousand applications for membership were received before the opening day — a very promising start.

At the opening ceremony the managing director, Mr. Bernard W. Sheppard, presided, supported by Sir Harold and Lady Bellman, Miss Joyce Cooper, and Messrs. H. Sheppard, F. E. Collinson, S. F. Meek, R. W. Oakden and A. E. Oakden (directors), and Mr. I. A. Reddall (secretary to the Board).

On behalf of Mr. Sheppard and his co-directors Sir Harold extended a cordial welcome to Miss Joyce Cooper, who was Britain's foremost lady swimmer. It was a

After standing derelict for some time permission was given for the erection of a multi-story hotel on the site in 1973.

great source of pride to the club that Miss Cooper was present to take part in the opening ceremony. He wondered if he dared congratulate Miss Cooper upon the married state which she would enter in about a month's time.

Miss Joyce Cooper expressed her great pleasure at being present and wished the club every success. She then switched on the cascade and declared the pool open.

An enjoyable musical programme was given during the afternoon by the Woodford Military Band.

The members of the club lost no time in sampling the new pool and many were the expressions of satisfaction at the comfortable warmth of the water in which they revelled joyously.

The Woodford Times, June 15, 1934

The nearest parallel one can draw to describe the evangelism of the 'world's most popular preacher', Gipsy Rodney Smith, MBE, would be to point out the latter-day example of Billy Graham. Gipsy Smith began his ministry at the invitation of General William Booth, founder of the Salvation Army. Gipsy was a great believer in the power of prayer and his open-air meetings, in which his sincere and brilliant oration brought countless devotees, must partly have sprung from his simple birth in a gipsy camp on Mill Plain.

'I'm not interested in your denomination my friend', Gipsy would say, 'it's your destination I'm concerned with.' He became a special missionary with the National Free Church Council from 1897 to 1912 and toured Australia, Canada and the USA. During the First World War he served with the YMCA in France, his great achievement being, it was said, that 'he made religion attractive'. During the Second World War Gipsy travelled all over North America, conducting meetings and telling his by-then world famous testimony of 'the gospel in the gipsy tent'. After his first wife Annie died, he had married again in 1938 and Mary worked tirelessly with him during his final years. He returned to England in 1945 and went to Epping Forest to see again the hornbeam tree beneath which he had been born in 1860. In his last two years, although his spirit was as lively as ever, bodily he was failing. In August 1947, then 87 years old, he sailed with his wife aboard the Queen Mary once again for America but, as the liner reached New York on August 4, Gipsy died. His wish was that his ashes should be buried beneath the tree 'from whence I came' and on July 2, 1949 Mary unveiled a four-foot-high memorial on the spot.

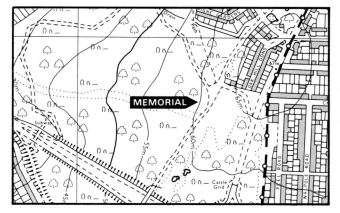

Unsignposted, the memorial is difficult to find tucked away on the boundary between Chingford and Woodford. We hope this map will be a help to readers wishing to visit the Forest's most poignant grave.

'It was an earthly paradise, in which the delightful harmony resulting from the perfect accord of duty and inclination were felt and enjoyed. Those who have been witnesses of our manner of living at Gilwell can vouch for the truth of what I say . . . God . . . best knows why that happy peaceful home where He was adored in fidelity and truth is now to be sold by public auction.' So wrote Margaret Chinnery on July 2, 1812 — forced to leave her home at Gilwell due to her husband's misappropriation of Government funds. The Crown seized the property and it was sold to help pay his debts. When purchased by Mr W. F. de Bois Maclaren for £10,000 to provide a camp site for the Scout Association in 1919 it was very dilapidated, having lain empty for years. This is the back view in 1919 showing the section of balustrade preserved from the old London Bridge. It had been erected on the bridge in 1760 when the shops were demolished and was moved to Gilwell in 1824.

The Chief Scout, Lieutenant-General Sir Robert Baden-Powell speaking at the dedication ceremony. The Hall itself was opened by Mr de Bois Maclaren cutting ribbons in the Scouts' colours stretched across the doorway.

A mass gathering of Scouts took place at Gilwell Park, Chingford, on Saturday, the occasion of its opening as a scoutmasters' training college, and as a camping and rallying centre for Scouts from all parts of London. Gilwell Park, comprising 55 acres of woodland adjoining Epping Forest, has been given to the Scouts by Mr. W. de Bois Maclaren, and Mrs. Maclaren performed the opening. General Sir Robert Baden-Powell complimented the 700 lads on their valuable acquisition and urged them to live up to the character given to them by the King, who said: 'Whenever you tell a Scout to do a thing you may be sure it will be done. The beauty of a Scout is that he never makes a mistake. I have never known a Scout to make a mistake yet.' — At the request of the French Government Sir Robert presented Scoutmaster Gregory with the Medaille Militaire for valuable services rendered in France.

The Essex Weekly News, August 1, 1919

Without noise or excitement our camp of Woodcraft training has started, and has started with a swing that means life and go in its future work and resultant life-blood in the Movement. There was a launching ceremony it is true, when Mrs. de Bois Maclaren scissored the ribbon and gave us entry into the institution that her husband had provided for us. But even while the central buildings were yet in the workmen's hands, the camps were alive with boys, and the first Scoutmasters' Training Class has been in full swing. I am consequently possessed with a tremendous belief in what Gilwell Park is going to do for us, especially when one realises the wonderful spirit which is already established there. Already some 150 Troops of Scouts have enjoyed the camping facilities amongst the surrounding beauties of Epping Forest. I only hope that they will not consider that the winter is a bar to their continuing their camping experiences. It should be part of our training that Scouts can take the rough with the

smooth and are not merely fine-weather campers. The place at any rate will be open to week-end bivouacs, with shelter handy within the building should it be necessary.

Headquarters Gazette, November, 1919

The line which standardises the world's time passed right through Epping Forest.

The Greenwich Meridian celebrates its centenary this year and the district is permanently to mark the line with trees at various sites.

It is proposed to plant Western Red Cedars — chosen because they are outstandingly hardy — at regular intervals at field boundaries and roadsides where practicable.

This will involve a maximum of 27 sites and Epping Forest Council is hoping to seek sponsorship and co-operation from land owners, Lee Valley Park Authority, parish and town councils and Gilwell Scout Centre.

Other district councils through whose territory the line passes are also being asked to join in.

Guardian & Gazette, April 13, 1984

One of the first, if not the very first, troops to camp at Gilwell — before the official opening — was Epping Forest's own, the 17th. This picture shows Mr Maclaren with the boys on May 10, 1919.

At 10.35 on the evening of Sunday the 18th June, during an alert which had lasted from 8.37 in the evening, a pilotless aircraft fell in the King George V Reservoir in the Chingford area, the first incident in the Borough in connection with this form of attack.

During the next few days it was decided by the Ministry of Home Security that this type of missile should be referred to in official reports as 'Flying Bomb,' but it was more popularly referred to by the public and the Press as the 'Doodle-bug.' . . .

In view of the unsettled weather which set in at the end of June, the enemy intensified this form of attack, losing no time in launching flying bombs against London and the South-East whenever the weather was cloudy. . . .

The fourth incident which occurred in Chingford was at 7.59 a.m. on Wednesday, the 28th June, when a flying bomb fell at Seymour Court, Whitehall Road. In this particular instance, the flying bomb appears to have struck a large tree at the rear of the block of flats numbered 37-48, and serious damage was caused to the rear of the two blocks of flats 25-36 and 37-48. Very extensive damage was caused to residential property in Courtland Avenue, Rosslyn Avenue, Whitehall Road, Forest Side and Forest Court.

No one was killed outright as a result of the incident, but Mrs. J. Morris, of 33, Seymour Court and Mrs. Ethel Smith of 32, Seymour Court died in hospital from injuries received.

A number of the flats were vacant at the time of the incident, otherwise casualties must have been more serious. Ten persons were conveyed to hospital and ten others were treated for injuries at First Aid Posts in the Borough. Eighteen of the flats in Seymour Court were demolished or had to be demolished, whilst twenty other flats and a number of properties in Courtland Avenue had to be evacuated for extensive repairs. Altogether some 500 properties were damaged by the incident.

Civil Defence Services were on the scene within a matter of ten minutes from the time the incident occurred and Rescue Parties were required to extricate a number of persons from the debris, one being a resident of one of the flats, who, at the time of the incident, was taking his morning bath.

Chingford at War, S. Warburton. July 1946

Back on the Ching which forms both the natural and official boundary in the north-eastern corner of the Borough. This is where the river crosses, or rather passes beneath, Whitehall Road. Seymour Court lies on the left.

Our rescue dogs in action in Chingford, photographed in the aftermath of the Seymour Court incident, most probably by Mr Alf Sparrow of Loughton. Could the bath be the one mentioned in the text, we wonder?

365

High Beach

High Beach. There is controversy as to whether this somewhat scattered village, on the west boundary of the Forest is correctly spelt 'Beach' or 'Beech'. Whilst generally supposed that it derives its name from the nature of the tree which is now the principal constituent of the surrounding woodlands, it is deemed by others to allude to a much earlier nomenclature. In early English, any gravel bank was a beach and the older inhabitants still 'go up to the Beach'. In an early poem, the oak groves on the 'beach' were praised and the fame remains in 'King's Oak'. For the recent map revision, the Ordnance Survey adopted 'Beach' as the correct spelling.

Epping Forest, Alfred Quist, 1971

Sir, — A terrible piece of destruction is about to take place in Epping Forest, at High Beech, Captain Sotheby, one of the Lords of the Manor, is, I am told, having 500 trees a day marked with a view to having them cut down shortly. Unless a commoner should obtain an injunction, one of the most beautiful parts of the forest will be completely spoiled. Chief Justice Cockburn and Mr. Baring are, I believe, both of them commoners. This piece of common contains 200 acres, and is more used for picnics than any

The Woodman, a wayside beerhouse near Sewardstone Green, was a much welcomed respite on the route from Chingford to High Beach. Today it has been replaced by a private house, the licence taken by the nearby West Essex Golf Club.

other part of the forest. Is no step to be taken to save it? D.C.L.

The Daily News, March 10, 1871

Some forty years ago a group of gravel-diggers were removing some of the sandy gravel which rests in patches on the clay of Epping Forest, on a site not far from High Beech, when one, more observant than the rest, picked up a flint having the appearance of being shaped by hand. It so happened that a frequenter of the forest — a Loughton geologist — passed by, and the workman showed him his curious find.

So by the merest chance one of the most astonishing archaeological discoveries of Essex came to light. The geologist minutely examined the area, and later reported the finding of many 'pigmy flints' in and around a hollow in the ground which, he said, might well be the site of a pit dwelling. He kept the locality secret from all but a handful of his closest friends, and it was not until his death that a systematic search was begun by the West Essex Archaeological Group.

Working in some of the worst of early spring weather in 1959, a small party of archaeologists marked out a portion of the area in metre squares. Then, with trowels and brushes, they removed the sandy loam inch by inch downwards. Within a week or two, upwards of 300 flint fragments had been unearthed from an area of ten square metres, all of which belonged to the type known as 'pigmy flints' or microliths. A great many were broken, obviously spoilt and discarded by the maker, but others were perfect examples of his craft. There were sharp and pointed little blades, scarcely an inch long; flint cores from which these small blades had been struck; and the curious thing called a 'burin,' which seems to be residue from which a tiny blade has been split off.

Here then was evidence that people of the Stone Age had squatted on this patch of Epping Forest and used it as a working floor for the manufacture of their tools and weapons. Who were these people, and what manner of life did they lead?

The answer to these questions is given in part by comparing the forest finds with others

in East Anglia, Sussex and Yorkshire. Laboriously the evidence has been built up by many archaeologists that these tiny flints were the work of Stone Age men who lived in Britain during the cold and cheerless period after the recession of the Ice Age. Britain was still joined to the Continent, and the North Sea was a wide, flat and marshy river bed. Across the land-link, and through the marshes, came migrating families of primitive hunters and fishers. Some settled on the coast, others kept to the river valleys, while a third group lived on the sandy plateaux. For many years they had free contact with the Continent, but eventually, 8,000 years or so ago, the land bridge was broken through, the North Sea flooded, and Britain became an island. For centuries to follow, those who were cut off by this great event evolved a way of life unaffected by any outside influences. They were truly the earliest Britons.

Their houses were of the most primitive kind: a shallow pit dug into the gravel and covered by a thatch of brushwood supported on posts. Nothing remains of these structures today except the post-holes, detected by an experienced eye by a slight difference in colour and texture from the surrounding soil.

These then were the earliest natives of Essex, roaming the barren gravel ridges in search of food and shelter and resting awhile on a sandy cap later to become a fragment of Epping Forest. They scattered around their simple homes the products of their industry, to lie undetected beneath the forest leaves for thousands of years. It seems incredible that these small flinty relics should have rested where the savage workman dropped them so long ago, barely covered by a thin layer of dead leaves, undisturbed by the passing pageant of Roman and Saxon, of the hunting retinues of medieval kings and the countless holidaying visitors of modern times.

E. A. Rudge, Essex Countryside

The most notable event to occur at High Beach has to be Queen Victoria's historic visit in May 1882. Although the occasion has been fully described earlier (pages 52-58, this chapter would not be complete without its mention. Her route ran from Chingford along Rangers Road to the junction with the Epping New Road, passing north for a few hundred yards before dropping down to the left through Fairmead Bottom. This engraving is titled 'The Royal Procession entering High Beech *(sic)* **Wood, the spot depicted is that** *below* **where the old road enters the Forest. Fairmead Bottom was closed off at its southern end in 1974 after several serious accidents at the almost blind junction with the New Road.**

There has been a surprise 'bonus' for the High Beech Green Belt Association in its struggle to preserve the calm of Epping Forest.

Without any persuasion by forest-lovers, Chigwell Council has decided to close off part of Fairmead Bottom to traffic. This will leave one of the more beautiful roads through the forest undisturbed by the roar of cars and the smell of exhaust fumes.

Actually the road will be closed only from its junction with Epping New Road as far as Palmers Bridge, but this will remove traffic from the forest where it disturbs the natural surroundings, and divert it back on to the A11.

The council made its decision after pressure was brought to bear by Essex County Council in view of the hazards involved in traffic turning right at the junction.

West Essex Gazette, February 1, 1974

Ben Hur comes to the Forest. The other event for which High Beach is famous is speedway. Although an earlier meeting is recorded as having taken place the previous year at Manchester, February 19, 1928 is generally accepted as the day dirt-track racing was born in the United Kingdom. The old running track behind the King's Oak was adapted by the Ilford Motor Cycle and Light Car Club. That Sunday thousands of local people packed the circuit to watch what must have been for many the most exciting thing they had ever seen — at least since Ben Hur had become the silent screen's biggest epic three years earlier. Here Fletcher and Smythe battle for the lead.

SPEEDWAY

Origins

Motorcycle racing on large dirt track surfaces has been traced back to 1902 in the United States. The first organized 'short track' races were at the West Maitland (New South Wales, Australia) Agricultural Show in November 1923. The sport evolved in Great Britain with small diameter track racing at Droylsden, Greater Manchester on 25 June 1927 and a cinder track event at High Beech, Essex, on 19 Feb 1928.

Guinness Book of Records, 1985

Over 3,000 people flocked here today to watch the first DTM races held in this country. There were thrills in plenty, motor cyclists tearing around the track with their knees almost touching the ground and, in some cases, landing on their heads when their machines skidded from under them. But the enormous size of the crowd which gathered at the Kings Oak Speedway provided the greatest surprise of all.

The races were timed to run from 10.30 until 4.30 and there were eight events with several 'heats' in each race. With such a feast of thrills offered, motor cyclists turned up in their thousands while motorists and others rolled up through the day. Considerable difficulty was found in accommodating this huge crowd as all spectators, owing to the danger of being run into by the machines, are supposed to be confined to the inside of the track only. As this was impossible, even the hundreds of stewards present, could not restrain the enthusiastic crowds from crossing the track and watching from the outside. Those who desired a 'grandstand' view climbed trees where, both in clambering and swinging from the branches they supplied as many thrills as the motor cyclists, to the huge enjoyment of the crowd.

Two Australian 'cracks' Mackay and Galoway were competing, all the others being Englishmen who had never ridden on a dirt track before.

Daily Mirror, February 20, 1928

The Motor Cycle Club held a dirt track meeting on Saturday at the Kings Oak Speedway, Loughton. Through the agency of the vice-president, Mr W. J. Cearns, the gathering were able to see the Australian cracks, Vic Huxley, who recently broke the world's record, and Cecil Brown, of the U.S.A. The International Speedway arranged for Huxley to travel by air from Naples. Huxley, who had not ridden a machine for three months, and had a strange motor to ride, managed to clip 3-5ths of a second off A. Frogley's record. Frogley did not beat the time set up by Huxley.

In the 300 cc. Class, R. Frogley won from M. Seiffert 2nd, with F. T. Law 3rd.

The Woodford Times, May 11, 1928

The Daily Mirror featured Billy Galloway's crash in two pictures — this is the third in the sequence. The Australian had come to Britain to demonstrate the new sport — something which he certainly accomplished in a spectacular way. After the first meeting it was said that 'a theory is mooted by some experts that this sport will prove to be a serious rival to greyhound racing', then all the rage but the subject of a fierce anti-dog racing campaign. (When this fight was lost the Walthamstow Stadium was erected in 1931 against much opposition from people in Chingford.)

371

At this time of the year members of the Veteran Dirt Track Riders' Association get down to reliving 'the good old days' usually with a Dinner-dance. That annual event was held last Saturday. On Sunday they'll all be trooping up to High Beech, near Loughton, to relive the memories of the first-ever meeting behind the King's Oak, which took place almost 40 years to the day — on Sunday, February 19th, 1928.

Stars of the sport — past, present and future — are all expected to gather in the heart of Epping Forest on Sunday for a big programme of events which will include displays of most of the leading trophies ever competed for in Speedway.

Secretary Peter Arnold has also arranged for displays of programmes, pictures and badges. 'In fact,' says Peter, 'nostalgia by the bucketful.'

One of the leading personalities to have a place of honour in the Cavalcade of Speedway, which gets under way at 2.15 p.m., will be Johnnie S. Hoskins. It was in November, 1923, that Johnnie first started the Speedway bug, as a special attraction for one of his agricultural shows in Newcastle, Australia.

Johnnie came over to England with the first wave of Australians and has been in the sport ever since. Now 75, Johnnie is at the moment actively engaged in opening a new stadium for Speedway!

Johnnie is to ride a 1919 belt-drive ex-DR Triumph in the Cavalcade — one of many vintage machines which it is expected to have on show.

It promises to be a great day, reserved in the main for the veterans of the sport. One thing is for certain, though, it will be an autograph-hunter's paradise!

Guardian & Gazette, February 16, 1968

Historic reunion. *Right:* **Ready to go are Phil Bishop, Jack Barnett and Sonny Wilson.** *Below:* **Geoff Pymar, Alex Slow, Fred Law, George Gower with Cyril Taft on the bike.**

More than 40 years ago, the roar of a massive coughing engine tore open the silence deep in Epping Forest.

A gang of young men shifted trees, laid down cinders and introduced a new creature to the woods — the motorcycle.

There, at High Beech, Loughton, a quiet corner of the forest was to give birth to a new sport and a crop of young riders who were to become almost legendary.

The year was 1928. The name of the sport — Speedway.

Credit for that first track goes to Mr. Lionel Wills, then secretary of the Ilford and District Motor Cycling Club. He heard from Australia of an activity called dirt track racing.

A friend supplied graphic details of the sport and said it was exciting, lots of fun — and highly dangerous.

Mr. Wills went to the King's Oak, High Beech. He knew that nearby, tucked in the trees, was a small running track falling into disuse.

With a little extending here and there, some cinders, a few trees removed and some eager motorcyclists, a trial could begin, he thought.

After preparation, he announced the meeting and invited any prospective motor-cycling dare-devils along to High Beech. By Easter, 1928, crowds of 20,000 were gathering to see Speedway.

One of the first to turn up at those meetings was a 19-year-old farmer's son from Hoddesdon, Roger Frogley. He earned only 30s per week — but, he owned a motor cycle.

Within a year, Roger Frogley was the British Champion and a household name in England and Australia. He became, in the words of daily newspapers at that time, Britain's first 'track star'.

Today, at 62, he is a successful business-man, being the managing director of the Herts and Essex Aero Club Co. Ltd., which is based at Stapleford Aerodrome, near Abridge.

That first ride at High Beech on his Rudge-Whitworth 500cc machine put him on the road to fame.

He said 'I remember that at that very first High Beech meeting, I broke my gearbox on the way, so I had to spectate. But you can bet that next weekend, I was there on the track.

'All the riders competed as individuals, there were no teams then. The whole thing — especially the technique used — was totally new to this country.'

The technique, in fact, was the now-famous broadside. For high speed cornering, this meant sliding the back wheel out sideways and steadying the other side of the machine with a leg.

Was it dangerous? 'Yes, at the speeds we travelled at it was' said Mr. Frogley. 'But then motorcycling was, and still is, damn dangerous anyway.'

With crowds of 20,000 at High Beech, it was soon realised that Speedway was a money-spinner.

With the onset of war, the track closed in 1941 but reopened in May 1945. However, by then both competitors and spectators were enjoying the superior facilities of purpose-built stadiums like West Ham and Crystal Palace, and the magic days of High Beach were over. Some budding 'leg-trailers' continued to practice the art into the late 1940s but as Jimmy Goldring, former ex-professional rider from Waltham-stow, recalls, 'only the tough survived because training sessions were held in the winter months and there was only one cold water tap to remove the day's grime'.

Young men came along to try their hand in a sort of club atmosphere. Cash was not the driving force.

As well as Roger Frogley, many of the big names in Speedway started at High Beech.

'There was Jack Barnet, Colin Watson — one time captain of Wembley — Buster Frogley, my own brother, and Jack Parker, who only packed up a few years ago at 55' said Mr. Frogley.

And the headlines went on 'High Beech Records Broken' 'Frogley Again!' 'King's Oak at its Best' and 'High Beech Man Scores Triple Success'.

By 1932, Mr. Frogley was a rare visitor to High Beech. He had reached the absolute top in Speedway, both at home and abroad and was on the verge of retiring to become a pro-fessional pilot.

This he in fact did and went on to teach flying, until 1935 but an urgent plea from his old club brought him back in that year. Eight Crystal Palace riders were out of the running after crashes — 'Fantastic Frogley' was needed again.

He went back for half a season, taking the place of three riders. It was during this time he noticed the lack of good up-and-coming Speedway men in the sport.

At the end of that season, he ended with Crystal Palace and planned to open the world's first ever Speedway School. He hired the High Beech track, put a large advert in the Daily Mirror and waited.

Two days later, 1,600 applications had been received and the project was under way.

'I bought about a dozen bikes, the sort that ran on nitro and dope fuel, sets of leathers and helmets, and got started.

'No person was ever killed at High Beech but it's surprising. There were so many ac-cidents'.

However, in the two years that the school lasted, only six made it to the professional track. None became well-known. Roger Frogley returned to flying, for good.

High Beech, the first milestone in the exciting history of British Speedway, fell into disrepair. Ponies occasionally came along for small shows, but little else happened.

Silver birches sprang up on the banks and poked through the roof of the old wooden grandstand. Grass covered the cinders.

And that is how it remained until a few weeks ago, when the last traces of the circuit were removed to create a field study centre for the Corporation of London.

What once echoed to the roar of motor-cycles has, perhaps rightfully, been restored to nature.

Guardian and Gazette, January 1, 1971

Britain's first, purpose-built Nature Conservation Centre is to be built in Epping Forest. The £70,000 proposal, which went before the Common Council yesterday (Thursday) aims at 'creating a centre to afford facilities for ecological studies in relation to the Forest'.

Mr. Alfred Qvist, superintendent of the Forest, said this week 'Not only have more people come to live around the Forest and therefore come to use it more, but there has been a growing interest in natural history subjects among townspeople everywhere in recent years.

'The survival of Epping Forest in its natural aspect is dependent upon a proper understanding of what is involved in its management, and a conservation centre, where the increasing interest in the natural history aspects of the Forest can be satisfied, will provide a means to that understanding.'

And it was to meet just this need — to safeguard Epping Forest as a natural beauty spot for the benefit of all Londoners — that the Corporation became trustees of the Forest in 1878. During the past 91 years the Corporation has run a multi-million pound programme of Forest improvement and this new centre is an extension of this development/preservationist policy.

The centre itself, to be sited at High Beech,

will be the first of its type in the British Isles. There are, at present, a small number of residential field study centres operating mainly for advanced student courses, but the Epping Forest project will concentrate on the younger age groups and also provide facilities for the natural history societies and groups of that kind for whom Epping Forest has always been an area of special interest.

Says Mr. Qvist 'Our object is simple: to provide a self-contained unit for the study of the flora and fauna of the Forest and thereby a better understanding of why we have to do what we do in its management.

'The scheme, I suppose, arose because we were being asked an increasing number of informed questions about the Forest by the public at large and also because of the interest shown by education authorities in making use of the Forest for informed instruction.'

When opened during the early summer of 1970, the centre will be a part of the Corporation's contribution towards European Conservation Year, 1970, and will also, slightly ahead of the actual date, mark the centenary of the law suit launched by the Corporation in August, 1871, by which Epping Forest came to be saved for the public.

The centre itself will include lecture theatres, laboratories and living quarters for the warden and his staff. Their work will be

mainly concerned with teaching up to 100 children per day (consisting of three primary and one secondary school classes) about natural history and the conservancy of the Forest. The centre will also be open for adult education, weekend and teaching training courses, and for use by natural history societies.

The Field Studies Council will manage the centre on behalf of the Corporation of London. They have been closely consulted throughout.

'At base this is primarily an educational project, for it is vital that with the increasing use of the Forest people understand that it has to be preserved and protected. One of the great difficulties at the moment is that by sheer weight of numbers people are threatening to destroy the thing they have come to enjoy', said Mr. Qvist.

'We hope that by teaching young people a little about natural history at the centre they will come to appreciate just what is involved in protecting our countryside for the future'.

Gazette and Guardian, January 17, 1969

From racing circuit to conservation centre — the King's Head has seen it all. This is the view from the roof looking east.

With its historic associations with racing High Beach has always had a problem with motorcycles. The rules governing the early meetings included the warning that 'The Speedway is at the King's Oak, not on the roads approaching same' but the pub has always had a magnetic attraction to bikers. When Ernie Saunders took the licence over on moving his Stag Restaurant from Buckhurst Hill to High Beach in 1979, he tried to enforce a 'no motorcycles' rule but he needn't have bothered: general disorder has always had its way at the King's Oak — ever since 1887!

At the Epping Petty Sessions on Friday last, the licence of the King's Oak Inn, High Beech, was transferred from Mr. Christopher Wm. Pfleger to Mr. James Hyams. The chairman (Mr. C. J. Bury) remarked to Mr. Hyams that the Bench hoped and trusted he would keep the house in perfect order. The place had been a regular nuisance to the neighbourhood and the Bench had had more trouble with it than with any other house in the division.

The Woodford Times, January 1, 1887

Nightspot boss John Simmons has vowed to fight a council decision which will close the late night disco he opened only last year.

Mr. Simmons opened Turpins, at the King's Oak, High Beech, in July 1983 after spending thousands on redecorating and improving the premises.

Now the public health committee of Epping Forest District Council has said it will not renew Mr. Simmons' music and dancing licence, which expires after Christmas.

The committee received written objections to renewing the licence from the Metropolitan Police, the Conservators of Epping Forest and the Epping Forest Conservation Centre.

The Metropolitan Police stated that Mr. Simmons was not considered to be a 'fit and proper person to hold an entertainments licence'.

It was claimed: 'There have been numerous incidents of disorder and violence inside and outside these premises and many serious assaults.

'The premises are a constant drain on already heavily committed police resources. It is not in the public interest that the licence be renewed.'

Yellow Advertiser, November 30, 1984

The King's Oak, High Beech, has won back its nightclub operating licence. The Sunday musical entertainments licence application was granted at an extraordinary meeting of Epping Forest Council's public health committee on Monday.

The King's Oak lost its operating licence for Turpins Disco last November and it ceased running in January this year. Since then changes have been made by owner. . . . 'It will be a place where couples can eat and talk with music to dance to if they want,' said Mr Simmonds. 'It is not a disco as such. It is an entirely different operation and I don't anticipate noise will disturb our neighbours.'

The police were represented by Superintendent Brian Plaxton, who told the committee: 'These fancy plans are no different. The same problems will occur again and there are not sufficient means of controlling them.

'Very little has occurred since the disco closed but you wouldn't expect much to happen. It would be quieter because the main focus of trouble had gone.'

For the Conservators, it was argued: 'There are gangs of motorbikes, noise and all sorts of problems . . . and these premises are the focus of these problems.'

Guardian & Gazette, April 19, 1985

In the early days the 'Oak' tried to compete with the nearby retreats (page 48) by opening its own Temperance Department alongside the pub. The corner of the verandah of Roserville Retreat can be seen on the left.

Noisy bikers are abandoning their haunt at High Beech — and it's all thanks to local special bobbies.

In a new police initiative started in May, the number of bikes at the trouble spot near the King's Oak pub on Sundays has dropped from an average of 150 to 20, a spokesman said this week.

And he praised the efforts of the MSC (Metropolitan Special Constabulary) for helping to man the area at the rate of up to 10 officers a day.

Some of these have been regular police but, said MSC Liaison Officer Robert Armstrong: 'It would have been impossible without the help of the specials.' This new tighter control on an area, which has caused complaints over several years, also involves closing the Wellington Hill slip-road.

Inspector Armstrong said results of the scheme, which continue until the end of the summer, had been difficult to evaluate until now because of bad weather.

But, he added, the extra policing 'has gone down very well with the public. It has had the effect of making it much more pleasant for people to go up there and enjoy the amenities of the forest.'

Guardian & Gazette, July 19, 1985

Left: Yanks in Epping Forest. Off duty and it was into The Owl for Sergeant Eric Robinson from Esmond, Rhode Island and Technical Sergeant Jack Abele of Boston, Massachusetts. Meanwhile Sergeant Albert Ouellette chats up the barmaid and is no doubt about to produce the PX nylons! These men were based at Lippitts Hill Camp opposite. *Above:* The old Owl — it is also featured on pages 366-367 — no doubt appealed to the Americans as 'quaint' but McMullen and Sons Ltd must have thought it rather outdated for they applied for planning permission in May 1974 to demolish and rebuild *(below).*

As a young GI away from home, Bill Callum was grateful for the friendship he found at the West Essex Golf Club, Chingford.

No mean hand at the game himself, he was welcome to play any time he could get away from his anti-aircraft base at Lippitts Hill, High Beech.

When the war ended and Bill returned home to North Carolina, he never forgot the English friends he had made.

Over the years he kept in contact, and whenever he and his wife Hannah visit these shores — which is fairly frequently — they also visit the club.

On Sunday, Bill had a particular reason for returning once again, 40 years after peace was declared.

He presented a bench seat he had specially made, with an inscription reminding present and future members of his appreciation.

It had been placed at the first tee so golfers can sit down while waiting to drive off.

Lippitts Hill is now the Metropolitan Police helicopter base, but Bill recalled the time he spent there in 1944.

'During the London bombing we used to shoot down the German aircraft,' he said.

'I was an army sergeant, but I was made so welcome at this golf club.

'I remember, too, that the English could not get wooden golf tees, so I got my wife to send over 5 lbs of them — and that's a lot of tees!'

Bill was reunited with his golfing friends when he returned for the first time 10 years ago.

Bill and his army colleagues left High Beech when they joined the D-Day invasion.

But as he told club members: 'It's great to be back and see my old friends.'

Guardian & Gazette. June 7, 1985

'In grateful appreciation of the many kindnesses shown to us in 1944 when billeted with the artillery unit of Lippitts Hill. Bill Callum & friends, N. Carolina, USA.'

From the Army camp on Lippitts Hill the first American guns to fire in the defence of London came into action in March 1944 during the mini-Blitz, manned by Battery B, 184th Anti-aircraft Artillery. The precise date is in dispute: this picture from US archives gives March 1 but the monument erected later recorded it as March 24.

At work . . . and rest. These two pictures were not released until August 7, 1947. *Left:* The gun is a 90mm (3.54 in) M1 which could fire a 24lb shell up to nearly 40,000 feet. It was towable: the platform folds up and the wheels can be seen on the right. *Right:* The crew pictured here in their quarters, L-R: Pfc. William O. Richasson of Macedonia, Illinois; Cpl. Edmund D. Kennedy of Aurora, Illinois; Pvt. Leonard T. Ruzicki of Nanticoke, Pennsylvania; Sgt. Clifton Voltz of Lake Geneva, Wisconsin; Pfc. Sherwood Swarthout of Rochester, New York; and Pvt. Harold Paulsen of West Branch, Iowa.

The Americans moved to France on June 16 and Lippitts Hill became a German POW camp. In 1960 the Metropolitan Police took it over as a training area, and an underground command centre was constructed for use in the event of a nuclear attack. The camp also serves as a wireless station and has landing and hangering facilities for the Air Support Unit (see also page 89).

Sir Stuart Mallinson (see pages 242-243) was chief welfare officer of the Essex Anglo-American Goodwill Association which was very active with American servicemen in the county, especially aircrews with the Eighth and Ninth Air Forces. Lippitts Hill was unique as it had been a US Army base and it was one of five sites selected for the erection of a memorial. The unveiling ceremony was performed by the wife of the US Ambassador, Mrs. Lewis Douglas.

This first memorial was badly vandalised and a more permanent monument in brick replaced it. Then in May 1976 an additional plaque was added to mark the 200th anniversary of American Independence, unveiled by General Ewan Rosencrans of the USAF assisted by chrome-helmeted Staff Sergeants Willie Wartham and William Poelinger.

Today the old army base echoes to the clatter of the police whirlybirds and gunfire on the target range but the former German occupants also left behind a remarkable memorial: this Teutonic figure carved out of a solid block of concrete by Rudi Weber during October 1946.

We discussed the connections Dick Turpin had with the neighbourhood in the chapter on Crime but this is what remains of his legendary cave. Legend or not, originally it was incorporated in the small pub bearing his name — a brick lining being necessary to stop it from collapsing. Being situated down a narrow track, accessibility had always been a problem and, after Charringtons closed Turpin's Cave, it was demolished and the plot redeveloped in 1973. Tony Giblett named his new home 'Turpin House' and it was he who added a concrete lining to the cave to preserve it. People still came from as far as New Zealand looking for the hide-out which they now found back in the open air in his front garden. Incidentally the roasting of the old woman at Loughton (page 76) by Turpin is reputed to have taken place at Gould's Trap's Hill Farm!

The story of Turpin's 'hideout' in Epping Forest is a well-known and authentic one. It was in 1737, two years before his execution, that he decided that it would be best for him to establish such secret headquarters that no one could possibly find him.

By this time there was hardly an innkeeper in the London area who would dare to house him for more than a few minutes, such was his brutal reputation. So Turpin, with a fellow-highwayman, Tom King, hit on the plan of 'burying' himself in the Forest. . . .

Their Forest retreat was not far from the main road near High Beech, and its supposed site is still an object of attraction to visitors in summer. They made a cave large enough to accommodate the two of them, together with their belongings and horses, and they covered the entrance with forest brushwood, ferns and other vegetation. Here Turpin's wife kept them supplied with food, and from here they sallied forth in search of fat merchants to rob on the London road, and likely looking coaches to hold up on their way to outlying Essex towns.

Not long after they had ensconced themselves snugly in their retreat, their whereabouts was discovered by a certain Thomas Morris, a Forest keeper's servant who, with a bold friend, decided to try and win for himself the reward for Turpin's arrest. When the highwayman saw them, he thought they were poachers, but he soon realised his mistake when Morris levelled his gun at him and told him the game was up.

Morris's friend, who was behind and could not see what was going on, called out to know what was the matter. Morris, gleefully realising that Turpin had mistaken him for a poacher, bellowed. 'I haven't got a rabbit, I've got a Turpin.'

But the crafty robber was unobtrusively backing towards his hideout. Turning swiftly, he grabbed a loaded gun and shot straight at Morris before the latter could lift a finger.

Morris was killed outright, and his companion made tracks for home at top speed.

Express and Independent, June 13, 1936

The Duke of Wellington nearby has changed but little.

I have been at this place all the year, with nothing but that muddy pond in prospect, and those two little sharp-barking dogs. . . .

What a thunderstorm we had the other night! . . . It lasted the whole night, and part of the previous afternoon. Lewis Fytche, who was with us then, was looking out of my window at half-past 11 o'clock, and saw a large fire-ball come up the valley from Waltham, till it seemed to come quite over our pond; it then according to his account grew on a sudden amazingly large. 'How large?' I asked him. He said: 'Like a great balloon, and burst with an explosion like fifty batteries of cannon.' I am so sorry not to have seen it, for it was a thing to remember; but I had just gone to my mother's room; she was grovelling on the floor in an extremity of fear when the clap came, upon which she cried out, 'Oh, I will leave this house; the storms are very bad here.' Such a scene, almost ludicrous in its extreme.

Tennyson to Emily Sellwood, 1839

In his first year at High Beach he contributed *St. Agnes* to *The Keepsake*, and *Oh! that 'twere possible*, one of his best lyrics, to Lord Northampton's volume, *The Tribute*. Part of *In Memoriam* was written at High Beach, including the stanzas inspired by the bells of Waltham Abbey — 'Ring out, wild bells.' *The Talking Oak* and *Locksley Hall* were both written in the Forest, and during the three years spent there his mind was being prepared for some of his most popular work, part of which must have been contemplated if not actually written at Beech Hill House. He must have begun if not completed in the Forest many of the poems that appeared in the 1842 volume. He was standing on the threshold of his great career. Throughout the forties his reputation steadily increased, until in 1850 he reached a peak of honours such as few poets have known, married Emily Sellwood at long last, and became Poet Laureate.

Epping Forest, William Addison, 1945

Alfred Tennyson — Poet Laureate of the Victorian age, knighted in 1884, spent three years of his life at High Beach.

The remains of Alfred Lord Tennyson's High Beech house will not be destroyed — despite the owner's plans for alterations.

Outer Lodge in Pynest Green Road is one of two buildings still standing which once formed part of the Victorian poet's home. Today it is owned by Eddy and Sonia Sibley, who moved in just three years ago and have tried hard to keep the period appearance of the house.

Now the couple are planning to make changes, with an extension giving the lodge 15 rooms in all, including three more bedrooms. But Mrs. Sibley assures me that this will not involve pulling down any part of the house that dated back to Tennyson's day. In fact the only part to be destroyed is a 25-year-old garage which, although built to look as old as the rest of the building, is really of no historical value at all.

The facts surrounding the history of Outer Lodge are rather obscure. Tennyson lived on what was then the Beech Hill Park Estate, in Beech Hall, from 1837-53. Today the two lodges are all that remain of the original house, and Outer Lodge itself seems to have been built in 1862, when the poet was long settled in the Isle of Wight.

However, legend and history merge in the 1860s when Tennyson is supposed to have spent some time at Beech House, the home of his friend Judge Arabin. The story goes that he wrote a poem in this house about the funeral of Prince Albert, mentioning the bells of Waltham Abbey.

It would have been at this time that he stayed in Outer Lodge, and Mr. Peter Watson, who lived there before the Sibleys, went to great lengths to find out the facts.

Today the old Beech Hill Park Estate has long since disappeared and Tennyson's house, too. Beech House is now Arabin House, Manor Road, and Beech Hall merely two lodges and some fields.

Nevertheless, the Sibleys would like to keep the romantic atmosphere of their historic home, but give it 20th century luxury.

Tennyson would almost certainly have approved.

West Essex Gazette, April 12, 1974

In 1836 Alfred met Emily Sellwood who was bridesmaid at her elder sister's marriage to his brother Charles. The following year they became engaged although Alfred moved south the same year from his native Lincolnshire to High Beach. There he settled in Beech Hill House, its name being changed to Beech Hill Park when it was greatly enlarged in 1850, the year he married Emily after a thirteen-year engagement.

Today Tennyson's house has gone — replaced by a modern dwelling on the same site. The original stable block remains.

John Clare, born in 1793, was one of England's finest poets, yet like so many artists, not recognised by his own age. He grew up in extreme poverty and after a brief glimpse of fame in 1820, success eluded him and he was forced to work as a farm labourer to support his large family. By 1835 he was suffering from fears and delusions, believing that his boyhood sweetheart Mary was his first wife, and his real wife Martha, the daughter of a neighbouring farmer who he married in 1820, was his second. In 1837, on the insistence of his publisher, he went into Dr Matthew Allen's asylum founded in Fairmead House at High Beach. After four years Clare escaped and walked the 80 miles to his home at Northborough. Within seven months he had been certified insane and he spent his final 23 years in St Andrew's Asylum in Northampton, writing during this period what is considered some of his finest work. Fairmead House closed in 1859 and was later demolished. Today the Sun Trap Maternity Home which replaced it is now a field study centre *(above)*.

The sadder story of another poet, John Clare, clings to Fairmead, close at hand. Fairmead House, in the year 1837, was a private lunatic asylum, surrounded by a large garden, and kept by a Dr. Allen, one of the first of the lunacy doctors who adopted the humane treatment of patients. Here poor Clare was brought in his forty-fourth year, a complete mental wreck. Within a few years he had tasted the sweets of popularity in London drawing-rooms and fashionable guinea 'Annuals,' and the bitterest adversity and humiliation. At Fairmead House, far away from his Northamptonshire home, he lived for four years, digging in the garden, or roaming at will through Epping Forest.

The Leisure Hour, Henry Walker, 1883

I love the Forest and its airy bounds,
Where friendly Campbell takes his daily
    rounds:
I love the breakneck hills, that headlong go,
And leave me high, and half the world below;
I love to see the Beech Hill mounting high,
The brook without a bridge and nearly dry,
There's Bucket's Hill, a place of furze and
    clouds,
Which evening in a golden haze enshrouds.

John Clare, 1793-1864

Sunday. Felt very melancholy; went a walk in the forest in the afternoon; fell in with some gipsies, one of whom offered to assist in my escape from the madhouse by hiding me in his camp; to which I almost agreed, but told him I had no money to start with, but if he would do so I would promise him fifty pound; and he agreed to do so before Saturday. On Friday I went again, but he did not seem so willing, so I said little about it. On Sunday I went and they were all gone. I found an old wide-awake hat, and an old straw bonnet of the plum-pudding sort was left behind. I put the hat in my pocket, thinking it might be useful for another opportunity, and, as good luck would have it, it turned out to be so.

Diary entry, John Clare, July 18, 1841

Dr Allen occupied three buildings at High Beach: one for the men; another for women under his wife's care, and a third for those requiring constant supervision. Each was specially adapted for its purpose with cubicles for those who had to be isolated. Lippitts Hill Lodge *centre* and Springfield Farm *below* still survive.

On the creation of the new ecclesiastical parish of High Beach in 1836, the church of St Paul *(left)* was erected on a small piece of level ground *(right)* between the Sun Trap and the keeper's cottage. The Lord of Sewardstone manor had contributed £1,000 towards its construction yet the choice of the low lying, poorly-drained site was unfortunate. Within thirty years the little church was in a bad state of repair and it was seen that it would have to be demolished and an alternative position should be found for a new building. Thomas C. Baring of Wallsgrove House offered to pay for the construction of the new church at the top of Church Hill as a memorial to his two sons who had died in infancy. Sir Arthur Blomfield (he was not actually knighted until 1897, two years before his death), the

great church architect of the Victorian age, was entrusted with the design in the Early English style and it was opened on Sunday, June 22, 1873. This of course was at the time of the intense campaigning for the preservation of Epping Forest and, under the provisions of the Act, all such unauthorised enclosures of Forest land were deemed to be illegal. At one stage it was feared that demolition of the new church might be ordered but fortunately the difficulties were resolved by a Deed of Conveyance dated June 7, 1879 which made over the church and the surrounding graveyard to the Ecclestiastical Commissioners. On August 18, 1883 it was consecrated and formally dedicated to the memory of the two young Baring children: the Holy Innocents.

The Holy Innocents has always been a favoured spot for weddings and many are the happy couples who have been photographed within its beautiful setting. However none could be more tragic than that which took place in the midst of the Battle of Britain. Philip David Lloyd was born in Loughton and attended Loughton School (also known as The Vincents) before starting work in the offices of the Chigwell Urban District Council. About the time of Munich he joined the RAF Volunteer Reserve, learning to fly at Stapleford Tawney aerodrome. At High Beach on Saturday, August 24, 1940, Sergeant Pilot Philip Lloyd married the girl he had known since his schooldays

but they were parted after two weeks when he took up his posting as a replacement pilot with No. 41 Squadron then resting at Catterick. Tuesday, September 3 saw the return of No. 41 to Hornchurch and the mounting fury of the battle. Over the next few weeks the squadron took heavy losses, but Sergeant Lloyd seemed to bear a charmed life. Then, in the early morning of Tuesday, October 15, the 23-year-old pilot set off on a routine coastal patrol from which he never returned. Twelve days later his body was washed up on the beach at Herne Bay and Philip Lloyd returned for ever to the little church where he had been married just two months before.

God's Acre — the 'cathedral in the forest' pictured by Dick Cramp. Many of the original windows commemorating members of the Baring family were destroyed when a V-2 exploded nearby in 1944, but some remain in the north transept.

Theydon Bois

Theydon Bois, a pretty mixture of rustic village and villa suburb, about a green much in favour for school treats, brought to its station by the Epping line.

Essex, A. R. Hope-Moncrieff, 1926

Theydon Bois — transformed with the permanent closure of the level crossing in Station Road in 1949 (see Chapter on Railways). The post office-cum-stationers stands on the right next to Sid Cottee's small cycle shop. In those days the village's claim to fame was its retreats — frequented by East-Enders in their thousands. The picture opposite shows the opposing view in 1926 — the small hut on the right being Barclays Bank, open only on Fridays between 10.00 a.m. and midday!

The coming of the Victorian iron road brought 'Railway Hotels' and 'Railway Arms' to countless towns and villages in Britain. Theydon Bois was no exception and the Railway Arms pub stands beyond the post office. In between, in the yard behind the cycle shop, was the blacksmith's shop, the proprietor in 1898 being Mr Flack.

ESSEX FIELD CLUB IN EPPING FOREST

The Essex Field Club held their first field demonstration of the season on Saturday last. The party assembled at Theydon Bois railway station, and had a pleasant excursion into the Forest in search of fresh water algae and mosses. The conductors were Mr. E. D. Marquand, of the Royal Herbarium, Kew, Mr. E. M. Holmes, F.L.S., curator of the Museum of the Pharmaceutical Society, and Messrs. William Cole and R. G. Cole, hon. secretaries. Some good specimens were collected, and the ramble ended at the Wake Arms inn, where tea was served. After tea the 168th ordinary meeting was held, and Mr. Marquand delivered a short lecture on 'Freshwater Algae: their structure, distribution, and relationships.' The lecture was illustrated by diagrams, and listened to with much attention.

Epping Monthly Record, April 1897

Mr Flack's advertisement is reproduced from the old Epping Monthly Record which served the district from December 1894-1900. It was delivered free 'by responsible men from house to house throughout the four parishes' with a circulation of 1,500 copies per month. Although there were county, London and national newspapers available, this was the first opportunity people had of really local news and all the notable events — such as they were — to occur in Theydon Bois were included. Over the last ten years, 'controlled circulation' publications, where the cost of production is entirely borne by the advertisers, have dropped through our letterboxes in increasing numbers but in 1894 it must have been a very bold experiment.

Two advertisers supported all 73 issues (W. Cottis & Sons and C. B. & A. Sworder, both of Epping). Alfred Davis had published his first newspaper, the West Essex Patriot, in 1890, followed by the Monthly Record printed at his Steam Printing Works, Epping. In the first month of the new century Mr Davis changed the format to that of a weekly newspaper: the direct forerunner of the West Essex Gazette of today. The news on Theydon in issue No. 1 of the Record was confined to a rather mundane account of the Parish Meeting; the extract reproduced here from No. 29 is rather more interesting although most folk in 1897 were preoccupied with the forthcoming Diamond Jubilee celebrations to be held in June.

387

The most celebrated inn in Theydon Bois, The Bull, formerly the Bull's Head dating from 1656. The old assembly room of the 1880s is now the lounge bar. In the seventeenth century Theydon Green Gate stood here. The building seen standing on the left just opposite the stocks was used as the local police office in 1886.

By 1928 when this view was taken Coppice Row was already being transformed into a busy 'High Street'. It can be seen that an extension has been added on the front of the 'police station' which functioned as a small confectionary shop called 'The Cabin'. Charles Wood, who opened the shop next door in 1888 as a draper's, began servicing motor cars around the turn of the century. A partner, George Krailing, joined him in partnership in 1918 (see page 408).

In 1952 an employee of Wood and Krailing's since 1927, Jack Farmer, purchased the garage and under his charge the premises were greatly modernised during the following ten years. Jack purchased 'The Cabin' in 1967 and continued the business until it was sold in 1972. The old building, originally the police office, was demolished shortly afterwards.

1931. This was the year of financial collapse in Europe. In January the Allied Military Control Committee for Germany was demolished; in May the bankruptcy of Credit-Anstalt in Austria began the crisis; in June President Hoover proposed a one-year moratorium on reparations and war debts; in July the bankruptcy of the Danatbank led to closure of all the German banks and in Britain the estimated budget deficit was given as £100 million. In August a Franco-US loan was agreed to Britain and that same month Prime Minister Ramsay MacDonald resigned to form a National Government. In September Government economy measures provoked riots and a naval mutiny; Britain abandoned the gold standard and the exchange rate dropped from $4.86 to $3.49. In October a General Election was called and Winston Churchill, Member of Parliament for the Epping District since 1924 (Colonel Mark Lockwood had left parliament when he became Lord Lambourne in 1917) visited the Cabin which was then serving as an election committee room. With him were his wife Clementine and daughter Diana.

About half a mile eastward from Debden Hall is Theydon Bois, which lies on the very confines of our survey, at the north-east angle of Epping Forest. It is a pretty village, and with its triangular green fringed with an avenue of oak-trees, has almost a foreign appearance. It is called Bois after a family who in early ages possessed the manor, and who, in their turn, doubtless bore that name from dwelling in the wood, which in Norman and French was *'le Bois'*.

Greater London, Edward Walford, 1883

THEYDON GREEN This, in a sense, is the Theydon Bois village green. It is noteworthy for the avenue of oaks by which it is divided and the pond on the east side. The Avenue, planted at about the time of Queen Victoria's accession, demonstrates how slow can be the growth of such trees in an exposed situation.

Epping Forest, Alfred Qvist, 1971

The Theydon Bois village sign, designed by Mr W. E. Large, a local commercial artist, was erected facing the Green in 1950 on the traffic island formed by the diversion of Station Road.

Like all of our Epping Forest villages, each has been faced with the threat of creeping urbanisation. As soon as communication links are introduced, be they the railways of the nineteenth century or the motorways of the twentieth, areas become vulnerable to the establishment of 'dormitory suburbs'. Theydon, just 40 minutes or so from the metropolis, was a prime target and development began apace during the 1930s. Although the opening of hostilities in 1939 brought an end to building, it was evident to some far-sighted local residents that 'once the war was over, the probability of indiscriminate development in the Theydon Bois area, with the renewal of the London sprawl into the Essex countryside was clearly foreseen

. . . and it was decided that no time should be lost in preparing to offer the strongest resistance to such threats'. Led by the late Bruce Goodchild, in 1943 the Theydon Bois and District Rural Preservation Society was formed. Essex County Council were no doubt mindful that Theydon Bois was in a vulnerable part of the Green Belt although, as we have seen earlier, this did not stop the establishment of Debden on Green Belt land a couple of miles to the south. Anxious to avoid the eventual linking of the new Loughton with old Theydon, the Society has fought several successful cases to protect the 'village'. Nevertheless the establishment of the new 'Estate' epitomised by the Soper developments brought the issue into sharp focus.

The passage of time has quelled the pre-war arguments about the impact the new properties would have on the former village way of life. *Above:* Forest Drive was cut across Baldocks Farm owned by Horace Morgan who had entered into partnership with William Soper et al to develop his land *below.*

Above: On the opposite side of the Green, Blackacre Farm can be seen on the left of this picture of Hill Road. In the 1960s it was offered for sale at auction but permission to use the whole site for housing was refused in 1967. Only selected development has been permitted alongside the road *(below).*

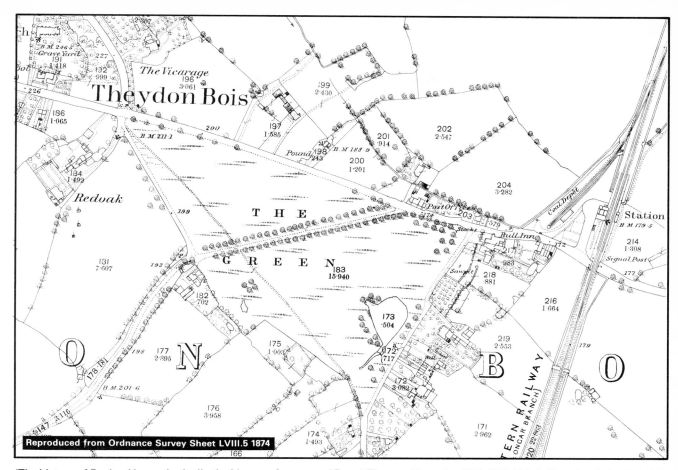

Reproduced from Ordnance Survey Sheet LVIII.5 1874

'The history of England is emphatically the history of progress.' Baron Thomas Macaulay 1800-1859. This is Theydon Bois 1874-1984.

Naturally the new estate required a new High Street and this imposing block surmounted by Bridgeland's clock had been completed by the time this picture was taken in 1936.

FIRE AT COPPICE ROW

On Saturday, the 28th ult., Mr. T. Keen's workshop and contents to the value of £250 were totally destroyed by fire. The outbreak was discovered between two and three o'clock in the afternoon. An alarm was quickly raised, the inhabitants hastening to render assistance in removing the furniture from Mr. Keen's and the adjoining house which were in great danger. A bucket service was soon organised, and the double pump and garden hose from Birch Hall was brought into action, and proved a most useful check on the flames that were threatening the premises next door. A telegram was despatched to the Epping Brigade, and, within ten minutes of the steam signal the engine and appliances were on their way to Theydon. On their arrival it was at once apparent that nothing could save the workshop, the roof having now fallen in. Capt. Saward directed the attention of the brigade to saving such portions of the contents that were of any value. Unfortunately the hydrants are not laid down in that part of Theydon Bois, the only available supply being a well 100 yards away. This was soon exhausted by the engine. The fire was then gradually got under by means of buckets and such water as could be obtained from two or three ordinary taps. The dwelling house, in which Mr. T. Keen resides, was damaged by the heat, the windows being broken and the sashes scorched. We understand that the property is insured, or partly insured in the Phoenix Office.

Epping Monthly Record, September 1895

We have heard that the need of effective hydrants was amply demonstrated at the recent fire at Theydon Bois. Although the water main is laid past the premises on to Abridge, not a single hydrant or fire plug is fixed within half-a-mile of this most populous part of the parish. The various parish councils could put in some good work by attending to this important matter, which, at times, resolves itself into a 'burning question'.

Epping Monthly Record, September 1895

The Herts and Essex Water Company are making provision against a water famine in Epping. Windmill Farm reservoir is nearly finished and it is expected that by next month the districts of Ivy Chimneys, Theydon Bois and Abridge will have the benefit of a plentiful supply of water without draining the town pipes. The new reservoir is being constructed under the superintendence of Mr. G. Smith (resident engineer) and Mr. W. Guest. It has a capacity of 120,000 gallons, which will be under a 40-lb. pressure — sufficient to force the water over the highest building if used through a hydrant. By-the-way, the Urban Council have provided the fire brigade with a new standpipe to fit the new hydrants that are being put in.

Epping Monthly Record, July 1897

On Monday evening Nov 5th, the Fire Brigade received a call from Mr. Avila's farm at Theydon Bois. On the steam whistle sounding, the firemen turned out very smartly and were on the road within six minutes. Fortunately the fire, which proved to be a stack, was got under before it became serious and the firemen had their drive for nothing. It is singular that the rule of mustering the brigade on Guy Fawkes Night was relaxed for the first time this year.

Epping Monthly Record, November 1900

This rural scene (see also pages 384-385) shows Coppice Row almost unchanged for 300 years. The weatherboarded building next to The Queen Victoria housed Theydon's first post office, later Gussin's the grocers and Barnes the bakers.

One of the prettiest groups of old buildings in Theydon Bois may disappear soon to make way for a new trio of shops.

The old buildings in Coppice Row, have for many years been used as shops, the best known being A. and J. Barnes, the bakers and confectioners.

The buildings are classified but only in Grade Three so the local authority has no power to prevent them being demolished. They are of Essex weatherboard.

'The last remaining feature of old Theydon,' a member of the Rural Preservation Society said at the parish council meeting last week.

The council was discussing an application made for outline planning permission for the three shops on the same site.

'The cottages are far prettier than anything that will be put there,' commented Miss Blanche Buxton.

Another worry came from the housewives on the council. 'What will happen to the bread?' they asked.

Barnes have a reputation throughout the village for excellent bread, but the housewives are afraid that redevelopment will mean a new oven and bread quite different to the crusty loaves so loved in the village.

Press report, September 1971

April 1963: Theydon Bois Preservation Society writes to Parish Council with plea for the preservation of the cottages. August 1963: cottages become listed Grade III. March 1969: planning permission to demolish them and build three shops and flats. December 1969: Essex County Council declare cottages 'not worth preserving'. January 1972: revised plans accepted for development as a supermarket. November 1974: the International superstore opens its doors.

'Such buildings are becoming all too few in number in Epping Forest due to the absence of an appreciation of what they represent — our link with the past.' So wrote the Theydon Bois Preservation Society about the demise of the old shops.

The Queen's Record Reign was celebrated at Theydon Bois, on Friday, June 25th. Notwithstanding the storm of the previous day very little inconvenience was felt in the matter of outdoor enjoyment. The committee elected at the public meeting was as follows: Rev. C. E. Campbell, Rev. W. P. Lillingston, R. F. Ball, R. T. Bell (chairman), G. Buxton, J. Cottee, A. Fitt, T. Keen, P. Mitchell, W. H. Nicholls, C. R. Parkes, T. Riggs, and C. Woodward. The amount of money collected was about £45. At 3 p.m. the children's races took place in Red Oaks field, kindly lent by Mr. P. Mitchell. It should be mentioned that great credit is due to Mr. Woodward for the manner in which he prepared the course — especially the impediments for the obstacle race. Owing to the number of entries some of the races had to be duplicated. At 5.15 a move was made to Riggs' Retreat for dinner. This, undoubtedly, was the event of the day to which invitations had been freely given to every parishioner irrespective of age. The popularity of this policy on the part of the committee was evidenced by the fact that 380 persons assembled at the festive board, and expressed their lively gratification. Mr. Gerald Buxton took the chair and Mr. R. T. Bell occupied the vice-chair. Grace was said by the Rev. C. E. Campbell.

In 1832, five years before Queen Victoria came to the throne, a fine avenue of 62 oak trees was planted across the Green by Robert Westley Hall-Dare (whose father owned the manor of Ilford Lodge and his wife that of Cranbrook). This is how they had grown by the time Theydon Bois celebrated the Queen's Diamond Jubilee.

Left: **The Green once boasted a fine horse trough and drinking fountain — one of the normal pieces of 'furniture' to be seen at the beginning of the century in every town and village in** Britain. *Right:* **By the 1930s all that remained was this miserable little structure by the junction with the road to the Wake Arms.** *Below:* **Today a litter bin marks the spot!**

Mr. T. Riggs, the well-known caterer, is to be congratulated upon the way in which he served up the repast. When it is borne in mind that, owing to the storm on the previous day he had lost a large number of appliances which it was impossible to replace in so short a time, it seems wonderful the way in which he surmounted all difficulties.

After dinner the company adjourned to the field where the sports for adults was carried out. Mr. A. Fitt acted as starter, Mr. Bell clerk of course, and Messrs. G. Buxton and Allfrey were judges. Prizes to the amount of £4 10s. were given. It is pleasing to note that those people who, through age or infirmity, were unable to attend the festivities were each presented with 2/6. There is no doubt that the celebration in Theydon Bois was one calculated to live long in the memory of those who were fortunate enough to take part in it.

Two gross of medals were distributed by Mrs. Campbell, the medals being the gift of Mr. Max Simon.

On Jubilee Day itself (June 22nd) many of the houses were decorated and illuminated, notably Mr. Skinner's and Mr. Martin's, and a large bonfire was lighted at 10 o'clock in the grounds of Mr. Bell.

Epping Monthly Record, July 1897

A second avenue of oaks was planned in 1935 to mark the Silver Jubilee of King George V. Mrs Gerald Buxton planted the first one at the top of Chapel Road (on the western side of the Green). Unfortunately only three have survived.

An effort is being made to form a Golf Club for Theydon Bois and the district. It is proposed to admit both lady and gentlemen members, and an effort is being made to obtain the use of the forest land known as 'Thames Valley,' which is considered a magnificent site and well suited for a nine hole course.

Epping Monthly Record, November 1897

We are pleased to hear that permission has now been obtained from the Forest Committee of the Corporation of London for the Theydon Bois Golf Club to play the game in the very picturesque part of the Forest known as 'Thames Valley,' but now more appropriately called 'Nightingale Valley,' lying between Piercing Hill and Bell Common. We understand that at the preliminary meeting of the Club held at 'Pine Mount,' the following gentlemen were elected:— President, Col. Lockwood, M.P.; vice-presidents, Rev. C. Campbell, Messrs. Gerald Buxton, W. H. Nicholls, E. J. Wythes, and Major Tait; hon. treasurer, W. H. Nicholls; captain, J. Carson; hon. secretary, L. N. Bamber, 'The Glen,' Theydon Bois (to whom application for membership should be made). The entrance fee for the first 50 members has been fixed at one guinea and annual subscription one guinea, but lady members are admitted without entrance fee. We are informed that the links are now being laid out and it is anticipated that members will be able to commence playing early in January.

Epping Monthly Record, December 1897

The new links, which have been recently laid out under the supervision of Mr. J. Braid, one of the champion professional golf players, were formally opened for play on the 5th inst. The attendance of members was very good, and several very close games were contested, more especially a foursome between Messrs.

Carson (the captain) and McGregor (Finchley), and Messrs Allfrey and Bamber (secretary), in which the former pair won by one hole. The latter, however, neatly turned the tables by winning the next game.

Epping Monthly Record, March 1898

Elsewhere tree growth has been more prolific. Compare the present-day sylvan scene *(above)* on the road to Epping with the open aspect of the golf links (created at a cost of £15 in 1897-98) as they appeared fifty years ago *(below)*.

Hard by the golf course lies Piercing Hill, also known as Church Hill *(above)* for obvious reasons. St Mary's, the parish church, is the third building to bear the name. The first *(below left)* stood for some 700 years a mile south-east of the village beside the Abridge road. It appears to be quite a normal mediaeval practice to build the church some distance from the village — we have already seen this at Woodford, Loughton and Chingford — the hearty walk no doubt serving to freshen up worshippers before their devotions! As the churches were normally sited alongside the manor house, his Lordship, on the other hand, could just stroll next door. (At Draycot, where Catherine Tylney Long of Wanstead Hall is buried, the 'family pew' is in fact a small curtained-off room complete with its own fireplace! The chimney can be seen in the picture on page 163.) At Theydon the old church lay beside Theydon Hall but when the Reverend George Hambleton was inducted in 1842 he decided that a larger church, nearer the village, was required. Two years later the original building was demolished; all that remains today to mark its passing being a few mouldering tombstones *(below right)*.

The church here has been transplanted, the original structure, which stood to the south on the high ground, having been pulled down, and its materials worked into the new structure — a tasteful little building, with a tall and tapering spire. One or two monuments and graves, with their contents, were transferred, among them some members of the Hall-Dare family, the squires and patrons of the living.

In the church is a well-preserved painting of the royal arms, and the initials 'J. R.' clearly denoting 'Jacobus Rex', our first English James. Below the escutcheon is a portrait of the king — an unmistakable Stuart, but more like Charles I than his father. It was probably owing to the remote position of the church in 'the woods' that this royal heraldry escaped the hands of the Parliamentary Roundheads of Cromwell's time. The old churchyard is still enclosed, and its tombs are carefully kept.

Greater London, Edward Walford, 1883

On Saturday, Sept. 25th, a window which has been put in the parish church to the memory of the late Miss Buss, founder of the North London Collegiate School for Girls, was publicly unveiled. The window was erected by

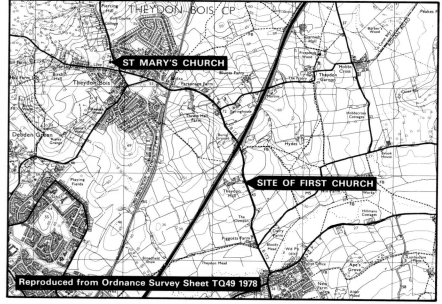

Reproduced from Ordnance Survey Sheet TQ49 1978

Miss Toplis and the girls of Montague House, one of the school boarding-houses in connection with the school, and illustrates the words from *The Pilgrim's Progress*: 'The interpreter called a servant of his called Greatheart. "Take these, my daughters," said he, "and conduct them to the house called Beautiful,"' A short service was conducted by the vicar, the Rev. C. E. Campbell, the Rev. Alfred J. Buss, and the Rev. Septimus Buss.

Epping Monthly Record, October 1897

The confirmation of the death of Capt. Horace Mann, of Theydon Bois, cast quite a gloom over the neighbourhood in which he was so well known. Capt. Mann, who was killed in action on Monday, June 11th, whilst serving with Thorneycroft's Mounted Infantry at the battle of Almond's Nek (also called Allemann's Nek), was the eldest surviving son of the Rev. Noel Mann, of Torquay, and St. Issey, Cornwall. He married, in 1889, Ada, daughter of Col. T. A. Pitt, R.A., of Maidstone. He entered the Army in 1882 joining the 1st Royal West Kent Regt., and served throughout the Nile expedition in 1884-5, for which he obtained the Medal with clasp and Khedive's Star. He obtained the Captaincy in 1890, and acted as Adjutant to the 1st V.B. Royal West Kent Regt. from 1892 to 1897, retiring from the service shortly afterwards. On the outbreak of the present war he went as a Volunteer to South Africa, where he served as aide-de-camp to Lord Dundonald, afterwards joining Thorneycroft's Mounted Infantry. He was present at Colenso and the action leading to the relief of Ladysmith.

The late Captain Mann was Churchwarden of St. Mary's, Theydon Bois, for two years previous to his departure to South Africa. It is intended to perpetuate his memory by means of a memorial in the parish church. Donations for this purpose may be sent to the Vicar or Churchwardens of Theydon Bois or to Mr. Alf. Cable, of Epping.

Epping Monthly Record, June 1900

We regret to record the death of the Rev. C. E. Campbell, vicar of St. Mary's, Theydon Bois, which took place on Friday morning October 26th. The deceased had officiated at St. Mary's for a period of 27 years, and was both loved and respected throughout the district. He was 74 years of age, having been born in 1826 at Killeigh, County Down, Ireland. He entered Trinity College, Dublin, in 1845, passed out with high honours, and was a theological and classical scholar and exhibitioner. Before coming to Theydon in 1874 the deceased held chaplaincies at Southall, and Chantilly, France.

Epping Monthly Record, November 1900

Land for the replacement church was given by the Hall-Dare family, which then owned the manor, and the new church, partly constructed from the demolished rubble of the old one to cut costs, was erected in 1843-44 for £1,310 by a builder from Norfolk. However there must have been cowboys around even in those days for within five years his shoddy workmanship had resulted in dangerous cracks and subsidence. The architect was found partly to blame and agreed to pay £400 compensation towards the cost of rebuilding — this being the only practical solution. Thus the second church was pulled down in 1849 and a fresh start made with a new architect, Samuel Smirke who had recently designed St John's at Loughton, and a new builder! St Mary's was consecrated on February 9, 1851.

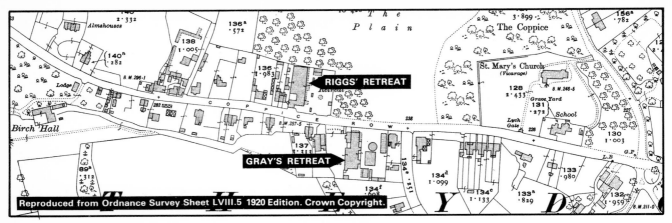

The third Riggs retreat in the forest was opened in 1882 in Coppets or Coppice Row, Theydon Bois. The retreat was on the north side adjacent to Theydon Plain. It was operated by John Riggs's son, Thomas, and it is of interest that in the period 1896 to 1900 he was advertising in Davis's Epping, Loughton and Ongar Almanack that he was prepared to supply and deliver in the surrounding areas potatoes and other root vegetables at a price of 3/- per hundredweight. An illustrated brochure shows that by 1911 the retreat was being managed for him by Mrs. Martha Turner whose husband was chauffeur to Mr. Gerald Buxton at Birch Hall. In 1915 or 1916 the Turners left the retreat and removed to Bath where one of their daughters was married in 1919. When they returned to the area, Mr. and Mrs. Turner became licensees at the Carpenters Arms at Thornwood Common.

By 1916, possibly because of war-time conditions, and because by then Thomas Riggs would have been near his sixties, the retreat passed into other hands and eventually was taken over by Edwin Yates. . . .

The Retreats of Epping Forest,
Bernard Ward

We have already discussed the retreats of Epping Forest in an earlier chapter but we must now return to the two at Theydon Bois as they are such a part of its history — both happy and tragic.

Green and white painted Riggs' Retreat on the northern side of road, also known just as the Theydon Retreat, became Yates' Retreat when taken over by Mr and Mrs Teddy Yates who were ably assisted by their five daughters who no doubt provided an additional attraction. The family lived on the first floor at the eastern end.

As part of their post-war survey of Britain, No. 541 Squadron photographed Theydon Bois on October 10, 1946. (Crown Copyright)

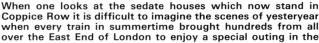

When one looks at the sedate houses which now stand in Coppice Row it is difficult to imagine the scenes of yesteryear when every train in summertime brought hundreds from all over the East End of London to enjoy a special outing in the country. We have nothing today which compares; they were more than just funfairs and, because Theydon lacked a village hall of its own, the retreats were also used for entertainments and all kinds of local events.

On Friday, May 21st, a dramatic entertainment was given at Rigg's Retreat in aid of the cricket club. There was a good attendance and a substantial balance was realised. The following programme was carried out:- 'Sunset': Lois, Mrs. Gerald Buxton; Joan, Miss Clare Buxton; Aunt Drusilla, Miss Theresa Buxton; Lawrence Leigh, Mr. Owen Hugh Smith; Azariah Stodd, Mr. Jocelyn Pelham; Mr. Rivers (Lois' father), Mr. J. Randall. 'Highwayman': Lady Betty Basset, Miss Ruth Buxton; Sir Harry Bellairs, Mr. J. Pelham. Violin, Mrs. Lloyd Pease; violoncello, Miss Claudia Pease; piano, Miss Clare Buxton and Mr. A. B. Walker.

Epping Monthly Record, May 1897

A peculiar outbreak of fire occurred at Riggs' Retreat on Tuesday morning last. Smoke was observed issuing from the flooring of one of the refreshment stands. On removing some of the boards it was discovered that one of the rafters was alight. It is thought that a lighted match or piece of paper must have fallen through a crevice and so started the fire. It is fortunate that it was discovered in time, and it brings to mind the entire absence of hydrants at Theydon Bois, which was painfully apparent some two years ago, when the firemen had to stand by and see Mr. Keen's workshop destroyed for the want of a hydrant. When the new reservoir is completed there will be a splendid supply of water under a high pressure, and we again urge the matter of hydrants upon the notice of the parochial authorities.

Epping Monthly Record, July 1897

Snowdrop Minstrels

An excellent local troupe of Negro minstrels has been formed under Mr. R. T. Bell's direction, and they gave their first performance on Wednesday, 27th ult., at Riggs' Retreat, before an audience numbering nearly 200. The entertainment went with a swing from beginning to end. There were 26 performers, including a band of six players. Mr. R. T. Bell was interlocutor, and superintended the arrangements generally. The 'bones' were Messrs. E. Brewer and J. Smith, and the tambourines, Messrs. A. Burton Walker and C. E. Purkiss. Miss Bell presided at the piano. In the farce 'Waxination Gratis', Mr. Burton Walker played capitally as the assistant of Senor Frangipanni (Mr. R. T. Bell). Mr. Powell made a great hit in his character, and Master Bell as Mrs. Greeneye played with remarkable ability, and delighted everybody.

Epping Monthly Record, May 1898

Monday, November 18, 1940 Place: Epping

At 0345 hrs this morning a parachute mine hit one of the wooden billets at Theydon Bois. The whole building was destroyed and there were 26 killed and many injured. The local defence services did admirable work in helping to clear the casualties to hospital, in rendering first aid, and in helping to search the debris.

Tuesday, November 19

Two more casualties have resulted from the explosion yesterday. New billets have been found for 'C' Coy. This involved moving part of the Essex Reg. out of Epping and the drawing of 'C' Coy. into their place.

Wednesday, November 20

Three more casualties. Some are still seriously ill.

Wednesday, November 27

H.R.H. The Duchess of Gloucester visited the battalion. She inspected 'B' and 'C' Coys. and part of HQ at Thornwood and then went to Theydon Bois to inspect 'A' Coy. After lunch in the Officers' Mess at Epping she visited those injured by the explosion at Theydon Bois and went to the companies at North Weald and Chipping Ongar.

War Diary, 6th Battalion, King's Own Scottish Borderers

The building involved in the explosion at Theydon Bois was Yates' Retreat. This building was a two-storied building occupied by 'A' Coy. HQ and two platoons of 'A' Coy. on the north side of the road from Theydon Bois to the main Epping-London road (Map ref O.S. Sheet 107 891182). It was almost entirely built of wood except for a small portion near to the road which was of brick. There were tall trees on two sides and a private house and garden on the west side. Slit trenches had been dug amongst these trees to accommodate the personnel living in the billet. The billet was large and personnel were well scattered in it.

The total number of men billeted in Yates' Retreat was 60, consisting of men from 7 Platoon, 8 Platoon and Coy. HQ, two Signallers and four Stretcher Bearers. Of these men, 7 slept on the upper floor.

The Coy. office, cookhouse and Coy. store were also in this building. One man slept in the Coy. office, nobody slept in the cookhouse, one in the Coy. store.

At approximately 0345 hrs on November 18, 1940 the sentry was walking from the billets of 9 Platoon which were some distance eastwards of Yates' Retreat, when he saw an object with a parachute attached, falling through the air in the direction of the billet. He loaded his rifle to shoot it, but came to the conclusion that it was a pilot baling out of his plane. He therefore withheld his fire. When it exploded he flung himself on the ground. He states that there were two explosions and after the second, flares were dropped. There is a crater in the neighbourhood at approximately

ATKINS, Pvt. Richard. Liverpool (Anfield) Cemetery, Sec. 9. Nonconformist. Grave 539.

BOYD, Pvt. Thomas Gosnell, Age 23. Glasgow (Sandymount) Cemetery, Old Monkland, Compt. T. Grave 693.

CLARK, Pvt. William. Age 19. Edinburgh (Mount Vernon) Roman Catholic Cemetery, Sec. P. Grave 49.

COLTMAN, L/Cpl. William H, Age 20. Hawick (Wilton) Cemetery, Grave 1484.

CROZIER, Pvt. Allan. Age 22. Newcastle-Upon-Tyne, (Byker and Heaton) Cemetery, Sec. I. N. Cons. Grave 131.

DAVIDSON, Pvt. David Stewart McQuillin, Age 19. Ettleton Old Churchyard, Castleton, Row 2. Grave 56.

DICKSON, Pvt. John Brunton, Age 20. Jedburgh (St John) Churchyard.

DOBSON, Pvt. Allan Brown, Age 19. Jedburgh (Castlewood) Cemetery, 1st Extn. Grave 222.

DOUGLAS, Pvt. Godfrey Dalgety, Brookwood Memorial to the Missing, Panel 11. Column 1.

DOUGLAS, L/Cpl. John Turnbull, Age 21. Melrose (Wairds) Cemetery, Sec. B. Grave 274.

GAY, Pvt. Charles, Age 21. Tynemouth (Preston) Cemetery, Sec. F. Uncons. Grave 11669.

GIBB, L/Cpl. Alexander, Kelso Cemetery, Compt. B. Grave 238.

GLANCY, Pvt. Paul F, Age 23. Edinburgh (Mount Vernon) Roman Catholic Cemetery, Sec. O. Grave 25.

GOFF, Pvt. Esmond John, Age 23. Edinburgh (Comely Bank) Cemetery, Grave N. 1224.

HAY, Pvt. Robert, Age 23. Edinburgh (Saughton) Cemetery, Sec. L. Grave 497.

HEWITT, Pvt. George Robert, Winlaton (St Paul) Churchyard Extension, Blaydon. Sec. E. South, Grave 59.

HUNTER, Pvt. John, Age 23. Melrose (Wairds) Cemetery, Sec. B. Grave. 90.

JAMESON, Pvt. Thomas William, Age 25. Berwick-Upon-Tweed Cemetery, Sec. C. A. Cons. Grave 1120.

KER, Pvt. James, Age 21. Kelso Cemetery, Compt. B. Grave 240.

LANNIGAN, Pvt. Michael, Liverpool (Ford) Roman Catholic Cemetery, Sec. A. B. Grave 547.

McCREADIE, Pvt. Samuel McClurg, Borgue Parish Churchyard, West Extn. Grave 122C.

McGUIRE, Pvt. James, Age 23. Edinburgh (Mount Vernon) Roman Catholic Cemetery, Sec. N. Grave 54.

MURRAY, Pvt. Robert Thomas, Age 21. Kelso Cemetery, Compt. B. Grave 239.

PROUDFOOT, Pvt. James Stevenson, Age 20. Castleton Churchyard, Grave 911.

PURVIS, Pvt. Joseph. Age 21. Jarrow Cemetery, County Durham, Sec. 17, Grave 52.

REED, Pvt. Selby Douglas, Age 21. Newcastle-Upon-Tyne (Byker and Heaton) Cemetery, Sec. 2. Grave 48.

ROGERS, Pvt. James. Age 23. Choppington (St Paul) Churchyard, Bedlingtonshire.

SHANKS, Pvt. David Wilson. Age 19. Bowden New Cemetery, Grave 268.

SHEARER, Pvt. Alan, Age 26. Portsoy Cemetery, Fordyce, Sec. B. Grave 24.

SKILTON, Pvt. Ronald Herbert, Age 29. Crystal Palace District Cemetery, Sec. V.11. Grave 17921.

According to the number of dead given in the KOSB war diary there would appear to be one further casualty although his name is not stated and his death is not recorded at Epping Registry Office. Army records (page 399) also state 26 deaths as having occurred on the 18th whereas 28 were recorded at Epping for that date. Lance Corporal Coltman is recorded as having died of injuries on November 19 and Private Hunter on November 20.

'They shall not grow old, as we that are left grow old. At the going down of the sun and in the morning we will remember them.'

Death and destruction at Theydon Bois. Both Yates' and Gray's suffered at the hands of the Luftwaffe yet by October 1946 the sites of both had been cleared in preparation for their subsequent redevelopment for housing.

898184. The aeroplane seemed to be above the clouds and the sentry did not see it.

The civil police state that they have found part of a mine and it is considered that it was a mine that fell near to Yates' Retreat. The crater is situated adjacent to the north-eastern end of the building. It is 30 foot diameter and twelve feet deep.

The explosion destroyed the entire building except for the brick part, which still stands.

The explosion also damaged the northern end of Gray's Retreat which is occupied by 'C' Coy. Part of the roof is shattered and damage has been done to the walls and upper storey making the building unfit for occupation.

The casualties of 'A' Coy. were 26 killed and 3 injured.

At 'C' Coy. there were three men injured.

Report of
Officer Commanding 6th (Border) Bn.
The King's Own Scottish Borderers

When the military took over the Retreats the first contingent of soldiers stationed there were the Welsh Guards. When they moved on we had other regiments, until about the latter end of 1940 the King's Own Scottish Borderers took over. These were a nice lot of chaps, but they drove our Air Raid Wardens up the wall because they were everlastingly showing lights during the night raids. Of course, our wardens had no jurisdiction over the Military and so could only protest. It is no satisfaction to me to say they paid dearly for their carelessness.

On the night of Sunday November 17th 1940, the sirens had sounded the warning as usual. It was customary at that time for a 'peacetime' crew and an A.F.S. crew to man the Fire Station on alternate nights. On this particular night the Auxiliaries were on duty and the Retained men were at their homes. The raid continued all night, but sometime afer 3.00 a.m. it was noticed that a 'plane was circling round, though of course we could not see it. At 3.36 a.m. precisely there was a terrific explosion followed almost immediately by another. Scarcely had this happened when the 'phone rang with PC Hart on the line reporting that an oil bomb had been dropped on Yates' Retreat. He can be excused his error for there were a number of fires started. Actually a parachute mine had scraped across Yates's Retreat roof, collided with the helter skelter and exploded. The second one — for there were two — dropped in the garden of Braeside, damaging all the property up Piercing Hill. . . .

400

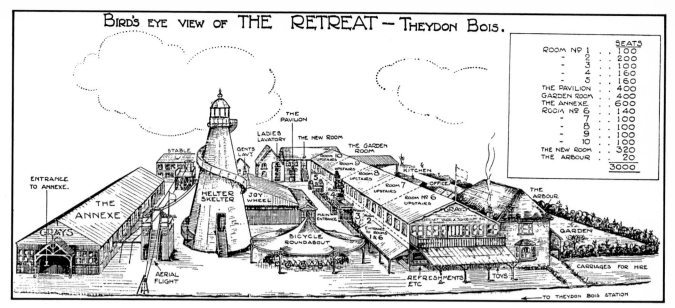

Bird's eye view of THE RETREAT – Theydon Bois.

	SEATS
ROOM Nº 1	100
— 2	200
— 3	100
— 4	160
— 5	160
THE PAVILION	400
GARDEN ROOM	400
THE ANNEXE	600
ROOM Nº 6	140
— 7	100
— 8	100
— 9	100
— 10	100
THE NEW ROOM	320
THE ARBOUR	20
	3000

The blast had lifted up the floor on which the men were sleeping, turning it completely over and trapping them in the foundation well beneath. We therefore had to be particularly careful to use the minimum of water, to avoid drowning them before they could be released.

The following Sunday morning, November 24th, a memorial Service was held at St. Mary's Church and the Kosby's Regimental band came down and assembled in Forest Drive. They started off in slow march time playing a lament. I have never seen or heard anything like it before or since, and I shall never forget it as long as I live.

Theydon Bois As I Knew It. Jack Farmer

Supplying Coffins to Thornwood Mortuary and St. Margaret's Hospital for men of the 6th King's Own Scottish Borderers killed in Air Raid at the Retreat, Theydon Bois, Nov. 18th, 1940.

Journal entry, Poulton & Sons, Undertakers, Epping

The retreats also served as convenient locations for meetings — this is Gray's (formerly Drossett's) on the south side of Coppice Row as it appeared in 1921.

Although also damaged in the blast of November 1940, Gray's was still habitable although Doug and Cath Gray decided to sell up in 1942, the auction taking place on May 27 and 28. Thereafter it was used by the Walthamstow Press to store paper until getting on for two and a half years later a flying bomb scored a direct hit during the V1 campaign. Fortunately this time there were no fatalities, a small boy slightly injured being the only casualty. This view shows the ruin of the Gray family house, visible on the right of the drawing at the top of the page.

Towards the end of the war, and for a short time afterwards, one of Pakes Farm's fields was rented by an aluminium firm in the Midlands. Every day huge lorries would arrive with damaged aeroplane fuselages, and these were dumped in the field. The engines and all the valuable fittings had been removed, and by the time deliveries ceased, there must have been several hundred there, piled on top of one another, four or five high. Most of the bodies were from Boeing B-17 Flying Fortresses, but there were some Liberators and the odd Marauder, etc. The firm contracted with R. J. Coley & Son, scrap metal merchants from West London, to cut up and load the aluminium into goods trucks at Theydon Bois Railway Station. Coley had all the other metals. They would light a large bonfire of self-sealing fuel tanks, wood, old cable, etc., and on top of this would put the Glycol

radiators and collect the solder from them at the bottom of the fire. This was very valuable even in those days, and these boys certainly knew their business! . . . Now, Pakes Way and parts of Green Glade stand on the site

The war had another striking impact on the village when R. J. Coley & Son, scrap metal merchants, began using part of Pakes Farm (see the aerial photo on page 398) to stockpile redundant aircraft for salvaging. These were cut up and the aluminium sent from the rail-head to the Northern Aluminium Company works at Adderbury, Oxfordshire, for reprocessing. It is quite possible therefore, that the replacement saucepan or kettle you purchased after the war is made from the wreckage of Theydon's aircraft! Only P-08 can be identified here — it was a B-26 Martin Marauder which served with the 575th Bomb Squadron of the 391st Bomb Group based at Matching airfield — part of the US Ninth Army Air Force.

and I'm sure queer looking objects are dug up from time to time in the gardens of the residents even today!

Theydon Bois As I Knew It, Jack Farmer

In 1972-73 permission to demolish Pakes farm, then classified as Grade III under the old listing system but now Grade II, and the nearby late-sixteenth century cottage on Poplar Row, was refused. The farm had been sold to a developer for £46,000 but housing was only allowed to infill between Green Glade and the viaduct.

Centrepiece of the development is Robert Daniels Court (the man himself appears on page 127), which provides sheltered accommodation for retired folk. Compare this picture by Ray Stebbings in 1966 with the one on page 391 taken in 1985.

Poplar Row runs in front of the farm down to Theydon Park Road. Originally this ended a mile short of any habitation in

Rectory Lane, Loughton: now the built-up area of the Debden Estate reaches to within a few hundred yards.

The remains of a Battle of Britain fighter shot down by an enemy plane were unearthed on Saturday.

The Hurricane aircraft was part of the 242 Fighter Squadron led by war hero Group Captain Douglas Bader.

It nose-dived 18 feet into the soil of a field in Theydon Bois on September 7, 1940, killing 25-year-old Pilot Officer Benzi of Winnipeg, Canada.

Parts of the Rolls-Royce Merlin Mark II engine were dug out by a team led by wartime planes expert Tony Graves and Loughton building contractor Gordon Bridgman.

Bones were also found in the wreckage. These are now in the hands of the police and will be analysed by pathology laboratory experts.

The casualty list at the Air Ministry is being consulted. The pilot was based at Debden, Essex, and listed on an unknown grave at Runneymede War Memorial.

Sixty-year-old Harry Smith of Buxton Road, Theydon Bois, was cutting a nearby hedge when the fighter plunged from the sky. He told the Gazette: 'It came over and clipped the top of a line of elm trees and then plunged into the ground. It hit the earth with such an impact all the leaves in the nearby wood fell. As it hit the field near Theydon Park Road little bits of plane fell like leaves.'

Mr Smith and other onlookers stood helpless. 'There was nothing we could do' he added. A few people ran out into the field — but all there was left was a mound and the scorched grass.

The engine was hauled from the ground by the recovery team — just a week off exactly 36 years ago when the unsuspecting pilot was cruising in the skies on the lookout for enemy aircraft. . . .

West Essex Gazette, September 3, 1976

It was on that intervening Green Belt land that another wartime drama was enacted . . . together with its post-war sequel. On September 7, 1940, some three hundred yards from the end of the road, an aircraft plummeted to earth after a combat which began over the Thames Estuary. No remains were recovered from the crash and the incident was all but forgotten until the London War Museum heard of it when excavating the German crash site at the Wake Arms (page 60). By a process of elimination (the Royal Air Force lost 17 pilots that day of whom 5 were listed as just 'missing in action') they believed the aircraft off Theydon Park Road was that of a Canadian, Pilot Officer John Benzie. Almost exactly 36 years after the crash, the site was investigated and, although human remains were discovered, there was no trace of any identification, either of pilot or machine. After an inconclusive Coroner's inquest at Epping, the remains were buried in the military cemetery at Brookwood as just an unknown pilot from the RAF — his nationality being confirmed by identifying pieces of wreckage as being parts of a Hurricane. Other amateur aircraft investigators were not satisfied that all had been done that could be done to identify the pilot, and in 1981 the site was re-excavated to try to find the aircraft serial plate as it was known from squadron records that John Benzie was flying Hurricane No. P2962 on his last patrol. However nothing more positive came to light and there the matter had to be left. However Pilot Officer Benzie, if it is he who is buried in Grave 1 of Row E of Plot 22 at Brookwood, is unique amongst all 'The Few' in that his countrymen

honoured his sacrifice by naming the largest of all memorials to casualties of the Battle of Britain: Lake Benzie.

Loughton Lane in the 1930s. One thing which has certainly not changed from that day to this is the street illuminations — or lack of them! Although gas reached the village in 1872 and the new-fangled electricity in 1928, the roads remain unlit and Theydon Bois must certainly hold some sort of record for holding out for so long against their introduction.

The ghost of the almost-forgotten Village/Estate split was to materialise once more in 1963, the year of the Great Street-Lighting Debate. This is recent history indeed, and the writer proceeds with caution.

For the benefit of newcomers: the campaign for street lights had its roots in the Estate and support for it grew rapidly there. This was not the first time that the issue had been raised; a similar attempt had been made before the war. Now the old arguments, pro and con, were brought out and dusted-off.

Once again, the correspondence columns of the local Press became the battle ground and much hot air was vented, both in print and at council meetings. Curiously, the din of battle reached the ears of the BBC in what was presumably a quiet week for news as they sent a camera crew down. They set up a pitch in Forest Drive, where shoppers could be seen crossing the road in a seemingly casual fashion, some towards and others away from the camera.

A beleaguered parish council called an extraordinary meeting for the airing of views, to be followed by a referendum. The meeting proved one of the liveliest in the council's history, with a massive turnout of ratepayers. The old Village Hall was packed to capacity, sitting and standing, while the overflow gathered outside around open doors and windows.

In a vigorous but mostly orderly fashion, members of the community put their points. Some hurtful things were said concerning people who chose to come to a village to live and then wanted to change everything when they got there . . . and so on. One compassionate villager told of benighted old age pensioners stumbling in potholes, which brought from another quarter the stout rejoinder that the thing to do with potholes was to fill them in, rather than to go to great expense to light them up. Unanswerable, really, and Theydon duly voted by a large majority for starlight and hand-torches. There the matter rests — until the next time.

About Theydon, David Phillipson

Do street lights save lives on busy roads, reduce burglaries, and allow your teenage daughter to walk home safely?

Or does a village like Theydon Bois manage quite well without them? Would lighting reveal dark secrets on the roads — or would it effectively detract from their charm?

These are just some of the questions that the people of Theydon Bois are going to have to weigh up in the coming month.

For on September 9 the parish council is to hold a public meeting on street lighting, to discuss the arguments for and against. Shortly afterwards, on a day to be fixed, a referendum will be held.

The issue has been sparked off by the new housing estate at Pakes Farm, described by Epping Forest Council lighting engineer Mr Geoff Pettit as a 'development with a large proportion of old people mixed with young families'.

He believes that both the young and the old have a particular need for street lights.

Mr Pettit is proposing 11 for the estate, and favours high-pressured sodium lamps, which give a white, though not harsh, light. They are, he says, 'The next best thing to daylight.'

The cost of installing them would be borne by the developer, while Essex County Council would foot the bill for maintenance and energy costs.

As for the cost to Theydon Bois residents, Mr Pettit estimates: 'They are paying between 0.2 and 0.5 pence in the pound on the rates for 90,000 street lights in the county. Eleven more are not going to push the rates. They are already paying for them.'

Mr Pettit summed up: 'If they don't want street lights good luck to them. But I feel all the parishioners should have the chance to say.'

West Essex Gazette, August 20, 1976

Theydon Bois villagers may be asked to vote for or against street lamps.

The commuter village, which consists mainly of inter-war and post-war estates, has stubbornly refused to light up, despite demands in the past from some residents.

Now another referendum or poll may be carried out.

The last ballot, in 1977, was a straight vote in the village hall. But those in favour of lights say the referendum then wasn't representative of the people.

The issue was raised again by a member of the public at last Thursday's parish council meeting.

Councillor Mrs Joy Wainwright claimed it would mean a burden on the rates for the village.

And Councillor Mrs Eileen Johnson said people who moved to the village had to put up with what was there — the forest, a rail link to London — and no street lamps, all attractions.

But Councillor Ron Barrows said it would not be unreasonable to have a referendum or poll, as the last one was seven years ago.

Parish clerk Mrs Jean Shephard said to demand a referendum or poll, 10 electors would have to support it, or a third of the members of public present.

West Essex Gazette, February 3, 1984

STREET LIGHTS FIZZLE OUT AGAIN

The parish council is not to call a special meeting to discuss street lighting in Theydon Bois.

Parish clerk Mrs Jean Shephard told last Thursday's meeting of the parish council street lights in the village would be likely to cost — up to £150 for each light, with a further £150 for connection.

These figures were given by Essex County Council, which confirmed it would not be prepared to contribute towards the cost.

Parish council chairman Bob Daniels said, after listening to the views of parishioners: 'I don't feel it is necessary to call a special meeting at the moment. It will be up to the new parish council if someone wishes to make a request in respect of street lighting.

'We have had some intimation of what the costs would be and I feel that there is no justification to call a special meeting.'

A large majority of Theydon Bois residents voted against street lights in a referendum in 1964 and at a special parish council meeting in 1976.

West Essex Gazette, April 6, 1984

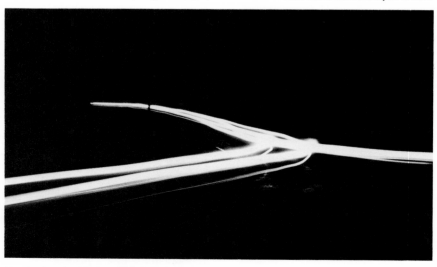

If only they had lights. This is in fact Loughton Lane if you could but see it!

As we have seen, Theydon's fight to preserve its rural character began to be lost before the war and far-sighted villagers perceived that the battle would really start once the war was over. The public meeting held in February **1944** to form what must have been one of the very first local preservation societies took place in the The British Restaurant, located in the Working Men's Club which stood alongside the western boundary of the car park of The Queen Victoria, one of the **16** listed buildings still standing in Theydon Bois today.

A large audience of Theydon Bois residents attended at the local British Restaurant on Saturday, and heard the case for the Theydon Bois and District Rural Preservation Society explained to them by experts.

Mr. H. G. Waterson, who presided, said that one might ask the need for the local association. Why not let the national organizations deal with the matter? The answer was that it was better for local feeling to be made felt through a local society.

Mr. Bruce J. Goodchild (acting honorary secretary and founder of the movement) read letters of support and commendation from such notable members of the community as Lieut.-Col. E. N. Buxton, M.C. (President) who expressed his regret at not being present, Mr. E. J. Wythes, J.P., Mr. Dudley Ward, Mr. Hugh Kemsley, and from Epping Rural District Council and the Chingford area group (Essex Branch) of the Council for the Preservation of Rural England, which body said the best countryside was in the Theydon and district section of Essex, and applauded this timely effort. This correspondence served to strengthen the hope that bricks and mortar would not pollute the green fields that, on both sides of the Atlantic, are thought of as England.

Express and Independent, March 4, 1944

The first annual meeting of the Theydon Bois Rural Preservation Society was held at the British Restaurant on Wednesday, Mr. H. G. Waterson presiding.

The annual report stated that, 'The possibility of oil-boring operations in the district has had the committee's closest attention and the matter was taken up with the Ministry of Fuel who admitted that licences had been granted for operations in Essex, but the particular areas in which the Society is interested formed only a small part on the fringe of an area of 195 square miles for which prospecting licences have been granted. The possibility of drilling operations taking place in the district is considered very remote.'

West Essex Gazette, November 22, 1946

A small group of beauty-lovers living at Theydon Bois in Essex are to present the Planning Minister with a scheme for making 100 square miles of Essex into a National Park for the use of Londoners.

They are the nine committee members of the Theydon Bois and District Rural Preservation Society (membership about 250) and the area is the country which includes part of Epping Forest and the ancient forest of Hainault.

The south-eastern boundary would run along the Romford-to-Chelmsford main road and the western boundary from Chigwell to Harlow. Sheering would be its northern limit and Hainault its southern limit.

'About six months ago we put the proposal before the Hobhouse Committee,' the secretary, Mr. Bruce J. Goodchild, said to-day, 'but it was turned down because it did not come within the committee's 'terms of reference'.

The Preservation Society does not claim that this section of Essex can approach the beauty of the National Parks selected by the Hobhouse Committee (which made its report in July after two years' work). But it does think it merits being among the 52 areas recommended 'for conservation and special treatment.'

Mr. Goodchild added: 'By getting the area recommended, we should stop any threat of building, agriculture would benefit, and London would have another place, along with Epping Forest, for its millions.'

The proposed area includes such Essex beauty spots as Chipping Ongar, the Roding villages, Good Easter and High Easter.

The Evening News, December 3, 1947

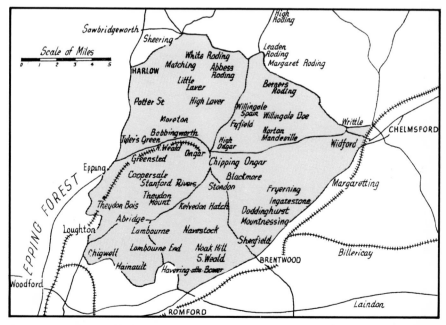

Today everyone is preservation conscious but forty years ago it was a brave new initiative — not that the Society was purely parochial in its outlook. Its greatest plan — never taken up — under its go-ahead secretary Bruce J. Goodchild was in **1947** for the creation of a National Park in Essex. National Parks were then all the rage — the first ten were promoted in a White Paper in **1945** but, as Mr Goodchild said at the time, 'The areas selected by the Committee for National Parks or Conservation Areas are too remote from London to be of value to the great majority of Londoners who, after all, form a large percentage of the population of the country'.

The old winding road to Abridge had been reconstructed just prior to the Second World War, linking up with the new viaduct over the railway line built under the 1935 plans for the eventual electrification of the Central London line and its extension northwards to Epping. In the event this did not take place until after the war but, nevertheless, the wide, new concrete swath was ready in time for it to play its part in easing wartime communications in an area largely made up of narrow country lanes. *Above:* This is Station Hill; the old bypassed lane still remaining to be seen today.

The old and the new. Lark Hill between Parsonage Farm and Coopersale Lane where another section of the old road remains.

Abridge

'Abridge, that most picturesque little old town, of red-brick gabled houses, with red-tiled roofs standing all huddled together in a circle, as if there were once walls round it. A strangely quiet town, which looks as if it had never even heard of the outer world, and took no interest in anything but itself.'

Essex, A. R. Hope-Moncrieff, 1909

Grade II
Road bridge over the River Roding

Bridge, late C18/early C19. Red brick, keystones of limestone. 3 round arches, the middle one wider than the outer arches. One keystone at each side of each arch. Shallow cutwaters both sides.

*Department of the Environment,
List of Buildings of Special Architectural
or Historic Interest, May 29, 1984*

And so we reach Abridge with its listed bridge: the only one in our area to have survived the attentions of highway engineers.

We sometimes refer with pride to the vast strides which have been made in the Baking Trade, as shown by gigantic bakeries which are found in our large centres of population. It is equally gratifying that in the smaller town businesses in the rural districts, the members of the Trade are alive to the desirability of having sanitary bakehouses, well equipped with labour-saving machinery and fitted with hygienic and cleanly ovens. The little Essex village of Abridge is picturesquely situated on the border of Epping Forest, and we have pleasure in showing the interior of the bakehouse of Mr. W. Krailing, which shows that in its erection excellent ovens have been installed and that the light and height have been well provided for. The white enamelled tiles on the outside of the ovens are also indication of the cleanliness and attractiveness of the place.

The British Baker, August 5, 1910

From bakers . . . to restaurant . . . to what? Krailing's old building, latterly the Roding Restaurant, was sold in September 1985. Prior to the First World War there was an influx of German bakers to the area: Ziegler at South Woodford, Scheffel at Woodford Green and Krailing at Abridge. With the outbreak of war any person or premises with a Teutonic sounding name risked an attack by the public, and families from the highest to the lowest in the land changed their names.

King George V, a member of the German House of Saxe-Coburg-Gotha, adopted the very British sounding name of Windsor, Ziegler became Sinclair (later Chalkleys) and the Scheffels took the name of Shepherd, still in being today in Epping. Krailing sold up and moved to Buckinghamshire. Meanwhile a relative, George Krailing, bravely kept his name when he teamed up with Charles Wood to form Wood & Krailing's Motor Works at Theydon Bois.

Gradually the village of Abridge is losing its rural atmosphere and is becoming more and more like a suburb. Now villagers, who have watched — bitterly — the Green Belt being slowly eaten away by building schemes, are fighting this expansion.

A Rural Preservation Society will be formed with the prime aim of keeping a very watchful eye on future building programmes for Abridge.

Within the next few days the Parish Council will hold a meeting with Mr. B. J. Goodchild — who founded the active Theydon Bois Rural Preservation Society — to discuss plans for forming an Abridge Society.

A public meeting will be called later so that the whole village can be put in the picture about the proposed work of the Society. A membership of about 500 would be enough thinks the new chairman of Lambourne Parish Council, Mr. Frederick Lee, of New Farm Drive.

'The chief purpose of the Society would be to gain prior knowledge of building proposals,' he explained. 'We always hear about new buildings after planning permission has been given,' Mr. Lee added.

'You can walk down a lane and see builders piling bricks on to a site and that is the first time you know that the land is to be developed. It is very hard to resist building at that stage.'

But, he added, if the Society found out about new building plans they could take necessary steps against development by stating their case at public inquiries.

'If we are not careful we will grow into a suburb like Barkingside,' warned Mr. Lee. 'What happened there could happen here!'

Left: **1916**: year of the Battle on the Somme yet in peaceful Abridge it is still life as normal for the Essex Hounds, pictured here just to the left of Krailing's. One rider is attired in Army uniform, another appears to be in civilian clothes with a trilby! *Right:* Not quite the same spot but latter-day members of the same Hunt in Abridge in more recent times.

Next to Stanford's, the general store and post office, lay Whitbread's brewery — the dray is just pulling out of the yard.

The Society will also try to put a stop to the 'old dodge' of a landowner buying part of the Green Belt for agricultural purposes and then erecting a house — then another house, and so on until his land is covered in property. The result: another few acres of the precious Green Belt has disappeared for good. This trick is defeating the purpose of the laws preventing individuals buying land for building one house on the Belt.

The restriction of tree-felling and the conditions of local footpaths will also be included among the Society's other concerns for the beauty and prosperity of the village.

Mr. Lee expects that the property owners in Abridge will be most enthusiastic for the success of the Society, as many of them have lived there for many years.

Press report, June 6, 1958

Nearly opposite the Blue Boar lay another of Riggs' retreats — this one rather more modest. Today it's the 'new' post office.

Looking from London Road towards the junction with Hoe Lane (on the right) where Ted Towers had his blacksmith's

shop. The large house is The Poplars — home of the Bayles family until pulled down in the 1960s.

Fred Bayles (right) outside his little grocer's shop which lay next to his house. With him is his assistant Tommy Edgar who lost his life in the Great War. The building was formerly the local mortuary and undertakers and, according to local legend, two children lie buried beneath the trees outside. Sadly the old shop, a part of Abridge's heritage, was pulled down in 1984 — helped on its way after a motor-cycle failed to negotiate the bend and crashed, through its front window!

'Let a bridge be built.' With those immortal words — so popular legend has it — Queen Elizabeth I named Abridge, now among the first villages outside London.

But, like all legends, it spans a mixture of truth and fiction. The earliest record of the name in its present form is in 1203, but a pre-Conquest map mentions Asserbugge — a name which means 'Ashes are burnt'.

Since earliest times, Abridge has been a centre of trade. It was originally one community with Lambourne End, 1½m to the east, where the village church still stands.

Change came when the countryside became safer for travel and traders moved down to the river where stagecoaches changed horses on the main London to Dunmow route.

Since then the village has remained a curious paradox — a centre of activity yet in the heart of the country.

Just 14 miles from Marble Arch, it was at one time nicknamed 'Little Sadom' because of its reputation for drunkenness and crime, especially among the poorer population.

It's not so long ago to Charlie Lister (84), who has lived in Hoe Lane since 1920, and was born in the village.

'If you had been in Abridge at the beginning of this century, you would have entered a world which was so different to the present day that it is difficult to imagine it has all happened in my lifetime.

'When we wanted to go out of the village we had to walk to Theydon or Chigwell and hire a horsedrawn cab, or perhaps ride a bicycle. There were no street lights, and the roads then were bad — they were just granite. In summer a water cart would fill up opposite the Maltsters Arms and spray the road to prevent the dust from blowing about.'

Charlie grew up in a world with no gas, electricity, plumbing, telephones or public transport. Hoe Lane had two cottages and the school. Stables opposite the Post Office kept horsepower for the long processions of brewers' drays which lined up in the village before taking beer to the surrounding pubs.

Charlie has seen the village slowly engulfed by new housing estates, but it is not the buildings that matter to him most — it's the people.

'It's no longer a village to me,' he says sadly. 'There was a time when I could tell you where everyone around here lived. Now, I don't even know their names. That's the difference.'

Guarded by rigid green belt regulations, one of London's nearest villages may not seem to be under threat. But while the fields remain, has the real Abridge been submerged, unnoticed?

Guardian & Gazette, June 15, 1984

One of the most amazing features of the village of old was its swimming pool — seen here being admired by a gathering including Lord and Lady Lambourne on the right.

It had been built by voluntary subscription and lay in a field beside the river. A wind-powered mill pumped in water from the Roding. Older residents remember the pool for its frogs . . . and the day a cow was found floating in it one morning. After the beast had been pulled out swimming continued as normal! Today the cattle have it all to themselves as yet another outdoor 'Epping Forest' swimming pool is lost.

Strictly speaking Lambourne is out of 'our' area (we have got to draw a line somewhere) but these pictures of a staff tea party were just too good to leave out. They were taken in 1895 and came to us via a roundabout route from the daughter of Mr Borkett, the photographer. The spot chosen to set up the table can be seen on the left of the picture at the top of the page. You can visit the same spot today if you wish, close to the church (see pages 8 and 9) and Lambourne Hall. (This was not the residence of Lord Lambourne who resided at Bishop's Hall not far away.)

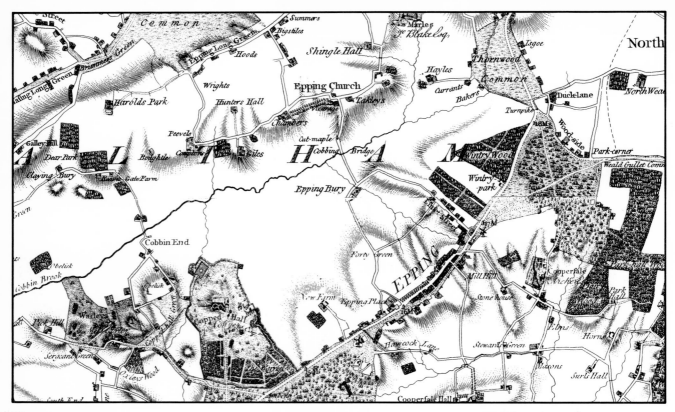

Epping

This large parish, extending north-east from Waltham Abbey, is above thirty miles in circumference; it lies on the borders of the forest, and is divided into Epping Upland, where the church is situated, and the Townside, where the town is built; consisting of one long and wide street, on a ridge of hills of considerable extent, north and south; it is of later origin than the church, and seems to have become more considerable after the turning of the road, which used to pass from Harlow to London, by the corner of Wintry Wood, across the forest to Abridge. In 1518, John Baker, mercer, of Epping, in his will charged his estate of Stonards, in Theydon Gernon, with payment of a sum of money for repairing the road between Harlow and London by Epping Street, for the purpose, as is supposed, which was ultimately effected, of inducing travellers to pass this way.

The History and Topography of the County of Essex, 1831

This illustration depicts Epping Street — the Epping of today — in 1669.

In the beginning the ancient parish of Epping was centred on what we now call Epping Upland. Here the manors fanned out almost like the slices of a cake — Gills, Campions, Chambers, Takleleys, Shingle Hall, Marles, Hayleys, Priestbury (most probably located by the 'cut maple' on this map of 1777), and Eppingbury — the capital manor of the parish. With the development of the London road in the Middle Ages, the focus of the parish moved south-east to Epping Heath, later called Epping Street, where Epping Place was the manor.

Dull and quiet appears this elongated, straggling little place, with its two irregular lines of houses stretching away from Epping Upland, by the church, down to Epping Townside, and Epping Street. But it was a bustling, busy, thriving place enough in the old coaching-days, as its many inns, open, or now turned to other uses, remind us. Then day and night, in quick succession, came coach after coach, with merry soundings of long horns, and jolly jingling of harness to the rhythm of beating hoofs, and the occasional explosive crack of some cheery coachman's long-thonged whip. Then hostlers and stable-helps abounded, and were proud of the magical celerity with which they substituted for steaming foam-flecked horses, the fresh, brisk, cloth-covered teams led out to take their places. Then the guard's horn awakened a responsive clanging of the inn-yard bell, and waiters, all listless, idle, and half-asleep, started into sudden life and activity. Then

excited people crowded to doors and windows to watch the coach go by, or gathered in gossiping and laughing knots to see the horses changed; while glasses were hurriedly emptied, and hastily ordered refreshments were rapidly consumed. Then all Essex gloried in the fame of Epping butter, and Epping cream; then Epping pork was of a mellow whiteness, a chicken-like tenderness, and a specially delicious flavour; and a basket of Epping sausages was a gift gracious and savoury. Then market-day brought country-folk in crowds, until all the big roomy old inns were overflowing with them, until the broad, long street was full of their noises, and the market-place was a farmyard fair.

But, alas! these glories are departing, not to return. Railways have diverted both the traffic and the trade of Epping, and something ails the place, it has grown so staid and dull.

Walks in Epping Forest. Percy Lindley, 1886

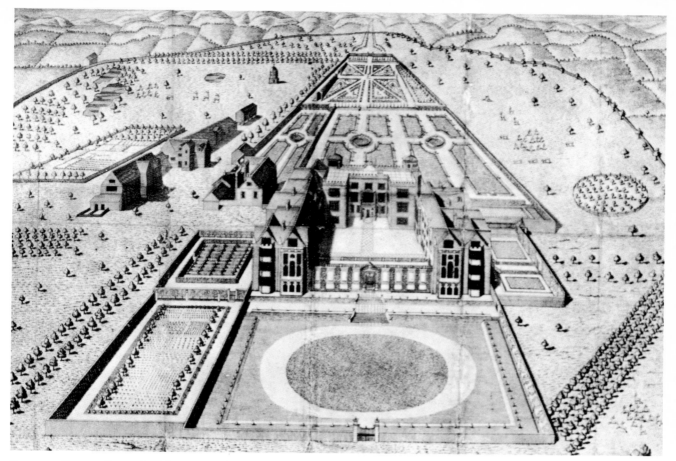

However it was Copped Hall which, by a succession of takeovers by its owners, eventually became the major manor in the parish although the house actually lay just within the parish of Waltham Holy Cross. The medieval building had stood since the twelfth century but when it came into the possession of Sir Thomas Heneage he rebuilt the hall between 1564-68.

If we go by road from London to Epping Town, we shall notice that, when first we enter the forest lands, the metropolis is giving disagreeable evidence of its proximity by the blackness of the trees. This gloomy effect gradually disappears, and before Epping Town is reached the sylvan effects are very pleasant. Marching with the old rural chase is the estate of Copped Hall, in mediaeval times the home of the FitzAucher family, who held the office of Foresters. It is a picturesque stretch of park and woodland, which is seen to spread itself out widely from the elevated ground whereon the house stands. The house is about a century and a half old, but it has recently been enlarged, surrounded by important architectural gardens, and its interior fitted and refurnished with much taste and considerable magnificence. Although this house is of some age, it is the successor of a still finer one which had, in its turn, replaced a yet older habitation. But the eighteenth century builder changed the site. The present house is in Epping Parish, whereas the little bit of ruin which alone remains of its sixteenth century predecessor, although it stands in the garden, lies within the bounds of the Parish of Waltham.

To the great monastic house that made that place famous much of the land hereabouts belonged, and both Epping and Copped Hall were in the list of its manors. Copped Hall, at one time held under them by the FitzAuchers, is afterwards described as 'a mansion of pleasure and privacy for the Abbots of Waltham'. So pleasant a spot was it that Henry VIII seems to have wished for it before his quarrel with Rome and his seizure of Church lands. We are told that 'some Years before the Dissolution, Robert, the last Abbot of Waltham, passed over the fair Seat of Copt Hall unto King Henry the Eighth, in hopes

The estate was purchased by the Member of Parliament for East Grinstead, Edward Conyers, in 1739 who had bought Eppingbury five years earlier. When his son, John I, inherited in 1842, he demolished the Heneage building six years later and constructed a new manor house 250 yards to the south-east in Epping Parish proper, adding Campions to the estate in 1761. In turn, his son, John II, added Chambers and Gills about 1796. When George Wythes took over the manor, then totalling about 2,800 acres, in 1869 he completed the acquisitions by incorporating Hayleys, Shingle Hall and Takeleys. (Only Marles held out under the ownership of the Arkwright family.)

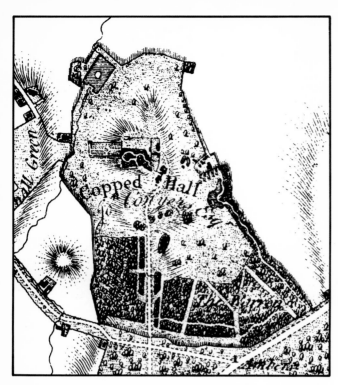

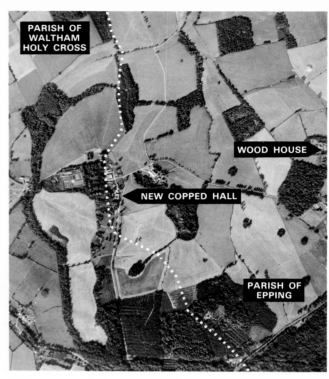

PARISH OF WALTHAM HOLY CROSS

WOOD HOUSE

NEW COPPED HALL

PARISH OF EPPING

When one compares a modern aerial survey photograph (taken by Aerofilms) with the map produced by John Chapman and Peter André (see also page 110), one can only marvel at the accuracy achieved by those men over 200 years ago with all the problems they must have faced. This is a blow up of a section of the map on page 414 showing the Copped Hall estate.

thereby to preserve the rest of his Revenues. However all would not do (so impossible it is to preserve what is designed for Ruin), for a few Years after, the Abbey with the large Lands thereof was seized on by the King.' Of Copped Hall he retained possession, and appears to have assigned it to the Princess Mary as one of her habitations, for a letter of hers is preserved in the British Museum dated 'from my poor house of Copped Hall', and here it was that some of her father's later bishops came to attempt to convert her to his new religious opinions. When she became Queen she annexed both the Epping and Copped Hall Manors to the Duchy of Lancaster, but her sister Elizabeth, a few years after her accession, granted them both to Sir Thomas Heneage. He was of the ancient Lincolnshire family of that name, and was her Vice-Chamberlain, her Chancellor of the Duchy of Lancaster as well as of her Privy Council. He it was who built a 'noble large House, with a Court in the middle' between the year 1564, when he obtained possession, and 1595, when he died.

Sir Thomas Heneage left a daughter only, who carried Copped Hall to her husband, Sir Moyle Finch of Eastwell in Kent. After his death in 1614 she was created Countess of Winchelsea, and this title descended to her son, who, succeeding in 1633, sold Copped Hall to the Earl of Middlesex. Ten years earlier Lionel Cranfield, Earl of Middlesex, as an unpopular Lord High Treasurer, had been tried and condemned by his Peers for bribery and neglect of duty. After a short period in the Tower he retired into private life, and as he was able to buy Copped Hall, it is evident that the fine he had been condemned to pay had not made a very great inroad into the fortune he had accumulated. When his younger son died in 1674 Copped Hall passed to his nephew, Lord Buckhurst, who afterwards succeeded his father as sixth Earl of Dorset. As he would then become possessed of Knole and other great houses, it is likely that he gave the Palladian touches that we notice about the sketch of Copped Hall immediately after his uncle's death. The old plan calls the wing on the right-hand side 'King William's apart-

ments', and the inference is that William III must have been the guest of the sixth Earl of Dorset and that the Palladian features, including the screen stretched across the open side of the court, had been added previously to this. Whether King William really occupied these apartments does not appear, but his sister-in-law, the Princess Anne, certainly on one occasion made a hurried and none too dignified visit to Copped Hall. After William's landing at Torbay in 1688, Anne deserted her father, and, taking refuge with Bishop Compton of London, rode down with him, some people say on the pillion behind him, to 'the Earl of Dorset's seat in Epping Forest'. Thence the Earl rode on with her to Nottingham.

The Earl was now finding Copped Hall an unnecessary possession, and he sold it, in the year 1700, to Sir Thomas Webster, a Yorkshireman whose father before him had settled in Essex and who himself represented the

county in Parliament after he had established himself at Copped Hall. In Farmer's *History of Waltham*, published in 1735, there is a large engraving of Copped Hall, including its outbuildings, gardens, park and the country beyond. It is described as the 'Seat of Sir Thomas Webster', but that description soon after ceased to be correct, for Sir Thomas sold it to Edward Conyers at some moment before the death of the latter in 1742. He was the third owner who had come down from the North, for he was sprung from the family of that name who, from the Conquest onwards for some centuries, played a considerable part in the counties of Durham and Yorkshire One Tristram Conyers, a cadet of the house, settled at Walthamstow somewhere about the time when Sir Thomas Heneage was building or his daughter Elizabeth was occupying the house at Copped Hall. Although he was a Yorkshire landowner and Lord of the Manor of Scarborough, it was probably commerce

This is the new home that John Conyers I built from 1751-58 to the design of John Sanderson. Kilns to bake clay for the bricks were actually set up in the grounds. In 1775-77 his son employed James Wyatt to redecorate the house, work which included new plasterwork and painted motifs.

416

that brought him South, and his son certainly was a London merchant.

The next generations, however, went in for the law, and Edward Conyers, fifth in descent from Tristram, was of the Middle Temple. He was the purchaser of Copped Hall, and left it to his son John, who pulled down the Heneage house and built the much smaller and much plainer Georgian edifice illustrated in Morant's *History of Essex*, where it is described as built 'in an elegant manner in 1753 by the present worthy owner, John Conyers Esq., who had adorned this work with a view of it'.

From the house that once was we will pass into the house that now is, approaching it from the east, where a forecourt is formed by a fine *clairvoyée* of stone piers and wrought ironwork. The entrance above leads into a hall that occupies the centre of the east elevation, on what the original plan calls the basement. We should now term it the ground floor, as the rooms on this storey are not sunk and are of considerable height. Although the house has been completely redecorated, the interior disposition has been very slightly altered and therefore the old plan still answers for today and shows the arrangement both of the entrance floor and that above. There is nothing now in the hall to remind us of John Conyers' 'elegant taste', but there are mementoes of the older house. The lower part of the mantelpiece dates from Sir Thomas Heneage's day. John Conyers put this mantel-piece into the housekeeper's room. Such objects were not worthy of his principal storey, and the height of his basement storey did not admit of the lofty upper part being used. It has therefore disappeared, and the present lower overmantle is modern work in the spirit of the old. The whole is now painted green and gold, and it is very probable that the lower part always was so, as such mantel-pieces were frequently coloured in Elizabeth's day.

On the opposite wall to the mantel-piece stands a very large table with cabriole legs. That, too, came from the old house, having stood in the great gallery, and dating from Sir Richard Webster's time. There is nothing in the get-up of the hall to remind one of the exterior architecture. The placing here of the Heneage mantel-piece gave reason to the introduction of a decorated plaster ceiling of Elizabethan character. The German cupboard of delicate inlay work belongs to the same age, but there has been no attempt to keep to a period. The door-frames have the great roll moulding of Wren's time, and besides good examples of English and German furniture, Italy is well represented by a set of late eighteenth century armchairs, gilt and upholstered in red silk, that came from the Borghese Palace.

Right and left of the hall are the study and the billiard-room. Both are full of interest, arising both from their decoration and their furnishing.

Passing out of the billiard-room, the morning-room is entered, from which a door gives on to the garden gallery leading to the great conservatory or winter garden, of which the great glass roof is certainly not an improvement to the general architectural composition of the place.

There is much fine furniture in the Copped Hall morning-room, and on the walls, which are hung with silk damask, are several admirable pictures by such Dutch masters as Hobema and de Hooghe, while the English school is well represented by Sir Joshua's [Reynold's] portrait of Lady Kent, who was related to the family of the present Mrs. Wythes. North of the morning-room the disposition of the old plan has been somewhat altered. The main stair, indeed, is untouched, but the remaining space is now arranged as chapel and ante-chapel. The latter is fully lighted by the windows but the chapel itself, being screened off and occupying the space up to the staircase wall, has a dim religious light

John Conyers II died in 1813 and his son Henry inherited the Hall in 1818. His first interest was hunting and he is reputed to have spent over £100,000 on his passion to the detriment of the estate. He died in 1853 and his eldest daughter Julia, who had married the Hon. Anthony Ashley, made it her home. When her husband died in 1867 she sold out to George Wythes of Bickley Hall, Kent — a self-made millionaire having made his fortune in the railway construction era of the Victorian age. This picture is believed to date from shortly after the sale.

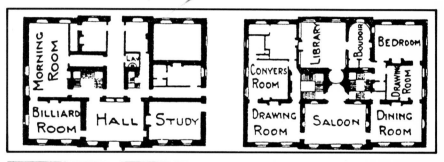

The building purchased by George Wythes in 1869 was rather nondescript and it became the home of his son, George Edward, who lived there until his death six years later. Followed by his eldest son, another George Edward, he died when only 20 years old leaving his younger brother, Edward James, to succeed to the title in 1887. Although then only nineteen, it was during his tenure that Copped Hall really reached its zenith. This engraving was published in 1883 — the year his grandfather (the purchaser of the hall) passed away aged 72.

The grandeur that was once Copped Hall. Country Life, the magazine which has become almost an institution for presenting the great houses and gardens of Britain, began in 1897. Two years previously, Edward Wythes had set his plan in motion to extensively improve the house and grounds to the designs of the architect C. E. Kemp of Lindfield. In 1910 the magazine featured the Hall in a two-issue article under its feature: 'Country Homes and Gardens, Old and New'. The photographic record made at the time still survives and provides a dramatic contrast to the scenes today after 70 years neglect following the disastrous fire in May 1917. *Above:* This is the entrance hall described on the previous page: the Heneage mantlepiece was one of the original fittings from the old house. The German cupboard can be seen on the right as well as the Italian armchairs from the Borghese Palace. (All contemporary pictures courtesy of Country Life.)

On the first floor was the richly decorated saloon, our comparison somewhat shakily taken from the top of a ladder as the floor is completely missing.

that appeals to the sentiments, and the effect when the altar candles are lit and the electric light shut off is very striking. It was a fitting opportunity for Mr. Kemp to give free scope to his love of richness and his affection for a seventeenth century decorative style, rather more Flemish than English.

The visitor will wish to linger amidst other fine furniture and fittings on the ground floor; but it is time we ascended the stair and entered the suite of lofty and sumptuous apartments which we shall find there. The disposition of the space between the two staircases is a really clever bit of designing, for which we must give full praise to John Conyers' architect. Robert Adam delighted in these little rounds and oblongs with domed ceilings, and it is possible he had something to do with this arrangement, though not with the planning and building of the house in 1753. The walls are hung with tapestry, designed by Mr. Kemp and carried out in Paris. Pillars, not unlike those on which the garden statues stand, rise from a balustrade and support an entablature, of which the frieze curiously enough also represents a balustrade. The intervening spaces are occupied by three-tiered fountains and swags and wreaths of ribboned leafage, while on the balustrade stand vases of flowers or sit children playing musical instruments or indulging in other sports and pastimes. The decorative manner of this tapestry is closely allied to much of Mr. Kemp's glass designs for domestic use, such as he himself introduced at his home at Lindfield. It is also in full harmony with that which he has placed in the saloon windows. Here he removed the sashes and introduced French casements with leaded quarries. The Essex landscape lies below you and the pictured glass has the sky for its background. Fanciful pedestals, composed of masks and boys and scrollwork, support little round platforms on which stand figures, over whose heads hang valanced baldachinos. The figures are, of course, emblematical. Music and the chase are represented, while a very appropriate panel shows us Hospitality standing behind the model of the west elevation of the house and having on a scroll above her head the legend: 'At first and last the hearty welcome'.

One of Mr Kemp's attributes was the design and making of stained glass. Through the bottom of the saloon windows the Essex countryside could be seen — as it still can from the empty openings today.

The dining-room lies north of the saloon. It is again a fine example of the craft of the wood-worker directed by Mr. Kemp. Walls and ceiling are alike veneered in walnut carefully chosen to show the figure of the wood at its best, and formed into geometrical figures by bands of a lighter wood. The walls are divided up into great panels or sections by twisted columns standing on bases, themselves composed of four such columns in miniature. These bases, however, are set on corbels, which have only flat pilasters below them, and the structural effect is perhaps not altogether satisfying. Apart from that nothing can be better as a modern rendering of the style chosen. It harmonises perfectly with the German inlaid furniture, of which there are such good examples in other rooms of the house besides the dining-room.

Balancing the dining-room on the other side of the saloon is the apartment called the drawing-room on the plan, and which was so until, quite recently, the claims of a growing family to abundant space and light and air caused it to be given over to the children's use. The paper on the walls must be a constant delight to them, for it is an extremely fine example in an excellent state of preservation of the great Chinese pictorial papers that were imported into England in the second half of the eighteenth century. This one represents the pleasures of life in China.

Next to this former drawing-room, where choice examples of lacquer furniture, in harmony with the wall lining, used to stand, is a bedroom richly got up, and with the walls hung with a considerable collection of portraits of the Conyers family and their connections.

Once the setting for select dinner parties — now the haven of creatures of the feathered kind.

The library, which, like the saloon, has a delightful little circular ante-chamber, is interesting as being the one room in the house that has not been redecorated under the present ownership, but is left to tell its tale of the past. As well as the Adam drawings for the saloon decoration, a set are preserved signed 'James Wyatt, 1775'.

A view to rival the Palace of Versailles: the garden from the first floor terrace — looking westwards towards Warlies Park.

The gardens as well as much of the interior decoration, are essentially creations of the late Mr. C. E. Kemp, the well-known designer and maker of stained glass. He was a man of great taste, but though his architectural outlook was by no means narrow, he was not really a Palladian, and least of all did he sympathise with that style when it took on the almost Quaker demureness which seems to have formed the 'elegant taste' of John Conyers. As a result there is a slight feeling of disconnection between Copped Hall and its garden. Certainly much was done to obviate such a defect, for the enrichment of the west front of the house and the added dignity given to it by great flights of steps have done much towards making the whole place hang together. But even now the house does not quite carry the

garden — does not by its mass or by its striking features claim the first and foremost attention. The eye is rather too quickly attracted away from it to the extent and diversity of the richly wrought garden architecture which lies before it. Each one of these features is well designed and the whole conception is large and coherent. But a suspicion of restraint in the garden would have improved the general effect, for the composition would have been more absolutely harmonious and satisfying if the house had been given a somewhat greater relative importance.

This said, criticism shall cease and praise be the order of the day. The scheme was to use the natural qualities and features of the site for a stately formal layout that should be convincingly fitting as a quite reasonable

outcome of the lie of the land. Old antiquarians puzzled much over the name of the place. But Morant's explanation that it is 'from Saxon Coppe, the *top* of a hill, it standing upon a high or copped ground' is at least a good description of the position of the house. Considering that Essex is a county of undulations rather than of steeps, Copped Hall stands on a most marked elevation and commands views all round. It is on something of a table-land, but an appreciable drop begins close to the west front. The height of the house itself is accentuated by the eighteenth century plan of placing the main suite of reception-rooms on the first floor. Copped Hall in size and disposition was not unlike Wolterton in Norfolk, designed by Thomas Ripley ten years earlier. That house

A somewhat different aspect — our comparison photography in 1986 coinciding with the second coldest February this century!

The majesty of the Great Causeway — focal point of the formal garden.

was planned for, if it did not at first possess, great stairways from the reception-rooms to the ground, and the elevation of Copped Hall as published by Morant shows that this idea was somewhat meanly carried out by John Conyers on the west front of his new house. When, however, the centre was recently recased, a much larger feature of the kind was substituted, taking the form of a balustraded terrace thrown out at first-floor height with descents of ample size and dignity sweeping down at either end of it. It forms an adequate beginning to the lay-out which lies wholly on this side, consists principally of a large oblong plat reached by these stairways, and has its western corners strongly marked by two stately garden-houses. The centre of this plat is projected westwards far beyond its general limit on a broad architectural causeway edged by a balustrade and ending with a lofty pair of gateposts and a wrought-iron gate, through which a segmental flight of steps leads down to the park. This long extension of the chief level of the garden is the most marked feature of the design, and its full value is insisted upon by allowing no break in the broad path which runs down it by any object standing centrally in the great plat.

Looking out from the raised house terrace, the eye is first carried along to enjoy the horizontal effect and the wooded landscape beyond. Then it turns right or left and seeks the relief of the vertical lines given by the statues, standing on tall sculptured columns that rise out of octagon basins, and by the garden-houses beyond, to which the pilasters, obelisks and dormer windows give an aspect of great height. The level is laid out as two

Our bird's-eye view shows better than any ground level picture the transformation since 1910; although the Causeway remains, its former beauty is extinguished.

balancing squares, of which the fountain basins form the centre and dictate the line of the paths and the form of the grass-edged beds, which are set partly with flowers and partly with topiary bushes. The western edge of this garden hangs above a lower level severed into two independent plats by the central causeway, from which ample flights of steps lead down to them; and as it might be wearisome to have to mount and descend these in order to get from one plat to another, a passage is afforded through a bridge-like arch under the causeway.

The basement storey of the garden-houses forms shelters at the corners of these gardens, as their main floor does to the upper plat. They are designed in a somewhat florid Palladian manner that has not quite lost Jacobean influence, the latter being specially marked by the pairs of obelisks at each corner, while the swags and drops of sculptured fruit and drapery are more in the decorative manner of Inigo Jones and Wren. This reliance on forms dating from rather different moments within the Renaissance period is again seen in the treatment of the octagon fountains. The columns that rise in the centre of the basins, and from which water drops into the pool below through beautifully wrought bronze spouts, are of that decorative type that flourished in Flanders at the beginning of the seventeenth century, being a Low Country rendering of Italian models.

The situation being high and exposed and the climate of Essex not the warmest in England, full advantage is taken of the shelter given by the retaining walls that separate the causeway and the main garden from the lower level south-west of them. The result is that spring is brightened here by the early flowering of shrubs, such as the Forsythias, while beautiful and none too hardy evergreen shrubs, like Choisya ternata and Azara microphylla, give welcome winter furnishing. In the summer sun-loving shrubs, like the Cistuses, and Californian plants, like Romneya Coulteri, make a gay display of bloom. The latter does particularly well here, and is very cleverly placed.

From the centre of the Causeway a diverging flight of steps descending to the lower level stretches its lower steps out on to the gravel path beyond the line of wall and balustrade, and the whole space between the two flights is filled in with the Romneya, which has the protection of the wall behind, but is allowed freedom for the natural display of its long graceful stems, grey-green themselves and bearing grey-green foliage, topped by the immense and elegant pure white poppy-like blooms. With such less usual plants rose and clematis are associated against the walls, while bush roses fill many a bed, although an abundance of herbaceous plants gives endless variety and a long blooming season to this part of the garden.

Garden houses with a difference: their magnificence fading with the passing of the years . . . fugit irreparabile tempus . . .

Renaissance at Epping: from creation to dereliction — a sad reflection on the recent history of Copped Hall.

The lower garden on the right hand or north side of the causeway has its northern boundary formed by a tall cut yew hedge, broken in places to give room for lead figures standing on stone pedestals. The openings are not merely large enough to hold these, but to form passage-ways on to a great stretch of lawn following the natural north-western slope of the grounds. It is set with great trees and bounded by woodland effects. The native oak plays the greatest part, but cedars and plane trees also find a place. The grounds here depart from the complete formalism of the William III period, and show that inclination towards Nature tempered by classic garden objects that prevailed under George II. It is here, looking out eastward and backed by trees, that is placed the charming little temple of which an illustration is given. Fluted columns of the Corinthian order carry the half-circle of the entablature and the little projections at the side. All this is in wood painted white, while the ribbed dome-like roof is of lead.

The lawn on its northward course modifies its natural lines, and gives way to a yew enclosed rose garden and bowling green. At the end of this, standing on its own green and

The introduction of statuary in this yew hedge accentuated the division of the formal garden on the right from the informal lawn leading to the sloping woodland. We can see in this picture (behind the garden house) the three-storied wing, lower than the main block, which Edward Wythes added on the northern side.

looking out towards the northern landscape, stands Pan playing his pipes. He is carved as a Terminal out of Travertine stone, and of the same material is formed the pedestal he stands on. Three bronze boys, one of them fawn-legged, dance round him to his music, linked by the ribbon they hold in their hands. Of bronze also are the rams' heads and bay wreaths that circle around the base as the boys do the statue above. There is an exactly right quantity, placing and balance of the metal features that by their dark colour, smooth texture and delicate treatment stand out against the plainer, lighter stone, which is broadly, massively, sketchily treated, its rough-hewn sculpture being in full harmony with its own rough grain, rich in tone and sprinkled with little cavities that preserve for it, even in its wrought state, something of the quality of the imperishable rock of its composition. Certainly the Pan at Copped Hall is one of the most admirable and successful of Countess Feodora Gleichen's creations.

A little east of it, half buried amid shrubs and ivy, stands the masonry that marks the site, and it is the only remaining fragment, of the old Heneage house. It consists of a block of brickwork and a stone pilaster, and must

Tucked away amid the trees was once the temple.

Immortalised in lead and stone: Pan and the dancing children.

When the fire broke out on the morning of May 5, 1917, members of the family were preparing to go to church. Although at first it was not considered serious, when the Epping Fire Brigade arrived aboard their recently-purchased Mercedes Motor Pump, wartime manpower shortage resulted in it being manned by only three men. As one man would be required to operate the steamer pump (seen here in tow), and due to the inadequate water supply, the fire soon gained hold. The town's old horse-drawn appliance was brought up as well but, in spite of the help of volunteers, the Hall was gutted.

have been part of the screen that stretched across the entrance of the quadrangle.

To linger about Copped Hall and to assimilate all that it has to teach is to learn in most agreeable fashion the lesson of the architecture and decorative arts in England from the sixteenth to the twentieth centuries. We still get a glimpse of the work done by Elizabeth's Captain of the Guard, and we deeply regret that there is so little left of his fine achievement. We are able, by occasional fragments and by pictorial representations, to understand what modifications were made to his home. We then reach the story of its destruction, and get a striking instance of the revolution in taste that ruthlessly destroyed that which the sixteenth and seventeenth centuries had so finely wrought and replaced it with what was mediocre even for its own day. We then come down to our own times, and we see the overwhelming dominance which knowledge and admiration of the past exercises over us. To collect old objects and old furniture and to reproduce former styles is our main object — learned, worthy, civilised, no doubt, but not heroic or self-reliant. At the same time, it is far wiser to adhere modestly to exact precedent and preserve lovingly what is old than to set out in an ill-equipped bark upon the stormy and shoal-set sea of originality. What has been done of late years at Copped Hall is typical of what we can do within the limitations of our own particular age and intellectual bent. But if it is typical it is also somewhat exceptional, for it is done in a really fine manner and on a large scale.

Country Life, October/November 1910

COPPED HALL DESTROYED

Walthamstow antiquaries will be particularly interested in the news that Copped Hall, near Epping, a historic landmark in Essex, was on Sunday morning completely destroyed by fire, although a large part of the valuable contents was salved.

The beautiful mansion was the country seat of Mr. E. J. Wythes, D.L., J.P., and overlooked one of the most lovely views in the county, while it was noted for its Italian gardens with terraces. . . .

*Walthamstow, Leyton, and Chingford
Guardian, May 11, 1917*

What memories you revive from time to time. . . . I was an unofficial fireman on the occasion of the great fire at the hall. An old pal of mine, Don Wilson (now dead), and I cycled with the old fire engine — drawn by two horses owned by Sadler's — to Copped Hall and helped the official firemen man the pumps, which were on both sides of the old engines. These were worked by four men each side. We two 'unofficials' helped while the regulars went into the hall to help bring out furniture and anything else they could.

I remember one of the men bringing out to us on the pump a five-gallon jar of wine — but it was too smoky to drink!

Now, if my memory serves me right, we were working hard to save everything that could be saved; but for us the fight was no doubt in vain — for one very good reason: the only available water supply in those days came out of the ponds on the grounds of Copped Hall, and I believe now that these ponds were pumped dry.

What a pity this beautiful home has been left in this state; perhaps there is still a chance that it may be restored and probably opened to the public at a small charge, as other places have?

P. E. JENKINS
30, Englands-lane, Loughton.

West Essex Gazette, June 5, 1964

These pictures are ironic — taken for posterity in 1938 they show the Epping Brigade equipment at the Hall just before the Fire Brigades Act came into force, handing over control to the local authority. Previously the brigades had been privately operated, sending bills to unfortunate householders for putting out their fires! The insurance company paid £20 4s. 6d. for use of the appliances at Copped Hall: Mercedes £4 4s. 0d.; Steamer £3 3s. 0d.; wear and tear on hose £10 0s. 0d.; petrol £2 17s. 6d.

A melancholy accident occurred at Little Copped Hall, near Epping, on Sunday the 31st ult. Mr. Samuel Fitch, the son of the occupier of the Hall, with a relative, went out about seven o'clock in the morning, for the purpose of bathing. Not returning to breakfast, Mr. Fitch, the father, proceeded to a pond just by, and there discovered some clothes hanging upon the rails, and his son's hat floating upon the water, with a book in it. Mr. Fitch immediately procured assistance, when the bodies of the two unfortunate young men were found, locked so fast in each other's arms, as to render it difficult to separate them; young Mr. Fitch having his clothes on. Doubtless Mr. Fitch had risked his own life in the attempt to save his relative, when in danger from cramp or some other cause. The jury returned a verdict under that impression.

Press report, 1823

This stately and elegant mansion, nearly in the centre of a large park, is a conspicuous object on grounds of considerable elevation, presenting grand and very extensive views, and enriched by a succession of groves and plantations, rising from the lower grounds, forming varied and boldly irregular scenery.

The park, with some other lands included in the estate, forms an enclosure of four thousand acres, of which above four hundred were some time ago an unprofitable waste, covered with hornbeam, pollards, and brushwood, and infested with lawless bands of wood and deer-stealers, whose forefathers, haunting the close covers of Epping Forest, had subsisted by plunder for centuries. By the praiseworthy exertions of the ancestor of the present owner of Copped Hall, a considerable number of these outcasts were reformed, and prevailed on to live in small cottages built on purpose for them, at a distance from each other, with a portion of garden ground to each. He also provided them with labour, and agreed to supply them with firewood. By this judicious plan, the idle have been inured to habits of industry, and a large tract of waste land rendered subservient to public utility. An important improvement was also effected in the cultivation of a piece of ground called the Warren, which consists of one hundred and one acres, and was, about seventy years ago, offered to a speculating farmer, on a lease of forty years, at two shillings and sixpence per acre. He, however, refused these terms, supposing the land absolutely unproductive. The ground was then ploughed, and sown with seeds of almost every kind of tree, thrown in indiscriminately, and left to the operations of Nature. The young plants sprung up, and without further attention, have thriven with so much vigour, as to form one of the finest and most valuable woods in this part of the country. Particularly one tree, a cedar of Lebanon, is deserving notice, on account of its rapid growth. It was sown in 1747. The girth of the bole, some time ago, measured upwards of twelve feet, and the extent of the branches on each side exceed twelve yards. The proprietor of Copped Hall is lord of the manor throughout the extensive parish of Epping.

The History and Topography of the County of Essex, March 1831

As we take our leave of Copped Hall, one cannot help feeling a sense of loss; that all Mr and Mrs Wythes' lavish care has come to naught ... 'tho perhaps our emotion should really be directed at the old house of Sir Thomas Heneage, demolished over two hundred years ago. That was the building, walked by many of our Kings and Queens, of which nothing now remains; yet in the chancel of St Margaret's, Westminster, can be seen one of its grandest features — a stained glass window depicting Catherine of Aragon and Prince Arthur, King Henry VIII's elder brother, her first husband. Believed to have been painted for Henry VII's chapel at Westminster, the window was purchased by Edward Conyers from New Hall, Boreham (where it had been placed when the monasteries were dissolved during the English Reformation) and incorporated in the chapel of the house by his son. St Margaret's bought it in 1758 when the Tudor building was pulled down.

To celebrate the wedding anniversary of Mr. and Mrs. E. J. Wythes, the men employed on the Copped Hall and Bickley Park estates (numbering 120) sat down to a capital dinner, presided over by Mr. Wythes. There were also present the Revs. E. Buckmaster, F. B. Johnston, and S. H. Hartley. The workmen's wives and families and also the cottage tenantry on the estate, to the number of 350, were invited to participate in the sports and amusements in the afternoon, and which they all thoroughly enjoyed; afterwards, doing justice to the good tea provided for them. Mr. H. Morris, of the 'Cock' Hotel, catered. The Epping Town Band enlivened the proceedings with some good selections and their efforts were heartily appreciated.

Epping Monthly Review, August 1895

Immediate action is to be taken to protect historic features in the grounds of Copped Hall, the ruined eighteenth century mansion near Epping.

Nature itself has begun to cause problems as trees have seeded themselves, to grow on 'ha-ha' walls surrounding the site and on a causeway in the nineteenth century formal garden.

If left unchecked, the trees would likely cause structural damage to the features so they will be removed.

'Ha-has' were popular in country houses of the period. Generally, trenches, fences or walls, they kept animals out of the gardens.

Their name comes from the fact that they couldn't be seen from a distance, fooling the onlooker to believe that the gardens continued unchecked into the landscape.

Epping Forest District Council and the Hall's owners have agreed on works which will include the removal of 13 young trees growing out of the walls and clearing scrub.

The operation will require hand felling the trees to ground level and chemical treatment of the roots to avoid harming the walls.

The estate's own staff, supervised by Copped Hall's agents, Messrs John D. Wood, will do the work as well as removing five young oak trees from the central causeway in the formal garden.

The site of Copped Hall was designated a Conservation Area by the District Council last year and further work will take place from time to time to protect the historical interest of the grounds.

Epping Forest Classified, January 31, 1985

Charles I went through Epping in 1634. In John Baker's Trust Account we read of a payment: 'For taking upp the stulpes and settinge upp the same upon the highway leading througe Wintrie Wood, for his Maties travelings that way.' We read also that 'The Protector lay last night in Epping.' Charles II dined at Copt Hall in June 1660, and William III, on his way to Newmarket, dined and stayed the night there on 4th April 1698. With Henry VIII, Mary, Elizabeth, Charles II, Anne, William III, and perhaps others, the first two Copt Halls had an impressive list of royal visitors. . . .

In 1688 the life of Princess Anne, afterwards queen, was believed to be in danger, and Sackville was called upon to arrange her escape. Dr. Johnson tells us that he conducted her to Nottingham under guard. Macaulay's account of the escape is the most romantic. 'That evening,' he says, 'Anne retired to her chamber as usual. At dead of night she rose, and, accompanied by her friend Sarah [Churchill] and two other female attendants, stole down the back stairs in a dressing gown and slippers. The fugitives gained the open street unchallenged. A hackney coach was in waiting from them there. Two men guarded the humble vehicle. One of them was Compton, Bishop of London, the princess's old tutor; the other was the magnificent and accomplished Dorset, whom the extremity of the public danger had roused from his luxurious repose. The coach drove instantly to Aldersgate Street . . . there the princess passed the night. On the following morning she set out for Epping Forest. In that wild tract Dorset possessed a venerable mansion [Copt Hall], the favourite resort, during many years, of wits and poets.'

Of this incident the earl's grandson relates that 'one of her Royal Highness's shoes sticking fast in the mud, the accident threatened to impede her escape; but Lord Dorset, immediately drawing off his white glove, put it on the Princess's foot and placed her safely in the carriage.'

Morant, Wright, and other historians of the Forest who have copied them, tell us that Princess Anne retired to Loughton Hall. As they do not also mention this escape to Copt Hall, and do not give any supporting evidence for the Loughton Hall story, it appears reasonable to conclude that the two halls have been confused, and that it was to Copt Hall, not Loughton Hall, that she escaped.

Epping Forest, William Addison, 1945

This crumbling piece of masonry is all that remains today of the original building.

Wood House, the large and elegant dower house of Copped Hall, Epping, and the main building of the estate since the hall itself was destroyed by fire in 1917, is to be sold by auction at the Thatched House Hotel on February 25th.

The house was started in 1898 and built for Ernest James Wythes, grandson of one of the most successful Victorian railway contractors, George Wythes, from whom he inherited a large fortune.

The design of the building was by Walter E. Tower and Charles Eamer Kempe, and the cost of the work is said to be far more than the original estimate by Mr. Tower of £9,400. Mrs. Joy Bergl said that the she would estimate it would cost at least £200,000 to build such a house today.

When Copped Hall was burnt down, Mr. Wythes moved into Wood House and gathered a fine collection of furniture, paintings, tapestry and china, which have passed on to his family.

Mr. Wythes died in 1949 and the house then became the property of his daughter Barbara, wife of an architect, Colonel Guy Elwes.

After living there for ten years they sold Wood House to Mr. and Mrs. Bergl.

The Bergls have redecorated many of the rooms to give them more light, and in some cases they have covered over the large open fireplaces, each tiled in blue and white Dutch tiles, to make space for a bookcase or a cupboard.

But none of the original fireplace fittings has been removed, and it could easily be restored to its former state, said Mrs. Bergl.

Much of the interior design is by William Morris, but some of his wall hangings have had to be replaced after examination by experts, because the effects of wood smoke and age have proved too much for them.

Mrs. Bergl said that the house was one of the finest of its kind. Its design was a reaction against the mechanisation and industrialisation of the 19th century and great emphasis was placed on craftsmanship.

It has over 30 rooms, including a family chapel with stained glass from Copped Hall itself, and a gunroom. It has 25 acres of land, with landscaped gardens and woodland.

The auctioneers are Messrs. Jackson-Stops and Staff, of London, and they told the Gazette they are expecting the sale price to be between £35,000 and £40,000.

West Essex Gazette, February 12, 1965

Secluded Wood House (see page 416) became the Wythes' home after the fire — and a retreat for Winston Churchill in later years.

John. At first we desir'd nothing of you, but Leave to go thro' the Town; we should have offer'd no Injury to any of you, neither would you have had any Injury or Loss by us. We are not Thieves, but poor People in distress, and flying from the dreadful Plague in *London*, which devours thousands every Week: We wonder how you could be so unmerciful!

They were soon made sensible of this, for two Days afterwards they found several Parties of Horsemen and Footmen also about, in pursuit of three Companies of Men arm'd, *as they said,* with Muskets, who were broke out from *London*, and had the Plague upon them; and that were not only spreading the Distemper among the People, but plundering the Country.

As they saw now the Consequence of their Case, they soon saw the Danger they were in, so they resolv'd by the Advice also of the old Soldier, to divide themselves again. *John* and his two Comrades with the Horse, went away as if towards *Waltham;* the other in two Companies, but all a little asunder, and went towards *Epping.*

When they came near *Epping* they halted, choosing out a proper Place in the open Forest, not very near the High-way, but not far out of it on the North-side, under a little cluster of low Pollard-Trees: Here they pitched their little Camp, which consisted of three large Tents or Hutts made of Poles, which their Carpenter, and such as were his Assistants, cut down and fix'd in the Ground in a Circle, binding all the small Ends together at the Top, and thickning the sides with Boughs of Trees and Bushes, so that they were compleatly close and warm. They had besides this, a little Tent where the Women lay by themselves, and a Hutt to put the Horse in.

It happened that the next day, or next but one was Market-day at *Epping;* when Capt. *John,* and one of the other Men, went to Market, and bought some Provisions, that is to say Bread, and some Mutton and Beef; and two of the Women went separately, as if they had not belong'd to the rest, and bought more. *John* took the Horse to bring it Home, and the Sack (which the Carpenter carry'd his Tools in) to put it in: The Carpenter went to Work and made them Benches and Stools to sit on, such as the Wood he cou'd get wou'd afford, and a kind of a Table to dine on.

They were taken no Notice of for two or three Days, but after that, abundance of People ran out of the Town to look at them, and all the Country was alarmed about them. The People at first seem'd afraid to come near them, and on the other Hand they desir'd the People to keep off, for there was a Rumour

The original drive to Copped Hall seems to have been from the south of the house to the Waltham Road. However, Mr Wythes altered the course of the later drive from the London Road, passing Wood House, erecting lodges flanking the entrance seen here on the right. These views date from 1909.

that the Plague was at *Waltham*, and that it had been in *Epping* two or three Days. So *John* called out to them not to come to them, *For,* says he, *we are all whole and sound People here, and we would not have you bring the Plague among us, nor pretend we brought it among you.*

After this the Parish Officers came up to them and parly'd with them at a Distance, and desir'd to know who they were, and by what Authority they pretended to fix their Stand at that Place? *John* answered very frankly, they were poor distressed People from *London*, who foreseeing the Misery they should be reduc'd to, if the Plague spread into the City, had fled out in time for their Lives, and having no Acquaintance or Relations to fly to, had first taken up at *Islington*, but the Plague being come into that Town, were fled further, and as they suppos'd that the People of *Epping* might have refus'd them coming

into their Town, they had pitch'd their Tents thus in the open Field, and in the Forest, being willing to bear all the Hardships of such a disconsolate Lodging, rather than have any one think or be afraid that they should receive Injury by them.

At first the *Epping* People talk'd roughly to them, and told them they must remove; that this was no Place for them; and that they pretended to be Sound and Well, but that they might be infected with the Plague for ought they knew, and might infect the whole Country, and they cou'd not suffer them there.

John argu'd very calmly with them a great while, and told them, 'That *London* was the Place by which they, that is, the Townsmen of *Epping* and all the Country round them, subsisted; to whom they sold the produce of their Lands, and out of whom they made the Rent of their Farms; and to be so cruel to the

This extract from Daniel De Foe's journal graphically imparts the feelings of people in the 1660s when faced by the scourge of the killer plague sweeping the country. Its cause and method of transmission then unknown, Londoners attempting to escape the Black Death were ostracised out of fear and ignorance. (One cannot help but compare their reaction with that to the recently-detected AIDS disease and to speculate on how we will respond to a similar threat.) The camp on the outskirts of Epping described by De Foe must have been quite near Bell Common.

Inhabitants of *London*, or to any of those by whom they gain'd so much was very hard, and they would be loth to have it remembered hereafter, and have it told how barbarous, how unhospitable and how unkind they were to the People of *London*, when they fled from the Face of the most terrible Enemy in the World; that it would be enough to make the Name of an *Epping*-Man hateful thro' all the City, and to have the Rabble Stone them in the very Streets, whenever they came so much as to Market; that they were not yet secure from being Visited themselves, and that as he heard, *Waltham* was already; that they would think it very hard that when any of them fled for Fear before they were touch'd, they should be deny'd the Liberty of lying so much as in the open Fields.'

The *Epping* Men told them again, That they, indeed, said they were sound and free from the Infection, but that they had no assurance of it; and that it was reported, that there had been a great Rabble of People at *Walthamstow*, who made such Pretences of being sound, as they did, but that they threaten'd to plunder the Town, and force their Way whether the Parish Officers would or no; That they were near 200 of them, and had Arms and Tents like Low-Country Soldiers; that they extorted Provisions from the Town by threatening them with living upon them at free Quarter, shewing their Arms, and talking in the Language of Soldiers; and that several of them being gone away towards *Rumford* and *Brent-Wood*, the Country had been infected by them, and the Plague spread into both those large Towns, so that the People durst not go to Market there as usual; that it was very likely they were some of that Party, and if so, they deserv'd to be sent to the County Jail, and be secur'd till they had made Satisfaction for the Damage they had done, and for the Terror and Fright they had put the Country into. . . .

Here they liv'd very comfortably, tho' coarsely, till the beginning of *September*, when they had the bad News to hear, whether true or not, that the Plague, which was very hot at *Waltham-Abby* on one side, and at *Rumford* and *Brent-Wood* on the other side; was also come to *Epping*, to *Woodford*, and to most of the Towns upon the Forest, and which, as they said, was brought down among them chiefly by the Higlers and such People as went to and from *London* with Provisions. . . .

But now these new Inmates began to be disturb'd more effectually, for the Towns about them were really infected, and they began to be afraid to trust one another so much as to go abroad for such things as they wanted, and this pinch'd them very hard; for now they had little or nothing but what the charitable Gentlemen of the Country supply'd them with: But for their Encouragement it happen'd, that other Gentlemen in the Country who had not sent 'em any thing before, began to hear of them and supply them, and one sent them a large Pig, that is to say a Porker; another two Sheep; and another sent them a Calf: In short, they had Meat enough, and, sometimes had Cheese and Milk, and all such things. They were chiefly put to it for Bread, for when the Gentlemen sent them Corn they had no where to bake it, or to grind it: This made them eat the first two Bushel of Wheat that was sent them in parched Corn, as the *Israelites* of old did without grinding or making Bread of it.

At last they found means to carry their Corn to a Windmill near *Woodford*, where they had it ground; and afterwards the Biscuit Baker made a Hearth so hollow and dry that he cou'd bake Biscuit Cakes tolerably well; and thus they came into a Condition to live without any assistance or supplies from the Towns; and it was well they did, for the Country was soon after fully Infected, and about 120 were said to have died of the Distemper in the Villages near them, which was a terrible thing to them.

On this they call'd a new Council, and now the Towns had no need to be afraid they should settle near them, but on the contrary several Families of the poorer sort of the Inhabitants quitted their Houses, and built Hutts in the Forest after the same manner as they had done: But it was observ'd, that several of these poor People that had so remov'd, had the Sickness even in their Hutts or Booths; the Reason of which was plain, namely, not because they removed into the Air, but because they did not remove time enough, that is to say, not till by openly conversing with the other People their Neighbours, they had the Distemper upon them, or, (as may be said) among them, and so carry'd it about them whither they went: Or, Because they were not careful enough after they were safely removed out of the Towns, not to come in again and mingle with the diseased People.

But be it which of these it will, when our Travellers began to perceive that the Plague was not only in the Towns, but even in the Tents and Huts on the Forest near them, they began then not only to be afraid, but to think of decamping and removing; for had they stay'd, they wou'd' ha' been in manifest Danger of their Lives. . . .

I have, since my knowing this Story of *John* and his Brother, enquir'd and found, that there were a great many of the poor disconsolate People, as above, fled into the Country every way, and some of them got little Sheds, and Barns, and Out-houses to live in, where they cou'd obtain so much Kindness of the Country, and especially where they had any the least satisfactory Account to give of themselves, and particularly that they did not come out of *London* too late. But others, and that in great Numbers, built themselves little Hutts and Retreats in the Fields and Woods, and liv'd like Hermits in Holes and Caves, or any Place they cou'd find; and where, we may be sure, they suffer'd great Extremities, such that many of them were oblig'd to come back again whatever the Danger was; and so those little Huts were often found empty, and the Country People suppos'd the Inhabitants lay Dead in them of the Plague, and would not go near them for fear, no not in a great while; nor is it unlikely but that some of the unhappy Wanderers might die so all alone, even sometimes for want of Help, as particularly in one Tent or Hutt, was found a Man dead, and on the Gate of a Field just by, was cut with his Knife in uneven Letters, the following Words, by which it may be suppos'd the other Man escap'd, or that one dying first, the other bury'd him as well as he could;

O mIsErY!
We BoTH ShaLL DyE,
WoE, WoE.

Journal of a Plague Year, Daniel De Foe, 1665

The Forest Ponds. — The Epping Forest Committee wrote with reference to the Council's application for permission to clean out and deepen the pond on Bell Common, with a view to water being used for highway purposes. The Conservators could only consent to allow the pond to be deepened three feet, upon the condition that a light fence was erected round the pond. — Referred to the Highway Committee.

Epping Monthly Record, June 1899

The second of Bell Common's ponds also received a facelift. The picture above was taken in 1915, that at the bottom of the page some time afterwards.

So we went to our Inn, and after eating of something, and kissed the daughter of the house, she being very pretty, we took leave, and so that night, the road pretty good but the weather rainy, to Epping, where we sat and played a game of cards, and after supper and some merry talk with a plain bold maid of the house, we went to bed. Up in the morning. Then to London through the forest, where we found the way good.

Samuel Pepys, February 1660

Coaches are ordered to lie on the Road at Epping, Hockerill, and Bourn-Bridge, to convey his Royal Highness the Duke of Cumberland to Newmarket on Monday Morning next.

Press report, 1753

There are some good houses of modern erection; and, besides the Episcopal chapel, which is an elegant building, there are places for public worship, belonging to the Independents, and to the Society of Friends. In the summer months this place is resorted to on account of its healthy and pleasant situation, and it is also well suited for schools, of which there are several, among which may be mentioned in particular a boarding school for boys, sons of the members of the society of Friends, opened in this town about thirty years ago, by Mr Isaac Payne, and during that period of time the number of scholars has been between sixty and seventy, without any variation worth mentioning; latterly, however, many children belonging to other religious sects have been admitted; a fact which may be regarded as a proof of the growing liberality of the age.

This town, though situated upon a ridge, is well supplied with water from land springs; but though several attempts have been made here, as well as in the neighbouring parishes, to procure a purer and more certain supply of this prime necessity of life, from what is termed the *main spring*, yet it is believed that they have in no instance succeeded. A well was sunk, a few years since, on Mr Payne's premises, to the depth of two hundred feet; boring was then commenced, and continued two hundred and twenty feet farther, but without reaching the main spring. The blue clay began to yield a lighter and more sandy substance, but it being found impracticable to keep out the water from the land springs, the undertaking was given over as hopeless, and the well covered in. At the end of five months it was found that the water had risen to within ten feet of the surface, and it has so continued. This water is limpid and soft. The well extends eighty feet below the bed of the

In June 1897 Epping celebrated Queen Victoria's Diamond Jubilee in 'capital' style, to use a word of the period. The High Street was decorated from end to end; there was a parade; a Thanksgiving Service; a dinner for the old folks; a march to the Plain on the northern outskirts; sports; a children's tea; bonfires; fireworks; and a torchlight procession at midnight to round off the gaiety of the day. One of the lasting tributes to the Queen's 60-year reign was the planting the following winter of Victoria Avenue on the eastern side of the London road just beyond the Bell. However, as the article from the January 1898 Epping Monthly Record shows, not all the townspeople were in favour of the scheme.

Thames, and rises three hundred and forty above its level.

The weekly market is on Friday, and a large fair for cattle is held on Tuesday, in Whitsun-week, and another on the 13th of November, which is well attended by graziers from the adjoining districts. Distant from London sixteen miles.

The History and Topography of the County of Essex, 1831

The Duke of Sussex, having been recommended a change of air for the benefit of his health, left Kensington Palace last week for Epping, and will take up his temporary abode at an Inn, on the brow of the forest for a short time.

His Royal Highness, has had a slight attack of his pulmonary complaint, which is generally removed in the summer by a change of air. In every other particular his Royal Highness enjoys excellent health.

Press report, 1835

Some twenty years since, than Epping a more lively or bustling town could not be found in the county of Essex, nor, in proportion to its population, we may say in the kingdom.

The number of coaches passing through were a constant source of excitement, and the employment they created caused a means of livelihood for numbers. The position of the town in relation to the Eastern Counties, it being on the main road to most of the Towns in them, caused an immense amount of traffic, and at the times of the Newmarket races, the posting houses obtained a perfect harvest. The result of this favourable situation was manifest in the flourishing condition of its innkeepers and tradespeople. But the invention of travelling by steam soon showed itself in the construction of the Cambridge and Norwich Railway and the Eastern Counties Railway. And then, 'What a falling off was there!' The coaches soon ceased running, and the town, that was so enlivened by 20 of them passing through daily, soon put on an appearance of mourning, and the large posting house, so many years known as 'Epping Place,' as such no longer existed.

own be compelled to leave the town for London on a winter's morning, almost before it is light, and then hurry back at night, or if their business be but trifling, be obliged to remain there from 10 a.m. till 4 p.m. Must any one walking in our streets at night, run the risk of falling over wheel-barrows, or breaking their legs or necks against the horse-less hay-carts, from the miserable darkness of our town?

The answer to these queries is very short. Notwithstanding the opposition of the aristocracy (and at the outset, of the Eastern Counties Railway Co) our Epping Railway will shortly be commenced; and in addition, some energetic gentleman or gentlemen, are about commencing the building of a gasometer, so that by another Christmas we hope to be able to travel the whole distance to London by rail, and be able also to wish any friend we may meet in our streets at night, a 'Merry Christmas,' without mistaking strangers for friends, or vice versa.

Bishop Stortford Observer and Epping Advertiser, January 4, 1862

we presumed that the fever, although raging severely in Epping, had not affected the heads of the people, except, perhaps, to cause them to be put together. The putting together of heads is not altogether a bad thing, especially when they have good ideas in them; at least, that is the conclusion we came to after walking down the broad High Street. Epping had got the fever, and badly, too! It was proud of it, and made the fact known to everybody having eyes. The main thoroughfare, from the church to the bank, and even a little way beyond, was all ablaze with colour. Never before has the town looked so gay, so happy, or so frivolous. From the windows of the smallest tenements, as well as from the larger windows of the business houses, flags and streamers were projecting. From tree to tree and from post to post lines of waving pennons, red, white and blue, were stretched on both sides and along the whole length of the street. The supports of the trees were decorated with paper flowers, paper chains, flags, and red bunting, and in amongst the foliage were placed Japanese lanterns. The fountain, which was erected ten years ago to celebrate the Queen's 50 years' reign, looked very smart, being adorned from

The avenue is clearly visible in this picture taken by Ray Stebbings, Epping chemist and photographer, in April 1963.

A stagnation in all kind of business soon followed, and from being the most lively town, than Epping a more dull one could not be found. Various proposals have been made to enliven it, but its principal support being the aristocracy, they, as they are so often wont to be, have proved themselves the opponents of any progressive measures for benefiting the mediocracy or lower classes. The tradespeople following in their rear, endeavoured to monopolize their businesses, and the poor suffered accordingly.

But things could not always remain so — an energetic grocer, from a neighbouring town, set the example by opening a business where all classes could be suited at fair and reasonable prices — competition in that respect brought things to an honourable level.

But that was not sufficient. Should Epping at a distance of only 15 miles from London remain without a railway? Must such of its inhabitants possessing no conveyance of their

It is quite warm, although the sun can scarcely be seen, and a gentle breeze rustles the leaves on the trees. The uphill walk from Epping railway station to the post office has made even a light jacket seem a burden, and it is necessary to stop for breath. When, after much effort, we do arrive at the top of Station Road and turn our gaze to the right we are quite overcome. The extraordinary sight which the High Street presents as we turn the corner quite takes our breath away, and also our speech. At last, having recovered from our open-mouthed, open-eyed astonishment, we venture to inquire, very meekly, of an inhabitant what might have happened to the town. 'It's only the Jubilee fever,' we were informed, 'it takes some people very suddenly, and if they have it badly they lose their heads.' Further enquiries showed that the epidemic had seized Epping some weeks ago, and that now the fever was at its height.

Seeing no headless people about the town,

top to bottom with bright-coloured paper flowers and pale green paper leaves. Nearly every shop front was decorated with either flags or bunting, the prevailing colours being red, white, and blue, while many were ornamented with coloured lamps and hanging lanterns, which gave a most effective illumination after dusk.

Essex Times, June 1897

At the Epping Petty Sessions yesterday, Mr. W. Patchett called the attention of the Bench to the preparations for tree-planting now being made on Bell Common, and which was, in his opinion, absolutely illegal, as they would not only obstruct one of the most beautiful views, but would also curtail the rights of the commoners. It was decided to write to the Forest authorities on the matter.

Epping Monthly Record, January 1898

Although Epping Cricket Club's original pitch was located on the Plain — later moved to Bury Lane — this would seem an appropriate point in our story to include mention of the threat faced by the Foresters Club's pitch on the southern outskirts a hundred years later. This picture taken in April 1983 shows the hallowed square (established after the Second World War) completely swept away by the M25 tunnel. Its reinstatement on the concrete roof can be seen illustrated on page 127.

THE CRICKET GROUND ON THE PLAIN
Shall it be abandoned?

A preliminary meeting of cricketers and others interested in the preservation of the old cricket ground on Epping Plain was held on Thursday last, when it was decided to make a vigorous and immediate effort to save the pitch from being destroyed. A committee was appointed to approach the Forest Commissioners upon the subject, and the following letter has been forwarded to the Forest superintendent, Mr. F. F. McKenzie:

Epping, March 12th, 1897

Sir, — We the undersigned, on behalf of a large number of inhabitants, having seen it stated in the public press that the Cricket Ground on Epping Plain has been abandoned by the Town Club, respectfully approach you with a view to retaining the ground for the use of cricketers of that portion of the town in proximity to it.

Having in mind the large amount of time and money expended in order to get the ground into its present grand condition we feel it would be a reflection, not only upon the lovers of the game, but the town itself, to have the ground destroyed.

We would undertake to provide the necessary funds to keep the ground in accordance with the regulations of the Forest Commissioners, and trust that our application will meet with your favourable and early consideration — especially as the contemplated moving of the present chains and posts will tend to destroy the work of so many years.

Your petitioners include some of the original promoters of the ground who would deeply regret its loss.

Attached to the above are the eight signatures of the committee. Just as we go to press we learn that a favourable reply to the above has been received and, in order to secure the ground, a club has been formed under the title of the 'Epping Mechanics' Cricket Club'.

Epping Monthly Record, March 1897

The fears of the cricketers who are trying to save the Plain have just been realised. On Friday last the posts and chains were removed, but, what is worse, the waggon used for carting the same was ruthlessly drawn right across the pitch. We hope that we shall not have to record the loss of this historic playground as one of the events of the Diamond Jubilee Year.

Epping Monthly Record, March 1897

In justice to the committee of the Epping Cricket Club we feel it incumbent upon us to correct the expression used in last month's *Record* with reference to the old ground on the Plain. 'Carelessly' or 'thoughtlessly' would have fitted the sentence more becomingly than 'ruthlessly,' as the cricket committee were in no way responsible for the cutting up of the ground.

We are glad to see that the posts and chains have been replaced round the pitch, and it is gratifying to know that the E.C.C. committee so readily consented to sell them to the energetic provisional committee of working men, who, after all said and done, really deserve credit for their prompt action in saving the ground from falling into the hands of an outside club, which was more than probable.

Epping Monthly Record, April 1897

The old cricket ground on Epping Plain was re-opened by the newly-formed club on Saturday, May 1st., in the presence of a large and enthusiastic gathering. The Town Band, under Bandmaster T. Smith, played a capital selection of music. The pitch was formally opened by a match of four overs by two old and two young cricketers of Epping, representing the past and future. The former were represented by Messrs. A. Monk and E. J. Jago, who played upon the same ground 60 and 49 years ago respectively; the Youngsters were represented by Masters F. Simpson and H. Hewitt. The juveniles proved victorious by three runs to two. Then followed a match between teams of 16-a-side, chosen by the captain (E. Hummerston) and vice-captain (W. Marrable), the latter winning a well-contested game. Messrs. H. B. Yerburgh and Jas. Nunn officiated as umpires. After the match a meat tea was served at the club house (Royal Oak) by host Shannon. The president of the new club (Mr. H. B. Yerburgh) occupied the chair and a company of 57 sat down. Mr. Yerburgh, amid applause, announced that he would give prizes for the best batting and bowling averages during the season. An excellent programme of toasts and songs was afterwards gone through under the chairmanship of Mr. Nunn.

Epping Monthly Record, May 1897

Not far away the Cottage Cafe — from Teas to Tandoori!

The road to Epping Upland — Bury Lane then and now.

Then and now — an Epping reverie

When seated in my fireside chair
I often think, while musing there,
Of Epping in the long ago,
When Epping was so quiet and slow.

No noise or bustle then was heard,
But oft the song of some sweet bird
Came softly o'er the summer air
From scented field, or woodland fair.

The distant whistle of a train,
The 'low' of cattle in the lane,
The rooks a-cawing in the trees
Were sounds that never failed to please.

And people *walked* — on their two feet,
And horses plodded down the street,
And cars were few and far between,
And Epping's air was fresh, and clean.

But now — in nineteen-sixty-three —
The roar of traffic deafens me,
And people hurry to and fro
As if they *must* keep on the go.

The reek of petrol taints the air,
To see a horse is very rare;
And no one serves us in a store —
We serve ourselves, pay at the door.

We cross the road with heart in mouth;
The traffic comes from north and south
And east and west and everywhere —
One has no time to stand and stare.

And big new buildings line the street,
And concrete lamp-posts light our feet,
And cockney tongues assail our ears —
So different from those bygone years.

Dear Epping of the long ago,
Dear country town we used to know,
No more we'll see you as of yore —
Goodbye, old town, for evermore.

SIDNEY HILLS, 1963

It will be a good thing when the application of the new county bye-laws regarding the playing of musical instruments on the highways is clearly defined and understood. At present it provides against annoyance caused by instrumental music within a certain distance of a dwelling house after a request to desist has been given. This is only right and proper, and might even go further by abolishing music of all kinds on any part of the highways on the Sabbath Day, but on ordinary days we fail to see why a well-played coach horn or cornet is to be considered a nuisance, whilst a German band may scrape away with impunity beneath your bedroom window within two hours of midnight.

Epping Monthly Record, June 1899

Once Hills Cyclists' Rest and Tea Gardens — now Tabletalk. The proprietor was found dead one day in the mid-1930s in tragic circumstances during a police raid on the premises.

In the mid-nineteenth century Epping had the highest death rate in the whole of Essex — from cholera, typhoid and related diseases — caused by insanitary conditions. There was no sewage disposal, and villagers were drawing their drinking water from polluted wells. A local doctor, Joseph Clegg, campaigned for over twenty years for something to be done, but ranged against him were two local landowners and the vicar of the parish church who considered Clegg's proposals for a water and sewage works to be too extravagant for such a small town. In 1867 the doctor petitioned the Home Office under the Sanitary Act, which had been passed by Parliament the previous year, and Epping became one of only seven places in the British Isles where the local authority had to be ordered to carry out the improvements.

Epping could lose one of its best known landmarks. The water tower, which influenced Epping Forest Council's choice of design for centralised offices, is going up for sale in four to six weeks' time — with no strings attached. Epping Forest Council's planning department has confirmed that the 100-year-old building is not listed.

Agents Taylor and Melhuish, of New Barnet, acting for the owner, Lea Valley Water Company, admitted there was no barrier to a purchaser pulling the building down. Spokesman Simon Scarisbrick said there could be 'no cast-iron guarantee' against loss of the tower. It would be up to the purchaser', he added. 'A tower of that age will require quite a lot of maintenance.'

Mr. James McGowan, speaking for Lea Valley Water company, said the tower and adjoining office was being sold because it was no longer useful. 'We were having problems in the town of Epping and carried out some mains laying in the area; now Epping is supplied from an alternative tower.'

A suggestion that Tower Garage might be interested in purchasing the site met with a denial from manager Denis Minihane. 'As far as I am concerned we are not looking for expansion,' he said. 'I have no interest (in the tower) either way at this stage.'

Guardian and Gazette, July 5, 1985

Prevarication, including the wholesale resignation of the district sewer committee, delayed completion of the water tower until 1872. The imposing structure became synonymous with the town and it was even used as a turning point in the 1st Aerial Derby around London in 1912 (see pages 440-441). Now its future hangs in the balance.

The nearby area was the subject of another controversial issue in 1985 — the erection of the Tesco supermarket, designed by

Michael Biscoe, on the site of the garage opened by Claude and Lionel Staples in 1931 and the old Green Line depot.

Pegrum's Dairy — another tea room and cyclists' rest. The whitewashed three-storey building with dormer windows, formerly Nos. 92-94 High Street but now Nos. 98-102, dates from the late seventeenth century and is listed Grade II.

The demise of so many old firms is one sad aspect running central to the Epping story — like the little smithy shop run by Walter Nunn, seen here after shoeing Vera Korte's horse Sherry in September 1964 . . .

. . . and like the builders F. N. Palmer & Son, established over 150 years, which stood on the corner of St John's Road.

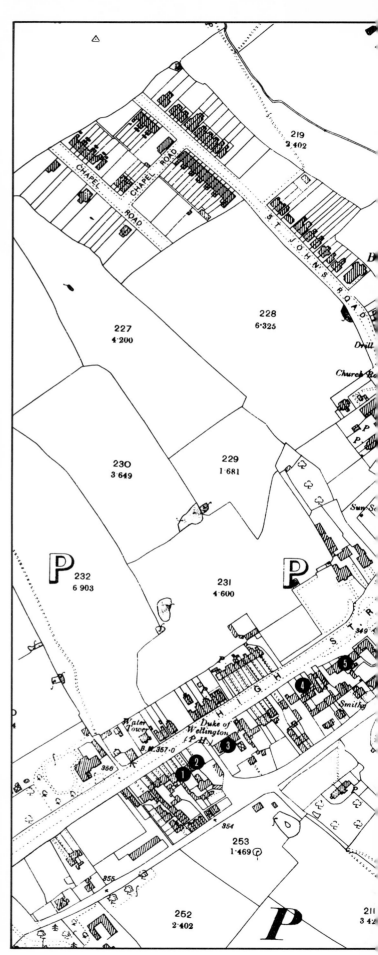

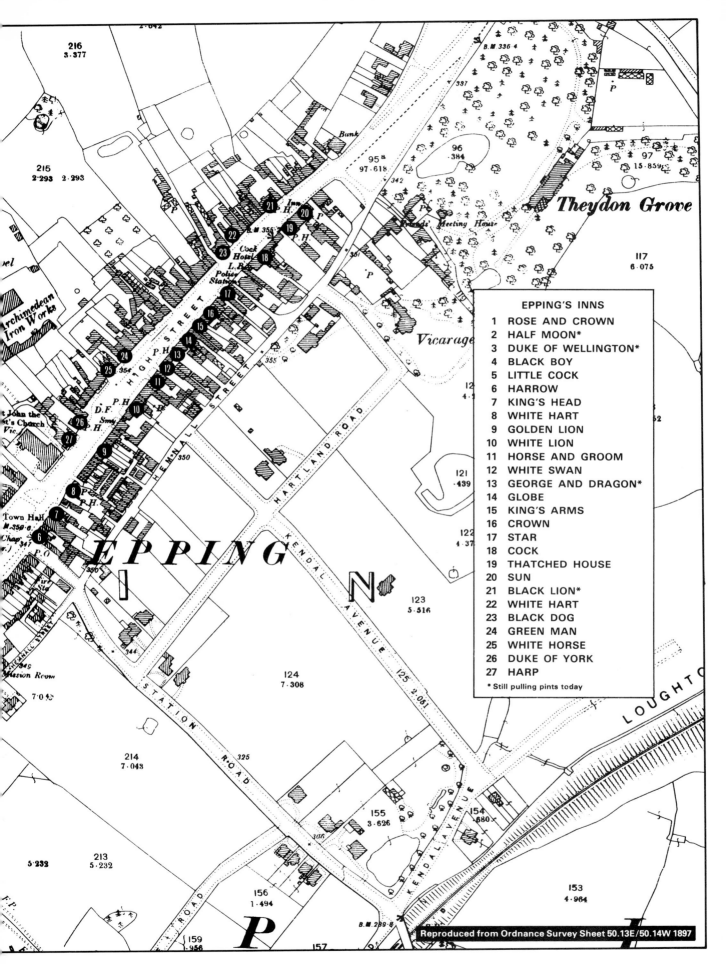

EPPING'S INNS

1 ROSE AND CROWN
2 HALF MOON*
3 DUKE OF WELLINGTON*
4 BLACK BOY
5 LITTLE COCK
6 HARROW
7 KING'S HEAD
8 WHITE HART
9 GOLDEN LION
10 WHITE LION
11 HORSE AND GROOM
12 WHITE SWAN
13 GEORGE AND DRAGON*
14 GLOBE
15 KING'S ARMS
16 CROWN
17 STAR
18 COCK
19 THATCHED HOUSE
20 SUN
21 BLACK LION*
22 WHITE HART
23 BLACK DOG
24 GREEN MAN
25 WHITE HORSE
26 DUKE OF YORK
27 HARP

* Still pulling pints today

Reproduced from Ordnance Survey Sheet 50.13E/50.14W 1897

The story of Epping's parish church begins at Epping Upland, two miles north of the town we know today. As we have seen (pages 93 and 99), this was the location of the Epping of old, and it was only in the 1600s that the focus shifted eastwards to Epping Street whose importance increased dramatically with the construction of the road from London to East Anglia. All Saints' church is claimed to date back to Edward the Confessor although the nave, the oldest part of the building still surviving, is probably of the thirteenth century. The church has undergone several restorations, the most major in 1878.

EPPING

The Old Chapel-of-Ease. — The last Sunday services were held in the old Chapel-of-Ease, St. John the Baptist, on Sunday, September 1st, previous to its demolition. The old place has many endearing associations to a large number of the inhabitants, who have attended its services for many years, but who have for the past few years become painfully aware that the building was too plain and old-fashioned for the present generation, who can only worship in beautiful temples, with ornate ritual. The services on Sunday were well attended, and appropriate sermons were preached by the vicar, who referred in feeling terms to the old associations connected with the present building, and earnestly invited his congregation to make the temporary iron Church their home whilst the new parish Church was in course of erection.

Press report, 1889

Wednesday was a day of exceptional interest in Epping, the occasion being the laying of the foundation stone of the new Church of St. John the Baptist, which, when dedicated, will become the parish church. The present parish church of All Saints' at Epping Upland is fully three miles from the town, and that, of course, is a serious disadvantage. It is true that for many years the chapel-of-ease of St. John the Baptist has existed in the town, but the feeling that the parish church should be in the centre of the population instead of occupying an isolated position has been steadily growing, and last year an Act of Parliament was obtained whereby the new Church of St. John the Baptist when consecrated will become the parish church, and the old church of All Saints' at Epping Upland will decline to the position of a chapel-of-ease. The bringing about of this desirable state of things is largely due to Miss Elizabeth Horsley Whiteman, formerly of Theydon Grove, who gave £3,000 for securing the Act of Parliament, and towards the building of the new Church.

The new church will occupy the site of the old chapel-of-ease, which has been pulled down, and a piece of land adjoining, given so long ago as 1848 for the purpose by Mr. John Clarmont Whiteman, then of Theydon Grove, Epping. The new church will be constructed of wrought Bath stone, finished in plaster inside. It will be covered by a wagon roof with moulded panels. The style of architecture will be gothic of the 14th century. It will be dignified rather than ornate in manner, and will be strictly English in character. It will consist of a nave and continuous aisles, and the original design provided for a tower at the west end of the south aisle, but, owing to lack of funds, it

The church in Epping Street, dedicated to St John in 1403, is first mentioned as existing in the previous century. From the mid-sixteenth century it seems to have been a chapel-of-ease to All Saints'. No illustrations appear to have survived prior to that *above* of the building which existed from 1784 to 1832. This engraving by J. W. Gear was made in 1822 and shows the stocks and whipping post and the market house beside the road beyond the church.

In 1832 the chapel of St John was rebuilt to a design by Mr S. M. Hubert incorporating a crenellated south-west front and central tower.

has been decided to postpone the building of the tower. When erected the tower will be connected with the church by a cloister-like passage. It is greatly to be desired that this part of the scheme may soon be carried out, as the long line of the church roof will need breaking, and the detached tower will be a striking feature in the town. The length of the church externally will be about 134ft. There will not be a chancel arch. The chancel will be an open one, divided by an oak open screen from the nave. A special feature will be the east window, consisting of a composition of seven lights, with delicate tracery. The building of the south aisle is for the present postponed. The church was designed by Messrs. Bodley and Garner, the builders are Messrs. Rudd and Son, of Grantham, and Mr. J. R. Streather is clerk of the works. The total cost of the work at present in hand is estimated at from £9,600 to £10,000, and the amount received and promised prior to the ceremony on Wednesday was £9,020. Until the new church is so far completed that it can be dedicated the services are being held in a comfortable temporary iron church. Very general interest was taken in the proceedings on Wednesday, and a thoroughly representative company, numbering about 2,000 people, assembled on and around the site of

With the growth of Epping Street into the modern Epping, what was once sufficient as a chapel-of-ease became inadequate for the burgeoning population. The reality of the changed situation was acknowledged in 1888 and the roles were reversed: St John the Baptist became the parish church of Epping and All Saints' was reduced to chapel-of-ease status. (It became a church again in its own right in 1912 when the parish was split into two.) As far as Epping was concerned, the Hubert-designed church was not suited to its new rôle and it was demolished in 1889 and the new St John's consecrated on April 7, 1891.

The Bodley and Garner-designed building had a nave, chancel and south aisle, but the planned north aisle was not added until 1908. The following year, through the generosity of Edward Wythes of Copped Hall, the imposing tower was erected on the

south-east corner. Before the building of the new tower in 1911-13 St John's only had one bell which had been given by William, Lord Grey, in 1650. This was re-cast and seven new ones added when the tower was completed.

the new church to witness the ceremony of laying the foundation stone.

Stratford Express, November 1889

Great interest attached to the consecration on Wednesday of the new parish church of St. John the Baptist, Epping. The day was observed as a holiday, and street decorations gave a festive appearance to the place. The building of the church has been an object dear to the residents of the town and neighbourhood, and people of all classes assembled to do honour to the occasion.

Essex County Chronicle, November 1889

Raise the roof of St. John's Church, Epping — and replace it with something better!

That's the plea to Epping pockets to be made on July 1, when the church council launches an appeal which could save this historic landmark from serious damage.

Causing concern are the 90-year-old roofing tiles, which are scaling (losing their outer surface so that they become porous) and allowing water to seep through. When this freezes the tiles then crack, causing further leakages.

The cost of repairs has been estimated at an initial £50,000 — but appeal chairman Michael Hepton says that the final amount needed could be three times as much.

Guardian and Gazette, June 28, 1985

This illustration is from a faded, uncaptioned postcard sent by 'Doris' to Miss Nicholls of Sidcup, Kent. Her cryptic message adds to the enigma: 'Thought you might like this P.C. for you see it has my pretty self in. You will guess when it was taken.' Posted on the afternoon of May 1, 1909, the date gives us the clue as it was shortly before, on April 28, that the new tower was dedicated by the Bishop of St Albans. Principal benefactor in the rebuilding of the church was Edward Wythes, lord of the manor, who donated £4,000.

When one remembers that the first successful powered flight in Great Britain had only taken place five years before (when Sam Cody flew about a quarter of a mile in his biplane at Farnborough), the courage of the early air pioneers, and the effect they had on the population, can well be appreciated. The Daily Mail soon established itself as a sponsor of many aviation exploits, one being the Aerial Derby around London. The water tower was the turning point on the north-east corner of the 94-mile course and thousands turned out at Epping to watch the spectacle. This was the scene in July 1912, the first time the race was held.

1913

August 27th. Bad luck happened to Mr. Hawker the 'airman' today. In his flight round Great Britain for the *Daily Mail* £5,000 prize, he had got to within 15 miles of Dublin (north) when his greasy boot slipping on the rudder bar, his waterplane 'side-slipped', turned over and fell 60 feet into shallow water below. The pilot escaped with a shaking, but Mr. Hanper, his passenger, broke his arm and injured his head and face. They were both rescued by fishermen, the passenger having to go to hospital. They started from Oban at 6.48 a.m., and at time of accident it was 1.00 p.m., doing 206 miles that day. 1,043 miles altogether were flown and 497 more to go to reach Southampton. Total distance around Great Britain (through Caledonian Canal) is 1,540 miles.

September 1st. *Androcles and the Lion* a comic play produced at St. James' Theatre tonight. It is by Bernard Shaw.

M. Santos Dumont the famous pioneer of flying has decided to return to his old labours after living in retirement for several years.

M. Pegoud, the French airman, 'looped the loop' in his Blériot monoplane at Paris today. He rose to a height of 3,000 feet, then purposely fell like a stone for 200 feet, then turned inwards till the aeroplane was flying on its back, afterwards rising perpendicularly upwards. He completed the circle by regaining his original position.

September 17th. Mr. Pemberton-Billing performed the remarkable feat of winning the Royal Aero Club's certificate in four hours 2 minutes at Brooklands today. He and Mr. Handley Page had wagered to learn to fly to gain this certificate in one day. The latter however did not get his certificate. Mr. Barnwell was the instructor of Mr. Pemberton-Billing.

September 20th. The 2nd Aerial Derby round London took place today for the £100 cup and 200 sovereigns offered by the *Daily Mail*. The first race took place in June last year and would have taken place in June again this year had not the Government prevented it by the 'Aerial Navigation Act'. However, special permission was granted for this particular race. The course was round Greater London, the start and finish being at the Hendon Aerodrome. The turning points were Kempton Park, Epsom Race Course, West Thurrock, Epping, Hertford and thence to Hendon again. The distance was 94 miles. Eleven competitors started and 9 finished the course.

Only 2 competitors who started failed to complete the course, E. Beauman who came down at Kempton Park owing to engine trouble, and Lieutenant Porte who descended at North Weald (Curr's farm) near Epping having lost his way. On restarting, the labourers who held his machine back let go too soon with the result that the propellor broke and the airman was then unable to proceed. At Epping all the airmen had to pass round the church tower (it was the water tower last year). Crowds came in to our little town and a large number of motors, motor bikes, brakes and bicycles were packed by the sides of the roads. However, I do not think there were so many people at Epping at the race this year as there were last. I stood in our field in St. John's Road where were a crowd of 200 or 300 and had a good view as the aeroplanes passed the church tower and sped away in the distance towards Hertford. These all passed Epping within 13 minutes. It was a grand and exciting race, especially when Hamel passed (underneath) another machine. Mr. D. J. Pearl stood in a field in Hartland Road opposite Mrs. Curnock's and had a good view from there. The race started at Hendon at 4.00 p.m. Hamel started at 4.12 p.m. and finished at 5.27¾. The airmen started one at a time, at minute intervals, the slowest machines first. The day was cloudy and damp but the rain kept off. At West Thurrock a cap to Hamel's petrol tank flew off and from there to home he had to plug it with his finger, steering with one hand. Hamel won the race last year.

September 25th. M. Pegoud the daring French airman is now in England giving exhibition flights on his Blériot monoplane at Brooklands. He flies upside down while strapped in his seat and descends in a corkscrew manner. He loops the loop in the air, and Brooklands Club is stated to have paid M. Pegoud for his engagement.

October 1st. Mrs. Stocks, the well-known airwoman, has just recovered consciousness after being 300 hours unconscious as a result of her fall in an aeroplane piloted by Mr. S. Pickles at Hendon Aerodrome on the 'Aerial Derby round London' day. She was kept alive by artificial feeding. Mr. Pickles is progressing towards recovery as well as can be expected.

October 17th. The world's greatest air disaster occurred today in Germany. The Zeppelin airship L2, the newest and most scientific of this class of airships, was on its way to take part in the national rejoicings at Leipzig when it exploded in mid-air, killing all its 31 occupants. The new building, the Battle of the Nations memorial, was to have been opened in the ceremonies.

1914

May 23rd. The *Daily Mail* Aerial Derby round London, 95 miles during which Epping was to be touched, was to have taken place today. Huge crowds gathered at all the controls and waited for the aeroplanes. They did not turn up however as the race was postponed on account of the misty atmosphere. J. and I standing in field in St. John's Road heard of postponement at 5.15 p.m. just when were were expecting the airmen. Buses came to Epping from London this afternoon. The 'Derby' of the air is to take place on June 6th.

A very sad catastrophe has happened which will take away somewhat of the interest of the coming race. Mr. Gustav Hamel, acclaimed by all to be Britain's foremost and most

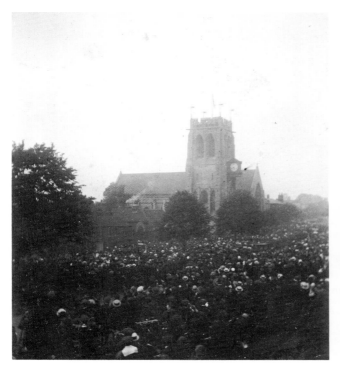

This was the dawn of the aviation age, and people everywhere were caught up in the excitement of the new era, none more so than Leslie Church, son of Stephen Church, the renowned Epping butcher of the period. These extracts from his diary, preserved and kindly made available by his nephew, Allan Church, impart the thrill of it all. With the second Derby in September 1913 the Epping marker was altered, giving the new St John's tower a purposeful, if unorthodox, christening. This picture shows Verrier, the fourth to arrive in the third annual race held in June 1914.

famous airman (and the handsomest as one paper puts it) and the favourite in the race around London, has disappeared. He set out from Hardelot in France this morning at 12.15 p.m. in a new Morane monoplane in which he hoped to win the race, to cross the Channel to England via Dover and thence on to Hendon. A cross-Channel steamer reported seeing an aeroplane in mid-Channel which was in all probability Mr. Hamel's. Since then all trace of him has disappeared. English warships and seaplanes were sent out tonight to search the Channel and a portion of the North Sea for the missing airman or for any wreckage of his machine. The seas were searched for two days but without result and it is presumed that Mr. Hamel has shared the fate of Cecil Grace by drowning in the Channel or the North Sea. As the wings of Mr. Hamel's monoplane were clipped short, they would not be of much use in keeping the machine afloat for more than 2 or 3 seconds. Mr. Hamel's disappearance has caused perhaps the greatest sensation in connection with aviation in this country and for one man perhaps in the whole world.

June 6th. The 3rd annual Aerial Derby round London took place today. The race was for the Daily Mail Gold Cup and also for the 'Shell' trophy of £200.

There were 60,000 people at Hendon to see the start and finish. Only 11 competitors out of 21 originally entered, started, and of these only 4 passed Epping. They passed over the church tower control in the following order:
1. W. L. Brock at 17½ mins past 5 (Morane monoplane)
2. L. Noel at 18½ mins past 5 (Morane monoplane)
3. R. H. Carr at 33 mins past 5 (Farman biplane)
4. P. Verrier at 40 minutes past 5 (Farman biplane)

After passing, the first two steered in quite opposite directions. Five competitors completed the course or nearly so, but Mr. L. Noel who was first back at Hendon was disqualified because he was not seen at West Thurrock or Hertford. Lord Carberry was also disqualified for not keeping to the course. The final result was:
1. W. L. Brock, 1 hr, 18 minutes, 54 seconds
2. R. H. Carr, 1 hr, 46 minutes, 27 seconds
3. P. Verrier, 1 hr, 49 minutes, 50 seconds

The speed of the winner was 72 miles per hour. Last year's winner's (the late Mr. Gustav Hamel, drowned in North Sea or Channel 2 weeks ago) speed was 76 miles per hour.

The others who flew in the race today were:
Mr. H. Pixton, landed near Croydon.
Mr. R. H. Barnwell and J. Alcock who landed at Brooklands.

Mr. W. Birchenough, landed at Richmond.
Mr. H. Bjorkland, landed at Epsom.
Mr. L. A. Strange, landed at West Wickham, Kent.

Most of these probably gave up on account of the thick mist which hung over the course. Myself, I think it was worse today than a fortnight ago when the race was postponed. Thousands of people were in Epping town or neighbourhood. I saw the machines from the field in St. John's Road where there were quite a crowd of people.

Unpublished diary, Mr. Leslie D. A. Church

Rain and mist marred the 1914 event: an unknown humourist has tried to brighten up the picture by the addition of a phantom flyer with the words: 'They were waiting near the church!'

We hear that the result of the protest from the freeholders in St. John's Road, relative to the making up of the road, will in all probability be made known on Friday next when the matter is down for hearing before the Justices at the Epping Petty Sessions. The few remaining plots of land in the above mentioned road have more than doubled in value since the first sale. This is doubtless due to a great extent to the excellent system of sewerage introduced by the Rural District Council, who evidently believe that a thing worth doing at all is worth doing well. A proper road and paths, together with a few lamps would undoubtedly make this portion of the town one of the most desirable.!

Epping Monthly Record, September 1895

St. John's Road. — The report of the Highways Committee stated that the contractor had completed the making-up of St. John's Road; and they therefore recommended that the final instalment of £52 be paid.— The Surveyor suggested that the Council should signify their intention of taking over St. John's and Chapel Roads at an early date.— Mr. Palmer asked whether the Surveyor was satisfied that the road had been rolled with a heavy roller? Mr. Trussell said the contractor was to keep the road in repair for three months, and during the greater part of that time both the Surveyor and the contractor thought that it would be useless to put the heavy roller on the road, as it was considered it might break the gas connections from the main to the lamps. Certainly it would not improve them; and he thought it would be wise to say no more about it.— Mr. Palmer said it appeared to him an excuse for not using the heavy roller. It looked as if it was not convenient.— The Chairman said that if a six-horse roller and animals were to trample about the road, they would disturb the pipes; but he thought a lighter roller might be used with advantage.— Mr. Sudul said there was no doubt that the contract had not been kept to the letter, but he thought the best that could be done under the circumstances had been done.— The report was agreed to.

Epping Urban District Council minutes,
June 22, 1898

The state of the streets, more especially those off the main roads, have, during the past few weeks, been wretched indeed. We notice that a large quantity of granite and gravel has been ordered, and will, doubtless, improve matters. Might we suggest that a few yards of road gravel or granite outside the gates of St. John's Church would add to the comfort of those worshippers who use the main entrance, and at the same time would add to the cleanliness of the slip of road over which there is more foot traffic than in any other part of Epping?

Epping Monthly Record, November 1900

The state of the road beside the church, formerly Chapel Lane but now taking its name from its patron saint, was the cause of much comment in the press just before the turn of the century. On the right can be seen the old Baptist church built in 1893 on a site given by one of the town's leading businessmen, William Cottis. It was demolished in June 1978, the replacement houses being called 'Cottis Court'.

AN EPPING BOY'S LAMENT

Dear Editor, — I am writing this letter to inform you and the townspeople that I do not think that the boys of St. Johns'-road are treated as they ought to be. Their piece of green grass on which they used to play is shut up by a fence, and then, again, if they go out into the road, and play in front of a house, the inhabitant comes out with a pail of water and threatens to throw it over them if they don't move on. They go up a little higher, and this time some old woman comes out with a horse-whip after them, and there they are to stand still and not move a limb. I think, dear Editor, some alterations should be made. I think there is one boy in particular, whom the people blame for everything.

I remain
Now, and for ever,

CARROT TOPS

The Loughton Gazette, January 24, 1903

442

A smile sometimes crosses the face of the more 'suburban' resident when he takes a trip out to Epping Town. He looks up and down the High-street, which, despite the advent of super petrol stations and garages, cars parked along its entire length and an oil-sheened road surface, yet retains much of its rural serenity. He may know that the population of the Epping urban district — which includes Coopersale and Ivy Chimneys — is not greatly in excess of 5,000.

'Epping Town', he echoes, with patronising emphasis on the 'Town.'

He thinks of great suburbs with populations running into hundreds of thousands, which have not the temerity to refer to themselves as towns; and he looks once more along the sleepy High-street, taking in at a glance the sentinel church tower, the concave roofs of historic inns, the 'village smithy,' the market place where pigs and sheep are still penned between old-fashioned hurdles tied together wtih string; he notes the narrow strips of land almost in the centre of the town, overgrown with grass, which the townsfolk call 'greens'; possibly he may see drovers hurling abuse at mountainous sows sitting in the middle of the road to the dislocation of a stream of traffic bound, not for Epping, but for the rolling plains of East Anglia. Epping Town!

There is in existence a document entitled 'The Patent Roll of the Seventeenth Year of the Reign of Queen Elizabeth' which in its seventh part refers to a charter granted by Henry III in the thirty-seventh year of his reign to 'the Church of the Holy Cross of Waltham and the Abbott' to hold one market on Monday in every week 'at the Heath of Epinge' and that they should have 'one fair every year to last three days, namely, on the Vigil, on the day, and on the morrow of the Ascension of Our Lord.'

The document continued that 'our well-beloved Thomas Heneage Esquire Treasurer of the Chamber, and Anne, his wife, to whom the right and interest of the said Market and Fair are now said to appertain, have given us to understand that the said Market and Fair for a long time were not used nor held by reason that the times days and places of the same were and had been inconvenient to the inhabitants there.'

Queen Elizabeth therefore granted to 'our dear beloved Thomas Heneage and Anne his wife' permission to hold the market on Friday's and two fairs during the year, together with a 'court of pie-powder' to be held at the same time as the fairs.

The practice of holding the market on Fridays has not persisted, for Monday is now, as in the days of Henry III, market day. Until 1845, the town had a market house which in that year was demolished. Epping, which has now no central meeting place, must regret its demise, but at the time, apparently, the inhabitants were not sorry to see it go.

A town historian records the happening thus: 'The Epping Market House was fifty-two feet long by twenty-four feet wide; and the lower part was fitted with chopping blocks and weighing scales. The upper part was used as a schoolroom, and on the holding of fairs was also used as a dance room.

'The market house was demolished at the end of June, 1845; and to commemorate the occasion a feast was given to, it is stated, nearly two thousand children.

'Tables were placed nearly the whole length of the town, and as the children poured into the town from neighbouring villages, the people of Epping rose to the occasion and brought out tables and chairs as well as food of every description, resulting in a day of remarkable festivity.

'An old inhabitant (one 'Jobber' Wright) stated that he had never seen or conceived of such a scene of activity and pleasure and never should see such a scene again.'

Express and Independent, June 13, 1936

In the twelfth century the manor of Epping was held by Waltham Abbey and its right to hold a market there was granted by King Henry III in 1253. Thus Epping's market heritage is steeped in antiquity, ownership of the rights to the market (and fairs) descending with the lord of the manor until the twentieth century. Originally trade centred around the market house but one was demolished in 1781 in favour of stalls and the one *above* (pictured in 1818) dismantled in 1845.

The annual fat stock sale held by Mr. Hugh Sworder on Friday, 10th inst., was a great success. A large number of buyers were present and business was decidedly brisk. Fifty beasts were entered and there was a large supply of pigs, but the supply of sheep was rather limited. The highest price realised for a bullock was £27 5s. which Mr. Howes purchased from Mr. Lyall's stock. A fine pig from Mr. Furze's stock sold for £4 7s. to Mr. Church.

The large attendance at the fat stock sale clearly shows that good business can always be done when there is stock to sell. There is not the slightest doubt that the co-operation of the farmers is all that is needed to make our market worthy of the town. The day (Friday) may be inconvenient for some buyers but it would be impossible to alter it to an earlier day in the week without clashing with other important markets in the immediate neighbourhood. In the matter of accommodation and facilities our market is well to the front compared with other towns.

Epping Monthly Record, December 1898

Before 1800 people automatically 'went to market' to purchase their necessities, but sometime after the turn of the century some bright tradesman thought up the idea of offering a service to deliver goods direct to his customers. The system soon gained such a hold that the market went into decline, the one at Epping becoming almost extinct after the second market house was pulled down — thereafter 'a single stall being a rarity'. Today of course we have seen the wheel turn full circle: the creation of the 'super'-market having led to the decline of the delivery system, milk rounds the only ones now holding out. However, as far as Epping was concerned, the coming of the railway brought new life to the town and a revival in the fortunes of the market. This picture was taken around 1900.

SALE OF A WIFE

At one time the Epping market sold anything — even wives!

On Friday the sale of a wife, with the approbation of her husband, took place at Epping. Between two and three o'clock on that day, Jane Brace, a good-looking female, of about 38 years of age, was led into the public market-place by her husband, with a long halter round her neck and waist. In a few minutes nearly the whole of the persons in the town were collected around the wretched woman, and a person named Godfrie, the master of the parochial workhouse, having appeared as auctioneer, after, in a most ludicrous manner adverting to her qualifications, put her up to the best bidder. Eighteen pence was first offered by James Bradley, a labourer, who gradually rose to half-a-crown, and there being no competition, he was declared the purchaser. He at once paid down the half-crown, as well as sixpence for market dues to the auctioneer, who handed the first-mentioned sum to the husband, and walked his bargain off to a neighbouring public-house, amidst the laughter and jeers of the assembled multitude.— The circumstances having reached the ears of the magistrates, who were sitting in petty session in the town at the time, they caused Brace, the husband, to be taken before them; and it having been sworn that he had deserted his wife and child, and left them burdensome to the parish, they committed him for one month to Ilford House of Correction. When taken before the magistrate, Brace, who has lived at several inns, was quite intoxicated, having spent at the time nearly the whole of the money which he had received for his wife in gin. He said that six years ago he was compelled to marry his wife by the parish officers of South Weald, she having swore at the time that a child of which she had been delivered was his. Since that time he had not lived with her, but it was well known that she had lived with Bradley, who had purchased her, and had had a child by him. The magistrates, Messrs. Marsh and Maitland, strongly reprobated his conduct, as well as that of all those concerned in the disgraceful transaction, and he was at once committed to prison.

Press report, 1833

Market day is on Monday, and although the market may be but a ghost of its former self, the town is a scene of much bustle and activity. Beneath the trees, beside the High Street, there are pens of cattle wedged between stalls of merchandise and fruit and vegetables, and all mixed up with cars and lorries. . . .

Epping Forest, J. A. Brimble, 1950

Most of the myriad small towns and villages that were once part of the forest have lost all their 'forest' atmosphere, and many have been swallowed up by the steadily increasing size of London. Epping, however, has retained much of its charm even in the face of present-day transport facilities. It is a bright and pleasant spot in beautiful surroundings and is deservedly popular as a semi-rural residential area. One of its attractive features and one which plays a large part in giving the town its rural atmosphere is its market . . .

The County Handbook, 1965

Dairy farming predominated around Epping, with Kelvedon Hatch, Navestock, Lambourne, Stanford Rivers, Ongar and the Theydons as its centres. It was already developing in 1700 and from 1750 quite large farms were devoted to it, such as Burroughs Farm at Stanford Rivers with its 120 acres of meadow and the 300-acre farm of an Ongar man whom Young described as 'one of the most successful graziers in Essex', outstanding for 'his ability and spirit of exertion'. Much arable was converted to pasture, a hundred acres on one Ongar farm, and several improvements were introduced. Buildings were sited north of the farmhouse for coolness, special lead-lined troughs were installed, and floors were paved on an incline and washed down daily. One Epping farmer's windows faced north and were latticed to admit air, his dairy house was always orderly and neat and his equipment 'perfectly clean'; he noted the less productive cows and sold them. Some made a by-product of the skimmed milk, feeding it to hogs with profitable results. While lesser producers sent

to Epping and Waltham Abbey markets, larger farmers supplied Clare Market in London by contract. 'Epping butter' won so wide a reputation that its name was usurped by Northamptonshire producers. Prosperity raised rents, a Coopersale farm being let at 33s. an acre in 1805 and one at Woodford at 60s. Success belonged to hard effort, and the farmer's wife, now a leisured person elsewhere in Essex, had here to work early and late.

Essex at Work 1700-1815, A. F. S. Brown, 1969

For 707 years there have been cattle in the stalls of Epping Market. But next Monday (market day) foot and mouth disease restrictions or not, there will be no cattle

Up to the end of the First World War, Friday was market day, but thereafter it reverted to the original day of Monday as decreed by King Henry. In 1955 the rights to hold the market were purchased by Epping Urban District Council from the Wythes family. (Ernest Wythes had died in 1949 and his wife Aline in 1951, leaving three daughters, Alexandrina, Barbara and Cecilia.)

market. It was learned this week that the Ministry of Agriculture has withdrawn its certifying officer — which virtually means that the market is closed.

Since the war fewer and fewer farmers have bought their beasts to the Epping market. In fact, with the widespread residential development in the area the number of farmers has been decreasing.

Development on the London side of the town has been so concentrated that now there

is practically no farmland left. On the Cambridge side, Harlow New Town had taken up most of the land.

A spokesman for Messrs. Ambrose and Son, who took over cattle sales at the market in 1946, said that in addition to the loss of land many farmers now sell cattle direct to butchers and send pigs to bacon factories. Often it would be much easier for them to adopt that course, but it all meant less support for the market.

The firm had kept the market open for two or three years now, although it had been uneconomic to do so, in the hope that it would continue, he said.

During the war Epping Market was used as a livestock collecting centre. In 1954, when meat was derationed it went back to its normal work as a commercial market.

In that year the Government decided to subsidise farmers against losses on the sale of cattle for slaughter.

The Minister of Agriculture's decision to withdraw his certifying officer means that beasts sold at Epping would not qualify any longer for that subsidy.

Townsfolk were even deprived of seeing the market operating for the last time on Monday. Foot and mouth disease has prevented Messrs. Ambrose from holding a market for the past three weeks.

But in any case there would have been little for people to see. During the past two years an average market has been 20 pigs, and during the spring and summer months, up to 20 sheep and lambs. There have been no steers.

In 1954, after derationing, an average market would include 12 to 15 steers, 100 pigs, 20 to 25 sheep, and 30 to 40 calves.

Express and Independent, February 12, 1960

With the building of Harlow New Town, 6,000 acres of pasture and farmland were lost, heralding the beginning of the end of the livestock side of the market. Farms in the area increasingly changed from animals to arable, and the collection of beasts for slaughter direct from the farm gate hastened its demise. Ambrose and Son attempted to keep auction sales going but the end came suddenly in February 1960: a sad day for all those who remembered it as it was in its prime.

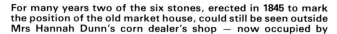

For many years two of the six stones, erected in 1845 to mark the position of the old market house, could still be seen outside Mrs Hannah Dunn's corn dealer's shop — now occupied by **Ambrose and Son. Only one uprooted stone remains to be seen today lying beside a lamp-post, having been moved from its original position, but who realises its significance we wonder?**

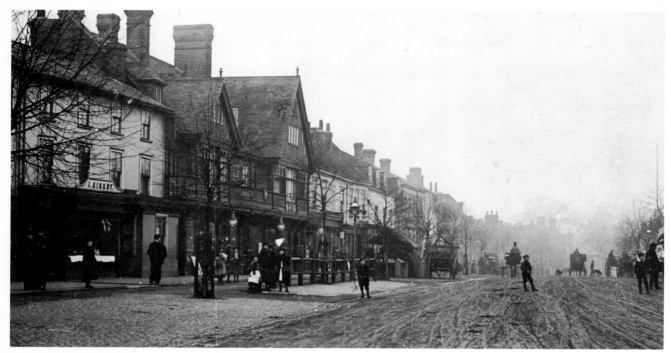

'Ancient Epping' is gradually disappearing before the onward march of modern enterprise. The old-time buildings in the main street are giving place to structures more in harmony with the characteristics and requirements of a growing market town. The old premises, until recently in the occupation of Mr. Jas. Wood, have been demolished and the site is to be occupied by a new shop, store rooms and offices, for the old-established business of Mr. A. B. Davis, next door.

In connection with the new building, an interesting incident took place last month. The discovery of a few old coins during the pulling down process, together with a recollection of the interest attending the finding of the 'Doubleday' jar at Mr. Hill's some time since, gave the idea that a suitable opportunity now presented itself for hoarding away some items of information that might be regarded as curious, if not valuable, in years, perhaps centuries, to come. Accordingly a short topographical history of the immediate surroundings, together with several details of every day life in Epping, was inscribed on vellum, and, accompanied by a *County Chronicle* giving an account of the great storm, a copy of Davis' Almanack and Directory, a copy of the *Record* and Jubilee Supplement, Jubilee medal, coins, etc., were placed in a jar and built into one of the walls.

Epping Monthly Record. September 1897

The new buildings in the Market Place. — A long discussion took place with reference to the gable projection in front of Mr. Davis' new premises in the Market Place — Mr. Trussell said that Mr. Davis was anxious to meet the council's wishes, and would do what they might suggest. — Ultimately it was decided to allow the building of the balcony and bay to be completed, keeping in view Mr. Egan's pledge to alter his plans so as to allow the setting back of the gable 16 inches if required. — The Chairman said the balcony and bay did not project appreciably beyond the building line, and the base line was three inches further back.

Epping Urban District Council minutes November 5, 1897

To celebrate the completion of the erection of Victoria Buildings, Mr. Alfred B. Davis entertained to dinner on Saturday, 9th inst,

The changes which have taken place to Epping High Street are many — one could virtually write a book on this subject alone. The present appearance of the frontages, several of which conceal earlier timber-framed structures, is largely as a result of development since 1800 — some of it not very complementary to those existing. One of the worst cases lies here — in a more or less central position on the western side. The gabled building, which certainly had character, was the Victoria Buildings, opened in a blaze of publicity in 1899. Instrumental in its construction was Epping printer and photographer, Alfred Davis, who took many of the contemporary illustrations in this chapter. It was built by James Whiffin of Epping, having been designed by Edmund Egan of Loughton who unfortunately never lived to see the culmination of his work. Downstairs lay Davis's printing works, a photographer's studio, a restaurant and estate agents, while upstairs the Victoria Hall was capable of seating about 200 people with an adjacent balcony overlooking the street for speakers at political meetings to address supporters gathered outside. Amongst the seventeen various rooms upstairs were ones used for smaller functions, committee meetings and those of the Urban District Council.

We leave our readers to judge if the replacement, approved in September 1967, constitutes an architectural improvement.

the whole of the workmen employed by the contractors together with his employees in the stationery and printing departments, and those who tenant various portions of the premises. The company numbered between 60 and 70, and included Mr. A. A. Tween and Mr. Horace White (architects), Mr. G. J. Creed, Mr. E. Allen, Messrs. G., A., and F.

Whiffin (builders), Mr. C. J. Cottis (W. Cottis & Sons), Mr. B. Cowlin (decorator), and Mr. F. Trussell. Mr. H. P. Brown (Victoria Restaurant) catered in capital style, the handsome interior of the Victoria Hall being gaily decked out with bunting and flowers.

Epping Monthly Record, November 1899

The Victoria Buildings featured in the cut and thrust of many political events. Winston Churchill became the MP for West Essex (including Epping) in 1922; who remembers one of his hecklers: 'Wot abaht Russia?' the man cried, 'Wot abaht fou'een eigh'een?' 'Let the man speak', Churchill replied.

From 1892-1917 Amelius Mark Lockwood sat as the Member of Parliament for West Essex which included Epping. Upon his creation as Lord Lambourne, Brigadier-General Sir Richard B. Colvin succeeded him until Churchill took over. Scene in January 1910 outside the police station — see pages 89 and 448.

Epping High Street is now a flesh-pot for speculators and developers, and a complete reappraisal of the urban council's policy regarding buildings listed as of architectural interest should be made.

This outburst was part of a long salvo delivered at the full council meeting on Tuesday by Mr. Ian Doyle, last year's chairman.

Mr. Doyle said he viewed with 'sorrow and alarm' the planning committee's decision to allow yet another supermarket in the High-street.

He was referring to plans to demolish the buildings around Slaters, the chemists, to make way for a Tesco supermarket, a Westminster Bank, and a new Slaters.

Tesco's new shop will be next door to the International Stores, and both will be close to the proposed London Co-op supermarket.

'I view it with sorrow because I think, and many others clearly agree, that the buildings have great charm and character. Buildings of this sort should be preserved, and only demolished when 'totally impracticable,' said Mr. Doyle.

'My alarm is because of the apparent ease with which a building listed as of interest can be replaced.

'Why do we have the list? If we allow this application, the door will be ajar for other similar applications,' Mr. Doyle continued.

He said there had recently been a gradual growth in the amount of destruction in the High-street, and he reminded councillors that in their election address they had said they would do their utmost to preserve the town's character.

The chairman of the planning committee, Mr. Michael Aldworth, said he too was keen to preserve the character of the High-street.

But, he said, the main part of the building was of a fairly common type put up in the last century, and the real charm — the façade — had been in place only since 1955, designed by the present owner.

The new plans, said the planning committee chairman, were quite acceptable, and included rather similar lines to the present buildings.

'The building is in a reasonably poor condition, and it is not viable as a trading concern,' said Mr. Aldworth.

Mr. Doyle came back and said any owner of a scheduled building could allow it to fall into ruin.

The Council asked the officers to prepare a complete list of scheduled buildings, and the members agreed to re-think their views on policy regarding listed buildings.

West Essex Gazette, August 2, 1968

In its coaching heyday, Epping boasted as many as 26 inns — now they can be counted on one hand. With the decline of coach traffic in preference to the iron road, many were converted into shops. This was the site of the Black Dog — demolished at the beginning of the 1960s. Allan Church recorded its demise . . . and its replacement . . . as a backdrop during the impressive march past of the 1st Battalion, the York and Lancaster Regiment on Sunday, November 24, 1968, on the occasion of their being granted the Freedom of the Town.

Probably the most famous of all the inns is, or rather was, The Cock. The brick façade was added early in the 1800s to the timber framed building behind, which probably dated from the sixteenth century. Modernised in July 1961, it was closed and boarded up from 1984-86 during its conversion into offices. Our comparison was taken in February 1986.

Monday, Aug. 22, at the Cock, Epping, sixteen Miles, to be ready at Ten o'Clock in the Morning: Here prepare cold Victuals and Fruit for twelve Persons, at the Rate of Half a Crown per Head, Wine excepted. At Hockerill, at the Crown, fourteen Miles, to be ready at Noon. At Chesterford, Mr. Gardiner's, thirteen Miles, at One o'Clock. At Cambridge, the Rose, ten Miles; here prepare warm Supper for twelve, seven Dishes, and Fruit, at the Rate of 10s. 6d. per Head, Wine excepted. Here will be wanted sixteen Beds for Noblemen and Gentlemen, eight for upper Servants, and eight for common ditto.

Press report, 1768

AN EXTRAORDINARY STAG HUNT.— A well-known sporting gentleman slept one night at the Cock Inn, Epping, preparatory to the last day's stag-hunt at that place; but going to repose, he was so full of the pleasures of next day's field, that he no sooner fell asleep than in imagination he entered upon the *chase* with his accustomed ardour. After running the first *burst* quietly enough *in bed*, he jumped up, in order, as he supposed, to take a leap over a stile; and to supply the want of a horse, he adroitly threw up the sash, and strided his supposed hunter; the window happened not to be far from *terra firma*, and by luckily catching hold of the curtain he landed safely on the other side of the *hedge*. Our sportsman then continued the sport with unabashed vigour, and had proceeded some considerable way towards Epping-place Inn, when he luckily met with a *check*; during his chase, he had kept the middle of the road, a privilege which he was by no means easily made to relinquish: however, he met with a broad wheel waggon, the driver of which perceived something in white before him, providentially stopped his horses, or the gentleman must have been materially injured. Hodge, still finding the ghost advance, and being a stout fellow, he stepped forward, and accosted him with 'Who's there?' No reply being made, he made bold to take him by the hand and shake him; it was not, however, till he had repeated this compulsory salutation two or three times, that the sportsman could

be made to relinquish his *pursuit*, and acknowledge that he was *thrown out*. When he came to himself, his astonishment is easier to be conceived than described: however, upon recollecting that he had been in bed at the Cock at Epping, and explaining the event to the astonished waggoner, he re-conducted him to the inn, and knocked up the landlord. The gentleman and his host immediately went to the room where he had slept, and there found the window and the curtain in the situation above described; the dream also recurring to the sportsman, the whole of this wonderful event was accounted for. He then went to bed again, had medical assistance, and continued at the inn several days, in consequence of the bruises he received in the fall from the window, and the cold he caught during the chase.

Press report, 1833

A day or two ago (writes a regular correspondent) I occupied a seat on board the 'Essex Express.' For once in a way the Clerk of the weather was kindly disposed, for he sent no rain to mar the day's outing, although it is as well to mention that old Sol failed to put in an appearance until late in the afternoon. He evidently does not know the rules which all good coaching men expect to see observed on the road. A large crowd assembled outside the Great Eastern Hotel, Liverpool Street, to witness the start-off, and I trust that the sightseers felt as glad to find a full load as all the passengers and I did. Every available seat was occupied by paying passengers — no dead-heads remember — and as half the number was composed of gaily bedecked members of the fair sex, the appearance of the whole turn-out was decidedly a gay one.

Young Mr. Whitehead, whose father is well known on most of the West End four-in-

Its demise can probably be traced to the construction of the M11 motorway, bypassing the town, which cut the number of travellers using the old A11 through Epping and its hotels as overnight staging posts.

hands, drove the team of skewbalds and pie-balds as far as the Crown at Hackney, the next stage being negotiated by Robert Bruce, the professional coachman, who, as readers of *The Road* will recollect, was formerly con-nected with Arthur Fownes' coaches. Bruce is an accomplished whip, and box-seat passengers will vote him excellent company. At Woodford the team was changed, and after a quarter of an hour's interval the journey was continued, Mr. Henry Balls, the proprietor of the coach, now occupying the dumping. As a rule the 'Essex Express' bears to the left when near the Bancroft Schools, and calls at the Royal Forest Hotel, at Chingford, for the purpose of picking up any passengers who may have booked there; but as the coach was already fully loaded, there was, of course, no necessity to make the detour.

Soon we passed the Robin Hood, and a little further on High Beach, where is to be seen a charming view over six or seven different counties. Personally, I could not see these counties; but the locals tell you that they are really visible, and what can you do but look in the direction they indicate and say 'Fancy!' or 'M'yes?' I selected the latter. At the King's Hotel, at High Beech, passengers alight for a few minutes in order to inspect and listen to the organ which is erected in the large dining-room. I could sit pleasantly for hours listening to that instrument. It is almost unique, as, indeed, it ought to be, seeing that it cost something like a thousand pounds.

Away we go again, passing through some of the most charming rural lanes, now catching a glimpse of the deer, then of the rabbits, proceeding through the long avenues of trees until we emerge again on the open road at the Wake Arms, the happy hunting ground of the wandering minstrel and the niggers, who for a penny — or more — will perform all sorts of wonderful tricks.

In less than five minutes we shall be in Epping, and as we canter along we think of the old days when, both day and night, in quick succession, came coach after coach. Now Epping has its one coach only; and will have to look to its laurels if it wishes to retain even this one remaining stage.

After luncheon at the Cock Hotel we again take our seats on the coach, and after a most enjoyable drive we reach Liverpool Street punctually to time, where Mr. John Finch and Mr. George Lacey, both capable whips, meet us. This season the Epping Road is worked better than ever, and it is gratifying to learn that Mr. Harry Balls is receiving a fair share of patronage. Once Hackney is left behind a more attractive route it would be difficult to find. W. Baddock, the guard, makes himself very useful in explaining to passengers the various places of interest passed en route, and he leaves nothing undone that can conduce to the comfort of those on board. Those readers, therefore, who are fond of forest drives should have a day on the 'Essex Express.' They will be sure to repeat the experiment.

The Road, August 1898

A similar fate befell the Thatched House. It too is listed Grade II, which hopefully assures us of its preservation — outwardly at least.

The most striking note of Epping, apart from the generous width of its street, is the extraordinary number of inns and places for all kinds of refreshment. Of these the Thatched House is the most notable, but is now no more thatched than is the 'Thatched House Club' in London. There is a baulking air of picturesqueness in the long view down Epping street, but taken in detail and analysed, it is evasive, and certainly most elusive when sought to be transferred to paper.

The Newmarket, Bury, Thetford and Cromer Road,
Charles G. Harper, 1904

EPPING LONDON 17. POP. 4,253.
E.C., WED
Market Day, MON.

HOTELS
YE OLDE THATCHED HOUSE, High Street. R.A.C. (Ap.): A.A. 6 bedrooms. R.B. and A. 8/6. Garage acc. 'Phone 6. Wires: Cooke.
COCK, High Street. 8 bedrooms. R.B.A. 7/-. Garage acc. 'Phone 5. Wires Cock.
BELL (Trust Houses, Ltd.). R.A.C. (Lis.). 2 bedrooms, R.B.A. 6/6. Garage acc. 'Phone 125.

The Dunlop Guide, 1925

On the opposite side of the road behind the second motor the Black Lion. Grade II, circa seventeenth century.

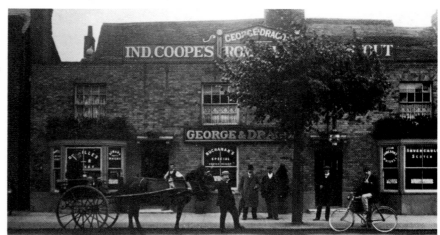

Waltham Abbey, May 5. On Wednesday the 3d was married, at the Quaker's meeting-house in this town, Mr. Robert Hayward, a noted Farmer of Kelvedon-hall, to Mrs. Alexander of Epping, a young widow, of 2000*l.* fortune, an agreeable person, and of so affable and obliging disposition as can't fail of rendering the conjugal state happy. Immediately after the nuptial ceremony was ended, the new-married couple, accompanied by a select number of their friends, went in carriages to Epping, where they were elegantly entertained at the Crown inn.

Press report, 1758

In a few weeks all vehicles passing along the highways of Essex will be compelled to carry lights at night. This regulation on the part of the County Council will doubtless be appreciated by all travellers, especially cyclists. It should be remembered that the C.T.C. and N.C.U. have for years been agitating for this very necessary reform.

The town Post Office has been practically re-built and forms another addition to 'modern Epping.' The telegraphic instruments have been removed to an adjoining room which affords increased convenience in the front office. A side entrance in Station Road admits the staff to the commodious sorting room which is fitted up on the most approved principles, especially as regards lighting and heating. Mr. Jas. Winter was the architect and Mr. J. Whiffin the builder.

The window clock is indeed a boon to the neighbourhood, and if the Urban Council can arrange to move the street lamp from the opposite corner to the Post Office corner, so that the time may be visible at night, it would, we feel sure, be a great improvement and as such appreciated by all.

Epping Monthly Record, September 1898

From post office to public house — a picture taken in the late 1950s. A good example of how many of the old buildings have received a stucco facelift is seen in the George and Dragon inn on the right. The picture *below* shows how the eighteenth century building looked at the beginning of the ninteenth.

EPPING DISTRICT AND THE WAR

The 1st of March, 1900, will long be remembered throughout the country as the day upon which the relief of Ladysmith was effected. The first telegraphic message was received in Epping shortly after 11 o'clock, and the townspeople immediately gave signs of their gladness at the relief of the long shut-up garrison under gallant General Sir George White. Flags and bunting were displayed at many of the shops, whilst the inhabitants generally were profuse in their expressions of delight, the news being the only topic of conversation.

The surrender of Cronje and the relief of

Ladysmith will always be looked upon as red-letter days in the history of the present war. The beginning of the end of the struggle is apparent, and it only requires another message — 'Mafeking Relieved' — to complete the success of the second stage of the War in South Africa.

The occupation of Bloemfontein commences the third stage, which will be completed by the entry of our army into Pretoria. Let us hope that this may be accomplished without the sacrifice of human life to the extent foretold by the stubborn leaders of the Boers.

Epping Monthly Record, March 1900

Above left: **Another inn no longer with us: the White Swan which lay alongside the Acme coach depot (later taken over by London Transport). Now the site is occupied by Messrs Goodrich (*below*).**

Also on the eastern side of the road, the Golden Lion Inn had become the Epping Restaurant by 1900 when this picture was taken, the country then in the throes of war. *Below:* **Now it's Shepherd's the bakers (see page 408).**

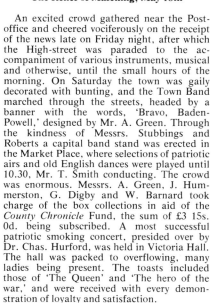

The Relief of Mafeking, May 18th

An excited crowd gathered near the Post-office and cheered vociferously on the receipt of the news late on Friday night, after which the High-street was paraded to the accompaniment of various instruments, musical and otherwise, until the small hours of the morning. On Saturday the town was gaily decorated with bunting, and the Town Band marched through the streets, headed by a banner with the words, 'Bravo, Baden-Powell,' designed by Mr. A. Green. Through the kindness of Messrs. Stubbings and Roberts a capital band stand was erected in the Market Place, where selections of patriotic airs and old English dances were played until 10.30, Mr. T. Smith conducting. The crowd was enormous. Messrs. A. Green, J. Hummerston, G. Digby and W. Barnard took charge of the box collections in aid of the *County Chronicle* Fund, the sum of £3 15s. 0d. being subscribed. A most successful patriotic smoking concert, presided over by Dr. Chas. Hurford, was held in Victoria Hall. The hall was packed to overflowing, many ladies being present. The toasts included those of 'The Queen' and 'The hero of the war,' and were received with every demonstration of loyalty and satisfaction.

Epping Monthly Record, June 1900

In the 1900s the Cottis family were to Epping what the Goulds were to Loughton. Commencing in 1858 with a single hardware shop, the business became the largest employer in the town with interests in ironfounding, manufacturing, retailing and brick-making. In January 1900 Mr and Mrs Crispus Cottis's son, Chris, became the town's first volunteer for the Imperial Yeomanry in the Boer War and he sailed to South Africa in the company of William Riggs from High Beach (see page 48). Chris's descriptive letters from the front, published in the Record, were a tremendous inspiration to local people and he and the other Epping boys were given a heroes' welcome when they returned home in 1902. Chris was pulled in an open landau from the railway station — here the cortège can be seen passing the old White Lion — seen also in the picture on pages 412-413.

The White Lion went in 1961 and the Duke of York, the white building on the opposite side of the road behind the fountain, in 1931 when the site was redeveloped for Barclays Bank.

On Monday night, Feb. 1, 1830, a small fire broke out in the Market House in the town of Epping, but it was soon put out. It broke out at the North East End.

On Saturday night, Jany. 1830, a small quarel arose between Samuel Champnesses, Carpenter, and H. Leah, Match Maker, at the Wite Lion publick house, which after some high words it was agread that Champnesses should make Leah a Coffin, and Leah should forgive him for all that he had said.

Accordingley Champnesses made the Coffin and took it to his house on Friday, Jany. 27, when he got in it, and said it fitted well. He gave Champnesses a shilling and he is to give him a shilling every month as long as he stayes in Epping.

His Book, January 29, 1830

Mr. Shissler, the Austrian hairdresser, who lately started in business opposite the church, was removed to the Brentwood Asylum on Sunday, 1st inst. Possessing a very excitable temperament, he was unable to stand against the petty annoyances to which he was thoughtlessly subjected, and as a consequence his mind became unhinged.

Epping Monthly Record, October 1899

Epping Water Supply. — The resolution passed by the Epping Parish Council respecting the water supply to houses at Twankhams Alley was laid before the Council. — Mr. Trotter pointed out that this Council

had applied to the Bench of magistrates asking them to close the well in Twankhams Alley on the grounds that the water was unfit for use, but the application had been dismissed. The Bench gave no reason for dismissing it. — Mr. Chisenhale Marsh said it was dismissed because this well had been in use twelve years, and there had only been one case of illness that was attributed to the use of the water from the well. They held that it was not injurious to health. —

Rural District Council meeting,
November 1895

Twankhams Alley. — The medical officer reported a case of scarlet fever in Twankham's Alley on the 1st inst. The child had been removed to the isolation hospital. The drainage and water supply of this alley was most defective, and it was not much more than 12 months since a similar outbreak occurred there. — Mr. G. H. Pegram (sanitary inspector) in his report upon this case said: The sanitary arrangements of this alley are very bad, and although I have reported fully upon it in my house-to-house visitations, it would, perhaps, be well to say that there are seven cottages here with 34 occupants — 15 adults and 19 children. There are two privies only for the use of all these people and there are three slop drain gullies for the seven houses. The

water supply, which is of doubtful quality, is from a well in the yard. — He also reported upon the insanitary condition of several cottages at Coopersale, some of which had no proper water supply, and owing to the brick floors being lower than the ground level and the absence of guttering to the roof, were extremely damp. — Reports referred to the sanitary committee.

Epping Monthly Record, February 1897

Water! Water! Water!!! — The committee recommended that an owner of property be served with notice to provide eighteen houses in Twankhams-alley with a proper supply of water. — Mr. Sudul hoped the council would go on and see that these people had what they should have had any time these ten years — a proper supply of drinking water. What they had at present was a well, situated in the midst of a number of cesspits. If that water was fit to drink, then all he had heard of sanitary matters was utterly wrong. — Mr. Palmer thought that while they were at it notices should be served on other owners. — The chairman said they would deal with them all in time. — The recommendation of the committee was adopted.

Epping Urban District Council minutes,
April 15, 1898

The most far-reaching event to change the face of Epping — a happening even reported around the world in the renowned Geographical Magazine — was the High Street Improvement Scheme by the Civic Trust in 1961. The image of the town was uplifted immeasurably by the complementary colour schemes devised for each individual building as part of an overall plan. Unfortunately no longer part of that picture was another of Epping's smithies, Clark's, right on the High Street next to the White Lion, demolished in August 1961. (Phil Clark, son of the family, still trades in Hemnall Street.)

Epping High Street Improvement Scheme

Mr. Ben Hiscott, clerk to the Council, said this week: 'Negotiations between members of the panel of architects and the owners and occupiers of premises affected by the scheme have in very many cases been completed. It is expected that work on the actual changes will soon begin.

'Improvements undertaken by Essex County Council and Epping Urban Council are proceeding apace, and the shape of things to come will gradually become apparent to the people of Epping.'

In the report of the Highways Committee a number of changes taking place were presented. Members heard that special efforts were being made to hurry up the removal of the market rails in the High Street and get the area resurfaced in time for the opening. It was stated that once work of widening St John's Road had been completed more seats would be installed alongside the original ones.

The bus shelter at St John's Church is to be removed and another one [is to] take its place. However, the Civic Trust report that London Transport Executive will not adopt the Norwich type shelter for this spot. Instead a prototype shelter which has been developed by the Timber Corporation in conjunction with the Civic Trust is hoped to be given a trial run in the town.

West Essex Gazette, February 7, 1961

Detail plans of the opening day of what has been described as 'the greatest communal venture undertaken in Epping' — the High Street Improvement Scheme — were released this week.

At a press conference on Monday it was announced that the Lord Mayor of London, Sir Bernard Waley-Cohen, will officially open the scheme at 3 p.m. on Saturday, May 27th.

In a written statement, the chairman of the Joint Committee which is behind the plan, Mr. D. F. Ritchie, says: 'The opening sees the culmination of an effort which is remarkable because of the length of time over which it has been sustained, because of the magnificent co-operation which has been forthcoming from so many people and, not least, because of the visible results of the enterprise.'

This week over 25 workmen are busy in the High Street working to complete the scheme.

Commented Mr. Ben Hiscott, clerk to the Epping Urban Council: 'The results of the scheme have exceeded our wildest hopes. At the beginning some concerns wanted nothing to do with the idea — but now everyone has joined in.

The clerk was asked what the total cost of the scheme would be to the town. 'No figure has been calculated — but it must run into several thousand pounds.'

Journalists were told that the biggest single change in the town was the removal of the market rails to make way for a car park.

What will happen after the opening day? Mr. Hiscott said: 'It is hoped to keep a committee in being to continue the co-ordination which has been achieved at present. What is envisaged is that traders should have their properties re-painted every three or four years so that the present effect is maintained over the years.'

Celebrations for Epping's 'big week-end' will begin on the Friday night with a civic ball at the Thatched House, Epping.

On Saturday the Lord Mayor will arrive in the town at 12.30 p.m. after having first made a private tour of Epping Forest.

After lunch, the Lord Mayor and his wife, accompanied by other guests, will walk along the High Street from the Half Moon inn and inspect the properties.

Following an inspection of the Guard of Honour provided by the 4th Battalion. The Essex Regiment, T.A., the Lord Mayor will perform the opening ceremony.

Shortly afterwards the procession will pass the dais, lasting about half an hour. Included will be 'Boadicea's Chariot and ancient Britons' (pupils of Epping Secondary School), a tableau depicting Epping's Market Charter (pupils of Epping Junior School), the Essex Hunt, Morris Dancers, a float from St Margaret's Hospital and veteran and vintage cars.

In the second half will be youth organisations and five artillery units, followed by trade exhibits.

Music — in the form of concerts by combined bands and a 'pop' dance for teenagers in the evening — will round off the day.

West Essex Gazette, May 5, 1961

The Big Day — Saturday, May 27, 1961 — and Allan Church was on hand in a vantage point above Barclays Bank to record the scene. *Left:* Here the Guard of Honour falls in before the dais facing the White Lion. As part of the town's facelift the opportunity had been taken to remove the rails from the market following its closure in February the previous year (see page 445). *Right:* The view southwards shows yet another of Epping's pubs, the White Hart, pulled down six years later. On the extreme left the notorious Twankhams Alley.

Official vandalism! In spite of the beneficial effect, did the 1961 improvements have to go quite so far? The water fountain, seen here decorated for the Diamond Jubilee of Queen Victoria's reign, had been erected to commemorate her Golden Jubilee in 1887. Seventy years later, without a thought of what it stood for in our ancestors' eyes, it was pulled down.

So another landmark must disappear from Epping. What right has the council to do away with these old and cherished landmarks, such as the fountain and now the water trough, without asking the opinion of the local residents?

Many people would have loved to have seen the fountain placed on one of our many greens, and then the trough could have been placed near it. Some villages use them for the planting of flowers.

With the price of petrol increasing, we may have the horse back with us and need the trough. No doubt the council would then pay thousands for one, instead of the few pounds which I expect was the cost of the one they are letting this farmer have.

Surely we could still have the trough placed on a green. Who will see it at Hobbs Cross? Certainly not the people who are interested in it.

It is now up to the farmer concerned to refuse what is morally Epping's property. — O.A.P., Epping (Name and address supplied to Editor).

West Essex Gazette, February 8, 1974

Stored in Messrs. Cottis's yard for many years, it was shovelled into a hole and buried en masse under the town lorry park. R.I.P. Thirteen years later it was the turn of the old horse trough which stood at the junction with the road to North Weald (see page 31), now to be seen at North Farm, Theydon Mount.

THE TOWN HALL

The Urban District Council of Epping have intimated that they cannot see their way to grant the request of a great number of ratepayers who signed a petition asking them to purchase the building known as the Town Hall, for the future use of the Council as well as for the benefit of the whole district. (It is only right to add that the Councillors themselves are very evenly divided in their opinions upon the subject.)

The reasons for the rejection of the proposal are chiefly that the Council may not spend money in acquiring a place of entertainment, solely; and also the expense would be too great to re-build in order to provide for the requirements of the Urban District — Council Room and Offices, Fire Engine House, and a yard for storage — and at the same time a large Public Hall with the necessary extra Rooms. In order to carry out such a comprehensive scheme as this, it might be requisite to purchase a larger piece of land at the rear of the Hall in Hemnall Street.

The memorial was signed by about 330 ratepayers, representing every class and the greater portion of the rateable value of the district; therefore it seems a pity that their wishes are not likely to be complied with.

Epping Monthly Record, March 1900

Whatever the fate of the Town Hall in the future, we must remember its past usefulness. For the long period of 37 years it has provided accommodation for public meetings and amusements, upholding in no small degree the dignity of Epping as a town.

Epping Monthly Record, April 1900

The long-neglected Town Hall has at last been restored and renovated. The much-needed improvements have been most efficiently carried out by the Company that has taken over the building. The walls and ceiling present a pleasing appearance, and with a little panelling the bareness will be entirely effaced. The floor has been re-laid with wood blocks forming a splendid surface for dancing, and the stage has undergone considerable alteration and improvement. A standpipe and hose is placed in the vestibule in case of fire. The heating apparatus will complete the comfort of the audiences who will doubtless attend this convenient place of amusement in largely increased numbers.

Epping Monthly Record, November 1900

What is now the Tesco supermarket was once Epping Town Hall. Built in 1863, the hall seated 500 people, and during the Gay Nineties was the town's main social and amusement centre. It was the headquarters of

On the right, Epping's Town Hall, built on the site of a pond in **1863** at a cost of **£1,700** by a Victorian property developer, G. J. Lawrence.

Epping Choral Society, whose guests included Dame Clara Butt.

About 1910 the hall became a roller skating rink. In 1912 it was due to open as Epping's first cinema, but shortly before the opening date it was gutted by fire. Later refurbished, it eventually opened showing silent films interspersed with second-rate musical hall acts.

The low structure in front of the Town Hall housed the dressing-rooms, when the stage was at the High Street end.

In 1923 another fire gutted the cinema building, but once more it was rebuilt, this time with the screen at the Hemnall Street end and with a red neon-lit 'Empire' sign over the entrance. The re-opening ceremony was performed by Ivor Novello. Talkies arrived in 1930 — Al Jolson in *The Singing Fool* — and the cinema flourished until 1954 when lack of patronage forced it to close its doors.

Guardian and Gazette, February 1985

Although it may never have aspired to its namesake in Leicester Square; it may not have had the spaciousness of the Majestic of Woodford (on page 187) or the atmosphere of the Century, Loughton (page 298), at least it was 'our flicks'. What does the future hold, we wonder? Will it go the same way as Palmer's yard — seen here being demolished in 1972.

455

Foodwise, without a shadow of a doubt, it is sausages for which Epping is renowned — even Charles Burdett remarked on it in his perambulation in 1900. This reputation is due to one man, Stephen John Church, who opened his first shop in 1888 (above) with capital of £20 and a pig given by his father! This marvellous picture was taken at Christmastide 1929. Stephen stands in the doorway with his son Cyril on his left. Over on the left are Fred Flack and Reg Sloper with Charlie Jaques and George Hewitt (the only one still alive at the time of writing) on the right.

Quite a different situation prevailed during the wars with the privations of rationing. These pictures are from the album of Allan Church, Stephen's grandson, who still runs the same shop next to the post office. The queue outside Church's in the Great War is paralleled by a comparison taken by Allan during the Second War period, the shop having been rebuilt in 1930.

Stephen's two sons Cyril and James both joined him in the butchering trade and two more shops in Epping were purchased to cater for expanding trade. *Above:* Around 1910 this shop was opened at the other end of town — Cyril is on the right in the white apron. *Below:* Then in 1919 J. Kirkby's, an existing butcher's shop on the opposite side of the road in Aberdeen House, was taken over and renamed. James stands on the left in the central doorway.

Epping, for butter justly famed, and pork in sausage popp'd,

Where winter time or summer time pig's flesh is always chopp'd.

Tom Hood

The forty-second annual show of the Essex Agricultural Society was held at Epping, on Friday and Saturday. The people of Epping 'rose to the occasion' thoroughly well, and gave the society as hearty a reception as it could well wish to have, and while the public generally supported the show in large numbers, the attendance would no doubt have been greater but for the competition of other shows at Richmond, Windsor, etc. The same competition no doubt also accounted for the absence from a very excellent all round exhibition of a number of animals, particularly horses. For all that there was keen competition for honors among some magnificent specimens alike of horses, cattle, and sheep. A great dog show, a beautiful flower show, a poultry and pigeon show, and other exhibitions all contributed towards a signal success, and the weather was very fine. Altogether the Society and the township of Epping are to be heartily congratulated. The management of the Show generally was good, the ability and foresight of Mr. Frank Whitmore, the secretary, Mr. Fred. Taylor, the assistant-secretary, and other prominent officials, being again conspicuous, while in Mr. E. J. Wythes, of Copped Hall, Epping, the Show had a President who proved as popular, as genial, and as generous as a President should be.

Essex Herald, June 1899

Mr. Hugh Sworder held his annual fat stock sale at Epping Market on Friday last, when there was a good attendance of buyers, and a capital sale transacted. Sixty-five excellent beasts were offered, amongst the consignees being Mr. Tolhunter, Mr. Lyall, Mr. Hugh Hart, Mr. Charles Hart, Mr. D. Christy, Mr. L. J. Furze, Mr. C. Cross, Mr. Sydney Furze, Mr. P. Pinch, Mr. John Smith, and Mr. Torrance. The highest price realised was £24 10s. Sheep made a fair show, and fetched from 65s. There was a good supply of pigs, and good prices were obtained. Some excitement was caused by a telegram posted just previous to the sale announcing the outbreak of foot and mouth disease at Hubbard's Hall Farm, Harlow, and naming the districts affected, but, apparently, the notice made little difference to the majority of buyers.

Epping Monthly Record, November 1900

After the Second World War Cyril and James were joined in the business by their sons, respectively Allan and Derek. In 1956 the original company of S. J. Church & Sons Ltd, founded in 1926, was continued by Derek at Aberdeen House (which had been largely rebuilt the previous year) (*below*), while Allan formed his own company, Church's Pork Butchers, based at Stephen's first shop which included the sausage factory. The other shop was sold in 1978 becoming Barbara Anne's *(top right)*.

Left: **William Cottis and Sons' first shop established in 1870 almost alongside Stephen Church's original pork shop.** *Right:* **The firm prospered and in 1906 the building was modernised with larger display windows.**

On Thursday evening, the 28th ult., the Fire Brigade received a call to attend a fire which was raging in the out-buildings at Gaynes Park. Fortunately some of the brigade were at the time preparing for the usual weekly drill, and the sound of Messrs. Cottis and Son's steam whistle soon brought every fireman to his post. A slight delay occurred owing to one of the horses being at the railway station, but this was amply compensated for by the speedy transport of the engine to the scene of the conflagration.

Epping Monthly Record, March 1895

On Monday, September 2nd, at 3.5 p.m., the Epping Brigade received a call to attend a fire at General Marter's. The steam whistle at Messrs. Cottis' foundry was the alarm signal, and in a few moments the firemen were mustered at their head-quarters in Station Road. Unfortunately some delay was caused through the horses, usually supplied by Mr. Flack, being engaged; however, through the kindness of Mrs. Sewell and Mrs. Savill, the difficulty was overcome, and William Flack took the team along in real professional style. On reaching the scene of the outbreak it was found that a hay stack was well alight and in dangerous proximity to another stack and buildings. No time was lost in getting the engine into position at a capital pond about 120 yards from the stack, Captain Saward directing the brigade in their operations, which were quickly and quietly performed. Mr. R. D. Trotter and Mr. H. H. Kemsley rendered most valuable and practical assistance to the brigade as did also many others, including several domestic servants from Walton, the residence of General Marter. The stack had to be cut all round, and the burning hay extinguished and carted away. About 12 loads were saved and by midnight all danger was at an end. The property was insured in the Atlas Company. It is much to be regretted that the strain upon the pumps placed the engine hors de combat after working a couple of hours. This has been the case at previous fires, and we have already called attention to the fact. It is anything but creditable that our excellent brigade should be handicapped with such an ancient and unreliable engine.

Epping Monthly Record, September 1895

Fire at Home Farm

At 1.45 in the afternoon of Monday, Nov. 1st, the steam syren at Messrs. Cottis' foundry sounded the fire alarm in response to a call from Mr. W. Willis, of Home Farm, Coopersale. Within eight minutes no less than ten firemen, fully equipped, were off under the command of Engineer Whiting. Thanks to the powerful brakes on the new engine, Driver Flack was enabled to negotiate both Station Road and Bower Hill at full gallop, and his skilful driving took the brigade to the scene of the outbreak in an incredibly short space of time. It was found that the fire had practically

Today that first building is occupied by the Nationwide Building Society and Smiths stationers. In the 1930s the business was transferred to larger premises behind the fountain (see page 454) close to their iron foundry. In 1962 the family sold their interest in the business which moved to new premises at No. 70 High Street under the management of two former employees. In the early years, the steam whistle at Cottis's doubled up as the rallying signal for Epping's firemen who, being volunteers, would have to be summoned from their regular jobs. The fire station in those days lay just across the road at the top of Station Road.

destroyed one of the timber-built store sheds and was just obtaining hold of the adjoining one. Without delay the engine was got into position at a roadside pond some 140 yards distant, the hose was connected, and in a few minutes the fire was practically under control.

The building, containing numerous farming tools, implements, and a large quantity of oil-cake, was totally destroyed and another building was slightly burnt.

Epping Monthly Record, November 1897

In the days when 'London prices' were obviously an attraction, this was the Victorian answer to the microwave — then 2/9 . . . now about £200!

Epping's Fire Stations. This was the first 'Engine House' (now Archer's) — the event depicted is the Diamond Jubilee parade on June 22, 1897. Two years later plans were formulated and land purchased for the erection of a purpose-built station.

It is a pity that the district bye-laws do not include measures against the dangerous practice of cleaning flues by means of allowing them to fire. A few days ago, in St. John's Road, there were to be seen two blazing chimneys within a few yards of each other.

Epping Monthly Record, March 1898

One of the few Epping institutions which really can give points to other towns is the Fire Brigade, of whose efficiency we have had ample illustrations. The results of the competition last week are eminently satisfactory, and we look forward to the time when they will be able to surpass even Ponder's End, and, as Capt. Horn said, take a part in the national competitions. At the pleasant little gathering which followed the competition, Dr. Fowler suggested a system of electric bells as a more satisfactory fire-call than the hooter, and he is right. When we get those we shall be up-to-date indeed.

The Loughton Gazette, October 8, 1904

The Epping Volunteer Fire Brigade had been formed in May 1894 — two years before Epping Urban District Council came into being. The new council purchased two possible sites, one at the top of Station Road for £250 and another on the corner of Clarke's Lane for £510. However in the absence of a firm decision to go ahead and build, the Brigade moved across the road into Flack's garage *(above)* where their horses were already stabled. The building still survives, the pump would have been parked in what is now The Paint Shop *(above right)*. In 1914, Harry Woore, works manager at Cottis's, was appointed chief officer and gradually the Brigade was 'taken over' by him as his personal organisation. Within three years he was attending fires in a private capacity, paying the Council for the use of the engine, while he was reimbursed by the unfortunate householder or insurance company as at Copped Hall in 1917 (see page 425). There was soon public disquiet over the unofficial use of the appliance, leaving the town denuded of fire cover, and by 1920 his relations with the Council were very strained. At this stage the Council decided to proceed with the long-delayed new building on the site on the corner of Clarke's Lane and the High Road only that the 'new' building became a second-hand army hut! *(below left)*.

By 1924 it appears that Woore's relationship with the Council had been patched up although he was still running the Brigade almost as a private concern. He built his own fire station in Hemnall Street, more or less behind the Council's station, and purchased his own fire appliance, adding three more to his fleet over the years until the Fire Brigades Act of 1938 effectively put him out of business. It was the end of a remarkable saga. The new Council-run Brigade operated from the old army hut which was replaced by the present building at a cost of £32,600 and opened in September 1974 *(above)*.

'It's a long way to Tipperary . . . ' Two girls in the Epping Stores admire the Epping 'Terriers' parading in the High Street.

A week after the Normandy landings in June 1944 the flying bomb attacks on London and the south-eastern counties commenced. There was no let-up in the weight of the bombardment for the following three months. VIs dived at random intervals throughout the twenty-four hours, seven days a week. Each bomb falling on a built-up area created very considerable damage to buildings, burying many people in the rubble of their homes or workplaces.

The National Fire Service had been reorganised to meet the new form of attack. As with other Civil Defence Units, the bombing resulted in long hours of removing masonry and tunneling into debris in search of those trapped. As they worked, flying bombs roared across the sky, sometimes flying over the city, at other times crashing close at hand, compelling rescue crews to rush for cover.

The strain of these arduous, dangerous and nerve-wracking duties began to show; personnel were seen to be in need of a complete break from the constant mental and physical

JULY 7, 1917
The second daylight raid on London

William Sowrey caught the bombers over Romford, but his B.E.12a was incapable of getting within 1,000 ft of their height, and two drums of Lewis at the tailmost machine had no effect. He maintained contact with the formation until it bombed, after which the Gothas climbed away and left him standing.

Ernest Gilbert, No. 39 Squadron, patrolling in a B.E.12a between Hainault and Joyce Green, engaged the inbound Gothas over the Ongar area with both guns, causing two of the pilots to start weaving. Then his Vickers jammed, and while he tried without success to clear the stoppage the bombers drew a long way ahead. He attacked again as they returned over the City, using all his remaining Lewis drums. Gilbert's report included the remarkable statement that the enemy formation was 'escorted by two or three small, dark-coloured scouts'. Having flown on the Western Front, Gilbert cannot have been completely ignorant of aircraft recognition, and his comment might have been an ironic suggestion that British fighters were not showing enough aggression — not realizing that some apparently 'escorting' were experiencing gun troubles, or out of ammunition.

Moulton-Barrett in one of the three S.E.5s recently allotted to No. 39 Squadron, spotted the enemy at 10.15 hr over north London and had no difficulty in overtaking. He fired at three Gothas in quick succession, then concentrated on one flying a little apart from the rest, giving it his last two drums of Lewis and seeing tracer enter the fuselage below the

Like all old soldiers they never die . . . they just fade away. Seventy years later their presence is only a memory.

nose cockpit. Out of ammunition, he flew on the north side of the formation as far as the coast, hoping to edge it within range of the Shoeburyness guns.

The No. 39 Squadron F.K.8 crewed by Haynes and Stoneham trailed the Gothas from Epping to central London and back to the coast without ever being able to close sufficiently for an effective attack, and a parting gesture of 37 rounds fired at the rearmost group of three produced no result.

The Air Defence of Britain 1914-1918, Christopher Cole and E. F. Cheesman, 1984

tension brought about by the barrage of V1s. Accordingly, a plan devised by senior fire officers was inaugurated early in September 1944. An area of countryside at Upshire, just north of the Wake Arms pub, was taken over for development as a camp site for firemen and women from the East End. It was an imaginative scheme, planned with a dual purpose in mind in which personnel were withdrawn from the operational area to enjoy a period of rest in the peaceful environment of Epping Forest, only a few miles beyond the boundary of the target area. Additionally, it provided an opportunity for a practice run in

Twenty-one years on and the sirens sounded once again over England but this time the horrors of war, instead of being largely confined to the battlefields, were to be brought to every corner of the land. The development of the aeroplane extended

the range at which an enemy could wage war and preparations had to be taken to combat the new threat to civilians. At Epping the Air Raid Precautions headquarters was set up in Ivy Lodge facing the Plain, now replaced by this block of flats.

460

exercising personnel in the problems involved in supporting a badly blitzed city, the purpose for which the Task Divisions had been formed.

Each Division comprised 100 fire-fighting pumps with a hose laying lorry carrying a mile of hose. A small administrative unit was included to take care of pay, welfare, provisioning and mobilising. Also included was a mobile kitchen carrying its own fuel for cooking and an accompanying stores van, with two complete crews of cooks and kitchen staff capable of providing cooked meals for the 1,000 personnel required to man the Division. There was a field telephone unit equipped with reels of telephone cable and portable exchanges for making the connections between operational centres and base.

Canteen vans were included to provide on-the-job refreshment to crews working at incidents and mobile workshops were available to repair any breakdown of equipment. In short, the Division would be equipped to live off its own fat without becoming a burden to the stricken city it had come to support.

Half a division at a time was withdrawn from the most heavily bombed areas and moved into camp at Upshire. Mobile kitchens had preceded the pumps and a hot meal awaited the troops as they moved in to the tented accommodation. Of all the restrictions imposed on NFS personnel in the autumn of 1944, none was more acutely felt than lack of sleep so, with the immediate prospect of an uninterrupted night's rest, with more to follow, weary crews promptly made up for lost time.

The improvement in physical well being and morale was astonishing after only one week in the country. All personnel attached to the Task Divisions in No. 36 Fire Force were given a week's respite in the peaceful environment of Epping Forest, returning to their stations mentally and physically refreshed for the task ahead.

Cyril Demarne, Letter to the Editor, 1985

Lord Dudley, Regional Commissioner for the Midlands, speaking of the relaxation of the black-out, Civil Defence duties, and fire watching, said at Birmingham yesterday 'It is possible, even probable, that the enemy will be able to launch something else at a longer range and a different type from V1. Therefore it is necessary for us to be on our guard. We must maintain full efficiency so as to be able to bring our defensive measures into operation at a moment's notice.'

The Times, September 11, 1944

From the Hague to Epping Green. In 1974 your Editor visited Holland to pinpoint the place from which the first two V2 rockets were launched against London . With the help of Colonel A. P. de Jong of the Royal Netherlands Air Force the precise spot where the launch pad had stood on September 8, 1944 was determined — here in the centre of Koekoekslaan.

Using mobile launchers, it had been planned to fire rockets from 45 unprotected positions between Calais and Cherbourg, but these areas were overrun by the advancing Allies before the V2 was ready for operation. By the end of August, 1944, a provisional plan had been made for launches against London and Paris from Belgium, between Tournai and Ghent; a day later this proposed launch area had to be moved north to Antwerp, because of the speed of the Allied advance. With the capture of Brussels on September 3, this area had been moved even further north to The Hague in Holland.

Two launch groups had been formed, Gruppe Nord to attack London and Gruppe Sud to prepare for attacks against France and Belgium.

The first offenseive V2 rocket was fired by a demonstration unit Lehr and Versuchs Batterie 44 at Paris at 8.30 a.m. on the morning of September 8. That evening Gruppe Nord fired its first rockets against London.

On Thursday, September 7, the SS had arrived in the Wassenaar district of the Hague and forced the civilian population to evacuate their property in Konijnenlaan, Koekoekslaan and Lijsterlaan within two hours, leaving windows and doors open. Electricity cables connected to the normal mains (380 volts), were laid via Rijksstraatweg and Rust En Vreugdlaan to the area of the seized houses.

Early the next day a column of six trucks

and launch vehicles arrived and began preparing for a double launch from the crossroads at either end of Koekoekslaan. Two rockets were set upright on their portable launch platforms fifty yards apart. Just after 6.30 p.m. in the evening, the first V2s were launched at England — the aiming point was the Fire Station in Southwark Bridge Road.

At 6.40 p.m. with a clap like thunder, the first rocket landed in Stavely Road, Chiswick, nearly 8 miles off target, where it killed three people and seriously injured another ten. Sixteen seconds later the second rocket fell harmlessly to earth near Epping, Essex, 18 miles from the aiming point. Within an hour the launch team had left Koekoekslaan leaving no trace of the launchings.

After the Battle, No. 6, 1974

At the end of August it seemed that our armies might expel the enemy from all territory within the two-hundred-mile range of the rocket from London, but he managed to hold Walcheren and The Hague. On September 8, a week after the main V1 bombardment ceased, the Germans launched their first two rockets against London. The first V2 fell at Chiswick at seventeen minutes to seven in the evening, the other at Epping sixteen seconds later.

The Second World War Volume VI, Winston S. Churchill, 1954

The two rockets were set up on their mobile launchers fifty yards apart. Both V2s missed their intended targets by some miles yet the resulting explosion here on the edge of Parndon

Wood put Epping firmly in the history books of the Second World War. Today the evidence of the explosion can still be seen in the blasted trees.

Before we leave the subject of the Second World War, mention must be made of another unique 'first', or rather 'last' for Epping. Historic Hill Hall was built by Queen Elizabeth I's Secretary of State Thomas Smith in 1558. Perhaps its greatest rôle in the war came in 1945 when it was used as a transit camp for the 8th Parachute Brigade and 1st Canadian Parachute Battalion and HQ for the 3rd Parachute Brigade for Operation Varsity — carried out by the US XVIII Corps (Airborne) in support of the crossing of the Rhine on March 24 and 25. The Hill Hall troops — in all some 1,400 officers and men — departed in their gliders from Chipping Ongar — US Station 162. At the end of the war Hill Hall became No. 116 Prisoner-of-war Camp and it was here that Obergefreiter Hans Teske, captured in North Africa in May 1943 and sent to the USA, was transferred in 1946. Never officially released or repatriated, he lives in England technically still Germany's — and Epping's — last prisoner-of-war.

In April 1946 I and other Germans were brought to England at gunpoint. It was almost a year after VE-Day. The purpose of the action was not clear until we arrived in Sudbury near Derby. Well after midnight, and in a peasouper of fog, a British officer told us: 'Gentlemen, you are now British prisoners-of-war. Don't try to escape. The guards are Poles who will shoot to kill'. We spent just a few days there to be registered as British POWs and I became No. B-272858. Once more we were on the move by rail. Destination Harlow. From there lorries took us to Epping's Hill Hall. Unlike Sudbury, which had a maze of barbed wire, Hill Hall had none at all on our arrival.

The camp was a fresh one for 'new category' prisoners, men who became British prisoners on orders of the British Government (Attlee) despite objections by the International Red Cross in Geneva. There had been an acute shortage of labour in agriculture and (I quote British Cabinet records) 'German POWs were cheap and they had to do what they were told'. Prior to our arrival in England our uniforms were taken from us and were replaced with black ones.

The camp consisted of a mixture of Nissen and wooden huts. Barbed wire was put up after our arrival. A small number of soldiers of the Essex Regiment were there to guard us.

Hans Teske had fought with the 5th Fallschirmjäger-Regiment in Tunisia and was awarded the Iron Cross Second Class for rescuing a British soldier while under fire (from the British!) and the First Class at a later battle. We traced him to Milton Keynes and in November 1976 took him back to Epping to match up photographs taken thirty years previously; Hans then and now a prisoner-of-war.

He showed us his favourite spot in the wire for escaping as he got out of the camp several times to roam the local countryside

. . . and enjoy himself in the company of the locally-based Land Army Girls!

Hill Hall later became a Home Office open prison holding such celebrity prisoners as Christine Keeler of Profumo fame, but it was during this period in its history that a fire broke out one night, sweeping through the old tinder-dry roof space and completely gutting the building.

Sergeant Flanders, of the Intelligence Corps, addressed us. The main points: No escaping. No fraternisation. No sex.

The first, and for a long time only positive gesture from British authorities was that we were allowed, for the first time since the war, to write to our families.

At first the relations between POWs and the local population were cool. The locals suspected us of being fanatical Nazis, because of the black uniforms, and we in turn took every citizen of Epping as stooges of the then British Government, which not only used us as forced, cheap labour (their words) and robbed us of our freedom, but was the same Government which was responsible for the mass-expulsion of 15 million Germans under the Potsdam Agreement, of whom 2½ million died as the result. (My family was one of the 15 million expelled, and my father was one of the 2½ million who died.)

As far as the guards were concerned we had no complaints. Lieutenant Blumenthal, a Jew, was very well liked and respected.

The food rations were rather small but some farmers were helpful and gave us extra food. In return the production on such farms increased. Uncooperative farmers in turn found uncooperative prisoners, to their cost. Non-fraternisation was a joke. Most of us were young men in our early 20s. The pundits in authority put us with girls of the Women's Land Army, girls in their late teens and early 20s. What more do I have to say.

By Christmas 1946 public opinion had turned in our favour, both locally and in Parliament, where the MP for Epping, Mrs. Leah-Manning, became one of our champions. Some restrictions were eased, limited freedom was given, and the dreadful yellow patch on the back of the jacket and on the trousers began to disappear.

Late summer of 1947 we were permitted to use public transport and go to cinemas, etc, yet with typical bureaucratic arrogance the orders of non-fraternisation remained in force.

In September 1947 I became the first POW of Hill Hall to be released on parole from there. However my official discharge from the German Forces never took place because of a bureaucratic error, which technically puts me in the unique position of being the last serving member of the old Wehrmacht, unfortunately unpaid! A repatriation programme to Germany had started a few weeks earlier at a trickle and gathered speed in early 1948. Likewise a number of POWs were released to

settle in the Epping Area and in late spring the camp at Hill Hall closed.

I think I can speak for all of us who were in that camp in saying to the people of Epping — and the WLA girls — a big thank you. To the British Government of the day (the Attlee administration) who robbed us of our freedom in peacetime and who robbed many of us of a return home for ever, the condemnation they deserve.

A Prisoner of War at Hill Hall, Epping. An unpublished manuscript by Hans Teske, 1985

The Government has rejected a proposal by the Prison Commission to use Thornwood War Department camp as a semi-secure prison for women.

They have decided that the prison should be built on a site at Hill Hall, Epping, the Minister of Housing and Local Government said today.

In his report to the Minister the Inspector who held a public inquiry on July 5th into the Thornwood proposal said that the main objection related to violation of the Green Belt.

To establish a prison would involve erecting many new buildings contrary to Green Belt policy. On balance the planning objections against the proposal should override the economic and operational advantages, though he recognised that the question would have to be considered in the light of national needs.

The Home Secretary and the Minister decided to accept the inspector's recommendations. At the inquiry the planning authority intimated that they would not offer any objection to the establishment of the prison on a site at Hill Hall, for although this was also within the Green Belt, development there would, in their view, be less obtrusive.

Guardian and Gazette, January 6, 1961

The doors of historic Hill Hall — last used as a women's prison — are to re-open.

But it will be the public, not prisoners, who will be filing in to look around.

Building work to smarten up the former open prison is planned. But it will not be open to the public this year, a spokesman for English Heritage said this week.

Hill Hall was built by Queen Elizabeth I's Secretary of State, Thomas Smith, in 1558. It burnt down in the 1960s.

Building plans include consolidating the main house and roofs of the remaining three open ranges.

The visiting public will also be able to see Elizabethan wall paintings.

The future of a more modern block on the Theydon Mount — formerly used by prison staff — is currently under discussion. Its possible uses are being explored by planning bodies and developers.

A spokesman for English Heritage denied a rumour that the block is being converted to holiday accommodation.

West Essex Gazette, January 10, 1986

Quite frankly we felt that in this day and age we could not have German wartime prisoners running around on the loose — it was just not good enough — so we had ex-Police Constable J622 Wilf Nicoll of Loughton 're-arrest' Hans at Ivy Chimneys on the exact spot where he had once been recaptured after one of his late-night amorous forays in 1946!

463

Although the County Planning Architect, the Area Planning Officer and Epping Urban Council's Surveyor all recommended an outline application to build on a 15½-acre site at Theydon Grove, Epping, the Council has turned it down.

The officers had told the council that adoption of the plan would result not only in a general improvement of the layout of the estate, but also the entrance to the town.

But the council decided against the plan because it would have meant building slightly beyond — towards the railway — the limit of the residential area laid down on the town map.

Instead it approved a second application by Dean Homesteads, Ltd., of Theydon Bois, to build on almost the whole site, with the exception of the pond.

West Essex Gazette, December 20, 1963

It is on the northern extremity of Epping that the most drastic development has taken, and is about to take, place. At this end of the town the major property was Theydon Grove, its name reminding us that the area to the east of the main road once lay in the parish of Theydon Garnon. It was once the estate of Miss Elisabeth Horsley Whiteman, 'founder' of the new St John's, but by **1960** was owned by Mr H. A. J. Silley, of Green & Silley Weir Ltd. Mr Silley was tragically killed in an air accident returning from a trip to the Isle of Wight and, subsequently, the property was sold. In **1964** the house was demolished and Dean Homesteads began to develop the site in stages with Georgian-style town houses.

A view about to undergo dramatic change. *Above:* **With the Theydon Grove estate on the left, the A11 (reclassified the B1393 in 1978) dips and rises towards the Plain. In former times that dip was even more pronounced resulting in constant flooding until it was raised by the infill of rubbish after the First World War. On April 1, 1974, consequent upon the reorganisation of local government, the Epping Forest District Council was created upon the amalgamation of the Chigwell Urban District, Epping Urban District, Epping and Ongar Rural District and the Waltham Holy Cross Urban District Councils.**

Office centralisation for Epping Forest Council took a step closer with councillors backing the draft design brief for the architectural competition.

The centralisation was first considered two years ago, and resulted in massive public opposition. The scheme was dropped when a public inquiry inspector said no to the plans, but now revised plans have been drawn up.

Architects have been told one of the main criticisms of the previous plans was that the building was out of scale with its surroundings. But the original building at the council offices, and the three derelict properties in Church Hill will be pulled down.

The plan is to have a civic suite, with a public gallery for 50 people plus committee rooms, offices for the seven departments of the council, car parking for 240 cars, and a canteen, recreation room and quiet area for council staff. Car parking may be underground, and may use parking facilities at Stonards Hill.

West Essex Gazette, December 23, 1983

Epping Forest Council has now approved the design brief for its office centralisation plans following a series of meetings with parish and town councils . . .

There are still 'a small minority of organisations' who do not accept the need for centralisation and refuse to be convinced, says the Council, which adds that it is recognised by others 'as being good sound common sense.'

An architectural competition for the design of the offices is now to be held, with members of the Eastern region of the Royal Institute of British Architects competing. They come from the Eastern Counties and London boroughs of Barking, Havering, Newham, Redbridge and Waltham Forest.

From the entries, six will be selected by an experienced and professional panel to go on to the second stage.

The design brief will be sent to all organisations who have made comments, and further meetings will be held to discuss the actual plan.

Guardian and Gazette, January 13, 1984

District councillor Ian Beattie faced a barrage of criticism over Epping Forest Council's plans at a meeting at Epping Hall last Thursday.

Angry residents packed the hall to speak out against the proposed offices — dubbed a 'monstrous carbuncle on the face of Epping' by a spokesman for North Epping Residents Association.

And the overwhelming message from the meeting was a loud NO to centralisation. Out of 190 votes cast, 98.2 per cent were for an Epping Society motion. This deplored the decision of Epping Forest Council to proceed with the selected building design 'because, in common with the previously rejected scheme, in our opinion, its scale and mass and associated traffic problems will have a seriously adverse effect, not only upon the Epping conservation area but on Epping as a whole. Accordingly we once again request the Secretary of State to call in the plans before EFDC grants itself planning permission.'

West Essex Gazette, March 29, 1985

The old Epping and Ongar Rural District Council offices were located at No. 323 High Street — a new office block on the right being opened in February 1971. The new Epping Forest District Council took the building over three years later.

As the site touches on the Epping Conservation Area, design considerations are important. One scheme in 1982 was rejected by a planning inspector who indicated what he thought was required in a local government offices design on the 323 High Street site. His conclusions and the results of extensive consultation have been brought together in a design brief for an architects' competition sponsored by the RIBA.

The winning design out of 51 entries is the basis for the planning application now submitted for approval. It has the support not only of the RIBA but also the Royal Fine Arts Commission and the Essex County Council on planning and highway grounds. Equal care to that given to the design has been taken to avoid any adverse effect on the Town Greens or traffic.

Epping Forest District Council, 1985

Amid heckling from a packed public gallery on Tuesday night the plans for centralised civic offices at Epping were given the go-ahead by the council's development committee.

The winning design by Richard Reid Associates — which was described as a 'toy town' design by one councillor — will now go before the full council in July for formal approval.

Members of the public often drowned out the voices of the councillors by clapping and cheering when anyone stated their opposition to the plans.

Cheshunt & Waltham Telegraph, June 27, 1985

The estimated cost of Epping Forest Council's centralisation scheme was officially revealed last week.

The appraisal shows that if centralisation was carried out now it should cost just over £4¼m. The likely cost is set at £4.9m, however, with £2m spent in 1986/7, £2m spent in 1987/8 and £900,000 in 1988/9.

The figures take inflation into account and are offset by estimated capital receipts from other Epping Forest Council sites to the tune of £1¾m at a conservative estimate.

West Essex Gazette, June 28, 1985

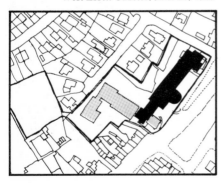

Central offices in Epping for Epping Forest District Council have been given the go-ahead.

At Tuesday's full council meeting a packed but surprisingly silent gallery heard planning consent for the controversial new complex given the official seal of approval by a comfortable majority of 10 votes.

Great emphasis was laid on arguments like the building's size, traffic increase and weight of public opinion, but Councillor Michaelman pointed out: 'People who objected to Tesco are already praising the building . . . If the Archangel Gabriel had produced this plan they would have opposed it!'

The design, he said, had been scrutinised by the RIBA and the Royal Arts Commission, and he argued that trade would be improved by the influx of workers to the town.

West Essex Gazette, August 2, 1985

Shortly after its creation, the new Council commissioned the Royal Institute of Public Administration to advise it on its future office requirements, the RIPA report stating that it recommended centralisation on a single site in the central town of the District: Epping. The chosen location was announced by the Council in 1975 as being adjoining the existing office block at No. 323 High Street.

Demolition work is going full-steam ahead at Church Hill, Epping, as part of the first step towards the centralisation of council offices.

Waltham Abbey contractors Pick Hill Demolitions are dismantling numbers 3, 5 and 7 Church Hill piece by piece.

An Epping Forest Council spokesman said the homes were being dismantled rather than knocked down to create less noise, dust and general nuisance.

Work started over two weeks ago, after the Department of the Environment gave permission for the houses to be pulled down.

Permission was needed because the buildings are in a designated conservation area.

The council spokesman pointed out that the homes would have been demolished regardless of centralisation plans because they were unsafe.

Guardian and Gazette, October 4, 1985

Although its intentions had been public knowledge for more than ten years, when the artist's impression for the new development was published in 1985 it aroused a storm of controversy — not only over the scale of the proposed design by Condor (Southern) Ltd., but bringing into question once again the actual cost effectiveness of the move. Although building work has not commenced at the time of writing (February 1986), the drawing shows the new town hall from the same north-easterly aspect as that in the aerial photograph taken by Ray Stebbings.

Above left and right: **An early resurfacing job on Maltman's Path, the road along the edge of The Green, now renamed Church Hill.**

It fell heavy in Epping, at midnight. At Mrs. Cowen's farm, in Linsel-street, it fired a barn, in which were two labouring men asleep, and three carts: the barn had been cleared out to receive the new corn, and had in it only bins full of chaff and some billet-wood. One of the men, in coming out of the barn, was twice struck down by the lightning, and much scorched and singed by the fire, besides the loss of cloaths which he could not go back to bring out. The wind happened to be in a most favourable direction; and plenty of assistance coming from the town and neighbourhood, together with the Epping engine, the rest of the barns and houses, though very contiguous, were preserved.

Press report, 1784

Apart from the High Street perhaps the oldest part of the town is Lindsey Street, a group of houses on the road to Epping Upland. The name of Lindsey Street, probably meaning 'inclosure at the top of the hill', goes back to 1200. In the 18th and 19th centuries this was the working-class quarter of the town, containing the maltings, the brewery, the workhouse, and the pest-house. At the east end of the street is still a small open green. On the south side of this is a roughcast building of timber framing and brick, with jettied gable to the east end. Nearby is the group composed of the former British School, built in 1845, and the Congregational church of late-17th-century origin, rebuilt in 1774 and re-fronted in 1887. Maltings Lane, which runs off the north-east corner of the green, contains a row of early-18th-century weather-boarded cottages.

Victoria History of the County of Essex,
Volume V, 1966

Below: **The building used from 1845 to 1875 for the British School still stands beside the Congregational Church.**

Lindsey Street leads round to Eppingbury Farm and on to Epping Upland.

The lake in the Lower Forest was dug as a result of a proposal by Mr H. B. Yerburgh to provide relief work for Epping's unemployed.

The lake on Epping Plain has an interesting history. The story goes back to the winter of 1893-4, which was 'very severe' by all accounts. Unfortunately many of the working men in Epping were thrown out of employment because of this. However, a group of people decided to start a fund with the object of relieving the sufferings of these unemployed. It would do this by providing them with work. A discussion was called and it was agreed that an artificial lake would be a fine acquisition to a town without a river or any natural sheets of water in its vicinity.

The intention was that the lake could serve as a swimming pool during the summer and as a skating rink in the winter. It appears that the weather could be relied upon in those days! It was not long before sufficient funds had been raised and the men could be set to work. In the following spring, as work neared completion, it was discovered that the response to the appeal had been such that there would be money in hand after the lake was finished. . . .

Peter Haining, Essex Countryside,
February 1962

On Wednesday, 21st June, Mr. C. Edgar Lewis, held an inquest at the Royal Oak Inn, Epping, concerning the death of George Edward Blatch, aged 14, who was drowned while bathing on the previous Monday.

Mrs. Elizabeth Chaddock, of Allnuts Estate, Epping, said the deceased was her son. She last saw him alive about seven o'clock on Monday evening, when he said he was going to the lake to bathe.

William Cuin, a boy, of Allnuts Estate, said he went with the deceased and others to bathe in Epping Lake. They had previously bathed there. Witness was in the water at the same time as the deceased. He could swim, but he did not know whether the deceased could or not. Witness swam across the lake, and the deceased attempted to do the same, only by a shorter way. His attention was called to the deceased by some young men who were standing on the bank. Deceased was struggling in the water, and witness swam to him and caught hold of his wrist. Deceased caught hold of witness by his body and right arm and drew him under three times. Samuel Foster held out a stick to witness and pulled him out, deceased having previously let go of him.

Charles Grout, of Brickfield Cottages, the Plain, Epping, said he saw the deceased and Cuin bathing in the lake. He saw deceased start from the deep side, and when about half-way across he appeared to be struggling in the water. Witness called to Cuin, who was bathing a short distance away. Cuin endeavoured to rescue the deceased, and was himself nearly drowned. Witness eventually walked into the water and fetched the deceased out.

Dr. Trevor Fowler said he was called to the deceased, who was lying on the bank of the lake. He was quite dead. Witness tried artificial respiration for a quarter of an hour, but without avail. Death was due to suffocation from drowning.

Forest-keeper John Little said he gave the boys permission to bathe, eight o'clock being the bathing time. He told them to stop at the spot where the water was shallow. About 8.15 p.m. he heard someone call out that a boy was going under the water. Witness saw a boy go to the assistance of the one in difficulty, as he went to get the rope. The rope was kept in a shed a few yards away, and witness had the key in his pocket. He procured the rope as quickly as possible and threw it to where the two boys were in the water. They both failed to get hold of it, but Cuin got hold of the end of a fishing rod which was held out to him.

Epping Monthly Record, June 1899

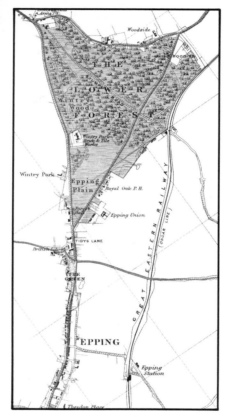

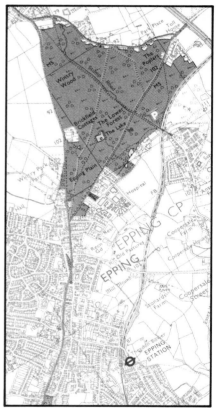

Before and after. Maps eighty years apart illustrate the lake-cum-bathing pool and the Royal Oak . . . and the growth of Epping from village to town.

468

The Royal Oak stood alongside the Epping Union Workhouse and Infirmary which opened in 1837 becoming St Margaret's, first used as a War Emergency Hospital in World War II. The 'Oak', one of Epping's most popular pubs, closed in 1915.

The sad death of the boy Blatch whilst bathing in the lake on the 19th June last reminds us that so long as three years ago we advocated the necessity of placing life-saving appliances near the deep end of the lake. Apparently a rope is kept *locked up* in the dressing shed. This is not sufficient security for the men and young lads who go there to bathe. What is necessary (and what probably will *now* be done) is that a life-belt, hooks, and rope should be placed where they can be immediately used if wanted. We learn from the Royal Humane Society that a complete outfit can be obtained at a cost of under £2.

All praise to the lad, W. Cuin, who so gallantly tried to save his comrade, and only desisted when he himself was like to meet a similar fate. The Misses Annie and Ada Johnson kindly undertook to raise a subscription on his behalf. The sum of £1 was collected with which a handsome writing desk was purchased and presented to him. This was supplemented by a gift of 10s. from an Epping gentleman.

Epping Monthly Record, July 1899

Dear Sir,

The lamentable fatality at the Epping Lake on the 19th of June last should serve to remind every one of the importance of 'First Aid' teaching. Although there was no lack of willing hands to attempt the rescue and to have carried out the proper methods for resuscitation after the body was recovered from the water, it does not appear that there was any one present who had ever had the benefit of 'First Aid' instruction. Ever since the Technical Instruction Classes have been held, the Epping Committee has very wisely constantly included the subject of 'First Aid to the Injured' in its programme; but, unfortunately, not more than about half the full number of persons have ever availed themselves of the opportunities thus afforded them. The last course was held in the spring of the present year, and although the Committee offered the Lectures free to certain classes of persons whom it was thought would be more especially interested in them, yet the attendance was not increased. Seeing how useful a little knowledge may be in such a matter

as this, it can scarcely be that the public are indifferent, and I have no doubt the difficulty in attending ambulance classes has been a very real one with many people. It needs to be pointed out, however, that when special facilities are offered to persons to become acquainted with the subject, it is a duty which they owe to their fellow-creatures to make an effort to take advantage of them.

I am, dear Sir, yours very faithfully,

TREVOR FOWLER
Epping, July 7th, 1899

Epping Monthly Record, Letter to the Editor

We are pleased to notice that the lake on The Plain is provided with a life-buoy, and, that illustrated examples of restoring animation by means of artificial respiration are placed in prominent positions in the shelter sheds.

Epping Monthly Record, August 1899

On Thursday afternoon, the 17th ult., Wm. Cuin, the boy who, on June 9th last, made such a gallant attempt to rescue his drowning companion, George Blatch, in the lake at Epping, was presented in the Boys' School

with the Royal Humane Society's Certificate, in recognition of his bravery.

Epping Monthly Record, September 1899

A smoking concert was held at the Royal Oak, Epping, on Thursday, Nov. 24th, under the auspices of the Epping Carnival Committee; and was well attended. The room had been effectively decorated by Mr. Albert Green; and Mr. E. G. Farnell illuminated it with fairy lights and Japanese lanterns. Mr. Avey presided, and Mr. F. W. Mott was in the vice-chair. The Secretary, Mr. Green, said he was very pleased that their second annual carnival turned out a great success, and he hoped that another year a more representative committee might be formed, so as to carry out a grander affair. He was sorry to say that there was a deficit of 15s., but their old friend, Mr. Shannon, had kindly cleared it off. (Applause.) A capital programme of songs, recitations, concertina solos, etc., was afterwards given by Messrs. W. Cuin, F. W. Mott, A. Green, H. Rowden, Dowsett, Wood, Doye and others; and the presentation of prizes to the winners at the carnival took place during the proceedings.

Epping Monthly Record, December 1898

Epping Plain. The open aspect at the turn of the century greatly contrasted by the present day encroachment of the Forest.

The official twinning of Epping and Eppingen took place with due pomp and ceremony at St John's Church, Epping, on Sunday.

Interest in the twinning was high, for the church was packed out and organisers ran out of programmes.

The twinning deed was signed by Epping town Mayor Peter Burns, Eppingen's Burgomaster Councillor E. Pretz, the chairman of the Epping association, Councillor Bob Hill, and the chairman of the Eppingen association, Councillor K. Zoller.

Sir William Addison, president of the association, made the vow of twinning. It promised to deepen the ties of friendship and collaboration between the two towns and to strengthen the European spirit through close co-operation. This would contribute to European unity and lasting peace between our countries.

The ceremony took place in German and English and was attended by 50 people from Eppingen, who stayed with host families from the association.

West Essex Gazette, November 6, 1981

'Epping twinned with Eppingen in West Germany' signposts have now been put up at all entrances to the town, two years after the towns were officially twinned.

The idea of twinning the towns came after an Epping man saw a signpost for Eppingen while on holiday in Germany. Mr Alan Swann, who has since died, followed the signs and visited this little town in the Baden-Wurtemburg region of West Germany, where he noticed that Eppingen bore some surprising similarities to his own town.

When he arrived home, he discussed the idea of twinning the towns with other local residents. After further exploratory trips and discussions with German counterparts, the towns were officially twinned in November 1981 in Epping, and June 1982 in Eppingen.

West Essex Gazette, October 28, 1983

It is here on the Plain that the visitor is reminded of more recent events.

The Convalescent Cottage, once a landmark on the main road, now replaced by the Wintry Park Service Station.

In Britain, perhaps more than in any other country, we find our way around the countryside via our inns and pubs. When one asks for directions to a certain place more often than not the route we are given to follow is: 'Turn left at the Duke of — ', or 'Go past the Royal — ' and so on. Our forebears, riding by coach or horseback, needed them even more as rest stops for both rider and horse in their long uncomfortable journeys. These pages have been sprinkled with pictures of many of those, both ancient and modern, which surround Epping Forest. We only wish there had been space to include them all.

And so, as we take our leave of Epping in order to begin the final chapter in our long journey around the Forest area, let us pause for breath at Epping Green. It seems an age ago that we began our journey at Forest Gate, and the temptation to rest awhile beside the village pond on an outdoor seat at the Travellers Friend with our ale beside us, is too much to resist.

Waltham Abbey

And so we end our journey at the great abbey church at Waltham, constructed on the orders of King Henry II from 1177 to 1242. George Campbell, our artist, gives us his impression of how it might have appeared when viewed from the north-west.

The whole parish of Waltham lay within the ancient Forest of Essex, known from the 14th century as Waltham Forest. In the Middle Ages the hundred of Waltham consituted a forest bailiwick, the forestership of which was held in serjeanty from the time of Henry II by Aucher the Huntsman and his successors, who were the lords of Copped Hall in Epping. In 1337 Aucher Fitz Henry sold Copped Hall and the forestership to Sir John Shardlowe. In 1358 Bartholomew Langridge quitclaimed the forestership of Shardlowe. Langridge's interest in it probably came from his ownership of Langridge, which may also have belonged to the Fitz Auchers. That interest does not appear to have been wholly extinguished until 1386, when Gillian, daughter of Langridge, and her husband John Fresshe, conveyed the forestership to Waltham Abbey. Waltham had bought Copped Hall from the Shardlowes in 1350. It is possible, therefore, that the abbey had acquired the forestership also before 1386, and that the conveyance of that year was merely to strengthen the title. The abbey retained the forestership until the Dissolution.

The Victoria History of the County of Essex. Volume V, 1966

The original Abbey Church of Waltham was built in the usual cathedral form, and consisted of a nave, transept, choir, ante-chapel, &c. It was a very considerable structure, and covered an extensive ground plan; of which some idea may be formed, when we find that the situation of Harold's tomb was about forty yards from the termination of the present building, in what is supposed to have been, at that time, the east end of the choir, or of some chapel beyond it. The intersection of the transept is yet visible. The ancient tower rose above this, and contained five large tuneable bells, which, on the suppression, were purchased of the King's commissioners. Part of the tower, having been

some time in a very decayed state, fell down soon after the surrender of the abbey, probably on pulling down the choir which, with the east chancel and transept, were entirely destroyed, leaving only the west end of the building, which constitutes the present parochial church.

This venerable relic of antiquity is rather large than handsome, and very dark within; yet it contains many curious and interesting specimens of ornamented columns, semi-circular arches, and other characteristics of Norman architecture. From the western entrance to the altar, the length of the building is ninety feet; and in breadth, including side aisles, it is forty-eight feet.

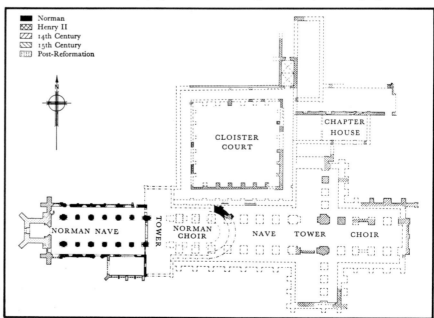

The abbey stood on the site of two earlier churches: one built by Tofig from 1016 and the subsequent rebuilding or enlargement by Harold, Earl of Wessex, in 1060. King Henry's church became an Augustinian abbey on the appointment of Walter de Gant as the first Abbot in 1184. Sometime that century a low dividing wall was built separating the monastic area of worship at the eastern end from that used by the local parishioners. Today only the architecture to the west of the wall remains.

Almost every vestige of ornamental grandeur, which anciently distinguished the exterior of this church, has been industriously demolished or defaced; and what remains owes its preservation chiefly to the durable nature of its materials. Much of the beauty of the original is obscured by modern reparations. The windows in the north aisle, which were once semi-circular, have in general been made square; a few are pointed. In other parts they retain their original shape, but their ornaments are filled up with plaster. In the inside, the hand of violence is less apparent, but every thing displays marks of the most wretched parsimony. The simplicity and grandeur of the ancient remains are much injured by the glare of whitewashing. The brasses are torn away from the grave-stones; the floor is badly paved, and the figures of the altar-piece disgrace the edifice in which they are placed. The south aisle is but little altered, and the windows retain their original forms: that on the north has been more modernised. Towards the east end, the arms of Philip and Mary are displayed on a handsome screen of wood; and near it there formerly stood a painting of the founder, Harold, on glass, which was destroyed by the puritanical zeal of the fanatics, in the beginning of the reign of Charles the First.

The History and Topography of the County of Essex, March 1831

It is dedicated to the 'Holy Cross,' and the origin of that dedication is found in an ancient legend which has its beginning 150 miles away at Montacute in Somerset.

In 1035 the sexton of Montacute had a dream in which he was told to go to the priest and bid him lead his parishioners to the top of the hill and dig until they found a wondrous cross. This they did and came upon an image of the crucified Saviour carved in black flint. The local landowner was Tofig, a standard bearer to King Canute, and he ordered the cross to be placed in an ox wagon and carried to 'wherever God willed.' After several unsuccessful attempts to persuade the oxen to move at the mention of places such as Glastonbury, Winchester and Durham, Tofig thought of Waltham, where he had an estate, and at the mention of that name 'the oxen moved off so easily that it appeared as if the wagon was drawing the oxen instead of they dragging it.' Eventually it arrived at Waltham, where the first church was erected, dedicated to the 'Holy Cross.'

A. J. Ford, writing in the Essex Countryside, Spring 1954

The only conventual building which has escaped destruction is a beautiful little chamber in the Abbey gardens. This fragment, which has been described as 'an architectural gem,' consists of a small apartment groined, in two bays, with quadripartite vaulting. The exterior is of rubble, the interior of squared ashlar, and the pointed bowtell occurs in the vault ribs. The ribs spring at the angles of the building from one shaft, and at the sides from clusters of three; the bases and capitals in these shafts are very curious. In the two centres of the beautifully groined ceiling, which is like that at the east end of Canterbury, portions of the ironwork still remain, with the ring for supporting pendant lights. The inside measurement is 29 feet 4 inches, by 14 feet 8 inches. It stands north and south, and is devoid of windows, but there is a doorway at the north end which still serves as the entrance. Another doorway at the south, now bricked up, appears to indicate that it originally gave access to the cloister court at the north-east angle, immediately to the east of the refectory or frater, and Mr Reeve has pointed out that 'the walls running west and south from this building must clearly mark

In March 1540 Waltham became the last abbey to fall under the dissolution decree of Henry VIII. The nave at the western end was retained for the parish church of St Lawrence and the Holy Cross while the remainder of the abbey, including the adjoining cloisters and chapter house, were abandoned or demolished. As a result, with its support on the eastern side removed, the great central tower fell down in 1553, the parishioners using the salvaged materials to build a new tower at the western end of the nave as a buttress to stop the building collapsing any further. A Lady Chapel was added on the south-east corner in the fourteenth century, beneath which the crypt was at one time used as the charnel house. This print dates from 1817 and shows the small, single-storey building added to the east end as a 'burying-out place'.

the north and east walls of the quadrangle.' The chamber, which evidently formed the ground floor of some important apartment, is now covered with a roof of thatch, which is in urgent need of renewal. Various conjectures have been made as to the ancient use of this interesting building. It has been referred to as a small chapel or oratory. Some archaeologists think it was the infirmary, but it does not appear large enough ever to have served that purpose. Others regard it as the parley chamber or frater, where the monks met for conversation when they were not on duty. Its appearance on the exterior, which is very rough, shows that it was attached to another building, which most probably was the abbot's mansion. It is therefore not unlikely that it was an antechamber in which the monks assembled and waited for their lord, the

Abbot, to join the solemn procession to the church. It has long since been shorn of all its ancient glory, and made to serve common uses. It is known now as the potato house or cellar, because it has been used as a storehouse for those useful vegetables. It has also been used as a woodshed, and in the production of mushrooms. The late architect, Mr. W. Burges, proposed at the restoration of the church in 1859-60 that it should be removed to the western bays of the north aisle in the parsonage garden, where it would be very convenient for use as the vestry. This good suggestion, unfortunately, was not carried into effect, and so the only fragment of the grand monastic buildings of Waltham Holy Cross, the loss of which would be irreparable, still remains in a condition of ruin and collapse.

This small building, the property of the Lord of the Manor, was demolished around 1828. Meanwhile the tower had been partially rebuilt the previous century.

473

SITE OF GRANGE FARM

'HAROLD'S BRIDGE'

ABBEY GATEWAY

CORNMILL STREAM

Above: **Beyond the abbey precincts the home farm of the monastery lay in the fields to the north-east. Called the Grange, the farm included the third largest barn in England, parts of which survived until the 1830s.** *Below:* **In 1970 construction began on a bypass for the town, the line of the new road running right through the site of the farm. The excavations thus gave the Waltham Abbey Historical Society a splendid** opportunity to record details of the barn, stables, dovecote and various outbuildings before they were lost beneath the tarmac. The only building now visible is the forge. The moat is believed to have been dug in the seventeenth century by the Earl of Norwich who occupied Abbey House, which had been built from the rubble of the abbey in about 1590. Aerofilms photographs taken in May 1968 and August 1974.

The ancient Abbey gateway was retained to serve as the entrance to the Abbey mansion, and is still in a fair state of preservation, although reduced to small proportions. There were originally two octagonal stone watch towers, flanking the entrance north and south, and projecting considerably before the walls, with loopholes commanding the gates, but a portion only of the south tower now remains. The north tower has disappeared altogether, and also a room over the doorway which it is said was used as a prison, until the middle of the last century. The remains of the original entrance into the monastery consist of two pointed arches, a south wall with doorway bricked up, and one watch tower, with porter's window also blocked. The gateway was approached by a drawbridge, but on the erection of the new Abbey house by Sir Edward Denny a single arch stone bridge was thrown across the stream, and this afterwards gave place to the modern bridge of three arches. In addition to the south wall near the gateway, there are numerous fragments of the ancient walls of the monastery in the Abbey gardens. These walls were erected in the reign of Edward III, and traces of the royal arms are still visible on the label of the large arch in the gateway. The monastic buildings stood in a quadrangular enclosure protected not only by these high walls, but by an extensive moat, the bed of which may still be seen on the inner side of the wall near the road to Holyfield, and on the north and west of the gardens.

SITE OF GREAT BARN

FORGE

MOAT

SITE OF ABBEY HOUSE

About 300 yards to the north-east of the Abbey gateway, and near the Abbey farm, an ancient stone bridge spans the cornmill stream. This bridge is evidently of great antiquity, and probably of contemporary date with the Church, as its traditional name of 'Harold's Bridge' appears to indicate. It is considered that this was the only passage across the stream in ancient times, and that not only Harold, but Tevi before him, used this bridge, or one occupying the same site, when proceeding to the royal forest of Waltham. At a later period it served the monks of Waltham as the approach from the Abbey precincts to their fish-ponds or stews, which may still be seen on the north-west of the bridge, although now filled with rushes, grasses, and wild flowers. Nearly half the structure has fallen into the stream below; and in all probability the remainder would also have disappeared during the heavy rains and floods of the past 18 months. It was, however, saved from extinction by lovers of antiquity in the neighborhood, who subscribed the necessary funds to ensure its safety, and it was thoroughly repaired by Mr. Churchwarden Bentley two years ago. In the field on the east of the bridge stood the old tythe barn, which was demolished about 60 years ago. The ancient roadway from the bridge to the monastery may be traced in dry weather, and it is affirmed that at certain seasons fragments of the foundations of some of the old monastic buildings are also exposed to view in this vicinity. The Abbey farmhouse, said to have served as the abbot's stabling in ancient times, stands on the north-east of Harold's bridge.

In the Middle Ages the River Lea was split into seven streams at Waltham. The waterway closest to the abbey on the western side was used to power the grinding mill; thus Cornmill Stream. *Left:* This engraving shows the old abbey bakery where today the river runs in a culvert *(right)*.

To cross Cornmill Stream a bridge was constructed here at the abbey's entrance. The gateway is attributed to the fourteenth century, circa 1370, although the bridge itself is of later construction.

To facilitate access across the river from Grange Farm, the abbey built a smaller bridge spanning Cornmill Stream. Some

600 years later, it still survives — more commonly referred to as Harold's Bridge.

The top of the church tower was rebuilt again in 1904-05 and restored in the 1970s. When seen from the market place the view is restricted by what is probably the only surviving mediaeval building in the town — The Welsh Harp inn — which forms a unique lychgate to the churchyard on its southern side.

After King Harold's great victory in the north at Stamford Bridge, he received news of the landing of Duke William of Normandy at Pevensey Bay, and hastened to oppose the invader. On his arrival at Waltham he rested for the night at his mansion in the park which still bears his name, the last house in which he slept on earth. A portion of the oak foundation of this old mansion is preserved with Harold's axe among other relics in the modern vestry. In the morning he proceeded to the church which he had founded, to pray for success, and from that holy house set out with his faithful warriors to wage war with the Pope's champion on behalf of the English Church and nation. According to the story received by the ancient chronicler from the lips of the old sacristan Turkill, who was present on this occasion, the figure of the Saviour on the wonderworking crucifix bowed the head, and this was regarded as an evil omen. The Dean and his Canons, in their solicitude for the King's safety, commissioned two of their number, Osgod and Ailric or Athelric, the childemaister, to attend on him, and in case their worst fears should be realised, they were instructed to bring back his body for Christian burial in the church which he had founded. On October 14th, 1066, after a most gallant and terrible

The quaint old lichgate at the entrance to the churchyard from the Market place, and on a line with the site of the central tower, is considered to be the oldest existing relic of domestic architecture in the parish, although the folding gates themselves are of no great antiquity. A second lichgate may have occupied a place at the western entrance to the churchyard, but no traces of it are now in existence.

An elm tree of large dimensions and great age stands near the churchyard path, almost facing the beautiful south doorway. It is supposed to have flourished here for at least five or six centuries. If this conjecture be correct, it must have been in its full prime at the dissolution of the monastery in 1540. It measures 22 feet round the base, 20 feet round the centre of the trunk, the height from the ground is twelve feet, and its foliage now spreads to a diameter of 63 feet. The main limbs were lopped off a few years ago, as they were considered unsafe, and the top of the trunk is now carefully protected from the ravages of the weather by a plate of zinc. It still shows signs of life and vigour in its widely extending branches which provide 'a shadow from the heat' for many an aged inhabitant and weary pilgrim.

The churchyard elm was reputed to be a silent witness to the demise of the monastery. Just before 1900 it was 'zinc-plated' (left) to protect it from water damage. Right: After having survived the ravages of centuries, it was killed by Dutch Elm disease in 1974. It was removed in June 1983 and its replacement, a Liriodendron Tulipifera — the beautiful flowering tulip tree — was planted the following year. The gravestones were removed in 1975.

struggle, the heroic patriot fell on the field of Senlac, about nine miles from Hastings, on the spot which was afterwards selected by the Conqueror as the site of the high altar of Battle Abbey, which he built in commemoration of his victory. His church has now entirely disappeared, although the remains of the monastery testify to the grandeur of his foundation. It is interesting to notice in this connection that Battle Abbey was purchased a few years ago for the sum of £200,000 by Sir Augustus Webster, the descendant of Sir Thomas Webster, a former owner, who also held the royal mansion of Copped Hall, then situated in this parish. The two Canons of Waltham, with the aid of Edith, the swan-necked, Harold's old love, found the body on the fatal battlefield, and although the Conqueror at first roughly ordered it to be buried under a heap of stones on the seashore, at the earnest entreaty of the Waltham Canons, which has been preserved in full, he relented, and granted them permission to convey it to Waltham, where it was at length interred with due honours in front of the high altar, about forty yards from the present east end, then the site of the ancient choir. In course of time a magnificent tomb of black marble or ironstone was erected over his grave, but this was destroyed with forty-five other monuments when the choir was demolished after the dissolution of the monastery. A fragment of this tomb once in the possession of the historian Dr. Fuller may still be seen in the Abbey Church, where an ancient battle-axe is also kept, which, according to a local tradition, was one wielded by the royal hero, when he fell with his brothers Gyrth and Leofwin, with the battle-cry of the English proceeding from his lips, and ringing in his ears, 'The Holy Cross of Waltham.' The ancient chronicler bears testimony to the burial at Waltham, for he had conversed with men who knew Harold and had been present at his funeral in our church. He also asserts that he remembers witnessing the translation of the royal remains when the coffin was deposited in its new resting place, before the high altar, on the extension of the choir in the reign of Henry I. The late Professor Freeman, a devoted admirer of our beautiful church and its historical associations, was so convinced that the great king, who was second only to Alfred in the Saxon line, was buried here, that he offered to find the coffin if he were allowed to explore the site of the ancient choir; but the necessary permission could not be granted on account of recent interments near the spot. We cannot but regret the loss of the tomb of the hero, to whom we owe so much.

The History of the Ancient Parish and Abbey Church of Waltham Holy Cross A lecture by the Reverend J. H. Stamp, 1904

Struck down by a Norman arrow, King Harold *(left)* was taken back to the church he had founded, together with his two brothers also slain in the battle near Hastings. Buried inside the original church, according to Edward Walford writing in 1883, his stone coffin was supposed to have been discovered by a gardener in the service of Sir Edward Denny, to whose grandfather the rectory and manor had passed at the Dissolution. The remains when exposed to the air mouldered into dust. When Sir Edward (then Earl of Norwich) died in 1637 he was succeeded by his grandson, James Hay, the 2nd Earl of Carlisle. According to Fuller writing circa 1655, Harold's tomb was 'where now the Earl of Carlisle's leaden fountain in his garden, then probably the end of the choir, or, rather some eastern chapel beyond it'. When he died, King Harold's reign had lasted a mere nine months.

In the beginning, Waltham — a derivation of 'wald' meaning forest, and 'ham', an enclosure — gave its name to what we now know as Epping Forest. In the beginning its church became the repository of the legendary Cross of Waltham — the Holy Cross of black stone. The abbey became a mecca for Christian pilgrims and a sealed-off flight of worn out steps in the present church, untrodden for 400 years, testifies to the many thousands who must have journeyed to seek out the miraculous qualities of the Cross. Its present-day whereabouts remain the Forest's greatest secret.

The Epping Forest Museums

The perfect setting for the first Epping Forest Museum — the 'Greate Standinge' on Dannetts Hill — the building we know now as Queen Elizabeth's Hunting Lodge.

A local museum need not necessarily be a dusty and depressing collection, formless and void of instruction, of savages and clubs, Indian snakes, dried lizards, and cracked Roman jars. On the contrary, it could be made the centre of intelligent curiosity respecting the district in which it stands, and as an educational agency second only to the reading room and public library. . . . Judging from their published pamphlet, some such ideas as these are present in the minds of the gentlemen forming the committee of the Essex Field Club, who are endeavouring to establish a small local museum in illustration of the natural history and antiquities of Epping Forest. As reported in our columns, a meeting was held some little time back in 'Queen Elizabeth's Lodge', in which some of those scientists best qualified to speak on the importance of local museums took part. Epping Forest, that magnificent heritage of modern London, is yearly frequented by countless troops of visitors of all classes, and in no place could the experiment of setting up a true local museum be better tried than in the old Tudor dwelling-house, in itself a most picturesque example, which stands just on the verge of the woodlands, near the village of Chingford. . . .

The Daily Graphic, April 26, 1894

On Saturday the 2nd inst., the Epping Forest Free Local Museum, established by the Essex Field Club, under the sanction of the Corporation of London, was formally opened in Queen Elizabeth's Hunting Lodge, Chingford, in the presence of a large and fashionable gathering, amongst whom we noticed Mr. E. J. Wythes, Mr. B. Winstone, Mr. E. N. Buxton, and others.

Owing to the limited space in the banqueting room of the Lodge, the meeting in connection with the opening ceremony was held in the dining room of Mr. Butler's Retreat, which adjoins, where speeches were delivered by Mr. David Howard, J.P., the Rev. A. F. Russell, M.A., and Sir William Flower.

Mr. Deputy Halse, in declaring the Museum open, said that as far back as 1883 many gentlemen who took an interest in the Forest assembled at the hospitable residence of Mr. E. N. Buxton, and application was made to the Corporation for the use of the Queen Elizabeth's Lodge for the formation of the museum, but at that time it was thought to be undesirable to nominally part with the control of the property to which they had succeeded. Although the notion of forming this museum had slumbered, the gentlemen interested did not sleep. Last year, application was made to his predecessors, Mr. James Salmon to bring the subject before the Forest Committee the negotiation resulting in the present gathering to witness the opening of the Museum.

The visitors then adjourned to the Museum and examined the interesting collection arranged by Messrs. W. and B. G. Cole, the secretaries of the Field Club, with assistance in certain sections from Mr. F. C. Gould, Mr. Walter Crouch, and others. The specimens exhibited at present, illustrate human history from the old stone age, geology, Romano-British pottery (found at Chigwell), flora, and fauna, insects, shell, &c. On the staircase are shown some useful maps and various views of the Forest, geological sections, plans, &c., presented by Mr. H. A. Cole, Mr. T. V. Holmes, Mr. Winstone, Mr. Stanford, Mr. Waller, the Epping Forest Committee, and others.

Epping Monthly Record, November 1895

Henry VIII, who held the Chingford manors in the mid-sixteenth century, converted part of the Forest between Chingford and Waltham into Fairmead Park furnished with 'standings' to afford grandstand views of the hunt. We began this book with New (or Fairmead) Lodge in existence since 1378, probably the earliest of the King's hunting lodges; and we now end it with a view of Great Standing, converted in 1899-1900 into the Epping Forest Museum.

Before any description of the contents of the Museum is given, it is desirable to offer some account of the old timber-framed and plastered building itself, which is worthy of more than cursory inspection as being an almost or quite unique example of a 'grand stand' of Tudor times, from whence the sport-loving sovereign and great ones of the land might conveniently witness a drive-past of the Forest deer.

Originally of late 15th century erection, the earliest known mention of the Lodge is in a Report, dated June 23rd, 1589, on two of Queen Elizabeth's houses in Waltham Forest, as Epping Forest was then called. One of these is therein referred to as the 'Greate Stand-inge' or 'lodg' on 'Dannet' or 'Dannetts' Hill, and has been satisfactorily identified with the building which we now know as 'Queen Elizabeth's Lodge': in the Report, the upper floors are described as serving 'for convenient standing to viewe the game.' At that time, as has been proved by expert examination during the re-construction, no glazed windows existed except on the Ground

The two stone mantlepieces are modern; that in the upper room is dated 1879, and bears in shields in the spandrils the arms of the City of London and the intertwined initials JTB in commemoration of J. T. Bedford, the energetic member of the Court of Common Council to whose efforts the saving of the Forest was largely due.

Since Tudor times, the old Lodge has been several times restored, the last occasion being in 1899-1900, when extensive alterations were carried out by the City Corporation, at a cost of over £1,000, to render it suitable for its present purpose. The picturesque half-timbered exterior with its elaborate-pierced bargeboard, is unfortunately only a sham modern veneer.

The great feature of the interior is the massive open timbered roof to the upper room; it consists of three bays divided by two bold curved and moulded roof-trusses, and with chamfered purlins and curved braces and boldly mounted wall plate: the roof over the square-neweled staircase is of similar construction.

At twelve o'clock midday on Friday, the 22nd October, 1944, the first long range rocket fell in the Borough. Fortunately, it fell on forest land, approximately 150 yards east of the Royal Forest Hotel and thirty yards north of Rangers road. Although it was a fine morning, there was apparently no one about at the time and, apart from two minor casualties caused by flying glass, the Civil Defence Services were not required. Some damage was caused to property, mainly of a minor character. Butler's Retreat was probably the worst affected, although much minor damage was caused to the Queen Elizabeth Hunting Lodge and the Forest Keeper's Lodge off Rangers road; damage was also caused to the Royal Forest Hotel and one or two buses standing outside the Hotel at the time suffered a little damage to windows.

This rocket made a very large crater some 60 feet across and about 20 feet deep, and several large boughs were blown off the oak trees nearby.

Chingford at War, S. Warburton, July 1946

Floor; on each of the upper floors the spaces between the main timber uprights, which are now filled in either with windows or with lath-and-plaster, were open above breast height on all sides, much like a racecourse stand of the present day. From here the Queen and her Court had an extensive view over all the surrounding country and could without fatigue watch the herds of deer which were driven past the Lodge for inspection: to drain off the rain which would drive in through these openings the floors were originally 'laid to fall.'

The original entrance to the staircase, up the solid oak steps of which, according to popular but unsupported tradition, Queen Elizabeth rode her palfrey, was by a door, which has now disappeared, in the East wall at the foot of the stairs.

The fireplaces and brick chimney are later, but still old-time, additions, made to fit the building for dwelling purposes: succeeding generations of Forest-keepers have been domiciled here, and the Lodge is still occupied, so far as the ground floor is concerned, by a keeper who acts as caretaker.

Were we to choose our seven wonders of Epping Forest, the Lodge, which escaped total destruction in 1944 by a hair's breadth, must surely be one of them, together with Ambresbury Banks, Loughton Camp, Waltham Abbey, Fairmead Lodge, the Fairlop Oak and, arguably, the ancient Stump Road.

The pleasing lead diamond-latticed casements in their Tudor-headed openings are, as already remarked, a later addition.

By the Epping Forest Act of 1878 (Sec. 8), the Lodge was transferred to the custody of the Corporation of London as Conservators of the Forest with the stipulation that it 'shall be preserved and maintained by them as an object of public and antiquarian interest.' It has now been approved by the Ancient Monuments Board for inclusion in the Schedule under the Ancient Monuments Act of 1913, so that the building is doubly safeguarded against wanton destruction or vandalism.

Essex Field Club, 1925

Prior to the war, the lodge was used as a museum and contained specimens of all the birds found in the forest, and, for the entomologist, a wealth of interest in the many cases of butterflies, moths, etc., with notes on their life, carefully compiled by the Essex Field Club. From the top floor of the lodge the spire of High Beach Church shows just above the trees in a northerly direction. Although the lodge is at present closed owing to war damage, it is hoped to re-open it on former lines as soon as repairs are completed.

Rambles in Epping Forest, F. H. Headley, 1948

An ancient building, known as Queen Elizabeth's Hunting Lodge, houses the Epping Forest museum, a collection of archaeological, botanical, zoological and other specimens of local associationship, founded by the Essex Field Club and now organised to complement the aims and objects of the Conservation Centre.

Epping Forest, Alfred Qvist, 1971

A 500-year-old timber framed house and its 200-year-old neighbour, once in grave danger of being pulled down, have been renovated to last a few more centuries.

For the two houses — 39 and 41 Sun Street, Waltham Abbey — have been completely done up to house the new Epping Forest Museum.

The doors will be thrown open to the public on Monday.

But on Friday the museum was packed with civic dignitaries, historians and other guests when the chairman of Epping Forest District Council, Cllr Dennis Morton, declared the museum open.

From 1975 until the early part of this year the ground floor of number 41 was used as a local museum by Waltham Abbey Historical Society and was run and staffed on a voluntary basis.

But now the two buildings have been combined to form the district museum and will be run by professionally qualified museum staff.

The pair of houses have been given an exciting new layout which reveals the medieval timbers but does not attempt to reconstruct the original building.

Cheshunt & Waltham Cross Telegraph,
November 13, 1981

Epping Forest District Council has recently taken advantage of its requirement to preserve two listed buildings to convert these into a permanent district museum. The two houses adapted are a sixteenth and an eighteenth century timber framed building with Georgian and Victorian additions.

One room is panelled entirely in a fine example of Renaissance oak panelling, carved early in the reign of Henry VIII, recovered by the Victoria and Albert Museum from a house in Green Yard, Waltham Abbey, and now generously loaned back. The collection includes items of local interest with early agricultural and other allied craft tools, but there will be temporary exhibitions of national interest and a small picture collection.

The garden of No. 41 features a Tudor herb garden with relevant displays in the main galleries, and related items for sale in the shop. Other sale items will be replicas, pottery, postcards and books. Coffee and herb tea can be bought to refresh visitors before they return to the displays.

Essex Countryside, January 1982

In 1946 Dr Robert Parkinson purchased No. 41 Sun Street, the historic old main street of Waltham Abbey. In 1966 the local authority had plans to demolish and redevelop the centre of the town and a compulsory purchase order was served on the house by Waltham Holy Cross Urban District Council. When the antiquity of Nos. 39 and 41 was appreciated, the Department of the Environment listed the property Grade II on October 25, 1973, thereby preventing its demolition.

After having stood empty for a year, the building was restored and opened in July 1975 as a local history museum by the Waltham Abbey Historical Society. That same year the recently-created Epping Forest District Council had begun their own museum in the rooms of the Recreation Department in Hemnall Street, Epping. As it was intended to expand the display area, studies were made during 1978-79 to find a suitable site, the final choice favouring Nos. 39 and 41 Sun Street. The new District Museum opened in November 1981 coincidentally with the pedestrianisation of Sun Street.